Lecture Notes in Computer Science 10298

Commenced Publication in 1973
Founding and Former Series Editors:
Gerhard Goos, Juris Hartmanis, and Jan van Leeuwen

More information about this series at http://www.springer.com/series/7409

Jia Zhou · Gavriel Salvendy (Eds.)

Human Aspects of IT for the Aged Population

Applications, Services and Contexts

Third International Conference, ITAP 2017
Held as Part of HCI International 2017
Vancouver, BC, Canada, July 9–14, 2017
Proceedings, Part II

 Springer

Editors
Jia Zhou
Chongqing University
Chongqing
China

Gavriel Salvendy
Purdue University
West Lafayette
USA

and

Tsinghua University
Beijing
P.R. China

and

University of Central Florida
Orlando
USA

ISSN 0302-9743   ISSN 1611-3349 (electronic)
Lecture Notes in Computer Science
ISBN 978-3-319-58535-2   ISBN 978-3-319-58536-9 (eBook)
DOI 10.1007/978-3-319-58536-9

Library of Congress Control Number: 2017939719

LNCS Sublibrary: SL3 – Information Systems and Applications, incl. Internet/Web, and HCI

Printed on acid-free paper

This Springer imprint is published by Springer Nature
The registered company is Springer International Publishing AG
The registered company address is: Gewerbestrasse 11, 6330 Cham, Switzerland

Foreword

The 19th International Conference on Human–Computer Interaction, HCI International 2017, was held in Vancouver, Canada, during July 9–14, 2017. The event incorporated the 15 conferences/thematic areas listed on the following page.

A total of 4,340 individuals from academia, research institutes, industry, and governmental agencies from 70 countries submitted contributions, and 1,228 papers have been included in the proceedings. These papers address the latest research and development efforts and highlight the human aspects of design and use of computing systems. The papers thoroughly cover the entire field of human–computer interaction, addressing major advances in knowledge and effective use of computers in a variety of application areas. The volumes constituting the full set of the conference proceedings are listed on the following pages.

I would like to thank the program board chairs and the members of the program boards of all thematic areas and affiliated conferences for their contribution to the highest scientific quality and the overall success of the HCI International 2017 conference.

This conference would not have been possible without the continuous and unwavering support and advice of the founder, Conference General Chair Emeritus and Conference Scientific Advisor Prof. Gavriel Salvendy. For his outstanding efforts, I would like to express my appreciation to the communications chair and editor of *HCI International News*, Dr. Abbas Moallem.

April 2017   Constantine Stephanidis

HCI International 2017 Thematic Areas and Affiliated Conferences

Thematic areas:

- Human–Computer Interaction (HCI 2017)
- Human Interface and the Management of Information (HIMI 2017)

Affiliated conferences:

- 17th International Conference on Engineering Psychology and Cognitive Ergonomics (EPCE 2017)
- 11th International Conference on Universal Access in Human–Computer Interaction (UAHCI 2017)
- 9th International Conference on Virtual, Augmented and Mixed Reality (VAMR 2017)
- 9th International Conference on Cross-Cultural Design (CCD 2017)
- 9th International Conference on Social Computing and Social Media (SCSM 2017)
- 11th International Conference on Augmented Cognition (AC 2017)
- 8th International Conference on Digital Human Modeling and Applications in Health, Safety, Ergonomics and Risk Management (DHM 2017)
- 6th International Conference on Design, User Experience and Usability (DUXU 2017)
- 5th International Conference on Distributed, Ambient and Pervasive Interactions (DAPI 2017)
- 5th International Conference on Human Aspects of Information Security, Privacy and Trust (HAS 2017)
- 4th International Conference on HCI in Business, Government and Organizations (HCIBGO 2017)
- 4th International Conference on Learning and Collaboration Technologies (LCT 2017)
- Third International Conference on Human Aspects of IT for the Aged Population (ITAP 2017)

Conference Proceedings Volumes Full List

1. LNCS 10271, Human–Computer Interaction: User Interface Design, Development and Multimodality (Part I), edited by Masaaki Kurosu
2. LNCS 10272 Human–Computer Interaction: Interaction Contexts (Part II), edited by Masaaki Kurosu
3. LNCS 10273, Human Interface and the Management of Information: Information, Knowledge and Interaction Design (Part I), edited by Sakae Yamamoto
4. LNCS 10274, Human Interface and the Management of Information: Supporting Learning, Decision-Making and Collaboration (Part II), edited by Sakae Yamamoto
5. LNAI 10275, Engineering Psychology and Cognitive Ergonomics: Performance, Emotion and Situation Awareness (Part I), edited by Don Harris
6. LNAI 10276, Engineering Psychology and Cognitive Ergonomics: Cognition and Design (Part II), edited by Don Harris
7. LNCS 10277, Universal Access in Human–Computer Interaction: Design and Development Approaches and Methods (Part I), edited by Margherita Antona and Constantine Stephanidis
8. LNCS 10278, Universal Access in Human–Computer Interaction: Designing Novel Interactions (Part II), edited by Margherita Antona and Constantine Stephanidis
9. LNCS 10279, Universal Access in Human–Computer Interaction: Human and Technological Environments (Part III), edited by Margherita Antona and Constantine Stephanidis
10. LNCS 10280, Virtual, Augmented and Mixed Reality, edited by Stephanie Lackey and Jessie Y.C. Chen
11. LNCS 10281, Cross-Cultural Design, edited by Pei-Luen Patrick Rau
12. LNCS 10282, Social Computing and Social Media: Human Behavior (Part I), edited by Gabriele Meiselwitz
13. LNCS 10283, Social Computing and Social Media: Applications and Analytics (Part II), edited by Gabriele Meiselwitz
14. LNAI 10284, Augmented Cognition: Neurocognition and Machine Learning (Part I), edited by Dylan D. Schmorrow and Cali M. Fidopiastis
15. LNAI 10285, Augmented Cognition: Enhancing Cognition and Behavior in Complex Human Environments (Part II), edited by Dylan D. Schmorrow and Cali M. Fidopiastis
16. LNCS 10286, Digital Human Modeling and Applications in Health, Safety, Ergonomics and Risk Management: Ergonomics and Design (Part I), edited by Vincent G. Duffy
17. LNCS 10287, Digital Human Modeling and Applications in Health, Safety, Ergonomics and Risk Management: Health and Safety (Part II), edited by Vincent G. Duffy
18. LNCS 10288, Design, User Experience, and Usability: Theory, Methodology and Management (Part I), edited by Aaron Marcus and Wentao Wang

Human Aspects of IT for the Aged Population

Program Board Chair(s): **Gavriel Salvendy, USA and P.R. China, and Jia Zhou, P.R. China**

- Panagiotis Bamidis, Greece
- Marc-Eric Bobillier Chaumon, France
- Julie A. Brown, USA
- Alan H.S. Chan, Hong Kong, SAR China
- Neil Charness, USA
- Shelia Cotten, USA
- Hua Dong, P.R. China
- Mireia Fernández-Ardèvol, Spain
- M. Anwar Hossain, Saudi Arabia
- Yong Gu Ji, Korea
- Jiunn-Woei (Allen) Lian, Taiwan
- Hai-Ning Liang, P.R. China

- Eugene Loos, The Netherlands
- Lourdes Moreno Lopez, Spain
- Lisa J. Molnar, USA
- Natalie Pang, Singapore
- Andraž Petrovčič, Slovenia
- Marie Sjölinder, Sweden
- Alvaro Taveira, USA
- António Teixeira, Portugal
- Wang-Chin Tsai, Taiwan
- Gregg C. Vanderheiden, USA
- Brenda Vrkljan, Canada
- Martina Ziefle, Germany

The full list with the Program Board Chairs and the members of the Program Boards of all thematic areas and affiliated conferences is available online at:

http://www.hci.international/board-members-2017.php

HCI International 2018

The 20th International Conference on Human–Computer Interaction, HCI International 2018, will be held jointly with the affiliated conferences in Las Vegas, NV, USA, at Caesars Palace, July 15–20, 2018. It will cover a broad spectrum of themes related to human–computer interaction, including theoretical issues, methods, tools, processes, and case studies in HCI design, as well as novel interaction techniques, interfaces, and applications. The proceedings will be published by Springer. More information is available on the conference website: http://2018.hci.international/.

General Chair
Prof. Constantine Stephanidis
University of Crete and ICS-FORTH
Heraklion, Crete, Greece
E-mail: general_chair@hcii2018.org

http://2018.hci.international/

Contents – Part II

Silver and Intergenerational Gaming

Aging and Learning, Working and Leisure

Contents – Part I

Product Design for the Elderly

Aging and User Experience

Digital Literacy and Training

Mobile and Wearable Interaction for the Elderly

How Do Users Interact with Mobile Devices?
An Analysis of Handheld Positions
for Different Technology Generations

Christina Bröhl[1]([✉]), Alexander Mertens[1], and Martina Ziefle[2]

[1] Institute of Industrial Engineering and Ergonomics,
RWTH Aachen University, Aachen, Germany
{c.broehl,a.mertens}@iaw.rwth-aachen.de
[2] Human-Computer-Interaction Center,
RWTH Aachen University, Aachen, Germany
ziefle@comm.rwth-aachen.de

Abstract. While interacting with digital information, input devices are varying widely as technology is constantly changing. The most successful input devices are currently touchscreens, as they combine information input and output on a single interface. The aim of the present research was to gain a basic understanding of how people hold their hands when interacting with handheld devices and how this interaction changes depending on task context. To gain a large sample size, the study was administered via an online questionnaire. Five different hand positions were evaluated with regard to three different tasks: typing short text, typing long text, and reading. When considering user characteristics with regard to technology, one of the most influential factors is the user's age. Therefore, the sample ($N = 1022$) was analyzed with regard to four different technology generations. Results show that there are significant differences in handheld positions with regard to different tasks and depending on the interaction with a smartphone or tablet PC. Furthermore, significant differences were detected between the four technology generations.

Keywords: Human-system interaction · Ergonomic design · Handheld devices · Usability · Ageing

1 Introduction

Smartphone and Tablet PCs are currently the most successful mobile devices. In 2015, 68% of U.S. adults had a smartphone and tablet PC ownership has increased 45% among adults (Pew Research Center). The operations of smartphones and tablet PCs are carried out via applications, or short apps that are primarily used through the devices' screen, which allows for bidirectional interaction. There are different apps for different tasks. The most basic apps, for example, are apps for checking e-mails, apps for web browsing or apps for taking notes. Thereby, the task in question and the size of the device may determine how the device is held in the hands, and information input might vary from just taping with one finger to typing text with two fingers. Knowledge about how users hold their hands when interacting with touchscreens can impact

© Springer International Publishing AG 2017
J. Zhou and G. Salvendy (Eds.): ITAP 2017, Part II, LNCS 10298, pp. 3–16, 2017.
DOI: 10.1007/978-3-319-58536-9_1

ergonomic interface design by designing apps that consider the handheld position people are most likely to use for interaction. The study presented in this paper focuses therefore on an analysis of handheld positions for three different tasks and considers age-related differences.

1.1   Handheld Positions

Touchscreen devices can be operated either vertically or horizontally, with one or both thumbs, or one or more fingers of the same hand or another one. Thereby, it is essential to differentiate between tablets and smartphones since they have different sizes, weights and shapes. Therefore, different requirements are laid down when designing user interfaces [1]. Research conducted so far investigated approaches of finger placement and hand grasp during touchscreen interaction. With regard to the interaction with tablets, Oulasvirta et al. [2] recommended a symmetric bimanual grip while holding a tablet in landscape orientation as being the most appropriate for ergonomic text input. Odell and Chandrasekaran [1] examined this position in order to measure the thumb reachable areas for two different grips and for different anthropometric measures. What those researchers found was that the reachable distance of the thumb on the tablet is larger on the side grip than on the corner grip and therefore it can be inferred that the hand grip on the sides should be preferred to the position of the hands at the corners. Regarding smartphone interaction, Wobbrock, Myers and Aung [3] studied a total of eight different postures, four different two-handed postures and four different one-handed postures. They found that the posture of the hand has a significant effect on users' touch performance and that interaction with the device should not only take place by placing fingers on the front of the device but also back-of-device performance should be investigated as a feasible means for interaction, which enables a richer set of finger and thumb interactions. This idea was studied by Le, Mayer, Wold and Henze [4]. Specifically, those researchers analyzed how users naturally position their hands for three different tasks aiming to develop ergonomic back-of-device interaction techniques. The tasks studied were derived from Böhmer, Hecht, Schöning, Krüger and Bauer [5], and involved writing a text message, reading a text, and watching a video. Thereby, writing and reading tasks were conducted in the portrait mode of the device, while watching a video task was conducted in the landscape mode. Since the sample consisted of ten right-handed subjects, results may lack reliability. In all tasks, it was found that the right hand touched the phone the most. Furthermore, a higher number of different hand positions was found for the landscape mode compared to the portrait mode, which let the researchers conclude that people might be less used to the landscape mode.

1.2   Perception of Peripersonal Space in the Elderly

The space surrounding the body that is within reach of the hands is called peripersonal space. Most interaction with handheld devices takes place within peripersonal space. Past studies have shown that there are differences in the perception of peripersonal space with regard to age. Bloesch, Davoli, and Abrams [6] studied reach-and-point actions, such as the movement needed to dial a phone, and found that distractor objects placed along a movement path slowed the performance of younger participants more than distractors outside the movement path. However, older subjects perceived interference in their movement when an object was placed in front of their body. The authors thus concluded that younger subjects adopt an action-centered reference frame, as peripersonal space has a different neural representation compared to the rest of the body. While using the hand to perform an action, this reference frame activates brain areas that allow the movement path to be planned and executed more accurately. Older subjects, however, may exhibit declines in those brain areas (parietal cortex [7] and intraparietal cortex [8]), which may make the use of an action-centered reference frame more difficult or impossible. As the older subjects' performances in reaching movements were slowed down when a distractor object was placed near their bodies, the authors concluded that older subjects make use of a body-centered reference frame. An explanation for an action-centered reference frame is the fact that individuals prioritize objects near their hands, as these may be candidates for potential actions and thus automatically encode the location of those objects in reference to their hands. As perihand space and the corresponding neural representations might become less accurate with age, the authors hypothesized that the dominant reference for spatial coding might move from the hand to the trunk, which may lead to a body-centered reference frame. In line with these findings, research by Gabbard, Cacola, and Cordova [9] that investigated mental models supports the assumption of age-related differences in action representation. These authors tested the ability of individuals to estimate whether an object is within reach or out of grasp. The results indicated that older subjects made significantly more errors and both age groups performed worse in extrapersonal space (beyond reach) compared to peripersonal space. Further evidence for an altered representation of perihand space in the elderly comes from studies by Ghafouri and Lestienne [10]. These authors studied three-dimensional arm movements and found that space representation changes with aging. In particular, subjects in the study were requested to draw ellipses in three spatial planes (sagittal, frontal, and horizontal) to measure the deviations in the orientation of the ellipses with regard to the planes. The results showed that older subjects made larger errors than the younger ones, supporting the assumption of an age-related representation of perihand space.

One of the key findings from these papers is that older people on average encounter more problems in performing actions in peripersonal space. Thereby these difficulties are not only present while performing actions but also when predicting actions in peripersonal space. This finding indicates that these effects are not caused by impairments in motor skills of elderly people but indicate tendencies to perceive peripersonal space in a different way than younger aged subjects do.

1.3 Technology Generations

Understanding user requirements is one essential part of design. Taking chronological age into account, however, is often not productive as aging processes are highly individual, resulting in ambiguous measurements. Therefore, considering the subject's age in combination with period and cohort effects seems promising. Age, period, and cohort effects must be considered as being interrelated, as it is impossible to deal with one without also dealing with the others. Age effects are the result of getting older and deal with specific effects in different age groups. Period effects are the consequences of influences that vary through time and are associated with all age groups simultaneously. Cohort effects are the consequences of being born at different times and are associated with variations in successive age groups in successive time periods (e.g. long-term habits or long-term exposures), so different generations are exposed to different factors. Estimating the effects of either one of those is not easy because the effects may be confounded with the others [11].

Building on existing theories regarding age-period-cohort models, the concept of technology generations was introduced by German sociologists in the early 1990s [12]. These researchers defined a technology generation as "groups of birth cohorts whose conjunctive experience with technology is differentiated by social change" (p. 493). The authors state further that technological change, and especially changes in basic technologies, enhances inter-cohort differences, thereby raising the likelihood of a conscious perception and description of differences as generational differences. The concept of technology generations includes technologically-related cohort effects and refers to cohort variations with regard to changes in the social and cultural environment.

A range of birth cohorts that show behavioral similarities or shared norms and values based on common sociological environments and predominant developments during the formative period (the period of time between adolescence and young adulthood, operationalized between 10 and 25 years) is called a generation. Studies about age cohorts have shown that after young adulthood, individuals are less likely to change their attitudes, norms and values. During the formative period, subjects undergo a number of crucial transitions, like from school to university or from parental home to independent living. Researchers found out that acquired norms, skills and values during that period tend to be constant and influence behavior later in life [13]. Sackmann and Weymann [12] point out that individuals experiencing the availability of the same types of products during the formative period display similar product usage many years later. Thus, different technology generations appear to behave differently with respect to technology, which is the result of differences in their experience gained in their formative years. Going further, Docampo Rama, Ridder and Bouma [14], whose approach consisted of distinguishing technology generations by interface usage, infer that generation-specific technology experience could induce differences in the usage behavior of current consumer products. Older people may be at a disadvantage in using present complex user interfaces, as they did not acquire that skill in their formative period earlier in life.

The question then arises where the boundary between different birth cohorts occurred. Following earlier investigators [15, 16], Docampo Rama et al. [14] define changes in basic technology causing generational differentiation as the point in time where 20% diffusion within the population has been reached. At that point, it is regarded as likely that persons who do not have such technologies themselves have experienced them in their social surroundings (e.g. in their families, with their friends or at work). In order to get information about the degree of diffusion of a technology, Sackmann and Weymann [12] used qualitative interviews, group discussions, surveys, and secondary data analysis to develop and test their concept of technology generations. As a result of this, Sackmann and Weymann [12] distinguished generations from birth cohorts that currently are displaying similar behavior with regard to technology based on technological achievements in their formative periods. Hence, four different technology generations were initially identified:

- the mechanical generation (born before 1939)
- the generation of the household revolution (born between 1939 and 1948)
- the generation of technology spread (born between 1949 and 1963), and
- the computer generation (born between 1964 and 1979).

In 2013, a new generation was added by the authors to this typology of technology generations:

- the internet generation (born in 1980 and later)

In summary, generation-specific experience with technology might influence the usage of currently available technologies, as older people did not encounter the complex interaction patterns that are necessary to handle modern technologies in their formative period. Therefore, age differences in this study are analyzed with regard to different technology generations.

1.4   The Present Study

While previous work provides some approaches of hand positions analyses, none of them takes a large group of users, a thorough differentiation of hand positions, and a comparison between smartphone and tablet PC interaction into account. Therefore, the study presented in this paper provides an analysis of handheld positions while interacting with smartphones and tablet PCs and differentiates between three different tasks. To obtain a large sample size, the study was administered via an online questionnaire. Participants were assigned to four age groups according to the four youngest of the five technology generations proposed by Sackmann and Weymann [12].

2   Method

2.1   Procedure

The questionnaire started with a short introduction of the study and demographic questions. After that, subjects were asked to specify how they would position their hands by choosing between five different positions:

(1) Holding the device vertically and interacting with the thumb of the same hand.
(2) Holding the device vertically with one hand and interacting with a finger of the other hand.
(3) Holding the device vertically with both hands and interacting with both hands.
(4) Holding the device horizontally and interacting with both thumbs.
(5) Holding the device horizontally with one hand and interacting with a finger of the other hand.

In order to simplify the answering process, images of the handholding positions were added to the questionnaire (Fig. 1).

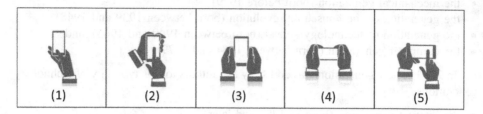

Fig. 1. Depiction of the handling positions studied

The tasks that were studied were inspired by those used by Böhmer et al. [5] and Le et al. [4], although not fully identical. The tasks were: typing short text, typing long text, and reading.

2.2   Participants

A total of 1022 subjects aged 20–77 took part in the online questionnaire. Their mean age was M = 48.08 years (SD = 12.03). The age structure was not equally distributed, but showed a middle age peak (Fig. 2). As people usually tend to use their dominant hand when operating their phone [17], we only included right-handed subjects in our analysis. For the analysis, participants were classified according to four age groups in accordance with the technology generations proposed by Sackmann and Winkler [18]. Due to a lack of participants, the fifth group could not be studied. The resulting age groups were as follows:

- The first group, called "the internet generation" and aged 19–36, consisted of N = 196 persons (M = 30.8, SD = 4.37)
- The second group, called "the computer generation" and aged 37–52, consisted of N = 457 persons (M = 45.21, SD = 4.63)

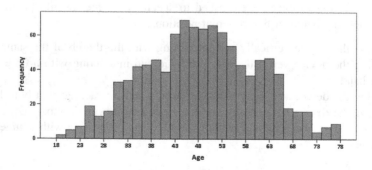

Fig. 2. Age distribution of participants

- The third group, called "the generation of technology spread" and aged 53–67, consisted of $N = 316$ persons ($M = 59.06$, $SD = 4.18$)
- The fourth group, called "the generation of the household revolution" and aged 68–77, consisted of $N = 52$ persons ($M = 71.63$, $SD = 3.0$)

3 Results

Chi-square tests were used to study the effects of handheld positions for the three different tasks separately, as the measurement was at the nominal level. The level of significance was set to $\alpha = 0.05$.

3.1 · Overall Age Effects

In order to analyze differences between the four age groups, chi square tests were analyzed for the three tasks and for smartphone and tablet interaction separately. An overview of the results is shown in Table 1. Overall, significant differences were found between the tasks with regard to the handholding positions for the four different age groups.

Table 1. Results of chi-square tests for overall differences between technology generations

Device	Task	N	df	Pearson chi-square	p-value
Smartphone	Typing short text	1009	12	128.28	.00
	Typing long text	982	12	115.37	.00
	Reading	977	12	52.89	.00
Tablet PC	Typing short text	972	12	51.65	.00
	Typing long text	979	12	49.64	.00
	Reading	984	12	39.22	.00

3.2 The Internet Generation

Smartphone Interaction
Results of the analysis of handheld positions with regard to smartphone interaction of the youngest age group showed significant effects for typing short text ($\chi^2(4, N = 193) = 169.46$, $p = .00$), typing long text ($\chi^2(4, N = 189) = 62.03$, $p = .00$), and reading text ($\chi^2(4, N = 186) = 95.13$, $p = .00$). The visual analysis of the bar graphs (Fig. 3) shows that for typing short text and reading, the most prominent position is holding the smartphone vertically and interacting with a finger of the same hand, whereas the most prominent position for typing long text is holding the smartphone vertically and interacting with a finger of the other hand.

Tablet PC Interaction

Results of the analysis of handheld positions with regard to tablet PC interaction of the youngest age group showed no significant effects for typing short text ($\chi^2(4, N = 184) = 6.87$, $p = .14$), typing long text ($\chi^2(4, N = 187) = 7.2$, $p = .13$), and reading text ($\chi^2(4, N = 189) = 8.65$, $p = .07$). The visual analysis of the bar graphs (Fig. 3) shows that the distribution of the handheld positions is rather evenly distributed, with a peak for the position of holding the tablet PC vertically and interacting with a finger of the other hand for all three tasks.

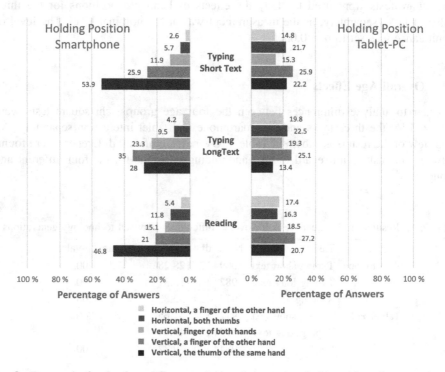

Fig. 3. Bar graphs for the three different tasks in relation to handheld positions for smartphone and tablet PC interaction for "the internet generation"

3.3 The Computer Generation

Smartphone Interaction

Results of the analysis of handheld positions with regard to smartphone interaction of the "computer generation" showed significant effects for typing short text ($\chi^2(4, N = 450) = 434.98$, $p = .00$), typing long text ($\chi^2(4, N = 432) = 401.91$, $p = .00$), and reading text ($\chi^2(4, N = 426) = 246.61$, $p = .00$). The visual analysis of the bar graphs (Fig. 4) shows that the most prominent position for all three tasks is holding the smartphone vertically and typing with a finger of the other hand, followed by holding the smartphone vertically and typing with a finger of the other hand for typing short text and reading, but not for typing long text.

Tablet PC Interaction
Results of the analysis of handheld positions with regard to tablet PC interaction of the "computer generation" showed significant effects for typing short text ($\chi^2(4, N = 424) = 175.18$, $p = .00$), typing long text ($\chi^2(4, N = 425) = 152.85$, $p = .00$), and reading text ($\chi^2(4, N = 431) = 95.65$, $p = .00$). The visual analysis of the bar graphs (Fig. 4) shows that the most prominent position for all three tasks is by far holding the tablet PC vertically and interacting with a finger of the other hand.

3.4 The Generation of the Technology Spread

Smartphone Interaction
Results of the analysis of handheld positions with regard to smartphone interaction of the "generation of technology spread" showed significant effects for typing short text ($\chi^2(4, N = 314) = 422.59$, $p = .00$), typing long text ($\chi^2(4, N = 309) = 449.72$, $p = .00$), and reading text ($\chi^2(4, N = 313) = 166.95$, $p = .00$). The visual analysis of the bar graphs (Fig. 5) shows that by far the most prominent position for all three tasks is holding the smartphone vertically and typing with a finger of the other hand.

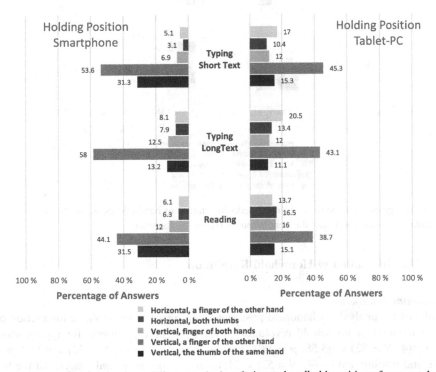

Fig. 4. Bar graphs for the three different tasks in relation to handheld positions for smartphone and tablet PC interaction for "the computer generation"

Tablet PC Interaction
Results of the analysis of handheld positions with regard to tablet PC interaction of the "generation of technology spread" showed significant effects for typing short text (χ^2(4, N = 312) = 157.52, p = .00), typing long text (χ^2(4, N = 315) = 150.57, p = .00), and reading text (χ^2(4, N = 312) = 70.95, p = .00). The visual analysis of the bar graphs (Fig. 5) shows that the most prominent position for all three tasks is by far holding the tablet PC vertically and interacting with a finger of the other hand, followed by holding the tablet PC horizontally and interacting with a finger of the other hand.

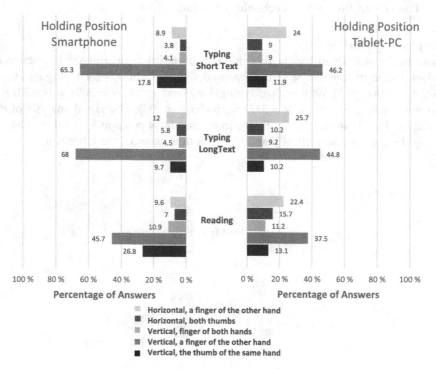

Fig. 5. Bar graphs for the three different tasks in relation to handheld positions for smartphone and tablet PC interaction for "the generation of technology spread"

3.5   The Generation of Household Revolution

Smartphone Interaction
Results of the analysis of handheld positions with regard to smartphone interaction of the "generation of household revolution" showed significant effects for typing short text (χ^2(4, N = 52) = 93.58, p = .00), typing long text (χ^2(4, N = 52) = 90.12, p = .00), and reading text (χ^2(4, N = 52) = 31.46, p = .00). The visual analysis of the bar graphs (Fig. 6) shows that once again, the most prominent position for all three tasks is holding the smartphone vertically and typing with a finger of the other hand.

Tablet PC Interaction

Results of the analysis of handheld positions with regard to tablet PC interaction of the "generation of household revolution" showed significant effects for typing short text ($\chi^2(4, N = 52) = 38.81, p = .00$), typing long text ($\chi^2(4, N = 52) = 27.81, p = .00$), and reading text ($\chi^2(4, N = 52) = 17.04, p = .00$). The visual analysis of the bar graphs (Fig. 6) shows that the most prominent position for typing long text and reading is holding the tablet PC horizontally and typing with a finger of the other hand, whereas for typing short text the most prominent position is holding the tablet PC vertically and typing with a finger of the other hand.

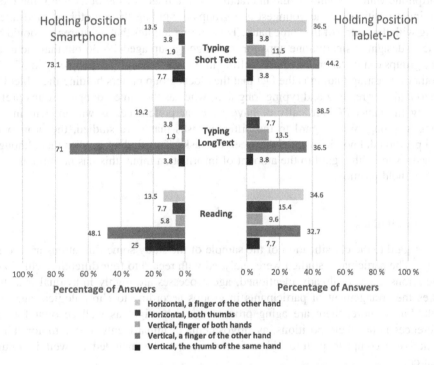

Fig. 6. Bar graphs for the three different tasks in relation to handheld positions for smartphone and tablet PC interaction for "the generation of household revolution"

4 Discussion

Developing ergonomic user interfaces requires to understand how users naturally hold their devices. The analyses presented in this paper show how users hold and interact with their smartphones and their tablet PC in three common tasks. To understand how different age groups interact with mobile devices, the results were analyzed for four different technology generations.

Overall, the results show significant differences in the way different technology generations hold their hands while interacting with smartphones and tablets as well as differences in the interaction patterns between smartphones and tablet PCs. While the most prominent positions when interacting with a smartphone are holding the phone vertically and interacting with a thumb or a finger, there is more variability in the results of the analysis of the interaction with a tablet PC. Specifically, the internet generation as the youngest age group shows no significant differences between the hand positions for interacting with a tablet PC, while the other three user groups do show significant differences. This implies that apps for tablet PCs that are used by younger people do not need to account for different hand positions but can be designed in such a way that they fit the needs of the older groups. Regarding smartphone interaction, the most prominent position for the three older-aged groups is holding the smartphone with one hand, while interacting with a finger of the other hand, the most prominent position for the youngest age groups is holding the smartphone and interacting with the thumb of the same hand. This finding implies that a difference should be made in designing smartphone apps for a younger group aged 19–36 but that the three older groups can be taken together resulting in the same design for people aged 37–77. Another interesting finding is the fact that the oldest group prefers holding the tablet PC horizontally for reading and typing long text, whereas the three younger groups prefer holding the tablet PC vertically or have no clear preference, as was evident in the youngest group. With regard to the different tasks that were studied, the prominent hand position did not differ much between the tasks. This finding implies that although the tasks vary with regard to the amount of information input, this has no influence on the handheld position.

4.1 Limitations

With regard to the classification of the sample of the study some limitations are worth noting. The participants studied were analyzed with regard to four different technology generations. As was already mentioned, age processes are highly individual and this makes the arrangement of participants in groups according to chronological age difficult. Furthermore, there are aging processes which might as well account for the differences in handheld positions, as amyosthenia or impairments in fine motor skills. To derive a complete picture, these factors need to be included as well in future research.

Another point of criticism is the fact that most research related to grouping of birth cohorts corresponds to studies that were done in highly industrialized European societies. Actually, the data had to be adapted to local technological spread patterns for other regions of the world in order to be reliable. Furthermore, with regard to the sample of our research, the group sizes of the technology generations were not equally distributed, and this might cause a bias in the data between the different age groups.

4.2 Conclusion

Overall, the results of the questionnaire study show significant differences in the way technology generations interact with their mobile devices. On the one hand, this supports the structure of those age groups and, on the other hand, this points out the importance of studying age effects in human-system interaction and does only partially support design for all approaches. With regard to interface design, the findings imply further research to test if interfaces that are designed taking the handheld position that they are used in into account profit positively with regard to ergonomic criteria.

Acknowledgements. This publication is part of the research project "TECH4AGE", which is funded by the German Federal Ministry of Education and Research (BMBF, Grant No. 16SV7111) supervised by the VDI/VDE Innovation + Technik GmbH.

References

1. Odell, D., Chandrasekaran, V.: Enabling comfortable thumb interaction in tablet computers: a Windows 8 case study. Proc. Hum. Factors Ergon. Soc. Ann. Meet. **56**(1), 1907 (2012). doi:10.1177/1071181312561278
2. Oulasvirta, A., Reichel, A., Li, W., Zhang, Y., Bachynskyi, M., Vertanen, K., Kristensson, P.O.: Improving two-thumb text entry on touchscreen devices. In: Mackay, W.E., Brewster, S., Bødker, S., (eds.) CHI 2013, Changing Perspectives, The 31st Annual CHI Conference on Human Factors in Computing Systems, Conference Proceedings, 27 April - 2 May 2013, Paris, France, p. 2765. ACM, New York (2013)
3. Wobbrock, J.O., Myers, B.A., Aung, H.H.: The performance of hand postures in front- and back-of-device interaction for mobile computing. Int. J. Hum Comput Stud. **66**(12), 857 (2008). doi:10.1016/j.ijhcs.2008.03.004
4. Le, H.V., Mayer, S., Wolf, K., Henze, N.: Finger placement and hand grasp during smartphone interaction. In: CHI 2016, pp. 2576–2584. ACM (2016)
5. Böhmer, M., Hecht, B., Schöning, J., Krüger, A., Bauer, G.: Falling asleep with Angry Birds, Facebook and Kindle. In: Bylund, M. (ed.) Proceedings of the 13th International Conference on Human Computer Interaction with Mobile Devices and Services, p. 47. ACM, New York (2011)
6. Bloesch, E.K., Davoli, C.C., Abrams, R.A.: Age-related changes in attentional reference frames for peripersonal space. Psychol. Sci. **24**(4), 557 (2013). doi:10.1177/0956797612 457385
7. Lehmbeck, J.T., Brassen, S., Weber-Fahr, W., Braus, D.F.: Combining voxel-based morphometry and diffusion tensor imaging to detect age-related brain changes. NeuroReport **17**(5), 467 (2006). doi:10.1097/01.wnr.0000209012.24341.7f
8. Kochunov, P., Mangin, J., Coyle, T., Lancaster, J., Thompson, P., Rivière, D., Cointepas, Y., Régis, J., Schlosser, A., Royall, D.R., Zilles, K., Mazziotta, J., Toga, A., Fox, P.T.: Age-related morphology trends of cortical sulci. Hum. Brain Mapp. **26**(3), 210 (2005). doi:10.1002/hbm.20198
9. Gabbard, C., Caçola, P., Cordova, A.: Is there an advanced aging effect on the ability to mentally represent action? Arch. Gerontol. Geriatr. **53**(2), 206 (2011). doi:10.1016/j.archger. 2010.10.006
10. Ghafouri, M., Lestienne, F.G.: Altered representation of peripersonal space in the elderly human subject: a sensorimotor approach. Neurosci. Lett. **289**(3), 193 (2000). doi:10.1016/ S0304-3940(00)01280-5

11. Robertson, C., Gandini, S., Boyle, P.: Age-period-cohort models: a comparative study of available methodologies. J. Clin. Epidemiol. **52**(6), 569 (1999). doi:10.1016/S0895-4356 (99)00033-5
12. Sackmann, R., Weymann, A., Hüttner, B.: Die Technisierung des Alltags, Generationen und technische Innovationen. Campus-Verlag, Frankfurt/Main (1994). ISBN: 3593351773. http://www.soziologie.uni-halle.de/sackmann/docs/die-technisierung-des-alltags.pdf.ger
13. Sroufe, L.A., Cooper, R.G., DeHart, G.B., Marshall, M.E., Bronfenbrenner, U.: Child Development: Its Nature and Course, 2nd edn. Mcgraw-Hill Book Company, New York (1992). English
14. Docampo Rama, M., de Ridder, H., Bouma, H.: Technology generation and age in using layered user interfaces. Gerontechnology **1**(1), 25 (2001). doi:10.4017/gt.2001.01.01.003.00
15. Rogers, E.M.: Diffusion of Innovations. Free Press of Glencoe, New York (1962). http://worldcatlibraries.org/wcpa/oclc/254636
16. Ryder, N.B.: The Cohort as a Concept in the Study of Social Change. Springer, New York (1985)
17. Arif, A.S.: A survey on mobile text entry handedness: How do users input text on handheld devices while nomadic? In: 4th International Conference on Intelligent Human Computer Interaction (IHCI), 27–29 December 2012, Kharagpur, India, pp. 1–6. IEEE, Piscataway (2012)
18. Sackmann, R., Winkler, O.: Technology generations revisited: the internet generation. Gerontechnology **11**(4), 493 (2013). doi:10.4017/gt.2013.11.4.002.00

Movement Analysis for Improving Older Adults' Performances in HCI: Preliminary Analysis of Movements of the Users' Wrists During Tactile Interaction

Lilian Genaro Motti Ader[1(✉)], Nadine Vigouroux[1], and Philippe Gorce[2]

[1] IRIT, Université de Toulouse, 118 Route de Narbonne, Toulouse, France
{genaro,vigourou}@irit.fr
[2] Handibio, Université de Toulon, Avenue de L'université, Toulon, France
gorce@univ-tln.fr

Abstract. In view of the adoption of touchscreen devices by older aged users, it is important to consider the comfort of use from an ergonomic point of view. We implemented an experimental study associating the analysis of the movements and performances of 15 older aged adults (65–84). The task consisted on positioning targets with drag-and-drop interaction on a tablet. Participants were equipped with a motion capture system. In this paper, we present a preliminary analysis of the movements of the users' wrist, characterized by a predominant radial deviation and extension of this articulation during interaction with their finger. We discuss the impact of the ergonomics of touchscreen interaction on the accessibility of interactive technologies for older people.

Keywords: Touchscreen interaction · Older aged users · Motion analysis · Wrist · Ergonomics

1 Introduction

The analysis of the movements of human users interacting with touchscreen devices have been used to study the ergonomics of devices and graphical interfaces. By recording the user's body postures and positions, it is possible to compare different situation of use of touchscreen devices [1] or interaction techniques [2], in order to identify postures that could cause lack of comfort or even musculoskeletal disorders [3]. Besides, the posture of the users' body in relation to the position of the devices can affect the performances of the users during the execution of interaction tasks [4]. For this reason, designers should also consider the analysis of the interaction with technologies from an ergonomics approach.

In view of the adoption of touchscreen devices by older aged users [5], it is important to consider the comfort of use of these technologies. The age-related changings in muscle, bones and articular cartilage may lead to a functional loss, affecting the movements the users need to perform during tactile interaction [6]. The analysis of the movements of older-aged users during interaction with touchscreen devices should provide

© Springer International Publishing AG 2017
J. Zhou and G. Salvendy (Eds.): ITAP 2017, Part II, LNCS 10298, pp. 17–26, 2017.
DOI: 10.1007/978-3-319-58536-9_2

some evidence of the difficulties this group of users may find when using these devices [7].

We implemented an experimental study associating the analysis of the movements and performances of fifteen older aged adults (65–84). The task consisted on positioning twenty-five targets with drag-and-drop gestures using their index finger, on a tablet. The movements of the participants were recorded through a motion capture system, providing data for the analysis of the postures of their bodies and articulatory angles.

In this paper, we present a preliminary analysis of the movements of the users' wrist. Previous studies demonstrate a great mobilization of the users' wrist during tactile interaction [8, 9]. In this study, the movements of the wrist represent the arrangement of the articulations of the users' upper limbs as the users move to execute the interaction task.

Results present the analysis of the articulatory angles we registered and a discussion about their consequences on the comfort of use of touchscreen devices. Additionally, the analysis of the performances of the participants for the interaction task discusses the possibility of the effects of ergonomics on the usability and accessibility of touchscreen interaction.

Finally, this paper discusses the use of movement analysis (A) for understanding the differences in performances for users with different functional capacities and the impact on accessibility of interactive technologies and (B) for identifying postures and positions of the users' bodies that could present a risk for developing musculoskeletal injuries for older and younger users.

2 State of the Art

In this session, we review some previous studies using motion capture systems to analyze the movements of the users during the use of touchscreen devices, most of them to evaluate the positions and postures of the body from an ergonomic point of view. Then, we discuss the mobilization of the user's wrist during interaction with touchscreen, in order to justify our choice for this articulation on the preliminary analysis we present in this study.

2.1 Movement Analysis During Use of Touchscreen Devices

The analysis of the movements of human users interacting with technologies consists on recording the user's body postures and positions during the execution of an interaction task. Mobile devices present the advantage of being adapted to different situations of use, at home, office or mobility. Consequently, we consider that mobile devices are particularly suitable for older aged users in regard of their possibilities of use at home, in institutions and in mobility.

However, it is difficult to provide ergonomic recommendations that could take into account the context of use of mobile devices. Besides, mobile devices are often equipped with touchscreen, which has being shown to be easier to learn and use for older aged users [7]. In order to evaluate the comfort of use of mobile devices and touchscreen interaction, the analysis of the users' movements seems fundamental.

Previous studies have used motion capture systems to study the ergonomics of devices and graphical interfaces for younger and adult users. Pereira et al. [2] compared pen and finger interaction for participants holding mobile devices at their hand. Bachynski et al. [1] evaluated and compared different screen sizes and situations of use of touch sensitive surfaces. In their study, the use of motion capture system allowed the definition of the groups of muscles and articulations participants employed during interaction. Additionally, data collected through the interactive systems can provide information about the users' performances, helping designers to compare different devices [10]. However, the studies we reviewed included only young participants. The ergonomics of touchscreen interaction for older aged users is yet to be investigated.

More than identifying the postures that could cause lack of comfort, the posture of the users' body in relation to the position of the devices can affect the performances of the users during the execution of interaction tasks. Pereira et al. [2] showed that users holding tablets with one hand should prefer small or median devices, so to improve usability and ergonomics. The association of the analysis of the users' movements and the usability of devices is necessary to provide recommendations for users and designers.

2.2 Mobilization of the User's Wrist During Interaction with Technologies

Studies that evaluated the movements of adult users during the use of touchscreen devices demonstrated a great mobilization of the users' wrist during tactile interaction. Young et al. [9] showed that wrist postures are affected by the position of the devices. In their study, they discuss that using cases for holding tablets tilted requires increased extension of the wrist. Jacquier-Bret et al. [8] demonstrated that adults adopt different strategies for accomplishing an interaction task, adapting the movements of their upper-limbs when using touchscreen devices horizontally placed on a desk. According to their analysis, some users present small movements of the wrist but increased mobilization of the elbow and arms, while others present little movements of elbow and arms but compensatory mobilization of the wrist, for allowing the fingers to reach to the targets presented on the touchscreen. Both studies alarmed us about the risks of musculoskeletal injuries for intensive or prolonged use of touchscreen interaction.

During touch interaction, users would try to optimize their performances, increasing velocities for example. An intensive use of touchscreen would be related to repetitiveness, which could also present a risk for musculoskeletal disorders [11]. An advantage of touchscreen devices is the sensitivity of the screen, that would reduce force of touch compared to traditional physical input devices [12]. However, wrists disorders are also related to the angle deviations and amplitude of movements of this articulation [11, 13]. It is though important to consider that the movements of the wrist articulation are affected by the natural aging process [14]. For this reason, evaluating postures and movements of the wrist can provide relevant information about the comfort of use of touchscreen.

3   Experiment and Equipment

Fifteen older adults, aged 65 to 84, were recruited for this study. Their mean hands' length was 18 cm (SD = 1.3) and mean index finger length was 8 cm (SD = 0.6). According to a pre-evaluation form and practice trials for the task, participants do not presented any motor, visual or cognitive loss that could hinder the interaction with touchscreen. They were right-handed. They were familiar to the use of computers and touchscreen devices.

The task consisted on positioning twenty-five targets with drag-and-drop gestures on a tablet (Samsung Galaxy Note 10.1 inches screen). The interactive system was set to display nine large and sixteen small targets and their sizes were: 46 × 35 mm for large and 35 × 27 mm for small targets on the tablet.

Participants were seated and the tablet was horizontally placed on the desk in front of them. The top of the device was 30 cm from the border of the desk. Participants executed three iterations of the task. They used their index finger to interact with the system. Figure 1 illustrates the set of the experiment.

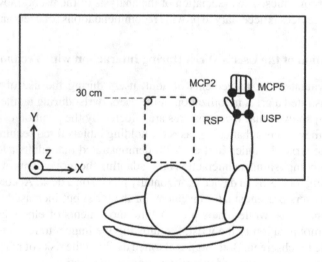

Fig. 1. Experimental set

The postures of the users have been captured through an optoelectronic motion capture system (Qualisys AB, Gothenburg, Sweden). This motion capture system was chosen because it is not invasive and do not disturb the movements of the users during the execution of the task. Four reflective markers were placed at the users' right hand and forearm: metacarpi 2 (MCP2) and 5 (MCP5), radial (RSP) and ulnar styloid process (UCP). The markers' positions were registered in three dimensions (X, Y, Z) at sampling rate of 200 Hz, tracking of the movements of the users' wrists.

4   Data Analysis

At total, 1125 gestures were registered (15 participants × 3 iteration series × 25 targets). Data from motion capture was synchronized with touch information registered from the interactive system (timestamp and coordinates).

In this paper, we present a preliminary analysis of the movements of the users' wrist. The articular angles were calculated through the coordinates of the anatomical markers MCP2, MCP5, RSP and USP in relation to the coordinates of the device, as illustrated in Figs. 2 and 3. Articular angles vary from neutral position (0 degrees) to increased deviations (negative or positive angles, until 45 degrees or over). Radial deviation is positive and ulnar deviation is negative as illustrated on Fig. 2. Extension angles are positive and flexion angles are negative, as illustrated on Fig. 3.

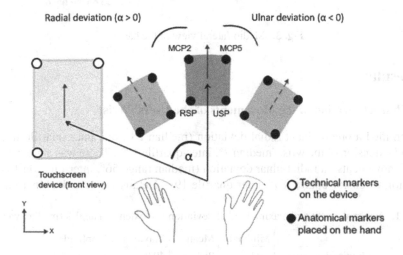

Fig. 2. Dorsal view of the hand

Median deviation angles (minimal, mean and maximal deviations) and median amplitudes of movements have also been calculated for each subject at each situation of the task. Then, for the analysis of the users' movements, we calculated the mean percent of time participants' wrist spent on different postures during the execution of the task.

For the analysis of performances, we calculated the median time for positioning a target and the median number of errors from data recorded by the interactive system.

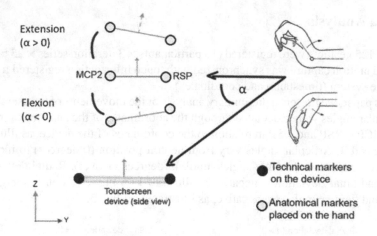

Fig. 3. Medio-lateral view of the hand

5   Results

5.1   Characterization of the Movements of the Users' Wrist

We identified a predominant radial deviation (median 28°, one inter-quartile interval 16°) and extension of the wrist (median 7°, inter-quartile 12°). There was a great amplitude of movements on radial-ulnar deviation (median range 56°, inter-quartile 19) and on flexion-extension angles (37°, inter-quartile 19°). Details are described in Table 1.

Table 1. Minimal, mean and maximal radial deviation and extension angles (median values)

	Minimal	Mean	Maximal	Amplitude
Radial deviation	−8°	28°	49°	56°
Extension	−6°	7°	32°	37°

Figure 4 describes the percent of time participants spent on radial or ulnar deviated postures of the wrist during the task. On average, radial deviation was most of the time characterized by an articular angle between 20° and 40° (52% of the time of interaction). Only 8% of the time the wrist was close to a neutral position (near 0°, between -5 and 5°). 28% of the time the radial deviation was inferior to 20° while 12% of the time there was a great radial deviation (superior to 40°). The users' wrist assumed an ulnar deviated posture 7% of the time during interaction.

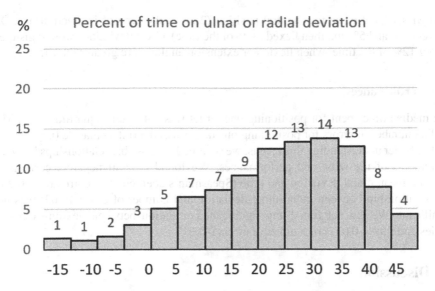

Fig. 4. Percent of time on ulnar (negative) or radial (positive) deviated postures of the wrist during interaction

Figure 5 describes the percent of time participants spent on flexed or extended postures of the wrist during the task. On average, the users' wrist were extended most of the time (61% of the time of interaction). Extension was characterized by small angles, between 5° and 15° during 45% of the time. The mobilization can be described by the

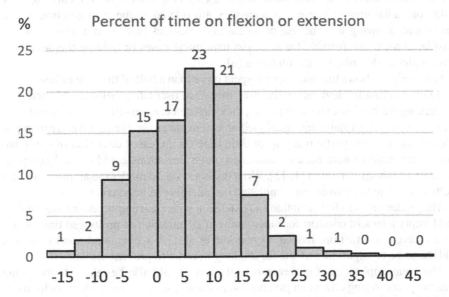

Fig. 5. Percent of time on flexed (negative) or extended (positive) postures of the wrist during interaction

time wrists spent close to a neutral position (32% of the time of interaction near 0°, between -5° and 5°) and then flexed (27% of the time). Great deviations were registered during 12% of the time, when flexion or extension angles were greater than 15°.

5.2 Performances

The median time spent for positioning one target was 4.4 s (inter-quartile 1.5 s). The median number of errors for positioning one target was 0.4 (inter-quartile 0.9).

For better understanding this results, we searched for possible relationships between movements of the wrist and performances. We found a small negative correlation between mean radial deviation and time (Spearman's coefficient of correlation -0.25). The relationship between radial-ulnar deviation and number of errors (0.03) was not significant. We did not found any significant correlation between flexion-extension angles and time (-0.07) nor number of errors (-0.01).

6 Discussion

In the present study, we used a motion capture system to assess the movements of older adults during interaction with touchscreen in order to find the relationship between their movements and performances for an interaction task. In this preliminary analysis, we evaluated the time users' wrist assumed deviations from neutral positions during interaction with finger on a tablet.

The time spent on different postures describes the movements of this articulation during the task. Median angles and amplitudes we observed demonstrate a predominant radial deviation and extension of the wrist with a great amplitude of movements (superior to 45° on radial-ulnar). These characteristics are related to the configuration of the experiment, showing that the use of touchscreen devices placed on a desk could be considered more comfortable for the wrist than using cases or holding the device on tilted angles as described in the literature [9].

Our analysis shows that participants spent more than a half of the time of interaction (52%) on fixed radial deviated postures of the wrist, oscillating between 20° and 40°. Concerning the flexion-extension angles, they variate between -10° and 10° about 64% of the time, which explains the small median extension angle. Despite the great amplitudes of movements, participants spent little time on increased deviation of the wrist. This is important to note because increased angle deviations could cause injuries or disorders of this articulation [11, 13]. Wrist disorders could hinder the abilities of older adults to execute the movements employed on touchscreen interaction.

The predominant radial deviation and extension with great amplitudes of movements could imply a lack of comfort for older adults after intensive or prolonged time of use of touchscreen interaction. Indeed, Dennerlein et al. [15] recommend users to do not hold the same configuration of use for too long in order to prevent discomfort.

The great amplitudes of movements of the wrist could also be related to the group of participants. Aging effects on psychomotor system can result on difficulties for users to execute or perceive the movements of the wrist [14], which could imply on bigger movements of this articulation for accomplishing the gestures of interaction. This hypothesis should be further investigated with another study, comparing older aged users with a younger group of people.

The values reported in this paper describes a general characterization for a group of older-aged adults. When evaluating users with different functional capacities, we would recommend to take into account the inter-individual differences such as minimal and maximal angular deviations of radial-ulnar or flexion-extension of the wrist. Further evaluations are needed for identifying postures and positions of the users' bodies that could present a risk for developing musculoskeletal injuries for older and younger users.

Our study demonstrates that assessing the users' movements during the evaluation of interaction with technologies should also be considered in order to provide recommendations for users with different functional capacities or users with special needs. Indeed, the analysis of the movements of the users could be used in order to better understand the causes of their difficulties and provide appropriate assistance.

7 Conclusion

In the present study we presented a preliminary analysis of the movements of the users' wrist during interaction with touchscreen. We demonstrated a predominant radial deviation and extension of this articulation and great amplitude of movements for older-aged adults. Participants executed drag-and-drop interaction with their index finger on a tablet, horizontally placed on a desk. The results we presented encourage the use of movement analysis for understanding the differences in performances for users with different skills and functional capacities.

Designers should consider the impact of ergonomics on the usability and accessibility of interactive technologies. In view of the adoption of touchscreen devices by older aged users, improve comfort of use could also determine a better user experience.

Acknowledgements. We cordially thank Julien Jacquier-Brett for his contribution during postures assessment and initial treatment of movement data. Lilian Genaro Motti has been supported by Phd Scholarship Ciências sem fronteiras, CNPQ, Brazil (#237079/2012-7).

References

1. Bachynskyi, M., Palmas, G., Oulasvirta, A., Steimle, J., Weinkauf, T.: Performance and ergonomics of touch surfaces: a comparative study using biomechanical simulation. In: Proceedings of ACM CHI 2015, Seoul, Korea, pp. 1817–1826 (2015)
2. Pereira, A., Miller, T., Huang, Y.-M., Odell, D., Rempel, D.: Holding a tablet computer with one hand. In: Proceedings Human Factors and Ergonomics Society 57th Annual Meeting, vol. 57, pp. 1634–1638 (2013)
3. Kim, J.H., Aulck, L., Bartha, M.C., Harper, C.A., Johnson, P.W.: Differences in typing forces, muscle activity, comfort, and typing performance among virtual, notebook, and desktop keyboards. Appl. Ergon. **45**, 1406–1413 (2014)

4. Young, J.G., Trudeau, M., Odell, D., Marinelli, K., Dennerlein, J.T.: Touch-screen tablet user configurations and case-supported tilt affect head and neck flexion angles. Work **41**, 81–91 (2012)
5. Mallenius, S., Rossi, M., Tuunainen, V.: Factors affecting the adoption and use of mobile devices and services by elderly people–results from a pilot study. In: 6th Annual Global Mobility Roundtable (2007)
6. Caprani, N., O'Connor, N., Gurrin, C.: Touch screens for the older user. In: Cheein, F.A. (ed.) Assistive Technologies, InTech (2012)
7. Motti, L.G., Vigouroux, N., Gorce, P.: Ease-of-use of tactile interaction for novice older adults. In: Zhou, J., Salvendy, G. (eds.) ITAP 2015. LNCS, vol. 9193, pp. 463–474. Springer, Cham (2015). doi:10.1007/978-3-319-20892-3_45
8. Jacquier-Bret, J., Gorce, P., Motti, L.G., Vigouroux, N.: Biomechanical analysis of upper limb during the use of touchscreen motion strategies identification. Ergonomics **60**(3), 358–365 (2014). (accepted to publication)
9. Young, J.G., Trudeau, M.B., Odell, D., Marinelli, K., Dennerlein, J.T.: Wrist and shoulder posture and muscle activity during touch-screen tablet use: Effects of usage configuration, tablet type, and interacting hand. Work **45**, 59–71 (2013)
10. Kim, J.H., Aulck, Lovenoor S., Thamsuwan, O., Bartha, Michael C., Harper, Christy A., Johnson, Peter W.: The effects of touch screen virtual keyboard key sizes on typing performance, typing biomechanics and muscle activity. In: Duffy, V.G. (ed.) DHM 2013. LNCS, vol. 8026, pp. 239–244. Springer, Heidelberg (2013). doi:10.1007/978-3-642-39182-8_28
11. Malchaire, J.B., Cock, N.A., Robert, A.R.: Prevalence of musculoskeletal disorders at the wrist as a function of angles, forces, repetitiveness and movement velocities. Scand. J. Work. Env. Heal. **22**, 176–181 (1996)
12. Irwin, C.B., Sesto, M.E.: Performance and touch characteristics of disabled and non-disabled participants during a reciprocal tapping task using touch screen technology. Appl. Ergon. **43**, 1038–1043 (2012)
13. Carey, E.J., Gallwey, T.J.: Effects of wrist posture, pace and exertion on discomfort. Int. J. Ind. Ergon. **29**, 85–94 (2002)
14. Wright, M.L., Adamo, D.E., Brown, S.H.: Age-related declines in the detection of passive wrist movement. Neurosci. Lett. **500**, 108–112 (2011)
15. Dennerlein, J.T.: The state of ergonomics for mobile computing technology. Work **52**, 269–277 (2015)

Investigation into the Discrepancies Between Writing on Paper and Writing on a Touchscreen Device

Yu-Chen Hsieh[1(✉)], Ke Jia Hung[1], and Hsuan Lin[2]

[1] Graduate School of Industrial Design, National Yunlin University of Science and Technology,
Douliu, Yunlin, Taiwan
chester.3d@gmail.com

[2] Department of Product Design, Tainan University of Technology, Tainan, Taiwan
te0038@mail.tut.edu.tw

Abstract. Due to the complexity of text in Asian languages and hence the complexity of input methods, demand for stylus-type input is higher in Asian than the Western world, prompting Asian tech brands such as Samsung and Sony to introduce smart devices with in-built stylus to cater to this group of consumers. To account for general usage, this research has opted to employ mobile devices with built-in stylus as test equipment. In addition, in order to account for the difference between various sizes of devices, the researchers have chosen three device dimensions: 5.7 in, 9.7 in, and 12 in, for the tests, and each size of device is compared to an identically sized piece of paper. In consideration of the locality of the behavior of users, the subjects are asked to input using Traditional Chinese text only. Results from the experiment showed, in terms of writing behavior, that almost all subjects put the device flat on a table for writing, and that the habit of spinning the paper to an angle for writing is transferred to writing on a device. The finger positions on a stylus change depending on the properties of the device, especially when writing on the 5.7 in, the smallest device, touching the stylus at the smaller supporting points or completely dangle the pen away from the palm occurs much more often than on the bigger device sizes. In terms of writing performance, writing time on a device is generally longer than that on paper. The words written on a device are bigger and grow in size as the device size increases on the devices, but on the different sizes of paper the words stay relatively the same size. Words written on a device are generally less legible than those written on paper.

Keywords: Mobile device · Touchscreen · Stylus · Writing performance

1 Purpose

Recent technology has brought about a new type of computer interface enabling new modes of operation which have impacted the user experience of computers. Since the pen was modified into an input instrument known as a stylus, a most quickly accepted and easily adapted type of pre-learned input instrument which has proven to be more effective at the task of selecting items than the computer mouse [1]. In addition to the mouse-like operations, the stylus provided a more intuitive way of computer input, and

© Springer International Publishing AG 2017
J. Zhou and G. Salvendy (Eds.): ITAP 2017, Part II, LNCS 10298, pp. 27–41, 2017.
DOI: 10.1007/978-3-319-58536-9_3

for certain parts of computer operation, the combination of voice and writing input were more efficient than the combination of the keyboard and the mouse [3].

The advancement of technology, however, has not affected people's dependence on the pen [11]; studies have likewise shown that writing with a pen is better for learning than the keyboard, exhibiting increase in cognitive understanding and longer memorative duration [10]. Mobile devices in recent years have reverted back to using handwriting as a primary means of operating the product, such as the Samsung Galaxy Note, the Microsoft Surface, or the iPad Pro, which have stressed handwriting and drawing as their primary features.

Nevertheless, due to technical limitations and tactile distinctions, a significant discrepancy in perception is still present between writing with a stylus on a mobile device and writing with a pen on paper. This research investigated the differences between writing Chinese text on various sizes of mobile devices and paper. Due to the structural complexity of Chinese characters, Typing in Chinese is much more complex than Western languages causing greater demand for stylus based writing than western countries. In addition, this research was conducted in Taiwan, and all of the participants use Chinese as their primary language. This research thus focused on the performance of Chinese text writing. The observations were divided into two criteria:

(1) Writing behavior: posture and habits, how the user holds the writing instrument, the points of pivot while writing, and the angle of rotation of the writing surface.
(2) Writing performance: writing time, the size of written Chinese text, neatness and legibility.

2   Literature

2.1   The Ergonomic of the Use of Stylus

Stylus-based input works by employing the habits of pen use onto a computer interface, which, when compared to using a mouse, is not only more intuitive, but also far more comfortable. While holding a stylus the elbow angle is about 45 degrees less than when holding a mouse, contributing to more relaxed muscles. The operating process also benefits from being able to utilize more parts of the arm for motor control, avoiding Repetitive Strain Injury (RSI) or Carpal Tunnel Syndrome which can result from overuse of wrist muscles. In addition, the development of multi-touch interface has made stylus use even more flexible and more preferable than the mouse [4]. Luo's [9] comparison of the dimensions of styluses on the market revealed that those with the combined dimensions of 140 mm long and 8 mm thick are ideal for use for all operating tasks on a screen, perhaps due to this specification being closest to that of pen and paper writing. Luo further suggests that the shaft of the stylus should be longer than 100 mm in order for users to hold it at the three optimal points of the hand: the thumb, index finger, and the crevice between the thumb and index finger. In addition, Huang's [5] investigation into the stylus shape concluded that styluses with a circular cross-section performs best for writing, ovals are best for drawing stability, and hexagonal are best for firm holding.

2.2   Writing Behavior

Stylus-based interface works by emulating writing with pen and paper on a device screen with a stylus, transferring the habits of holding a pen and writing with it on paper onto doing the same on a digital surface [3, 12]. Conventional writing can be discussed in three categories: writing environment, position of paper, and method of holding the pen. For a person to have a suitable writing environment, the following criteria need to be met: (1) consolidate the height of the seat (chair) and the writing surface (table) for the table height to be no taller than the elbow. (2) the body should be 10 cm away from the edge of the table, the distance between the eyes and the paper should be maintained at around 30 cm, and the forearm should rest halfway on the table. (3) A sufficiently bright light source should be to the above-left of the paper (above-right for left-handed individuals).

The position of the paper should have a rotation of 10–20° to the left. so that the upper-right corner is slightly higher than the upper-left corner, in order to compensate for how the arm exerts force according to ergonomics, where the wrist tilts to the upper-right instead of being parallel to the upper edge of the table [7]. The pen should be held with a three-point pinch for normal sized pens, and a lateral pinch would be used for styluses with smaller dimensions [14]. In addition, when writing with the stylus, the user typically avoids contact between the screen and the palm or finger, resulting in two primary pivot points of the hand on the screen which differs with the writing surface (Fig. 1). Luo [9] therefore proposes the design of dedicated supports to improve stylus writing.

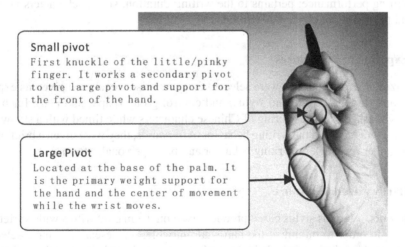

Small pivot
First knuckle of the little/pinky finger. It works a secondary pivot to the large pivot and support for the front of the hand.

Large Pivot
Located at the base of the palm. It is the primary weight support for the hand and the center of movement while the wrist moves.

Fig. 1. Two pivot points used for writing

According to Chien's [2] research, 72% of stylus users will retain the way they hold conventional pens when holding a stylus, but the positions they hold the stylus may be somewhat lowered, with increased muscle intensity to maintain stability. In addition, the wrist and the pinky may be used as support to keep minimum contact between the palm and the screen.

2.3   Writing Performance

Henderson's [13] research discovered that when the written content is more simplistic, readability is not affected by writing pace, but when content complexity or quantity of writing increases, the pace of writing can affect the quality of the words written as well as the flow of writing. Li [8] also discovered in her research that the speeds of transcribing common words and uncommon words are significantly different. Discretion was therefore prudent during design of the writing performance test, otherwise the experiment result would be adversely affected. In terms of readability, Chinese character strokes are not simply made up of a combination of stroke lines; when the strokes are out of order, the writing speed and aesthetics can be affected. The readability of Chinese text is associated with the Chinese character structure and the continuity between the characters. Character structure can affect readability by having incorrect overlapping, addition, or omission of strokes, or the spread of character blocks or their incorrect position or proportioning. Continuity between characters pertains to the text size, text spacing, the horizontal evenness, and general layout neatness [6].

3   Research Method

This research is divided into writing behavior and writing performance for investigation.

(1) Writing behavior: pertains to how the user holds the writing instrument, the points of pivot while writing, and the angle of rotation of the writing surface.
(2) Writing performance: pertains to the writing duration, size of characters written, and the quality of characters written.

3.1   Experiment Procedures

Three sizes of writing surface were selected for comparison, each size given its experiment group (mobile device and stylus) and control group (paper and pen). Each test subject was asked to write a string of Chinese characters while timed with a stopwatch while a camera recorded the writing behavior. Afterwards, they were given a brief interview to gather feedback on writing behavior and basic personal information.

3.2   Hardware and Software

Equipments.   Various stylus based products exist on the market with a wide variety of hardware. In order to minimize the hardware variable, our researchers have selected Samsung mobile devices which include electromagnetic induction styluses for the experiment. Their specifications are as Fig. 2.

Samsung Galaxy Note pro, 12.2"   Samsung Tab A, 9.7"   Samsung Galaxy Note 3, 5.7"

Fig. 2. Mobile devices for the experiment

Software used for experiment. This research selected 'MyScript Smart Note' for the experiment as depicted in Fig. 3. Compared to the free-writing app 'S Note' pre-installed in all Samsung devices, 'MyScript Smart Note' provides a superior writing experience, whether it be decreased lag-time or smoother pen-stroke display. The app has an additional 'write mode' which recognizes written character and is therefore able to digitize the written content and save it as a text file. The stylus included in the device is also fully compatible and functionally supported. The above reasons resulted in the app's selection for use in the experiment.

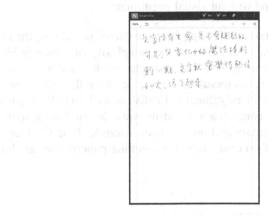

Fig. 3. MyScript smart note interface image

Writing instruments. The selection of writing instruments require a digital writing instrument and a paper based writing instrument. For writing on paper, the popular 'Penrote NO.6506' black ballpoint pen was chosen to match the color of stroke trails displayed by the digital app [2]. For digital writing, the 'S pen' stylus built into each of the three mobile devices was used, as depicted by Fig. 4.

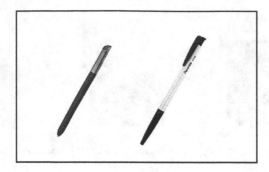

Fig. 4. The writing instruments for the experiment (left: S pen, right: Penrote NO.6506)

Environment and participants. The experiment took place in a well lit interior prepped with desks and chairs for the participants. The seat of the backrest-equipped chairs is 430 mm off the ground. The seat surface area is 360 mm x 420 mm. The desk is 730 mm tall. The experiment contains three sets of dimensions of writing surfaces, each dimension is assigned 30 participants for a total of 90 participants who conducted the writing task on both pen and paper as well as stylus on mobile device. The participants consist of college graduates and post-graduates between the ages of 18 and 24, whom have all had at least one year of experience on a mobile device or tablet PC, and all of whom are right handed and without visual impairment.

Experiment text. Due to the research having been conducted in Taiwan, the primary language used for the participants is Chinese, the complexity of which is ideal for researches to observe during writing how the character strokes and structural form change when writing Chinese. It has therefore been selected for this experiment even though most participants are sufficiently fluent in English as well. In order to ensure the straightforwardness of the test content, a word string was chosen from a sixth grade elementary Mandarin supplementary text book 'Smart Lifestyle' from Chapter 1 'The Magic of Words' consisting of 40 characters, not counting punctuation, as shown in Fig. 5.

Experiment Procedure.

(1) The participants were seated followed by a briefing on the experiment purpose and necessary precautions.

(2) A projector screen displays the experiment text for every participant to see and transcribe once on to a mobile device, and once on to paper, for a total of two transcriptions. To minimize familiarity, the order of paper and device is randomized. A break of 5 min is taken before the second transcription.

(3) After the writing experiment is completed, the participants are given a brief interview to gather feedback.

文字沒有生命的，

是不會說話的，

只要仙女的魔法杖輕輕一點，

文字就會變得熱情如火，

活了起來。

Fig. 5. Writing experiment text (translated into English: *"Words are lifeless; they don't talk. However, with the tap of the fairy's magic wand, the words become passionate and alive"*)

Data collection and analysis. The experiment supervisors performed observations and measurements, and corroborated information gathered using the recorded videos. The observations made emphasized the following:

(1) Writing habit: the pivots of the hand on the writing surface, whether pivots were used and where they were.
(2) Rotation: Observations were made as to whether the participants rotated the writing surface, and videos were made and used to determine the angle of rotation, whereby rotation within 5° were considered none.
(3) Size of written text: a font size chart is used to determine the size of text produced by the participants.
(4) Quality of written text: In order to maintain an objective standard of critique of the quality of written text, this research employed a focus group consisting of four Mandarin instructors to evaluate the written text in 3 categories: strokes, proportion, blank space.
    Stroke: pertains to the correct stroke order of the written text as well as neatness of the strokes.
    Proportion: pertains to the size and position of the character blocks in relation to each other.
    Blank Space: pertains to the straightness of the written words and their indentation to other strokes. In short, neatness of layout.

The panel of four Mandarin experts were asked to score the writings from each group from 1-point to 5-points.

4   Results

Of the 90 participants of the experiment, 41 individuals have had experience in writing or drawing with a stylus (45.5%) while the other 49 individuals have not (54.5%). The results of the observations and measurements are as following.

4.1 Writing Behavior

Rotation of writing surface. 90 participants produced 180 text samples, of which 133 samples (74%) were written while rotated. Tilted papers consisted of 72 samples, 80% of all paper samples, and tilted devices consisted of 61 samples, 68% of all device samples, revealing a 12% higher ratio of rotation of paper to that of devices (see Fig. 6). The results also revealed that those with the habit of tilting the paper while writing were the ones who rotated the device, with 85% of paper rotaters maintaining the habit while writing on the device. In addition, medium-sized surfaces were rotated the most, followed by small and then large surfaces. This revealed that the habit of rotating the device can present on either digital or paper surfaces, but participants are slightly less likely to rotate a digital surface. Furthermore, no participant was found who rotated the digital device without also rotating the paper. 9.7 in writing surfaces experienced the least variation; participants given medium sized writing surfaces exhibited the least change in habit of rotation between the two surfaces.

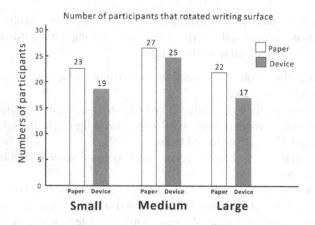

Fig. 6. Number of times writing surface was rotated

Use of pivots. When writing on paper, all participants used both large and small pivots of the writing hand, which is resting almost the entire bottom edge of the hand on the paper. When writing on a digital device, on the other hand, 19 participants used only the small pivot or suspended the hand entirely. The ratio of changing pivoting patterns from small to large devices were 40%, 10%, and 13% respectively, revealing the highest change in pivoting habits happened on small devices. The small devices group had 9 participants who used only the small pivot for writing, which is much greater than other device groups (see Fig. 7).

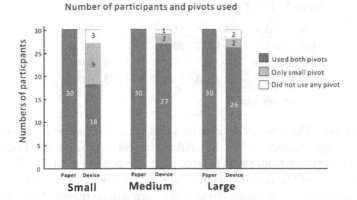

Fig. 7. Participants usage of large and small pivots during writing for various sizes of devices

4.2 Writing Performance Results

Writing time. The average writing time for each groups are indicated in Fig. 8. Comparing the same sizes together, writing on paper was faster than writing on a screen for each size, and the difference in speed on paper increased as surface size became smaller, while 9.7 in device screen performed best in terms of speed. ANOVA analysis of surface size to writing speed did not reveal a significant difference, but T-test analysis of the difference in writing time revealed a significant difference between small and medium sized surfaces, indicating the effect of the properties of the writing surface were more prominent on these two sizes, but not as much on the large devices (Table 1).

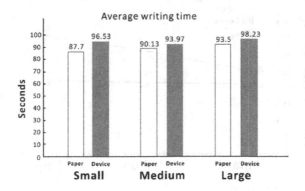

Fig. 8. Writing time of various sizes of both surface types

Table 1. Pair T test for writing time of paper and device

Paper vs device	M	SD	t	Sig.
Large size	−4.733	20.596	−1.259	0.218
Medium size	−3.833	8.175	−2.568	0.016*
Small size	−8.833	10.011	−4.833	0.000*

* $P < 0.05$ significant

Written text size. The changes in the written text size of the groups are as indicated in Fig. 9. The change in paper surface area did not have a significant effect on text size. The average in text size from small to large paper surfaces were 21.5 → 21.6 → 21.9 exhibiting a growth of less than 0.4 pts. A significant growth of average written text size is experienced, however, on digital devices as screen size increased. Average text size from small to large devices was 25.9 → 31.5 → 36.1 exhibiting a growth of over 10pts. In addition, text sizes on digital devices were significantly larger than text sizes on paper overall, making this finding the most significant as well as the most interesting difference between paper and digital device. Further ANOVA comparing the text sizes revealed that the difference between text sizes on paper was not significant ($F(2, 87) = 0.095$, $p = 0.910$), indicating no effect of paper size on text size, but that difference on digital devices was significant for all sizes ($F(2, 87) = 16.105$, $p < 0.001$) as the text size increased with the size of digital device (Tables 2, 3). T-test analysis also revealed a significant difference between paper and digital device for each of the three tested sizes, where the text size on digital devices were all significantly larger than that on paper, consistent with findings (Table 4).

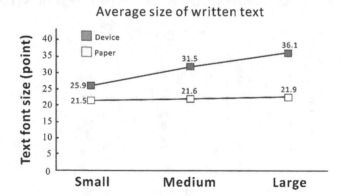

Fig. 9. Text size results for all test groups

Table 2. ANOVA analysis for written text size

		SS	df	MS	F	Sig
paper	Between groups	2.156	2	1.078	0.095	0.910
	Within groups	988.167	87	11.358		
	Total	990.322	89			
Devices	Between group	1565.600	2	782.800	16.105	0.000*
	Within groups	4228.800	87	48.607		
	Total	5794.400	89			

*The mean difference is significant at 0.05 level

Table 3. Post hoc test by Tukey for written text size of device

	Size (I)	Size (J)	Mean Difference(I-J)	Sig.
Paper	Large	medium	0.267	0.950
		Small	0.367	0.907
	Medium	Large	−0.267	0.950
		small	0.100	0.993
	small	Large	−0.367	0.907
		medium	−0.100	0.993
Devices	Large	medium	4.600*	0.033
		small	10.200*	0.000
	Medium	Large	−4.600*	0.033
		small	5.600*	0.007
	Small	Large	−10.200*	0.000
		medium	−5.600*	0.007

*The mean difference is significant at 0.05 level

Table 4. T-test for written text size for paper and device in different size

Size	M	SD	SEM	t	p
Small	−4.367	2.606	0.476	−9.177	0.000*
medium	−9.867	5.361	0.979	−10.081	0.000*
Large	−14.200	8.310	1.517	−9.359	0.000*

* P < 0.05 significant.

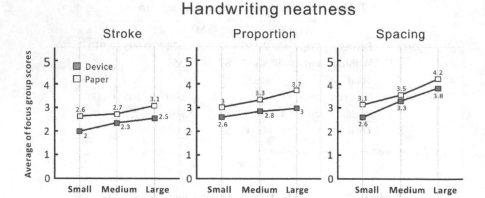

Fig. 10. Comparison of writing neatness

4.3 Writing Neatness

The scores of the categories of neatness of handwriting is as depicted in Fig. 10. From the scores of the three categories it can be seen that paper based writing groups performed superior to the digital writing groups. In addition, increase in size of both paper and digital device produced ever better neatness. It can thus be speculated that the size of the writing surface directly affects writing neatness, even though writing on paper is still superior to writing on digital device.

5   Discussions

5.1   Smaller Screen Has Greater Change to Influence Writing Behavior

From the experiments in this research, it can be observed that a large portion of users have the habit of rotating the writing surface (around 70–80%) and those with the habit of rotated writing may transfer the habit onto writing on a digital device. It is interesting to note that there were no participants who rotated the digital device but not the paper. The medium writing surface (9.7 in) showed the least change of behavior, suggesting that it is the size that least alters the habit of rotated writing. As to how the writing instrument is held, results from this research were similar to the study conducted by Chien [2], where the majority of users held a stylus the same way they held a pen. This research further found that when writing on a digital device, particularly for small device users, more than half of the participants write with only the small pivot or even a suspended hand. The subsequent interview revealed the reason to be an apprehension to unintentionally triggering unwanted functions if the palm makes contact with the device screen. Therefore, it is suggested that this psychological element be taken into account during the design of small devices to alleviate the accidental triggering of functions in order to avoid forcing a change of writing habit for the user.

5.2   The Size of the Device Affects Writing Time

In all size groups, writing on digital surface cost more time than writing on paper, with writing on a medium digital surface taking the least amount of time. On the other hand, the larger the paper surface size, the longer the writing time became. Our researchers speculate that the techniques and habitual motions of writing on paper were the same, and therefore the size of the text characters would be similar, meaning that the additional time was due to the increase in paper size enlarging the spacing between words, prompting increased displacement between characters, increasing total writing time. Due to the properties of writing on a digital device, users may change writing behavior resulting in bigger characters being written in a less fluidic manner, slowing down writing speed. The small screen can be challenging to use if the user tries to avoid triggering unwanted functions by using different hand pivots or none at all. On the other hand, a large screen surface prompted the production of larger fonts and bigger displacement of the strokes as well as the hand position, producing the slowest writing speed of all the groups. Our researchers speculate that the apprehension of touching the screen undesirably, the non-rotated writing surface due to the bulk of the larger device, and the abundance of screen writing space on the larger device prompted the user's writing behavior to produce larger writing. All in all, writing on screens too small can cause difficulty, and writing on larger screens suffered from enlarged text and increased displacement of the hand, making the medium sized digital interface the most suitable size for writing.

5.3   Stylus Based Writing Needs to Be Provided with More Writing Space

This research has shown that writing on different sized paper resulted in consistent written text size, with text size having variation of less than 1.8% and the text size between 21.5 pt and 21.9 pt. Comparatively, writing on digital devices can cause unintentional enlargement of text size, increasing with screen size. Compared with paper of the same size, words on 5.7 in, 9.7 in, and 12.2 in devices grew by 20%, 46%, and 66%, respectively. It can therefore be speculated that when writing with a stylus on a device, the properties of such constraints forced users to make maximum use of available space, and when not given lines or a grid to write on, will adjust writing according to one's own intuition, as can be seen by how the text size of writing on digital devices grew from 20% to over 60% depending on the device size. Interface designers are therefore encouraged to consider this phenomenon and provide more fitting interface features, such as suitably sized writing lines similar to paper notebooks, or space for signatures or making notes on e-books.

5.4   Paper Based Writing Is Superior to Digital Device Writing Overall

Overall, results indicate that writing performance can be affected by the constraints of the properties of the writing hardware as well as the digital interface, such as when the apprehension of unintentional screen contact alters how the stylus is held for writing, or when the bulk of the writing device stops users from rotating it to a more suitable angle for writing, which can all result in the decrease of writing speed on digital devices to that of on conventional paper. In terms of writing neatness, writing on paper is superior to writing on digital surfaces as well, possibly also due to the way the stylus is held and the properties of digital devices. However, the writing neatness on both paper and digital devices improved with the increase of size, which our researchers speculate to be related to the ample available space which allowed users to more freely conduct movements of the hand for writing and thus produced smoother and more proportional pen strokes to form the Chinese characters. The factor of making text more immaculate is therefore the size of the writing surface, and larger surfaces allow users to write neater characters.

6 Conclusion and Recommendations

Despite technology having advanced greatly closing the gap between digital device and paper, The properties of digital devices as well as user habits continue to keep the performance gap of the two types of writing open. All in all, writing on paper is significantly better than writing on screen; writing speed on paper can decrease with increasing size of paper, meaning that smaller paper sizes are better for writing, while medium sized digital devices can be the quickest device for writing. For writing neatness, paper based writing produces better looking texts than digital writing for any size, but both paper and digital device can result in neater writing with increase in size. What's more interesting to note is the difference in text size, where the increase in digital device size can inadvertently trigger an increase in text size, as an increase between 20% to over 60% was observed in the experiment.

Designs henceforth would benefit from consideration of this phenomenon, and include into different devices an interface more suitable for writing, such as properly spaced lines for guidance and a more suitable blank area for writing. This paper was focused on Chinese text due to cultural constraints. In the future research can be done in the language of English or observing writing neatness for different specs of styluses.

References

1. Buxton, W., Scadden, L., Roulds, R., Shein, F., Rosen, M.J., Vanderheiden, G.: Human interface design and the handicapped user. In: Proceedings of CHI 1986, pp. 291–297 (1986)
2. Chien, L.S.. Exploring the stylus design through operation behaviors. Master thesis, Shih Chien University, 10.24-25.39.47, p. 58 (2012)
3. Frankish, C., Morgan, P., Noyes, J.: Pen computing: some human factors issues. In: IEEE Colloquium on Handwriting and Pen-Based Input (1994)
4. Glans, M.: Drawing Tablet – A Perfect Ergonomic Mouse Alternative? Office Orbiter, Ergonomics Office Gear, 21 April 2015
5. Huang, C.W.: A study on the writing and drawing performance affected by the cross-section of the stylus for the tablet PC. Master thesis, Department of Industrial Design, Tatung University, Taipei, Taiwan (2008)
6. Hsu, C.F.: A study on usability and interface design of table apps for learning chinese character writing. Master thesis, National Yunlin University of Science and Technology, Yunlin, Taiwan (2015)

7. Jheng, W.B.: Basic techniques for writing beautiful word. Beboss Industry. Taiwan, pp. 8–9 (2013). ISBN:9789868624023
8. Li, Y.T.: The cognitive components relating to handwriting performance of students with and without Chinese handwriting difficulties. Master thesis, National Taiwan Normal University, Tainan, Taiwan (2001)
9. Luo, S.: Performance and innovation of touch pens for computer inputs. Master thesis, Department of Industrial design, National Chen Kung University, Tainan, Taiwan (2005)
10. Mueller, P., Oppenheimer, D.M.: The pen is mightier than the keyboard: advantages of longhand over laptop note taking. Psychol. Sci. **25**(6), 1159–1168 (2014)
11. Parush, S.: Ergonomic factors influencing handwriting performance. Work **11**(3), 295–305 (1998)
12. Raynaerts, D., Brussel, H.V.: Design of an advanced computer writing tools. In: Sixth International Symposium Micro Machine and Human Science, pp. 229–234 (1995)
13. Rubin, N., Henderson, S.E.: Two sides of the same coin: variations in teaching methods and failure to learn to write. Spec. Educ. Forward Trends **9**, 17–24 (1982)
14. Yang, J.C.: A study on the usability of stylus location and design for smart phone. Master thesis, Department of Industrial design, Tatung University, Taipei, Taiwan (2010)

A Conceptual Design for a Smart Photo Album Catered to the Elderly

Hui-Jiun Hu[1(✉)], Pei-Fen Wu[2], and Wang-Chin Tsai[3]

[1] Department of Visual Arts, National Chiayi University, Chiayi, Taiwan
momo@mail.ncyu.edu.tw
[2] Department of Information Management,
National Changhua University of Education, Changhua, Taiwan
[3] Department of Product and Media Design,
Fo Guang University, Yilan, Taiwan

Abstract. As Taiwan becomes an aged society, the problems caused by memory and cognitive impairments have added to the enormous medical care costs, increasing the burden placed on the next generation. Medical studies have found that adding brain-protective factors into daily life and engaging in mental activities that stimulate brain function, creative activities, or regular exercise can significantly prevent mental and memory loss. Therefore, this study used the concepts within reminiscence therapy to develop a smart photo album in order to improve elderly memories and ability to feel happiness. The user-centered design focused on care for the elderly to accomplish the conceptual design. Observation and interviews were first conducted to explore the needs and ideas of the elderly had regarding photographs (the discover step). Then, the key factors for design were analyzed and defined by affinity diagram (the define step). We founded 4 affinity factors relating to the mental ideals of the elderly: Memories (k1), Sharing (k2), Emotion (k3) and Lack (k4). Next, the scenario story was used to generate rich and innovative conceptual designs and to integrate new technologies (the develop step). In this study the smart photo album was named Fond Memories that presented two features: "Image memory sharing" and "Emotion detection". These shared memories create empathy, relieve depression, and allow the elderly to enjoy memories with their families.

Keywords: Smart photo album · Reminiscence therapy · Conceptual design

1 Introduction

Population aging has become an inevitable global trend; coupled with the extremely low birth rate, Taiwan has quickly become an aging society where the elderly will soon comprise the majority of society. People's bodies, senses, memories, and cognitive functions deteriorate as they age, and these the elderly often experience frustration, difficulties, and distress as they adjust. Hsieh (2002) found that the problems and obstacles the elderly face regarding their emotional adjustments are often ignored or underestimated. This may be due to the fact that their mood disorder is expressed by physical symptoms of aging, thus becoming masked depression. A 2006 survey taken by Global Views Monthly found that adults over the age of 70 are Taiwan's loneliest

© Springer International Publishing AG 2017
J. Zhou and G. Salvendy (Eds.): ITAP 2017, Part II, LNCS 10298, pp. 42–52, 2017.
DOI: 10.1007/978-3-319-58536-9_4

age group, comprising 20.3% of the total population. It was reported that the lack of companionship was the cause of their loneliness (Chiang 2006).

IEK (2011) also found that the environments in which Taiwanese senior citizens are typically active comprise at their home (87.7%), nearby parks (66.4%), and activity centers (34.5%) (IEK 2011). These statistics suggest that Taiwanese senior citizens prefer to stay at home. These citizens, who comprise men and women who lack exercise or are recovering from strokes, are more prone to the loss of memory and cognitive functions, even increasing the chances of contracting Alzheimer's disease (AD). However, the elderly in addition to physical disease and physiological function of the decline, their mental health can be not ignored such as Dementia, Depression, Anxiety, Stress, and Low self-esteem. Without immediate help and treatment, the Well-being of the elderly can be seriously damaged, and even their quality of life may be affected.

In recent years, a study conducted at the University of New South Wales also found that the elderly who watched more programming on the National Geographic Channel and documentaries on natural ecosystems scored significantly higher on tests for language and cognitive skills. Dr. Haruyama Shigeo (1996) also pointed out that sustained positive emotions release a type of β-endorphine in the brain that can help retain youthful and happy feelings and can even fight cancer cells. This sort of happy hormone can significantly improve memory, immunity, and spiritual happiness. Psychologist Dr. Enomoto Hiroaki (2013) found that the results of memory training using interactions between the five senses were the best and that memories related to feelings were the least likely to be forgotten (emotional effect).

Furthermore, Psychologists used memory therapy to improve the mental state of the elderly, improve self-esteem, reduce depression, improve their life satisfaction, reduce stress, have a significant impact (Haight and Burnside 1993; Matteson and Munsat 1982; Nugent 1995). Therefore, this study is based on the benefits of memory therapy to develop a smart album. We will explore the feelings and needs of the elderly when viewing photos, and then propose conceptual designs that integrate ICT. Smart albums look forward to meeting the wisdom of life, and to achieve a more comfortable, safer orange technology as the goal.

2   Research Method

An analytical framework based on user experience assist researchers and designers in understanding the thinking patterns and logic of users. In addition, this framework further allows researchers to objectively identify problem patterns, assisting them in accurately designing user-centered products. Numerous related studies show that the users interact with systems to pursue the feelings and psychological satisfaction provided by the products based on the consideration of basic functionality and the satisfaction of usage. This further suggests that users no longer place their focus solely on needs, but also emphasize their desired, which complies with the theory of Norman (2004), who contended that the satisfaction of desire can better facilitate the success of a product than that of needs. And consistent with presented by Weinschenk (2010) that products are easier-to-use when the product's conceptual model resonates with the user's mental model.

This study used the concepts within reminiscence therapy to develop a smart photo album in order to improve the elderly memories and ability to feel happiness. The user-centered design focused on care for the elderly to accomplish the conceptual design. Observation and interviews were first conducted to explore the needs and ideas of the elderly for photographs (the discover step). Next, the critical factors for design were analyzed and defined (the defined step). Finally, the scenario story was used to generate rich and innovative conceptual designs and to integrate new technologies (the develop step).

- **The discover step**: observation interviews were first conducted to explore the needs and ideas the elderly had regarding photographs. Six elderly over the age of 65 were interviewed in this study. Three of the participants were male and three were female, and their average age was 74.8. Table 1 shows the participants' basic information. The participants were asked to provide five of their favorite photographs and describe their memories, thoughts, and feelings regarding the content of each picture. Meanwhile, the emotions and expressions of the participants were observed. The interview time was approximately 1.5 h and the content was recorded as five categories: A(Activities), E(Environments), I(Interactions), O (Objects), and U(Users).
- **The define step**: the key factors for design were analyzed and defined. The collected qualitative data was written on individual post-it notes. Then, bottom-up inductive and axial coding to cluster similar concepts into a concept group, forming the aforementioned affinity factors. Coding is an operation process that first decomposes and conceptualizes data, and then reconstructs the concepts using alternative novel methods. Through coding, complex theories can be grouped and classified (Strauss and Corbin 1990). Subsequently, the affinity diagram method proposed in the book authored by Young (2008), Mental Models: Aligning Design Strategy with Human Behavior, was employed to extract the mental models of the research subjects. Young elaborated that mental models is a tool that can establish intangible thinking patterns using organized frameworks and present these patterns using visual lists or tables. Thus, affinity can effectively compile complex data and systematically present the current important clues and areas of interest regarding the photo memories of the elderly.
- **The develop step**: according to the results of the discover step and the define step, converted into design criteria. And then used scenario story to develop the conceptual design of a smart photo album. Scenario story are fictional stories, with characters, events, products and environments. They allow us to explore product ideas and key themes in the context of a realistic future. The most typical example are ID TWO design company and Richardson Smith design company, together for Fuji Xerox to develop photocopiers panel design. More successful cases proved that whether it is to create a simple children's toys, or the development of e-commerce have a good effect (Kelley et al. 2001).

Table 1. Profile of participants

No	Title	Sex	Age	Occupation	Living conditions	Symptoms	Characteristics
A	Mr. Lee	M	83	Barber	Live alone, son and daughter live nearby	Hypertension, Heart disease, gout	Opening at eight am, closing at seven pm; sometimes dizziness uncomfortable; drinking tea; reading newspapers and chatting with the elderly neighbor; three meals a day to take care of himself; occasionally sing karaoke OK
B	Mr. Liu	M	77	Farmer	Live with family	Stomach	Plowing in the morning, drinking tea, chatting and playing chess in the afternoon
C	Mr. Chen	M	65	Worker	Live with family	Diabetes	55 years old had diabetes, change eating potato, easily swollen limbs, wound difficult to heal, can not long standing and walking
D	Ms. Pan	F	75	Housekeeper	Live with family	Lumbar	Get up early, go walking and stretching exercises in the morning
E	Ms. Cheng	F	85	Housekeeper	Live alone	Foot arthritis	About 70 years old with his family eat vegetarian, now the knees more and more weak rarely go out
F	Ms. Chiang	F	67	Housekeeper	Live with family	Foot arthritis, presbyopia	Optimistic personality, bad memory, long-term medication

3   Data Analysis and Concept Design

3.1   Data Analysis

First, we used AEIOU to record the thoughts and feelings of six elderly on the photo. The result was shown in Fig. 1. The participants pointed to the photo and excited about the interesting story:

> *I like seeing pictures of myself together with my family, but before cameras were expensive, so we didn't take that many pictures (A06). I don't like taking pictures because I don't have anything nice to wear (B11). This was taken at your uncle's wedding (C09). They all look so similar; I forget who is who (D21). This is my eldest grandson; he's so cute; he's much more handsome now, but I don't have a more recent picture (E13). This is the house I grew up in; the bathroom was built so far from the house (F04). This picture was taken when I was in the army (F08) ...*

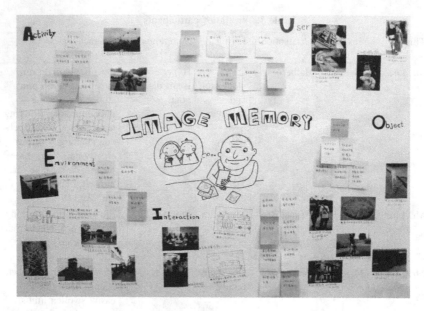

Fig. 1. Data collation using the AEIOU

Then, affinity diagramming was then used; the collected qualitative data was written on individual post-it notes for two rounds of categorization and coding. Finally, we founded 4 affinity factors relating to the mental ideals of the elderly. Memories (k1): seeing the photos of people, things, objects and places, can evoke a lot of memories (evoke memories), but some memories are fuzzy (vague memories). Sharing (k2): sharing happy story on photo, and enthusiastically introduced their families. Emotion (k3): think of the good things in past, feel happy (good mood). Think of the dead relatives or dislike the man, felt sad (sad mood). Lack (k4): at that time lack of resources (lack of resources), a rare opportunity or occasion can take pictures. Because the old photos lack, many scenes don't remember.

The collected data were organized and coded based on the affinity diagram proposed by Young (2008). The results obtained during the context observation process were compiled and converged, transforming abstract thinking patterns into physical solutions. Then, the mental models of senior citizens were compiled into lists and tables using a visualization method, as shown in Fig. 2.

The sorted categories clearly highlight important clues and areas of interest regarding the photo memories of the elderly. The results in Fig. 2 point out that photographs give importance to "Memories", "Sharing" and "Emotion" for the elderly. And, for over 65 years of age the elderly, because of the "Lack" of resources, each photograph for they more have a special significance.

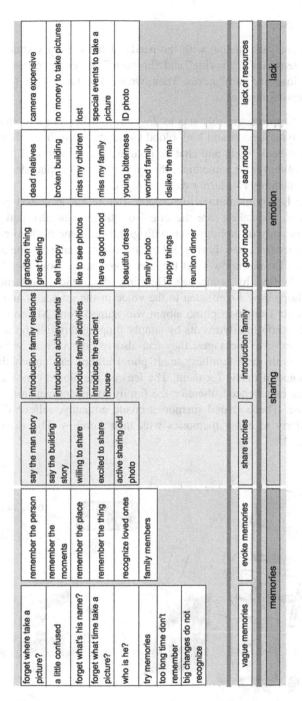

Fig. 2. Affinity diagramming of the elderly' memories

3.2 Concept Design

After the above analysis, in line with the needs of the elderly's smart photo album, should have a "Memories", "Sharing" and "Emotion" design standards. And meet their expectations of "love and care" needs. Then, we used scenario story to create rich and innovative conceptual design.

- **Characters mapping**: the role sets to 73 years old Lee grandmother. She is easy anxious; has hypertension and high blood sugar; currently lives alone; her son and grandson come back to eat and chat on holiday; knees more and more weak; poor memory and often forgot something; the spirit is not good and sleep at night poor; feel boring; watching TV during day and night.
- **Storyboards**: Lee grandmother lives alone. Before her grandson goes to the elementary school, she takes care the grandson single-handedly and they are very close. But now only on holiday, son with grandson come back to eat and to chat. Weekday life becomes very boring. When she misses grandson, she always looks at the old photos. Do not know what they are doing now? How high? How weight? Will not be bullied by someone? Thinking about the mood more and more depressed. I hope now I can listen to the voice of the grandson and see his smile.
- **Design concept**: The smart photo album was named Fond Memories. The elderly can stay updated on family events by simply flipping through the album of family pictures and real-time messages; they can also record voice or write messages to communicate with their families; smart photo album can automatically play the children's choice of music for them; The lens on the album can detect and record their emotions experienced, therefor the family members can immediately understand and care. These shared memories create empathy, relieve depression, and allow the elderly to enjoy memories with their families. The sketch design was shown in Fig. 3.

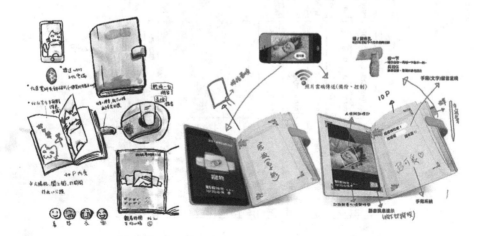

Fig. 3. Sketch design

Then, the modified conceptual design is shown in Fig. 4. The advantages of smart photo album: (1) To provide a dedicated image communication platform. (2) The traditional way to flip the page, don't need to learn. (3) One-touch operation. (4) Any time with family, don't feel alone. (5) Image stimulation to enhance memory.

Fig. 4. Fond Memories concept design

The ICT technologies include: mobile device App development technology, cloud storage technology, wireless communication technology, community network technology, flip-flop device technology, music recommendation technology and emotion-awareness technology. Figure 5 illustrates the architecture of Fond Memories. Table 2 presents the scenarios for using Fond Memories.

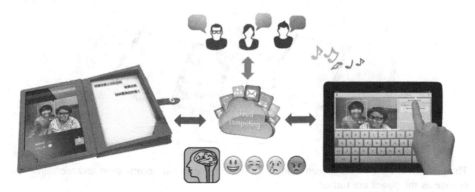

Fig. 5. The architecture of Fond Memories

Table 2. The scenarios for using Fond Memories

Scenario & Description

Family members can use mobile devices to access the cloud photo management system to add, delete, manage, and respond to messages. When a new picture is added, a light on the album will flash and notification sound will play. The elderly can simply turn the pages to view pictures and leave messages.

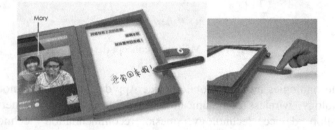

Name labels for those pictured can deepen the elderly' impressions of their families. Messages for each picture can be recorded or hand written in this platform for family interaction.

The pictures shown on the screen along with the corresponding information and messages change as the pages are turned.

(continued)

Table 2. (*continued*)

Scenario & Description

The lens on the album can detect and record their emotions experienced and give music suggestions, increasing the feeling of happiness felt when viewing pictures. Family members are automatically notified when the elderly feel melancholy.

- Mobile device App development: the family members can manage the cloud album through the mobile App, set music, set people name labels.
- Cloud storage: save photos, sound and messages, and keep in sync with mobile device and smartphone.
- Wireless communication: use Wi-Fi or Bluetooth to communicate with the cloud.
- Community network: to establishment family network of community, to enhance the elderly and their families to share and interaction.
- Flip sensor: combined with electronic paper sensor technology, the photos and information is real-time updated when flip left and right page.
- Emotional Sensing: records the mood of the elderly when they are viewing the album and sends a message to inform the family.

4 Conclusion

The process of recording, remembering, and sharing photos can improve older adults' willingness to interact with others and provide them with means to recall, discuss, and share past experiences in order to improve confidence and self-esteem, relieve depression, and prevent mental and memory degradation. Families can use this shared platform to archive mutual feelings and memories. Each time these image memories are recalled and shared shortens the time interval between the event and the present and improves interactions and relationships between older adults and their families.

In this study the smart photo album presented two features: "Image memory sharing" and "Emotion detection".

1. **Image memory sharing**: The concepts within reminiscence therapy allow family members and the elderly to collect and record shared memories so that the elderly can improve their verbal expression, interpersonal interaction, memory reinforcement, and emotional state.
2. **Emotional detection**: the elderly's emotional responses are often carelessly overlooked and forgotten and minor changes in their emotions are difficult to distinguish. The elderly frequently do not know how to express their feelings and needs; thus, the lens on the smart photo album can be used to measure the emotional responses of the elderly so that family members are more able to provide care and communicative support

Acknowledgments. The researchers of the present study would like to extend their gratitude to the Ministry of Science and Technology (MOST), for their grant (Program No. 102-2218-E-415 -002-)

References

Center, I. E. a. K. R.: Investigation on the Consumer Behavior of Cross-Strait Senior Citizens, July 2011. https://www.itri.org.tw/chi/news/detail.asp?RootNodeId=060&NodeId=061&NewsID=544

Hsieh, C.J.: Who lit "melancholy" Bomb? Teacher Chang Monthly **289**, 14–18 (2002)

Chiang, I.C.: Lonely index survey in 2006: how lonely in Taiwan? Global Views Monthly **238**, April 2006. http://store.gvm.com.tw/article_content_11920.html

Haight, B.K., Burnside, I.: Reminiscence and life review: conducting the processes. J. Gerontol. Nurs. **18**(2), 39–42 (1993)

Hiroaki, E.: Life will not forget, amazing mnemonics: Beautiful Art Academy Club (2013)

Kelley, T., Littman, J., Peters, T.: The Art of Innovation: Lessons in Creativity from IDEO, America's Leading Design Firm. Crown Business, New York (2001)

Matteson, M., Munsat, E.: Group reminiscing therapy with elderly clients. Issues Ment. Health Nurs. **4**(3), 177–189 (1982)

Norman, D.A.: Emotional Design: Why We Love (or Hate) Everyday Things. Basic Books, New York (2004)

Nugent, E.: Try to remember … reminiscence as a nursing intervention. J. Psychosoc. Nurs. Ment. Health Serv. **33**(11), 7–11 (1995)

Shigeo, H.: Brain revolution: Brain hormones create a different life: Creative force culture Ltd (1996)

Strauss, A.C., Corbin, J.: Basics of Qualitative Research: Grounded Theory Procedures and Technique, 2nd edn. SAGE Publications, Thousand Oaks (1990)

Weinschenk, S.: The Secret to Designing an Intuitive UX: Match the Mental Model to the Conceptual Model, 08 April 2010. http://uxmag.com/articles/the-secret-to-designing-an-intuitive-user-experience

Young, I.: Mental Models: Aligning Design Strategy with Human Behavior. Rosenfeld Media, New York (2008)

Development of a User Experience Evaluation Framework for Wearable Devices

Young Woo Kim[✉], Sol Hee Yoon, Hwan Hwangbo, and Yong Gu Ji

Department of Information and Industrial Engineering, Yonsei University, Seoul, Korea
gugstarac@naver.com, yoonsolhee@yonsei.ac.kr,
dieonesus@gmail.com, yongguji@yonsei.ac.kr

Abstract. Wearable devices such as smartwatch, tracker, and head-mounted display devices are commonly used along with the advance of IT. Users face novel user experiences owing to the "wearing" nature of wearable devices. However, until now there is no framework to assess the overall UX of a wearable device. Therefore, the objective of this study is to provide a systematic framework that assist in the evaluation and design of wearable devices. In this study, a framework was presented consisting of design space, evaluation factors, and context of use. It could classify each area into several subcategories based on the previous research. We carried out a case study of expert evaluation and user evaluation to investigate the applicability of the framework. For two types of wearable devices, HMD and smartwatch, the experts evaluated the correlation between the design spaces and the evaluating factors. Users also assessed the association between the two areas through questionnaires. Results showed that relation in between design space and evaluation factors alter by varying products. Although there are limitations on the number of subjects and UX factors, this study has significance in that it enables quick and systematic evaluation of wearable devices.

Keywords: Wearable device · User experience · Design space · Evaluation factors · Smartwatch · Head-mounted display

1 Introduction

Wearable devices such as smartwatch, activity tracker, and head-mounted display refer to the electronic devices that transmit information in real time to the body. Since wearable devices can communicate at the closest distance to the user than any other device, they provide a new user experience in some aspects. For example, wearable devices, along with functional aspects such as traditional smartphones, have expressive aspects; accessories or clothing, for example. In addition, since user has to "wear" the product, factors such as comfort became important which were not considered before.

According to Gartner (2016), the number of wearable devices will be over to 322.7 million by 2017, with more than 20% of them being covered by smartwatch. The growth of such wearable devices is closely related to the development of the Internet of Things environment, and devices such as activity trackers are good examples. Activity Tracker tracks user behavior, sends it to the computing environment, and provides feedback to

© Springer International Publishing AG 2017
J. Zhou and G. Salvendy (Eds.): ITAP 2017, Part II, LNCS 10298, pp. 53–67, 2017.
DOI: 10.1007/978-3-319-58536-9_5

the user in real time. This process is similar to that of the desktop environment, but there is a fundamental difference in that the desktop user uses the device stationary (Lumsden and Brewster 2003). Thus, a wearable device is required to have a different evaluation framework than a traditional computing environment because it is more influenced by the context, or the user's value, as well as the function of the device.

However, until now, researches related to evaluation of wearable devices have been evaluated in the field of usability such as the accuracy of control or efficient input method. Of course, the usability-oriented viewpoint should be performed during the whole product design process of the high-end product, but it should be accompanied with the consideration as to what user value the wearable device can provide. Therefore, designers and manufacturers should design a product with a sufficient understanding of the user experience (UX) in wearable devices, and a development of a user experience evaluation framework for wearable devices is required to reduce the time and cost burden in the evaluation process.

The research objective of this study is to provide a systematic framework that assist in the evaluation and design of wearable devices. For this, we first defined features and functions of wearable devices. Based on this, we constructed three core areas of UX evaluation: design space, evaluation factors, and context of use. The relationship between design space and evaluation factors was examined through a case study by applying the developed evaluation framework.

2   Related Works

2.1   Framework for Understanding Product UX

Although the definition of UX is different for each researcher, according to ISO DIS (2008), it is defined as '*a person's perceptions and responses that result from the use and/or anticipated use of a product, system or service*'. It is said that the UX is inherently variable because it can change according to the characteristics and context of use of the product and the external environment. Therefore, UX should evaluate not only values of interaction with the subject, but also values of the interaction before and after inter-action with the subject (Vermeeren et al. 2010). In order to evaluate these long-term and changing experiences, we thought that we needed to include user values and contextual factors in the evaluation framework.

Prior to the evaluation framework of UX, we highlighted the differences between usability and UX for this study. Some studies suggested that usability can be inter-changed with UX, but in general, UX is seen as a larger concept involving usability (Saffer 2010). Usability begins with a consideration of how easy it is to use design elements of interacting products (Heo et al. 2009). Therefore, usability differs from UX in that the issue is related to task performance regardless of user's emotional state or attitude (Kaye 2007).

In order to measure or evaluate the UX of wearable devices, it is necessary to identify the factors that directly and indirectly affect it (Schulze and Krömker 2010). In Wech-sung (2014)'s framework for evaluating multimodal interactions, for example, they classified factors that affect UX as user, context, and system. User referred to the user-level variables that interact with the product, including demographic information, personality, needs, abilities, and emotional states. Context included environmental factors and service factors while system was divided into functional factors and agent factors. In order to create the evaluation framework, the design principles are collected and reconstructed according to the subject.

Design principles have been developed for good product design, but they can also be effective guidelines for evaluating objects. Also, when evaluating new products that have not existed before, it is necessary to present new evaluation factors in accordance with the product. In addition, it is important to determine which design spaces should be evaluated and how to evaluate them to build a user experience framework (Heo et al. 2009).

2.2 Features of Wearable Devices

It is important to understand the specific characteristics of wearable devices to evaluate UX. Wearable devices basically share properties with mobile devices as they are mostly used mobile. Mobile devices enable to provide information by themselves presenting the following three main characteristics: (1) they usually work in the hands of users, (2) they mostly operate without a physical connection like a cable, and (3) they provide additional features such as new applications and internet connectivity (Weiss 2003). On the other hand, the characteristics of wear for wearable devices can be summarized in two ways: the user must always be with them, and their appearance is exposed.

Characteristics of mobile devices changes in the environment of wearable devices. That is, they are no longer used by holding it in one hand, as they do not need to be hold body of the device since it is already worn by the user. On the other hand, the rest two mobile devices characteristics can be considered as more emphasized in wearable devices, where the non-linear characteristics are directly related to the battery and communication speed of the device. As devices become more compact, designers intensively deploy multiple technologies within smaller devices. Likewise, in order to provide additional functions, the wearable device usually operates by providing the application itself or by operating the application in cooperation with the smartphone.

In recent mobile computers, such as smartphones or tablet PCs, weight reduction of the product was an essential factor. However, since the wearable device is in direct contact with the user's skin, weight factors as well as comfort factors are important. For example, if you are playing a game or watching an image through a Head-Mounted Display, this can provide a greater immersion experience than interacting with an existing desktop monitor. However, over-heavy display weight and eye fatigue due to fast screen switching can interfere with user engagement and provide a negative user experience. The characteristic of being exposed is a feature that restricts the form and wearing manner of the wearable device because the device should not cause the device to have a sense of heterogeneity. For example, smartwatch, which is the most widespread wearable device at present, suggests a way to replace the watch as its name suggests, and its shape is also a form that does not deviate greatly from the existing form of the watch.

Further, since the form of the product can be determined from its function, it is necessary to search for the function of the wearable device. The development of various wearable devices has also diversified its functions. However, the wearable device must basically provide the role that the existing product performs, such as time confirmation and vision adjustment. In addition, wearable devices require display because they provide common mobile product functions such as dialing, sending messages, scheduling, and running applications.

Although wearable devices evaluated in our study are smartwatches and HMDs, these interface features and functions are similarly defined in other types of wearable devices. Of course, there will be a few differences between them because there will be so many different wearable devices and they will be released. Products that do not provide their own output, such as a fitness tracker, differ in appearance from functional differences, such as small or no display, when compared to smartwatch. Despite these small differences, however, we can provide a consistent design space for constructing our evaluation framework in the context of a product's wear and movement.

3   Evaluation Framework for Wearable Devices

Figure 1 shows the overall evaluation framework for wearable devices which is based on the product design space and evaluation factors. The framework enables to explore user value from the product and evaluate them. We aimed to propose an evaluation framework taking into consideration aspect of user values as evaluation factors, design space of wearable devices as well as context of use.

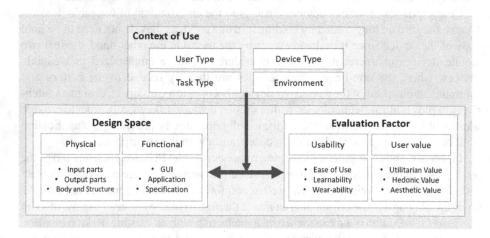

Fig. 1. Evaluation framework for wearable devices

Context of use is the area to be considered in product development apart from the above two areas, and includes external factors related to the user experience. From the proposed framework, it is able to create an evaluation table that shows the relationship between UX evaluation factors and design space. In this way, it enables designers to quickly identify UX problems and modify correctly in the according design spaces that need improvement.

3.1 Design Space

Wearable devices share design spaces with the mobile device. In previous research, the design space of mobile device has been divided into Linguistic User Interface (LUI)/ Physical User Interface (PUI)/Graphic User Interface (GUI) dimension or Hardware and Software dimension (Heo et al. 2009; Kim et al. 2008). LUI is a concept that includes menus and navigational structures as interfaces related to information content and structure for task execution. A GUI is an interface that displays task-related information graphically or visually, such as icons or fonts. A PUI is an interface that can be physically touched, such as a keypad and a microphone, and the user actually performs the task through the PUI.

As shown in Table 1, in this study, the design spaces of wearable devices are divided into physical and functional aspects by reconstructing the sub-categories of existing studies. The physical design space refers to an external aspect of a product that a user can physically touch or perceive. Physical design spaces are divided into three sub categories: input, output, and body and structure. The input refers to the part used by the user to operate the product, such as a controller. In the traditional computing environment, the mouse and the keyboard were used for input manipulation. However, with the birth of the touch screen, introduction of the gyro sensor and the improvement of the speech recognition rate have made it possible to manipulate the device with finger, voice and gesture. The output means the part where the user receives the sensory feedback from the product like the display. In recent wearable devices, auditory feedback and tactile feedback are often provided together. Finally, the body and structure refers to the rest of the product's exterior, excluding the input and output parts, such as the shape of the device or strap.

The functional design space refers to an area that actually functions based on a software system. It consists of three categories: GUI, application, and specification. The application of a wearable device is defined as a set of functions that a wearable device provides by itself or in cooperation with another device. In addition, the GUI means an icon on the screen, audio feedback, etc. in which functions are output. Finally, specification means the parts inside the product and how they work together.

3.2 Evaluation Factors

Since we have classified the UX into the dimension of user value along with the concept of usability, we reviewed the usability evaluation factors of the existing mobile and wearable products, and studies on the user value that can be obtained through the products. Table 2 shows the evaluation factors of the evaluation framework defined in this study. Usability dimension is a very important evaluation factor from the existing computer interaction environment and we classify it as the ease of use, learnability, and wearability. In addition, user value is a factor that increases the merchandise in terms of marketing. User value dimension of wearable device is divided into utilitarian value, hedonic value, and aesthetic value.

In ISO 9421-11 (1998), usability is defined as: *the extent to which a product can be used by specified users to achieve specified goals with effectiveness, efficiency and*

Table 1. Design space of the evaluation framework

	Category	Description	Example
Physical design space	Input	Hardware components used to transform user action or commands into electronic signals	Touchscreen, controller
	Output	Hardware components used to deliver data received from the system to the user	Screen, speaker
	Body and Structure	Physical shape and components unrelated to the communication of information	Straps, frame
Functional design space	GUI	Graphical interface that enables the visual communication with the system	Icons, images
	Application	Programs or functions that the system provides	Messenger, alarm
	Specification	The structural and essential characetristic of the system	Memory capacity, battery

satisfaction in a specified context of use. In the evaluation area of this study, usability factors were derived by focusing on the meaning of effectiveness. The reason for this is that efficiency shares a lot of scope with the Utilitarian value in the user value domain, and satisfaction is regarded as the overall result of the user experience (Joo et al. 2011).

The ease of use of the wearable device as usability factor is the degree to which the user believes that using the device from free to effort (Davis 1989). This factor may be considered similar to the effectiveness of usability, and it measures how easily and accurately the user can perform a given task. According to Nielsen (1994) usability model, learnability can be said to be the degree to which novice users can easily master the system. Learnability includes sub-principles such as familiarity, consistency, and predictability, and is considered as an important usability evaluation factor in many studies. Likewise, learnability should be considered to be one of the most important indicators of wearable device usability, because most users have not or have not used a wearable device. Based on the research of Gemperle et al. (1998), we defined wearability of a system as the degree to which the user could wear it without disturbing. In their research, guidelines were provided to improve the wearability of wearable products. Principles such as weight and human movement were used in this study to measure the wearability of the device.

Table 2. Evaluation factors of the evaluation framework

Dimension of Evaluation	Factors	Description	Reference
Usability	Ease of Use	The degree to which an user believes that using the device would be free from effort	Davis (1989)
	Learnability	The degree to which novice users can easily master the system	Nielsen (1994)
	Wearablity	The degree to which the user can comfortably and easily wear it	Gemperle et al. (1998)
User Value	Utilitarian value	Value that the user receives from functional and task-related benefits	Babim et al. (1994)
	Hedonic value	Value based on the personal experience of fun and playfulness	Babim et al. (1994)
	Aesthetic value	The pleasure that emanates from looking at a product without evaluating utility	Holbrook (1980)

Understanding the user value is needed to define the relationship between user experience and user value domain. The user value, second evaluation area of our framework, refers to the experience and benefits that users gain by consuming products (Holbrook 1999). In particular, since the value will affect the experience of interacting with products and services, this relationship should be considered from the outset of the product design process (Kujala and Väänänen-Vainio-Mattila 2008). In this study, we divide the user value dimension into utilitarian and hedonic dimensions according to existing studies (Babin et al. 1994). We also added aesthetics as a new dimension of user value.

The utilitarian value is a value that the user receives from functional and task-related benefits (Babin et al. 1994). A utility system has its purpose in a design that enhances user's performance and productivity (Van der Heijden 2004), For example, the design of smartwatch for utility value has value in that smartwatch can quickly handle the tasks that smartphones need to handle, such as receiving notifications. According to Kivetz and Simonson (2002), users tend to think utilitarian value is more important than hedonic value when satisfactory function is not satisfied. In other words, utilitarian value is a value expressed when the product meets the minimum functions that must be met to have value.

On the other hand, hedonic value is defined as that value based on the personal experience of fun and playfulness (Babin et al. 1994). The purpose of the hedonic system is to make the product enjoyable and sustainable for the user (Van der Heijden 2004). For example, if a user continues to use a product through challenging content, such as competing through the number of steps measured by a smartwatch, it can be said that the product has a hedonic value. The user feels hedonic value is more important than practical value when the functional minimum level of product is met. Positive experience on hedonic value causes feelings like cheerfulness and excitement (Chitturi et al. 2008)

Finally, the aesthetic value describes the pleasure that emanates from looking at a product without evaluating utility (Holbrook 1980). In some studies, aesthetic value is regarded as a sub-factor of hedonic value (Chitturi et al. 2008). In this study, two concepts were separated to evaluate the role of wearable devices as clothing. Especially, according to Hekkert et al. (2003), it can be seen that the appropriate combination of prototypicality and novelty increases the aesthetic appreciation, which shows that wearable devices can benefit from maintaining the appearance of existing clothes.

3.3   Context of Use

As shown in Fig. 1, the context of use can be defined as a combination of user, task, device, and environment while the users are using the product and achieving their intended goals (Baber 2009). The combination of these contextual information helps to construct multiple evaluation tables. Defining the context of use in the evaluation process has the advantage of enabling a focused approach and providing the basis for developing a replicated evaluation plan (Maguire 2001).

The user type is a factor indicating the familiarity level of the user with respect to the wearable device, and can be classified into the novice and expert level. The type of task means the activity performed by the user during the UX evaluation, and the type of task may vary depending on the purpose of the device or the purpose of the evaluation. The type of environment refers to the ambient conditions of the environment in which the actual product is used and can be divided into field/laboratory. Finally, the types of wearable devices can be divided into smartwatches, HMD devices, smart glasses, and fitness trackers.

4   Case Study

We carried out a case study to investigate the applicability of the developed evaluation framework. The case study was conducted in two parts, the expert evaluation and user evaluation.

4.1   Expert Evaluation

The purpose of the expert evaluation is to discover the relation of the evaluation factor and design space in a relatively short time using heuristic method, thus finding the design space needing improvement. For expert evaluation, we need to create the association table. The rows and columns of the association table contain the evaluation factors and design space defined in the evaluation framework. Strong (S), moderate (M), and low

(L) are used to present the correlation between the evaluation factors and design space. The degree of relevance between each design space and the evaluation factor was scored using a five-point scale, and based on the results of the score, those having arithmetic average exceeding 3 was presented as moderated, and more than 4.5 as strong. In this study, two HCI experts with sufficient knowledge about smartwatch and HMD scored the evaluation table.

4.2 User Evaluation

User studies were carried out to investigate the factors affecting actual user wearable device satisfaction and to identify usability problems that were not found yet. Since the user does not have a clear concept of each evaluation factor, the relationship between the evaluation factor and the design space should be identified through an indirect method. In this study, we tried to clarify the relationship between the two areas through self-reported metrics.

Participants. For the user study, 12 university students with high knowledge in Information Technology (IT) were recruited. Data were obtained from eleven subjects except one subject who complained of dizziness during HMD device evaluation. The data of the abandoned subjects were collected only for four devices except PS VR. The subjects consisted of ten males and two females. Age ranged from 17 to 28 years with an average of 23.6 and a standard deviation of 2.52.

Apparatus. In order to evaluate the user experience of wearable devices, we conducted experiments with two smartwatches and three HMDs (Table 3). The biggest difference between the Apple Watch 2 and Huawei Watch was the difference in the operating system, and there were other differences, such as the shape of the watch and the display. Likewise, three Virtual Reality (VR) systems also showed differences in PUI, drive system, and wearing style.

Table 3. Apparatus used for the case study

Device	Apple watch 2	Huawei watch	Gear VR	Oculus Rift	Playstation VR
Image					
OS/Drive system	watchOS 3.0	Adroid Wear OS	Smartphone	PC	Playstation 4
Input method	Touch screen, digital crown, MIC	Touch screen, button, MIC	Touchpad, Back button	Xbox controller	Playstation controller
Output method	Display, speaker, vibration	Display, speaker	Display, speaker	Display, headset, vibrarion	Display, speaker, vibration

Design of the Experiments. The experiment was conducted in a laboratory environment with a within subject design. HMD devices were evaluated after assessing smartwatches data, because the HMD may cause motion sickness which could influence on the results of smartwatches. The order in the device type was randomly assigned to each subject and after each device a short questionnaire was conducted asking participant to score with a 7-point likert scale to gather data on satisfaction as well as design space and evaluation factor.

The tasks selected for the user study were primarily based on functions that are common for both devices which are considered the most frequently used functions when the product is first introduced or by results of user surveys. The major functions selected for smartwatch were largely classified into application setting and management, communication, and health management. Application setting and management task asked participants to set up and manage the app such as changing of watch face and app install. Communication function were tasks such as confirming and replying to messages or notifications through the actual smartwatch, and confirming/correcting the schedule. Finally, health management were functions like setting the target momentum, tracking the exercise information/physical information, and designing such tasks as the use during the move to be able to evaluate the factors such as the normal wearing comfort at the same time. The task selected for the HMD device was set based on the basic function of the device which were navigation and option setting, video viewing, game activity. The navigation and option tasks asked participants to set up setting such as avatar or profile directly on the main screen. In video viewing, participants watched a 360degree VR video provided without actual operation. The game activity was evaluated through a racing game in which the user directly controlled and accomplished the goal.

Questionnaires were designed to evaluate UX factors and device satisfaction which were generated based on previous papers on usability and user values (Lund 2001; Knight and Baber 2005; and Vosset al. 2003). All users' evaluation factors were categorized into two questions. Satisfaction scores were evaluated with satisfaction of overall device and satisfaction of each design space. We also interviewed at the end of the experiment and collected qualitative data on specifically satisfied or unsatisfied items. Correlation analysis was performed to analyze the relationship between device satisfaction and evaluation factors.

5   Results

5.1   Results from Expert Evaluation

The results of the expert evaluation for smartwatches and head-mounted display are shown in Tables 4 and 5. For smartwatches, there was a strong correlation between input and ease of use, and body and structure and wearability for usability evaluation factor and physical design space. Moreover, only one strong correlation between physic design space and user value was encounter: body and structure and aesthetic. In the case of smartwatches, there were more strong correlation between functional design space with evaluation factor of usability and user value. For instance, GUI and Application showed strong correlation with ease of use (Table 4).

Table 4. Results of expert evaluation for smartwatches

Evaluation factor		Design space					
		Physical space			Functional space		
		Input	Output	B&S	GUI	App	Spec
Usability	Ease of use	S	L	L	S	S	M
	Learnability	M	L	L	M	M	L
	Wearability	L	L	S	L	L	L
User value	Utilitarian	M	M	M	M	S	M
	Hedonic	L	M	L	M	S	L
	Aesthetic	M	M	S	S	M	L

S = strong correlation, M = moderate correlation, L = low correlation

Table 5. Results of expert evaluation for head-mounted display

Evaluation factor		Design space					
		Physical space			Functional space		
		Input	Output	B&S	GUI	App	Spec
Usability	Ease of use	S	M	M	M	M	L
	Learnability	S	L	M	M	M	L
	Wearability	M	L	S	L	L	L
User value	Utilitarian	L	M	L	M	S	S
	Hedonic	M	M	M	L	S	M
	Aesthetic	S	M	S	S	M	L

S = strong correlation, M = moderate correlation, L = low correlation

For the results of the expert evaluation for head-mounted display, it is possible to see that there is difference with respect to the results of the smartwatches. For instance, there are more strong correlation between physical design space and evaluation factor (Table 5). Input was rated to have strong correlation with ease of use and learnability, while body and structure showed strong correlation with respect to wearability. For the user value evaluation factors, aesthetic aspects were considered to have strong correlation with input and body and structure physical space (Table 5). No strong correlation was found between functional space and usability evaluation factor, however, functional space showed strong correlation with user value evaluation factor.

5.2 Results from User Evaluation

Results of the user evaluation can be divided into two parts. First, we show the score of satisfaction and evaluation factors for usability and user value for the difference devices (Table 6).

Table 6. Results of User questionnaire on smartwatches and head-mounted display

Devices	Satisfaction	Usability			User value		
		EOU	LN	WR	UV	HV	AV
Apple watch	3.67	3.79	4.5	5.33	4.04	3.42	5.08
Huawei watch	4.08	5.04	5.33	4.75	4.54	3.42	4.29
Samsung Gear VR	4.5	4.71	5.29	4.71	4.46	5.63	5.13
Oculus Rift	5.42	5.58	5.88	4.58	5.17	6.17	5.67
Playstation VR	5.91	5.86	6.05	4.68	4.77	6.36	5.59

Results from the correlation between satisfaction of design spaces and evaluation factor for smartwatches are shown in the following table (Table 7). Satisfaction on physical design space for input is strongly correlated with ease of use, learnability, and aesthetic. For output, there is a strong correlation for ease of use, learnability, utilitarian value, and aesthetic value. Lastly, for body and structure, there was only significant correlation with respect to wearability. For the functional space, GUI had significantly strong correlation with ease of use and learnability. Application was the one having the most number of evaluation factors significantly correlating, which were ease of use, learnability, utilitarian value, hedonic value, and aesthetic value. Aesthetic value was shown to be significantly correlated for all of the evaluation factors (Table 7).

Table 7. Correlation matrix of user evaluation for smartwatches

Evaluation factor		Overall SAT	Satisfaction on design space					
			Physical space			Functional space		
			Input	Output	B&S	GUI	App	Spec
Usability	Ease of use	0.688^b	0.765^b	0.681^b	0.105	0.571^b	0.766^b	0.696^b
	Learnability	0.700^b	0.580^b	0.684^b	0.321	0.615^b	0.642^b	0.733^b
	Wearability	0.293	0.121	0.450^a	0.498^a	0.249	0.122	0.181
User value	Utilitarian	0.629^b	0.467^a	0.602^b	0.074	0.349	0.783^b	0.448^a
	Hedonic	0.527^b	0.414^a	0.451^a	0.108	0.336	0.693^b	0.483^a
	Aesthetic	0.610^b	0.533^b	0.556^b	0.662^b	0.592^b	0.497^a	0.702^b

Sig. at a: $p < 0.05$, b: $p < 0.01$

For the overall satisfaction, usability evaluation factors like ease of use and learnability were found to be significantly correlated. Evaluation factors of user were all found to be significantly correlated with satisfaction of users.

Table 8 shows the results from the correlation analysis between user evaluation factors and satisfaction of design space for head-mounted display. The results of the overall satisfaction show that satisfaction is significantly correlated to all of the evaluation factors selected: ease of use, learnability, wearability, utilitarian value, hedonic value, and aesthetic value. The strongest correlation was between satisfaction and hedonic value ($r = 0.691$), followed by aesthetic value ($r = 0.557$) (Table 8). For the physical design space, input and output, all the evaluation factors of usability and user value were shown to have significant correlation between both. However, in the case of body and structure physical design space, there were significant correlation with respect to learnability ($p < 0.05$), wearability ($p < 0.01$), and aesthetic value ($p < 0.05$) (Table 8). In the case of the functional design space satisfaction, there were less significant correlation with evaluation factors. That is, GUI satisfaction was significantly correlated with user value evaluation factors (utilitarian, hedonic, and aesthetic values). For the application satisfaction, all of the evaluation factors were found to have significant correlation except for wearability ($r = 0.227$). Lastly, the specification functional design space was found to be significantly correlated with utilitarian, hedonic, and aesthetic value.

Table 8. Correlation matrix of user evaluation for head-mounted display

Evaluation factor		Overall SAT	Satisfaction on design space					
			Physical space			Functional space		
			Input	Output	B&S	GUI	App	Spec
Usability	Ease of use	0.544^b	0.596^b	0.496^b	0.306	0.230	0.435^b	0.380
	Learnability	0.441^b	0.424^a	0.425^a	0.386^a	0.260	0.482^b	0.371
	Wearability	0.390^a	0.465^b	0.395^a	0.450^b	0.327	0.227	0.246
User value	Utilitarian	0.544^b	0.483^b	0.444^b	0.311	0.354^a	0.469^b	0.452^b
	Hedonic	0.691^b	0.635^b	0.546^b	0.170	0.400^a	0.382^a	0.536^b
	Aesthetic	0.557^b	0.565^b	0.597^b	0.375^a	0.466^b	0.476^b	0.461^b

Sig. at a: $p < 0.05$, b: $p < 0.01$

6 Discussion and Conclusion

The research aimed to present a framework for user experience evaluation of wearable devices based on evaluation factors and design space. Based on previous researches, we presented a framework that explains the importance of separating the design space of the product in physical and functional space since they refer to different aspect of the product. Also, we divided the evaluation factors of the product in usability evaluation factors, which are commonly used by previous studies, and added the user value evaluation factors that are more related to the user experience throughout the usage stage of the product.

Two evaluation process were presented in this study which consisted on an expert evaluation and a user study. The proposed expert evaluation enables to understand that expert on the field are also enabled to score and evaluate the relation between evaluation factors and design space. In this way, the presented method might provide a fast way of encountering design issues and importance of design space aspect for the development and design of a product. The second method used in this research consisted on a user evaluation. User evaluation results also showed that there exists different relation between design space and evaluation factors for different product even in the same product group such as wearable devices. These methods allow to get a more detailed analysis on the results of the correlation and know how users rate importance and satisfaction of each of the area.

With the results obtained from the expert evaluation and user evaluation case study, we can conclude that there is a necessity to divide and categorize the design space of the product and evaluation factor; for better understanding the needs of the user and help designs to improve the product. The framework presented in this research can be used as basis for future research to develop a more systematic evaluation tool of user experience. Moreover, this research enhance researcher to be aware and continue researching and investigating the need to develop new form of evaluation for user experience in product design and development.

This research has limitation in three aspects. First, the research was conducted with small number of participants which might have bought biases on the research. However, it is important to note that different products are categorized in the same product family as wearable device; which needs to consider on different design space as well as evaluation factor. Secondly, the research only takes into consideration three evaluation factors for usability evaluation and three for user value. This might be reinforced in future researches, adding more evaluation factors relevant for the product design and perception of user experience. Finally, in this research, there was lack of contextual consideration as well as user factors consideration. Therefore, future research might be conducted by adding contextual factors for the development of the evaluation framework as well as user factors such as age and gender.

Acknowledgements. This work was supported by the Ministry of Trade, Industry & Energy (MOTIE, Korea) under Industrial Technology Innovation Program. No.10060517, 'Development of user-centered product design support system based on cognitive and affective information'.

References

Baber, C.: Evaluating mobile human-computer interaction. In: Mobile Computing: Concepts, Methodologies, Tools, and Applications, pp. 225–239. IGI Global (2009)

Babin, B.J., Darden, W.R., Griffin, M.: Work and/or fun: measuring hedonic and utilitarian shopping value. J. Consum. Res. **20**(4), 644–656 (1994)

Chitturi, R., Raghunathan, R., Mahajan, V.: Delight by design: the role of hedonic versus utilitarian benefits. J. Mark. **72**(3), 48–63 (2008)

Davis, F.D.: Perceived usefulness, perceived ease of use, and user acceptance of information technology. MIS Q. **13**, 319–340 (1989)

Gartner Inc (2016). http://www.gartner.com/technology

Gemperle, F., Kasabach, C., Stivoric, J., Bauer, M., Martin, R.: Design for wearability. In: Second International Symposium on Wearable Computers, Digest of Papers, pp. 116–122. IEEE, October 1998

Hekkert, P., Snelders, D., Wieringen, P.C.: 'Most advanced, yet acceptable': typicality and novelty as joint predictors of aesthetic preference in industrial design. Br. J. Psychol. **94**(1), 111–124 (2003)

Heo, J., Ham, D.H., Park, S., Song, C., Yoon, W.C.: A framework for evaluating the usability of mobile phones based on multi-level, hierarchical model of usability factors. Interact. Comput. **21**(4), 263–275 (2009)

Holbrook, M.B.: Some preliminary notes on research in consumer esthetics. In: Olson, J.C. (ed.) NA-Advances in Consumer Research, vol. 07, pp. 104–108. Association for Consumer Research, Ann Abor (1980)

Holbrook, M.B.: Consumer Value: A Framework for Analysis and Research. Psychology Press, London (1999)

ISO DIS 9241-210:2008: Ergonomics of human system interaction - Part 210: Human-centred design for interactive systems (formerly known as 13407). International Organization for Standardization (ISO) (2008)

ISO 9241-11: Ergonomic requirements for office work with visual display terminals (VDTs). The international organization for standardization, vol. 45 (1998)

Joo, S., Lin, S., Lu, K.: A usability evaluation model for academic library websites: efficiency, effectiveness and learnability. J. Libr. Inf. Stud. 9(2), 11–26 (2011)

Kaye, J.J.: Evaluating experience-focused HCI. In: CHI 2007 Extended Abstracts on Human Factors in Computing Systems, pp. 1661–1664. ACM, April 2007

Kim, H.J., Choi, J.K., Ji, Y.: Usability evaluation framework for ubiquitous computing device. In: Third International Conference on Convergence and Hybrid Information Technology, ICCIT 2008, vol. 1, pp. 164–170. IEEE, November 2008

Kivetz, R., Simonson, I.: Earning the right to indulge: Effort as a determinant of customer preferences toward frequency program rewards. J. Mark. Res. 39(2), 155–170 (2002)

Knight, J.F., Baber, C.: A tool to assess the comfort of wearable computers. Hum. Factors 47(1), 77–91 (2005)

Kujala, S., Väänänen-Vainio-Mattila, K.: Value of information systems and products: understanding the users' perspective and values. JITTA J. Inf. Technol. Theory Appl. 9(4), 23 (2008)

Lumsden, J., Brewster, S.: A paradigm shift: alternative interaction techniques for use with mobile & wearable devices. In: Proceedings of the 2003 Conference of the Centre for Advanced Studies on Collaborative Research, pp. 197–210. IBM Press, October 2003

Lund, A.M.: Measuring usability with the USE Questionnaire 12. Usability Interface 8(2), 3–6 (2001)

Maguire, M.: Context of use within usability activities. Int. J. Hum Comput Stud. 55(4), 453–483 (2001)

Nielsen, J.: Usability Engineering. Elsevier, Amsterdam (1994)

Saffer, D.: Designing for Interaction: Creating Innovative Applications and Devices. New Riders, Berkeley (2010)

Schulze, K., Krömker, H.: A framework to measure user experience of interactive online products. In: Proceedings of the 7th International Conference on Methods and Techniques in Behavioral Research, p. 14. ACM, August 2010

Van der Heijden, H.: User acceptance of hedonic information systems. MIS Q. 28, 695–704 (2004)

Vermeeren, A.P., Law, E.L.C., Roto, V., Obrist, M., Hoonhout, J., Väänänen-Vainio-Mattila, K.: User experience evaluation methods: current state and development needs. In: Proceedings of the 6th Nordic Conference on Human-Computer Interaction: Extending Boundaries, pp. 521–530. ACM, October 2010

Voss, K.E., Spangenberg, E.R., Grohmann, B.: Measuring the hedonic and utilitarian dimensions of consumer attitude. J. Mark. Res. 40(3), 310–320 (2003)

Wechsung, I.: An Evaluation Framework for Multimodal Interaction. T-Labs Series in Telecommunication Services. Springer International Publishing, Cham (2014). doi: 10.1007/978-3-319-03810-0

Weiss, S.: Handheld usability. Wiley, Chichester (2003)

A Field Experiment on Capabilities Involved in Mobile Navigation Task

Qingchuan Li and Yan Luximon[✉]

School of Design, The Hong Kong Polytechnic University,
Hung Hom, Kowloon, Hong Kong
qingchuan.li@connect.polyu.hk, yan.luximon@polyu.edu.hk

Abstract. An increasing usage of mobile technologies has been seen among diverse age groups of users in recent years. The limited screen size and multiple interaction styles inevitably produce much more workload on mobile technologies use; thus it is necessary to investigate the possible capabilities involved in mobile navigation tasks. The particular interests of this study are the cognitive capabilities, namely spatial ability, short-term memory and processing speed and attention, as well as the visual abilities including vision acuity and visual perception of digital screens. Fifteen participants who covered a wide age range attended in this field experiment to complete several navigation tasks with three levels of complexity using an experimental mobile application. The results suggest that the capability of processing speed and attention is more important than the other capabilities for navigation performance and subjective preference. Specifically, the capability of processing speed and attention is significantly correlated with user characteristics, including age, education experience, and technology experience. The results can help designers to address the major capabilities involved in mobile navigation tasks to make relevant allowance to include more possible users, such as elderly people.

Keywords: Mobile technology · Navigation task · Capability · User characteristics · Aging

1 Introduction

An increasing usage of mobile technologies has been seen in recent years, especially among the older adults who aged 65 years old and above [1]. Mobile technologies can provide improved mobility, better security and advanced functions that benefit users from diverse age groups; thus it becomes more convenient for users to manage social relationships, monitor health status as well as learn and search online information [2, 3]. However, the features of contemporary mobile technology make it inevitably produce much more workload on technology use. In the same time, the declines in capabilities with aging could also slow down the human information processing cycle from information perception to response execution. For instance, the small multi-touch screens normally come with hidden buttons or menus, complicated information structures, as well as changeable interaction modes, which proposes more mental requirements for the mobile

© Springer International Publishing AG 2017
J. Zhou and G. Salvendy (Eds.): ITAP 2017, Part II, LNCS 10298, pp. 68–78, 2017.
DOI: 10.1007/978-3-319-58536-9_6

navigation tasks, especially for older adults. Thus it is necessary to investigate possible capacities involved in technology use and examine relevant limitations to maintain a proper workload when design mobile technologies, in particular considering the process of aging.

Designers should be aware of the typical changes with aging in terms of cognitive functions and visual facilities, such as attention, memory, processing speed, and visuospatial functioning [4]. For instance, the declines of cognitive capabilities may harm the process of paying attention to multiple resources, encoding of new information and retrieval of information from memory. The declines in visual abilities buffer the process of executing technology tasks, such as information seeking [5, 6]. Studies demonstrate that most of the cognitive capabilities have started to decline as early as mid-fifties, and then present a very fast decrease since the seventies [7]. In this way, with aging, people are experiencing more difficulties in ignoring the irrelevant information, dividing attention to different resources, recalling and recognizing the information when doing technology tasks. Particularly, spatial ability is reported to be an important determinant in technology usage especially menu navigation [8–10]. Users with higher spatial ability are expected to have better mental model to understand the underlying website structures to search the information efficiently [5, 11, 12].

While considerable studies have been conducted to investigate the effects of individual characteristics on computerized web-navigation that utilizing larger screens and mouse controlling, there is a distinct lack of research into the situation when navigating and browsing by advanced mobile technologies. The issue of user experience exists at different levels, from the user interface design to various task demands. Much of the current studies are concentrated on the menu and interface design [13, 14] as well as web browsing styles [15]. However, considering of wider range of possible users and increased task demands, it is also essential to examine how user capability make an impact on mobile navigation tasks. This study aims to explore the effects of cognitive and visual abilities on users' task performance and subjective preference in mobile navigation tasks. Three kinds of cognition capabilities were emphasized, namely short-term memory, spatial ability, and processing speed and attention. Vision acuity and visual perception of digital screens were measured by test performance and self-reports. The results give some insights into the possible capabilities that involved in mobile interface navigation with different levels of task complexity.

2   Methods

In order to investigate the role of related capabilities in mobile navigation tasks, a field experiment was utilized to measure user's mobile navigation performance and collect their subject preference among fifteen participants. Since this study aimed to include a wider age range of users, participants were recruited from different age brackets from 20s to 80s. In this situation, the field experiment allows for flexible arrangement considering of older adults' security and mobility issues. All the experimental environments were separated from the outside and kept quiet and tiny; the disturbing factors were controlled in an acceptable range.

2.1 Participants

Fifteen participants were recruited from the community center and university in Hong Kong. Participants were selected without any cognitive and visual impairments. Of all the participants, experience of using advanced mobile technologies was reported, such as smartphones, tables or smart watches. Participant's demographic information was collected, including age, gender and education level. In addition, prior technology experience was evaluated because of the high importance reported in previous studies [16, 17]. It is also notable that the experience with previous generations of technology may also matter when interacting with new technologies, especially for older adults [18]. Thus, the technology experience was measured by computer experience and mobile technology experience. Specifically, mobile technology experience was evaluated by technology exposure (e.g. duration of use, intensity of use, diversity of use) and technology competence.

2.2 Capability Measurement

Before the experiment, three particular cognitive capabilities in terms of working memory, spatial ability, as well as attention and processing speed, were measured by a modified Mini-Cog^{TM} test [19] and symbol digit modalities test [20] respectively. The Mini-Cog^{TM} test was composed of a word recall test (WRT) and clock drawing test (CDT). The spatial digit modalities test (SDMT) was administered to measure participants' attention and processing speed. Additionally, visual abilities were evaluated in terms of visual acuity and self-reported visual perception of digital screens.

Word Recall Test (WRT). The word recall test was used to evaluate the participants' short-term memory. In this test, participants were required to remember 5 unrelated words and then complete the following clock drawing test (CDT). After finishing the CDT test, they were instructed to tell the 5 previously stated words. The number of correctly recalled words was recorded as the test performance. Thus, the result scale was from 0 to 5.

Clock Drawing Test (CDT). The clock drawing test was employed to evaluate participants' spatial ability [21]. Provided with a circle on a paper, participants were first verbally instructed to draw the number to display the clock face, and then were asked to draw the hands of clock to read the time of 09:20. Each point was given to the participants if they correctly instructed the numbers on the circle or drew the hand of the clock to indicate correct time. Thus, the result scale was from 0 to 2.

Spatial Digit Modalities Test (SDMT). The spatial digit modalities test was administered by asking participants to correctly match 9 pairs of symbols and numbers (e.g., "(" and "1", "#" and "2", ">" and "3", …, "&" and "9"). They were asked to complete as many as paired symbols and numbers in 90 s. The number of correctly matched pairs was recorded as user performance. Result scale is from 0 to 90.

Vision Acuity (VA). This study used Tumbling E chart that calibrated and showed by a 2048 × 1536 display screen. Participants were asked to read the chart from 1.9 meters' distance with corrections. Starting from the biggest row, each participant was tested three letters in each row. The vision acuity results were calculated and noted as the minimum visual angel of each participant.

Self-reported Visual Perception (SVP). The participants were asked about their ability of reading and recognizing the characteristics on a 2048 × 1536 display screen, such as "is it easy for you to read or recognize the characteristics on this screen". The responses were marked as 1–5 from very difficult, difficult, neutral, easy and very easy.

2.3 Experimental Design

In order to reduce the influence of experience with specific mobile applications, a new iOS mobile application was designed and built using Unity. To facilitate user's real experience of using mobile technologies, this application was simulated to remind participants to take specific medicine in time. Participants were instructed to navigate between a menu navigation page and four sub-pages to complete serval tasks. Totally, three levels of task complexity were designed to simulate the real situations that the users would face in different kinds of tasks.

Specifically, this study concerned the task complexity according to the cognitive workload and requirements of the task. It was defined by how many information sources the participants need to remember or integrate when doing the mobile navigation tasks. For instance, the task complexity of level 1 didn't require participants to remember or integrate information at all; whereas, the task complexity of level 2 required for some memory load when completing tasks. When coming to the task complexity of level 3, users needed to remember some information as well as search for the relevant information to integrate useful resources and make decisions.

Participants' navigation performance was measured by their completion time, correctness rate, and the number of return steps and incorrect clicks. Following each task, the participants were asked to evaluate their subjective preference. They need to evaluate in terms of ease-of-use from very difficult to very easy (ranking 1–5), the disorientation from very disoriented to not disorientated at all (ranking 1–5), the effort needed from many efforts needed to few efforts needed (ranking 1–5), and overall satisfaction from very dissatisfied to very satisfied (ranking 1–5).

2.4 Procedure

Participants were provided with a brief experimental instruction and instructed to fill the consent form upon arriving. Then they were required to answer some questions and complete several tests according to the questionnaire. The first part of questions was concerned participants' age, gender, education level and technology experience. Following that, several paper-based assessments of short-term memory, spatial ability, and processing speed and attention were administered. The Tumbling E chart was then used to measure participants' vision acuity and a digital display was showed to ask about their visual perception of reading and recognizing texts.

Finally, participants were provided with a smartphone with a 1080×1920 digital screen. Experimenters instructed them to use the application first and participants could try and use the application freely. Then, participants were required to complete three trials by themselves. With no questions or doubts, the experiment began. For each participant, 9 tasks were assigned to them in the randomized order. The background system recorded all the click data automatically.

3 Results

3.1 Participants Description

In order to analyze the mobile navigation behavior among a wide age range of users, we recruited fifteen participants aged from 24 and 81 years old. They averagely aged at 47.73 years old, with an average education experience of 15.47 years. The participants reported that they had the experience of using computer for 11.10 years averagely and have been adopted mobile technologies for about 5.19 years in average. They normally use the mobile technologies for 22.03 hours per week. High diversity of use was reflected by the number of functions that used by these participants. On average, they used 4.80 functions or applications, mainly for maintaining social relationships (100%), some basic functions (93.33%), managing healthcare status (73.33%), information searching (73.33%) and entertainment (46.67%). When asked how confident they feel when using mobile technologies, the majority participants reported they had a medium technology competence level of 3.53.

3.2 Analysis of Capability Assessments

Three categories of cognitive capabilities were measured, namely short-term memory, spatial ability, and processing speed and attention. Visual ability was assessed by the participants' vision acuity and self-reported visual perception. The details of assessment results are shown in Table 1. Basically, most of the participants indicated a normal level of short-term memory and spatial ability in the Mini-Cog^{TM} test, with no significant declines or impairment reported. The results of SDMT test varied a lot between different participant, which may be because the total scores had wider range. For visual abilities, no significant difficulties were reported from the participants with corrections when reading on the digital screens.

Table 1. Capability assessment results (n = 15)

	Cognitive capability			Visual ability	
	WRT	CDT	SDMT	VA	SVP
Mean	4.93	1.93	46.07	1.12	4.73
Standard deviation	0.26	0.26	19.23	0.48	0.59

To further analyze the relationship between participants' capabilities and their demographic factors, as well as the technology experience, the Spearman Test was employed. Results showed that the SDMT results indicated a significant correlation with participants' age ($p = 0.000$), education experience ($p = 0.001$), computer experience ($p = 0.020$), duration of use with mobile technologies ($p = 0.003$), intensity of use with mobile technologies ($p = 0.028$), and competence of use with mobile technologies ($p = 0.031$). The visual abilities were also found some significant relationships with demographic factors and technology experience. Specifically, the minimum visual angel was found to be positively correlated with age ($p = 0.003$) and negatively correlated with duration of use with mobile technologies ($p = 0.001$). The self-reported visual perceptions were found to be negatively related with age ($p = 0.034$), and positively related with education experience ($p = 0.036$) and duration of use with mobile technologies ($p = 0.031$). However, there is no correlation found in the other two capability assessment results. The details of relevant correlations are shown in the following Fig. 1.

3.3 Capabilities Involved in Navigation Tasks

The descriptive data of navigation performance of participants are shown in Table 2. For navigation performance, participants outperformed when the level of task complexity was lower (level 1 and level 2). They needed nearly half of the completion time, had higher correctness rate, and less return steps and incorrect clicks. However, for subjective preference, no significant differences were reported between different levels of task complexity.

In order to investigate the capabilities involved in mobile navigation tasks, the relations between capabilities and navigation performance as well as subjective preferences were analyzed by spearman test. The results showed that, for task complexity of level 1, there were significant correlations between the SDMT results and completion time ($p = 0.000$), as well as the correctness rate ($p = 0.007$). For the task complexity of level 2, significant relationship was found between SDMT results and completion time ($p = 0.000$). The similar relationships were also found when the task complexity was level 3. Specifically, significant correlations were found between the SDMT results and completion time ($p = 0.000$), as well as correctness rate ($p = 0.000$). Details are further shown in Figs. 2 and 3.

The correlation between capabilities and subjective preferences were also analyzed by the spearman test. The results are as follows. For task complexity of level 1, there is a significantly positive correlation between SDMT results and effort used ($p = 0.037$), and a significantly negative correlation between SDMT results and satisfaction ($p = 0.008$). The significantly negative correlation was also found between SDMT results and satisfaction ($p = 0.026$), when the task complexity was at level 3.

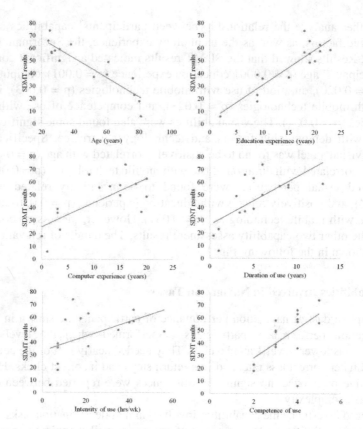

Fig. 1. Correlations between SDMT results and demographic factors and technology experience

Table 2. Descriptive data of navigation performance and subjective preference (n = 15)

Task complexity		Mean (Standard deviation)		
		Level 1	Level 2	Level 3
Navigation performance	Completion time	31.24 (21.30)	30.80 (19.03)	62.49 (37.86)
	Correctness rate	93.89 (9.16)	93.89 (13.16)	85.56 (18.49)
	Return steps	0.29 (0.47)	0.24 (0.39)	1.44 (1.24)
	Incorrect clicks	0.07 (0.14)	0.02 (0.09)	0.18 (0.28)
Subjective preference	Ease-of-use	3.87 (0.80)	4.02 (0.62)	4.36 (0.77)
	Disorientation	3.98 (0.97)	4.11 (0.65)	4.29 (0.73)
	Effort	3.58 (1.03)	3.75 (0.95)	4.02 (0.81)
	Satisfaction	3.58 (0.94)	3.76 (1.08)	3.73 (0.83)

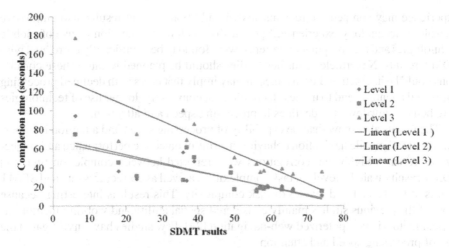

Fig. 2. Relationship between SDMT results and completion time

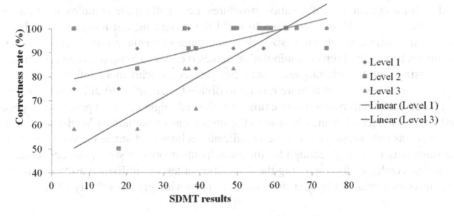

Fig. 3. Relationship between SDMT results and correctness rate

4 Discussion

Mobile navigating in a small touch-screen is a complex process. Thus, knowing different users' capabilities and limitations can help in reducing workload in mobile technology usage. This study is highlighted in the situation that a wider age range of users are adopting mobile technologies in the modern society [22]. The present results provide a number of interesting insights about mobile navigation behavior among participants with a wide age range.

Results indicate that age, education experience, and technology experience have significant correlations with SDMT results. The results supplemented previous studies that showed age and education are important for cognitive capabilities [5, 23]. With aging, users suffer from declined processing speed and attention; while longer education experience may compensate relevant loss. In addition, current results also emphasize the role of technology experience. Specifically, both of the duration of use of mobile technologies and the computer experience were found to be significantly correlated with SDMT results. Nevertheless, further studies should be planned because these correlations could be interactive. For instance, it may imply that users with declined processing speed and attention tend to use less technologies; conversely, longer use of technologies may help to slowdown the declines in processing speed and attention.

The results also show that the capability of processing speed and attention is important for users' mobile navigation behavior in terms of objective performance and subjective preference. Significant correlations were reported between completion time and SDMT results at all the levels of task complexities, as well as correctness rate and SDMT results at the level 1 and level 3 of task complexity. This result is interesting because most of the previous studies mainly considered spatial ability and working memory as critical factors in computerized web-navigation [24]. Few studies have investigated the role of processing speed and attention.

The possible reason may lie at two aspects. First, it may be because of the difference between computerized web-navigation and mobile interface navigation. For computerized web-navigation, the information structures are usually quite complex with flat or hierarchical layers. Thus, users need to build the correct mental model to search for useful information, which emphasizes the importance of spatial ability [24]. However, the interaction style of direct manipulation makes it easier to jump between each pages when using mobile technologies. Users can get access with more information with shorter time. Therefore, it is more crucial to divide the attention to different resources and process more information at one time, which needs higher level of processing speed and attention. Second, it may be due to the limitations of method of Mini-Cog^{TM} test. The test was only sensitive for some significant declines or damage of cognition; thus the sensitivity is not high enough for the participants in present study. Further research should be conducted by improving the difficulties of tests or utilizing various performance tests for spatial ability and short-memory to provide greater validity [25].

5   Conclusion

The field experiment outlined in this article found that the capability of processing speed and attention is important for mobile interface navigation. Users with higher processing speed and attention is more likely to find the information and complete the navigation task efficiently and effectively. The capability in terms of processing speed and attention is related to users' age, education experience, and technology experience with mobile technologies and computers. By investigating the capabilities involved in mobile interface navigation, designers could better understand a wider range of users' capability and limitation with different age, education experience and technology experience. In this way, it allows for including more possible users, such as elderly people.

The current results generate curiosity for some directions for future studies. First, more participants should be included to add the validity of participant's data. More age groups should be settled to further analyze the effects of individual characteristics on the mobile navigation behavior. Second, it would be interesting to explore the reason of how the processing speed and attention influence user's navigation behavior on small screens of mobile technologies. It is also important to investigate how to design the interface to compensate this capability lost. Third, other performance tests of spatial ability and short-term memory should be utilized to further analyze their possible effects on mobile navigation behavior.

Acknowledgements. The authors would like to thank the Research Grants Council for the UGC Funding Scheme from the Hong Kong Polytechnic University.

References

1. Harada, S., Sato, D., Takagi, H., Asakawa, C.: Characteristics of elderly user behavior on mobile multi-touch devices. In: Kotzé, P., Marsden, G., Lindgaard, G., Wesson, J., Winckler, M. (eds.) INTERACT 2013. LNCS, vol. 8120, pp. 323–341. Springer, Heidelberg (2013). doi:10.1007/978-3-642-40498-6_25
2. Gao, Q., Ebert, D., Chen, X., Ding, Y.: Design of a mobile social community platform for older Chinese people in urban areas. Hum. Factors Ergon. Manuf. Serv. Ind. 25(1), 66–89 (2015). doi:10.1002/hfm.20523
3. Zhou, J., Rau, P.L.P., Salvendy, G.: Use and design of handheld computers for older adults: a review and appraisal. Int. J. Hum. Comput. Interact. 28(12), 799–826 (2012). doi: 10.1080/10447318.2012.668129
4. Drag, L.L., Bieliauskas, L.A.: Contemporary review 2009: cognitive aging. J. Geriatr. Psychiatr. Neurol. 23(2), 75–93 (2010). doi:10.1177/0891988709358590
5. Wagner, N., Hassanein, K., Head, M.: The impact of age on website usability. Comput. Hum. Behav. 37, 270–282 (2014). doi:10.1016/j.chb.2014.05.003
6. Dommes, A., Chevalier, A., Lia, S.: The role of cognitive flexibility and vocabulary abilities of younger and older users in searching for information on the web. Appl. Cogn. Psychol. 25(5), 717–726 (2011). doi:10.1002/acp.1743
7. Schaie, K.W.: Handbook of the Psychology of Aging. Academic Press, San Diego (1996)
8. Ziefle, M., Bay, S.: Mental models of a cellular phone menu. comparing older and younger novice users. In: Brewster, S., Dunlop, M. (eds.) Mobile HCI 2004. LNCS, vol. 3160, pp. 25–37. Springer, Heidelberg (2004). doi:10.1007/978-3-540-28637-0_3
9. Chen, C.: Individual differences in a spatial-semantic virtual environment. J. Am. Soc. Inf. Sci. 51(6), 529–542 (2000). doi:10.1002/(SICI)1097-4571(2000)51:6<529:AID-ASI5>3.0.CO;2-F
10. Sein, M.K., Olfman, L., Bostrom, R.P., Davis, S.A.: Visualization ability as a predictor of user learning success. Int. J. Man-Mach. Stud. 39(4), 599–620 (1993). doi:10.1006/imms.1993.1075
11. Ahmed, I., Blustein, J.: Influence of spatial ability in navigation: using look-ahead breadcrumbs on the web. Int. J. Web Based Commun. 2(2), 183–196 (2006). http://dx.doi.org/10.1504/IJWBC.2006.010309
12. Westerman, S.J.: Computerized information retrieval: individual differences in the use of spatial Vs nonspatial navigational information. Percept. Motor Skills. 81(3), 771–786 (1995). doi:10.2466/pms.1995.81.3.771

13. Yu, N., Kong, J.: User experience with web browsing on small screens: experimental investigations of mobile-page interface design and homepage design for news websites. Inf. Sci. **330**, 427–443 (2016). doi:10.1016/j.ins.2015.06.004
14. Murano, P., Sander, M.: User interface menu design performance and user preferences: a review and ways forward. Int. J. Adv. Comput. Sci. Appl. **7**(4), 355–361 (2016). doi:10.14569/IJACSA.2016.070447
15. Roudaki, A., Kong, J., Yu, N.: A classification of web browsing on mobile devices. J. Vis. Lang. Comput. **26**, 82–98 (2015). doi:10.1016/j.jvlc.2014.11.010
16. Langdon, P., Lewis, T., Clarkson, J.: The effects of prior experience on the use of consumer products. Univ. Access Inf. Soc. **6**(2), 179–191 (2007). doi:10.1007/s10209-007-0082-z
17. Hurtienne, J., Horn, A.M., Langdon, P.M., Clarkson, P.J.: Facets of prior experience and the effectiveness of inclusive design. Univ. Access Inf. Soc. **12**(3), 297–308 (2013). doi:10.1007/s10209-013-0296-1
18. Rama, M.D.: Technology generations handling complex User Interfaces (Doctoral dissertation). Technische Universiteit, Eindhoven (2001)
19. Borson, S., Scanlan, J., Brush, M., Vitaliano, P., Dokmak, A.: The Mini-Cog: a cognitive 'vital signs' measure for dementia screening in multi-lingual elderly. Int. J. Geriatr. Psychiatr. **15**(11), 1021–1027 (2000). doi:10.1002/1099-1166(200011)15:11<1021:AID-GPS234>3.0.CO;2-6
20. Benedict, R.H., Smerbeck, A., Parikh, R., Rodgers, J., Cadavid, D., Erlanger, D.: Reliability and equivalence of alternate forms for the symbol digit modalities test: implications for multiple sclerosis clinical trials. Multiple Sclerosis J. **18**(9), 1320–1325 (2012). doi:10.1177/1352458511435717
21. Agrell, B., Dehlin, O.: The clock-drawing test. Age Ageing **27**(3), 399–404 (1998)
22. Li, Q., Luximon, Y.: Older adults and digital technology: a study of user perception and usage behavior. In: Goonetilleke, R., Karwowski, W. (eds.) Advances in Physical Ergonomics and Human Factors. AISC, vol. 489, pp. 155–163. Springer, Cham (2016). doi:10.1007/978-3-319-41694-6_16
23. Biswas, P.: Survey on inclusive human machine interaction issues in India. In: Biswas, P., Duarte, C., Langdon, P., Almeida, L. (eds.) A Multimodal End-2-End Approach to Accessible Computing. HIS, pp. 23–41. Springer, London (2015). doi:10.1007/978-1-4471-6708-2_2
24. Juvina, I., Van Oostendorp, H.: Individual differences and behavioral metrics involved in modeling web navigation. Univ. Access Inf. Soc. **4**(3), 258–269 (2006). doi:10.1007/s10209-005-0007-7
25. Johnson, D., Clarkson, J., Huppert, F.: Capability measurement for inclusive design. J. Eng. Des. **21**(2–3), 275–288 (2010). doi:10.1080/09544820903303464

Shape Design and Exploration of 2D and 3D Graphical Icons

Hsuan Lin[1(✉)], Yu-Chen Hsieh[2], and Wei Lin[3]

[1] Department of Product Design,
Tainan University of Technology, Tainan, Taiwan
te0038@mail.tut.edu.tw
[2] Department of Industrial Design, National Yunlin University
of Science and Technology, Yunlin, Taiwan
chester@yuntech.edu.tw
[3] Department of Interior Design,
Hwa Hsia University of Technology, Taipei, Taiwan
weilin@cc.hwh.edu.tw

Abstract. Due to the rise of the app market, icon design is highly valuable to app marketing. Currently, with a wide range of icons in the main menu, users can not immediately identify their needed interface or function, thus encountering operational problems. In the past, almost all relevant studies mainly focused on visual recognizability and shape features of 2D icons, not on those of 3D icons. Therefore, this study probed comprehensively into the design elements of 2D and 3D icons. The design elements include icon composition, border, polarity, shade, and shadow. After that, the design elements of 2D and 3D icons were extracted which may serve as a practical and scholarly reference in the field of icon design in the future.

Keywords: Icon composition · Border · Polarity · Shade · Shadow

1 Introduction

With the vigorous development of the app market, applications are nowadays commonly found in everyday life. From the perspective of app marketing, outer shapes of graphical icons seem to act as silent salespersons. Icon design plays a key role in app marketing, for icon presentation is the most prominent feature that attracts customers' attention. Thereafter, customers are induced to interact with the app involved and to purchase it in the end. Evidently, graphical icons have become a standard function of most graphical user interfaces(GUI) [1]. Also, GUI's have been widely used in computers and mobile devices, such as kiosks, ATM, tablets, and dashboard cameras [2, 3], in addition to other specialized areas like cash registers, medical environments, and operating industrial machinery [4]. In practical operation, users click or touch the GUI on a screen to receive and process large quantities of numerical as well as graphical data [5]. In that way, users can intuitively input instructions and interact with the device [6]. Well-designed icons enable users to search rapidly, minimizing errors. Consequently, icon design is an important part of GUI design.

© Springer International Publishing AG 2017
J. Zhou and G. Salvendy (Eds.): ITAP 2017, Part II, LNCS 10298, pp. 79–91, 2017.
DOI: 10.1007/978-3-319-58536-9_7

Graphical icons have standardized functions, enabling users to locate the needed instruction or program among a wide variety of icons [1]. In consequence, well-designed graphical icons effectively help users to handle large numbers of alphanumeric symbols. Alternatively, on a low-resolution screen, like that of a smartphone, users can easily find the needed function or target which is presented in a relaxing way [4]. On the other hand, designers tend to create increasingly complex icons so that they may provide a lot of information in a limited space and catch users' great attention [2]. Besides, with diversified presentation modes of icons today, users cannot find their needed interface or function instantly while searching for a particular icon on the main menu. In other words, they are faced with some operational problems.

GUI's allow users to operate computers and execute program instructions with the help of graphical icons [7]. Hence, graphical icons play an important role in communication between users and interfaces. An icon is not just an identifiable image of an object but also has a border, background, and label interpreting the image [8]. Moreover, the memory of an icon lasts longer than that of a printed word [9]. Graphical icons are now widely used for such interfaces as menus, thumbnails or symbols in a window, representing certain particular functions in the system and transmitting visually implicit messages to users [8]. Gittins suggested that the outline of an icon should be solid, closed, sharply-contrasting, and smooth [10]. An open figure should be avoided, for users tend to mistake it for being closed. The contrast of the icon should be clear and steady, but using color to produce contrast should be avoided. Though the icon itself has no meaning, it will possess a consensual meaning through human association and recollection. Only after some particular contents are combined with specific ideas does the icon convey a meaningful message. Therefore, the psychological factors of humans exert a significant effect [8].

Good icons help to achieve such positive results as reducing operational errors, shortening the mission time, and enhancing users' satisfaction level [5]. A well-designed icon is capable of conveying the intended message properly to users. In addition, different styles of icon design affect users' operation, recognizability, and satisfaction level [2]. For that reason, many researchers explored the influences of icon operation and screen size on users in the hope that operational efficiency might be improved [11, 12]. The distance between icons and icon size affect how fast users scan the GUI. Moreover, an icon put at the corner of a touchscreen affects its operation [5]. A target measuring 9.2 to 9.6 mm is large enough to be manipulated on a small touchscreen [13]. Instead of the visible size of the key, average users prefer a key measuring 20 mm^2, which falls within the identifiable range of touch [14]. The optimum viewing angle for a touchscreen is between 19° and 54.5° [15]. As for color, it not only draws users' attention but has different implications in different situations. For example, red may connote attractiveness (positive) or shockingness (negative) while blue may mean renovation (positive) or arrogance (negative). Therefore, while an icon is operated by a user, the appeal of color is a crucial principle [16]. A good interface which can use feedback effectively will definitely attract users' attention and enhance their operational performance [17].

It has long been the chief concern of researchers and interface designers to utilize the shape features of 2D and 3D graphical icons in a complex main menu. Thus, clear information can be offered to users, visual interference be lowered, users' recognition be improved, and overall performance be enhanced. At present, the research on graphical icons mainly concentrates on size, distance [2, 18–20], contrast [20], and users' subjective satisfaction level [19]. On the other hand, there is little research on the shape features and presentation modes of 3D icons. In view of that, this study analyzed the shape features of 2D and 3D icons, investigating their design elements, viewing angles, and depth comprehensively. In the end, the main design components of 2D and 3D icons were identified. The findings herein can serve as a reference for icon designers and researchers in the future.

2 Design Elements of 2D and 3D Icons

The shape composition of a figure is an important characteristic of design. Different ways of composition produce different visual effects [21]. An icon is a graphical interface with meaning that can convey messages quickly and be remembered easily. The icon is composed of figures whose qualities are multiple, including shape composition, color, and texture. There are three types of shape composition: point, line, and plane composition. Overlapping relationships include direction, position, space, distance, connection, and grouping. Direction is divided into three types: horizontal, vertical, and angular direction [21]. Consisting of points and lines, the icons available on the modern market are divided into two types: 2D icon (Fig. 1) and 3D icon (Fig. 2). To capture users' attention, many icons provide versatile visual effects, so various icons have distinct modes of presentation with different results [22].

Fig. 1. 2D icon   **Fig. 2.** 3D icon

2.1 Icon Composition

Before the widespread use of computers, research on icon design was relatively meager, primarily concerned with public information symbols. There are no more than two kinds of figures used for public information symbols, i.e., outline figures and solid figures [21]. A solid figure refers to one whose area surrounded by the outline is fully painted in a single color while an outline figure is composed of the outer lines, with the area surrounded by the outline being left blank. Solid figures are composed of planes while outline figures are composed of line-composed, imaginary planes. Outline figures have more details than solid figures; namely, the former are more complex than the latter. Outline figures are usually used to weaken the prominence of an icon; that is, a contour line is employed to form the icon shape instead of filling the icon with color to highlight it. Outline figures are intended to make the icon visible without highlighting it excessively. Easterby [23] and Sanders and McComick [24] think that solid figures are more eye-catching than outline figures.

The above is chiefly concerned with icon design in public information symbols or books. Horton [8] suggested that icons can be divided into two types: outlines and silhouettes. The outline style uses lines to draw prominent inner details while the silhouette style fully colors the area surrounded by the outline, with a solid color contrasting with its background. Silhouettes are generally used for roads and packaging signs. Outlines are less emphatic while silhouettes are overly emphatic [8]. Regarding the icons on electronic devices, Lin et al. suggested that there are two kinds of icon composition: line composition and plane composition [25]. Line-composed icons (Fig. 3) refer to outline figures consisting of lines while plane-composed icons (Fig. 4) refer to solid figures consisting of planes [24, 26]. In the former, the areas surrounded by the outline are left blank while in the latter, the areas surrounded by the outline are fully painted in a single color. According to the findings of Lin et al., plane composition is more eye-catching than line composition [25].

Fig. 3. 2D line-composed icon

Fig. 4. 2D plane-composed icon

Like 2D icons, 3D icons are divided into two types: line composition (Fig. 5) and plane composition (Fig. 6). Yet, presentation of 3D icons is more complex than presentation of 2D icons. It is because the way to present depth of 3D icons varies with different shapes.

Fig. 5. 3D line-composed icon   **Fig. 6.** 3D plane-composed icon

2.2 Border

Borders are used to limit the range of an image, being an active element of icon design [8, 27]. Consistent borders provide all icons with a uniform shape and size while individual images do not [8]. An icon with borders not only attracts a user's attention but also guides his or her sightline to the icon [28]. However, if the icon border is used improperly, distractors are likely to increase, which will lower search speed [29]. As a result, while an icon is being designed, its shape must be devised carefully. Meanwhile, borders should be added so that users may spot the icon easily and clearly, with search time shortened [1]. At present, some of the icons have borders (Fig. 7) while the others do not (Fig. 8). Furthermore, borders should be designed in accordance with the shape of an icon. There have been a lot of studies on icon borders. One of the findings indicated that non-border, round borders, and square borders show no significant difference in terms of search time [4]. Another study on the CRT monitor indicated that diamond borders are more difficult to detect than round or square borders [22]. In terms of correct response time, triangular borders take a longer time than round borders [28].

Fig. 7. 2D icon with border   **Fig. 8.** 2D icon without border

Likewise, some of the 3D icons have borders (Fig. 9) while the others do not (Fig. 10). Generally speaking, 2D icons employ borders to highlight themselves so that users may detect the range easily and clearly. However, 3D icons rarely use borders, for borders may occlude the icons, causing disturbance to users.

2.3 Polarity

There are two types of polarity displayed on the screen: positive (Fig. 11) and negative polarity (Fig. 12). Positive polarity refers to black images on a white background while negative polarity refers to white images on a black background [30]. Besides, Horton suggested that icons may be presented in two other modes: positive contrast and negative contrast [8]. Positive contrast means that the icon is brighter than its background while negative contrast means that the icon is darker than its background. Positive polarity performs better than negative polarity in terms of search time [31]. Shieh and Ko investigated how the color combination of the target/background and single/simultaneous

Fig. 9. 3D icon with border

Fig. 10. 3D icon without border

Fig. 11. Positive polarity

Fig. 12. Negative polarity

presentation affect preference for VDT icons [32]. Their findings indicated that black targets (black-on-white or black-on-yellow) and black backgrounds (red-on-black or yellow-on-black) are best-liked, followed by white targets (white-on-red or white-on-black) and white backgrounds (blue-on-white or red-on-white). What's more, regarding recognizability of icons, colorless targets (black-on-white or white-on-black) and color targets show no significant difference in preference. As for subjective preference, white-on-black and black-on-white icons are preferred by average users [33]. By combining two characteristic elements of icons, i.e., polarity and border, Lin et al. got the new element called the background, which was divided into three types: positive background (Fig. 13), negative background (Fig. 14), and non-background (Fig. 15) [25]. In terms of

Fig. 13. Positive
background

Fig. 14. Negative
background

Fig. 15. Non-background

attention, negative background performs the best, positive background ranks second, and non-background performs the worst.

2.4 Shade

The side of an object facing a light source is called the light-receiving surface while the side backing onto the light source is called the shady surface, or the shade. The shade of a 3D cylinder is presented differently from that of a cuboid. There are two ways to present a shade: plane and gradient shades. Typically, plane shades are used to present the 3D effects of cuboids (Fig. 16), gradient shades are used to present cylinders (Fig. 17), and diffusive gradient shades are used to present balls (Fig. 18). In general, 3D line-composed icons have no shades, so lines are used to separate thickness. By contrast, 3D plane-composed icons can use bright or dark shades to present different sides; however, cuboids, cylinders, and balls are presented in different ways.

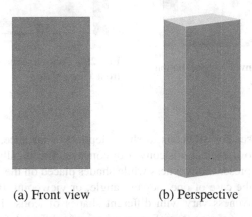

(a) Front view   (b) Perspective

Fig. 16. Plane shades of cuboids

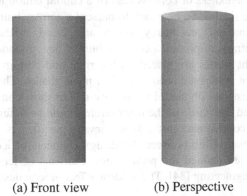

(a) Front view   (b) Perspective

Fig. 17. Gradient shades of cylinders

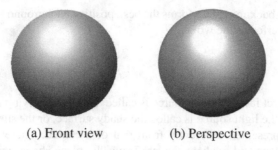

(a) Front view   (b) Perspective

Fig. 18. Diffusive gradient shades of balls

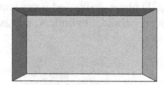

Fig. 19. Convex cuboid button in front view

Fig. 20. Concave cuboid button in front view

Shades can be used for 3D icons to show depth. For instance, shades used for a cuboid button can show whether it is convex or concave. Specifically, shades placed on the right and bottom present convexness while shades placed on the left and top present concaveness [7]. In the case of one viewing angle, or viewpoint, the ways to present convexness or concaveness vary with different shapes of icons. That is, the way to present convexness or concaveness of a round icon is different from that to present convexness or concaveness of a cuboid icon. Take the buttons frequently used for a GUI for example. Convexness or concaveness of a cuboid button is presented through heavy and light plane shades. To be exact, to present a convex button, light shades are placed on the left and top, and heavy shades are placed on the right and bottom (Fig. 19). On the contrary, to present a concave button, heavy shades are placed on the left and top, and light shades are placed on the right and bottom (Fig. 20). As for a round button, gradient shades are used instead of plane shades. The shade of the inner circle should be consistent with that of the outer circle to show convexness in the front view (Fig. 21). Instead, the shade of the inner circle should be different from that of the outer circle to show concaveness in the front view (Fig. 22).

To explore the relationship between the design elements of icons and visual aesthetics, Gaun and Chen defined the presentation elements of icon design under the concepts of Kansei engineering [34]. The shadow effect of icon design was divided into

Fig. 21. Convex round button in front view

Fig. 22. Convex round button in front view

three types: non-shadow, plane shadow, and gradient shadow. To achieve a certain shadow effect, gradient shadows and non-shadow can be employed to enhance the positive rating for aesthetics. Furthermore, Gaun et al. investigated how different local features, such as presentation modes and design techniques, affect users' Kansei images of the whole icon [35]. Their findings indicated that shadow effects have the greatest influence on perception of "bold-aesthetic" vocabulary. In other words, plane shadows are suitable for bold Kansei images.

2.5   Shadow

A shadow is the range produced by an object obstructing a light. The image of a shadow is two-dimensional, and its size and shape vary with the angle of the light. Generally, the shadow plays an auxiliary role in icon design. Its main function is to provide observers with clues about the direction and location of the light source. There are four kinds of shadows in a 2D icon: non-shadow, cast, drop, and back shadow. Non-shadow means that there is no shadow of the icon (Fig. 23). A cast means that the light source illuminates the object vertically from above, causing its shadow to contact the bottom of the object and appear on the surface below (Fig. 24). A drop means that the light source also illuminates the object vertically from above, but the bottom of the object does not contact its shadow, creating the illusion of the object floating in the air (Fig. 25) [8]. The back shadow means that the light source illuminates the object from the front and that its shadow contacts the back of the object, with part of the shadow visible (Fig. 26). Similarly, shadows of 3D icons are divided into four types: non-shadow (Fig. 27), cast (Fig. 28), drop (Fig. 29), and back shadow (Fig. 30).

Fig. 23. 2D non-shadow

Fig. 24. 2D cast

Fig. 25. 2D drop

Fig. 26. 2D back shadow

Fig. 27. 3D non-shadow

Fig. 28. 3D cast

Fig. 29. 3D drop

Fig. 30. 3D back shadow

3 Conclusions

This study investigated the shape features of 2D and 3D icons comprehensively, including design elements, viewing angles, and depth. The design elements covered are icon composition, border, polarity, shade, and shadow. Shades and shadows are used differently for 2D and 3D icons. Specifically, 3D icons use shades to present light or dark sides. Besides, the ways that shades are presented on cuboids, cylinders, and balls are different. Cuboids use plane shades to present different sides, cylinders use gradient shades to present lightness or darkness, and balls use diffusive gradient shades to present cubic effects. Therefore, the ways that shades are presented on icons are greatly different. However, many 2D icons use gradient or diffusive shades to achieve particular effects. This causes much confusion to viewers, so it should be avoided.

The modern world is faced with an increasingly aging population, so the demand and market of the aged have expanded rapidly. The authors suggest researching the icons suitable for the elderly. The findings herein identify design elements of 2D and 3D icons and may serve as a reference for those engaged in icon design and research in the future.

Acknowledgements. The authors hereby extend sincere thanks to Ministry of Science and Technology (MOST) of the Republic of China (ROC) for their financial support of this research, whose project code is MOST 105-2221-E-165-004. It is thanks to the generous patronage of MOST that this study has been smoothly performed.

References

1. Fleetwood, M.D., Byrne, M.D.: Modeling icon search in ACT-R/PM. Cogn. Syst. Res. **3**, 25–33 (2002)
2. Albinsson, P.-A., Zhai, S.: High precision touch screen interaction. In: Proceedings of the SIGCHI Conference on Human Factors in Computing Systems, pp. 105–112. ACM (2003)
3. Wu, F.-G., Lin, H., You, M.: Direct-touch vs. mouse input for navigation modes of the web map. Displays **32**, 261–267 (2011)
4. Huang, H., Lai, H.-H.: Factors influencing the usability of icons in the LCD touchscreen. Displays **29**, 339–344 (2008)
5. Lindberg, T., Näsänen, R.: The effect of icon spacing and size on the speed of icon processing in the human visual system. Displays **24**, 111–120 (2003)
6. Wu, F.-G., Lin, H., You, M.: The enhanced navigator for the touch screen: a comparative study on navigational techniques of web maps. Displays **32**, 284–295 (2011)
7. Näsänen, R., Ojanpää, H.: Effect of image contrast and sharpness on visual search for computer icons. Displays **24**, 137–144 (2003)
8. Horton, W.K.: The Icon Book: Visual Symbols for Computer Systems and Documentation. Wiley, New York (1994)
9. Rosbergen, E., Pieters, F.G.M., Wedel, M.: Undirected Visual Attention to Advertising: A Segment-Level Analysis. University of Groningen (1995)
10. Gittins, D.: Icon-based human-computer interaction. Int. J. Man Mach. Stud. **24**, 519–543 (1986)

11. Beringer, D.B., Peterson, J.G.: Underlying behavioral parameters of the operation of touch-input devices: biases, models, and feedback. Hum. Factors J. Hum. Factors Ergon. Soc. **27**, 445–458 (1985)
12. Sears, A.: Improving touchscreen keyboards: design issues and a comparison with other devices. Interact. Comput. **3**, 253–269 (1991)
13. Parhi, P., Karlson, A.K., Bederson, B.B.: Target size study for one-handed thumb use on small touchscreen devices. In: Proceedings of the 8th Conference on Human-computer Interaction with Mobile Devices and Services, pp. 203–210. ACM (2006)
14. Colle, H.A., Hiszem, K.J.: Standing at a kiosk: effects of key size and spacing on touch screen numeric keypad performance and user preference. Ergonomics **47**, 1406–1423 (2004)
15. Schultz, K.L., Batten, D.M., Sluchak, T.J.: Optimal viewing angle for touch-screen displays: is there such a thing? Int. J. Ind. Ergon. **22**, 343–350 (1998)
16. Götz, V.: Color & Type for the Screen. RotoVision, Berlin (1998)
17. Lansdale, M.W., Ormerod, T.C.: Understanding Interfaces: A Handbook of Human-Computer Dialogue. Academic Press Professional, Inc., San Diego (1994)
18. Legge, G.E., Pelli, D.G., Rubin, G.S., Schleske, M.M.: Psychophysics of reading—I. Normal vision. Vision Res. **25**, 239–252 (1985)
19. Legge, G.E., Rubin, G.S., Luebker, A.: Psychophysics of reading—V. The role of contrast in normal vision. Vision Res. **27**, 1165–1177 (1987)
20. Näsänen, R., Karlsson, J., Ojanpää, H.: Display quality and the speed of visual letter search. Displays **22**, 107–113 (2001)
21. Wong, W.: Principles of Form and Design. Wiley, New York (1993)
22. Hollands, J., Parker, H., McFadden, S., Boothby, R.: LCD versus CRT displays: a comparison of visual search performance for colored symbols. Hum. Factors J. Hum. Factors Ergon. Soc. **44**, 210–221 (2002)
23. Easterby, R.S.: The perception of symbols for machine displays. Ergonomics **13**, 149–158 (1970)
24. Sanders, M.S., McCormick, E.J.: Human Factors in Engineering and Design. McGRAW-HILL Book Company, New York (1987)
25. Lin, H., Hsieh, Y.-C., Wu, F.-G.: A study on the relationships between different presentation modes of graphical icons and users' attention. Comput. Hum. Behav. **63**, 218–228 (2016)
26. Shieh, K.-K., Huang, S.-M.: Effects of pictorial size and circle-slash thickness on glance legibility for prohibitive symbols. Int. J. Ind. Ergon. **33**, 73–83 (2004)
27. Houde, S., Salomon, G.: Working towards rich and flexible file representations. In: INTERACT 1993 and CHI 1993 Conference Companion on Human Factors in Computing Systems, pp. 9–10. ACM (1993)
28. Huang, K.-C., Chiu, T.-L.: Visual search performance on an LCD monitor: effects of color combination of figure and icon background, shape of icon, and line width of icon border. Percept. Mot. Skills **104**, 562–574 (2007)
29. Mohr, W.: Visuelle Wahrnehmung und Zeichenfunktion: Untersuchungen zur Grundlage des Kategorieneffekts bei der Wahrnehmung von Buchstaben und Ziffern. Roderer (1984)
30. Chan, A., Lee, P.: Effect of display factors on Chinese reading times, comprehension scores and preferences. Behav. Inf. Technol. **24**, 81–91 (2005)
31. Gould, J.D., Alfaro, L., Finn, R., Haupt, B., Minuto, A.: Reading from CRT displays can be as fast as reading from paper. Hum. Factors J. Hum. Factors Ergon. Soc. **29**, 497–517 (1987)
32. Shieh, K.-K., Ko, Y.-H.: Effects of display characteristics and individual differences on preferences of VDT icon design. Percept. Mot. Skills **100**, 305–318 (2005)

33. Wang, A.-H., Chen, C.-H.: Effects of screen type, Chinese typography, text/background color combination, speed, and jump length for VDT leading display on users' reading performance. Int. J. Ind. Ergon. **31**, 249–261 (2003)
34. Guan, Sing-Sheng: H.-Y.C.: A study on icon design applied Kansei engineering. J. Sci. Technol. **13**, 33–43 (2004)
35. Guan, S., Tong, D., Hsieh, C.: A study of partial feature attributes affecting holistic kansei for icon design. J. Sci. Technol. **17**, 149–158 (2008)

The Effects of the Transparency of the Guiding Diagrams on the Phone Interface for the Elderly

Shuo Fang Liu, Po Yen Lin[✉], and Ming Hong Wang

Department of Industrial Design, National Cheng Kung University, Tainan, Taiwan
liusf@mail.ncku.edu.tw, henry6812@gmail.com, wming0403@gmail.com

Abstract. This study aims to explore the elderly users' preference for the transparency of the guiding diagrams in the phone interface and their use of the interface. In the one-to-one interview and the questionnaire survey, the subjects compared the guiding diagrams of two levels of transparency, and the statistical software was adopted to analyze and process the data obtained from the questionnaire. According to the results of the statistical analysis of the interviews and questionnaire survey involving 20 elderly people, there is no significant difference in the preference for transparency among the elderly users, and the effects of the transparency of guiding diagrams on the use of the phone are insignificant. The findings can provide reference for phone interface designers in the process of interface design.

Keywords: Touch screen · Elderly · Assisting diagrams · Transparency

1 Introduction

As the proportion of the elderly people in the developed countries becomes larger, old people have become an indispensable group in the consumer market. According to the 2012 UN report on aging population, the aging rate of the developed countries has climbed from 12% in 1950 to 33% in 2050. Additionally, the investigation report of The International Data Corporation shows that there had been a year-on-year increase of 85% in the sales volume of cell phones by the first quarter of 2011, but the growth rate was merely 11% among the elderly. According to the above data, the sales volume and smart phones and the number of the elderly have increased, but corresponding growth has not been found in the elderly people's use of smart phones.

As has been revealed in the literatures about interface design, interface design and guiding diagram are two main factors which influence the experience of the users; however, many manufacturers pay relatively less attention to the design for specific groups because only by quickly delivering products to consumers can they make profits from the sale. At present, most products are aimed at young consumers, but manufacturers neglect the fact that it is the elderly who have great impact on the future trend of the whole market. Because of physiological decline, vision is the part which is the most sensitive to physical change. Therefore, this study adopted the interview approach and the questionnaire survey to probe into the effects of the presentation of guiding diagrams on the elderly users. The purpose of this study is to explore the effects of the guiding

© Springer International Publishing AG 2017
J. Zhou and G. Salvendy (Eds.): ITAP 2017, Part II, LNCS 10298, pp. 92–100, 2017.
DOI: 10.1007/978-3-319-58536-9_8

diagrams in the phone interface on the elderly users as well as the difference in the preference for guiding diagrams and the use of the interface; moreover, the possible reasons for the difference were discussed to offer some reference for the design of phone interface.

2 Relevant Studies

To date, there have been a large number of studies on the phone interface for the elderly, but the quantity of the studies on the operating gesture and on the transparency of assisting diagrams is rather small. Despite this, it is still useful to get acquainted with the features of the elderly and the design factors of phone interface with the help of the previous studies. In consideration of the topic of this study, the literature review was divided into three parts: the experimental exploration into phone interface, the design guidelines, and the visual decline and feelings of the elderly.

Some studies involved an experiment on the elderly people's use of cell phones. In the experiment by Rock Leung, 18 elderly subjects aged over 65 and young subjects aged between 20 and 37 were asked to recognize a series of phone diagrams. The results of the experiment indicated that the elderly were outperformed by the young in the recognition and understanding of diagrams. Besides, the diagrams with written illustration were more helpful for the elderly than the young. Similar studies have also been done on the computer interface. In the experiment by Min-Ju Liao, 12 elderly and young subjects were asked to express their views on complexity. The results showed that more colorful or complex diagrams had greater effects on the elderly than on the young.

Other studies investigated the elderly users' feelings about the computer interface. By conducting a survey on 300 elderly subjects who had never used the computer, Tracy L. Mitzner tried to achieve some insights into the improvement of the computer interface. The results showed that the factor which had the greatest influence on the intentional use of the elderly resided in the experience of using technological products and in the openness to fresh things. Therefore, Tracy L. Mitzner suggested helping the elderly to develop positive use experience and enhance their use of interface through appropriate training. The study most relevant to this study is the one by Silvana Maria Affonso de Lara in 2015, where the acceptance and use of the website interaction aids of 313 subjects (44% of them were elderly) were explored. The findings showed that the website interaction aids indeed promoted the interaction between the elderly and websites and between the young and websites.

Some studies focused on the guidelines for interface design. With emphasis on the buttons in the phone interface, Qin Gao invited 40 elderly and young subjects to participate in the experiment. After analyzing the size of button, gesture and the gap between buttons, he proposed a series of design guidelines. Jeff Johnson also offered some guidelines for interface design to create better visual effects for the elderly. As visual decline affects the cognition of the elderly in the use of smart phones, attention must be paid to the following aspects in the initial stage of interface design: (1) use a pure background color; (2) pay attention to blue, green and yellow and other similar colors; (3) use different color zones to distinguish the link which is being used from the ones which have not been used; (4) don't base differentiation on color alone; (5) use highly contrastive colors; (6) enable users to make adjustment and comparison.

The studies on the interface for the elderly focused on the visual decline and feelings of the elderly. Color is an essential factor which influences visual and interface design. For individuals and groups, the feeling about the same color is subjective, and the difference in the feeling about colors may be attributed to ethnic group, culture, age and even personal experience. Due to physiological influence, the elderly would have a weak ability to distinguish colors. As they age, they show more preference for red and green but less preference for blue (Dittmar 2001). The visual effects on the elderly include (1) uncomfortable about dazzling, (2) declining visibility and (3) weaker sensitivity to blue light. As one grows older, his lens would gradually become yellow, which will result in weaker sensitivity to blue, purple and green. To help the elderly see these colors clearly, stimulus is needed (Nguyen-Tri 2004). Visual decline would affect the cognitive ability of the elderly in the use of smart phones.

3 Experimental Design

After the above literature review, we have had a deeper understanding of the development of human computer interaction (HCI). Nonetheless, few studies on the transparency of guiding diagrams have ever been done so far. For that reason, emphasis was placed on the transparency of guiding diagrams in the experiment of this study. By asking the elderly subjects to compare the guiding diagrams of two levels of transparency, we tried to find out the needs of the elderly.

To get acquainted with elderly people's preference for the transparency of guiding diagrams, we conducted a pre-test, where 10 phone users aged over 50 were interviewed. Specifically, 4 of them preferred to transparent diagrams while 6 were more interested in opaque ones. In consideration of this study and others on the visual decline of the elderly, we proposed the following hypotheses: (H1) The elderly prefer to opaque guiding diagrams; (H2) The transparency of guiding diagrams has effects on using cell phones to browse websites; (H3) The elderly pay more attention to the transparency of guiding diagrams than other design factors when buying a cell phone.

3.1 Experimental Design

The subjects of this study were 23 smart phone users aged over 50, including 8 males and 15 females. Two subjects were removed for not having used a cell phone, and one for being aged below 50. Therefore, there were 20 qualified subjects in this study. The average age of the subjects was 60.2, and the average time of using smart phones was 4.35 years. To exclude possible variance, all the subjects were right-handed.

3.2 Experimental Site

The subjects of this study received the interview and filled the paper questionnaire in the quiet rooms of the Department of Volunteer Work at National Cheng Kung University Hospital.

3.3 Experimental Method

To get acquainted with the interviewee's opinion on certain object through dialogue, the interviewer has face-to-face communication with the interviewee, with the former attempting to know the thoughts and feelings of the latter. In this study, the authors interviewed the subjects aged over 55 in the Department of Volunteer Work at National Cheng Kung University Hospital, so as to know the subjects' views on the existing phone interface. Additionally, a questionnaire survey was conducted in this study. As an approach of collecting information, questionnaire survey is often adopted to measure personal behavior and attitude. With questionnaire, we can summarize and analyze the thoughts of several people and get to the essence of problems. The Likert scale, ranged from "1" to "5", was adopted to design the questionnaire and explore the elderly subjects' preference for guiding diagrams of different levels of transparency and the use of interface.

3.4 Experimental Method

In this study, the one-to-one interview and the questionnaire survey were adopted to obtain qualitative and quantitative data. To ensure that the subjects had a full understanding of the experiment, the research fellows interpreted the meaning of the guiding diagrams; then, the subjects were shown the guiding diagrams of two levels of transparency on a cell phone for a comparison (as is shown in Fig. 1). After that, the subjects expressed their views on the existing phone interface in the interview and filled in the questionnaire. Finally, the data obtained from the interview and the questionnaire survey were analyzed.

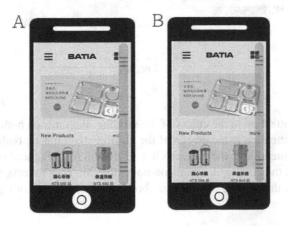

Fig. 1.

3.5 Questionnaire

The questionnaire consists of three parts. Part 1 comprises 3 items, which aims to get the subjects' opinions on the transparency. Part 2 and Part 3 focus on the comparison between opaque and transparent guiding diagrams. The 5-point Likert scale was applied to measure the preference of the subjects. The details of the questionnaire are shown in Figs. 2 and 3.

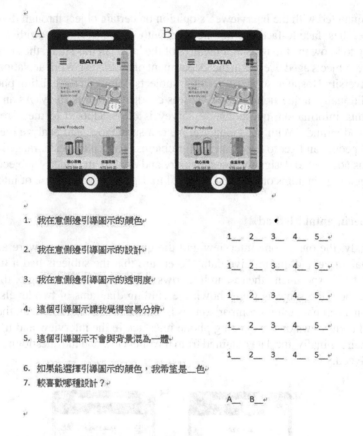

1. 我在意側邊引導圖示的顏色

   1__ 2__ 3__ 4__ 5__

2. 我在意側邊引導圖示的設計

   1__ 2__ 3__ 4__ 5__

3. 我在意側邊引導圖示的透明度

   1__ 2__ 3__ 4__ 5__

4. 這個引導圖示讓我覺得容易分辨

   1__ 2__ 3__ 4__ 5__

5. 這個引導圖示不會與背景混為一體

   1__ 2__ 3__ 4__ 5__

6. 如果能選擇引導圖示的顏色，我希望是__色
7. 較喜歡哪種設計？

   A__ B__

Fig. 2.

Example

1. Do you pay attention to the colors of the guiding diagrams on both sides?
2. Do you pay attention to the design of the guiding diagrams on both sides?
3. Do you pay attention to the transparency of the guiding diagrams on both sides?
4. Do you think the guiding diagrams on both sides are easy to recognize?
5. Do you think the guiding diagrams on both sides cannot be distinguished from the background?

1.我想我會願意使用有這個引導圖示的網頁
　　　　　1__ 2__ 3__ 4__ 5__
2.我覺得這個引導圖示過於複雜
　　　　　1__ 2__ 3__ 4__ 5__
3.我想我需要有人幫助才能使用這個引導圖示
　　　　　1__ 2__ 3__ 4__ 5__
4.我認這個引導圖示很容易使用
　　　　　1__ 2__ 3__ 4__ 5__
5.我覺得這個引導圖示的功能符合我的需求
　　　　　1__ 2__ 3__ 4__ 5__
6.我對這個引導圖示的功能感到困惑
　　　　　1__ 2__ 3__ 4__ 5__
7.我可以想像大部分的人很快就可以學會使用這個引導圖示
　　　　　1__ 2__ 3__ 4__ 5__
8.我覺得這個引導圖示使用起來很麻煩
　　　　　1__ 2__ 3__ 4__ 5__
9.我有自信能明白這個引導圖示的意思
　　　　　1__ 2__ 3__ 4__ 5__

10.我需要學會很多額外的資訊，才能了解這個圖示的意義
　　　　　1__ 2__ 3__ 4__ 5__
11.這個圖示能很好的傳達他的功能
　　　　　1__ 2__ 3__ 4__ 5__
12.這個圖示能幫助我更好地了解手勢的使用
　　　　　1__ 2__ 3__ 4__ 5__
13.這個引導圖示能讓我有更好的網頁瀏覽體驗
　　　　　1__ 2__ 3__ 4__ 5__

Fig. 3.

6. Were you allowed to select the colors for guiding diagrams, what colors would you choose?
7. Which one do you prefer, Design A or Design B?

4   Research Results and Conclusion

The paired sample T test was adopted to test the hypotheses about the two levels of transparency, and the ANOVA was used to detect the difference in the attention to the color, form and transparence of guiding diagrams among the subjects (Tables 1 and 2).

Table 1. Numbers of years of smart phone usage

Numbers of years of smart phone usage	Numbers of sample
1 ~ 3	10
4 ~ 6	4
7 ~ 9	4
More than 10	2
Total	20

Table 2. Age

Age	Numbers of sample
50 or less	1
50 ~ 55	6
56 ~ 60	4
61 ~ 65	5
66 ~ 70	2
More than 70	2
Total	20

Table 3.

Paired sample T test		
	Variable 1	Variable 2
Mean	3.15	3.45
Variance	1.923684211	0.892105263
Sample	20	20
Pearson's product-moment correlation coefficient	0.066291127	
Degree of freedom	19	
P value (one tail)	0.209695686	
P value (two tail)	0.419391372	

4.1 Discussion on the Preference for the Transparency of Guiding Diagrams

The questionnaire item "I think I would like to use the website with such a guiding diagram" was taken for the paired sample T test. According to the result of the test, there was no statistical significance when the significant level was 5% (p-value = 0.209695686). This indicated that the elderly didn't show special preference for the transparency of guiding diagrams.

4.2 Discussion on the Use of Interface According to Transparency of Guiding Diagrams

The items about the use of transparency in the questionnaire were used for the paired sample T test to explore the effects of transparency on the use of the interface among the elderly. The result showed that there was no statistical significance when the significant level was 5% (p-value = 0.370536326). This demonstrated that there is no difference in the use of guiding diagrams of two levels of transparency (Table 4).

Table 4.

Paired sample T test		
	Variable 1	Variable 2
Mean	3.25	3.35
Variance	1.460526316	1.50263158
Sample	20	20
Pearson's product-moment correlation coefficient	0.399685113	
Degree of freedom	19	
P value (one tail)	0.370536326	
P value (two tail)	0.741072652	

4.3 Discussion on the Attention to the Transparency of Guiding Diagrams

Finally, the items about the design of guiding diagrams in the questionnaire were used for the analysis of variance to explore the difference in the attention to these factors (the color, form and transparency of guiding diagrams) among elderly users. According to the result, there was no statistical significance when the significant level was 5%. This showed that there was no difference in the attention to the color, form or transparency of guiding diagrams. Also, it revealed that the elderly don't attach particular importance to guiding diagrams and that they wouldn't pay too much attention to the transparency of guiding diagrams when buying a cell phone (as is shown in Table 3) (Table 5).

Table 5. ANOVA

ANOVA						
Source	SS	DF	MS	F	P-Value	Critical
Between	4.9	2	2.45	1.97385159	0.14830271	3.158842719
Within	70.75	57	1.24122807			
Total	75.65	59				

5   Conclusion

Despite the increasing aging around the world, most elderly people still find it difficult to use the existing phone interface. As far as the transparency of guiding diagrams is concerned, this study shows that there is no significant difference in the attitude towards the transparency of guiding diagrams among the elderly and that the elderly don't pay special attention to the transparency. We assumed that the elderly would prefer to opaque guiding diagrams because of visual decline, but the investigation showed what was different from the assumption. For the elderly, the visual decline makes it more difficult to notice the difference in transparency. According to the follow-up interview, the elderly pay more attention to the contrast between guiding diagrams and background than guiding diagrams. Therefore, the designers of guiding diagrams should attach greater importance to the relationship between background and guiding diagrams. Because of the limitation on time, this study merely focuses on transparency in the experiment. It is hoped that future studies will probe into the contrast between background and guiding diagrams.

Acknowledgements. The authors would like to appreciate that this research is financially supported by MOST (Ministry of Science and Technology) at Taiwan, R.O.C, under the project number: MOST 105-2221-E-006 -124 -. All invited subjects and designers are also appreciated very much.

References

de Lara, S.M.A., de Mattos Fortes, R.P., Russo, C.M.: A study on the acceptance of website interaction aids by older adults. Univ. Access Inf. Soc. **15**(3), 445–460 (2015)

Mitzner, T.L., Rogers, W.A., Fisk, A.D.: Predicting older adults' perceptions about a computer system designed for seniors (2014)

Liao, M.-J., Wu, Y., Sheu, C.-F.: Effects of perceptual complexity on older and younger adults' target acquisition performance (2013)

Leung, R., McGrenere, J., Graf, P.: Age-related differences in the initial usability of mobile device icons (2009)

Gao, Q., Sun, Q.: Examining the usability of touch screen gestures for older and younger adults. Hum. Factors **57**(5), 835–836 (2015)

Dittmar, M.: Changing colour preferences with ageing: A comparative study on younger and older native germans aged 19–90 years. Gerontology **47**(4), 219–226 (2001)

Nguyen-Tri, D., Overbury, O., Faubert, J.: The role of lenticular senescence in age-related colour vision changes (2004)

Johnson, J., Finn, K.: Designing for an Aging Population: Toward Universal Design (2016)

UNFPA United Nations Population Fund (UNFPA). Population Ageing and Development (2012). http://www.unfpa.org/resources/population-ageing-and-development-2012

The International Data Corporation(IDC). http://www.idc.com/

Aging and Social Media

Exploring Storytelling for Digital Memorialization

Grace Ataguba$^{(\boxtimes)}$, Samantha Penrice, and John Shearer

University of Lincoln, Lincoln LN6 7TS, UK
{gataguba, spenrice, jshearer}@lincoln.ac.uk

Abstract. Memories are an interesting part of everyday lives and memorialization through storytelling is an important way to share memories. The increased use of digital devices in the society has brought about a shift suggesting that people are willing to use technologies to remember the dead. With a view to designing devices and platforms to support memorializing through storytelling we explored how willing and comfortable people are sharing stories about the deceased. Our results revealed longer stories were told about younger people who had been dead for longer. This paper reports on our findings of an exploration of stories told by the bereaved and considers design implications for future work.

Keywords: Memorialization · Storytelling · Natural language processing · Death

1 Introduction

This paper focuses on memorialization and storytelling through the lens of the continuing bonds theory. Memorialization and storytelling provides a sense of connecting community with the deceased while recounting memories [1, 2, 16, 26]. Memorialization is a process of remembering and creating a continuing bond with the dead [19]. It is also an intentional act of preserving the memory of a person or an event [18, 23]. Storytelling is a shared communication that requires three elements: the narrator, the subject and audience [16]. Therefore, digital storytelling in this context involves engaging the memories of the dead using technologies such as: CD's, social networks, E-mail, mobile phones, tangible digital devices and so on [15]. Digital technology can keep reminders, record wills, keep lifetime pictures etc. and hence the HCI community has considered ways digital technology will impact on memorialization [5, 19, 23], although there is a concern that *"digital memorabilia ... seem to lack salience"* [24]. Current designs around memorialization adopt participatory approaches, so an understanding of target groups is necessary to develop positive and ethical designs. With a view to designing and exploring storytelling for memorialization through physical, digital artefacts we wished to understand when and how people tell stories about the deceased and how other factors are responsible for how they tell their stories. We were particularly interested in anecdotal stories – i.e. short stories from the daily lives of people and we wanted to explore how the former two can present to the latter.

J. Zhou and G. Salvendy (Eds.): ITAP 2017, Part II, LNCS 10298, pp. 103–113, 2017.
DOI: 10.1007/978-3-319-58536-9_9

1.1   Death Digital Memorialization and Storytelling

Death brings about a barrier in the physical contact between loved ones, but the bereaved continue feel the bonds of those relationships [8] and the need to continuously establish these bonds has led to the process of memorialization. This is explained by the *continuing bonds* theory as proposed by Klass, Phyllis & Steven [13]:

> *"The bereaved remain involved and connected to the deceased and the bereaved actively constructs an inner representation of the deceased that is part of the normal grieving process."*

The bereaved make this representation through their expressions about the deceased. *Continuing bonds* expression is one of the most effective ways of coping during the grieving process and helps in mood regulation [9]. Mood regulation is focused on gaining positive experiences through certain activities [10].

The *continuing bonds* expression can also be seen from the memorialization perspective [17] as discussed by [4] which explains how the attachment needs of an individual are satisfied through symbolic representation of the memories of their deceased as they serve as sources of security and comfort. The attachment needs of an individual vary – being dependent on the size of their attachment network and their age. The attachment network as explained by the theory of socio-emotional selectivity proposed by [3] relates to how older adult attachment network reduces in size and is targeted towards a few friends and family they prefer to share emotional comfort with.

Memorialization through storytelling is influenced by various parameters and demographic data; including: time since death, relationship to the deceased, years of relationship with the deceased, closeness to the deceased, story about the deceased (i.e. deceased identity) and the storyteller [8, 25]. These measures play a role in the *continuing bond* expression and an understanding of these relationships will benefit future interventional technologies.

It's been suggested that *"Future systems need to ... target specific types of human memory"* [24] as there are at least 200 human memories types described in the literature. For human memory, [21] presented five memory types which technologies could support: recovery; recollecting; reminiscing; remembering intentions and reflecting. Memorialization is a conscious activity of the human memory, and with an underlying continuing bonds theory and an understanding of the relationships between demographical data memorialization technologies could leverage these properties of human memory.

2   Related Work

Recent work on memorialization and technologies has shown great potential of future systems, with so far only a few scientific works reported.

De Vries and Rutherford [8] presented findings of a typical memorialization process by measuring relationships that exists between demographic data and content of online memorials which revealed that: a higher proportion of females write memorials compared to males. [8] also reported the frequency distribution of whom memorials were written about: child (70%), friend (above 30%), family group (above 20%), grandchild (above 20%), parent (20%), siblings (above 10%), other relatives (above 10%) and spouse (below 10%) as well as varying content of the memorial which includes: letter to the deceased, emotional expressions, tributes, obituary, cause of death and others. Musambira, Hastings and Hoover [20] also reported (in online memorials) a higher participation of the females compared to the males.

Massimi and Baecker [15] revealed that younger generations hold more digital than non-digital remains and tangible assets were shared among household with a strong emotional attachment of the bereaved to digital/non-digital inheritance due to aesthetics. These findings suggested novel ways to designing technologies that will serve inheriting generations, support the bereaved and address existing life-logging technologies and has further informed designs using digital and non-digital remains.

Phylactery (Fig. 1) was designed by Cowling *et al.* [7] to record and play back stories of objects placed on it, asking the question *"What would the world look like if the IoT wasn't about rendering our physical world tractable to computational systems and was instead about the preservation of the unique personal meanings that accumulate around our material objects?"* It was designed to *"explore the possibility space for an Internet of Meaningful Things"*, and we suggest that preserving memories for memorialization is particularly meaningful.

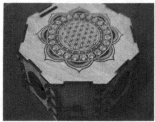  

Fig. 1. Phylactery: A tangible *object* that record stories of tagged objects. (Source [7], p. 44)

Fig. 2. Story *Shell*: A bespoke memorial system. (Source [19], p. 474)

Fig. 3. Pensieve *Box*: A bespoke memorial system that beeps during anniversaries associated with the deceased life time. (Source [5], p. 400)

Moncur *et al.* [19] developed a *Story Shell – "a bespoke, tangible, digital memorial"* that collects artefacts in the form of photos, music, books in addition to stories about the deceased (Fig. 2), finding that the very act of engaging participants in the design of these artefacts did itself serve as a memorial for those individuals. *Pensieve Box* is a similar implementation, developed by Chaudhari *et al.* [5] – a bespoke application that collects materials of the deceased such as photos and is set to beep during particularly anniversaries connected to the deceased, such as birthdays, wedding and death (Fig. 3).

A variation from the western context norm of designs around memorialization was the focus of Uriu and Odom [23] – *Fenestra* is a domestic memorialization technology that uses a wireless mirror display, photo frame and candle light based on the concepts of *butsudan* – a Japanese Buddhist home altar that supports mourning culture in Japan. They found that *"participants drew on Fenestra as a resource for their everyday memorialization practices in valued and, at times, unexpected ways"*.

Digital memorialization has also explored some potentials of the spaces holding the physical remains of the deceased. This was illustrated in Spomenik a geo-located audio based mobile memorial system for Slovenia's World War II victims linked between communities (local and diaspora) by Kirk, Reeves and Durrant [14] in death space. Their work presents some initial observations and reflects on "the challenges of designing digital ubiquitous technologies for culturally sensitive spaces".

3   Present Study

The goal of the study was to understand the relationships between the following factors: storyteller's age and gender, comfort of storyteller, years of relationship to the deceased, deceased age, length of story, time since death and relationship to the deceased in a memorialization practise. The years of relationship to the deceased was selected as a proxy for measuring the closeness of an individual to the deceased. The following research questions emerged to understand relationship between these variables:

1. What is the relationship between the storyteller and their comfort in storytelling, and the deceased?
2. What affects the length of the story?

4   Method

We designed a mixed method – qualitative and quantitative – study to explore our research questions. Research in the study of grief as explained by [13] shows a methodological consistency in the use of qualitative and quantitative methods. We designed an anonymous online survey, echoing the common usage of online memorials and social media, which was described by [2] as a naturalistic setting for grief expression.

This questionnaire was designed to provide participants with an opportunity to write and edit their stories without time or social pressures. Data collected includes:

- Participant demographics
  - age
  - gender
- Time since death
- Comfort of the storyteller
- Years of relationship with the deceased
- Deceased age
- Anecdotal stories
- Length of story
- Relationship to the deceased

The survey was made available for the period of two months: August-September and was deployed fully anonymously, with consent built in to the survey to ensure privacy and openness. Recruitment of participants (N = 90) was carried out using the snowball technique [6], advertisements and flyers. Incomplete data were omitted leaving 36 valid entries – sufficient for analysis [9, 12].

4.1   Story Themes

Stories told by participants were varied (as illustrated in the Word Cloud in Fig. 4), and participants frequently told non-anecdotal stories even though they were explicitly asked for anecdotal stories. Within these stories causes of death and the emotions around bereavement were common, as were descriptions of the personal characteristics of the deceased without any narrative. These stories reflect varying ways participants were willing to describe the deceased. We describe these major themes in the following subsections, along with some related quotes.

Fig. 4. Word cloud overview of story extracts from the dataset

4.2   Cause of Death

The cause of death was a common theme in the stories, even though non-solicited. For example, one of the recently bereaved participants (#26, time since death < 1 year) said "...the lady in question used to have a medical condition called low blood pressure... has been battling with it for a long time". Another person (#27, time since death = 6–10 years) wrote "...died some years ago after suffering from cancer..."

4.3   Personal Characteristics of the Deceased

The stories also reflected attributes that described the kind of person the deceased was – how the participants perceived them. Participant (#41, time since death = 11–15 years) said "... She was very kind...". Another participant (#23, time since death = 6–10 years) expressed that the deceased was "incredibly active and very physically strong *well into his 70s...His sheer determination to do things himself and not waste anything came from his tough youth during WWII when he was only 15 when war broke out".* Participant (#28 time since death = 11–15 years) said *"a very jovial and exciting person...I was able to ride a bicycle in my late teens because of him".*

4.4   Emotions Around Bereavement

Stories often included feelings of bereavement and reflected the emotional connection of participants to how the death occurred. For example Participant (#5, time since death = 21+ years) wrote *"Though I had lost Grandparents previously I was most affected by the sudden death of my best friend James when we were 15 years old.....died on Saturday evening..... It seemed unfathomable that he was no longer with us,.....bright, wonderful boy had gone......."* Participant (#22, time since death = 21+ years) recalled that *"It all began with a light feverish condition...as the night was fast approaching his health condition degenerated into severe body pains with nauseating and vomiting".*

5   Results

Participant Demographics
The participants (n = 36) comprised of 16 males (44.4%) and 20 females (55.6%) of 18 to over 75 years (Median age = 27 years).

What is the relationship between the storyteller and their comfort in storytelling, and the deceased?
The majority of participants told stories about family members (84%). Comfort of the storyteller measured on a Likert scale of 1 (not comfortable) to 5 (extremely comfortable) was higher amongst family than non-family (coded as others) (Fig. 5). This relationship is approaching significance (Kruskal Wallis, p = 0.056), but the number of non-family participants was low. Family relationships includes: parent, spouse, child/grandchild/great grandchild, siblings, and aunt/uncle/other relatives. The others-group includes non-family related relationships such as friend/family friend, neighbor and co-worker/colleague.

The comfort of the storyteller was not affected by the time since death, the length of their relationship with the dead, the storytellers' age or their gender (Kruskal Wallace, p > 0.05 in all cases). There was no bias caused by the respondent age and their likelihood to talk about deceased who they had known for longer (p = 0.408) or who were older (p = 0.35).

What affects the length of the story?
The length of the story, measured by number of words, varied substantially (mean 73.7, standard deviation 89.4). The age, gender and comfort of the storyteller did not affect the length of the story, neither did the type or length of the relationship with the deceased (ANOVA, all p > 0.05). This illustrates that although a storyteller may be uncomfortable, this comfort/discomfort does not influence the length of story they tell.

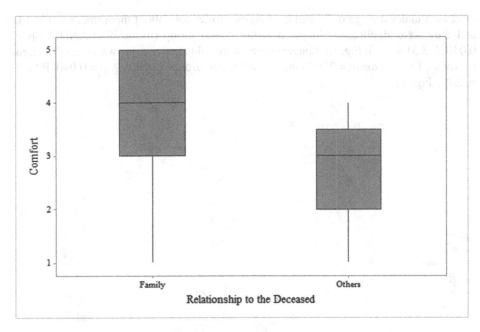

Fig. 5. Family members reported higher levels of comfort than non-family in storytelling (median/mean 4/3.867 and 3/2.8 respectively)

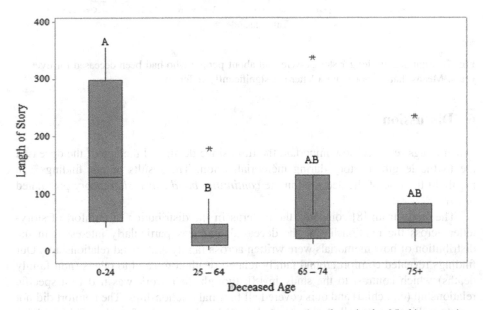

Fig. 6. Stories about young people are significantly longer than those in the 25–64 categories, means that do not share a letter are significantly different.

Deceased under the age of 24 had the longest stories told about them (mean = 166.6), and they were significantly longer than the 25–64 group (mean 39.4; ANOVA p = 0.040, F 3,31 = 3.13; Fig. 6). Longer stories were told about people who been deceased for over 21 years (mean = 229.7) than all other age groups (ANOVA p = 0.040, F 5,34 = 2.70; Fig. 7).

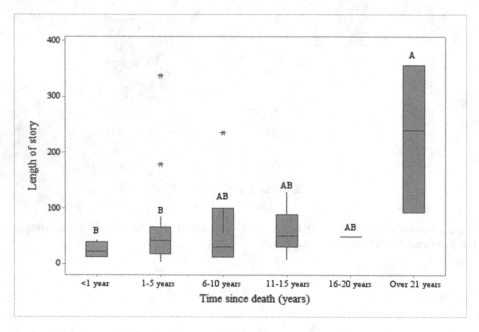

Fig. 7. Significantly longer stories were told about people who had been deceased for over 21 years. Means that do not share a letter are significantly different.

6 Discussion

Our findings revealed how important the time since death and the age of the deceased are to the length of story during memorialization. The results of our findings can highlight the role of the deceased in the *continuing bond expression* theory postulated in [9].

The study from [8] compared the patterns in the distribution of comfort of storyteller across the relationship to the deceased and was particularly interested in the distribution of how memorials were written across family and friend relationships. Our findings revealed comfort around family-related death compared to others (non-family deaths) which contrast to the study in [8], though their work was tied to a specific relationship (e.g. child) and ours covered all familial relationships. The comfort did not impact willingness to tell stories, as evidenced by the length of stories. This explains that grief (measured by comfort) may not prevent a storyteller from participating, supporting the continuing bonds theory.

Another measure of how a storyteller will participate in memorialization is the length of the story, which was characterised more by the deceased than by the story-teller. This supports the identity preservation aspect of storytelling, the storyteller is driven more by the need to preserve the identity of the deceased than by their own relationship and comfort, as explained by socio-emotional selectivity theory proposed by [3].

7 Limitations of the Study

One of the challenges and perhaps because of the sensitive nature of the study was the recruitment technique – snowballing although existing work adopted similar approach, it is likely to be restricted to a certain characteristic of the population only. Ideally, we'd want a good representation across the age demographic (and others), however, a small explorative study about the practices and parameters was sufficient to gain an understanding of the area to inform future work of the research team.

This study examined the emotional state based on text input only – since studies have shown great potential from online memorials where text is usually exchanged during memorialization and the bereaved decide when to post and what to post a priori. The emotional state based on *speech* memorialization technologies was not covered, but could be particularly effective. Similarly, due to the small nature of the exploratory study, data was collected via an online survey and was thus fairly low in content, longer form methods such as interviews could generate more data and longer stories, though inevitably introducing bias from the research team.

This study identified relationships between parameters involved in the memorial-ization process. The causality of these relationships could be based on other forms of closeness to the deceased (e.g. emotional closeness) which was not included in our survey because of the complexity and uncertainty of the measurement scale [22].

8 Implications for Design

We view memorialization as identity preservation to continue bonds with the deceased. The place of the deceased is continually reconstructed through means which people keep the deceased "alive": by calling up good memories; reinterpreting bad habits; and continuing in activities that were shared together [2, 26].

In future work we wish to design devices and platforms to support memorializing through storytelling. Our results suggest that the drive to tell stories about the deceased is sufficiently strong that people will tell these stories even when uncomfortable, with the direct implication for design that we could deprioritise making people comfortable, as long as the situation allows for effective story telling – allowing focus on other areas. Further, the findings that there is no relationship between comfort and demographic data other than perhaps familial vs. non-familial mean that selecting specific demo-graphics who would be more comfortable telling stories about the deceased is non-plausible – an avenue that we had previously considered. The especially important implication is that people are willing to share stories of the deceased even for recent bereavements – a group of people we thought would be unwilling to participate, who we believe memorialization support would be particularly powerful for – perhaps even assisting in the bereavement process.

The strong result that the stories told about people who died young are significantly longer is particularly interesting, and suggests a possible direction. As does the result of longer stories about people who died many years previously. The latter could be interpreted as even after a long time, people still wish to talk about those deceased people, and perhaps that need is underserved – leading to the longer stories in our sample. The understanding of interfaces as a medium makes it imperative to think about both users and storytellers [10, 11] in these contexts.

Overall, we find that these results support the *continuing bonds theory* as a lens for research into memorialisation technologies; that story telling seems powerful; and that even whilst talking about the deceased is perhaps inherently fairly uncomfortable, people are still willing to tell these stories – suggesting that digital memorialization though storytelling may be powerful and have real meaning for their users.

Acknowledgements. We appreciate the contributions of staff, field experts, authors, colleagues, family and volunteers for their support and comments. We particularly thank all the anonymous story tellers who took part in our study.

References

1. Benavides, W.J.J.: Remaining friends with the dead: emerging grieving practices on social networking sites (2013)
2. Brubaker, J.R., Kivran-Swaine, F., Taber, L., Hayes, G.R.: Grief-stricken in a crowd: the language of bereavement and distress in social media. In: ICWSM (2012)
3. Carstensen, L.L., Isaacowitz, D.M., Charles, S.T.: Taking time seriously: a theory of socioemotional selectivity. Am. Psychol. **54**(3), 165 (1999)
4. Cicirelli, V.G.: Attachment relationships in old age. J. Soc. Pers. Relat. **27**(2), 191–199 (2010)
5. Chaudhari, C., Prakash, A., Tsaasan, A.M., Brubaker, J.R., Tanenbaum, J.: Penseive box: themes for digital memorialization practices. In: Proceedings of the TEI 2016: Tenth International Conference on Tangible, Embedded, and Embodied Interaction, pp. 398–403. ACM (2016)
6. Cocciolo, A.: Mobile technology, oral history and the 9/11 Memorial: a study of digitally augmented remembrance. Preserv. Digit. Technol. Culture (PDT&C) (2014). http://www.thinkingprojects.org/Digitally_Augmented_remembrance_for_web.pdf. Accessed 4 Oct 2016
7. Cowling, M., Tanenbaum, J., Birt, J., Tanenbaum, K.: Augmenting reality for augmented reality. Interactions **24**(1), 42–45 (2016). https://doi.org/10.1145/3019008
8. De Vries, B., Rutherford, J.: Memorializing loved ones on the World Wide Web. OMEGA-J. Death Dying **49**(1), 5–26 (2004)
9. Field, N.P., Gao, B., Paderna, L.: Continuing bonds in bereavement: an attachment theory based perspective. Death Stud. **29**(4), 277–299 (2005)

10. Gross, J.J., Richards, J.M., John, O.P.: Emotion regulation in everyday life. In: Emotion Regulation in Couples and Families: Pathways to Dysfunction and Health, vol. 2006, pp. 13–35 (2006)
11. Jacko, J.A. (ed.): Human Computer Interaction Handbook: Fundamentals, Evolving Technologies, and Emerging Applications. CRC Press, Boca Raton (2012)
12. Johanson, G.A., Brooks, G.P.: Initial scale development: sample size for pilot studies. Educ. Psychol. Measur. **70**(3), 394–400 (2010)
13. Klass, D., Silverman, P.R., Nickman, S.: Continuing Bonds: New Understandings of Grief. Taylor & Francis, Washington, DC (2014)
14. Kirk, D.S., Reeves, S., Durrant, A.: Spomenik: augmenting memorials in the woods. In: Proceedings of 2nd All Hands Meeting for the Digital Economy (2011)
15. Massimi, M., Baecker, R.M.: A death in the family: opportunities for designing technologies for the bereaved. In: Proceedings of the SIGCHI Conference on Human Factors in Computing Systems, pp. 1821–1830. ACM (2010)
16. Massimi, M., Baecker, R.M.: Dealing with death in design: developing systems for the bereaved. In: Proceedings of the SIGCHI Conference on Human Factors in Computing Systems, pp. 1001–1010. ACM (2011)
17. Mikulincer, M., Shaver, P.R.: An attachment perspective on bereavement (2008)
18. Moncur, W., Kirk, D.: An emergent framework for digital memorials. In: Proceedings of the 2014 Conference on Designing Interactive Systems, pp. 965–974. ACM (2014)
19. Moncur, W., Julius, M., van den Hoven, E., Kirk, D.: Story shell: the participatory design of a bespoke digital memorial. In: Proceedings of 4th Participatory Innovation Conference, pp. 470–477 (2015)
20. Musambira, G.W., Hastings, S.O., Hoover, J.D.: Bereavement, gender, and cyberspace: a content analysis of parents' memorials to their children. OMEGA-J. Death Dying **54**(4), 263–279 (2007)
21. Sellen, A.J., Whittaker, S.: Beyond total capture: a constructive critique of lifelogging. Commun. ACM **53**(5), 70–77 (2010)
22. Servaty-Seib, H.L., Pistole, M.C.: Adolescent grief: relationship category and emotional closeness. OMEGA-J. Death Dying **54**(2), 147–167 (2007)
23. Uriu, D., Odom, W.: Designing for domestic memorialization and remembrance: a field study of Fenestra in Japan. In: Proceedings of the 2016 CHI Conference on Human Factors in Computing Systems, pp. 5945–5957. ACM, May 2016
24. Van Den Hoven, E., Sas, C., Whittaker, S.: Introduction to this special issue on designing for personal memories: past, present, and future. Hum. Comput. Interact. **27**(1–2), 1–12 (2012)
25. Williams, E.M.: Death of a child to Tay-Sachs or other progressive neurological disorders: long-term impact on parents' emotional and personal lives. Doctoral dissertation, Brandeis University (2014)
26. Wojtkowiak, J., Venbrux, E.: From soul to postself: home memorials in the Netherlands. Mortality **14**(2), 147–158 (2009)

My Interests, My Activities: Learning from an Intergenerational Comparison of Smartwatch Use

Mireia Fernández-Ardèvol(✉) and Andrea Rosales

Internet Interdisciplinary Institute (IN3), Universitat Oberta de Catalunya (UOC), Barcelona, Catalonia, Spain
{mfernandezar,arosalescl}@uoc.edu

Abstract. We analyze smartwatch use from an intergenerational perspective to garner non-stereotypical reflections on ageing. The research questions are: (1) How do personal interests shape, and how are they shaped by, first-time use of a smartwatch? (2) To what extent do tracked data help in interpreting the relationship between the user and the device? We analyze two older and two middle-aged adults involved in a one-year case study, and combine log data and reported activities for richer empirical evidence. The older adults showed higher levels of smartwatch activity than the middle-aged. The key services they used were notifications and the pedometer. We found that smartwatch uses and forms of appropriation are as diverse as the four participants are and that the ways in which such watches are adopted are shaped by personal circumstances and interests. The tracked data helped to illustrate smartwatch uses, providing acceptably accurate pictures of activities. However, the low number of participants in the case study magnified the data's limitations, which illustrate issues to be taken into account when working with tracked data – or big data in general.

Keywords: Smartwatches · Log data · Older adults · Middle-aged adults

1 Introduction

With the release of Android Wear and smartwatches by several big brands, including LG, Samsung and Motorola, 2014 was the year of the wrist revolution. There was quite a bit of expectation about how this wearable would allow the public to access and interact with personal information. The first results regarding smartwatch usage began to appear in 2015 (e.g. [1–4]), but these studies have not included older people nor have they made a generational analysis of the data. Following a common strategy in ICT studies, teenagers and young people constitute the reference generations, as they help identify main trends of adoption and use [5]. However, this negative correlation between age and ICT use, so persistent in digital divide studies [6], reinforces older people being overlooked. The increasing demographic and social importance of older people in Europe and other developed countries [7], together with the heterogeneity of older people [8, 9], should lead us to question this traditional approach. Of particular interest from among this group of older people are the active ICT users making specific use of digital technologies (e.g.

© Springer International Publishing AG 2017
J. Zhou and G. Salvendy (Eds.): ITAP 2017, Part II, LNCS 10298, pp. 114–129, 2017.
DOI: 10.1007/978-3-319-58536-9_10

[10, 11]), and we should not ignore them if we want to have an accurate picture of the ways our societies – as a whole – appropriate digital technologies.

Thus, in this study we address the issue of how older people use smartwatches from a generational perspective [12], in order to garner non-stereotypical reflections related to age. To do so, we analyze the experiences of two older adults and two middle-aged adults using smartwatch logs along with five interviews over the course of 12 months. Specifically, we used tracked data as material during the later interviews to spark discussion about user experiences. Therefore, beyond trying to provide descriptive statistics of smartwatch usage, as is common in big data analysis, we present in this paper the dialogue between tracked data and user experiences.

Multipurpose digital devices such as the smartwatch offer a set of possibilities that users adopt if they match their individual interests. Thus, in this study we approach two main research questions regarding this new digital product:

RQ1. How do personal interests shape, and how are they shaped by, first-time use of a smartwatch?
RQ2. To what extent do tracked data help in interpreting the relationship between the user and the device?

2   Related Work

Back in the 1990s, wearables were visualized as an opportunity to access personal information on the go, thus acting as "visual memory prosthetic(s) and perception enhancer(s)" [13] p. 23, capable of changing cultural concepts of everyday life [14]. However, since the irruption of different smartwatches onto the market in 2014, few studies on smartwatch use have been able to validate such an assumption. Similar to users of conventional watches [15], style-based choices constitute a relevant part of the smartwatch experience [1, 2]. Most studies highlight the use of notifications, fitness apps and – more recently – GPS [1–3]. Some users question the limited features of smartwatch apps compared to smartphones [1], and, similarly, [3] reports on the interest of users in replacing their smartphone with a smartwatch. While early studies argue that it is faster to access a wrist-mounted device than a device stored in the pocket [16], recent studies go even further, saying that smartwatch notifications distract less than smartphone notifications [3] and that they reduce smartphone dependency [2]. However, accessing smartwatch notifications while driving present no less of a risk as accessing smartphone notifications [4]. None of these studies includes older people or make an intergenerational analysis. Therefore, as of yet it is not possible to know if smartwatches have different meanings for users of different ages.

Most of the research on smartwatches in the field of human-computer interaction (HCI) focuses on new interaction paradigms, showing how smartwatch design is a vibrant area under development. Some examples include: exploring the interactive design within the limited space available on a smartwatch screen [17, 18]; exploring gestures to interact with a smartwatch, including beating gestures [19] and spatial gestures [20]; the limits of tactile patterns [21] or proximity-based hand input [22]; and exploring text input [23, 24] – for example with crowd-assisted writing [25]. A few other studies focus on the design of new smartwatch apps, e.g. for scratch recognition [26]. Again, these new interaction paradigms and smartwatch apps do not consider older people's interests and do not include older people in their conceptualization, design or evaluation.

Some of the problems for which wearable technologies are seen as a possible solution are often related to older people, such as managing emergencies, controlling health indicators, encouraging physical activity or fighting isolation. Some smartwatch developments give accounts of this trend, e.g. regarding homecare [27] and fall detection [28]. We suggest adopting a broader outlook in order to see how smartwatches can be connected to personal interests and activities and to understand to what extent such technologies are appropriated at different ages.

3 Empirical Data and Methodology

The empirical evidence presented here comes from a case study originally designed to analyze the processes of smartwatch adoption and appropriation by older people during one year. We provided a Moto G 360 smartwatch to participants, all of whom had to have a compatible Android smartphone. Participants had to be 65 or older. They needed to be active users of smartphones already, demonstrate strong engagement to follow the study, and not have a smartwatch. They could choose between the Moto G 360 1st generation (1.6'' screen) and the Moto G 360 Sports 2nd generation (1.37'' screen), models available on the market during the initial recruitment process. Participants received monetary compensation for time spent in interviews and will be able to keep the smartwatch at the end of the fieldwork. Following approved ethical protocols, participants could stop their collaboration with the project at their convenience.[1] Some members of the research team also started wearing the smartwatch to better understand, on the one hand, its affordances and limitations and, on the other, the actual meaning of the log data to be collected. This gave them the opportunity to analyze their experience as users under conditions similar to those of the senior participants. We inserted ourselves in the collection of data and our personal experiences with the smartwatch are included in our interpretation of the results, taking an analytical ethnography [29] approach.

We adopted a mixed-method strategy by combining quantitative and qualitative methods [30] in a flexible design [31] to address the research questions. On the one hand, we collected the smartphone logs. To do so, we developed and launched the Wear Monitor app on Google Play [32], which works with Android watches. All partakers installed it as part of their commitment to the project. To respect privacy, users could stop the tracking app for a period of time, at their convenience. The logs were periodically uploaded to our university server, where the information is securely stored. Among other features, Wear Monitor collected the date and duration of smartwatch app activities as well as the geolocation of these activities, if available. It also tracked if the phone

---

[1] In fact, two participants in Barcelona left the project at the beginning of the fieldwork and were immediately replaced.

was connected to the watch during each activity, and what kind of Internet connection the phone was using at that moment. Transmitted information, such as text or images, was not collected to respect users' major privacy issues. When the app was installed, a short survey collected basic demographic information including age, gender and level of education.

On the other hand, we conducted five semi-structured interviews, one every two or three months, with participants. We also provided some training sessions and offered support if they had problems with the wearable. The first semi-structured interview, conducted before the device was delivered, revolved around the expectations created by the smartwatch. The second and third interviews looked at smartwatch use in everyday life, once the participants had increased their level of experience with the smartwatch. The fourth and fifth conversations, conducted once enough log data had been collected, established a dialogue between the tracked logs – depicted as figures or geolocated maps – and the perceived and reported use of the smartwatch.

Partakers could decide when not to wear the smartwatch. The older participants could share the smartwatch with whomever they decided, while the middle-aged researchers shared it within the team or with technicians for exploratory purposes (i.e. to conduct specific observations or to address particular technical issues).

Tracked data were analyzed with basic tools, mostly the graphical depiction of time series (the daily activity of the smartwatch, average accesses per hour or geo-located activities, among others). In the two last semi-structured interviews, we discussed a set of figures with each participant to determine to what degree they identified with the personal information gathered. In preparing this paper, the authors read and reread the interviews with participants, transcribed verbatim, and conducted a thematic analysis [33] to identify common topics relevant to the research questions. The comments received from participants during the recruitment process, training sessions and personal support were also taken into account. The researchers followed a similar strategy to reflect on their own data. They took notes of their experiences with the watch and shared them with the rest of the team in different meetings. Of particular interest for this paper were the design of the figures we discuss in the next section and the subsequent validation of the data based on the researchers' experience.

The smartwatch users involved in the research project were, on one hand, nine older adult participants: four women and five men aged between 65 and 80 at the beginning of the study (average age 71.3, standard deviation 4.7). On the other, four middle-aged researchers: all of them women between 38 and 44 (average age 41.0, standard deviation 2.1). Fieldwork, conducted in Barcelona and Rome, was carried out over a little more than a year between winter 2015 and winter 2016/7 and was drawing to a close at the time we write this paper.

This paper focuses on the smartwatch experiences of four users, two older adults and two middle-aged adults, all living in Barcelona, to get more detailed nuances, enrich the analysis and inspire further analysis. Focusing on this small subset of partakers allows an in-depth investigation of the ways (if any) the smartwatch shapes – and is shaped by – personal interests and everyday life activities. Also, this reduced sample favors a critical analysis of the tracked data's potentialities and limitations to identify the activities conducted with the wearable. Neither the case study nor the subset is meant to provide representative data, but rather to create a discussion supported by substantive empirical evidence: it is an explorative study. This strategy looks for non-stereotypical reflections related to age, as we understand this is one of the most powerful outcomes of intergenerational comparisons.

The four users we reflect on in this paper are: Carme (female, 80 years old; secondary education); Pedro (male, 70; primary education or lower), who participates in the interviews together with his spouse, Rosa (female, 65, primary education or lower); and Irene and Laia (females, 41 and 44; university degree or higher). We use fake names to guarantee anonymity. In quotations, we will indicate the number of the interview preceded with an "i" (i.e. Pedro_i2). For log data analysis we selected a 3-month period, from March 1st to July 31st, five months after starting to use the watches, when partakers had already surpassed the first stages of use and, therefore, had reached more stable use in everyday life situations.

4 Results and Discussion

4.1 Perception of Use and Activities

In her 80s, **Carme** is a very social person with a fairly busy agenda during weekdays and weekends. Among other activities, she regularly attends different courses and works as a volunteer. She also has an extended personal network – family and friends – with whom mediated communication is essential.

When it comes to talking about digital technology, she loves being up-to-speed with the latest trend and being told that she acts much younger than her age. Regarding the smartwatch, she reports:

Carme_i5: *With the nephews, you feel a little bit conceited, full of yourself. [I tell them,] "What do you think? That you know a lot?" They tell me, "You are not the typical 80-year-old woman," and this makes me feel good.*

During the selected period of tracked data, Carme's smartwatch reported logs for less than half of the days (42%). She did not use it during some holidays in the beach or without internet access, and afterwards some days when it was not working properly. However, on the days she used the watch, she seemed to show the highest level of engagement, with 134 interactions per day on average (see Table 1 and Fig. 1). To her, wearing the smartwatch became "a force of habit... it goes with me". However, although she is the person who seemed to interact more frequently with the smartwatch – when she wears it – she does not think she uses the device too much. According to her, this result must have to do with the fact that she wears it many hours a day, and that she has a lot of incoming notifications from her social circle. Indeed, she explains how she handles notifications:

Carme_i3: *It's not that I use it too much. I mean, I don't get obsessed, but I use it. ... Yes. Also, when you get used to it, it's convenient, because suddenly, a beep. Let's see. What's that? Is it an email, a WhatsApp? ... And then, well, it's a WhatsApp, then you go to the phone and answer, if you have to answer... That's it... It's practical.*

Table 1. Daily use of the smartwatch during the selected 3-months period

	Older adults		Middle-aged adults		
	Carme	Pedro	Irene	Laia	Average
Smartwatch use, days (N)	39	92	43	73	61.8
% of use (days)	42%	100%	47%	79%	67%
Interactions per day (based on N)					
Average	133.8	84.9	84.6	58.7	84.3
Standard deviation	48.8	28.2	62.5	34.6	47.5
Median	128	82	79	56	81
Min.	5	28	1	1	1
Max.	241	175	264	134	264

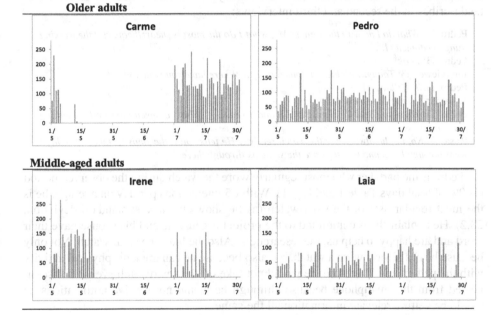

Fig. 1. Smartwatch, number of daily activities during the selected 3-month period

Finally, even though she "always wear[s] it", she clearly states that there are times when she would not put it on. The moments she would opt to wear a conventional watch include, firstly, when she wants or has to dress up; secondly, on vacations when she will not have Internet access; and thirdly, when the smartwatch disconnects from the smartphone and she will have to wait for more than a day to have a Wi-Fi connection so she can pair them up again.

Pedro, 70 years old, loves watches. He likes being in control of time. He and his wife Rosa liked the idea of participating in a technological project and using a new digital device while helping us, the researchers, to fulfill our goals. They share a smartphone, so when Rosa received the smartwatch, they decided Pedro would be the one to wear it. They also agreed that Rosa could "play" with the device whenever she wanted.

The arrival of the smartwatch changed their daily dynamic. Pedro has a great deal of stamina, and it is important for him to take long walks. He has a long walk in the city every morning, Monday to Friday, and Rosa is very open about how this is a must for him. He used to bring the mobile phone with him so he could track his walks, but as the phone was so big, they decided he could just wear the smartwatch instead. Now during his morning walks Pedro has no way of communicating with home – something Rosa is not happy about – but he has been able to ensure two very important aspects: control over time and control over his physical activity. He explains how he likes checking the number of steps every day and looks to see whether the same path on a different day results in the same step count. He is proud to explain how much he walks, and the number of steps he has taken has become part of his everyday discourse about his activities, as he describes in the second and third interviews:

> Pedro_i2: *What do I do with the watch? Me, what I do the most is [heart]beats and the walking thing [pedometer]...*
> Pedro_i3: *Look.*
> Interviewer_i3: *Today... Eighteen kilometers?! ... Where have you gone today?*
> Pedro_i3: *To [Place A].*
> Rosa_i3: *... Like almost every day.*
> Pedro_i3: *There are 18,248 steps... In 2 h and 15 min. ... Which is seven thousand-something per hour.*
> Rosa_i3: *No, no, he always has the watch ready... He tells you... the steps he takes: "Today I went through here, and the steps are the same as through there."*

Pedro is the partaker who most regularly wore the watch during the observed period (100% of total days Table 1 and Fig. 1). With 85 interactions per day on average, he is the most regular user of the smartwatch (as he shows the lowest standard deviation, 28.2). He explains he is committed to the project because he and his spouse gave their word and are happy to help us, the researchers. Also, he likes the smartwatch. Not only because he has always worn a watch, but also because he can track his physical activity with the pedometer. Therefore, he would not take off the smartwatch even if it disconnected from the smartphone because although he would not receive notifications he would be getting relevant information all the same.

The two middle-aged adults, Irene and Laia, are the enthusiastic researchers who designed the case study. They were partly inspired by their notion that it would be interesting to have a smartwatch and explore the use of a new digital device. **Irene** in particular felt that wearables would allow for a more natural interaction with information, expecting to be able to carry out the activities she usually did with the smartphone without having to hold a device in her hands. Irene, just like Carme, had a vacation during the observed period. This, together with a work trip during which she had limited access to a plug adaptor to charge the smartwatch, resulted in her using it 47% of the days (Table 1 and Fig. 1). Her number of interactions per day, 85, is similar to Pedro's but she shows more extreme values of use (standard deviation above the average, 63). This could be because, even though on some days she was not wearing the watch, it kept receiving notifications when it was close enough to the smartphone to connect to it.

Finally, **Laia** ranks second in wearing the smartwatch (79% of total days, Table 1). Laia started to use the smartwatch's pedometer and found it an interesting feature. She liked having the notifications on her wrist, as this allowed her to "ignore" the smartphone without missing any important incoming communication. While she found some of the new features convenient, Laia started wearing the smartwatch on and off – more often at the end of the period. She had issues with the watch battery, which drained very often. On these occasions, she would either leave the watch at home – this would happen mainly during weekends – or wear it even though it was off and charge it once she got to a place with a plug – usually the office or home. In fact, she had been asked more than once about the "black-screen watch" she was wearing and had to tell the person asking that the watch had lost its charge, which led to further (negative) comments.

She defines herself as "lazy" when it comes to keeping the smartwatch running, which could explain why she has the lowest number of interactions (59 per day of use, Table 1). In addition, Laia did not feel it necessary to wear the smartwatch during the weekend, even more so if she stayed at home. In terms of the daily activity of her smartwatch, this led to her having scattered zero values close to columns with very low values (Fig. 1). Based on what we learned during our fieldwork, columns with values close to zero typically respond to days on which the watch's battery was drained or the watch was turned off after midnight followed by at least one day in which the smartwatch was not turned on. Laia used to shut the watch down at night because she would put her smartphone on airplane mode. As she did not expect to have to use it, it made sense to go for this small, environmentally friendly gesture.

4.2 Hourly Distribution of the Smartwatch Activities

We explored and commented on with participants the hourly distribution of the smartwatch activities (see Fig. 2). The figures give a sense of the activity engaged in during the day and provide clues about how time is arranged socially – with less activity at night and, in some cases, during lunch time. They depict the average hourly smartwatch activities for each participant. **Carme** told us that she took off the smartwatch at night and left it outside the room, next to the charger. She would charge the watch when she got up, and after her morning routine – which included some physical exercise – she would put the watch on. The hourly distribution of Carme's smartwatch use is consistent with the fact that, out of the four partakers, she is the one who most interacts with the device.

Pedro and Rosa found that the figure reflected his activity:

Pedro_i4: *Me, when I check it the most is when I go walking, [I do it] every now and then ... I usually check it when I get to [place B]... And then when I arrive to [place A – his final destination]... There ... I check the time it took me ... and the steps to get there.*
Rosa_i4: *And then, all the days it is the same... time. ... When he gets home he shows it [the smartwatch pedometer] to me... This is why I say that, yes [we recognize ourselves in the figures], because [he usually would go] "look how much I walked today".*

Irene also felt that the figure reflected her activity both night and day. At night she kept both the phone and the watch turned on. Thus, the nighttime smartwatch activity should be due to the incoming notifications she receives while sleeping. She indicated

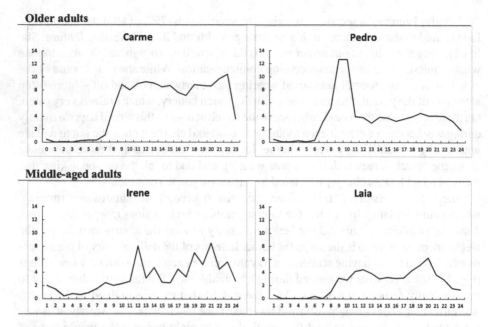

Fig. 2. Hourly distribution of smartwatch activities (average values per hour, 3 months)

that the high daytime peaks were due to the fact that she took her watch on and off during the day because of ergonomic and family issues. Of particular interest are ergonomic matters relating to the size and weight of the smartwatch, which causes discomfort when typing on the computer.

Laia used to take off the watch at dinner time – around 9 or 10 pm. Because of this and the fact that she would turn it off before going to sleep, she expected to have a low level of reported activity at night. In this regard, she considered the figure to be good reflection of the way she uses the watch. However, she expected higher numbers during office hours, as she was under the impression that she used to "touch it a lot" while at work. But it was in the evening that there was a spike in activity, which could have been related to incoming notifications regarding social and family life. Finally, the lower levels of activity on her smartwatch are in line with the results obtained in Fig. 1.

4.3   Smartwatch Geo-Located Activities

The logs include the geolocation of each smartwatch activity, but only when the GPS is activated. The maps in Fig. 3 show the geolocated activities tracked on the four smart-watches in the city of Barcelona. Other locations are excluded in this paper to guarantee greater privacy. Non-geolocated activities are not represented, nor are the days of non-use during the three months of observation. Therefore, it is not possible to compare the number and distribution of smartwatch activities among partakers.

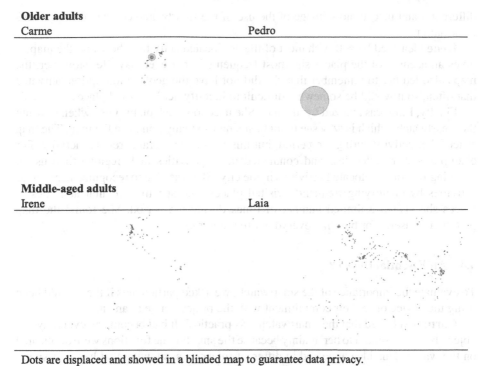

Dots are displaced and showed in a blinded map to guarantee data privacy.

Fig. 3. Geolocated smartwatch activities in the city of Barcelona (3 months)

Carme usually has the GPS activated, resulting in most of her smartwatch activities being geolocated. She admits that the map gives an account of the usual places she frequents in her life, as well as an account of other locations less frequently visited. Although not shown here, her map included sites in the same province – usually due to weekend activities – and more distant locations – usually trips to visit acquaintances or for vacation. On vacation she ended up taking off the smartwatch. Therefore, these activities are underrepresented on the map. Also, despite the fact she was already aware that we had access to such information, she was impressed with the maps and emphasized how sensitive the log data were: "We [participants] are under your control".

Conversely, **Pedro**'s map shows he did not have the GPS activated on a regular basis. Although he always wore the watch, there was almost no geolocated information in the watch logs. In fact, he had the watch disconnected – or unpaired – from the smartphone very often (data not shown here).[2] Also, instead of using the Wi-Fi connection, he and his spouse tended to use exclusively the mobile Internet connection for their mobile devices. This is particularly true for the smartphone they have paired with the smartwatch and shows that Pedro and his wife have control over the services they use in their everyday life. That is, they decided to switch off the GPS and Wi-Fi most of the time, switching it on only in specific situations. This resulted in a map with a decidedly

---

[2] This did not affect the ability to gather log data.

different – and inaccurate – image of the use of the smartwatch compared to previous information.

Irene identified herself with most of the geolocated activities shown on the map. It gives an account of the places she most frequents in her everyday life. However, the maps also led her to remember that she did not have the geolocation option activated that often, so it would be somewhat difficult to identify her less usual places.

Finally, **Laia** was amazed by the map. She used to switch on the GPS when wearing the smartwatch, which is why she thought she had so many points on the map. The map reflects her activity during the period, but this is not her average, regular activity. For example, she travelled less and conducted more activities in Barcelona than usual, resulting in more geolocated activities in the city. She was able to recognize her regular activities by identifying frequently visited places, and specific irregular activities in places she visited a limited number of times during the period. She found the map particularly useful for building everyday life memories.

4.4 An Essential Device?

To evaluate the importance of the smartwatch, we asked participants if they would keep using the device once their commitment with the project came to an end.

Carme explained that the smartwatch was practical. It had become an everyday life object, but not essential to her, mainly because the smartphone functions were duplicated on the watch. This idea appeared in different interviews, showing that her assessment of the new device did not change during the months she wore it.

Carme_i2: *Well, I look less at the phone... because I have notifications here [on the smartwatch]. Not much more. ... Look, I think the smartphone is useful for everything. And the watch, well, it's wonderful. ... It's beautiful. It's cute. ... You show it to anyone "Wow, what a watch you wear, how cutting-edge you are!" ... But not much more.*

Carme_i5: *It's more like a hobby. For somebody it could be useful, for me, too. For me, a regular watch is ok. You can follow the steps here [on the phone]; you can see the pictures, the bus information, the maps [on the phone]. Sometimes, it's a duplicate. In some moments it's ok to have it [this information] on the wrist.*

After some experience with it, in the third interview she explained she would not buy a smartwatch on her own. Although she was a happy user of the watch, in the last interview she explained her future plans for the device:

Carme_i5: *When the project is over, I think I'll give the watch to my nephew, for his birthday. I'll give this to him and it will be the coolest thing ever.*

Pedro, on the contrary, said he would keep using the smartwatch after the project. Rosa confirmed this, indicating that he was a fan of the device. As he explained at different times, for him "the steps (counter)" was extremely useful. The usability of the smartwatch was also key, as he preferred wearing it over having the smartphone in his pocket when he went on his morning walks. He has stopped using the smartphone's pedometer and only checks the information on the smartwatch. Therefore, when asked in the fifth interview, he explained that he "would consider buying a new one" if the smartwatch got broken.

According to **Irene**, the watch was a useful device, mainly for social purposes, particularly so that her personal network could reach her. Without the watch, she would have missed most of her phone calls and would not have received messages on time. She thought that she would keep using the watch after the project. However, wearing it all the time was uncomfortable; the watch was too big and heavy for her. Two particularly uncomfortable situations were wearing it while typing on the computer and wearing it with winter jackets, which tend to have tight-fitting sleeves for the dimensions of the smartwatch, during outdoor activities.

When she decided to put it on, **Laia** got accustomed to wearing the watch the entire day. She agreed that it was uncomfortable to wear while typing, but she found ways to get around this. She encountered a number of trade-offs with the smartwatch. For instance, when checking the time, she liked the big numbers and appreciated having the "official local time" provided through the mobile operator network. However, she found the need to touch the black screen each time she wanted to look at the time useless. She therefore tried to familiarize herself with the wrist movement feature to turn the screen on, but she never mastered it. She finally decided to keep the screen black as much as possible, as, in some contexts, the smartwatch could show unwanted information – a very prevalent concern when wearing short sleeves. These trade-offs, coupled with the battery issues, led to a feeling of relief when she had to (temporarily) lend the smartwatch to another partaker due to technical issues.

In summary, personal interests define digital activity no matter the age of the user. We found that in some instances new digital devices can foster the achievement of these interests, while in others they have no effect at all. The smartwatch is incorporated when it proves useful, particularly in comparison to the screen against which it competes: that of the smartphone. For the participants in the study, tracked data created a new way of depicting daily activities.

5   Conclusion

Smartwatches still have significant market possibilities, even though they might need to undergo a redesigning to meet users' needs better. At present, potential users are already highly accustomed to wearing a wristwatch and the concept of gathering information from it, such as the date or time. Moreover, watches are fashion accessories, often worn to express personal style [15]. For the analyzed participants, older and middle-aged adults, it was quite easy to integrate an augmented watch into their everyday lives. It allowed for more natural interaction [34] and provided them with a wearable extra screen that complemented the smartphone. However, a key point for becoming a long-term user was the cost-benefit balance, or the trade-offs, that accompanied the device. In this sense, participants evaluated the smartwatch's usability mainly in comparison with that of the smartphone – e.g. in situations in which the user could have also kept the phone in their pocket to complete a given task. Another important dimension, the new services only available on the smartwatch and not on other devices, such as the heartbeat monitor, appeared less prominently in this study.

To obtain better insight into the processes behind the adoption of this new digital device, we applied a mixed-method approach that combined log data and interviews during a one-year fieldwork case study and focused on four users, two older adults and two middle-aged adults. The smartwatch, a multipurpose digital device, served as the entry point through which to explore two main research questions.

- RQ1. How do personal interests shape, and how are they shaped by, first-time use of a smartwatch?

On the one hand, we observed that personal interests might lead to stop using the device. Carme, Irene, and Laia all appreciated easy access to notifications to ensure their connectivity; it was a feature that matched their interests. However, only Irene said she would keep using a smartwatch "if it were lighter." Carme planned to give the smartwatch to a nephew once the project is over, and Laia felt relieved when she had to pass the watch on to another project partaker. Pedro adapted the use of the smartwatch to his personal interests, as he loved the pedometer. Moreover, he appreciated being able to look at it all the time. Pedro's use of the smartwatch also made sense when unpaired with the phone, and he plans to keep using the device after the project. To our understanding, Pedro is the participant who had the best experience with the device, as he found a specific feature – the pedometer – that substituted the smartphone.

On the other hand, one case illustrates the way in which the introduction of the smartwatch shaped personal interest – even though this did not necessarily equate to the adoption of the smartwatch in the long term. Laia had never shown an interest in using her smartphone's pedometer, but she started to use the smartwatch's, since it was one the apps these wearables promote the most. She got encouragement from regular push messages. As a result, she got used to the pedometer and kept using it even when not wearing the smartwatch, since the app was also available on her smartphone.

- RQ2. To what extent do tracked data help in interpreting the relationship between the user and the device?

Tracked data provided significant insights into the relationship participants had with the smartphone. We were able to confirm the levels of use of the device: Pedro wore it every day, while the rest of the participants did not. Participants found that the figures we compiled reflected their use of the device in terms of number of daily activities and average activities broken down by hour. The geolocated map was also a fairly accurate representation of Laia's and, to some extent, Carme's and Irene's activities. However, Pedro's geolocated activity delivered biased information due to the way he uses his smartphone, namely with the GPS usually switched off. Based solely on the map, we could infer extremely motionless use, attributing this to technical problems or, following a stereotype – as the user is an old person – to the person being in a situation of dependency that prevents them from leaving the home. Applying the mixed-method approach allows us to establish a very different picture: an old person who uses the smartwatch mostly as a pedometer to track his high levels of daily walking activity, but for which geolocated data is not able to provide good quality information due to the device settings defined by the user.

In closing, smartwatch uses and forms of appropriation are as diverse as the four participants in our study. Ways of adoption are shaped by personal circumstances and interests, and tracked data help illustrate those uses – at least to some extent. Of particular importance is that the older users, Carme and Pedro, showed higher levels of smartwatch activity than the middle-aged ones. Furthermore, one of the older adults will most certainly keep using the smartwatch and one of the middle-aged adults might keep using it.

6   Limitations and Implications for Future Research

The small size of the case study magnified the limitations of tracked data, an issue that must always be taken into account, regardless of sample size. These limitations pose a greater problem than the lack of generalizable results common to qualitative case studies, as the quality of the tracked data depends on a number of factors that may go undetected. For instance, without the qualitative approach, we would not have been able to understand the motivations of the lack of movement in Pedro's data, since we would not have discovered that he hardly activated the geolocation option. Other limitations involved the technological affordances of the tracking process, as the system only provided information about the watch's activities. That is, we were only able to find out when the screen turned on, but it was impossible to determine whether this activity was generated by the user or by an incoming notification. In the first case, the interaction with the device would be expected to be intentional, something not applicable in the second case. Without specific information on how the activity was generated, we as researchers lose part of the (expected) richness of the data. These two examples show that log data – the raw material for big data approaches – face limitations that must be taken into account, as data affected by non-explicit biases result in badly informed decisions.

In response to this challenge, in a future paper we plan to develop an analysis of the biases gathered log data face and how they impact on both the interpretation of the available variables and the results. Our understanding is that, as proven in other fields, by understanding the limits of the method we will contribute to strengthening it.

Acknowledgments.   The authors are indebted to all participants in the study. Alexandre Dotor Casals and Jessica Zambrano supported the technical aspects of the study. This project received partial funding from the Ageing + Communication + Technology project http://actproject.ca/ (ref. 895-2013-1018, Social Sciences and Humanities Research Council of Canada).

References

1. Schirra, S., Bentley, F.R.: "It's kind of like an extra screen for my phone" understanding everyday uses of consumer smart watches. In: Extended Abstracts of the SIGCHI International Conference on Human Factors in Computer Systems – CHI 2015 EA, pp. 2151–2156 (2015). doi:10.1145/2702613.2732931
2. Cecchinato, M.E., Cox, A.L., Bird, J.: Smartwatches: the good, the bad and the ugly? In: Extended Abstracts of the SIGCHI International Conference on Human Factors in Computing Systems - EA CHI 2015, pp. 2133–2138 (2015). doi:10.1145/2702613.2732837

3. Pizza, S., Brown, B., McMillan, D., Lampinen, A.: Smartwatch in vivo. In: Proceedings of the SIGCHI International Conference on Human Factors in Computer Systems – CHI 2016 (2016) doi:10.1145/2858036.2858522
4. Giang, W.C.W., Shanti, I., Chen, H.-Y.W., Zhou, A., Donmez, B.: Smartwatches vs. smartphones: a preliminary report of driver behavior and perceived risk while responding to notifications. In: Proceedings of the International Conference on Automotive User Interfaces and Interactive Vehicular Applications, pp. 154–161 (2015). doi:10.1145/2799250.2799282
5. Castells, M., Fernández-Ardèvol, M., Linchuan Qiu, J., Sey, A.: Mobile Communication and Society: A Global Perspective. The MIT Press, Cambridge (2006)
6. Helsper, E.J., Reisdorf, B.C.: The emergence of a "digital underclass" in Great Britain and Sweden: changing reasons for digital exclusion, pp. 1–18. New Media & Society (2016). doi: 10.1177/1461444816634676
7. United Nations, Department of Economic and Social Affairs, Population Division: World Population Prospects: The 2015 Revision, Key Findings and Advance Tables. Working Paper No. ESA/P/WP.241 (2015)
8. Neugarten, B.L.: The young-old and the age-irrelevant society. In: Neugarten, B.L. and Neugarten, D.A. (eds.) The Meanings of Age: Selected Papers of Bernice L. Neugarten, pp. 47–55. The University of Chicago Press, Chicago (1996)
9. Stone, M.E., Lin, J., Dannefer, D., Kelley-Moore, J.A.: The continued eclipse of heterogeneity in gerontological research. J. Gerontol. Ser. B Psychol. Sci. Soc. Sci. 72, 162–167 (2016). doi:10.1093/geronb/gbv068
10. Rosales, A., Fernández-Ardèvol, M.: Smartphones, apps and older people's interests: from a generational perspective. In: Proceedings of the International Conference on Human Computer Interaction with Mobile Devices and Services – MobileHCI 2016. doi: 10.1145/2935334.2935363
11. Rosales, A., Fernández-Ardèvol, M.: Generational comparison of simultaneous internet activities using smartphones and computers. In: Proceedings of the Conference on Human Aspects of IT for the Aged Population – HCII 2016 (2016). doi:10.1007/978-3-319-39943-0_46
12. Loos, E.F.: Generational use of new media and the (ir)revelance of age. In: Colombo, F., Fortunati, L. (eds.) Broadband Society and Generational Changes, pp. 259–273. Peter Lang, Berlin (2011)
13. Mann, S.: Wearable computing: a first step toward personal imaging. Computer 30, 25–32 (1997). doi:10.1109/2.566147
14. Martin, T.L.: Time and time again: parallels in the development of the watch and the wearable computer. In: Proceedings of the International Symposium on Wearable Computers, ISWC 2002, pp. 5–11 (2002)
15. Lyons, K.: What can a dumb watch teach a smartwatch? In: Proceedings of the ACM International Symposium on Wearable Computers - ISWC 2015, pp. 3–10 (2015). doi: 10.1145/2802083.2802084
16. Ashbrook, D.L., Clawson, J.R., Lyons, K., Starner, T.E., Patel, N.: Quickdraw: the impact of mobility and on-body placement on device access time. In: Proceedings of the SIGCHI International Conference on Human Factors in Computing Systems – CHI 2008, pp. 219–222 (2008). doi:10.1145/1357054.1357092
17. Ashbrook, D.L., Lyons, K., Starner, T.: An investigation into round touchscreen wristwatch interaction. In: Proceedings of the International Conference on Human Computer Interaction with Mobile Devices and Services – MobileHCI 2008, p. 311 (2008). doi: 10.1145/1409240.1409276

18. Xu, C., Lyons, K.: Shimmering smartwatches: exploring the smartwatch design space. In: Proceedings of the International Conference on Tangible, Embedded, and Embodied Interaction - TEI 2015, pp. 69–76 (2015). doi:10.1145/2677199.2680599
19. Oakley, I., Lee, D., Islam, R.: Beats: tapping gestures for smart watches. In: Proceedings of the SIGCHI International Conference on Human Factors in Computer Systems – CHI 2015, pp. 1237–1246 (2015)
20. Chen, X. A., Grossman, T., Wigdor, D.J., Fitzmaurice, G.: Duet: exploring joint interactions on a smart phone and a smart watch. In: Proceedings of the SIGCHI International Conference on Human Factors in Computing Systems - CHI 2014, pp. 159–168 (2014). doi: 10.1145/2556288.2556955
21. Lee, S. C., Starner, T.: BuzzWear. In: Proceedings of the SIGCHI International Conference on Human Factors in Computing Systems – CHI 2010, p. 433 (2010). doi: 10.1145/1753326.1753392
22. Müller, F., Günther, S., Dezfuli, N., Khalilbeigi, M., Mühlhäuser, M.: ProxiWatch: Enhancing smartwatch interaction through proximity-based hand input. In: Proceedings of the SIGCHI International Conference on Human Factors in Computer Systems – CHI 2016, pp. 2617–2624 (2016)
23. Oney, S., Harrison, Ogan, A., Wiese, J.: ZoomBoard: a diminutive qwerty soft keyboard using iterative zooming for ultra-small devices. In: Proceedings of the SIGCHI International Conference on Human Factors in Computer Systems – CHI 2013, pp. 2799–2802 (2013)
24. Dunlop, M.D., Komninos, A., Durga, N.: Towards high quality text entry on smartwatches. In: Extended Abstracts of the SIGHCI Conference on Human factors in Computing Systems - EA CHI 2014, pp. 2365–2370 (2014). doi:10.1145/2559206.2581319
25. Nebeling, M., To, A., Guo, A., Freitas, A.A. De, Teevan, J., Dow, S.P., Bigham, J.P.: WearWrite: crowd-assisted writing from smartwatches. In: Proceedings of the SIGCHI International Conference on Human Factors in Computer Systems – CHI 2016 (2016)
26. Lee, J., Cho, D., Song, S., Kim, S., Im, E., Kim, J.: Mobile system design for scratch recognition. In: Extended Abstracts of the SIGCHI Conference on Human Factors in Computing Systems - EA CHI 2015, vol. 2, pp. 1567–1572 (2015). doi:10.1145/2702613.2732820
27. Ehrler, F., Lovis, C.: Supporting elderly homecare with smartwatches: advantages and drawbacks. Stud. Health Technol. Inform. **205**, 667–671 (2014). doi: 10.3233/978-1-61499-432-9-667
28. Casilari, E., Oviedo-Jiménez, M.A.: Automatic fall detection system based on the combined use of a smartphone and a smartwatch. PLoS ONE **10**, 1–11 (2015). doi:10.1371/journal.pone.0140929
29. Anderson, L.: Analytic Autoethnography. J. Contemp. Ethnography **35**, 373–395 (2006). doi: 10.1177/0891241605280449
30. Creswell, J.W.: Research design: qualitative, quantitative, and mixed method approaches. SAGE Publications, Thousand Oaks (2003)
31. Maxwell, J.A.: Qualitative Research Design: An Interactive Approach. SAGE, Thousand Oaks (2005)
32. UOC: Wear Monitor. https://play.google.com/store/apps/details?id=edu.uoc.mobtech.monitor.monitor&hl=en
33. Braun, V., Clarke, V.: Using thematic analysis in psychology. Qual. Res. Psychol. **3**, 77–101 (2006). doi:10.1191/1478088706qp063oa
34. Rosales, A., Sayago, S., Blat, J.: Beeping socks and chirping arm bands: wearables that foster free play. IEEE Comput. **48**, 41–48 (2015). doi:10.1109/MC.2015.168

Understanding the Motivations of Online Community Users - A Comparison Between Younger and Older People

Jiunn-Woei Lian[✉]

Department of Information Management,
National Taichung University of Science and Technology,
129 Section 3, San-min Road, Taichung 40401, Taiwan
jwlian@nutc.edu.tw

Abstract. With the arrival of an aging society, the major users of social network services include not only young people, but also older persons. The purpose of this study is therefore to understand the motivations of online community users. Data from younger and older people were compared; both quantitative and qualitative data were collected. This study first reviewed the literature regarding the purposes of using an online community. Second, based on the literature, a survey was conducted among college students. Finally, interviews were conducted with both younger and older people. The results were summarized and compared between the different age groups. First of all, the major motivations of young people to use SNSs include maintaining interpersonal interconnectivity, entertainment value, and purposive value (especially for homework and learning). Second, the major motivations of older adults to use SNSs are to contact friends and share information and knowledge. Finally, the major difference between young people and older adults' motivations is the use of SNSs by the young for entertainment purposes and to kill time. These findings will contribute toward understanding the motivations of online community users across different age groups.

Keywords: Online community · Motivations · Older people · Age

1 Introduction

In recent years, social network services (SNSs) have become major communication tools. Among these services, the growth of Facebook has been particularly fast around the world, Taiwan being no exception. According to the official Facebook figures (http://newsroom.fb.com/), Taiwanese have the highest Facebook stickiness rate in the world. Young and old people both like to use it as a social platform. However, most previous studies have focused on users in Europe and America. Ji et al. (2010) found that users' behavior within online social communities varied across different national cultures. Kim et al. (2011) also proposed similar opinions. Additionally, most of these studies examine younger users, while little research focuses on older adults.

Therefore, the purpose of this study is to understand the motivations of online community users and to compare younger and older users. Both quantitative and

© Springer International Publishing AG 2017
J. Zhou and G. Salvendy (Eds.): ITAP 2017, Part II, LNCS 10298, pp. 130–137, 2017.
DOI: 10.1007/978-3-319-58536-9_11

qualitative data were collected. First of all, this study reviewed the literature regarding the purposes of online community use. Second, based on the literature, a survey was conducted among college students. Finally, interviews were conducted with both younger and older people. The results were summarized and compared between different age groups. The findings can contribute toward understanding the motivations of online community users across different age groups. The three research questions of the present study are as follows:

1. What are major motivations of young people to use SNSs?
2. What are major motivations of older adults to use SNSs?
3. What are the differences between young people's and older adults' motivations in using SNSs?

2   Literature Review

Why is it critical to understand behavioral motivation? Teo et al. (1999) indicated that different motivations will affect users' online behavior in different ways. From the perspective of motivation theory, Ridings and Gefen (2004) found that people have various motivations to participate in communities and that these motivations affect their behaviors in these communities, online communities being no exception. Lin and Lu (2011) proposed a similar viewpoint. Therefore, understanding the motivations for using SNSs is becoming critical for forum management.

Table 1 summarizes the motivations for using SNSs proposed by previous studies. We can see that most previous related studies are focused on younger users from the United States and Europe. Studies that examine older people's motivations for using SNSs are particularly rare. Besides, Table 1 also indicates that the top three motivations proposed by previous studies include social purpose, entertainment, and kill time.

Table 1. Motivations for using SNSs (order by published year)

Authors (Year)	Motivations of using SNSs
Lee et al. (2015)	Social interaction, archiving, self-expression, escapism, and peeking
Wang et al. (2015)	Social interaction, entertainment
Holton et al. (2014)	Seeking and sharing (seek information by linking from other users)
Park and Lee (2014)	Entertainment, relationship maintenance, self-expression, and communication
Wang et al. (2013)[a]	Maintain relationships, extent social network, seek popularity, express emotions, get information, entertainment, kill time
Welbourne et al. (2013)	Informational and emotional support
Nadkarni and Hofmann (2012)	Belonging requirement and self-expression
Moradabadi et al. (2012)	

(*continued*)

Table 1. (*continued*)

Authors (Year)	Motivations of using SNSs
	Information sharing, free communication, information distribution, information control, the principle of equal, information requirement, entertainment
Alhabash et al. (2012)[a]	Social connection, sharing (pictures, content…), social network, update status
Dogruer et al. (2011)	Self-expression, applying media, kill time, search information, personal status, maintain relationships, entertainment
Cheung et al. (2011)	Social presence
Lin and Lu (2011)[a]	Enjoyment, number of peers, usefulness
Hew (2011)	Maintain relationships, meet more people, fashion, make oneself becoming more popular, kill time, self-expression, learning
Kim et al. (2011)	Seeking friends, social support, entertainment, information, and convenience
Ross et al. (2009)	Personality
Pempek et al. (2009)	Interact with the friends in the real world, expression personal identification
Ridings and Gefen (2004)	Exchange information, social support, friendship, entertainment

[a] Conducted in Taiwan

3   Research Methods and Results

This research is divided into two parts. Both quantitative (survey) and qualitative (interview) methods were employed. Study 1 undertakes a survey of college students, while study 2 employs the interview method for ten college students and four older adults. Following are the details and results.

3.1   Study 1: Quantitative Investigation

Study 1 is an online questionnaire survey of college students in Taiwan. Measurements are adapted from Cheung et al. (2011) and divide the motivations into hedonic and utilitarian categories. Nineteen items are included, comprising purposive value (9 items); self-discovery (2 items); maintaining interpersonal interconnectivity (2 items); social enhancement (2 items); and entertainment value (4 items) (see Table 2). A 7-point scale is employed in this study; each variable ranges from 1 to 7. The higher the value, the more important the variable.

At this stage, 209 valid questionnaires were finally collected. Among the respondents, 123 (58.9%) were female and 86 (41.1%) were male; 82.8% of subjects indicated that they used Facebook for 1–6 h daily on average. Using CR value >0.7, AVE >0.5, and Cronbach's alpha >0.7 as criteria, the results indicate that the measurements

Table 2. Measurements and values of study 1

Variables	Item numbers	List of items	Value (1–7)	Order
Purposive value	9	1. To get information 2. To learn how to do things 3. To provide others with information 4. To contribute to a pool of information 5. To generate ideas 6. To negotiate or bargain 7. To get someone to do something for me 8. To solve problems 9. To make decisions	4.7	3
Self-discovery	2	1. To learn about myself and others 2. To gain insight into myself	4.4	4
Maintaining interpersonal interconnectivity	2	1. To have something to do with others 2. To stay in touch	5.3	1
Social enhancement	2	1. To impress 2. To feel important	4.1	5
Entertainment value	4	1. To be entertained 2. To play 3. To relax 4. To pass time away when bored	5.1	2

have acceptable validity and reliability. Therefore, the following analysis can be conducted. From Table 2, we find that the order of the motivations for young people to use SNSs is maintaining interpersonal interconnectivity (mean = 5.3); entertainment value (mean = 5.1); purposive value (mean = 4.7); self-discovery (mean = 4.4); and social enhancement (mean = 4.1). Additionally, the mean and standard deviation (S.D) of each item is listed in Appendix. The top 5 critical motivations include to get information, to pass time away when bored, to stay in touch, to relax, and to have something to do with others.

3.2 Study 2: Qualitative Investigation

Interview research was employed in study 2. Two groups were interviewed: ten younger college students (five males and five females) and four older adults (two males and two females) among "evergreen" college students. Open-ended questions were employed to understand their motivations in using SNSs. Each interviewee was asked to share their experience of using SNSs such as LINE or Facebook. The questions

Table 3. Results from older adults interviewing

Interviewee	A	B	C	D
Gender	Female	Female	Male	Male
Age	61	73	69	65
Job before retired	Homemaker	Business (Bookstore)	Government employee	Stone sculptor
SNSs using experience	4–5 years	4–5 years	4–5 years	4–5 years
Most commonly used SNSs	Line and Facebook	Line and Facebook	Line and Facebook	Line and Facebook
Major motivations for using SNSs	Contact community members	Contact community members	Share creative writing and knowledge of everyday life	Share photography

examined both user motivations and user behaviors (frequency, interaction patterns with online friends, perceived advantages and disadvantages). The interviews were conducted by the author and research assistants. After recording and analyzing the content, we find the following results.

Results from young people. Ten college students participated voluntarily in this stage. Overall, the results of this stage confirmed the findings of study 1. Three major motivations are proposed in this phase, including maintaining interpersonal interconnectivity, entertainment value, and purposive value (especially for homework and learning). However, self-discovery and social enhancement as reported in study 1 are not found in study 2.

Results from older adults. The demographic data of the four interviewees are summarized in Table 3. The four interviewees are ranged from 61–73 years old. All of them have 4–5 years in using SNSs.

From Table 3, we find that older adults from Taiwan like to use LINE and Facebook in their daily life. Additionally, the major motivations for using these SNSs are contacting friends and sharing information and knowledge.

3.3   Comparison

The results of this study are summarized in Table 4, including the results from the literature review, survey, and interviews. Table 4 indicates that the major difference in the motivations to use SNSs between younger people and older adults is in the tendency for the young to use these services for entertainment purposes and to kill time. Additionally, both age groups, use SNSs to keep in contact with friends and share information. However, the content which they share is varied. For college students, the focus is on learning related information. However, older adults focus on sharing their work such as creative writing, photography, and so on. Finally, both younger and older people uses SNSs to maintain their interpersonal connections.

Table 4. Results comparison

	Literatures	Study 1	Study 2	
Methods	Content analysis	Quantitative	Qualitative	
Country	From different countries	Taiwan	Taiwan	
Subjects	Majority younger people	Younger people (ranged from 1 to 7)	Younger people	Older adults
Results (Motivations)	Social purpose, entertainment, kill time	Maintaining interpersonal interconnectivity (mean = 5.3), entertainment value (mean = 5.1), purposive value (mean = 4.7), self-discovery (mean = 4.4), and Social enhancement (mean = 4.1)	Maintaining interpersonal interconnectivity, entertainment value, and purposive value (especially for homework and learning)	Contact friends, share information and knowledge (Share personal works such as creative writing, photography, and so on.)

4 Conclusion

Based on the three proposed research questions, this study makes following findings and conclusions. These findings will contribute toward understanding the motivations of online community users across different age groups.

1. First of all, the major motivations of young people to use SNSs include maintaining interpersonal interconnectivity, entertainment value, and purposive value (especially for homework and learning).
2. Second, the major motivations of older adults to use SNSs are to contact friends and share information and knowledge (share personal works such as creative writing, photography, and so on).
3. Finally, the major difference between young people and older adults' motivations is the use of SNSs by the young for entertainment purposes and to kill time. Besides, although both of the groups use SNSs to share information and knowledge, but the sharing targets are different.

   Although this study proposes the different motivations of using SNSs across different age groups, but this study only interviewed four older adults, this is the major limitation. Therefore, we suggest that future study can make more interviewing of the older people or conduct a survey of older adults to make the conclusions more rigorous. Besides, cultural effect (Kim et al. 2011) is not considered in this study, this is also one of the critical issues in the future. Finally, more and more different kind of SNSs appeared on the Internet such as Instagram, the motivations of using different kinds of

136   J.-W. Lian

SNSs may also be various (Lee et al. 2015; Choi 2016). Future study can also consider the effects of this difference.

Acknowledgement. The author would like to thank the Ministry of Science and Technology of Republic of China, Taiwan, for financially supporting this research under Contract No. MOST 103-2410-H-025-024-).

Appendix - Younger Peoples' Motivations to Use SNSs

Item	Means	S.D	Order
1. To get information[a]	5.77	1.00	1
2. To learn how to do things	4.38	1.52	14
3. To provide others with information	5.07	1.23	7
4. To contribute to a pool of information	4.61	1.38	12
5. To generate ideas	4.60	1.43	13
6. To negotiate or bargain	3.44	1.48	19
7. To get someone to do something for me	4.91	1.30	8
8. To solve problems	4.81	1.25	10
9. To make decisions	4.70	1.64	11
10. To learn about myself and others	4.89	1.45	9
11. To gain insight into myself	3.89	1.46	17
12. To have something to do with others[a]	5.11	1.58	5
13. To stay in touch[a]	5.48	1.06	3
14. To impress	4.32	1.39	16
15. To feel important	3.89	1.50	17
16. To be entertained	5.10	1.40	6
17. To play	4.37	1.66	15
18. To relax[a]	5.14	1.35	4
19. To pass time away when bored[a]	5.59	1.21	2

1. [a] Top five motivations of younger peoples' motivation to use SNSs.
2. Each item ranges from 1 to 7. The higher the value, the more important the variable.

References

Alhabash, S., et al.: Exploring the motivations of Facebook use in taiwan. Cyberpsychology Behav. Soc. Network. **15**(6), 304–311 (2012)
Cheung, C.M.K., Chiu, P.Y., Lee, M.K.O.: Online social networks: why do students use Facebook? Comput. Hum. Behav. **27**, 1337–1343 (2011)
Choi, J.: Why do people use news differently on SNSs? an investigation of the role of motivations, media repertories, and technology cluster on citizens' news-related activities. Comput. Hum. Behav. **54**, 249–256 (2016)

Dogruer, N., Menevis, I., Eyyam, R.: What is the motivation for using Facebook? Procedia Soc. Behav. Sci. **15**, 2642–2646 (2011)

Hew, K.F.: Students' and teachers' use of Facebook. Comput. Hum. Behav. **27**(2), 662–676 (2011)

Holton, A.E., et al.: Seeking and sharing: motivations for linking on Twitter. Commun. Res. Rep. **31**(1), 33–40 (2014)

Ji, Y.G., et al.: The influence of cultural differences on the use of social network services and the formation of social capital. Int. J. Hum. Comput. Interact. **26**(11–12), 1100–1121 (2010)

Kim, Y., Sohn, D., Choi, S.M.: Cultural difference in motivations for using social network sites: a comparative study of American and Korean college students. Comput. Hum. Behav. **27**(1), 365–372 (2011)

Lee, E., et al.: Pictures speak louder than words: motivations for using instagram. Cyberpsychology, Behav. Soc. Network. **18**(9), 552–556 (2015)

Lin, K.Y., Lu, H.P.: Why people use social networking sites: an empirical study integrating network externalities and motivation theory. Comput. Hum. Behav. **27**(3), 1152–1161 (2011)

Moradabadi, Y.N., Gharehshiran, M.A., Amrai, K.: What is the motivation student of Iranians for using Facebook? Procedia Soc. Behav. Sci. **46**, 5192–5195 (2012)

Nadkarni, A., Hofmann, S.G.: Why do people user Facebook? Personality Individ. Differ. **52**(3), 243–249 (2012)

Park, N., Lee, S.: College students' motivations for Facebook use and psychological outcomes. J. Broadcast. Electron. Media **58**(4), 601–620 (2014)

Pempek, T.A., Yermolayeva, Y.A., Calvert, S.L.: College students' social networking experiences on Facebook. J. Appl. Dev. Psychol. **30**(3), 227–238 (2009)

Ridings, C.M., Gefen, D.: Virtual community attraction: why people hang out online. J. Comput. Mediated Commun. **10**(1) (2004). doi:10.1111/j.1083-6101.2004.tb00229.x

Ross, C., et al.: Personality and motivations associated with Facebook use. Comput. Hum. Behav. **25**(2), 578–586 (2009)

Teo, T.S.H., Lim, V.K.G., Lai, R.Y.C.: Intrinsic and extrinsic motivation in internet usage. Omega **27**, 25–37 (1999)

Wang, et al.: Facebook motivation scale: development and validation. J. e-Business **15**(3), 319–352 (2013)

Wang, J.-L., et al.: Predicting social networking site (SNS) use: personality, attitudes, motivation and internet self-efficacy. Personality Individ. Differ. **80**, 119–124 (2015)

Welbourne, J.L., Blanchard, A.L., Wadsworth, M.B.: Motivations in virtual health communities and their relationship to community, connectedness and strew. Comput. Hum. Behav. **29**, 129–139 (2013)

Visual Representations of Digital Connectivity in Everyday Life

Wendy Martin[1(✉)] and Katy Pilcher[2]

[1] College of Health and Life Sciences, Brunel University London,
Uxbridge, Middlesex UB8 3PH, UK
`wendy.martin@brunel.ac.uk.at`
[2] School of Languages and Social Sciences, Aston University,
Birmingham, B4 7ET, UK
`k.pilcher@aston.ac.uk`

Abstract. This paper draws on data from the empirical study *Photographing Everyday Life: Ageing, Lived Experiences, Time and Space* funded by the ESRC, UK. The focus of the project was to explore the significance of the ordinary and day-to-day and focus on the everyday meanings, lived experiences, practical activities and social contexts in which people in mid to later life live their daily lives. The research involved a diverse sample of 62 women and men aged 50 years and over who took photographs of their different daily routines to create a weekly visual diary. This diary was then explored through in-depth photo-elicitation interviews to make visible the rhythms, patterns and meanings that underlie habitual and routinized everyday worlds. The data was analysed using the software Atlas Ti. The analysis highlighted: (1) the increasing importance of digital connectivity and the ways in which people in mid to later life actively engage (and resist) technologies of communication in their daily lives; and (2) the significance of embodied co-presence and the immediacy of shared space and/or time. Exploring the routines, meanings, and patterns that underpin everyday life has therefore enabled us to make visible how people build, maintain and experience their social and virtual connections, and the ways in which digital devices and information technologies are being incorporated into (and resisted) within daily life.

Keywords: Ageing digital · Everyday life · Social connections · Space and time

1 Introduction

The 21st century has been characterized by a proliferation of digital devices, information technologies and mediated systems of communication within global and networked societies. Digital technologies permeate everyday life more and more [1] and have become interwoven with our identities, narratives, social relationships, social networks, lifestyles and societies. As people grow older their everyday lives will therefore become increasingly mediated by the proliferation of digital technologies and have a profound influence on the social worlds of people in mid to later life [2, 3]. At the same time there have been concerns that there is a digital divide in which older people are excluded from

J. Zhou and G. Salvendy (Eds.): ITAP 2017, Part II, LNCS 10298, pp. 138–149, 2017.
DOI: 10.1007/978-3-319-58536-9_12

participation [4–8] and the extent to which the digital is mainly focused on younger people. From a review of the literature on Information and Communication Technologies (ICT) older people are moreover often framed as 'passive' and 'dependent' receivers of new technologies and issues of surveillance and control predominate amongst the oldest old [3, p. 442], see also [9]. Whilst the digital divide may now be narrowing, except amongst the oldest old [3, 10], there is limited research into the ways in which people in mid to life incorporate digital technologies and communications into their daily lives and their own meanings and experiences of the digital as they grow older.

This paper draws on data from the empirical study Photographing Everyday Life: Ageing, Lived Experiences, Time and Space funded by the Economic and Social Research Council (ESRC) in the United Kingdom. The focus of the project was to explore the significance of the ordinary and day-to-day and focus on the everyday meanings, lived experiences, practical activities, and social contexts in which people in mid to later life live their daily lives. In particular, the project focused upon the very ordinariness and mundanity of daily living; and the day-to-day practical activities and personal meanings embedded within the personal, domestic and working lives of the participants. In order to make these everyday lives visible, the project involved visual methods (photographic diaries) and in-depth interviews (photo elicitation) with people aged 50 years and over who had different types of daily routines. In this context, the research aimed to be much closer to lived experiences and how people give meaning and engage with their own everyday lives in their own terms. As Gubrium and Holstein [11] argue a focus on daily life can generate important insights into 'how people themselves interpret and discern what it's like to grow older and be old in today's world' (2000, p. 3). Exploring the routines and patterns that underpin the everyday lives of people growing older have moreover enabled us to make visible how people build, maintain and experience their social and virtual connections.

2   The Research Project

The research involved a diverse sample of participants who took photographs of their different daily routines to create a weekly visual diary. Within the study there were 42 women and 20 men who participated aged between 52 and 81 years. There was a variety of routines amongst the sample, which included some participants who had retired, others who were in full and part time paid employment, some working as volunteers, and a number of the participants who had a combination of these roles. We recruited participants in the South of England, through a range of organizations and social groups aimed at people aged 50 years and over, as well as a variety of workplaces, sports and leisure centres, and social venues. In total there were 4471 visual images created by participants across the project, and interviews lasted for an average of about 46 min. Ethical approval was gained from Brunel University London, College of Health and Life Sciences Ethics Committee (Reference 10/04/STF/08).

The first stage of the study involved a researcher meeting with a participant to explain more about the project, hand over a digital camera, and to give appropriate support and guidance on how to use the camera. Participants then took photographs that depicted important aspects of their daily lives for one week. This was a participatory approach in the sense that participants are in control of the cameras and they can decide what to photograph (or not). In this sense the photographs act as a 'visual diary' of a participant's life and their daily routines across one week. The second stage of the research involved a researcher meeting the participants (usually in their own home, office, or a private area), to engage in a photo-elicitation interview. The photographs were uploaded onto a laptop computer at the start of each interview and were used as a resource to facilitate conversations. The photographs provided a reference point to focus and 'prompt' discussion during in-depth interviews in which we explored meanings, activities, roles, relationships, space, time, and participants' reasons for taking the photographs and the context of their visual diary.

The data was analyzed using Atlas Ti software as it enabled the incorporation and comparison of visual and textual data. We coded and thematically analyzed both the photographs and textual data to explore aspects of daily lives, time and space. For a more in-depth exploration of the methodological and ethical issues encountered within the research project see Pilcher et al. (2016) [12]. In this paper we focus on one dimension of an emergent theme - social connectivity and relationships – that highlighted an increasing presence of digital technologies and the active engagement of the participants with new technologies of communication within their daily lives.

3   Connectivity, the Digital and Everyday Life

It is argued that contemporary and global societies are characterized by changes in meanings and experiences of time and space, in which there has been a move from predominately face to face relationships in which time and space are inextricably linked, to an increasing separation of time and space resulting in more disembedded and distanciated social relationships [13, 14], a process that has further deepened in a network society in which connectivity is immediate and global [15, 16]. Massey [17] criticizes the dualist tendency of conceptualizing space and time as bounded and separate, and instead states that space and time are intimately interconnected, and are constructed out of social relations, within a context in which social relations are dynamic and changing. A focus on social relations further highlights the ways in which a proliferation of digital technologies can influence the ways we create and experience social connectivity in our daily lives [18]. It has been through a focus on daily life, and an exploration of the ways in which age and ageing are culturally mediated and subjectively experienced [19, 20], that has provided important insights into positive and negative dimensions of social connectivity as people grow older in a digital world.

Data from the *Photographing Everyday Life* research project illustrated the importance of connectivity, that is connections with family, partners, friends and the locality, as well as wider inter/national communities, amongst the participants. These social connections were interspersed throughout the daily lives of the participants. Social connections were maintained or created virtually (for example, social networking, emails, video calls) and in shared space and/or time (for example, the telephone, living or working together, visits). Participants portrayed how they incorporated a diverse range of digital, computer and mobile technologies via the images from their visual diaries, for example, mobile phones, smartphones, tablets, laptops and computers:

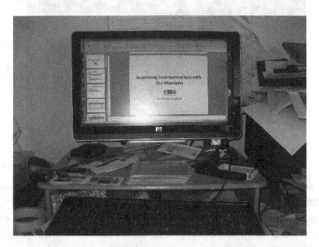

The digital and networked technologies were located in the participants' domestic spheres and their homes, including the lounge / front room, bedroom, study and kitchen; in public spaces, such as libraries, meeting rooms / halls, and at social events; in the work environment; and as mobile devices that were carried with the person.

The materiality of the digital and networked devices were evident, as objects and as screens, and can be seen to have become incorporated into the everyday infrastructure and daily rhythms and routines of most of the participants [21]. Many participants described the ways in which the use of online and digital resources, as a means to create and maintain social connections, were embedded and interspersed throughout their daily routines:

> And also I realised how much the thread of the day, because I sort of observed you know, for a week before of the kind of, sort of life, it was quite a reflective thing really to see what my week was.. And I realised how much of it, also revolved round the computer, which we've set up upstairs. We have a kind of bedroom office, in terms of e-mailing and with the phone next to it, keeping in touch with people. So I suppose somewhere in the day I'd spend at least an hour on the computer, either sending or replying to e-mails or looking up e-mails and there's a great sort of teetering pile of stuff that is either to be read or dealt with. (Hannah, aged 68 years, married)

The place and location of computers and laptops were part of the social and material fabric and were noticeable within the domestic and work environments of many of the participants and often provided significance and meaning about the use of space within their everyday lives:

> Yes, that's my office. I've got my printer and my computer and everything else, yes. But it's quite cool. You close the door and you know, everything goes away. (Victoria, 61 years, divorced)

The participants described that despite the prominence of digital and networked devices, there was predominately a purpose for their activities and practices when engaging with digital and online media and communications, that included enhancing social and virtual connections by communicating with family, friends and social groups, to search and find information, as part of their paid or voluntary work, and for enjoyment and pleasure, such as music, videos, games and chatrooms:

Yes, I think a lot of time. if I am alone I might be reading or on the computer. Sometimes chatting, very, very little. Not much. But usually just looking something. If I have a new thing then, then reading a book, if I find some then I'll go and go to Wikipedia things like that. (Zuberi, aged 66 years, divorced)

The nature and role of social relationships, their living arrangements, such as living alone, and the proximity of friends and family of the participants influenced the types of media and communications, the extent and meanings of engagement and the ways participants experienced and used digital technologies. Some participants described how social media enabled them to maintain social identities and be involved in the everyday worlds of their family across the generations, as well as with friends and family who live at a distance:

And I'm back on my Facebook you see..... I am. I'm on usually at least twice a day. Just to see.... Because I have a large family. There's [er] I'm Mother Nature I suppose. I have four children, eight grandchildren and I've got six great grandchildren. So my four children and my eight grandchildren are all going on Facebook. And that's all... and a couple of friends I connect to. So all the time I can see what's going on. (Annabel, aged 65 years, lives with partner)

Different types of social media, including Facebook and online forums, and video calls, such as Skype, enabled participants to engage virtually with and participate in intergenerational connections and keep updated on the daily lives of significant relationships. This was especially important when important family members lived at a distance, such as adult children and grandchildren:

We SKYPE or phone. I mean the baby's two, but yes, he's that's not... I don't mind them being away but I think it would be nice to see them at least once a month because... And the point of SKYPE is really good. It makes such a huge difference. To be able to see who you're talking to at the same time, and, because again when we're in France, we can say to them oh the sun flowers are out, and oh look, you know, and show them the sunflowers. (Mark, 66 years, married)

The visual dimensions of and the immediacy of seeing one another on video calls was especially highlighted by some participants as a means to sustain meaningful social connections:

I use skype quite a lot to keep in touch with my family, one of my sons lives in Qatar and they don't have a phone line or postal service so we talk on skype, or I talk to my grandchildren who live in England, I can also use the video with them and see them on the screen. (Dorothy, age 73 years, widow)

And if you've got Skype you know, why do you need to be visiting all the time? You can see your grandchildren on Skype and talk to people on Skype. We talk to a lot of people on Skype. The wife talks to a lot of her friends in Hungary on Skype. So we don't go into Facebook and Twitter. We're not twittering people I'm afraid and so that's you know. (Christopher, 75 years, married)

For some participants the significance of digital and networked technologies was the potentiality of time and ability of 'being there' if and when needed. This could relate to key roles and relationships associated with care:

Yes, friends a lot, family, work, everybody really through the phone. It's kind of constantly there. I've an elderly auntie whose a bit like my Mum, and because my Mum's dead and she's got dementia, so I keep the phone pretty close to me, because she does phone me up sometimes with odd and unusual requests. So I need to keep an eye on that, you know, in case she phones.... She phoned me up the other day to say where was she going for the weekend, and I said what do you mean, and she said well I've packed my bags but I'm not sure where I'm going. And I realised it was because we'd been talking about Christmas arrangements and she'd be going away. She'd packed her bags about four weeks too early. (Samantha, 53 years, divorced)

Or alternatively some participants would undertake other practical domestic and work activities whilst anticipating social and digital communications and connections, in particular, with family members. Naomi, for example, described how she was ironing while awaiting a potential and possible video call from her son:

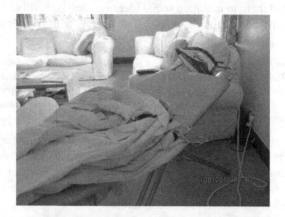

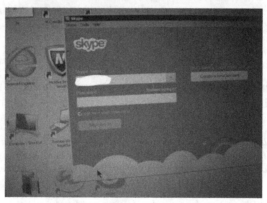

I also put on Skype, as I think I've mentioned before, some of my sons are abroad. … And the youngest one whose in Corsica at the moment, said that he would be skyping us. So I put skype on … but he didn't call … But it was in the room next to where I was ironing. I had it on just in case, you know, he did say…. So that's another way that I keep in touch with them when they're away. (Naomi, aged 55 years, married)

Some participants would also portray and describe how they use multiple sources of media, digital and networked devices and communications at the same time, and / or move between different media:

So yes, I would be watching the telly and if it was something that he was watching then I'd be checking my e-mails and stuff on my iPad. I love my iPad. (Catherine, 58 years, married)

I get my e-mails on it. I get loads of texts on it. I keep my diary on it. Got Facebook and Twitter and YouTube and things and some music on it I have some music on it. (Samantha, 53 years, divorced)

Whilst there were many positive dimensions and opportunities, there were some limitations and difficulties expressed about the amount and type of virtual connections and online activity amongst some participants. A key issue for some participants was that not all the people or social groups that a participant would want to communicate with had digital and networked devices. In this context age and generation were often identified as significant factors and dominant imageries of age and ageing were at times drawn upon:

Irene: *I talk to my friends on the phone constantly, during the day, any* time.

I: *So more on the phone rather than e-mail?*

Irene: *Yes. Yes. Not all of my friends have e-mail ... and I'd sooner talk to people then e-mail them.* (Irene, 68 years, divorced)

Phillip: *So I actually bound it together as a report and send it out in the post.*

I: *Okay.*

Phillip: *But normally. But not everybody's got e-mail. About 15% of our members aren't on e-mail…. Which is still quite. But one of the problems is people use that as an excuse not to move into the electronic era.*

I: *Okay yes.*

Phillip: *We can't do that because some people can't do e-mails. Well as long as they get it some other way it doesn't matter.*

I: *Yes.*

Phillip: *You know, all of our new members, the members who are showing up now who are in their late 50s 60s who are joining expect us to be using e-mail. They expect us to have. Which we can do. We can send out the programme and the newsletter by e-mail but that's how they expect us to communicate with them.* (Phillip, 68 years, married).

Other concerns that participants highlighted about using new media and networked devices were their own perceptions of not having sufficient technological skills and knowledge and /or safety concerns when online, that can include identity theft, sharing and loss of control of personal information and potential financial fraud:

I: *Do you use social networking or something like that at all or is it mainly the e-mail*

Jennifer: *No I don't go on the, I don't like Facebook or Twitter or anything like that. I don't think they're safe* (Jennifer, 68 years, married)

Moreover, whilst there were perceived to be many constructive and meaningful dimensions to digital communications and connections, many participants emphasized the continuing importance of locality and embodied co-presence, that is being in the same place at the same time as others including family, friends, work colleagues, neighbours and local social connections:

Irene: *Every month we go for lunch with U3A* [University of the Third Age]… *Different places. The, the lunch club [um] organises and susses the places out and then we just go and enjoy the meal and good company. That's it, some more people from the lunch. That's me having lunch and a glass of wine I hasten to add, with the lunch. Because I went into Abingdon on the bus.*

I: *So it looks like you quite enjoy going out for meals?*

Irene: *I do. Yes. It's nice to have company. When you live on your own its good to have company. To eat with someone else instead of eating on your own.* (Irene, 68 years, divorced)

The significance of embodied co-presence and social connectivity involved many varied and diverse activities including regular coffee mornings with neighbours, talking on the telephone, walking clubs, exercise classes, dog walking in the locality, participating in social groups, voluntary work, and sharing meals:

Oh this is more dogs. As I say I don't expect you to keep these, but this is just how many we meet up with. All these people every morning have got owners. So we all have a chat and it's quite a community actually. (Patricia, 70 years, widow)

4   Concluding Comments

Photographs from a visual diary depict 'a sequence of … frozen moments, each of which is exceptional by the fact of being singled out' by a participant, in which the images portrayed are "heightened' ordinary moments' of daily life [22, p. 35]. The images from the visual diaries can be seen to represent moments, rhythms, environments and practices that are meaningful within the ordinary, mundane and everyday routines of the participants. The increasing presence of digital devices and screens portrayed in the visual diaries as people grow older was therefore significant. The daily lives of people in mid to later were not only mediated, experienced and enacted in relation to digital and networked devices but digital objects and screens have increasingly become central to the everyday fabric of material and social domestic and working environments. Social connectedness was enhanced as people in mid to later life were able to create, build and maintain social relationships in the context of their everyday life. This included communications between different generations and with family, friends, colleagues and social groups both at a distance and in the locality; and the interconnectedness of time that was experienced and perceived as separate, simultaneous and/or immediate. The incorporation of digital and networked technologies has therefore influenced the context of social relationships and meanings and experiences of time and space. The significance of embodied co-presence, of being in the same shared space and time was prominent within the visual diaries and the meaning of being in immediate and direct connection with others as we grow older cannot therefore be under-estimated. The narratives of the participants moreover portrayed an *active* engagement with digital devices in which people in mid to later life made *active* choices about the opportunities and possibilities, as well as at times *actively* resisting being drawn into the increasing pace and predominance of digital and media technologies.

To conclude, we recognize the limitations in our portrayal of the visual and lived experiences of digital technologies in everyday life as social connectivity and the increasing presence of digital and networked technologies was an emergent theme and not the main focus of the research. The research has however highlighted the dynamic and changing context of social connectivity in a digital world that is experienced and understood as meaningful and significant in the daily lives of people in mid to later life which does therefore open up the possibility for future research.

Acknowledgements. This research was supported by funding from the Economic and Social Research Council / ESRC [grant number RES-061-25-0459] in the United Kingdom. We would like to thank our research participants for the generosity of their extensive time taken to participate in this research. Pseudonyms are given in this paper. Thank you also to our advisory group for their support and guidance, to Dr Veronika Williams who worked on earlier parts of the project, and to Dr Christina Silver for her invaluable technical and analytical support.

References

1. Lupton, D.: Digital Sociology. Routledge, Abington (2014)
2. Loos, E.F., Haddon, L., Mante-Meijer, E.A. (eds.): Generational Use of New Media. Ashgate, Farnham (2012)
3. Jones, I.R.: Connectivity, digital technologies and later life. In: Twigg, J., Martin, W. (eds.) Routledge Handbook of Cultural Gerontology. Routledge, Abingdon (2015)
4. Jaeger, B.: Trapped in the digital divide? Old people in the information society. Sci. Stud. **17**, 5–22 (2004)
5. Gilleard, C., Higgs, P.: Internet use and the digital divide in the english longitudinal study of ageing. Eur. J. Ageing **5**, 233–239 (2008)
6. Loos, E.F.: Senior citizens: Digital immigrants in their own country? Observatorio (OBS*) J. **6**(1), 1–23 (2012)
7. Loos, E.F.: Designing for dynamic diversity: Representing various senior citizens in digital information sources. Observatorio (OBS*) J. **7**(1), 21–45 (2013)

8. Olphert, W., Damodaran, L.: Older people and digital disengagement: A fourth digital divide? Gerontology **59**, 570–574 (2013)
9. Peine, A., Faulkner, A., Jaeger, B., Moors, E.: Science, technology and the 'grand challenge' of ageing - Understanding the socio-material constitution of later life. Technol. Forecast. Soc. Chang. **93**, 1–9 (2015)
10. Gilleard, C., Jones, I.R., Higgs, P.: Connectivity in later life: The declining age divide in mobile cell phone ownership. Sociol. Res. Online **20**(2), 3 (2014)
11. Gubrium, J., Holstein, J. (eds.): Aging and Everyday Life. Blackwell, Oxford (2000)
12. Pilcher, K., Martin, W., Williams, V.: Issues of collaboration, representation, meaning and emotions: Utilising participant-led visual diaries to capture the everyday lives of people in mid to later life. Int. J. Soc. Res. Methodol. **19**(6), 677–692 (2016)
13. Giddens, A.: Time-Space distanciation and the generation of power. In: A Contemporary Critique of Historical Materialism. Power, Property and the State. MacMillan, London (1981)
14. Giddens, A.: Modernity and Self Identity. Polity Press, Cambridge (1991)
15. Castells, M.: The Rise of Network Society: Information Age: Economy, Society and Culture. Blackwell, Oxford (1996)
16. Castells, M.: Communication Power. Oxford University Pres, Oxford (2009)
17. Massey, D.: Space Place and Gender. Polity Press, Cambridge (1994)
18. Chayko, M.: Techno-social life: The internet, digital technologies and social connectedness. Sociol. Compass **8**(7), 976–991 (2014)
19. Twigg, J., Martin, W.: The challenge of cultural gerontology. Gerontologist **55**(3), 353–359 (2015)
20. Marshall, B., Katz, S.: How old am I? Digital culture and quantified ageing. Digit. Cult. Soc. **2**(1), 145–152 (2016)
21. Horst, H.: New media technologies in everyday life. In: Horst, H., Miller, D. (eds.) Digital Anthropology. Bloomsbury Academic, London (2012)
22. Chaplin, E.: My visual diary. In: Knowles, C., Sweetman, P. (eds.) Picturing the Social Landscape. Routledge, London (2004)

Novel Functional Technologies for Age-Friendly E-commerce

Xiaohai Tian[1,2(✉)], Lei Meng[1], Siyuan Liu[1], Zhiqi Shen[1], Eng-Siong Chng[2], Cyril Leung[1], Frank Guan[1], and Chunyan Miao[1,2]

[1] Joint NTU-UBC Research Centre of Excellence in Active Living for the Elderly (LILY), Nanyang Technological University, Singapore, Singapore
`tian0063@e.ntu.edu.sg`
[2] School of Computer Science and Engineering, Nanyang Technological University, Singapore, Singapore

Abstract. In this paper, we present an age-friendly E-commerce system with novel assistive functional technologies, aiming at providing a comfortable online shopping environment for the elderly. Besides incorporating human factors for the elderly into the design of user interface, we build an age-friendly system by improving the functional usability. First, to improve the searching experience, we design a multimodal product search function, which accepts image, speech, text and the combination of them as inputs to help the elderly find products easily and accurately. Second, we develop a product reputation function to provide an objective evaluation of products' quality, which helps the elderly filter out low-quality products while saves their energy in product comparison. Additionally, to reduce the elderly's visual burden when browsing the Web, a personalized speech feedback function is designed to provide speech assistant for the elderly. Our system has been testified using real-world E-commerce data, and the result demonstrates its feasibility.

Keywords: Age-friendly E-commerce · Elderly · Usability · Multimodal search · Personalized speech feedback · Product reputation

1 Introduction

E-commerce (electronic commerce), a transaction of buying or selling online, has grown over years. These business transactions occur in four business models: business-to-business, business-to-consumer, consumer-to-consumer or consumer-to-business[1]. Online shopping, also named as electronic retail, is a form of E-commerce which allows consumers to directly buy goods or services from a seller over the Internet using a web browser. Because of its convenience, it has been reshaping the attitude and behavior of customers for purchasing products.

A success online shopping procedure consists of four steps, including (1) product searching, (2) products comparison and selection, (3) confirmation and payment for the product, and (4) products delivery. In order to complete an online

---

[1] http://searchcio.techtarget.com/definition/e-commerce.

© Springer International Publishing AG 2017
J. Zhou and G. Salvendy (Eds.): ITAP 2017, Part II, LNCS 10298, pp. 150–158, 2017.
DOI: 10.1007/978-3-319-58536-9_13

shopping loop, customers must access to the Internet and complete the first three steps. Although it attracts the younger generation who can quickly reach such requirements, the senior population shows less interests in shopping online. Most of the current E-commerce websites do not fully cover the requirements of the elderly. Some of these websites are not clear and intuitive enough, inevitably bringing difficulties for the elderly who suffers from age-related impairments or unfamiliar with computer. It is observed that the elderly are more reluctant to use information technologies [13]. Moreover, a study indicated that the users aged over 65 years old were over 40% slower than the younger generation in using the Internet, and were more likely to give up their trials [14].

In the past decades, the world population is aging at an unprecedented rate. According to the report of An "Aging World: 2015" [16], the number of older people has increased more than 60% in just 15 years. The aging population will continue growing in the following 35 years. By 2050, the number of persons aged 65 years and above will reach 1.6 billion, which is over double size of this population in 2015. Hence, there will be a huge potential E-commerce market for elderly, in turn how to adapt the E-commerce system for the elderly to improve their living quality has become an important research topic.

1.1   Related Works

There are several barriers for the elderly using E-commerce. One of the most important reasons is the declining of physical and cognitive functions of the elderly [1]. A number of previous studies are focus on the evaluation and development of age-friendly browser design [1,4,5,9,10]. In [9], the age-friendly design principles in terms of the usability were introduced. In [8], 36 websites were evaluated by older adults in items of 25 "senior-friendly" guidelines recommended by the National Institute of Aging. In [5], the authors investigated the web search and navigation system for the elderly. The study [10] evaluated the usability of E-commerce website and highlighted the importance of clear and smart navigation design for senior customers. In [4], the author proposed a Non Browser design for older novice users.

Unfortunately, the barriers of elderly using online shopping not only come from the developer side. There are also some difficulties caused by the inexperience of old users. A well-designed training program is one of the ways to reduce such problems. However, it hardly cover all the possible conditions and is time consuming. Another way is to develop age-friendly functions to improve the usability of an E-commerce website for the elderly [3]. In [2,15], speech technology was adopted for products search. The study [7] presented a study on using voice demands for the elderly when browsing websites. In [12], we also designed three age-friendly functions, crowd-improved speech recognition, multimodal search and personalized speech feedback, to improve the elderly's online shopping experience.

1.2 Contributions of This Paper

To improve the usability of the age-friendly website, in this work, we improve and integrate our previous designed functions into our E-commerce system. Different to previous works focusing either on the UI design or on functional module development, we consider both aspects to improve the usability of the E-commerce system.

We extend our previous work in [12] with following aspects: (1) An age-friendly UI following the human factor design for the elderly, such as simplicity and intuitive, is designed for our E-commerce system; (2) we integrate the previous developed functions, namely multimodal search and personalized speech feedback, into our proposed system; (3) we develop the product reputation module to further improve the online shopping experience of elderly. With these integrated function modules, our age-friendly E-commerce system provides users with the benefits of flexible multimodel search, personalized speech feedback and high-quality search results.

The rest of the paper are organized as follows. Section 2 discuss the problems in existing age-friendly E-commerce system. We then present our proposed age-friendly E-commerce system in Sect. 3. Section 4 is the conclusion and future directions.

2 Problem Statement

The decline of physical and cognitive functions may cause inconvenience for older people when using the Web and shopping online. Particularly, contrast discriminations and color perception decline with age increase [6]. Hence, past studies usually focus on the problems of visual crowding and the text font choice in terms of size, style, and color [1,4,5,9].

In general, it is commonly agreed to use bigger font size and list fewer items in a single page to increase the age-friendliness of a website. Although such UI designs can make an E-commerce website age-friendly to some extent, how to improve the usability is still an open problem. In this work, we mainly focus on the following aspects of an age-friendly E-commerce system.

- Product Searching: Search accuracy of an age-friendly website is crucial for the user experience. Most elderly, however, are relatively poor at searching. They use search queries that are either too broad or too narrow. This could easily make them frustrated if irrelevant search results occupy the first several places.
- Feedback: Due to the visual impairments and cognition changes, it may be difficult for the old user to access the information of search results they care.
- Products Selection: The products comparison and selection is also a problem for elderly, who are less experience of filtering out the irrelevant or low-quality results.

3   Proposed Age-Friendly E-commerce System

3.1   System Overview

Our previous work [12] presents three standalone techniques, namely the crowd-improved speech recognition, the multimodal product search, and the personalized voice feedback. In this work, we organically integrate them into two engines, i.e. the multimodal search engine and the personalized speech engine. Beyond them, we further incorporate a product reputation engine to help re-rank and filter out the low-quality search results. To effectively integrate these functional modules into a practical system, we implement them using Python language, which can be linked together through Django platform.

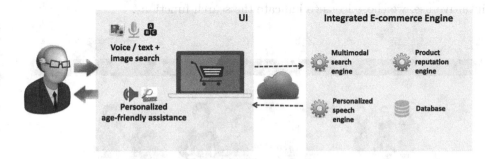

Fig. 1. Architecture of the proposed system for age-friendly E-commerce.

As shown in Fig. 1, our age-friendly E-commerce system contains two parts: (1) UI design, and (2) integrated E-commerce engine. In UI design part, similar to previous studies, our system adapt the UI of E-commerce website to assistant old users having visual and cognitive impairments. In the integrated E-commerce engine part, to improve the usability, three E-commerce engines, namely the multimodal search engine the personalized speech engine and the product reputation engine, are integrated into our system.

With age-friendly UI design and functional modules, our website provides users with the benefits of following properties,

- Our integrated system improves the flexibility of searching. User can search products using any combination of image, text, and voice as inputs;
- The informative feedbacks are returned to users in a personalized voice for them better understanding the results they are searching for;
- The product reputation engine re-ranks the results based on the user feedbacks of the products to help user to filter out the irrelevant products. This will help the users to select their desired products;
- Due to the unified implementation of all engines, our system become more robust and efficient.

In general, our integrated age-friendly E-commerce system provides a variety of adaptations, therefore meeting the needs of elderly.

In the following subsections, we will present the UI design and the integrated functional engines of our system.

3.2 UI Design

In this section, we will briefly introduce the age-friendly UI design of our system.

In order to adapt our UI to the old user, we incorporate of human factors for the elderly into the UI design of our system. As shown in Fig. 2, big font sizes with contrastive color (i.e. white text on dark backgrounds) are chosen to improve the visibility of our web browser, and fewer items are listed in a single page for simplified layouts. Additionally, to make the UI of our system more intuitive use, we chose icons to indicate the search functions.

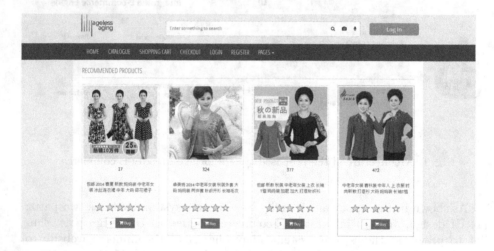

Fig. 2. Illustration of our age-friendly E-commerce UI design.

3.3 Integrated E-commerce Engine

In this section, we will present the three integrated functional engines of our system.

Multimodal Search Engine. The multimodal search engine provides multiple ways to users for searching the products. This engine is built upon an online multimodal co-indexing adaptive resonance theory (OMC-ART) [11] and crowd-improved speech recognition (CISR) function [12]. The OMC-ART is in charge of multimodal co-indexing and retrieval of weakly labeled web images. Thus, the OMC-ART enables both image- and/or text-based search. And the CISR function translates the users' voice into text, then realize the voice search function by feeding the recognized text to the search engine. Both the efficiency and accuracy of OMC-ART and CISR function have been proved in [12].

Fig. 3. Illustration of the difference between text search and multimodel search. (a) The search results use text as input only. (b) The search results use both text and image as input.

In our system, user can search by a part of speech, an image from camera or internet. As such, user is able to find the desired products more accurately with comparable time of previous search function. The example shown in Fig. 3 demonstrates the search results of our system with only text and the combination of text and image as input. Assuming the elderly found a picture of desired coat via internet, traditionally, they need to search via a text query. The searching accuracy highly depend on how well the elderly can describe the item. As shown in Fig. 3(a), the first several results may not hint the spot. While by adding the image for searching, it will be easier for them to find the desired item. As shown in Fig. 3(b), the coat, similar to the input picture, appears at the first place of the results. This example demonstrates the effectiveness our multimodel search function. The details of multimodal search function can be found in [12].

Personalized Speech Engine. For inexperience users, it may not be easy to notice all the information of the search results. In order to access the important information of search results for the old users, a personalized speech feedback engine is developed. When the product search is finished, the summary of the search results will be presented to the user with voice. A personalized voice can be generated by the engine for the old user better understanding the speech feedback. Personalized speech engine is built on voice conversion technology, which can transform one speaker's speech as it was uttered by another speaker with limited training data. Although text-to-speech (TTS) can also realize the similar function with better speech quality, long-time recording of the target speaker is required to build such a system. Hence, voice conversion is a more cost-efficient way to achieve this goal.

Fig. 4. Illustration of the personalized voice feedback function.

As shown in Fig. 4, after the product searching, a summary of search result is showed in the web page. Our speech feedback is used to help the elderly to access this information easily. Moreover, the elderly can also choose or create the voice they are prefer for better understanding. They can also replay the speech by click the audio button. The technique details can be found in [12].

Product Reputation Engine. Products comparison and selection of the searching results also might be a problem for elderly. To improve the searching accuracy and filter out the irrelevant products, a product reputation engine is developed in our system. Product reputation engine is responsible for calculating the reputation and re-ranking the products searching results based on the products quality. Three aspects of user's rating and feedbacks, namely temporal, similarity and quantity, are considered into quality calculation [11]. The reputation is calculated using the fuzzy-logic reputation engine to give a final score of the product.

Figure 5 demonstrates the product reputation function in our age-friendly E-commerce system. After searching, there is a reputation indicator below the products, which is used to re-rank the searching results. Specifically, the products with higher reputation score will be given higher rank. In this way, product reputation function ensures a robust performance in product search and benefits users for products comparison and selection.

Fig. 5. Illustration of the product reputation function.

4   Conclusion and Future Work

In this paper, we present an age-friendly E-commerce system with novel assistive functional technologies. Besides the age-friendly website design, our system integrates three functional engines, namely the multimodal search engine, the personalized speech engine and the product reputation engine, into Django platform. The multimodal search function integrate both the speech recognition and image searching techniques and enable the elderly to search for desired products using either speech, images, texts, or any combination of them. The personalized speech feedback presents the summary of search results with personalized voices, which helps the elderly better access and understand the searching results. The product reputation re-ranks the searching results based on the products quality, which improves the searching accuracy and filter out the irrelevant and low-quality products. We have shown the usability of our proposed age-friendly E-commerce system with the real-world E-commerce transaction data from REC-TMALL dataset[2].

While, it is noted that this is a preliminary study, the design for usability requires testing and iteration. Hence, in future, we will conduct a series of user study to evaluate the system. Additionally, more assistive techniques, such as personalized recommendation function, will be developed to further improve the usability of the system.

Acknowledgments. This research is supported by the National Research Foundation, Prime Minister's Office, Singapore under its IDM Futures Funding Initiative.

---

[2] https://tianchi.aliyun.com/datalab/index.htm?spm=5176.100075.2368.2.5czf7X.

References

1. Becker, S.A.: A study of web usability for older adults seeking online health resources. ACM Trans. Comput. Hum. Interact. (TOCHI) **11**(4), 387–406 (2004)
2. Biadsy, F., Moreno, P.J., Jansche, M.: Google's cross-dialect arabic voice search. In: IEEE International Conference on Acoustics, Speech, and Signal Processing (ICASSP 2012), pp. 4441–4444 (2012)
3. Chen, L., Gillenson, M.L., Sherrell, D.L.: Consumer acceptance of virtual stores: a theoretical model and critical success factors for virtual stores. ACM Sigmis Database **35**(2), 8–31 (2004)
4. Dickinson, A., Gregor, P., McIver, L., Hill, R., Milne, S.: The non browser: helping older novice computer users to access the web. In: Proceedings of the 2005 International Conference on Accessible Design in the Digital World, p. 18. British Computer Society (2005)
5. Dickinson, A., Smith, M.J., Arnott, J.L., Newell, A.F., Hill, R.L.: Approaches to web search and navigation for older computer novices. In: Proceedings of the SIGCHI Conference on Human Factors in Computing Systems, pp. 281–290. ACM (2007)
6. Hanson, V.L., Crayne, S.: Personalization of web browsing: adaptations to meet the needs of older adults. Univ. Access Inf. Soc. **4**(1), 46–58 (2005)
7. Hanson, V.L., Richards, J.T., Lee, C.C.: Web access for older adults: voice browsing? In: Stephanidis, C. (ed.) UAHCI 2007. LNCS, vol. 4554, pp. 904–913. Springer, Heidelberg (2007). doi:10.1007/978-3-540-73279-2_101
8. Hart, T.A., Chaparro, B.: Evaluation of websites for older adults: how "senior friendly" are they? Usability News **6**(1), 12 (2004)
9. Holzinger, A., Searle, G., Kleinberger, T., Seffah, A., Javahery, H.: Investigating usability metrics for the design and development of applications for the elderly. In: Miesenberger, K., Klaus, J., Zagler, W., Karshmer, A. (eds.) ICCHP 2008. LNCS, vol. 5105, pp. 98–105. Springer, Heidelberg (2008). doi:10.1007/978-3-540-70540-6_13
10. Kang, L., Dong, H.: B2C websites' usability for Chinese senior citizens. In: Kurosu, M. (ed.) HCI 2014. LNCS, vol. 8512, pp. 13–20. Springer, Cham (2014). doi:10.1007/978-3-319-07227-2_2
11. Liu, S., Yu, H., Miao, C., Kot, A.C., Theng, Y.L.: A fuzzy logic based reputation model against unfair ratings. In: Proceedings of the 12th International Conference on Autonomous Agents and Multiagent Systems, pp. 821–828 (2013)
12. Meng, L., Nguyen, Q.H., Tian, X., Shen, Z., Chng, E.S., Guan, F.Y., Miao, C., Leung, C.: Towards age-friendly e-commerce through crowd-improved speech recognition, multimodal search, and personalized speech feedback. In: Proceedings of the 1st International Conference on Crowd Science and Engineering (ICCSE 2016) (2016)
13. Niehaves, B., Plattfaut, R.: Internet adoption by the elderly: employing is technology acceptance theories for understanding the age-related digital divide. Eur. J. Inf. Syst. **23**(6), 708–726 (2014)
14. Nielsen, J.: Seniors as web users. Nielsen Norman Group. https://www.nngroup.com/articles/usability-for-senior-citizens/. Accessed Aug 2013
15. Schalkwyk, J., Beeferman, D., Beaufays, F., Byrne, B., Chelba, C., Cohen, M., Garret, M., Strope, B.: Google search by voice: a case study (2010)
16. Wan, H., Daniel, G., Paul, K.: An aging world: 2015, Issued March 2016. https://www.census.gov/content/dam/Census/library/publications/2016/demo/p95-16-1.pdf

Participatory Human-Centered Design of a Feedback Mechanism Within the Historytelling System

Torben Volkmann[1](✉), Michael Sengpiel[2], and Nicole Jochems[1]

[1] Universität zu Lübeck, Ratzeburger Allee 160, 23562 Lübeck, Germany
{volkmann,jochems}@imis.uni-luebeck.de
[2] Humboldt University of Berlin, Unter den Linden 6, 10099 Berlin, Germany
michael.sengpiel@hu-berlin.de

Abstract. This article describes the procedure and results of two workshops conducted following interviews with potential users within the development process of a feedback component for the Historytelling system, a cooperative interactive website for older adults. For the development of the Historytelling system we follow a Human Centered Design for aging (HCD+) process, gathering requirements and designing first prototypes of this component. Workshop results show that the most important element of the feedback component is the personal, context sensitive acknowledgement of the stories which can be enriched with multimedia contents to provide more palpable appreciation.

Keywords: Aging users · Human-Centered Design (HCD+) · Design thinking workshops

1 Introduction

With the demographic change the percentage of older adults within society increases steadily [1]. At the same time, the rapid advances in information and communication technology (ICT) offer great potential benefit for older users – but they can also bring about severe usability issues. Thus, human centered design for aging (HCD+) gains importance in the design of useful and usable products [2]. Goal of the "Historytelling" project is the human centered development of a cooperative interactive website with and for older adults. The following scenario introduces its functionality:

Carol Mayer has been retired for five years and lives by herself since her husband has died two years ago. She has experienced a lot in her lifetime and likes telling her grandchildren about it: the time after the war, her youth, holidays with her husband and children. Sadly, there seems never enough time to tell them when they visit. Her friend told her about "Historytelling" and she decided to give it a try. Here she can write down her stories and pinpoint the exact time and place on a map. She really likes the fact that she can also discover other people's stories attached to that place and/or time and that it is so easy to use – it really seems to be made for her! And if she wants, she can add her old pictures and unlock the stories for her grandchildren only. After her grandchildren liked some of her stories and left enthusiastic comments, she realized that as witness to history as she has experienced it, she can provide an important contribution to her

© Springer International Publishing AG 2017
J. Zhou and G. Salvendy (Eds.): ITAP 2017, Part II, LNCS 10298, pp. 159–169, 2017.
DOI: 10.1007/978-3-319-58536-9_14

family and to society. This has really boosted her participation in the "Historytelling" platform and she now has more meaningful contact to her own biography, to her grand-children, and even to other people she meets on the website.

Developing the "Historytelling" platform in a human centered design for aging (HCD+) process [2], we integrated methods for analysis and design as illustrated in Fig. 1.

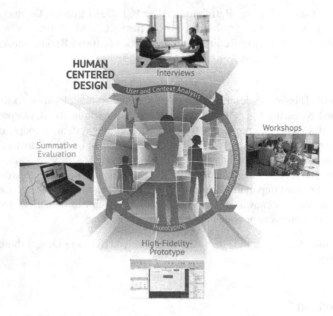

Fig. 1. Overview of the human centered design for aging (HCD+) process in the development of the "Historytelling" platform

To ensure high utility and usability for potential older users, they were included in the design process from the start. This also yielded valuable insights applicable for ICT design for aging in general. In the beginning of "Historytelling" development, an inter-view study with potential users was conducted to analyze user needs and context. Besides aspects of fear and motivation of older adults to use the Historytelling system, one of the main results of the interview study was the pivotal role of feedback within the system, leading to the following research questions for its design: Which kind of feedback motivates older people to post more stories? How will older users feel appre-ciated after contributing a personal story [3]?

This paper describes the development of suitable feedback components for the "Historytelling" system, focusing on two design thinking workshops with older adults aiming to "design with and for the Elderly". Results of these workshops directly informed the design of a first prototype.

2 State of the Art

Much has been published about user participation in the design process, including older users [4–7]. Since older adults often have less experience with ICT, including them in the design process can prove very effective to achieve high ICT usability. Because they might not know about current developments, they might foster technologically infeasible ideas or insist on older, well established technologies [8]. Yet while older research in this field of HCI focused on deficit-oriented design [9], newer research tries to include positive aspects of aging to design software that respects the users' abilities, needs and preferences. Some point out that sketching user interfaces is more difficult for older adults, yet criticizing existing UIs or imagining their use is easier [10]. Also, when conducting workshops with older adults it is paramount to create an atmosphere that encourages participants to enjoy the time and express their honest opinions, e.g. by explaining that their expertise is important for system development [11].

3 Method

Within the HCD+ requirements analysis, two workshops were conducted with older potential users, aiming to develop suitable feedback mechanisms for the Historytelling system, focusing on sharing stories in private and public. Feedback mechanisms were to be developed in abstract form first, before transferring them to a digital prototype by combining workshop results with guidelines for designing for older adults.

3.1 Participants

A total of 16 older adults, 14 women and two men, aged between 51 and 81 years (M = 66.63, SD = 7.94) took part in the workshops. They were selected for their declared interest and engagement in the cooperative development of the Historytelling software. A questionnaire indicated their potential interest in technology. Ten participants owned a tablet-PC and/or smartphone and used it regularly. All participants but one used the Internet, mainly for surfing and email.

3.2 Procedure

The workshops took place in a laboratory of the Institute for Multimedia and Interactive Systems of the Universität zu Lübeck. They lasted about 3,5 h and were conducted by one scientist, while another wrote the protocol. Figure 2 overview of the workshop procedure shows an overview of the procedure. After the introduction, participants filled in a questionnaire on technology use and were introduced to two scenarios that were chosen to counteract possible technology anxiety and to allow for a smooth initiation to the topic. Scenario one provided a general introduction into storytelling while scenario two and three focused on private and public sharing of stories, respectively.

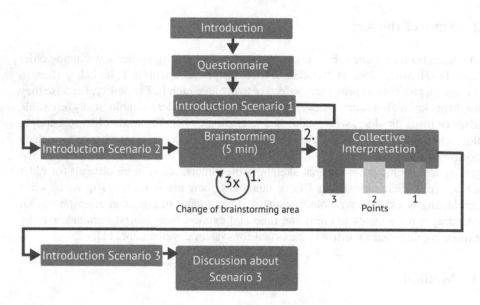

Fig. 2. Overview of the workshop procedure

Scenario one: General introduction. In the world that we imagine, people can tell their stories for as long as they want. If they desire feedback, they can push a button to receive it from their audience, be it text, pictures or anything imaginable.

Scenario two: Private sharing. You sit at home on the couch and tell your 12-year old grandchild one of your favorite personal stories. He listens attentively and when you are done you can invite him to provide feedback by pushing a button. How should your grandchild react? What should he or she say or do? What would you imagine?

Scenario three: Public sharing. Your grandchild invited you to an event where people want to hear your stories and those of other people your age and you are looking forward to the young audience. You imagine telling them a story from your life that you would not mind sharing publically. After telling the story you get immediate feedback at the push of a button again. How should people react? What should they say or do? What would you imagine?

Brainstorming. The brainstorming method was used for idea generation and discussion in the context of scenario 2. Participants were divided into three groups and the brainstorming process was split into three runs lasting five minutes each. In a first step, every group created its own ideas for the scenario and wrote them on post-its. Two post it colors were offered – yellow for abstract ideas and blue for ideas for technical implementation. After five minutes the groups changed positions to work with the ideas of another group. Then they could read the written post-its and develop new ideas based on the ideas of the previous group. This procedure was repeated once more so that every group could read the initial ideas of every group. Then the post-its were clustered with all participants. The moderator read all post-its out loud, wrote the topics discussed within the group on cards and put them above the related post-its, creating an elaborated hierarchy. Finally, the categories were rated by the participants regarding their importance for the Historytelling project.

4 Results

4.1 Brainstorming Results (Scenario 2)

In the first workshop, 108 post-its were created and clustered in 13 categories and 20 subcategories (Table 1). Figure 3 shows a group of participants in the brainstorming session and first results on post-its. Three categories that received the highest ratings and informed the further feedback-component development are as follows:

1. **More information on earlier days (15):** Were you bored without having a computer? How was your childhood in the 1950s?
2. **Visualization (14):** Grandchild wants to see a picture with the story or paint one, flight simulation instead of photo album, do you have pictures of this?
3. **Deeper questions (12):** Have you loved one another? What do you remember still today? How did you meet?

Table 1. Elaborated categories and subcategories

Category	Post-it points
More information about time	• Broad questions
	• Difference past and present
	• Link to other stories
	• Link to other information
	• Deeper questions
	• Place
	• Time
	• circumstances
Visualization	Demanding visual media
	Linking photos and maps
	Design ideas
Deeper questions	
Realization	Archiving
	Empathy
	Distribution
Inquiry	Difference past and present
	Deepening questions
	Emotions
Request	Direct request
	Photos and pictures
	Regional aspects

Fig. 3. A group of people in a brainstorming session (left) and first results on post-its (right)

In the second workshop, 52 post-its were created and clustered in 11 categories. As above, the three most important categories are as follows:

4. **Implementation/ develop something new (10):** Turn it into a game, I experienced something similar once, paint a picture about it
5. **Request (5):** Grandpa, tell me more stories, find photos for the stories, Why don't we talk about it more often?
6. **Inquiry (4):** Have you slept at your grandparents once? Who were your friends? How did your classroom look?

4.2 Discussion Results (Scenario 3)

The second workshop was based on the third scenario and consisted of a discussion about ideal feedback for publicly shared stories (see Fig. 4). Central themes from discussion were:

- Emotionality and intimacy of information, in particular for the public sharing of stories,
- The relation of feedback for public sharing and blogging,
- The purpose of memory books asking grandparents questions about their life,
- The target audience for private/public stories

Participants argued that the expected target audience for stories being close family or the wider public would have an impact on the amount and depth of information provided. They also saw a relationship between blogging and the public sharing of stories in the Historytelling system. They indicated that people writing a blog might be more willing to share stories publicly, motivated by the same reasons.

Memory books proved to be a controversial issue: Participants without experience with such books declared they would be happy to receive such books from their relatives.

Fig. 4. Participants of the first workshop during a discussion

However, those who had experience with them, mentioned three main concerns: (1) Questions are often very banal and can be answered with a single sentence. (2) Questions are often very intimate. (3) The book itself is not interested in the person.

Participants also saw issues of authenticity in automatic questioning, as they are not asked as family members would and the actual interest of the audience remains unclear. Also, they cast doubt on public interest for their private stories, thus further diminishing any interest in public story sharing. Additionally, discussed topics include: sharing options, story copyright, financial interests and trust in the Historytelling system, as well as options for an intelligent system which understands context, asks questions and adds information automatically when necessary (and available).

4.3   Prototyping Results

In the next step, (abstract) workshop results were combined with design learnings for reminiscence systems (e.g. by Thiry und Bosson [12]) and general design guidelines [13, 14] to create prototypes. Accordingly, the system requirements pictured in were derived (Fig. 5).

Then, low fidelity prototypes were built using the software "Balsamiq" ([15] - Fig. 6 shows an example) that were iteratively redesigned into a clickable prototype with the software "AxureRP" [16].

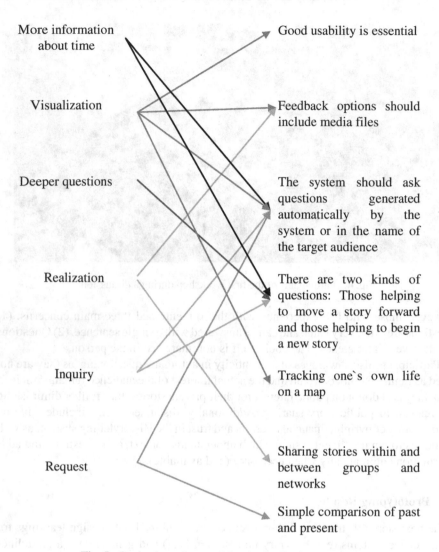

Fig. 5. Derived requirements for the feedback component

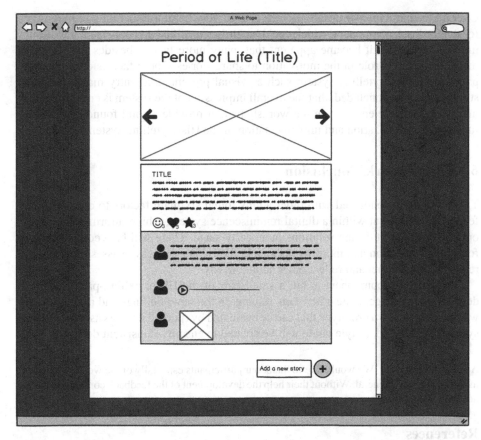

Fig. 6. Low fidelity prototype of the feedback component

5 Discussion

The Historytelling system component described in this article aims to provide feedback options designed to encourage the storyteller to share more stories. Prior interviews have shown that (perceived) appreciation for the story teller is a key component for (public) sharing. Thus, the system should support the storyteller by making the audience appreciation palpable. Questions should be placed in context and show the close relationship to the story, connecting the story with personal information and experiences. Thus, one original idea of integrating general questions without context into the feedback-component to automate asking seems not viable. However, perhaps semantic story content filtering could help to avoid this dilemma in the future.

In the workshops, a stimulating atmosphere was very important to the participants – they even contributed their own food and drink to enhance it. Particularly quieter participants did benefit from this atmosphere to talk to others. Participants are sometimes bound to digress from a given topic in brainstorming and discussion – they sometimes talked about other aspects of the Historytelling system besides the feedback component.

Overall, the participatory design process proved very helpful in defining requirements for the feedback component, which could be further specified and translated into design implications. Also, it became apparent that many more factors besides the feedback mechanism play a role in the motivation to share stories. These factors concern other parts of the Historytelling system such as visual presentation, entry masks and data storage. It can be concluded, that the overall impression of the system is crucial and that many aspects have emerged in the workshops that provide a solid foundation for the further conceptualization and implementation of the Historytelling system.

6 Future Work/Conclusion

Two workshops conducted with older adults found six main factors to consider for a feedback component within a digital reminiscence system, which informed the development of different design solutions in an early stage. There will be a comprehensive formative evaluation and more workshops in the HCD+ process to assess whether the requirements are met and reflect older adults' needs.

The feedback component is but a small part of the Historytelling-project. Future design cycles will generate other parts relying on the same findings and principles and will be merged into a prototype that can be evaluated by (potential) users as an integrated system. To that end, a style guide will be created to ensure a consistent design.

Acknowledgement. We would like to thank our participants especially of the workshop but the involved people in general. Without their help the development of the feedback component would not have been possible.

References

1. Preißing, D.: Erfolgreiches Personalmanagement im demografischen Wandel. Walter de Gruyter GmbH & Co KG, Berlin (2014)
2. Jochems, N., Sengpiel, M.: Introduction to the special issue on design for aging. i-Com **15**, 1–2 (2016)
3. Volkmann, T., Sengpiel, M., Jochems, N.: Historytelling: a website for the elderly a human-centered design approach. In: Proceedings of the 9th Nordic Conference on Human-Computer Interaction. pp. 100:1–100:6. ACM, New York (2016)
4. Wille, M., Theis, S., Rasche, P., Bröhl, C., Schlick, C., Mertens, A.: Best practices for designing electronic healthcare devices and services for the elderly. i-Com **15**, 67–78 (2016)
5. Lindsay, S., Jackson, D., Schofield, G., Olivier, P.: Engaging older people using participatory design. In: Proceedings of the SIGCHI Conference on Human Factors in Computing Systems, pp. 1199–1208. ACM, New York (2012)
6. Ellison, N.B., Vitak, J., Gray, R., Lampe, C.: Cultivating social resources on social network sites: Facebook relationship maintenance behaviors and their role in social capital processes. J. Comput. Mediat. Commun. **19**, 855–870 (2014)

7. Vines, J., Blythe, M., Lindsay, S., Dunphy, P., Monk, A., Olivier, P.: Questionable concepts: critique as resource for designing with eighty somethings. In: Proceedings of the SIGCHI Conference on Human Factors in Computing Systems, pp. 1169–1178. ACM, New York (2012)
8. Davidson, J.L., Jensen, C.: Participatory design with older adults: an analysis of creativity in the design of mobile healthcare applications. In: Proceedings of the 9th ACM Conference on Creativity & Cognition (2013)
9. Lorenz, A., Mielke, D., Oppermann, R., Zahl, L.: Personalized mobile health monitoring for elderly. In: Proceedings of the 9th International Conference on Human Computer Interaction with Mobile Devices and Services (2007)
10. Massimi, M., Baecker, R.: Participatory design process with older users. In: Proceedings of UbiCoomp2006 Workshop on Future Media (2006)
11. Eisma, R., Dickinson, A., Goodman, J., Syme, A., Tiwari, L., Newell, A.F.: Early user involvement in the development of information technology-related products for older people. Univ. Access Inf. Soc. **3**, 131–140 (2004)
12. Thiry, E., Rosson, M.B.: Unearthing the family gems: design requirements for a digital reminiscing system for older adults. In: CHI 2012 Extended Abstracts on Human Factors in Computing Systems, pp. 1715–1720. ACM, New York (2012)
13. Leavitt, M.O., Schneiderman, B.: Research-Based Web Design & Usability Guidelines. U.S. Dept. of Health and Human Services (2006)
14. Kurniawan, S., Zaphiris, P.: Research-derived web design guidelines for older people. In: Proceedings of the 7th International ACM SIGACCESS Conference on Computers and Accessibility, pp. 129–135. ACM, New York (2005)
15. Balsamiq Studios, LLC. https://balsamiq.com/
16. Axure Software Solutions, Inc. https://www.axure.com/

Research on New Media Usage Behaviors, Influencing Factors and Social Contact Mode of the Elderly

Minggang Yang[✉], Mingliang Dou, and Yinan Han

School of Art, Design and Media, East China University
of Science and Technology, M.BOX 286, No.130, Meilong Road,
Xuhui District, Shanghai 20023, China
yangminggang@163.com, enal211@163.com,
jackiedou@yeah.com

Abstract. The elderly should not become burden of the society. They still have strong sense of participation and sense of contribution in society through convenient high-efficient new social media, exploring social values of the elderly and making them a strong impetus of social development. Considering the population growth of the elderly and the increasing popularization of new media-based social contact in the current age, new media usage behavior data of the elderly were collected through questionnaire survey and in-depth interview. Factors of new media usage behavior of the elderly were analyzed by SPASS and four main influencing factors were concluded: serviceability, usability, value and willingness (SUVW) of the elderly using new media-based social contact. Next, the media-based social contact model of the elderly was constructed by the theoretical model approach based on SUVW. The new-media social contact mode of the elderly verified and discussed through some cases of china. Finally, shortcomings of this study were disclosed and the some reflections and prospects were proposed according to the large fuzzy improvement space in this field. These deserve further deep researches in future.

Keywords: The elderly · New media · Usage behaviors · Influencing factors · Social contact mode

1 Introduction

Both developed countries and developing countries pay more and more attentions on a series of advantages brought by demographic dividends in recent years. The population of the longevity old increases gradually as economic living standard improves increasingly. On one hand, China's two-child policy which was issued in the last year is beneficial for maintaining the labor's scale reasonably. On the other hand, it is good to decrease aloneness of the elderly. Meanwhile, with the continuous development of internet and mobile internet, the new media-based social communication which has characteristics of digitization, interaction and mobility becomes more and more popular. New social media orients to more and more population groups, from pupils to the elderly.

© Springer International Publishing AG 2017
J. Zhou and G. Salvendy (Eds.): ITAP 2017, Part II, LNCS 10298, pp. 170–180, 2017.
DOI: 10.1007/978-3-319-58536-9_15

Considering degraded visual and hearing senses, weakened cognitive ability and difficulty in accepting new things of the elderly, new media-based social contact of the elderly shall pay more attentions on studying new media usage behaviors and social contact mode of the elderly. This research topic emerges at the right moment. Firstly, existing researches on the elderly using new media social services were reviewed in this paper. Secondly, influencing factors against the elderly to use new media for social contact were analyzed and summarized through questionnaire survey and in-depth interview. Finally, a set of flow system to optimize the elderly using new media-based social services and innovate the service design mode was established based on these variable factors.

2 Literature Review

2.1 Connecting Older Adults

Robert Steele (2013), an informatics professor from the University of Sydney, led a team to study the program of "connecting older adults", concluding that social media could be used as an effective tool to decrease aloneness of the elderly. This research involves 150 respondents of 55 years old or higher and most were older than 65 years old. Before the experiment, researchers made a short training to the elderly. About 80% older adults answered that they would continue to use social media after the experiment and 65% agree or strongly agree that social media are very convenient.

By comparing data before and after the experiment, researchers found that older adults using social media feel significantly less lonely. Most respondents also reported that the usage of social media helps them to deepen connection with the community and participation in community activities.

2.2 Usage Behaviors of the Elderly for Social Contact and Influencing Factors

There is a strong intrinsic logicality between new media usage behaviors of the elderly and its influencing factors. Usage behaviors are the basis of service design and service design is the perfection and supplementation of usage behaviors. They supplement each other. The social contact design for the elderly could better and the elderly could participate in social activities better as long as paying high attentions to media usage behaviors by the elderly and analyzing corresponding influencing factors.

Most of existing researches on media usage behaviors of the elderly focus on the computer end and exploring the relationship between usage behavior data and user experience and interests. For example, based on the psychological knowledge-internal drive theory, Lucas (2006), an American scholar, found that the internet surfing behavior of older users is closely related with their interests on the webpage content. On this basis, he suggested to describe such correlation by the linear regression model. Based on this research result, Buultjiens (2008), an Australian scholar, proposed the combination of 6 types of users' minimum browsing behaviors. Furthermore, two internet surfing behaviors that influence interests of older users were acquired through mutual conversion of three types of behaviors, thus disclosing the quantitative relation between UE and key behaviors.

Additionally, with the continuous updating and development of mobile internet, many scholars focused on new media as the mobile end and attempted to study behavioral habits of the elderly and interaction design related with cell phone from. Relationship between behavioral habits and mental satisfaction of the elderly using social media services was analyzed by collecting data about cell phone using habits of older adults. Van Biljon et al. (2010) put forward the cell phone acceptance model of the elderly based on the technology acceptance model (TAM) and explored various factors that influence the elderly using cell phones, especially objectivity and procedure influencing factors. Later, Conci et al. (2012) established the TAM of the elderly to cell phone by combining the behavioristics and used perceived safety, self-actualization and enjoyment as the internal willingness. They found that social impact influences the perceived serviceability and willingness to some extent, whereas cell phone supports have some influences on willingness and perceived usability. These reveal that the internal willingness is important. Gobel (2013) concluded the two-factor model theory. In this theory, technological anxiety and perceived changes of the elderly are used as internal and external factors to explore the elderly make social contact based on cell phone. It found that resistance of older users will influence perceived serviceability. The technological anxiety is negatively correlated with perceived usability and is positively correlated with resistance behaviors of the older users, but the resistance changes are negatively correlated with perceived usability and are positively correlated with resistance behaviors of the older users. On this basis, Stamato et al. (2015) concluded the internal relationships of the elderly using cell phone with context of users, perceived serviceability, perceived usability and willingness. Finally, based on statistics, psychology and artificial intelligence, Lin Chuang et al. (2016) preliminarily explored the evaluation model of user satisfaction based on behavioral habit and pointed out relationships of subjective factors of human and objective factors of environment with user experience and social contact service quality.

To sum up, researches on usage behaviors and influencing factors of the elderly using new social media as well as how to improve interaction still have a large fuzzy space. No targeted and systematic researches have been reported yet. Combining above mentioned and more associated research results, four main factors (SUVW) that influence the elderly using new social media were analyzed and summarized in this paper. Based on SUVW, a theoretical model for optimizing new media usage of the elderly for social contact was constructed.

3   Research Methods

3.1   Main Research Methods

Firstly, numerous researches on usage behavior of new social media and user satisfaction of the elderly using new media were reviewed and analyzed. Secondly, related influencing factors were disclosed by combining psychology, statistics, behavioristics and human-computer interaction design. Thirdly, a questionnaire was designed by combining these information factors and 425 older users were interviewed. Questionnaire survey results and interview results were compared to further disclose other influencing factors. Finally, correlation between SUVW and older users' satisfaction to new media was analyzed by SPASS and a primary theoretical model of new media-based social contact of the elderly was constructed.

3.2 Questionnaire Design

In this paper, basic information of respondents were collected firstly (Table 1). Next, a series of problems related with the elderly using new social media were designed carefully to measure impacts of social media based on EXCEL descriptive analysis of 1012 questionnaires on older users' satisfaction to new media (Table 2), which were used to measure relationship between SUVW and usage behaviors. Correlation between answers of another 425 respondents and SUVW was analyzed by SPASS. All variables were masurd by the Likert scale (1–5). The SUVW were scored from 1–5 and the final mean of each factor was acquired. Since these variables belong to grading and sequencing variables, Spearman's rank correlation coefficient which is deduced by Spearman (An English psychologist and statistician) is appropriate to "two-variable correlation" analysis:

Table 1. Basic information of the elderly

Age	55–59	60–64	65–69	Over 70
Gender	Male		Female	
Education	≤ Primary	Junior	Senior	≥ College
Retirement	Yes		No	
Living Alone	Yes		No	
Work Out	Never	Seldom	Sometimes	Often
Use Social Medium	Yes		No	

Table 2. Correlation analysis between SUVW and user satisfaction

Variables	Questions	1	2	3	4	5
Serviceability	1. New media helps me to communicate with others more conveniently.					
	2. The diversified development of new media enriches my daily life (e.g. shopping and medical service).					
	3. New media helps me to make more friends with similar people.					
	4. New media is useful to me.					
Usability	5. New media is easy to operate for me.					
	6. New media makes it easy to communicate with my friends.					
	7. New media helps me a lot to make friends.					
Value	8. New media makes my life meaningful.					

(*continued*)

Table 2. (*continued*)

Variables	Questions	1	2	3	4	5
	9. New media helps me to know the latest situations of my friends.					
	10. New media will leak my privacy security.					
	11. New media disturb my life.					
Willingness	12. I will encourage more peers to use new media.					
	13. I wouldn't use new media more, because it brings me a lot of troubles.					
	14. I want to use new media more in future.					

('1 = Strongly Disagree, 2 = Little Disagree, 3 = Agree, 4 = Little Agree, 5 = Strongly Agree')

$$r_s = 1 - \frac{6 \sum_{i=1}^{n} D_i^2}{n(n^2 - 1)} \tag{1}$$

Where n is number of variable data pairs, D = xi−yi (i = 1, 2, 3,...n)(X_i and Y_i are ordinal number of value of each case on X, Y.) Spearman coefficient of rank correlation ranges between $-1 \sim +1$. When $r_s > 0$, two variables are positively correlated. When $r_s < 0$, two variables are negatively correlated. The higher the absolute value is, the stronger correlation between these two variables. Scores of these factors are shown in Fig. 1.

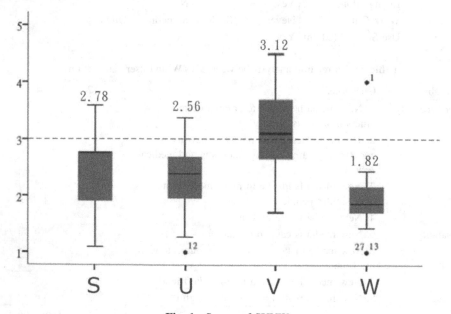

Fig. 1. Scores of SUVW

4 Impact Factor

A total of 1462 respondents were selected for the in-depth interview and questionnaire survey (425 for in-depth interview. 1012 questionnaires were sent offline and online, including 25 invalid questionnaires.). According to the investigation process and results, 83% older users' satisfaction to usage of current social media is lower than the mean value, which is attributed to different factors (Fig. 2).

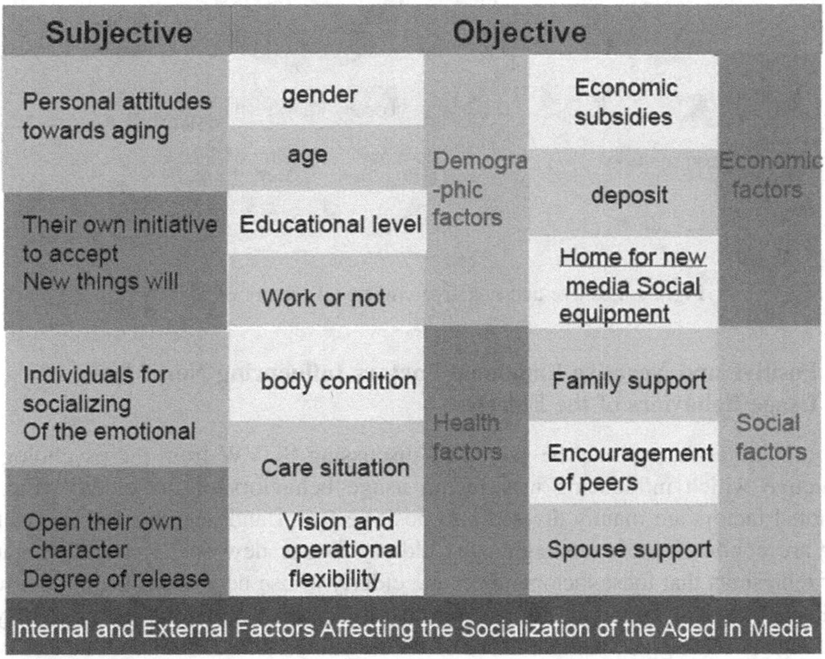

Subjective		Objective	
Personal attitudes towards aging	gender		Economic subsidies
	age	Demogra-phic factors	deposit
Their own Initiative to accept New things will	Educational level		Home for new media Social equipment
	Work or not		
Individuals for socializing Of the emotional	body condition		Family support
	Care situation	Health factors	Encouragement of peers
Open their own character Degree of release	Vision and operational flexibility		Spouse support

Economic factors

Social factors

Internal and External Factors Affecting the Socialization of the Aged in Media

Fig. 2. 17 influencing factors of new media usage behavior of the elderly

4.1 Classification of Subjective and Objective Influencing Factors

Influencing factors of the elderly using new social media which were gained from literature review and practice survey were classified into subjective and objective factors. The research framework is shown in Fig. 3. Subjective factors refers to attitude and emotions of older users to new social media, including individual attitude to aging, intention to accept and learn new things, individual emotion to social contact, and open-minded degree. Objective factors cover four aspects, including demographic factors, health factors, economic factors and social factors. There are 17 subjective and objective influencing factors. Finally, these 17 factors were classified into SUVW from the perspective of new media usage behavior of the elderly.

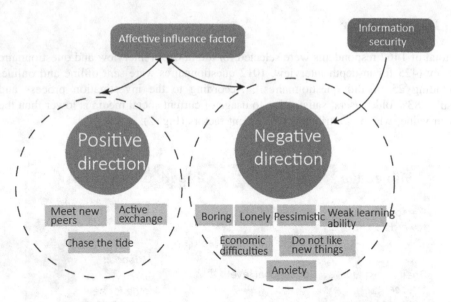

Fig. 3. Positive and negative emotional factors of SUVW

4.2 Positive and Negative Emotional Factors Influencing New Media Usage Behaviors of the Elderly

Some emotional factors may be gained by discussing SUVW from the psychological perspective which influencing new media usage behaviors of the elderly (Fig. 3). Emotional factors are mainly divided into positive factor and negative factor. Positive factor are conducive to encouraging the elderly to use new social media. Negative factor represents that these factors hinder the elderly to use new social media. Sense of security is the most important influencing factor. Sense of insecurity of the elderly to new things is the biggest internal cause of the negative factor. Emotional factors were not analyzed thoroughly and shall be further discussed in future researches.

5 Results

5.1 Research Results Analysis and Establishment of New Media-Based Social Contact Mode of the Elderly

Among 1462 random samples, only 17% older users are very satisfying with the usage of new social media, 52% express concerns to safety of new social media, and 31% haven't used new social media due to various reasons, such as economic factors, cognitive learning factors, physical health factors, etc. Based on relationships between SUVW and satisfaction, a primary theoretical model of new media-based social contact mode of the elderly was established (Fig. 4).

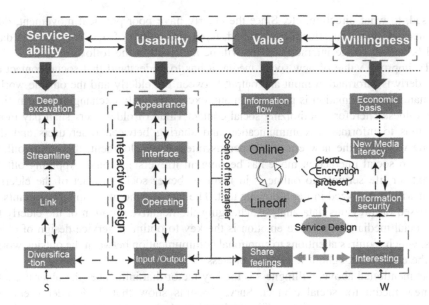

Fig. 4. SUVW model

The SUVW model is established by combining associated literature review and survey results. It constructs the theoretical new media-based social contact model of the elderly mainly from SUVW. Serviceability, usability, value and willingness supplement each other. Among them, willingness is the most important factor that influences new media-based social contact of older users.

When optimizing serviceability of new social media to older users, demands of older users for new social media shall be explored deeply. Next, these demands shall be simplified. Simplification of these demands covers two meanings. One is to eliminate all unnecessary and tedious application steps for older users. The other is to deepen rest demands thoroughly through design. Subsequently, linkage of new media-based social contact shall be improved. Such linkage also includes two meanings. One is to increase communications among older users through new social media, that is, man-man linkage. The other is to let older users to get contact with different new things through new social media, that is, man-thing linkage. Finally, the optimization goal of "serviceability" is to improve diversified life of the elderly, thus bringing the elderly a more colorful life.

Usability is mainly improved from interaction design, including appearance, interface, operation and information input/output. New media equipments for the elderly mainly refer to computer and cell phone. Appearance design of these products shall better conform to life and usage characteristics of the elderly. Interface of new social media equipments for the elderly shall be designed simple and clean, which is determined by the significantly weaker visual perception of the elderly compared to young population. Besides, more attentions shall be paid to man-machine interaction of new social media for the elderly. For example, interface switching shall consider page turning of the elderly comprehensively, such as how to slide pages, which fingers shall be used, to what direction, etc. Since the elderly have poor physical movement, dull response and low educational background, input and output of new social media data shall be mainly voice interaction. This will be analyzed in the following case.

To improve value of new social media, it has to understand that social contact of the elderly is information input and output between the elderly and the outside world. The nature of information is propagation and exchange. Only exchanging information have values. Therefore, optimizing social contact value of older users shall pay more attentions to information communication and sharing between older users and the outside world. In the new era of prosperous internet development, the online-offline integrated social interaction mode has become an irreversible trend. Applying offline context for life services to online is in favor of better social contact of the elderly, which will be analyzed in the following text. The last and the most important points is that based on previous data analysis, changing the negative emotion of the elderly to new social media into positive emotion is the key to optimize service design of older users, which requires attentions to emotional communication between the outside world and the elderly throughout the design process.

As mentioned above, willingness is the key factor that influences the older users to use new media for social contact. Survey results show that 31% older users are reluctant to use the new social media, which is directly caused by economic limitations. It is difficult to let more older adults to experience the new social media without economic subsidies from the society and the government. Caring the elderly is an indispensable virtue. Furthermore, strengthening the media education to the elderly is the premise of the elderly using new social media. Improvement of media education covers two aspects: one-to-one teaching and mutual environmental influences. The key to increase the willingness is to enhance interesting of social media, which is also the best expression and propagation mode of emotional communication. It can let the older users to enjoy themselves in the new social media, thus converting most negative emotions into positive emotions directly.

5.2 Application Case of Related Modes

The WeChat applet of China's Tencent and iFlytek Input of the Iflyteck Co. Ltd gave us good enlightenments on new media-based social contact of the elderly. On November 30th, 2016, Zhai Jibo of the Iflyteck Co. Ltd created a record of voice conversion of 400 Chinese characters per minute and maintaining 97% accuracy rate under external environmental disturbance. As mentioned above, with respect to usability of new social media, older users who have degraded vision, stubby fingers and slow response prefer voice input/output. Voice input can bring older users emotional intimacy and interesting of usage. However, older users are inconvenient to accept voice information in some special occasions and voice information must be converted into characters. iFlytek Input solves this interaction design problem well.

Older users are afraid of processing problems with complicated steps, which is caused by the degradation of different physiological mechanisms. Lapse of memory, poor ability of learning new things and worry on leakage of personal information restrict usage of new social media by the elderly. The WeChat applet of China's

Tencent also brings us some good enlightenment. The service flow of the WeChat applet is "Scan and Go". Users can apply the offline scenes of life to online through the "Scan" function of WeChat. For example, users can choose seat, order dishes and settle accounts in canteens by scanning the 2-dimensional bar code of the canteen, thus saving queuing. The scanned applications are stored in WeChat as applet and won't occupy memory of the device. Users can leave after the usage and no advertisements are offered. The WeChat applet can offer many references to service design optimization of new social media for older users. The cloud encryption protocol of the third party protects individual social interaction information of older users. The application of offline life services to online enrich the diversified life of older users through new media-social contact, increases their positive emotions, and strengthens interesting of life, which are good for the older users to make contributions to the society.

6 Conclusion and Future Work

With the prosperous development of new social media in the background of prosperous development of new media and annual growth of the elderly population in the background of gradual improvement of people's living standard, this paper discloses four influencing factors (SUVW) against the elderly using new media for social contact. Based on SUVW, the theoretical model of the elderly using new media-based social contract is constructed. Due to inadequate or rare research data on usage of new social media by older adults, this study reviews researches on social contact of the elderly, new media interaction design, service design and products for the elderly to analyze usage behavior of new media by the elderly, influencing factors as well as their relationships. Four influencing factors (SUVW) are concluded and used to establish the theoretical model of new media-based social contact of the elderly. Finally, feasibility, innovativeness and fuzziness of the established SUVW model are verified by related case studies in China.

Of course, this study also has some shortcomings, such as territory limitation of samples, sample size, subjective privacy of users in filling the questionnaire, etc. All of these will influence the summarization of factors that influencing new media usage by the elderly, thus further influencing integrity of the new media-based social contact mode of the elderly. Hence, future researches can focus on following aspects:

1. Explore emotional demands of the elderly deeply. The elderly use new social media is to make emotional communication of the elderly more harmonious and convert more negative emotions into positive ones. As a result, exploring emotional demands of the elderly can lay a solid foundation for the follow-up design.

2. Strengthen interaction design of new social media for the elderly. The gradual degrading physiological mechanism of the elderly determines the important role of interaction design in their new media-based social contact behaviors. This requires man-machine interaction simpler and more humanized.

3. Perfect service design of new social media for social contact of the elderly. The theoretical SUVW model of the elderly using new social media is explored preliminarily, which pays attentions to application of offline life services to online scenes and deep development of interesting. They can enrich the life of the elderly.

New media usage behaviors of the elderly, influencing factors and new media-based social contact mode of the elderly are meaningful. There is still a big practice fuzzy space in this field.

References

1. The elderly users social investigation 2016-iresearch (2016). http://www.lnrzj.com
2. David: The digital divide under the perspective of Chinese Internet use disorder in the elderly. Textile university press, Wuhan (2012)
3. Ma, N., Lin, Q.: Mobile SNS user mental models and interact in the research and application of compatibility. Tianjin university industry design press, Tianjin (2013)
4. Lee, B., Yang, H.: The elderly life form research and analysis on the user model, 30(05), 65–69. Northeast Forestry University, Packing Engineering press (2013)
5. Chen, Y., Lee, Y.: Abroad to white wave of new media strategy enlightenment to our country. Academic Exchange 201(01), 35–39 (2011)
6. Zhang, S.: Research to the influential factors of Chinese urban elderly new media use _ based on the investigation of Beijing Chaoyang district. The south's population (06) (2014)
7. Zhao, Y., Ci, Y.: Mobile social network service innovation factors affecting the empirical research. Practice research, Wuhan University (04), 79–85 (2016)
8. Deng, X., Huang, R., Yuan, M.: Based on the service quality gap model of social media service quality evaluation_WeChat, for example. Hunan University: View on publishing (02), 25–29 (2015)
9. Lu, Z., Wang, H., Lee, F., Zhang, Y.: The application of social network analysis in the social media research. Fund project (08) (2016)
10. Zhang, J.: Emotional care design based on service design research_to_Zhang Jingwen city empty nester for example. Huawei technologies co., Ltd. press, Zhejiang 25(04), 32–35 (2016)

Online Privacy Perceptions of Older Adults

Eva-Maria Zeissig[1(⊠)], Chantal Lidynia[1], Luisa Vervier[1],
Andera Gadeib[2], and Martina Ziefle[1]

[1] Human Computer Interaction Center (HCIC),
RWTH Aachen University, Aachen, Germany
{zeissig, lidynia, vervier, ziefle}@comm.rwth-aachen.de
[2] Dialego AG, Aachen, Germany

Abstract. Nowadays, the majority of people is connected to the world-wide web. Online services are included into everyday life to such a degree that non-use is almost impossible. Not only the young digital natives are online, also older users employ more and more online services. The amount of data created is vast but not without risks in terms of privacy behaviors. The present research addresses age differences in terms of attitude towards online privacy and privacy protection behaviors. Moreover, factors that can predict protection behavior and privacy concern, respectively, are examined. Via an online survey in Germany (N = 200), privacy concerns, trust in online companies, awareness of and experience with online data misuse, as well as their self-efficacy regarding protective measures was explored, contrasting younger and older users. It was found that older users significantly differ in their awareness of privacy issues and protect their data more actively than younger users. Furthermore, it was found that said protection behavior is mainly influenced by privacy self-efficacy, followed by privacy concern and trust. Privacy concern, in turn, is predicted through awareness and previous experience with data misuse.

Keywords: Online privacy · Privacy awareness · Privacy concern · Privacy protection behavior

1 Introduction

The digital world has become ubiquitous for many users. More and more formerly offline areas of live are going online and every online action generates "Big Data" [1]. This provides opportunities not only for the individual and companies, but also for society, and healthcare (ibid). In Germany – an average country concerning internet use in Europe [2] – only 55% of those older than 65 years are using the internet, compared to almost 100% of the so-called generation of the "digital natives", that was upraised with digital technologies [3, 4]. This world-wide phenomenon has been labeled the "grey" digital divide [5].

The online world offers an enormous potential for the older generations, those sometimes referred to as the "silver surfers" [6, 7]. Not only can older adults stay socially connected with those they have not seen in decades, with friends and families living far away, or get to know new people with similar interests [8, 9]. Digital technologies also offer opportunities for "aging in place" by supporting daily activities,

© Springer International Publishing AG 2017
J. Zhou and G. Salvendy (Eds.): ITAP 2017, Part II, LNCS 10298, pp. 181–200, 2017.
DOI: 10.1007/978-3-319-58536-9_16

or alerting family members in case of emergency [9]. Access to health-related information as well as expanded opportunities for lifelong learning are more advantages, that show how the quality of life of the older generations can be improved through digital technologies [8].

However, there are also drawbacks and reasons why people do not use digital technology. Van Dijk [10] distinguishes four kinds of barriers which restrict the access. He calls it the "material access" (no possession of computer or network connections), the "skill access" (lack of digital skills), "usage access" (no usage opportunities), and the "mental access" (e.g. no interest). The latter describing personal attitudes. As such, concerns about privacy when using online services are high (e.g., [4, 11–13]). For ambient assisted technologies, those technologies designed to help people staying independent in older age, privacy and security concerns have even been identified as one of the main barriers for acceptance [14, 15]. Privacy perceptions and behaviors have been extensively studied in the last decades (e.g., [16–18]) and the phenomenon of the privacy paradox, i.e. users reporting to be concerned about privacy but behaving contradictory by divulging a lot of information, has been discussed excessively (e.g., [19, 20]). The "digital natives" make use of many different online services while protecting their privacy (e.g., [21, 22]), thus, being able to profit of the digital world as they are reassured to have reduced the risks. Older internet users have been reported to be even more concerned about privacy risks [23–26], but also to use fewer protective measures [23, 25, 26]. This seems paradoxical, as concerns usually motivate protective behavior [27].

Older adults represent a special group concerning the usage of information and communications technologies. They are usually more cautious in adapting new technologies and often less experienced [28]. They also show less confidence in dealing with the internet and privacy protection (e.g., [26, 29, 30]). So far, technological developments, innovations and services have mainly been designed for generally younger target groups. Older people are catching up with the usage of digital media but they still lag behind [4]. In empirical research the focus has been predominantly put on younger users and their privacy attitudes (e.g., [22, 23]). In order to narrow the empirical state of the art of older users and their approach to digital media, we especially focus on the older user and their attitudes concerning internet usage. The question arises if the perceptions and evaluation of private information differs from those of younger generations. Therefore, this study is designed to gain insights into the privacy perception – mainly privacy concerns, trust and protection behaviors – of older adults. In the following section we focus on the theoretical background concerning the concept of online privacy and privacy attitudes and behaviors.

2 Privacy, Attitudes, and Behavior in the Online Context

First, a definition of the term *privacy* will be given. Then an introduction follows to establish the concepts of the *privacy paradox* and *privacy protection behavior*. Summarizing existing studies effects of age on behavior and attitude are then described.

2.1 The Meaning of Privacy

A multitude of definitions for the construct privacy exists from various scholarly fields. Some define privacy as a right, others as a state or even as a commodity [18]. Boundary regulation theory by Irwin Altman defines privacy as the process of "selective control of access to the self" ([31], p. 8) According to this theory, individuals use a dynamic process of boundary regulation to achieve the optimal level of privacy in each situation. Altman describes behavioral mechanisms that individuals can use to regulate privacy, e.g., territorial behavior and verbal content. These relate to the interaction of individuals with each other. In the online context, the individual is confronted with several addressees, e.g. other users, but also online companies. Logically, territorial behavior usually constitutes no mechanism for privacy regulation online. Still the notion of privacy exists also in this context, with types or *dimensions* of privacy differing. Burgoon, for example, differentiates between social, psychological, physical and informational privacy [32]. In the online context, focus lies on the dimension of informational privacy – "the ability to control who gathers and disseminates information about one's self or group and under what circumstances" ([32], p. 134). Hereafter, privacy is used synonymously for information privacy.

Just as multifaceted as the definitions of privacy are also the possibilities to measure the latent concept. Empirical research has mostly focused on the concept of *privacy concern* (e.g., [17, 33, 34]). Privacy concerns are experienced when an individual's actual state of privacy does not match the desired state of privacy [35]. Privacy concern can be very specific to one situation, but in this study the focus lies on general privacy concern, "which measures a person's overall perception of privacy risks on the Internet" ([35], p. 32). Many different scales for measuring privacy concern have been developed over the years [17, 36]. One popular example is the Internet Users' Information Privacy Concerns (IUIPC) scale by Malhotra et al. [37]. It consists of three subscales – control, awareness, and collection – which also illustrate the multidimensionality of this construct.

2.2 Attitudes vs. Behavior

Research in the field of privacy concern accelerated since the turn of the millennium. One phenomenon has gained much attention: the so-called *privacy paradox* [19].

Several studies report high levels of information privacy concern in the online context (e.g., [4, 11, 13, 38]). Logically, one would assume that this leads to the internet users being very careful in order to reduce their concerns. However, actual usage behavior, e.g., public self-disclosure on social network sites (SNS), shows that users do not behave accordingly. Empirical studies even demonstrate that personal information is traded for very small monetary rewards [39, 40]. This discrepancy between attitudes and behavior is usually referred to as *privacy paradox* [19].

According to Altman's theory, Internet users that are concerned about privacy should regulate their behavior to gain the optimal level of privacy. One regulating mechanism is to not use online services or to not disclose personal information. But it seems that not many users refrain from using services or from disclosing information.

Luckily, the online context gives users additional possibilities for privacy protection, e.g., using protective software or providing false information. This protection behavior is often not included in empirical studies concerning the privacy paradox, but it needs to be taken into account to fully understand users' privacy management.

Protection motivation theory by Rogers assumes that protection behavior is triggered by a risk evaluation [27]. Thus, again, a high level of concern should motivate internet users to protect their privacy. Recent studies confirm the assumption, as privacy concerns are positively correlated with protection behavior [41, 42]. But protection motivation theory includes other factors as well: Protection is only motivated when, first, the individual perceives the protective measures to be effective, and, second, feels competent in applying them [27]. The latter, self-efficacy in applying protective measures, matches the self-efficacy to protect one's privacy in the online context. Some scholars have already taken privacy self-efficacy or similar concepts into account when studying privacy attitudes and behaviors. Wohn et al. [43] and Chen & Chen [44] report that self-efficacy in privacy management and behavioral control does influence privacy protection behaviors.

Young internet users are often perceived as very vulnerable due to their excessive internet use and self-disclosure on SNS (e.g., [21, 22]). They have therefore been studied extensively (e.g., [22, 23]). Existing research also points out that young people are the internet users that exhibit much knowledge and self-efficacy regarding protective measures [26, 29, 45, 46]. Correspondingly, studies report that young internet users apply privacy protection behaviors, e.g., adjusting privacy settings on SNS [22, 23, 25, 26]. But what about older internet users? Do concerns motivate older internet users to either refrain from using internet technologies or to protect their privacy extensively? If they show low privacy self-efficacy does this lead to refraining? Are older users even aware of privacy issues and protective measures?

In the next section, we summarize what we already know about attitudes and behavior of older Internet users based on literature.

2.3   Older Adults' Privacy Attitudes

Privacy concern: The concept of privacy concern has been addressed in many studies, but results concerning age differences are contradictory. No significant differences in the level of privacy concern between older and younger internet users were reported by Hoofnagle et al. [47] and Taddicken [48]. Higher levels of concern for older adults were found, e.g., in studies by [23–26]. Sheehan [49] and Paine et al. [50] reported older internet users to be either very concerned or not concerned at all, respectively. That differences in privacy concern also depend on context was shown by Bergström [51]. She found older adults to be more worried concerning data misuse about credit cards, whereas younger users worry more about privacy on SNS (see also [46]).

Trust: Trust is a factor closely related to privacy concern. Rousseau et al. define trust as "a psychological state comprising the intention to accept vulnerability based upon positive expectations of the intentions or behavior of another" ([52], p. 395). Empirical studies have, in the past, considered trust as an antecedent, a consequence, a mediator, or moderator to privacy concern and the intention to use technologies, respectively. Regarding age differences, Blank and Dutton [53] found that older people are trusting the internet less than younger people.

2.4 Older Users' Privacy Behavior

Privacy protection is not black and white. There exist many ways of protection that provide different security. Apart from using protective technologies (Privacy Enhancing Technologies), users can, for example, refuse to use services and disclose information, provide false information, or adjust privacy settings of applications and services (e.g., [41]). Previous studies reported that young internet users show much more protection behavior than older internet users [22, 23, 25, 26]. Altman's and Rogers' theories suggest that privacy concerns motivates protection behavior [27, 31]. With some studies reporting higher privacy concern in older adults (see Sect. 2.3), their lower protection behavior is paradoxical.

2.5 User Characteristics Influencing Privacy Concern and Protection Behavior

Most privacy theories assume that attitudes influence behavior [54]. However, there are other variables that play important roles as well. Included in this study are *experience*, *awareness*, and *privacy self-efficacy*. Additionally, effects of gender are examined.

Privacy Self-efficacy: Privacy literacy [55], data protection confidence [45], or privacy self-efficacy [22]: several names have been used in the literature to describe the confidence users have in their ability to control privacy settings and to protect their data. Older users are in general often less confident in using new technologies (e.g., [28, 56–58]). That this holds true also for privacy protection has been shown by several authors, e.g., [26, 45, 46]. Privacy self-efficacy has also been shown to affect privacy protection behavior [43, 44].

Awareness: Privacy awareness - "the extent to which an individual is informed about organizational privacy practices and policies" [59] – has been shown to influence privacy concerns, such that high awareness raises concerns. (e.g.: [18, 59, 60]).

Experience: Experiences shape people's attitudes and beliefs. Individuals who experienced violations of privacy in the online contexts show a higher level of privacy concern (e.g., [11, 35, 61]). Debatin et al. [62] also report that personal experiences of privacy invasion motivated participants to change their privacy settings in online social networks.

3 Questions Addressed and Logic of the Empirical Approach

The present study is designed to gain insights into older users' (> 54 years old) privacy attitudes and behaviors regarding the use of internet technologies in general. A national survey was conducted to answer the following research questions: (1) Do older internet users differ in their privacy attitudes and privacy protection behavior from younger users? (2) Which constructs can predict protection behavior and privacy concern, respectively? The focus lies on privacy concern and trust as well as on privacy protection behavior when using online technology. As explanatory variables, *experience, awareness*, and *privacy self-efficacy* are included as well. Figure 1 depicts the empirical approach with the relevant variables under study.

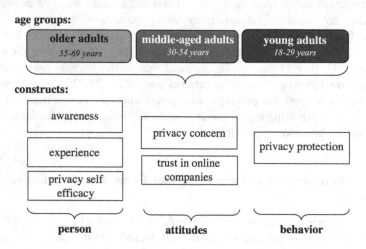

Fig. 1. Empirical approach and studied variables.

3.1 Hypotheses

Based on Rogers' protection motivation theory [27] it is assumed, that online privacy protection behavior is motivated by privacy concern and privacy self-efficacy Also it is inferred that trust reduces motivation to protect privacy. Privacy concern is hypothesized to be positively influenced by awareness of privacy issues as well as experience with privacy violations. Differences between age groups are hypothesized based on previous studies and theory (cf. Sect. 2). Our hypotheses concerning age differences read as follows:

> *H 1: Older adults report a higher level of privacy concern than younger age groups.*
> *H 2: Older adults report less trust in online companies than younger age groups.*
> *H 3: Older adults scale higher on protection behavior than younger age groups.*
> *H 4: Older adults report less privacy self-efficacy than younger age groups.*
> *H 5: Older internet users report a higher level of awareness than younger age groups.*
> *H 6: Older internet users report less experience with privacy violations than younger age groups.*

4 Method

In a quantitative approach, a study was conducted in the form an online questionnaire. The questionnaire study focused on older users' privacy attitudes in conjunction with their privacy behavior. Items used were based on literature and a prior focus group study. The questionnaire was distributed by a market research company. It was delivered online to their panel and took about 20 min to complete. Participants were remunerated by the market research company as by their practice.

4.1 The Questionnaire

Participants were invited to take part in the study by the market research company. First, a screening was conducted to select participants across all age groups with symmetrical gender distribution. The questionnaire itself consisted of three parts: user characteristics (1), online behavior (2), and privacy attitudes (3). All items are listed in Table 1. Scales from literature were partly changed after translation due to comprehensibility in the German language, consistency with the overall style of items, and adaption to the context of general internet use. Additionally, some scales were abridged.

User characteristics: Age, gender, education level, privacy self-efficacy, experience and awareness were assessed. To measure *privacy self-efficacy,* items of the scale "locus of control when interacting with technology" [63] and the subscale "competence" of Karrer et al.'s "technical affinity" scale [64] were adapted to the context of privacy settings and protective privacy measures. *Experience* was assessed with three items measuring experience with online privacy violations that have been adapted from [65] and translated into German. The scale *awareness* was developed based on [59] to measure awareness of online privacy issues in society and media.

Behavior: First, participants selected which of the following widespread online services they use: social networks, location-based services, chat applications, video chat applications, online banking cloud services and e-commerce (*usage of online services*). Second, they evaluated four items indicating whether they actively use measures to protect their online privacy (*protection behavior*).

Attitudes: A scale measuring *privacy concern* was developed from an extensive literature search by comparing and paraphrasing existing items. The new German scale contains three items translated and adapted from [40, 47, 48]. *Trust in online companies* was assessed via the 3-item subscale *Benevolence* (institution-based trust) by [68]. Additionally, participants evaluated five statements concerning the reasons why they do or do not protect their online privacy, as taken from the preceding focus group study.

All scales were measured on a 5-point Likert scale ranging from "I agree" to "I do not agree." The only exception was the use of online services for which the answers were either "I use this kind of service" or "I do not use this kind of service."

Table 1. List of items used in the questionnaire with their source. The respective scale's reliability is listed as Cronbach's α.

Item	Scale	
I believe that my online privacy was invaded by other people or organizations [65]	**Experience** α = .746	**Person**
I have had bad experiences with regard to my online privacy before [65]		
I experienced misuse of data from friends or family		
I follow the news and developments about privacy issues and privacy violations [59]	**Awareness** α = .637	
I cannot comprehend the relevance of the issue privacy because I do not care about it		
I pay closer attention to privacy issues and privacy violations since they have become so prominent in media		
I know most privacy settings of the applications I use (adapted from [64])	**Privacy self-efficacy** α = .691	
Because I have had no problems with privacy settings so far, I am confident for future privacy tasks (adapted from [63])		
I do not read privacy policies because I do not understand them (adapted from [63])		
I always change my privacy settings when I start using a new device (adapted from [63])		
I always change my privacy settings when I start using a new application (adapted from [63])		
I feel helpless with privacy settings and measures, so I do not change anything (adapted from [63])		
In general, I am concerned about my privacy when I am using the internet (adapted from [66])	**Privacy concern** α = .686	**Privacy attitudes**
I do not see risks when providing data in the internet (adapted from [59])		
With some type of information collected in the internet I do not feel comfortable (adapted from [67])		
I feel that most online companies would act in a customers' best interest [68]	**Trust in online Companies** α = .858	
If a customer required help, most online companies would do their best to help [68]		
Most online companies are interested in customer well-being, not just their own well-being [68]		
I use every option that I know to protect my online privacy (e.g., deleting cookies, anti-virus software)	**Protection behavior** α = .686	**Behavior**
I specifically search for more options to protect my online privacy		
I use the default settings of my devices and applications without changing them		

(continued)

Table 1. (*continued*)

Item	Scale
I use the default settings of my devices and applications without installing additional software to protect my privacy	
Privacy protection does not work. Whoever wants to can still access my data	Additional attitudinal items
I feel comfortable providing data on the internet because I get rewards (e.g., individualized advertisement, information from friends)	
I do not have enough time to keep informed and apply privacy protection	
Privacy protection has become so complex that I do not know how to protect my privacy anymore	
Friends and family tell me to be (more) careful with providing data on the internet	

Cronbach's α was calculated for a reliability analysis. Results and items are illustrated in Table 1. Except for experience and trust in online companies, all scales included at least one reverse coded item. The number of items ranged from 3 to 6. The reverse coded items and small number of items per scale contribute to a small Cronbach's α. Thus, values of α > .6 are assumed acceptable and indexes were calculated.

4.2 Participants

In total, 200 German internet users between the age of 18 and 69 (M = 44.8, SD = 13.7) took part in the study (of which 50.5% were male and 49.5% female). Data was collected in December of 2016. The overall goal was to get a heterogeneous sample with regard to age, gender, and education level. The education level varied across all participants: 38% reported a university degree and 16.5% a vocational training but between the age groups, the level of education did not differ significantly. However, the familiarity with using the internet was high as all participants are test persons in the panel of the online market research company and, thus, they use the internet regularly, at the very least for taking part in studies.

For analysis of age-effects, the sample was split into three age groups. The group of "older adults" was formed by 59 persons between 55 and 69 years of age (M = 61.0, SD = 4.7), often referred to as the "silver surfers" [6, 7]. A base group of the "middle-aged" consisted of 100 people between the ages of 30 and 54 years (M = 43.1; SD = 6.9), sometimes classified as the "digital immigrants" [3, 7]. For contrast, also a group of "young adults", or so-called "digital natives" [3, 7], was formed with 41 persons aged between 18 and 29 years (M = 25.5, SD = 3.1).

4.3 Data Analysis

Grouped differences were analyzed by ANOVA procedures which are quite robust even when the assumption of standard distribution is violated. Nevertheless, non-parametric tests were used for comparison and revealed the same results. Therefore, only the ANOVA findings are reported. Moreover, data was analyzed by multiple linear regression.

Significance level was set at 5%. For post-hoc procedures, either Hochberg's test was used for unequal group sizes or Games-Howell post hoc test, if homogeneity of variance could not be assumed. To quantify the different scales, overall scores were calculated as the average of single ratings of the items.

5 Results

In this section, the descriptive results for the group of "older adults" and differences between age groups will be presented. Then, regression results will be shown.

5.1 Differences in Privacy Attitudes and Online Behaviors

Usage of online services: Figure 2 depicts the percentage of participants using popular types of online services. The group of older adults uses, on average, less online services than young and middle-aged adults. The usage of e-commerce, online banking, location-based services, cloud services, and video chats does not significantly differ between the age groups. But significantly more young adults use social networks (83%) than do middle-aged (59%) and older adults (58%) do ($\chi^2(2) = 8.43$, p < .05). Chat applications are popular with young (80%) and middle-aged adults (76%), but significantly fewer older adults use them (42%) ($\chi^2(2) = 23.22$, $p < .001$).

Privacy Concern: Privacy concerns are reported to be on average 3.68 out of 5 points ($SD = 0.82$), see Fig. 3. As hypothesized, concern seems to be higher with older internet users, but there are no significant differences (Hypothesis 1). The pie charts in Fig. 4 show how many percent of participants of each age group did fully, partly or not at all agree to have concerns about their online privacy. No respondent reported to be free of any privacy concerns, but 11.5% fully agreed with all statements. 15% of the older adults, 12% of the middle-aged, and 5% of the younger adults are very concerned.

Trust: Trust in online companies on the other hand, was reported lower than the midpoint, with $M = 2.80$ ($SD = 0.93$) (see Fig. 3). Middle-aged participants reported the lowest trust on average ($M = 2.71$, $SD = 0.97$) and young participants the highest ($M = 2.96$, $SD = 0.8$). However, the differences are not significant.

Protection Behavior: Protection behavior is high on average in the sample (*M* = 3.67, *SD* = 0.86), see Fig. 3. Older adults show a significantly higher protection behavior (*M* = 3.99, *SD* = 0.87; *F*(2,197) = 7.63, *p* < .001) compared to young (*M* = 3.35,

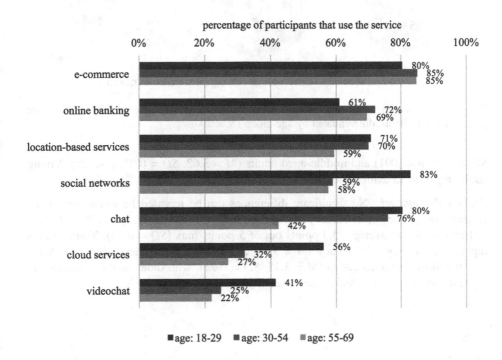

Fig. 2. General usage of popular types of online services in percent differentiated by age group (N = 200).

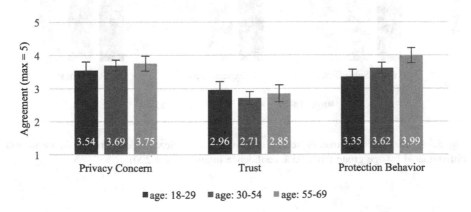

Fig. 3. Mean values of overall scores of privacy concerns, trust, and protection behavior differentiated by age group (with 95% confidence intervals; N = 200).

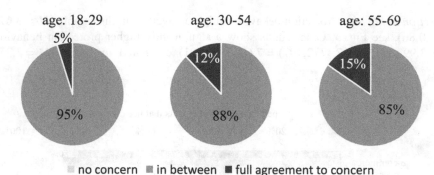

age: 18-29   age: 30-54   age: 55-69

no concern ■ in between ■ full agreement to concern

Fig. 4. Percentage of participants that do not agree at all, partly agree or fully agree to the privacy concern items; differentiated by age group (N = 200).

$SD = 0.71$, $p < .001$) and middle-aged adults ($M = 3.62$, $SD = 0.85$, $p < .05$). Young adults reported to exhibit the lowest protection behavior.

Privacy Self-efficacy: No significant differences can be reported between age groups concerning privacy self-efficacy (Welch-Test $F(2,110) = 2.87$, $p = .06$). Privacy self-efficacy is, on average, 3.3 points out of 5 points max ($SD = 0.74$). Young adults report less privacy self-efficacy ($M = 3.14$, $SD = 0.49$) than older ($M = 3.39$, $SD = 0.80$) and middle-aged adults ($M = 3.35$, $SD = 0.71$), with older adults reporting the highest level of privacy self-efficacy, see Fig. 5.

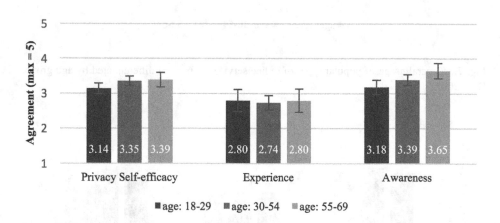

■ age: 18-29   ■ age: 30-54   ■ age: 55-69

Fig. 5. Mean values of overall scores of privacy self-efficacy, experience, and awareness differentiated by age group (with 95% confidence intervals; N = 200).

Experience with privacy violations: Experience with privacy violations averages to $M = 2.77$ out of 5 points max and shows with $SD = 1.1$ more variation than the other constructs (variation between $SD = 0.70$ (privacy self-efficacy) and $SD = 0.94$ (trust) with the maximum of 5 for all scales). No age differences could be found.

Awareness: Awareness of privacy issues is reported to be $M = 3.4$ out of 5 points max ($SD = 0.79$) and there is a significant effect of age on level of awareness (F $(2,197) = 4.63, p < .05$). Figure 5 shows that young users report the lowest ($M = 3.18$, $SD = .65$) and older adults the highest level of awareness ($M = 3.65$, $SD = 0.83$). Hochberg's post hoc test reveals the difference between young and older adults to be significant with $p < .01$.

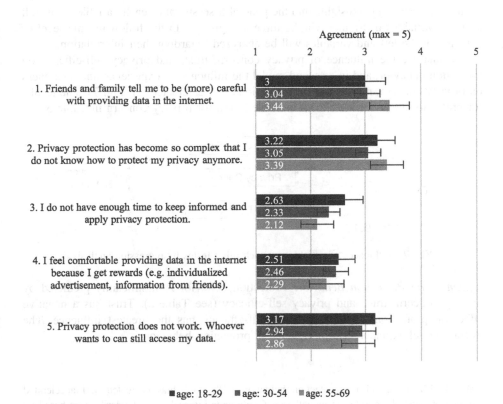

Fig. 6. Mean values for each statement differentiated by age group (N = 200).

Additional attitudinal items: In addition to the standardized constructs, five statements describing different attitudes towards privacy protection were evaluated by the participants. The results are depicted in Fig. 6. Older adults agree more than the other age groups that friends and family caution them to be more careful (Item 1: *"Friends and family tell me to be (more) careful with providing data in the internet"*) and that privacy protection is too complex (Item 2: *"Privacy protection has become so complex that I do not know how to protect my privacy anymore"*). In the opposite direction, older adults agree less that time is too short for privacy protection (Item 3: *"I do not have enough time to keep informed and apply privacy protection"*), that rewards outbalance concern (Item 4: *"I feel comfortable providing data in the internet because I get rewards (e.g. individualized advertisement, information from friends"*), and they are also less resigned considering the effectivity of protection measures (Item 5: *"Privacy protection does not work. Whoever wants to can still access my data"*). However, none of these differences is statistically significant.

5.2 Regression Analysis

So far, the results gave insights into the general assessment of each variable or overall score of variables distributed via the three age groups. In the following, the level of content will be left and variables will be analyzed regarding their interrelation.

To analyze the influence of privacy concern, trust, and privacy self-efficacy on protection behavior, and in a second model the influence of experience and awareness on privacy concern, multiple linear regressions was calculated (cf. Fig. 7). The results for protection behavior are shown in Table 2 and for privacy concern in Table 3.

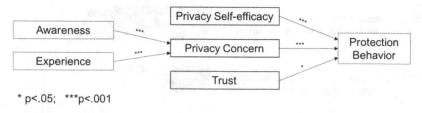

* p<.05;   ***p<.001

Fig. 7. Influences of variables on each other testes by regression analysis

Influences on Protection Behavior: Protection behavior is significantly predicted by privacy concern, trust, and privacy self-efficacy (see Table 2). Trust has a negative effect on protection behavior. Privacy self-efficacy has the greatest influence. The overall model explains 43% of variance in protection behavior.

Table 2. Linear model for protection behavior, with 95% bias corrected and accelerated confidence intervals reported in parentheses. Confidence intervals and standard errors based on 1000 bootstrap samples.

	B	SE B	β	t	p
Constant	1.049 (0.395, 1.686)	0.314		3.225	.001
Privacy concern	0.259 (0.132, 0.369)	0.063	.249	4.261	.000
Trust	−0.122 (−0.225, −0.025)	0.052	−.134	−2.411	.017
Privacy self-efficacy	0.606 (0.456, 0.764)	0.078	.499	8.763	.000
$R^2 = .43$, $F(196,3) = 48.62$, $p < .001$.					

Influences on Privacy Concern: Awareness and experience significantly predict privacy concern, with awareness showing a greater influence (see Table 3). The model explains 31% of variance in concern.

Table 3. Linear regression model for privacy concern, with 95% bias corrected confidence intervals reported in parentheses. Confidence intervals and standard errors based on 1000 bootstrap samples.

	B	SE B	β	t	p
Constant	1.597 (1.098, 2.105)	0.276		6.199	.000
Awareness	0.395 (0239, 0.537)	0.076	.249	5.995	.000
Experience	0.217 (0.110, 0.317)	0.053	−.134	4.669	.000
$R^2 = .31$, $F(196,3) = 29.21$, $p < .001$.

6 Discussion

With the ever more prevalent inclusion of online services into everyday life, possible benefits as well as risks of misuse and abuse of the available digital data gain more importance. Therefore, a study was conducted to gain insight into the prevailing assumptions and behaviors people exhibit when dealing with digital services. For the present article, the focus was put on the influence of age on constructs such as privacy concern, trust in online services, awareness of and experience with online data misuse, as well as their self-efficacy regarding protective measures. Based on the literature, and a focus group study, different hypotheses have been formulated and tested with an online questionnaire.

The findings revealed both, patterns related to age and related to other variables. Regarding privacy concerns, the results show that older adults do not report a significantly higher level of privacy concerns than younger adults (rejecting Hypothesis 1). Perhaps it is, as Sheehan [49] and Paine et al. [50] have reported, that the group of older adults consists of either very concerned or not at all concerned internet users. On the other hand, it could be hypothesized that, with the more and more widespread use of internet technologies also by the older adults, the so-called "grey" digital divide is getting narrower. To fully resolve this issue, previous studies should be repeated using the same research design to get up-to-date results and the latest baseline for the relevant and often cited phenomenon of the digital divide.

Even though other studies report older adults to be less protective of their data than younger adults, our study showed them as more protective, thereby confirming Hypothesis 3. Furthermore, it could also be shown that the more concerned an individual, regardless of age, is for their privacy, the more protective behavior is exhibited. This is in line with previous research as well as with Rogers' [26] theory that risk evaluations motivate protection behavior. No paradox can be reported in this study.

However, in contrast to the actual protection behavior, the present study examined a somewhat relative protective behavior. Instead of measuring if every available possibility to protect data was utilized, our sample confirmed to using "everything I know of." This operationalization measures the intention and motivation to protect privacy more than actual behavior – in other words, it is more the wish to protect than the actual protection. Thus, the results show that older adults are trying their best to protect their privacy. A next step would be to relate actual protection behavior to our construct and include knowledge of privacy protective measures as well. If the trying is high but actual protection is low, it is not the intention that is lacking but probably the knowledge. Other reasons should be further investigated as well. It is very much possible that protective measures are very complex in their application and easy to understand guidance is lacking. Also, it could be possible, that older adults are perfectly aware of the importance of adaptive protection behaviors in the internet, however, they could have a different understanding of which information is private, and thus, worth protecting, and which information can be shared from their perspective. The latter refers the fact that the meaning of quality of life is different from that of younger persons ([69–71]). Here, future research has to explore the privacy motives of seniors and reasons to protect or share digital information. Furthermore, research into the perception of the sensitivity of different types of information is interesting, especially concerning age differences.

The present study has also confirmed that trust and privacy self-efficacy also influence protection behavior. The more persons trust in online companies in general, the less they pay attention to protection behavior. No differences in trust levels between the age groups could be reported. Self-efficacy could explain the most variance in protection behavior in our data: The more confident users are in protecting their privacy the more protection behavior was reported. This is again in line with previous studies and with Rogers' protection motivation theory [26]. Against our hypothesis (H4), privacy self-efficacy was highest with the older adults and lowest with the younger participants. Again, this could be an effect of relativity: Confidence in the own protection abilities is not equivalent with the comprehensiveness and completeness of these abilities. Thus, again, the relation of privacy self-efficacy and actual protection abilities needs to be studied further. In line with the above hypothesis, that applying protective measure is complex, also evaluating the effectiveness of what one has done is hard. This could be one possible explanation for a discrepancy between abilities and confidence in these abilities.

Nonetheless, the considerations up to this point do not include one important restriction: The present data is based on a sample of participants, that are used to participate in market research via the internet and, thus, may consist of more technically experienced, affine, and confident people than the average population – especially concerning the older age group. This could have veiled potential age differences in a less technically affine sample. Nevertheless, the data shows older adults to be even more confident and protective than younger age groups. Furthermore, trust in online companies in general was relatively low with all age groups and privacy concern was, on the other hand, still high.

The present study also investigated awareness of privacy issues and previous experience with privacy violations as antecedents of privacy concern. Regarding age, no differences between groups could be found for experience, but awareness was much higher with older adults and the lowest with younger adults. In regression analysis, it could be confirmed that both variables predict privacy concern, with awareness being the better predictor. Protection motivation theory by Rogers' assumes an evaluation of risks as the central element to motivate protective behavior [26]. Perception of risks is in this study operationalized as privacy concern and awareness of risks is a precondition for these concerns. But we know that concern is influenced by many different factors, not the least being the personality and disposition of individuals to worry and to feel a need for privacy (e.g., [11, 59, 65, 72]). Awareness of privacy issues may be the very first step to motivate privacy protection behavior. This study took a very general approach to all constructs in the context of general internet use. Further investigation should be done to get a better understanding of how being aware of specific risks motivates people in different contexts to take protective measures.

We live in an ever more networked world where not being online is, for many people, no feasible alternative anymore. Apart from numerous benefits, data collection also brings about risks and the internet does not forget. Older users have, in the past, been more reluctant to participate in online activities, but they are catching up on using different online services. Increasingly more studies conclude that privacy is still very important to most and privacy concerns are especially high with the older adults. Taking protective measure could reassure users and, thus, yield more online participation. But the privacy paradox phenomenon shows that there is a missing link somewhere between attitude and behavior. At the same time, taking protective actions mostly lies in the responsibility of each individual internet user, regardless of the actual awareness or capability to protect oneself. It is very important to study people's motives and barriers to internet use but also to privacy protection behavior, so that the digitalized world can utilize its full potential, without leaving many behind or vulnerable to harm. Our results are a precursor and impulse for more detailed research into the relationships between awareness, privacy self-efficacy, concern, and behavior.

Acknowledgments. The authors would like to thank Christiane Dahm and Elisabeth Pusch for their help in developing and distributing the online questionnaire. This project is funded by the German Ministry of Education and Research (BMBF) under project MyneData (KIS1DSD045).

References

1. Sagiroglu, S., Sinanc, D.: Big data: a review. In: 2013 International Conference on Collaboration Technologies and Systems, pp. 42–47 (2013)
2. European Commission, The Digital Economy & Society Index (DESI). https://ec.europa.eu/digital-single-market/en/desi#the-digital-economy-and-society-index-desi. Accessed 1 Mar 2017
3. Prensky, M.: Digital natives, digital immigrants. Horiz **9**(5), 1–6 (2001)
4. Private Haushalte in der Informationsgesellschaft - Nutzung von IKT (2016)
5. Millward, P.: The 'grey digital divide': perception, exclusion and barriers of access to the internet for older people. First Monday **8**(8) (2003)
6. Patalong, F.: Silver Surfer: Ganz oder gar nicht, Spiegel Online, 8 Oct 2010
7. Media Use Index 2014 - Das Smartphone schlägt alle. Y&R Group (2014)
8. Schreurs, K., Quan-Haase, A., Martin, K.: The older adults digital literacy paradox: aging, media discourse, and self-determination. Canadian J. Commun. **42** , 1–35 (2017)

 9. Bercovitz, K., Pagnini, F.: Mindfulness as an opportunity to narrow the grey digital divide. In: Villani, D. (ed.) Integrating Technology in Positive Psychology Practice, pp. 214–228. IGI Global (2016). http://doi.org/10.4018/978-1-4666-9986-1.ch009
10. Van Dijk, J.: The one-dimensional network society of Manuel Castells. New Media Soc. **1** (1), 127–138 (1999)
11. Bansal, G., Zahedi, F.M., Gefen, D.: The impact of personal dispositions on information sensitivity, privacy concern and trust in disclosing health information online. Decis. Support Syst. **49**, 138–150 (2010)
12. Rainie, L., Kiesler, S., Kang, R., Madden, M.: Anonymity, Privacy, and Security Online (2013)
13. European Commission, Data protection Eurobarometer (2015)
14. Wilkowska, W., Ziefle, M.: Perception of privacy and security for acceptance of E-health technologies: exploratory analysis for diverse user groups. In: 2011 5th International Conference on Pervasive Computing Technologies for Healthcare Work, pp. 593–600 (2011)
15. Wilkowska, W., Ziefle, M.: Privacy and data security in E-health: requirements from the user's perspective. Health Inf. J. **18**(3), 191–201 (2012)
16. Bélanger, F., Crossler, R.: Privacy in the digital age: a review of information privacy research in information systems. MIS Q. **35**(4), 1–36 (2011)
17. Li, Y.: Empirical studies on online information privacy concerns: literature review and an integrative framework. Commun. Assoc. Inf. Syst. **28**(28), 453–496 (2011)
18. Smith, H.J., Dinev, T., Xu, H.: Information privacy research: an interdisciplinary review. MIS Q. **35**(4), 989–1015 (2011)
19. Norberg, P.A., Horne, D.R., Horne, D.A.: The privacy paradox: personal information disclosure intentions versus behaviors. J. Consum. Aff. **41**(1), 100–126 (2007)
20. Kokolakis, S.: Privacy attitudes and privacy behaviour: a review of current research on the privacy paradox phenomenon. Comput. Secur. **2011**(2013), 1–29 (2015)
21. Steijn, W.M.P.: Developing a sense of privacy: an investigation of privacy and the differences between young and old in the context of social network sites [s.n.] (2014)
22. Youn, S.: Determinants of online privacy concern and its influence on privacy protection behaviors among young adolescents. J. Consum. Aff. **43**(3), 389–418 (2009)
23. Van den Broeck, E., Poels, K., Walrave, M.: Older and wiser? Facebook use, privacy concern, and privacy protection in the life stages of emerging, young, and middle adulthood. Soc. Media + Soc. **1**(2), 1–11 (2015)
24. Zukowski, T., Brown, I.: Examining the influence of demographic factors on internet users, information privacy concerns. In: SAICSIT (2007)
25. Blank, G., Bolsover, G., Dubois, E.: A new privacy paradox: young people and privacy on social network sites (2014)
26. Miltgen, C.L., Peyrat-Guillard, D.: Cultural and generational influences on privacy concerns: a qualitative study in seven European countries. Eur. J. Inf. Syst. **23**17(2), 103–125 (2014)
27. Rogers, R.W.: Cognitive and physiological processes in fear appeals and attitude change: a revised theory of protection motivation. In: Cacioppo, R.E., Petty, J.T. (eds.) Social Psychophysiology: A Sourcebook, pp. 153–174. Guilford Press, New York (1983)
28. Lee, C., Coughlin, J.F.: Older adults' adoption of technology: an integrated approach to identifying determinants and barriers. J. Prod. Innov. Manag. **32**(5), 747–759 (2014)
29. Maaß, W.: The elderly and the internet: how senior citizens deal with online privacy. In: Trepte, S., Reinecke, L. (eds.) Privacy Online, p. 235. Springer, Heidelberg (2011)
30. Park, Y.J.: Digital literacy and privacy behavior online. Commun. Res. **40**(2), 215–236 (2013)
31. Altman, I.: Privacy - a conceptual analysis. Environ. Behav. **8**(1), 7–29 (1976)

32. Burgoon, J.K., Parrott, R., Le Poire, B.A., Kelley, D.L., Walther, J.B., Perry, D.: Maintaining and restoring privacy through communication in different types of relationships. J. Soc. Pers. Relat. **6**(2), 131–158 (1989)

33. Dinev, T., Hart, P.: Internet privacy concerns and their antecedents - measurement validity and a regression model. Behav. Inf. Technol. **23**(6), 413–422 (2004)

34. Smith, H.J., Milberg, S.J., Burke, S.J.: Information privacy: measuring individuals' concerns about organizational practices. Manag. Inf. Syst. Q. **20**(2), 167–196 (1996)

35. Li, Y.: A multi-level model of individual information privacy beliefs. Electron. Commer. Res. Appl. **13**(1), 32–44 (2014)

36. Preibusch, S.: Guide to measuring privacy concern: review of survey and observational instruments. Int. J. Hum. Comput. Stud. **71**(12), 1133–1143 (2013)

37. Malhotra, N.K., Kim, S.S., Agarwal, J.: Internet users' information privacy concerns (IUIPC): the construct, the scale, and a causal model. Inf. Syst. Res. **15**(4), 336–355 (2004)

38. Rainie, L., Kiesler, S., Madden, M.: Anonymity, Privacy, and Security Online (2013)

39. Carrascal, J.P., Riederer, C., Erramilli, V., De Oliveira, R.: Your browsing behavior for a big mac: economics of personal information online. In: Proceedings of the 22nd International Conference on World Wide Web, pp. 189–200 (2013)

40. Beresford, A.R., Kübler, D., Preibusch, S.: Unwillingness to Pay for Privacy: A Field Experiment, WZ Discuss. Pap. No. SP II 2010-03 (2010)

41. Son, J., Kim, S.S.: Internet users' information privacy-protective responses: a taxonomy and a nomological model. MIS Q. **32**(3), 503–529 (2008)

42. Lutz, C., Strathoff, P.: Privacy concerns and online behavior – Not so paradoxical after all? Multinatl. Unternehm. und Institutionen im Wandel – Herausforderungen für Wirtschaft, R. und Gesellschaft, pp. 81–99 (2013)

43. Wohn, D.Y., Solomon, J., Sarkar, D., Vaniea, K.E.: Factors related to privacy concerns and protection behaviors regarding behavioral advertising. In: Extended Abstracts of the ACM CHI 2015 Conference on Human Factors in Computing Systems, vol. 2, pp. 1965–1970 (2015)

44. Chen, H.-T., Chen, W.: Couldn't or wouldn't? The influence of privacy concerns and self-efficacy in privacy management on privacy protection. Cyberpsychol. Behav. Soc. Netw. **18**(1), 13–19 (2015)

45. Park, Y.J.: Do men and women differ in privacy? Gendered privacy and (in)equality in the internet. Comput. Hum. Behav. **50**, 252–258 (2015)

46. Kowalewski, S., Ziefle, M., Ziegeldorf, H., Wehrle, K.: Like us on Facebook! – analyzing user preferences regarding privacy settings in Germany. Procedia Manuf. **3**, 815–822 (2015). Ahfe

47. Hoofnagle, C., King, J., Li, S., Turow, J.: How different are young adults from older adults when it comes to information privacy attitudes and policies? New York **4**(19), 10 (2010)

48. Taddicken, M.: The 'Privacy Paradox' in the social web: the impact of privacy concerns, individual characteristics, and the perceived social relevance on different forms of self-disclosure1. J. Comput. Commun. **19**(2), 248–273 (2014)

49. Sheehan, K.B.: Toward a typology of Internet users and online privacy concerns. Inf. Soc. **18**(1), 21–32 (2002)

50. Paine, C., Reips, U.-D., Stieger, S., Joinson, A., Buchanan, T.: Internet users' perceptions of 'privacy concerns' and 'privacy actions'. Int. J. Hum. Comput. Stud. **65**(6), 526–536 (2007)

51. Bergström, A.: Online privacy concerns: a broad approach to understanding the concerns of different groups for different uses. Comput. Hum. Behav. **53**, 419–426 (2015)

52. Rousseau, D.M., Sitkin, S.B., Burt, R.S., Camerer, C.: Not so different after all: a cross-discipline view of trust. Acad. Manag. Rev. **23**(3), 393–404 (1998)

53. Blank, G., Dutton, W.H.: Age and trust in the internet: the centrality of experience and attitudes toward technology in Britain. Soc. Sci. Comput. Rev. **30**(2), 135–151 (2012)
54. Li, Y.: Theories in online information privacy research: a critical review and an integrated framework. Decis. Support Syst. **54**(1), 471–481 (2012)
55. Trepte, S., Teutsch, D., Masur, P.K., Eicher, C., Fischer, M., Hennhöfer, A., Lind, F.: Do people know about privacy and data protection strategies? Towards the 'online privacy literady scale' (OPLIS). Reforming Eur. Data Prot. Law **20**, 333–365 (2015)
56. Brauner, P., Ziefle, M.: Exergames for Elderly in Ambient Assisted Living Environments, pp. 145–150 (2015)
57. Heidrich, F., Ziefle, M., Röcker, C., Borchers, J.: Interacting with smart walls: a multi-dimensional analysis of input technologies for augmented environments. In: Proceedings of the 2nd Augmented Human International Conference, pp. 1:1–1:8 (2011)
58. Wilkowska, W., Ziefle, M.: Which factors form older adults' acceptance of mobile information and communication technologies? In: Holzinger, A., Miesenberger, K. (eds.) USAB 2009. LNCS, vol. 5889, pp. 81–101. Springer, Heidelberg (2009). doi:10.1007/978-3-642-10308-7_6
59. Xu, H., Dinev, T., Smith, H.J., Hart, P.: Examining the formation of individual's privacy concerns: toward an integrative view. In: International Conference on Information Systems (2008)
60. Brecht, F., Fabian, B., Kunz, S., Mueller, S., Fabian, B., Kunz, S.: Are you willing to wait longer for internet privacy? (2011)
61. Bansal, G., Zahedi, F.M., Gefen, D.: Do context and personality matter? Trust and privacy concerns in disclosing private information online. Inf. Manag. **53**(1), 1–21 (2016)
62. Debatin, B., Lovejoy, J.P., Horn, A.K., Hughes, B.N.: Facebook and online privacy: attitudes, behaviors, and unintended consequences. J. Comput. Commun. **15**(1), 83–108 (2009)
63. Beier, G.: Kontrollüberzeugungen im umgang mit technik. Rep. Psychol. **24**, 684–693 (1999)
64. Karrer, K., Glaser, C., Clemens, C., Bruder, C.: Technikaffinität erfassen – der Fragebogen TA-EG. Der Mensch im Mittelpkt Tech. Syst. 8. Berl. Werkstatt Mensch-Maschine-Systeme **8**, 196–201 (2009)
65. Li, Y.: The impact of disposition to privacy, website reputation and website familiarity on information privacy concerns. Decis. Support Syst. **57**(1), 343–354 (2014)
66. Joinson, A.N., Paine, C.B., Buchanan, T.B., Reips, U.R.: Measuring Internet privacy attitudes and behavior: a multi-dimensional approach. J. Inf. Sci. **32**(4), 334–343 (2006)
67. Dinev, T., Xu, H., Smith, H.J.: Information privacy values, beliefs and attitudes: an empirical analysis of web 2.0 privacy. In: Proceedings of the 42nd Hawaii International Conference on System Sciences, pp. 1–10 (2009)
68. McKnight, D.H., Choudhury, V., Kacmar, C.: Developing and validating trust measures for e-commerce: an integrative typology. Inf. Syst. Res. **13**(3), 334–359 (2002)
69. Bowling, A., Banister, D., Sutton, S., Evans, O., Windsor, J.: A multidimensional model of the quality of life in older age. Aging Ment. Heal. **6**(4), 355–371 (2002)
70. Bowling, A., Gabriel, Z., Dykes, J., Dowding, L.M., Evans, O., Fleissig, A., Banister, D., Sutton, S.: Let's ask them: a national survey of definitions of quality of life and its enhancement among people aged 65 and over. Int. J. Aging Hum. Dev. **56**(4), 269–306 (2003)
71. Sarvimäki, A., Stenbock-Hult, B.: Quality of life in old age described as a sense of well-being, meaning and value. J. Adv. Nurs. **32**(4), 1025–1033 (2000)
72. Korzaan, M.L., Boswell, K.T.: The influence of personality traits and information privacy concerns on behavioral intentions. J. Comput. Inf. Syst. **48**, 15–24 (2008)

Examining the Factors Influencing Elders' Knowledge Sharing Behavior in Virtual Communities

Xuanhui Zhang[✉] and Xiaokang Song

School of Economics and Management, Nanjing University of Science and Technology,
Nanjing, China
zhangxhdo@163.com, sxksxk666@163.com

Abstract. The development of Information and Communication Technology (ICT) reduces the cost of communication, and the emergence of a large number of virtual communities to promote more frequent knowledge sharing behavior. However, there are still great differences in knowledge sharing behavior among different age groups in virtual communities. Through long-term observation we found that whether it is a large virtual community, such as WeChat, micro-blog, Zhihu et al., or a virtual community which is designed for the elderly, such as The lovely old man, The home of old man, Sunset Forum et al., the old people's participation and enthusiasm for knowledge sharing are not high in China. The purpose of this paper is to explore the motivation of the elderly to participate in knowledge sharing in virtual communities. We select participants through various virtual communities, and using the grounded theory to carry out conceptual analysis and coding. To understand the motivation of the elderly to participate in knowledge sharing in the virtual community, so as to provide some reference for the development of the elderly human resources.

Keywords: The elderly · Knowledge sharing · Virtual community · Grounded theory

1 Introduction

As we all know, in the late nineteenth Century, the aging of the population began to appear in some developed countries. Nowadays, the aging of population has become a global phenomenon due to the decrease of birth rate and the improvement of people's life (Lee 2003). According to "The China Statistical Yearbook 2016" released by the National Bureau of Statistics of the People's Republic of China, the number of people over the age of 65 in China reached 143 million 860 thousand by the end of 2015, accounting for about 10.5% of the total number of people in China (The China Statistical Yearbook 2016). China has become one of the most populous countries in the elderly. The traditional "negative aging" takes a large number of elder people as a burden on society, it argues that in the economic field, the aging of the population may affect economic growth, savings, consumption, investment, labor market, tax, etc., on the social level, the aging of the population may affect health care, family structure, living arrangements, housing and population mobility, etc. (Liu and Jiao 2015). However, in

© Springer International Publishing AG 2017
J. Zhou and G. Salvendy (Eds.): ITAP 2017, Part II, LNCS 10298, pp. 201–213, 2017.
DOI: 10.1007/978-3-319-58536-9_17

the course of their lives, the elderly have accumulated a lot of valuable knowledge, experience, professional skills, social resources and wisdom. If the knowledge of the elderly can be expressed and passed on, it will not only enrich the lives of the elderly, but also bring about a sense of accomplishment, and will also play a guiding role in young people. Active aging suggested that the old man should not be regarded as a burden on society, and we should pay more attention to the discovery and excavation of the social value of the elderly. Older people can make more contributions to society.

With the rapid development and popularization of the Internet and information communication technology (ICT), it creates the space and environment of knowledge sharing. Virtual community provides users with online communication platform, such as asking questions, post sharing or discussion issues; it reduces the cost of communication. Knowledge sharing in network virtual community has become an important way to develop the social value of the elderly gradually. Worldwide, older people are the fastest growing computer and Internet user group in many cases (Wagner et al. 2010). More and more older people are beginning to integrate online media into their lives. China Internet Network Information Center (CNNIC) released the "thirty-ninth China Internet development statistics report" shows that by the end of 2016, China's Internet users reached 731 million, and mobile phone users reached 695 million, among them 60 years old and above Internet users have accounted for 29 million 240 thousand, accounting for the total number of Internet users by 4% (CNNIC 2017). It can be seen that the number of Internet users in China is very large. A large number of elderly people participate in various virtual communities, at the same time, there are many virtual communities designed for the elderly. Through long-term observation we found that the old people's participation and enthusiasm are not high. Therefore, it is necessary to study the motivation of the elderly to participate in knowledge sharing in the virtual community, which will help to develop their social value and contribution ability.

This study is based on user motivation. We conducted in-depth interviews with 21 older adults, and analyzed the motivation factors of knowledge sharing in the virtual community by using the grounded theory so as to put forward some suggestions on how to improve the participation of the elderly.

2 Literature Review

With the increase of the number of elderly people, the attention of this group is gradually increasing. Scholars in many fields have done a lot of research on the elderly. In this paper, we mainly investigate the demand for Internet, the use of virtual community and the sharing of knowledge among the elderly study. These arrangements will help us better understand the motivation of Internet knowledge sharing.

For the elderly, the growth of age leads to a series of changes in physiology and psychology. Physically, they have different degrees of hearing, vision, memory, limb activity, etc.; psychologically, they tend to suffer from anxiety, tension, depression and fear of death. In addition, old people like to be quiet but they are afraid of loneliness, and they are reluctant to accept new things and new ideas. In the face of these physiological and psychological changes, the needs of the elderly are: safety needs, belongingness and love needs, esteem needs, self actualization needs, etc. Liu's study (2014) found that the majority of older people think that information is important to them, and a considerable number of elderly people are still willing to accept information technology. Sharit (2008) reported that health is one of the most important themes of the elderly, and using the Internet to acquire health knowledge is a demand for the elderly. He found that the knowledge structure and cognitive ability of the elderly had an impact on the acquisition of knowledge. The elderly mainly use social networks to share photos, participate in group discussions, contact old friends, keep in touch with their children and develop personal interests (Leist 2013). Some scholars study the factors that affect the use of the Internet in the elderly. Compared with older men, female participants were more familiar with the term "online social network" and used more frequently, in addition, age, gender, and education appear to be the most important factors affecting the use of activity of the elderly in the online community (Vošner et al. 2016). Old people's willingness to use the Internet will be affected by three factors: attitude, subjective norm and perceived behavior control. However, due to the differences in personality, past experience and living environment, the influence of the three factors on the willingness of the elderly to use the network is different. Among them, the use of attitude will be affected by the perceived ease of learning, perceived usefulness, trust and fear of the network; Subjective norms are mainly from children, grandchildren and peer group; Perceived behavioral control was mainly influenced by self-efficacy, perceived control, past experience, social support, and website design (Xie 2014).

Virtual community is an online collection of users with common interests or similar purposes and emotional communication with each other (Koh and Kim 2003). In the virtual community, users often discuss various topics, participate in specific activities, and establish a certain network of interpersonal relationships. Due to the support of the information technology, the virtual community has got rid of the restriction of the geographical position, which makes the scattered individuals not to meet, but also to participate in the exchange and discussion of the problem, and gradually become the platform of knowledge and information sharing. In the process of interaction, the members of the community can find out the active degree of different users in the virtual community, so as to find some positive or similar users. Similar hobbies make them feel familiar with each other, and the sense of belonging to a community may be stronger, thereby enhancing their sense of virtual community (Koh and Kim 2003). The use of virtual community has a positive impact on the elderly, especially the community forums designed for the elderly, and it can meet the needs of different elderly people. Forum members can help each other, and provide emotional support, is a new source of social support for the elderly after retirement. The elderly participate in virtual communities often hope to obtain some harvest, such as, maintain relationships with relatives and friends, get news, health and medical information, consumer information and online courses, shopping, travel and financial management, or game and cultivate virtual hobbies, etc. (Nimrod 2010). Elderly people are very willing to share their experience in the forum and blog, their community stickiness is strong, and will not easily leave a community generally. When communicating with other people in the virtual community, the elderly prefer to use relatively formal expressions, and less use of fashionable network language (Pfeil et al. 2009).

Bouty (2000) puts forward the knowledge sharing behavior among individuals. In today's Internet environment, knowledge sharing has been widespread, people are accustomed to sharing fragmentation knowledge in a variety of virtual communities. Zhou (2015) compared the differences of different user groups in the virtual community, and finds that compared with the elderly, young people have higher expected returns and self-efficacy. However, there is no significant difference in knowledge sharing. It indicating that the elderly are eager to knowledge sharing behavior, and their expectations of returns is lower than that of young people, which is very useful for the development of the elderly human resources. Chen and Hung (2010) divided the factors that affect the individual knowledge sharing into two categories: individual cognitive factors and environmental factors. The former includes personal traits and attitudes, such as expert sense, reputation, self-efficacy and internal motivation; The latter is mainly the virtual community environment, such as the rules of the community, the location of the nodes in the network, the social interaction with other users and community participation etc.

Through the collation and analysis of relevant research, we initially summarized the initial motivation model for the elderly to participate in the virtual community knowledge sharing, as shown in Fig. 1:

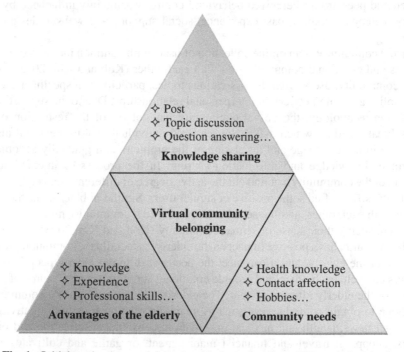

Fig. 1. Initial motivation model for the elderly to participate in knowledge sharing

To sum up, at present, many scholars have done a lot of research on the elderly. The research on the Internet demand and the use of virtual community has been a certain foundation, but there is less research on the knowledge sharing of the elderly. In this paper, we study the motivation of the elderly to participate in the virtual community knowledge sharing, which will have a certain significance for the effective development of the elderly human resources.

3 Research Design

3.1 Methods

A grounded theory methodology was chosen for the qualitative analysis because it is a highly structured method of inquiry and is well established (Bisogni et al. 2012; Ponterotto 2005; Lovell 2016). In this study, we employed the grounded theory methodology to explore the motivation of knowledge sharing among the elderly in the virtual community for two main reasons. (a) Although there are many researches on knowledge sharing, there is little research on the motivation of knowledge sharing among the elderly in the virtual community. So, there are many issues worthy of further analysis, suitable for qualitative research methods to carry out exploratory research. (b) The development of the aged human resources is a new research direction, and the most direct method is to access the data from the interview for qualitative analysis. This study adopted the Strauss (1990) analysis method, the method step by step through open coding, axial coding and selective coding analysis data, until the concept is saturated(Heath and Cowley 2004).

3.2 Participants

Now generally defines people over the age of 65 as the elder. Prior studies have shown that internet and broadband use drops off significantly after age 75 (Zickuhr and Madden 2012). Therefore, the elderly aged between 65–75 years old were selected as the subjects. According to data presented in Fig. 2, from the recruitment of participants to finish data collecting, we totally used 45 days. First, we posted in various elderly virtual communities for recruiting participants. About two weeks later, we received a response from the 43 volunteers to show that they were willing to participate in the study. Second, we emailed the volunteers with some survey questions (such as how old are you? How many years of knowledge sharing experience have you had in the virtual community? etc.) Eligibility based on: (a) age 65–75 years, (b) volunteers who experienced in knowledge sharing in the virtual community for more than one year, (c) fluent in Mandarin. A total of 43 questionnaires were distributed, and 41 questionnaires were returned, of which 12 persons less than 65 years old and 5 persons lack of knowledge sharing experience. Of 24 participants, 21 got in touch with, while 3 persons were not contacted. Third, we conducted semi-structured in-depth interviews of the 21 participants, each interview lasted between 30 and 50 min in length, the purpose of interview is primarily to explore the elder's cognition degree of knowledge sharing in virtual community, and the motivations for knowledge sharing. Hence, data from 21 interview records were analyzed.

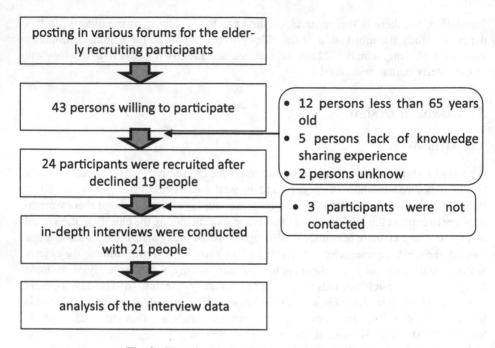

Fig. 2. Flowchart indicating sampling for the study.

4 Data Analysis

4.1 Open Coding

Open coding is the process of breaking dawn, examining, comparing, conceptualizing and categorising data. This process of coding yields concepts, which are later to be grouped and turned into categories (Strauss and Corbin 1990). Analysis began with open coding by the manual, which involved the identification of raw statement units, small sections of text representing a certain idea or concept (Strauss and Corbin 1990). 21 interview records for a total of 38714 words. Due to the large number of initial concepts, and there is a certain degree of cross duplication, we have to make some consolidation. We merged repeat crossover concepts, and excluded the concept which repeated less than 3 times. Consequently, 15 concepts were proposed (Table 1).

Table 1. Open coding interview and dimension

Concepts	Explanation	Raw data examples
The sense of honor	The elderly can feel honorable through knowledge sharing in virtual community	"Others often praise highly of my writing, I feel very proud."
Improve the reputation	Knowledge sharing can improve the reputation in the virtual community	"I spent two years as the moderator of the forum, and I already have more than and 100 fans."
Self-realization	Knowledge sharing makes old people feel their value	"I don't feel old, my brain is still very young, I hope I can help more people with what I can, and realize the value of my own life."
Helping others	In order to help others to share knowledge	
Active community	To share knowledge in order to make virtual community more active	"Sometimes I feel lonely when I at home,…I would like to share knowledge on internet, some people would actively participate in"
Interest	Share knowledge of interest	"I like to tell everybody what I know."
Make friends	Knowledge sharing in virtual community is to meet people with similar interests	"Our forum has many old man who likes to sing. We like communicate with each other."
Acquire knowledge	Knowledge sharing is to gain more knowledge from others	"I am interested in history, I like to post comments on historical events, and then cause others to discuss, I will learn sth."
Get help	Knowledge sharing is to get the help of others in the future	"One day, my flower is ill, I don't know how to do,…As a result, my friends in the forum helped me."
Material reward	Sharing knowledge will get material rewards	"1000 points can be exchanged for 10 online shopping coupons."
Collection	Write the knowledge to facilitate the future view	"I like to write out what I know, afraid of forget in the future."
Interaction with others	Knowledge sharing can interact with others on the content sharing	"Interact with others let me not feel lonely"
Game design	Game design can encourage the elderly to knowledge sharing	"I ranked fifth now; I want to squeeze into the top three next week."
Sense of ritual	Sense of ritual can encourage the elderly to knowledge sharing	"A bunch of people to discuss a problem in the BBS, feeling like a workshop on major issues."
Peer influence	Peer influence can encourage the elderly to knowledge sharing	"Many friends around me is here to share all kinds of knowledge."

4.2 Axial Coding

Axial coding based on open coding, both the function are different, but not completely independent, sometimes the relationship between the concepts can emerge in the open coding. Axial coding is a set of procedures whereby data are put back together in new ways after open coding, by making connections between categories. This is done by linking codes to contexts, to consequences, to patterns of interaction, and to causes (Strauss and Corbin 1990). In general, we through two ways for axial coding: (a) Interviewees directly describe categories, (b) researchers based on the analysis of the conceptual. Because the interviewees of this study are elders whose Chinese tends toward the colloquial, this study focuses on using the second method.

During axial coding we identified the relationships between initial concepts into categories and to sort similar categories into summary categories. The categories include satisfaction, sense of mission, enjoyment, resource exchange, the expected benefits, virtual community design, peer influence. And the summary categories included psychological motivation, cognitive motivation, and external motivation. Summary categories, categories and concepts are shown in Table 2.

Table 2. Axial coding results

Summary categories	Categories	Concepts
Psychological motivation	Satisfaction	The sense of honor
		Improve the reputation
		Self-realization
	Sense of mission	Helping others
		Active community
	Enjoyment	Interest
		Make friends
Cognitive motivation	Resource exchange	Acquire knowledge
		Get help
	The expected benefits	Material reward
		Collection
		Interaction with others
External motivation	Virtual community design	Game design
		Sense of ritual
	Peer influence	Peer influence

4.3 Selective Coding

Selective coding is the procedure of selecting the core strategy, systemically relating it to other categories validating those relationships, and filling in categories that need future refinement and development. A core category is the central or focus around which all other categories are integrated (Strauss and Corbin 1990). The purpose of this study is to explore the motivations of the elderly knowledge sharing in virtual community; the core category is what motivations will make old people for knowledge sharing. Therefore, this study put the "elders' knowledge sharing in virtual communities" as the core category. The structure of the summary categories is shown in Table 3.

Table 3. The structure of the summary categories

Relationship	Relational structure	Explanation
Psychological Motivation → Knowledge Sharing	Causality	The elderly get satisfaction, a sense of mission and enjoyable when using the virtual community is the psychological motivation for knowledge sharing, which is the intrinsic motivation for knowledge sharing.
Cognitive Motivation → Knowledge Sharing	Causality	and expected benefits when using virtual community is the cognitive motivation for knowledge sharing, which is the intrinsic motivation for knowledge sharing.
External Motivation → Knowledge Sharing	Causality	The design of virtual community and peer influence is the external motivation for the elderly to share knowledge
External Motivation → Knowledge Sharing	Mediated	The design of the virtual community and peer influence will directly affect the elders' cognition for knowledge sharing, and then affect their knowledge sharing behavior.

Based on grounded theory research results, we can found that the psychological motivation, cognitive motivation, and external motivation would affect elders' knowledge sharing behavior in virtual communities together. Hence, on this basis we proposed the theoretical model which indicates the motivation of knowledge sharing among elders in virtual communities (Fig. 2). However, the theoretical model was based solely on interview data and not on previous theoretical structure. This is also the deficiency of this study (Fig. 3).

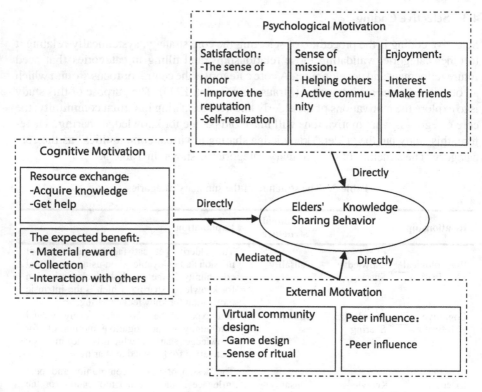

Fig. 3. Theoretical model

5   Discussion

According to social cognitive theory and motivation theory, individuals tend to participate in the activity which may bring benefits. Elders' motivation in knowledge sharing
is explored from the perspective of inherent motivation in participation including
psychological and cognitive motivation as well as other external factors supporting or
encouraging participation. Based on the data analysis in part 4, some key research
findings have been drawn from the analysis.

5.1   Psychological Motivation

This study found that the elders' motivation of knowledge sharing is not much different
from that of young people. For example, sense of honor, improve the reputation, Self-
realization, make friends or just for fun. Among all the 21 participants, there were
13(62%) elders mentioned they hope to realize self-value, and 8(38%) elders said they
want to try their best to help others, show that older people tend to contribute to society
and others, and then helpful to their self-realization. The discovery provides a reference
for the realization of active aging and the development of elderly human resources.
Moreover, 11(52%) elders expressed the reason they do knowledge sharing is to make

friends, and 5(24%) to active community. The data shows that most old people are afraid of loneliness; on the contrary, they like a lively atmosphere and more like-minded friends. Based on the above psychological motivations, knowledge sharing in virtual communities can bring the elder contentment and entertainment.

5.2   Cognitive Motivation

Cognitive motivation refers to the elderly based on their own understanding and consideration of the participation of knowledge sharing motivation in virtual communities, this part of the motivation mainly include resource exchange and the expected benefits. There were 5(24%) elders expressed they shared knowledge in the virtual communities because they could acquire more knowledge from the comments, and 3(14%) is to get help in the future. On the one hand, if you want to get more knowledge in a certain field, you must first launch related topic for others to discuss; on the other hand, ordinarily, people give back (reciprocate) the kind of treatment they have received from another, this is called reciprocity that is a social rule that says people should repay, hence, most of the participants thought they actively help others to solve the problem, others would repay. Moreover, 4 participants mentioned material reward, show that the elders keen on gaining petty advantages. And 10 participants said they like to interact with others, mapping out the elders were very lonely generally.

5.3   Extrinsic Motivation

Extrinsic motivation refers to the elderly to stimulate inspired by external factors involved in virtual community knowledge sharing motives, this part mainly includes virtual community design and peer influence. 6(28.5%) participants said the design of the virtual communities, such as leaderboards, badges, and points, etc. drives of motivational of knowledge sharing. In other words, the traditional game elements can affect elders' knowledge sharing in virtual communities positively. Furthermore, it is worth noting that 3(14.3%) participants referred to the virtual community bring them sense of rituals is their motivation for knowledge sharing. For example, they have hundreds of fans call them teacher, whenever the Chinese New Year or other holidays these fans will give their blessing. In other words, the sense of rituals makes the elders have high self-esteem. Last, peer influence also a very important motivation for elders to share knowledge in virtual communities.

6   Conclusion

In summary, our goal was to investigate the motivational affordances of elders' knowledge sharing in virtual communities. We use the in-depth interviews to get the data and use the qualitative grounded theory method to analyze it. In fact, many elder people have rich experience and wisdom, which is a valuable asset, can effectively help solve the shortage of human resources in China. As an aging country, both academic and business must pay close attention to this problem.

However, our study was not without limitations. The motivational theoretical model was based solely on interview data and not on previous theoretical structure. Furthermore, its underlying motivational affordances were not addressed. In future work, we will conduct some quantitative studies to extend and validate our findings.

References

Lee, R.: The demographic transition: three centuries of fundamental change. J. Econ. Perspect. **17**(4), 167–190 (2003)

National Bureau of Statistics of the People's Republic of China. The China Statistical Yearbook 2016 (2016). http://www.stats.gov.cn/tjsj/ndsj/2016/indexch.htm

Liu, W., Jiao, P.: Study on active aging in an international perspective. J. SUN YAT-SEN Univ. **55**(1), 167–180 (2015)

Wagner, N., Hassanein, K., Head, M.: Review: computer use by older adults: a multi-disciplinary review. Comput. Hum. Behav. **26**(5), 870–882 (2010)

China Internet Network Information Center: Thirty-ninth China Internet development statistics report (2017). http://www.cnnic.net.cn/hlwfzyj/hlwxzbg/hlwtjbg/201701/P020170123364 672657408.pdf

Liu, Z.Y.: Survey on status quo of urban elderly's information literacy. J. Inf. Res. **4**(4), 45–50 (2014)

Sharit, J., Hernández, M.A., Czaja, S.J., Pirolli, P.: Investigating the roles of knowledge and cognitive abilities in older adult information seeking on the web. ACM Trans. Comput. Hum. Interact. **15**(1), 3 (2008)

Leist, A.K.: Social media use of older adults: a mini-review. Gerontology **59**(4), 378–384 (2013)

Vošner, H.B., Bobek, S., Kokol, P., Krečič, M.J.: Attitudes of active older internet users towards online social networking. Comput. Hum. Behav. **55**(PA), 230–241 (2016)

Xie, L.L.: Study on the factors influencing the elderly's internet usage based on the planned behavior theory. J. Sci. Res. Aging **4**(2), 50–59 (2014)

Koh, Joon, Kim, Y.G.: Sense of virtual community: a conceptual framework and empirical validation. Int. J. Electron. Commer. **8**(2), 75–94 (2003)

Nimrod, G.: Seniors' online communities: a quantitative content analysis. Gerontologist **50**(3), 382–392 (2010)

Pfeil, U., Arjan, R., Zaphiris, P.: Age differences in online social networking – a study of user profiles and the social capital divide among teenagers and older users in myspace. Comput. Hum. Behav. **25**(3), 643–654 (2009)

Bouty, I.: Interpersonal and interaction influences on informal resource exchanges between R&D researchers across organizational boundaries. Acad. Manage. J. **43**(1), 50–65 (2000)

Zhou, J.: Knowledge contribution in virtual communities: a comparative research between different sub-groups. Manage. Rev. **27**(2), 55–65 (2015)

Chen, C.J., Hung, S.W.: To give or to receive? factors influencing members' knowledge sharing and community promotion in professional virtual communities. Inf. Manage. **47**(4), 226–236 (2010)

Bisogni, C.A., Jastran, M., Seligson, M., Thompson, A.: How people interpret healthy eating: contributions of qualitative research. J. Nutr. Educ. Behav. **44**(4), 282–301 (2012)

Ponterotto, J.G.: Qualitative research in counseling psychology: a primer on research paradigms and philosophy of science. J. Couns. Psychol. **52**(2), 126–136 (2005)

Lovell, J.L.: How parents process child health and nutrition information: a grounded theory model. Appetite **97**, 138–145 (2016)

Strauss, A., Corbin, J.M.: Basics of qualitative research: grounded theory procedures and techniques. Mod. Lang. J. **77**(2), 129 (1990)

Corbin, J.M., Strauss, A.L.: Basics of Qualitative Research: Techniques and Procedures for Developing Grounded Theory. SAGE, Thousand Oaks (1998)

Heath, H., Cowley, S.: Developing a grounded theory approach: a comparison of glaser and strauss. Int. J. Nurs. Stud. **41**(2), 141–150 (2004)

Zickuhr, K., Madden, M.: Older adults and internet use. Pew Internet & American Life Project, pp. 1–23 (2012)

Silver and Intergenerational Gaming

Digital Gaming Perceptions Among Older Adult Non-gamers

Julie A. Brown[✉]

Ohio University, Athens, OH, USA
brownj14@ohio.edu

Abstract. A report published by the Entertainment Software Association in 2013 stated that nearly half of persons aged 50 years and above play digital games. To better understand the characteristics of this growing marking, audience studies have been conducted. However, there is a dearth of research that specifically assesses the underlying qualities that characterize older adult non-gamers. As a direct extension of a study that examined older adult gamers and resulted in the generation of theory, this study sought to understand the older non-gamer audience. In particular, this study aimed to identify aspects that occurred over the course of the adult's life that hindered digital game engagement. By individually interviewing eleven non-gaming older adults (age 60 to 89), three notable themes emerged and provided supportive evidence for the validity of the theory. By gleaning insight from the full spectrum of the population (gamers to non-gamers), game scholars and developers may a have better understanding of how to meet the needs of a wide range of older adults.

Keywords: Older adult gamers · Older adult Non-Gamers · Audience study · Life course · Play

1 Introduction

The most current demographic findings within an industry report generated by the Entertainment Software Association (ESA) indicate that 26% of digital game players are persons age 50+ [1]. Furthermore, an additional assessment conducted by ESA reported that nearly half (48%) of persons aged 50+ play digital games, and among that gaming population, 80% play on a weekly basis [2].

Indeed, digital games – an encompassing term that includes video, console, and computer games – have grown in popularity among older populations. It is challenging to identify a primary catalyst in this shift, yet it has been suggested that the introduction of Nintendo's Wii console in 2006 helped to spur the popularity of digital games among the older consumer market [3]. However, it must be kept in mind that as time progresses, the characteristics and collective life experiences of this population becomes redefined.

This evolving shift was highlighted in a large qualitative study that explored the characteristics of older gamer populations [4]. The majority of the older adult gamers within the study (those age 60+ years) began playing digital games in their adulthood

© Springer International Publishing AG 2017
J. Zhou and G. Salvendy (Eds.): ITAP 2017, Part II, LNCS 10298, pp. 217–227, 2017.
DOI: 10.1007/978-3-319-58536-9_18

years. This is natural being that early console systems became available to the public when they were adults.

However, a number of the middle-aged gamers within the study (those aged 40 to 59 years old) shared stories of how they were first introduced to or began playing digital games when they young (e.g., early adolescence). For example, at the time of this writing, a 14-year-old adolescent who played an Atari console game in 1980 is now 50 years old. This means that today's middle-aged cohort, will be the first older adult generation to have been exposed to digital games for the full span of their life – from childhood to older adulthood.

It was also found within the study that some of the older adult gamers who are now in their 60s began playing digital games when they were in their 20s. Thus, they, too, have been playing for decades and gaming has been a major component of their play identity.

With the proliferation of digital games into the American culture of play, it may be difficult to imagine how an average adult would *not* have been exposed to digital games at one point or another in their life. Yet, even once that encounter occurs, one may question why the individual fails to adopt the technology when there is evidence that there can benefit to engaging with digital games. This study sought to explore the variety of factors that hinder gameplay among older adults

2 Review of the Literature

There has been an increase in the amount of scholarly attention that has been paid to older adult gamers (i.e., those who regularly play digital games). Even within the past five years, there has been a notable increase in the number of studies that specifically target older gamers. This is in comparison to those studies that were identified by DeSchutter, Brown, and Nap in a comprehensive literature review where – at the time of their writing – roughly a dozen articles were identified that focused on this niche [5].

With respect to those few audience studies that specifically explore the characteristics of the older gamer [e.g., 4, 6], most research within this realm (i.e., older gamers) have an eye to identifying how or to what extent older adults may benefit from game engagement.

One of the more popular approaches that have received much attention is the potential influence of digital gameplay on the cognitive ability of the older adult. Positive associations have been suggested with aspects such as visuospatial ability and processing speed [7–11]. Other approaches have included how digital games have come to serve as tool for socialization [4], a source of challenge [12] and improved emotional well-being [e.g., 13].

In comparison, the majority of the research that pertains to older adults and digital games tends to focus on older adults as a potential user of gaming technology (e.g., for rehabilitative purposes). For example, approximately five years after the Nintendo Wii was released to the public, there was a proliferation of studies that assessed it as a potential intervention for rehabilitation or to aid in balance among older non-gamers (e.g., 14–19]. And still, even in the last year, the Wii has been a primary platform to assess these aspects among older populations [e.g., 20–22].

Overall, there appears to be a positive relationship between digital games (or at least the potential for digital game use) and older persons. However, it is worth investigating the other half of the population who do not engage in regular digital gameplay – the older adult non-gamers.

There is a dearth of research that specifically examines older non-gamers as a distinct audience. One such study sought to examine both older gamers and non-gamers with respect to psychological functioning [23]. Overall, the findings indicated that occasional and regularly playing older gamers fair better in terms of well-being, social functioning, and depression.

Despite the promising findings of the aforementioned study, there is a lack of research that probes the defining characteristics of older adult non-gamers in comparison to older gamers. The study presented herein aims to serve as a springboard for a new chapter in this niche of audience studies. It is a continuation of the larger (parent) study described within the introduction [4, 24]. The parent study focused on two populations: Middle-Aged Gamers (age 40–59) and Older Adult Gamers (age 60+) and employed a life course perspective as a means to situate the individual in their personal and historical context. That research resulted in the generation of theory – *Engagement in digital gaming in old age is a life course extension of play that is a function and mediation of a person's motivation, experience, and ability.*

The three identified domains refer to: *the strength of an aging gamer's (1) motivation to play digital games, (2) experience with digital games (including platforms) and (3) functional ability to interact with the digital game.*

The following study was conducted as a means to test the domains by exploring those qualities among older adult non-gamers. Although an abundance of findings were gleaned, this manuscript hones in on the identification of aspects that hinder digital gameplay among this population.

3 Methods

Because this study is an extension of a larger, prior study, the same methodology was used to promote continuity. With that in mind, a grounded theory approach was used [25–27]. This methodology is typically employed when there is limited knowledge on a subject matter.

Also, similar to the parent study, there was an eye toward the role of a temporal perspective of life events that related to "play" and "digital games". This lends to the application of a life course lens, as it highlights the importance of individual life experiences [28, 29]. By asking participants to share their own story and perceptions, there is a greater opportunity to have a richer understanding of the origin and development of personal themes. In addition, pertinent aspects can be compared among those interviewed.

This writing focuses on one primary question that was asked of the older adult participants who do not play digital games:

What factors hinder older adult from engaging with digital games?

3.1 Participants

The parent study consisted of two groups of participants: *Older Gamers*, Age 60 to 77 (19 females, 11 males) and *Middle-Age Gamers*, Age 43 to 59 (16 females, 10 males). However, this study honed in on the older of the two groups by exploring characteristics of *Older Non-Gamers* – persons age 60 years and older. (A future study will examine *Middle-Age Non-Gamers*.)

3.2 Inclusion Criteria and Recruitment

Candidates for this study had to meet the following requirements:

- Be at least age 60 or older
- Not currently play digital games on a regular basis
- Report having at least a "fair" health status

To identify candidates, a range of recruitment strategies was employed. The initial search consisted of snowball sampling information about the study was shared and passed along to persons within the community. This included individuals promoting this opportunity with others via social media. A flier was also distributed to members of local senior organizations and an advertisement was placed in a local emeriti newsletter. Interested persons were instructed to contact the primary investigator via email or office phone so that the details of the study could be reviewed, including the candidate's eligibility. It merits noting that the term "digital game" was explained and described on advertisements as "any game that is played on an electronic device, such as a smartphone, tablet, or computer."

For those who met the inclusion criteria, a meeting time was arranged to be held at either the participant's house, a quite public location (e.g., a reserved room at a library), or the investigator's office to share further details about the study. And, if preferred by the participant, the study proceeded with the interview.

3.3 Interview Guide

Nearly identical to the parent study, a semi-structured interview guide was created to explore the notion of "play" and "digital games" throughout the life of the participant by exploring its role or integration at different life stages. This pertains to childhood (up to age 19), young adulthood (ages 20–39), middle adulthood (ages 40–59), and older adulthood (ages 60 and above) [30].

The interviews began by creating a general timeline of their life. Participants were asked when and where they were born, aspects related to family characteristics and structure (both in childhood and adulthood), and education and career milestones.

The participants were also encouraged to share any additional aspects that they deemed worthy to create their personal timeline. By doing so, this provided a template for being aware of the individual's general position or circumstances in life when exploring a certain stage. For example, this may include their occupation at that time and family structure.

After establishing a general timeline, the participant was asked to define "play", as it is a very subjective concept. Next, each participant was asked to recall how he or she engaged in play at each developmental stage and the factors that contributed to play engagement.

Although none of the participants reported being a current digital game player, they were asked if they had been exposed to or played digital games (or digital game technology) at any point. This also included asking the participant about self-identified barriers or hindrances to digital game engagement, if it did not already surface organically within the interview. Finally, the interview was concluded by asking participants if they anticipated any circumstance where they may play digital games in the future.

3.4 Analysis

All interviews were digitally recorded and transcribed verbatim. To aid in validity and accuracy, member checking was employed by providing a copy of the interview to each respective participant and asking each to provide any feedback they deemed appropriate. Next, interviews were uploaded into a qualitative analysis software program (NVivo 10) to identify and categorize themes. A variety of coding techniques were used to assess each interview – open, axial, and selective – along with the application of the constant comparison technique [25–27]. This process was employed concurrently throughout the study so that findings could help shape and guide subsequent interviews.

4 Findings

A total of eleven participants were individually interviewed (3 male, 8 female) and ranged in age from 60–89. All but one of the participants reside within the immediate vicinity of a university-based, small town in Ohio. In addition, all participants reported having at least a high school education, yet most reported having a college education.

The interviews ranged in length of time, mostly depending upon the time availability of the participant. On average, they were two hours in length and most occurred either in the participant's home or in the primary investigator's office.

Review of the transcripts and codes resulted in select themes that reflect the reason why the participants within this sample do not currently engage in digital gameplay.

4.1 Theme I – Limited Knowledge of Game Platform Technology

All of the participants shared stories that highlighted some level of exposure to gaming technologies even if they did not use that platform for gameplay. This was explored with participants as a means of understanding if there was an association between access to platforms and comfort with engaging with that technology to play a digital game.

In most cases, the technologies discussed were in reference to computers, tablets, and smartphones. However, this does not mean that the participant owned or owns multiple platforms in which a game could be played. And, in most cases, introduction to and personal interaction with these types of technologies typically began within their workplace.

Only one participant, (male - age 66) expressed that he has had minimal exposure to game-related technologies, which he attributed to his former career as a mechanic. Ironically, he owns a smartphone, yet only uses it for basic phone calls because he is unaware of its features and capabilities. When asked about his experience and comfort level with such technologies, he responded with the following.

> I'm almost to the point, I guess, you would call "electronically challenged people." Probably, what I need to do is get involved in [taking courses to] introduce [me] to modern technology, some of the stuff that's out there. I have difficulty playing with new cell phones.

Six other participants expressed that they have experience with game-related technologies and their familiarity is what regard as "the basics" (i.e., emailing and/or texts). A female (age 76) believes that her age is related to her limited experience and comfort with game-related technologies.

> I'm a relic of the past and I'm also mechanically and technology challenged. I don't function well in that world. I do better doing the things I've always done and know how to do.

Some of the additional reasons the participants provided as to why they have limited interaction with these technologies relate to (1) limited exposure when they were employed (i.e., pre-retirement) and (2) poor internet access. A male (age 73) cited both of those for being primary barriers for his knowledge of game-related technologies. Although his former job as a guidance counselor required some computer use, he only knew how to perform what he regarded as basic duties (e.g., looking up a student's name.) He later shared that he heavily relied upon his secretary to compose correspondences and other tasks that required greater computer familiarity. He expressed that this kind of reliance was typical, so there was no need for him to learn much beyond his basic level of computer literacy.

> I never really have become engaged in that [computers]. Keep in mind that the closest we came to anything like that when I was in high school was typing [on a typewriter], back then was called "typing".... As a guidance counselor I had to use computers to look up things and typing schedules and things like that... Our computer set up here [at home] is still a dial-up type thing so we can't do a lot on that.

4.2   Theme II: Digital Game Engagement is too Challenging

Another issue that was brought up among participants pertains to perceived barriers related to the actual game or platform, which hinder engagement. Those who reported an attempt at playing digital games at some point voiced that they had problems with one of the following: (1) game controller manipulation, (2) the pace of the game, and (3) functional ability issues that thwarted gameplay.

A female (60) shared that she once tried playing with family members and found the fast-pace nature of the game was too challenging for her to keep up. Ultimately, this frustration was enough to forego any future play.

> Then I'd look at these video games that they're watching. They're so virtual worlds. They almost make me dizzy how fast that they go through them, whether this character is going through this tunnel or not and he's shooting this character… I would try with those nephews to sit down and play video games with them. It was really hard.

Similarly, another female participant (age 67) reported that she had difficulty in manipulating the game controller, specifically the buttons, and her ability to keep up with the pace of the game. Ultimately, this experience strongly influenced her opinion of digital games and she did not attempt to play again.

> It was too frustrating. It was like too quick with the buttons. I couldn't get the left or right… Oh I got the wrong hand, so it's frustrating and not being competitive. I don't want to master this so I could not run into a something on a video screen, I'd rather read. I'd rather watch a dumb TV show and knit at the same time.

This participant also expressed that it can be difficult for her to interact with a platform's screen due to visual impairment. "I think it's a physiological thing with my eyes. I'd much rather have that book in my hand." Similarly, another female (age 60) has vision problems, yet she wants to play digital games on her computer. She ultimately expressed that this functional impairment is a significant barrier from her gaming even though she once enjoyed it.

> When my computer was up and running, I did play *Solitaire* but that's about the only thing that I did play. Sometimes, you can just sit there and gaze at that screen. I've got an eye disease that's an inherited thing. The numbers all merge. The words all merge together. It's not good for my eyes. That's probably a deterrent to me, too, to want to use a computer.

4.3   Theme III: Digital Games are not of Interest

There were numerous times during the interviews when participants expressed that they were simply not motivated to play any kind of digital game. When this kind of sentiment was expressed the primary investigator encouraged them to elaborate further in an attempt to identify the exact barrier. In most of these cases, the overall feeling towards digital games were contemptive. Specifically, digital games were referred to as a "waste of time". This is noteworthy because this may associated with a decreased likelihood of engage in this activity.

A female participant (age 67) was asked of her opinion of digital games and she gave thought to her own mother who played, and still plays, digital games. Although she acknowledged that playing may be beneficial for some, it had no place in her life.

> They [digital games] just don't speak to me at all. They're sort of a waste of time but my mom when she was my age, she really got into Tetris…. I know that's good for your brain. She is also a bridge player, my mom. She played Duplicate Bridge for a year. She's a master bridge player, all these gold points… there's nothing in me that would want to do that.

Another female (age 72) who also expressed that it was a waste of time, later admitted that she used to play *Spider Solitaire* regularly on her computer before bedtime.

Yet, she also expressed that she did not think that playing a card game on her computer would constitute a "digital game." Thus, this also relates to the older non-gamer's understanding of what a digital game is or what it fully encompasses. This female was one of the seven participants who did not seem to grasp the full scope of digital gaming, especially in relation to traditional games (e.g. card games) that can now be played digitally or games that are typically associated with younger populations of gamers.

> It's a waste of time... *Spider Solitaire* was something that I played usually just before I went to bed [most nights] and it relaxed me... I'd play a few games and then go to bed... It wasn't a waste of time because I was doing it to get ready for bed.

Two of the participants regard digital games as violent in nature and generally referred to them as "shoot 'em ups", yet acknowledged that there could be more genres out there than they were aware of. Contrary to her peers in the sample, one of the two participants (female, age 69) shared her that she had limited awareness of digital games, yet after discussing the topic, was open to learn more. In fact, she acknowledged that she may even enjoy playing but noted that her interest was strongly related to whether or not there was a social component. This is worth highlighting because she is unaware that games can be played within a social context [1].

> I haven't sought [digital] games. The only thing I really hear about or see are the shoot 'em up type things. There is a lot of other things out there that I don't know anything about... Maybe it would be something I'd like to do, but generally I think it is the social contact with somebody else that's more important to me than spending time [on digital games.]

Another participant, a female who is 89-years-old, is not interested in playing digital games because she believed it is impersonal. Although she was aware that games could have social component, she would prefer to engage with persons one-on-one. It is worth noting that she was unaware that some digital games can include that one-on-one component by engaging multiple persons in the same room (e.g., Wii Bowling). She, along with four other participants, was largely unaware of how digital games could facilitate in-person socialization.

> Well for those that enjoy it they should do it, but it just doesn't appeal to me. I don't ever ever play game on a computer or on my Kindle or anything - never. I have two sons who played chess on the computer and I watched them but I had not participated in them. Doesn't really appeal to me. They really like it, they can play with people all over the world, and they can have teams, there's something there for everyone. Just isn't my cup of tea... [because] I guess I'd just be by myself.

5   Discussion

This study described the prominent themes that surfaced when asking older adults non-gamers about their perceptions of and lack of engagement with digital games. When considering the theoretical domains that surfaced in the original study of middle-aged and older gamers, there is a connection with the themes that provide support to the theory. Although a participant may not have expressed a deficiency in all three areas, all of the participants provided information that suggested that they may be "weak" in at least one domain.

The first theme discussed, *Limited knowledge of game platform technology*, relates to the domain – "experience with digital games (including platforms). Participants varied in their experience levels with game-related technologies. Yet, those who had limited knowledge (and comfort) with these technologies suggested this as a reason for why they do not play games.

Theme II, *Digital game engagement is too challenging*, is associated with the domain – "functional ability to interact with the digital game." Aspects that were brought up within that theme revolved around physiological and cognitive considerations. These negatively influenced the ability to keep up with the pace of a motion-based game, the successful manipulation of a game controller, and the ability to see critical elements of the game (i.e., visual impairment). Similar to the first theme, the barriers discussed within this theme can decrease the strength of this domain.

The final theme, *Digital games are not of interest*, is associated with the remaining domain – "motivation to play digital games." Some of the older non-gamers saw little to no value in playing digital games, as it was seen as a waste of time. Yet, it is worth noting that if the social element that is available in some forms of gameplay becomes apparent, then the motivational strength may be sufficient to prompt engagement. Finally, the aversion to "shoot 'em ups" as a deterrent to gameplay is consistent to prior research conducted on older adult attitudes toward "shooter" gamers [31].

6 Conclusion

This study examined the characteristics of 11 older adult non-gamers, ranging in age from 60 to 89. As an extension of a larger one that focused on exploring the character-istics of middle-aged and older gamers, this current study aimed to identify hindrances to gameplay. In addition, the findings were compared to the theory that was developed within the parent study to assess its validity.

The three primary themes that surfaced from the proposed research question supports the theoretical domains and gives reason to probe this line of inquiry further. In addition, there is a dearth of studies that specifically target older non-gamers within the context of "audience studies" research. This would be a valuable departure being that ample game-related research has been conducted with this population, yet none hone in on identifying the underlying elements that distinguish them from their gameplaying coun-terparts.

The current study would have benefited with interviewing more older non-gamers and by spending an even greater time on deciphering not only the theme-related elements, but also their origin within a life course context.

In addition, it is important to recognize that the vast range of characteristics that are attributed to both the older gamers and non-gamers will continue to modify over time as individuals age into this this stage of life. And, although it is likely that there will be a greater proportion of older gamers in the coming years, it is necessary to understand the life course events and transitions that distinguish them as a unique and dynamic market.

References

1. Essential Facts about the Computer and Video Game Industry (2016). http://essentialfacts.theesa.com/Essential-Facts-2016.pdf
2. Gamers Over 50: You're Never Too Old to Play (2013). http://www.theesa.com/wp-content/uploads/2015/02/Elder-Gamer-Fact-Sheet-FINAL.pdf
3. Theng, Y.L., Dahlan, A.B., Akmal, M.L., Myint, T.Z.: An exploratory study on senior citizens' perceptions of the Nintendo Wii: The case of Singapore. In: Proceedings of the 3rd International Convention on Rehabilitation Engineering & Assistive Technology. ACM (2009). doi:10.1145/1592700.1592712
4. Brown, J.A.: Let's play: Understanding the role and significance of digital gaming in old age. Dissertation at the University of Kentucky (2014)
5. De Schutter, B., Brown, J.A., Nap, H.H.: Digital games in the lives of older adults. In: Predergast, D., Garattini, C. (eds.) Ageing and the Digital Life Course, pp. 236–256. Berghahn Books, Brooklyn (2015)
6. De Schutter, B., Malliet, S.: The older player of digital games: A classification based on perceived need satisfaction. Communications 39(1), 67–88 (2014)
7. Basak, C., Boot, W.R., Voss, M.W., Kramer, A.F.: Can training in real-time strategy video game attenuate cognitive decline in older adults? Psychol. Aging 23(4), 756–777 (2008)
8. Boot, W.R., Basak, C., Erickson, K.I., Neider, M., Simmons, D.J., Fabiani, M., et al.: Transfer of skill engendered by complex task training under conditions of variable priority. Acta Psychol. 135, 349–357 (2010)
9. Lee, H., Boot, W.R., Basak, C., Voss, M.W., Prakash, R.S., Neider, M., et al.: Performance gains from directed training do not transfer to untrained tasks. Acta Psychol. 139(1), 146–158 (2012)
10. Stern, Y., Blumen, H.M., Rich, L.W., Richards, A., Herzberg, G., Gopher, D.: Space fortress game training and executive control in older adults: A pilot intervention. Aging Neuropsychol. Cogn. 18(6), 653–677 (2011)
11. Whitlock, L.A., McLaughlin, A.C., Allaire, J.C.: Individual differences in response to cognitive training: Using a multi-modal, attentionally demanding game-based intervention for older adults. Comput. Hum. Behav. 28(4), 1091–1096 (2012)
12. De Schutter, B.: Never too old to play: The appeal of digital games to an older audience. Games Cult. J. Interact. Media 6(2), 155–170 (2011)
13. Rosenberg, D., Depp, C.A., Vahia, I.V., Reichstadt, J., Palmer, B.W., Kerr, J., Jeste, D.: Exergames for subsyndromal depression in older adults: A pilot study of a novel intervention. Am. J. Geriatr. Psychiatry 18(3), 221–226 (2010)
14. Ackerman, P.L., Kanfer, R., Calderwood, C.: Use it or lose it? Wii brain exercise practice and reading for domain knowledge. Psychol. Aging 25(4), 753–766 (2010)
15. Bainbridge, E., Bevans, S., Keeley, B., Oriel, K.: The effects of the Nintendo Wii fit on community-dwelling older adults with perceived balance deficits: A pilot study. Phys. Occup. Ther. Geriatr. 29(2), 126–135 (2011)
16. Bell, C.S., Fain, E., Daub, J., Warren, S.H., Howell, S.H., Southard, K.S., Shadoin, H.: Effects of Nintendo Wii on quality of life, social relationships, and confidence to prevent falls. Phys. Occup. Ther. Geriatr. 29(3), 213–221 (2011)
17. Hsu, J.K., Thibodeau, R., Wong, S.J., Zukiwsky, D., Cecile, S., Walton, D.M.: A "Wii" bit of fun: The effects of adding nintendo Wii Bowling to a standard case regimen for residents of long-term care with upper extremity dysfunction. Physiotherapy Theory Pract. 27(3), 185–193 (2011)

18. Hurkmans, H.L., Ribbers, G.M., Streur-Kranenburg, M.F., Stam, H.J., van den Berg-Emons, R.J.: Energy expenditure in chronic stroke patients playing Wii Sports: A pilot study. J. NeuroEng. Rehabil. **8**(38), 1–7 (2011)

19. Miller, C.A., Hayes, D.M., Dye, K., Johnson, C., Meyers, J.: Using the Nintendo Wii Fit and body weight support to improve aerobic capacity, balance, gait ability, and fear of falling. J. Geriatr. Phys. Ther. 1 (2011). doi:10.1519/JPT.0b013e318224aa38

20. Kwok, B.C., Clark, R.A., Pua, Y.H.: Novel use of the Wii balance board to prospectively predict falls in community-dwelling older adults. Clin. Biomech. **30**(5), 481–484 (2015)

21. Nicholson, V.P., McKean, M., Lowe, J., Fawcett, C., Burkett, B.: Six weeks of unsupervised nintendo Wii fit gaming is effective at improving balance in independent older adults. J. Aging Phys. Act. **23**(1), 153–158 (2015)

22. Whyatt, C., Merriman, N.A., Young, W.R., Newell, F.N., Craig, C.: A Wii bit of fun: A novel platform to deliver effective balance training to older adults. Games Health J. **4**(6), 423–433 (2015)

23. Allaire, J.C., McLaughlin, A.C., Trujillo, A., Whitlock, L.A., LaPorte, L., Gandy, M.: Successful aging through digital games: Socioemotional differences between older adult gamers and non-gamers. Comput. Hum. Behav. **29**(4), 1302–1306 (2013)

24. Brown, J.A.: Let's play: understanding the role and meaning of digital games in the lives of older adults. In: Proceedings of the International Conference on the Foundations of Digital Games, pp. 273–275. ACM, May 2012

25. Charmaz, K.: Constructing Grounded Theory: A Practical Guide Through Qualitative Analysis. Sage Publications Ltd., Thousand Oaks (2006)

26. Corbin, J.M., Strauss, A.: Grounded theory research: Procedures, canons, and evaluative criteria. Qual. Sociol. **13**(1), 3–21 (1990)

27. Glaser, B.G., Strauss, A.L.: The Discovery of Grounded Theory: Strategies for Qualitative Research. Aldine, New York (1967)

28. Elder Jr., G.H.: Perspectives on the life course. In: Life Course Dynamics, pp. 23–49 (1985)

29. Elder Jr., G.H.: Time, human agency, and social change: Perspectives on the life course. Soc. Psychol. Q. **57**(1), 4–15 (1994)

30. L'Abate, L.: The Praeger Handbook of Play Across the Life Cycle: Fun from Infancy to Old Age. Praeger/ABC-CLIO, Santa Barbara (2009)

31. McKay, S.M., Maki, B.E.: Attitudes of older adults toward shooter video games: An initial study to select an acceptable game for training visual processing. Gerontechnology **9**(1), 5 (2010)

My Grandpa and I "Gotta Catch 'Em All."
A Research Design on Intergenerational Gaming
Focusing on *Pokémon Go*

Francesca Comunello[1](✉) and Simone Mulargia[2]

[1] Department of Humanities, LUMSA University, Rome, Italy
`f.comunello@lumsa.it`
[2] Department of Communication and Social Research, Sapienza University of Rome, Rome, Italy
`simone.mulargia@uniroma1.it`

Abstract. Intergenerational gaming is gaining growing scholarly attention, as it can be considered a means of fostering relationships between younger and older players, a way of overcoming real or perceived differences between generations, a chance to (re)negotiate norms and roles, and a way to question age-related stereotypes. In this paper, we conduct a literature review on intergenerational gaming and pervasive gaming and present a research design to conduct an intergenerational gaming study focusing on *Pokémon Go*. We aim at exploring gaming practices, role negotiations, and the presence/absence of age-related stereotypes. To reach our goals, we elaborate and evaluate different research methods and tools, discussing their strengths and weaknesses and designing further research steps.

Keywords: Intergenerational gaming · *Pokémon Go* · Location-based mobile gaming · Augmented reality games

1 Introduction

In recent years, scholars have started devoting growing attention to intergenerational gaming practices, while video gaming itself is undergoing a "mainstreaming" process, which is enabled by the diffusion of both specific devices and new gaming practices.

Intergenerational gaming can be considered a means of fostering relationships and connections while producing positive emotions for both generations [1]. As underlined in the context of social network games, playing together among family members can enrich the family's existing relationships [2] and overcome (or positively exploit) real or perceived differences in digital skills among young and older people [3], thus contributing to playful interactions, appealing to both grandparents and grandchildren [4–6].

In this paper, we analyze intergenerational gaming practices, focusing on *Pokémon Go*, which has been massively adopted worldwide by both young children and adults. From a conceptual perspective, we rely on literature analyzing intergenerational gaming and focusing on mobile, location-based, and augmented reality gaming, also considering literature addressing the "social side" of video gaming. After exposing our theoretical framework (which builds on literature addressing both intergenerational gaming, and

J. Zhou and G. Salvendy (Eds.): ITAP 2017, Part II, LNCS 10298, pp. 228–241, 2017.
DOI: 10.1007/978-3-319-58536-9_19

location-based gaming), we describe the design of a research project aimed at analyzing intergenerational gaming practices involving grandparents and their young grandchildren (age up to 11) playing *Pokémon Go*. More specifically, we briefly describe the game and the reasons we decided to focus on it; specify our goals and research questions; and elaborate on research methods and the tools to be used to answer our questions, also considering recruiting issues and ethical concerns. We conclude by critically addressing both the goals and the methods in the broader framework of the proposed background and by discussing our further research steps, as well as the research project's limitations.

2 Background

2.1 Intergenerational Gaming

Intergenerational gaming represents a promising but controversial area of application of video games to promote social interactions between different age cohorts. On the one hand, video games could represent "an interactive environment where collaboration and cooperation occur" [7, p. 48] among different generations of users, thus contributing to lessening age segregation and consequently ageism [8]. More specifically, playing video games can facilitate intergenerational relationships and offers a playful context of interaction through which a new equilibrium can be negotiated in terms of social roles, thus contributing to mutual respect between young people and the elderly [9]. On the other hand, a stereotypical representation of older people [10, 11] seems to affect the public debate on video games and the elderly, as underlined by De Schutter and Abeele [12] in their "gerontoludic manifesto". In this context, video games are framed as useful tools to improve older people's skills, or they are considered only in terms of features aimed at reducing age-related limitations, disregarding the playfulness associated with gaming and implicitly depicting the elderly as a monolithic social group [12].

To avoid a deterministic approach, it is necessary to carefully evaluate advantages and disadvantages, refusing to consider video games as the "panacea" for intergenerational relationships but avoiding disregard of their potentiality. As underlined by Chua et al., "perceptual changes between different groups are not assured by mere contact or interactions but depend on a series of factors" [9, p. 2304], even if "video games can be an effective facilitator to enhance intergenerational perceptions when members from different age groups are paired to play video games together as a novel leisure activity, as compared to daily routine activities used to facilitate intergenerational bonding" [9, p. 2308].

Several studies have addressed the topic on a participatory-design level, allowing both older and young people to take an active role in designing video games that can facilitate mutually satisfying interactions. As a result of this approach, a series of recommendations for intergenerational gaming design are now available [6]. Besides the need to create an *ad hoc* intergenerational video game, such recommendations offer a manifold theoretical framework to better refine our project. As summarized by Costa and Veloso [13] in a recent literature review, intergenerational video games have to promote peer-to-peer mentoring, taking advantage of specific age-related skills and avoiding unidirectional knowledge transfer; they also have to offer communal activities, trying to balance skills and challenges, thus fostering individual well-being. In this respect, intergenerational video games can represent a shared context hosting social interaction, prioritizing physical mixed-reality (i.e., the integration of physical objects and digital communication tools) [13] to properly address older people's potential concerns with digital interfaces. In line with these recommendations, Rice et al., as a result of intergenerational game design workshops, outline that intergenerational games have to build on users' intrinsic qualities, sustain mutual engagement, balance challenges to promote long-term commitment, and exploit public spaces for community engagement [14]. Siyahhan et al. [15], observing pairs of players composed of parents and children playing *Quest Atlantis* (a multiuser 3D educational video game), focus on specific characteristics of the dyads (i.e., being a novice vs. an expert). Key points in fostering intergenerational exchange are the convergence of intentions among players and a fruitful negotiation of norms and roles that can potentially reveal opportunities to question the traditional roles of adults and children.

If these recommendations apply to a wide variety of intergenerational games and video games, a more specific interest in game experiences that mix traditional games and video games (augmented games) or physical and digital environments (as in the case of augmented reality games) is growing among scholars. Al Mahmud et al. [16] experimented with an augmented table-top game for intergenerational gaming, observing that technology played a special role in enhancing young people's gameplay experience. As a result of their experiment, the authors outline that children involved in the project liked their own customized (in terms of references to a fantasy universe) version of the game more than the adults' version, while the adults were quite unconcerned about specific game versions. To promote gratifying social interaction among participants, special attention has to be paid to games' rules, exploiting uncertainty as a means of maintaining interest in the game but also trying to balance immersion with social interactions (as young users tend to focus more on the game than on their partners) [16]. The analysis of Khoo et al. [17] of the process leading to the prototype of *Age Invaders* (a so-called intergenerational social and physical game) offers useful insights about mixing physical and digital games for intergenerational interactions. In this respect, as older people can potentially be intimidated by traditional interfaces, such a game exploits the physical space as an interface (users move on an LED-enriched roof that recognizes their movements through RFID technologies), thus stimulating older people's motivation to play while engaging young users through the well-known metaphor of a traditional video game like *Space Invaders*. Allowing users to naturally interact in the same physical environment, mixed-reality games seem to offer a naturalistic setting for intergenerational interactions, promoting face-to-face conversation and body-language expressions during the game, thus acting as a stage that hosts users' performances [17]. Despite these promising examples, researchers have devoted scarce attention to alternate reality games (ARGs) in the context of intergenerational gaming [7]. To contribute to the debate, Hausknecht et al. [7] illustrate some potentiality of ARGs and point out some design considerations. ARGs can act as intergenerational learning tools promoting collaboration among adults and young people and stimulating counterfactual thinking (enacted by users to solve quizzes and puzzles embedded into the ARG's narrative). In this respect, ARGs can offer possible gaming situations where different age cohorts have to exchange their own points of view and negotiate roles and positions of power [7]. Moreover, as discussed by Costa and Veloso [18], relying on Bonsignore and colleagues' analysis of ARGs in the context of 21st-century literacy skills [19], ARGs can promote specific core literacies that can be beneficial for both adults and children. To actualize these potentialities, game designers must find a balance between the canonical trajectory of the game's narrative (i.e., the narrative path imagined by the game creator) and the participant trajectory, creating an equilibrium in the openness of the game. Specific characteristics of users need to be capitalized on, and ARGs can potentially exploit users' prior knowledge and their former experiences as gamers, thus promoting a satisfying division of labor in the case of young and older people playing together [7].

Despite these optimistic considerations about ARGs' potentialities to promote and facilitate intergenerational interactions and collaborative learning among different age cohorts, Hausknecht et al. [7] and Costa and Veloso [18] express cautious concerns. More specifically, as outlined by Costa and Veloso, playing ARGs can result in "(a) addictive experiences; (b) identity crises; and (c) disparities in (grand) child–(grand) parents' relationships of authority" [18, p. 5]. In more general terms, as underlined by Iversen in her application of the Foucauldian concept of discourse to digital game research and older adults, the growing interest in older people and video games is characterized by a utilitarian approach that tends to depict old age as a problem to solve, implicitly considering older people unproductive subjects who can be re-assimilated in the system as consumers through video games: "Digital games in this regard are both offered as training equipment for body and mind and more implicit markers of youthfulness" [10, p. 17].

2.2 Mobile, Location-Based, and Augmented Reality Gaming in the Urban Playground

In recent years, scholars have devoted growing attention to a particular set of digital games that are designed to be played on mobile devices, exploiting urban environments as a playground and incorporating, at various levels, augmented reality features as well as relational practices between players. While "pervasive gaming" has been proposed as a unified label to address such a broad set of games [20, 21], several partially overlapping definitions have been used to describe the different features, as well as the different gaming practices, related to such games, including mobile games, location-based games, augmented reality games, and so on.

One of the first attempts to historically and theoretically contextualize digital gaming practices in urban spaces was proposed by De Souza e Silva and Hjort [22], who focus on the term "mobile gaming," underlining how "location awareness and global positioning system (GPS) devices embedded in mobiles turn them into interfaces to navigate physical spaces" [22, p. 603]. Even before mobile devices spread, the social construction of urban spaces could be considered "inherently playful" [22, p. 603], as several playful usage forms of such spaces can be documented historically (the authors include, as relevant examples, Baudelaire's *flâneur*, the situationist idea of *dérive*, and the subculture of *parkour*).

A broader framework for contextualizing similar processes can be identified in literature analyzing locative media, as well as in the concept of "geomedia" [23]. The term "locative media" was "first used by Karlis Kalnins in 2003 in Latvia to set apart 'the corporation use of location-based services from artistic propose' (...) [and] is defined as a 'mobile media with geographical positioning and context sensitivity'" [24, p. 2]. Geomedia, in contrast, can be defined as platforms that "merge existing electronic media +the Internet+location-based technologies (or locative media)+AR (augmented reality) technologies in a new mode of digital composite imaging, data association and socially maintained data exchange and communication" [23, p. 14].

The first generation of experimental location-based mobile games was developed in the late nineties and aimed at transforming urban spaces into playful places [25]. Early pervasive games were often oriented toward educational applications, as well as toward reshaping previous digital games. Early literature on the topic, in contrast, focused on chances to bridge the physical and digital domains [20], consistent with more general trends in Internet research, underlining how networked individuals seamlessly operate between the physical and digital worlds [26, 27].

Scholars have proposed several attempts at the categorization of pervasive games. For instance, De Souza e Silva and Hjort distinguish between urban games (UGs), "games that use the city space as the game board. UGs are often multiplayer games played out in the streets of the city" [22, p. 612]; location-based mobile games (LBMGs), "games played with cell phones equipped with location awareness (...). Like UGs, LBMGs use the city space as the game environment. However, they additionally allow the linking of information to places, and players to each other via location awareness" [22, p. 614]; and hybrid reality games (HRGs), which "have an online component, represented as a 3D virtual world, so they take place simultaneously in physical and digital spaces. It is the shared game experience among multiple users that creates the hybrid reality" [22, p. 618].

When analyzing *Ingress* (a game that can be considered a predecessor of *Pokémon Go*), Hulsey and Reeves describe it as combining different game design genres: it is "a multiplayer location-based mobile game (LBMG) [...] that also incorporates augmented and alternate reality" [28, p. 390], underlining the centrality of hybrid spaces [29] in its game design and practices. Similarly, Chess [30] refers to *Ingress* as a game combining geomedia [23] and AR, negotiating "complex relationships between community and space on both global and regional levels" [30, p. 1105]. From such a perspective, the player is bound to proximity (several actions can be performed only when one is next to a physical place), to the digital layer overlapping the physical world (the gaming arena displayed on mobile devices), and to a broader social and gaming context, at a regional or even at a global level (the evolving *Ingress* storyline, as well as the overall scores, are related to the global performances of the two opposing factions operating in the game). In such a context, the AR layer both allows and "forces" the player to see the world differently, pushing him to notice regional points of interest [30, p. 1107]. According to Chess, furthermore, *Ingress* should also be considered through the lens of the ARG model [30], which is an immersive form of gaming "that combines narrative, collaborative storytelling, mixed media, and puzzle solving" [7, p. 52].

Addressing the debate surrounding pervasive game definition, Kasapakis highlights several game genres that can be defined as "contiguous" with pervasive games, underlining that most authors propose genre-focused categorizations. Among the most commonly proposed genres are AR games; mixed-reality games; LBMGs; trans-reality games; and cross-media games [21, p. 24]. Kasapakis' proposes a definition for pervasive games that elaborates on Huizinga's [31] concept of "magic circle," which refers to the (conventionally agreed upon) boundaries between the game and ordinary life. More specifically, in Kasapakis' definition, "pervasive games expand the spatial, temporal or social borders of the magic circle while also utilizing pervasive technologies" (p. 23). Other authors [22, 25, 32] rely on such a concept, exploring the ways in which such boundaries are blurred in pervasive gaming. Majorek and du Vall, for instance, underline that,

> Today, games intended for mobile phones using AR technology have given a completely new meaning to the magic circle. [...] when dealing with applications using AR technology, it is important to note that they lead to a certain connection between the virtual world and the real world, and these two dimensions become nearly identical [32, p. 674].

While several scholars struggle in attempting to categorize pervasive games, mainly distinguishing between different genres (or features), others, such as Hjorth and Richardson [25], propose a comprehensive framework for analyzing the convergence between social, locative, and mobile media gaming, underlining that such a distinction is a heuristic strategy [25, p. 2] rather than an intrinsic characteristic of game design and gaming practices. On the contrary, "in contemporary game practices, we would more commonly experience a variable intersection of these features [25, p. 2]. The authors also underline how

> Mobile networked technologies not only transform how we understand place in everyday life, they also remind us that place is more than just physical geographic location; it is constructed by an ongoing accumulation of stories, memories, and social practices (...) This is particularly the case within the realm of urban mobile gaming, which seeks to challenge everyday conventions and routines that shape the cityscape [25, p. 6].

Furthermore, while mobile gaming has traditionally been associated with "casual gaming" practices, the traditional distinction between "casual" and "hardcore" gamers needs to be overcome. Following Consalvo, the pervasiveness and mainstreaming of mobile gaming practices in everyday life means that mobile phone gamers "defy categorization" [33, p. 193], underlining the need to overcome the conventional distinction between casual and hardcore gamers to build a more nuanced picture that, as may be the case for *Ingress* and *Pokémon Go*, supports both gaming attitudes, leaving to each player room for calibrating his/her engagement with the game according to various situational, attitudinal, and contextual considerations.

While the first generation of LBMGs was mainly oriented toward serious applications, with a main focus on educational outcomes, the following generations dedicated more emphasis to playful attitudes and to the social side of gaming [25]. This does not mean that such attention toward serious outcomes has been dismissed, as shown by several applications in the fields both of education and of "exergames" [34].

Literature on pervasive gaming, as well as the few articles analyzing *Ingress*, or *Pokémon Go* [35], highlight several themes that are relevant to our research, also considering their broader social implications.

The first area is related to the relation between players and the urban space. In this regard, the literature explores the ways in which players negotiate their presence between different realms and their understanding of the domains they are operating in: on the one hand, the physical and the digital realms and, on the other hand, the local, regional, and global levels that might be implied in pervasive gaming [30]. Furthermore, relying on the concept of "ambient play" helps "to reconcile the cyclic debates around intimacy and co-presence" in digital media scholarship [25, p. 62], reshaping the very concept of presence [22, p. 618]. Moreover, an analysis of data from mobile networks in Santiago, Chile highlighted the effects of *Pokémon Go* on the pulse of the city, resulting in more people being outside at certain times, and, in more general terms, in people slightly adapting their daily routines to play [36]. Both the reshaping of presence and the negotiation of space and place, on the one side, and the modification of daily routines and itineraries through the city are relevant aspects to be explored through the lens of intergenerational practices.

Moreover, the game offers the chance to coordinate, at various levels, with other players to achieve relevant goals with teammates (from conquering a single gym to "controlling" a neighborhood) or with general players (i.e., taking profit from lure modules) or even just to experience a more enjoyable and playful gaming practice [35]. This implies, on the one hand, that young children are commonly in need of adult supervision when interacting with strangers through the game and, on the other hand, that this relational dimension adds further layers to the role-taking and negotiating processes taking place around gaming practices.

Finally, even the growing consumption of mobile data (see [36]) might translate into a need for adult assistance and is likely to be an arena for intergenerational negotiations.

3 Presenting a Research Design for an Empirical Intergenerational Gaming Study

In this section, we present a research design for an empirical intergenerational gaming study, focusing on *Pokémon Go*. After briefly presenting the game and the motivation for the choice to focus on it, we discuss our goals and research questions, and elaborate on research methods and the tools to be used to answer our questions, also considering recruiting issues and ethical concerns.

3.1 *Pokémon Go*

Pokémon Go (Niantic) is a location-based AR game available for iOS, Android, and Apple Watch devices. The gamer uses his/her smartphone's GPS tool to move his/her own avatar through a game map representing the real physical space. As a result of users' explorations, virtual creatures, called Pokémons, appear on the map when the user is physically close to a specific location. The main goal of the game is to locate, capture, battle, and train these virtual creatures. The game calls for physical space exploration, as the gamer has to move into the (real) playground to find new Pokémons and obtain game resources. More specifically, game maps are characterized by the presence of points of interest (i.e., Pokéstops that provide gamers with items such as eggs, Pokéballs, berries, and potions and gyms that can be conquered and defended through Pokémon matches). The game also allows for social interactions, as the users are called to join a specific worldwide team (i.e., red for Team Valor, blue for Team Mystic, or yellow for Team Instinct) in a collaborative and competitive struggle for gym conquest.

A relevant share of intergenerational gaming literature analyzes *ad hoc* video games (i.e., games created for research purposes). In our research, we decided to focus on a widespread commercial video game to observe interactions in a "natural," non-research-driven setting. Indeed, playing a well-known game that has received a great deal of coverage even in mainstream media, is likely to activate users' relational networks (talking with friends and relatives who know the game), which, as already observed in the case of mobile phone usage practices among the elderly [37], plays a relevant role in motivating older users in digital media adoption, providing a richer social context to their practices.

Furthermore, *Pokémon Go* is an interesting case study because (a) the game promotes face-to-face social interaction between players [35]; (b) young children, even if they have access to a smartphone, need adult support to safely move in the urban space; (c) compared to serious games (or games developed for research purposes), such a successful commercial game allows researchers to observe interactions that take place in a "natural" (i.e., not a research-driven) setting; (d) the large user base potentially allows researchers to reach a significant number of respondents.

3.2 Goals and Research Questions

Relying on both intergenerational gaming literature and pervasive gaming literature, the overall goal of our research is to explore intergenerational gaming practices related to *Pokémon Go* taking place in Italian urban areas. In this regard, we aim at observing usage practices and motivations, specific usage patterns, goals and achievements, and so on.

Besides this overall goal, we aim at observing particular aspects of intergenerational gaming practices. More specifically, our research questions are as follows:

- Did interacting with and through the game contribute to setting shared game-related goals? If so, to what extent?
- What are the negotiation practices related to goal-setting and gaming strategies?
- Did game-related interactions contribute to shaping the mutual role recognition of both the young child and the older adult (with regard to both representational level and storytelling practices)? If so, to what extent? If so, how were such representations built?
- What is the user attitude toward the game? Does it change over time?
- Are there any age-related stereotypes at stake? If so, how do respondents elaborate on them? Do such stereotypes evolve over time?

In such a context, participants quitting the game, as well as any unpleasant experience with the game itself or with the research protocol, will also be considered as highly meaningful.

3.3 Research Methods: Participant Selection

To explore the aforementioned dimensions (see Sect. 3.2), we decided to focus on children age 6–11 and to their older adult relatives (generally grandparents). The age range was chosen to include children attending primary school, who are likely to be used to adult supervision for most of the activities they conduct outside their homes. Nevertheless, as some of the oldest children in this age cohort might also be experiencing growing levels of autonomy, a preliminary informal interview with children's family members or teachers will aim at verifying whether the hypothesis of playing with an older family member might match the children's needs and routines (mainly regarding the need for adult supervision to move in the urban context or to use mobile data).

As for older participant selection, we decided not to set a fixed age range. In this case, participants will be chosen from among each child's older family members. In general terms, we aim at recruiting grandparents, but other older family members (e.g., great uncles, great aunts, etc.) can also be involved if they are older than the child's parents.

We decided to focus only on major urban areas in Italy. This decision is related to both game-specific considerations (urban areas offer a higher Pokéstop and gym density, as well as higher chances to meet and coordinate with other players) and broader contextual considerations (young children living in urban areas are commonly more likely to need adult supervision to move through the city).

A major choice needs to be made with regard to participant recruitment. We might decide to recruit only people already playing *Pokémon Go* ("players"), to recruit only people who have not already played it ("non-players"), or to recruit both types of people. On the one hand, recruiting people who have never played *Pokémon Go* might ensure higher uniformity in game progression, allowing us to observe the early gaming stages, during which identity performances, gaming goals and strategies, and time allocation are negotiated. However, such a strategy would have some drawbacks: our intervention would "force" the adoption of a game that has no explicit educational overcomes and has been the target of criticism addressing several aspects, including its pervasiveness and its highly time-consuming nature. After evaluating the advantages and disadvantages of the two options, we decided to include both categories (players and non-players), using slightly different research tools to address the two cohorts, and being aware of their peculiarities when conducting interviews and analyzing research results.

Participant recruitment might be performed by involving schools, community organizations, or game-related informal groups (such as local Facebook groups or Telegram channels related to the gameplay). The first contacts will be established with adults, while children will be interviewed only after their parents or legal guardians have signed the informed consent form, approved by the Ethical Committee at the first author's university and specifically designed for conducting research with young children. Participant recruitment will be stopped once we reach saturation.

3.4 Research Methods and Tools

Ours is an exploratory study aimed at understanding user perceptions, motivations, sense-giving processes, and negotiation strategies. Therefore, we rely on qualitative research techniques, among which a major role is played by a set of semi-structured interviews to be integrated by focus groups and/or a diary.

We decided to rely on semi-structured interviews as our main research technique because we are interested in grasping the particularities of each dyad (child + older adult) involved in the research. Having different characteristics, as well as being likely to follow different game progression stages, each dyad will likely develop specific game practices as well as game-related negotiation strategies. A focus group will be employed as an integration method to better address the broader social considerations implied in gaming practices. Interviews will be administered at different stages to both dyads and individuals (subject to express parental – or a legal guardian's – authorization in the case of young children).

While interviews will cover the same topics when addressing both players and non-players interview timing will differ for the two groups. More specifically, we plan to conduct two interviews with players and three with participants who did not play before participating in the project. The interview scheduling and content will be as follows:

First interview (day 1)

- Shared content (both players and non-players)
  - Socio-demographic dimensions
  - Digital media usage
  - Video gaming activities
  - Leisure and mobility
  - Shared experiences between the child and older adult
  - Overall opinions toward the other age cohort as they emerge when exploring digital media ideologies [38] and social representations
- Only for players
  - Gaming experience (*Pokémon Go*)
  - Experience playing with others
  - Previous intergenerational gaming experience
  - Cognitive walkthrough of the player's profiles (user profile, achievements, favorite Pokémons, collected objects, diary, etc.)

After this first interview, players will be assigned specific tasks to be performed by playing together. Tasks will be selected according to participants' gaming levels from among those that are more likely to activate negotiations and interactions between the child and the older adult.

Second interview for non-players (at least one month after the first interview)

- Gaming experience (*Pokémon Go*)
- Experience playing with others
- Previous intergenerational gaming experience

- Cognitive walkthrough of the player's profile (user profile, achievements, favorite Pokémons, collected objects, diary, etc.); thinking aloud

After this first interview, players will be assigned specific tasks to be performed by playing together. Tasks will be selected according to participants' gaming levels from among those that are more likely to activate negotiations and interactions between the child and the older adult.

Second interview for players, third interview for non-players (at least one month after tasks have been assigned)

- Gaming experience with *Pokémon Go*, with regard to:
  - Shared goal setting
  - Game-related negotiations (with regard to playing times, areas, activities to be carried out); role negotiations in child/older adult relations
  - Attitude toward the game
  - Cognitive walkthrough of the player's profile; thinking aloud
  - Overall opinions toward the other age cohort as they emerge when exploring digital media ideologies [38] and social representations

Such interviews will be integrated with focus groups, aimed at emphasizing the social negotiation aspects related to gaming practices (social norms and roles, shared representations and practices, etc.). Furthermore, some users might be involved (on a voluntary basis and only if highly motivated) in keeping a game-related diary, structured around specific questions and open fields, with the goal of keeping track of long-lasting processes. The diaries will be compiled online and commented on during the final interview.

4   Conclusion

This paper presented the early steps of an ongoing research project aimed at exploring intergenerational gaming practices related to *Pokémon Go* and taking place in Italian urban areas. More specifically, we built the theoretical framework of the paper, discussing literature addressing both intergenerational gaming and pervasive gaming, and designed the research question and methods.

From a conceptual perspective, literature reviewed in this paper proposed that video games can be, under certain conditions, powerful tools for intergenerational interaction. In such a context, as age-based stereotypes are also related to age-cohort segregation, video game-mediated interaction can play a role in overcoming them. More specifically, mixed-reality games can represent an interesting playground for intergenerational interaction, as gamers need to deal with both the digital and the physical worlds, thus experimenting with game practices as well as role negotiations that are typical of both domains.

When considering intergenerational interaction, we are willing to dismiss any patronizing attitude toward both young children and older people. Moreover, we are not conceptualizing the transmission of knowledge in a unidirectional way. We believe that it does not occur just from one individual to the other (e.g., from the older individual to the younger, or vice-versa): on the contrary, it represents a complex phenomenon that could challenge traditional assumptions related to both young and old people (in their relationship to each other, as well as with regard to their interaction with digital technology and with the physical world).

In this respect, to problematize the implicit functionalist approach that partially characterizes the debate on intergenerational gaming, we do not consider *Pokémon Go* a "tool to solve problems" (as implicitly assumed in literature focusing on "exergames" or on the educational outcomes of video games) but, instead, an environment that can potentially host meaningful interactions. More specifically, we elaborate on the difference between, on the one hand, approaches focusing only on games as tools to reach goals that are completely external to the game experience (such as exercising or cognitive training) and, on the other hand, approaches aimed at focusing on the social and relational practices that can be enabled by the gaming practice. The latter case refers to specific forms of gratification that are actually looked for by a relevant number of gamers, particularly if we consider pervasive games. Consequently, we aim at "giving voice" to the respondents instead of trying to set external goals or to adopt any form of patronizing approach toward respondents themselves.

As we aim to deal with representations, motivations, and role negotiations, a set of qualitative approaches appears to be the best option to reach our goals. Nevertheless, future projects, building on qualitative research results, should also gather and analyze quantitative data. Furthermore, different local contexts (different countries and smaller town or villages), as well as different age cohorts, should also be explored to build a more comprehensive picture of the phenomenon.

References

1. Osmanovic, S., Pecchioni, L.: Beyond entertainment motivations and outcomes of video game playing by older adults and their younger family members. Games Cult. **11**(1–2), 130–149 (2016)
2. Boudreau, K., Consalvo, M.: Families and social network games. Inf. Commun. Soc. **17**(9), 1118–1130 (2014)
3. Aarsand, P.A.: Computer and video games in family life: the digital divide as a resource in intergenerational interactions. Childhood **14**(2), 235–256 (2007)
4. Davis, H., Vetere, F., Francis, P., Gibbs, M., Howard, S.: "I wish we could get together": exploring intergenerational play across a distance via a magic box. J. Intergenerational Relat. **6**(2), 191–210 (2008)
5. Loos, E.F.: Designing meaningful intergenerational digital games. In: Proceedings of the International Conference on Communication, Media, Technology and Design, Istanbul, pp. 46–51 (2014)
6. Loos, E.F., Simons, M., De la Hera, T., Gevers, D.: Setting up and conducting the co-design of an intergenerational digital game (submitted a)
7. Hausknecht, S., Neustaedter, C., Kaufman, D.: Blurring the lines of age: intergenerational collaboration in alternate reality games. In: Romero, M., Sawchuk, K., Blat, J., Sayago, S., Ouellet, H. (eds.) Game-Based Learning Across the Lifespan. AGL, pp. 47–64. Springer, Cham (2017). doi:10.1007/978-3-319-41797-4_4

8. Hagestad, G.O., Uhlenberg, P.: The social separation of old and young: a root of ageism. J. Soc. Issues **61**(2), 343–360 (2005)
9. Chua, P.H., Jung, Y., Lwin, M.O., Theng, Y.L.: Let's play together: effects of video-game play on intergenerational perceptions among youth and elderly participants. Comput. Hum. Behav. **29**(6), 2303–2311 (2013)
10. Iversen, S.M.: Play and productivity: the constitution of ageing adults in research on digital games. Games Cult. **11**(1–2), 7–27 (2016)
11. Loos, E.F., Kubinsky, P., Romero, M.: The misrepresentation of older players in the world of digital games: grandparents trying to play a digital game (submitted b)
12. De Schutter, B., Abeele, V.V.: Towards a gerontoludic manifesto. Anthropol. Aging **36**(2), 112–120 (2015)
13. Costa, L., Veloso, A.: Being (grand) players: review of digital games and their potential to enhance intergenerational interactions. J. Intergenerational Relat. **14**(1), 43–59 (2016)
14. Rice, M., Cheong, Y.L., Ng, J., Chua, P.H., Theng, Y.L.: Co-creating games through intergenerational design workshops. In: Proceedings of the Designing Interactive Systems Conference, pp. 368–377. ACM (2012)
15. Siyahhan, S., Barab, S.A., Downton, M.P.: Using activity theory to understand intergenerational play: the case of family quest. Int. J. Comput. Support. Collaborative Learn. **5**(4), 415–432 (2010)
16. Mahmud, A., Mubin, O., Shahid, S., Martens, J.B.: Designing social games for children and older adults: two related case studies. Entertainment Comput. **1**(3), 147–156 (2010)
17. Khoo, E.T., Merritt, T., Cheok, A.D.: Designing a mixed reality intergenerational entertainment system. In: Dubois, E., Gray, P., Nigay, L. (eds.) The Engineering of Mixed Reality Systems, Human-Computer Interaction Series, pp. 121–141. Springer, London (2010). doi:10.1007/978-1-84882-733-2_7
18. Costa, L., Veloso, A.: Alternate reality games and intergenerational learning. In: Videojogos 2014 Conferência de Ciências e Artes dos Videojogos, pp. 1–6 (2014)
19. Bonsignore, E., Hansen, D., Kraus, K., Ruppel, M.: Alternate reality games as platforms for practicing 21st-century literacies. Int. J. Learn. Media **4**(1), 25–54 (2013)
20. Benford, S., Magerkurth, C., Ljungstrand, P.: Bridging the physical and digital in pervasive gaming. Commun. ACM **48**(3), 54–57 (2005)
21. Kasapakis, V.: Pervasive role playing games: design, development and evaluation of a research prototype. Ph.D. thesis, University of Aegean (2016)
22. De Souza e Silva, A., Hjort, L.: Playful urban spaces: a historical approach to mobile games. Simul. Gaming **40**(5), 602–625 (2009)
23. Lapenta, F.: Geomedia: On location-based media, the changing status of collective image production and the emergence of social navigation systems. Vis. Stud. **26**(1), 14–24 (2011)
24. Weng, E.: Observing the impact of locative media on the public space of contemporary cities. Polymath Interdisc. Arts Sci. J. **2**(2) (2012)
25. Hjorth, L., Richardson, I.: Gaming in Social, Locative and Mobile Media. Springer, London (2014)
26. Wellman, B.: Physical place and cyberplace: the rise of personalized networking. Int. J. Urban Reg. Res. **25**(2), 227–252 (2001)
27. Rainie, L., Wellman, B.: Networked. The New Social Operating System. MIT Press, Cambridge (2012)
28. Hulsey, N., Reeves, J.: The gift that keeps on giving: Google, Ingress, and the gift of surveillance. Surveill. Soc. **12**(3), 389–400 (2014)
29. Gordon, E., De Souza e Silva, A.: Net Locality: Why Location Matters in a Networked World. Wiley-Blackwell, Malden (2011)

30. Chess, S.: Augmented regionalism: ingress as geomediated gaming narrative. Inf. Commun. Soc. **17**(9), 1105–1117 (2014)
31. Huizinga, J.: Homo Ludens: A Study of the Play Element in Culture. Beacon, Boston (1955). Original work published 1938
32. Majorek, M., du Vall, M.: Ingress: an example of a new dimension in entertainment. Games Cult. **11**(7–8), 667–689 (2016)
33. Consalvo, M.: Slingshot to victory: games, play and the iPhone. In: Snickars, P., Vonderau, P. (eds.) Moving Data: The iPhone and the Future of Media, pp. 184–194. Columbia University Press, New York (2012)
34. Laine, T.H., Suk, H.J.: Designing mobile augmented reality exergames. Games Cult. **11**(5), 548–580 (2015)
35. Clark, A.M., Clark, M.T.: Pokémon Go and research. Qualitative, mixed methods research, and the supercomplexity of interventions. Int. J. Qual. Methods **15**(1), 1–3 (2016)
36. Graells-Garrido, E., Ferres, L., Bravo, L.: The effect of Pokémon Go on the pulse of the city: a natural experiment. *arXiv preprint* arXiv:1610.08098 (2016)
37. Comunello, F., Fernández-Ardèvol, M., Mulargia, S., Belotti, F.: Women, youth and everything else: age-based and gendered stereotypes in relation to digital technology among elderly Italian mobile phone users. Media, Culture and Society (2016). doi: 10.1177/0163443716674363. Article first published online
38. Gershon, I.: The Breakup 2.0. Disconnecting Over New Media. Cornell University Press, Ithaca (2010)

Socioemotional Benefits of Digital Games for Older Adults

David Kaufman(✉)

Faculty of Education, Simon Fraser University, Burnaby, BC, Canada
dkaufman@sfu.ca

Abstract. Older adults are the fastest growing population in the world, with the number of those over sixty years old expected to grow to more than two billion by 2050. In recent years, discussions have focused on programs aimed at fostering socioemotional factors, such as social connections, subjective wellbeing, life satisfaction, and levels of loneliness of older adults, to maintain their quality of life. This paper reviews the literature on socioemotional benefits and the impacts of digital games on this factor. Three examples are given from recent studies carried out in Canada that demonstrate the impacts of digital games on social connectedness.

Keywords: Older adults · Seniors · Digital games · Socioemotional benefits · Social connectedness

1 Introduction

Older adults are the fastest growing population in the world, with the over sixty years age group projected to grow to more than two billion by 2050 [1]. Canada is following this global trend. Today, approximately three in 10 Canadians are members of the baby boomer generation, those born between 1946 and 1961 [2]. The average life expectancies for those born in 2012 were 84 years for Canadian women and 80 years old for Canadian men, up from 81 and 74 years, respectively, in 1990 [3]. These increases will require greater resources to support individuals' aging process.

Aging older adults face challenging conditions as they experience declines in physical and cognitive abilities, changed living arrangements, loss of lifelong friends and partners, and increasing likelihood of chronic and debilitating illness [4]. Recent evidence shows that the quantity and/or quality of social relationships in western societies are decreasing. For instance, the data shows fewer cases of intergenerational living, greater social mobility, dual-career families that decrease the time available for the elderly, more single-residence households, and increased age-related disabilities [5, 6].

In recent years, discussions have focused on programs aimed at fostering socioemotional factors for older adults, such as social connections, subjective wellbeing, life satisfaction, and reduced loneliness, to maintain their quality of life [7]. Social engagement (also referred to as social connectedness) has been shown to be an essential component of successful aging [8]. For overall wellbeing, social engagement may be more important than physical health [9], as it has been shown to be associated with a variety of health indicators [10]. Social engagement is an important component of

© Springer International Publishing AG 2017
J. Zhou and G. Salvendy (Eds.): ITAP 2017, Part II, LNCS 10298, pp. 242–253, 2017.
DOI: 10.1007/978-3-319-58536-9_20

positive aging [8, 11]. Earlier epidemiological, cross-sectional, and longitudinal research has shown that older adults with greater levels of social interaction report more positive wellbeing. Glei et al. [12] examined how changes in cognition over time are related to social participation and the extent of social networks. Data drawn from this population-based, longitudinal study revealed that respondents who engaged in one or two social activities failed 13% fewer cognitive tasks than those with no social activities, and those who participated in three or more activities failed 33% fewer cognitive tasks. Glei et al. also assert that social interaction outside the family may have a bigger impact on cognitive function than social contacts with family. Social engagement also provides opportunities for older adults to deal with stress and receive social support and connect with friends.

Rowe and Kahn [13] included social engagement as one of the three major elements of successful aging. Rowe and Kahn [7] defined social engagement as being involved "in activities that are meaningful and purposeful" and "maintaining close relationships." On the opposite side, social isolation and cognitive decline are two potential negative effects of the aging process and have consistently been identified by older adults as some of their main concerns about aging [11, 14–18]. Previous studies have shown that a lack of communication and social connection to others can contribute to isolation and loneliness [19–21], which in turn can result in problems such as depression and cognitive decline for older adults. Furthermore, loneliness may lead to many other negative health effects, such as feelings of not belonging, elevated systolic blood pressure, less restorative sleep, and diminished immunity [22–24]. A number of lifestyle factors associated with the aging process have been shown to be associated with feelings of loneliness, such as spouses dying [25] and declines in physical health [26, 27]. In addition to the complexity of social wellbeing and cognitive functioning in older adults, research has found these two factors to be associated with one another.

1.1 Older Adults and Digital Games

Digital games have the potential to support seniors in creating meaningful and enjoyable ways to enjoy life and the company of others [28]. Researchers have identified older adults as prominent digital game players and have been evaluating the benefits they receive from engaging in digital games as a leisure activity. Thirty-four percent of older adults over 55 years old in Canada played digital games in 2014 [29], and as younger generations who grew up with digital games grow older, this number is expected to increase. Research in this area is in its early stages, but studies are uncovering evidence to support various benefits associated with playing digital games [30, 31].

Older adults play games to satisfy diverse needs [32–34]. The ability to interact socially with other players is one affordance that draws older players to engage in gameplay is [35, 36]. Research has shown that digital games have the potential to enhance the social life of older adults [37] and to exert a positive influence on an individual's sense of wellbeing [38]. Playing digital games with others has been found to increase older adults' social connectedness, defined as a person's feelings of belonging and being able to relate to others, and to decrease feelings of loneliness [36, 39, 40]. When played with one or more other people, games have a social element that can enhance wellbeing.

Playing digital games offer a venue for meeting people, staying connected and coping with loneliness [39].

The social context surrounding older adult players has been largely neglected by researchers until recently [42]. Modern digital gameplay can be carried out in many different social contexts, locations, and modes of play, including online co-playing with other players and with virtual game agents. Social events during gameplay directly affect players' enjoyment in a social gameplay session [42].

Research investigating the impact of digital games on older adults' social wellbeing is showing promising results. Researchers have suggested that digital games hold great promise for enhancing older adults' quality of life by improving their subjective well-being, enhancing their social connectedness, and offering an enjoyable way of spending time [43, 44]. Increasingly, digital game playing involves social interaction [45]. However, while these findings are encouraging, they are found under special circumstances. Researchers have set up programs in retirement communities, assisted living facilities, and community centres. They have provided the equipment and trained participants to use the game, thereby creating a social environment in which the older adults can engage. Without the support of researchers and other assistants, the older adults in those studies may have not obtained these positive benefits.

1.2 Online Games and Social Connectedness

Massively Multiplayer Online Role-Playing Games (MMORPGs) such as *World of Warcraft* (*WoW*) offer immersive worlds that are based on social interaction with other players in persistent, online virtual worlds. In an online survey study of older adult *WoW* players, Zhang and Kaufman [46] found a connection between enjoyment of relationships with the game and the development of online bridging and bonding social capital that they used to build and sustain their social networks. The researchers also reported that playing MMORPGs offered older adults ways to nurture off-line relationships with family and real-life friends and to create new meaningful and supportive relationships with friends in the game [47]. These results show that it is important to provide opportunities in which older adults can share their experiences and build relationships with their peers in a supportive social environment.

Online games offer a venue for interacting with other people and enjoying leisure activities; this can have positive impact on wellbeing and successful aging. Nimrod's analysis of 50,000 posts, collected from online social games, showed that participants reported that online games offer meaningful play, an opportunity for practice, a venue to demonstrate their abilities, and a means for coping with ageing [48]. Nimrod noted that "regulars" "knew" one another and had interpersonal dialogues, mostly relating to the game. Nimrod also found play and active entertainment were important goals for those who participated in social online games. Also, those who played digital social games frequently were often involved in sociable conversations. Players identified each other, exchanged personal information and experiences and had their own "group humor." The main categories of subjects in the postings —funny stories, jokes or other comments— fostered connectedness among players and provided enjoyable interaction, and to a certain extent, a sense of belonging.

Studies have shown that social interaction that takes place when playing digital games is important to older players [41, 49, 50]. Playing digital videogames promotes positive health outcomes associated with alleviating depression, and reducing feelings of loneliness, and isolation [50]. Digital gaming also provides a venue for developing social capital that strengthens strong social ties both online and offline [51].

More recently, older adults have begun to experience online communities as a medium for enjoyable social interactions. In a study of one online community, Nimrod found that the majority of posts were part of online social games, including cognitive, associative, and creative games [52]. In another study [48], Nimrod concluded that because online communities offer both leisure activity and an expanded social network, participation in these settings could contribute to the wellbeing of older adults.

Recent research suggests that training in technology use can enhance older adults' cognitive functions as well as facilitate their social interaction and support [53]. Astell [54] suggests that games and social/ interaction technologies offer both cognitive stimulation and social connection, particularly for older adults with dementia. Older adults are currently the fastest growing segment of society with regard to active technology use and should be able to readily learn and use digital games [55]. *ELDERGAMES* [56] and *HERMES* [57] showed promise for improving cognitive function. Regarding older adults' social interactions, Whitcomb [44] identified several early studies in which older adults had positive social experiences when playing computer games. In the *ELDER-GAMES* project, participants identified social interaction, defined as the "opportunity to create and maintain new relationships," as that game's biggest benefit.

Kari [58] conducted a review of systematic reviews in this field and drew the following conclusion:

"The results indicate that exergaming is generally enjoyed and can evoke some benefits for physical fitness and physical activity, but the current evidence does not support the ability of exergaming to increase physical fitness or physical activity levels sufficiently for significant health benefits. This systematic review also revealed several gaps in previous research. Additional high-quality research and systematic reviews concerning exergaming are needed" (p. 59).

Researchers agree that much additional work is needed to establish whether and in what forms digital games can best and most efficiently benefit older adults. This issue has been addressed by IJsselsteijn et al. [37], who identified four potential areas for games to contribute to improving the quality of life for older people: (1) relaxation and entertainment, (2) socializing, (3) sharpening the mind, and (4) more natural ways of interacting. Our current knowledge of older adults' needs suggests that many of today's commercial games pose usability challenges for older adults [32, 41, 57], although tablets and larger mobile phones offer great opportunities for improved ease of use.

2   Some Examples

2.1   Older Adult Game Player Survey

In a recent survey of 463 Canadian older adult digital game players aged from 55–89 years [4] recruited from shopping malls, community centres, long-term care centres, and assisted living facilities, there was a broad spread in number of years respondents had played digital games, with almost one-third (31%) reporting that they had played for 10 years or more. Most (84%) had played in the past month and almost one-quarter (23%) had played every day in the past month. Most (88%) reported that they had played at least one day or more per week on average. Nearly all (93%) had played between 2 and 5 h per day on average when they played, and more than one-quarter (27%) had played social games with other players.

Table 1 shows participants' gameplay patterns. Most participants played digital games alone (81.2%) and a minority played either social games (27.5%) or role-playing games (9.5%) online with other players. A majority of older adults reported that they played digital games alone, but about a third played with family members and almost a quarter played with friends.

Table 1. Results of social gameplay patterns

Social gameplay patterns	% Respondents
Played social games online with other players	
Yes	15.3
No	84.7
Who do you play digital games with?	
Alone	81.2
Family members	34.3
Friends	22.5
Members of a club/association	5.2

Table 2 lists participants' opinions about the benefits and difficulties of playing digital games. Mental exercise was the most commonly selected benefit of digital game playing (83.0%), with the next most common selection being enjoyment (fun) (70.7%). More than 25% of respondents saw social interaction and a general escape from daily life as additional benefits.

Table 2. Benefits of playing digital games (n = 463)

Benefits	% Selecting
General benefits	
Mental exercise	83.0
Enjoyment (fun)	70.7
Social interaction	25.9
Escape from daily life	25.7
Reported increases in socioemotional areas	
Developing self-confidence	41.9
Dealing with loneliness	34.5
Connecting with family	32.5
Connecting with various age groups	28.1
Connecting with current friends	26.6
Developing new friendships	25.6

When asked to what extent they experienced playing digital games as leading to specific socio-emotional and/ or cognitive changes, no participants reported a decrease. They most frequently reported increases in the socio-emotional areas of developing self-confidence (41.9%), dealing with loneliness (34.5%), and connecting with family (32.5%). The lowest-rated benefit, dealing with depression, was still reported by 23.9% of participants.

These results show that a minority of older adults report playing with others and therefore these players report fewer socio-emotional benefits than cognitive benefits from playing digital games.

2.2 Wii Bowling Study

This study investigated the impact of playing digital games on the social life of both gamer and non-game older adults by implementing a citywide Wii Bowling tournament at a number of centers in the metropolitan area [59]. The primary research question was: Does playing a digital game, Wii Bowling, with peers in a tournament, decrease older adults' feelings of social isolation and loneliness?

This research focused on a digital game that many have played or are familiar with, Wii Bowling, published by Nintendo in 2006. The Wii remote device contains sensors that detect body movements that are mirrored within the game play itself. Through our mixed methods approach, data collected included quantitative survey results that included 73 players and recorded interviews with 17 participants.

During each Wii Bowling session, research assistants ensured that the teams of 3–4 participants played two full games of Wii Bowling. The research assistants recorded the scores and posted them on a tournament website and announced the next game date and time. They also encouraged practice during the week between sessions. The sites' social coordinators extended invitations encouraging others to attend as audience members at the weekly Wii Bowling sessions.

Of the 73 participants in the experimental group, there were 52 female (71.2%) and 21 male (28.8%) participants. A paired-samples t-test was conducted to compare loneliness before and after game playing. There was a significant decrease in the score of loneliness (M = 2.21, SD = 0.53) before game playing and (M = 2.04, SD = 0.54) after game playing; t (70) = 3.52, p = 0.001. The effect size was .42, which suggests that the loneliness score of older adults decreased moderately after two months of game playing. A paired-samples t-test was conducted to compare social connectedness before and after game playing. There was a significant increase in the scores for social connectedness (M = 3.41, SD = 0.53) before and (M = 3.53, SD = 0.49) after game playing; t (72) = −2.18, p = 0.033. The effect size was .25. The results show that the social connectedness score of older adults increased significantly, with a low to moderate effect size, after two months of game playing.

The primary theme uncovered through the qualitative analysis coding process was social connectedness. The main codes were: team experience, interaction with others because of playing Wii Bowling, better social connections, and conversations with family and friends about playing Wii Bowling. For example, one participant commented:

"Getting to know your teammates, right. Then, you know, when you see them, you sort of well, you feel part of them Right? So it brings the camaraderie between you, you know."

A number of older people are often lonely [60, 61]. Those who are at the greatest risk of loneliness include widows and widowers, the oldest of the old, those living in institutions, and those with problems with hearing and vision. Older adults who are single or widowed made up 75.3% of participants in the quantitative study and all participants in the qualitative sample. Eight of the 17 in the qualitative study were 75 to 84 years old. Participants' comments indicated that they found playing in the tournament with others whom they may have known or been acquainted with before had social benefits for them.

Playing Wii Bowling appeared to have expanded their social network, and although these contacts involved fairly casual relationships, they were thought to be enjoyable and satisfactory encounters. The results of this study have contributed to a deeper understanding of the role that digital games could play in helping older adults who are dealing with feeling of loneliness and a diminished sense of social connectedness.

This quantitative study included a larger sample than some earlier studies and included an older demographic group not studied to the same extent as younger age groups. The larger sample size, combined with the rich descriptions of personal experience, uncovered insights into the social process related to digital game playing that reached beyond prior work that had primarily been focused on cognitive and physical advantages. The results suggest that playing Wii Bowling might extend relationships beyond the confines of the game playing activity itself to those who watch the game, play the game with them, or simply enjoy the conversations they have with others about the game.

2.3 Bingo Study

Marston [62] found that older adults identified a number of motivating benefits for digital games, including social enjoyment, competitiveness, feeling connected, and education for oneself and other players. She recommended integrating both player interaction and learning content into digital games, supported by multiple levels of game tasks and positive feedback to aid in learning and improving self-confidence.

To test this approach, a study investigated the embedding of learning content to better understand both gameplay outcomes and players' gameplay experiences with a multi-player, educational digital game. Fifty older adults (aged 60+ years) in co-located groups played the customized online educational game "Bingo Nutrition and Health" [63] in assisted living homes and community centres. The quantitative results revealed that participants experienced statistically significant increases in social connectedness and in their knowledge about nutrition and health.

Qualitative results described players' social and learning experiences. Three of the themes generated from the coding of interview transcripts, together with their respective sub-categories, were used to provide a description of players' social experience: social co-playing, gameplay excitement, and making new friends. Two sample quotes are given below.

"... you're meeting new people. And if you don't know them in person, perhaps there's a connection where you form it."

"Yes, I like playing with the group, you are talking to them, playing and sitting with them, you feel comfortable."

This study provided a better understanding of the learning and social gameplay experience of older adults (60 years and above), when playing an educational game that embeds learning content into the game. A digital game that offers an objective that is relevant to what the older adults want (in this case, learning about nutrition and health in a social co-playing setting) has the capability to provide them with a good social and learning experience. When digital games present a combination of enjoyment, social interaction, and learning, they engage to older adults by offering them cognitive and social benefits.

3   Conclusions and Future Research

Several studies have demonstrated that the social interaction that takes place when playing digital games is very important to older players [41, 49, 50]. Playing digital games has the potential to promote positive health outcomes associated with alleviating depression, and reducing feelings of loneliness and isolation [50]. Digital gaming also provides a venue for developing social capital that strengthens strong social ties, both online and offline [51].

We are continuing our research on the socioemotional impact on the oldest old, i.e. those over 80 years of age, of playing digital games. Marston, Freeman, Bishop, and Beech [64] concluded in their scoping review that no studies focused directly on the oldest old population. Therefore, we are investigating various questions such as whether these oldest players experience a greater decrease in loneliness and a greater increase in social connectivity than their younger counterparts? We are also investigating the potential of intergenerational gameplay as a method for overcoming ageism and changing the stereotypes between youth and older adults.

This is a challenging area to investigate as there is so much variability in the group that we refer to as 'older adults' or 'seniors'. The differences between 60 year-old and 80 year-old adults can be enormous along several dimensions, e.g., cognitive abilities, physical health. Also, the life experiences of older adults vary and there can be huge variability among adults within the same age range, e.g., computer skills, educational background. Future research studies need to better describe the participants and should avoid placing everyone over the age of 55 years in the same category.

Acknowledgments. We thank the AGE-WELL NCE Inc., a member of Canada's Networks of Centres of Excellence Program, and the Social Sciences and Humanities Research Council of Canada (SSHRC) for their financial support for this research.

References

1. He, W., Goodkind, D., Kowa, P.: An Aging World: 2015. International Population Reports. United States Census Bureau, Washington, DC (2015). https://www.census.gov/content/dam/Census/library/publications/2016/demo/p95-16-1.pdf
2. Statistics Canada: Population by Sex and Age Group. Statistics Canada, Ottawa (2015). http://www.statcan.gc.ca/tables-tableaux/sum-som/l01/cst01/demo10a-eng.htm
3. World Health Organization: World Health Statistics 2014. World Health Organization, Geneva, Switzerland (2014). http://apps.who.int/iris/bitstream/10665/112738/1/9789240 692671_eng.pdf
4. Kaufman, D.: Aging well: can digital games help older adults? In: Bastiaens, T., Marks, G. (eds.) Proceedings of World Conference on E-Learning in Corporate, Government, Healthcare, and Higher Education 2013, pp. 1943–1949. AACE, Chesapeake (2013)
5. McPherson, M., Smith-Lovin, L., Brashears, M.E.: Social isolation in America: changes in core discussion networks over two decades. Am. Sociol. Rev. **71**(3), 353–375 (2006)
6. Putnam, R.D.: Bowling Alone: The Collapse and Revival of American Community. Simon & Schuster, New York (2000)
7. Rowe, J.W., Kahn, R.L.: Successful aging. Gerontologist **37**(4), 433–440 (1997)
8. Ristau, S.: People do need people: social interaction boosts brain health in older age. Generations **35**(2), 70–76 (2011)
9. Giummarra, M.J., Haralambous, B., Moore, K., Nankervis, J.: The concept of health in older age: views of older people and health professionals. Aust. Health Rev. **31**(4), 642–650 (2007)
10. Novek, S., Menec, V., Tran, T., Bell, S.: Social Participation and Its Benefits. University of Manitoba Centre on Aging, Winnpeg (2013)
11. von Faber, M., Bootsma-van der Wiel, A., van Exel, E., Gussekloo, J., Lagaay, A.M., van Dongen, E., Knook, D.L., van der Geest, S., Westendorp, R.G.: Successful aging in the oldest old: who can be characterized as successfully aged? Arch. Int. Med. **161**(11), 2694–2700 (2001)
12. Glei, D.A., Landau, D.A., Goldman, N., Chuang, Y.L., Rodríguez, G., Weinstein, M.: Participating in social activities helps preserve cognitive function: an analysis of a longitudinal, population-based study of the elderly. Int. J. Epidemiol. **34**(4), 864–871 (2005)
13. Rowe, J.W., Kahn, R.L.: Successful Aging. Pantheon Books, New York (1998)
14. Duay, D.L., Bryan, V.C.: Senior adults' perceptions of successful aging. Educ. Gerontol. **32**(6), 423–445 (2006)
15. Reichstadt, J., Depp, C.A., Palinkas, L.A., Folsom, D.P., Jeste, D.V.: Building blocks of successful aging: a focus group study of older adults' perceived contributors to successful aging. Am. J. Geriatr. Psychiatry **15**(3), 194–201 (2007)
16. Reichstadt, J., Sengupta, G., Depp, C., Palinkas, L.A., Jeste, D.V.: Older adults' perspectives on positive aging: qualitative interviews. Am. J. Geriatr. Psychiatry **18**(7), 567–575 (2010)
17. Laditka, S.B., Corwin, S.J., Laditka, J.N., Liu, R., Tseng, W., Wu, B., Beard, R.L., Sharkey, J.R., Ivey, S.L.: Attitudes about aging well among a diverse group of older Americans: implications for promoting cognitive health. Gerontologist **49**(51), 530–539 (2009)
18. Tate, R.B., Swift, A.U., Bayomi, D.J.: Older men's lay definition of successful aging over time: the Manitoba follow-up study. Int. J. Aging Hum. Dev. **76**(4), 297–322 (2013)
19. Cacioppo, J.T., Patrick, L.C.: Loneliness: Human Nature and the Need for Social Connection. Norton, New York (2008)
20. Rook, K.S.: Social relationships as a source of companionship: implications for older adults' psychological well-being. In: Sarason, B.R., Sarason, I.G., Pierce, G.R. (eds.) Social Support: An Interactional View, pp. 219–252. John Wiley & Sons, New York (1990)

21. Rook, K.S.: Gaps in social support resources in later life: an adaptational challenge in need of further research. J. Soc. Pers. Relat. **26**(1), 103–112 (2009)
22. Hawkley, L.C., Browne, M.W., Cacioppo, J.T.: How can I connect with Thee? Let Me count the ways. Psychol. Sci. **16**(10), 798–804 (2005)
23. Hawkley, L.C., Preacher, K.J., Cacioppo, J.T.: Loneliness impairs daytime functioning but not sleep duration. Health Psychol. **29**(2), 124–129 (2010)
24. Pressman, S.D., Cohen, S.: Does positive affect influence health? Psychol. Bull. **131**(6), 925–971 (2005)
25. Dykstra, P.A., de Jong Gierveld, J.: Gender and marital-history difference in emotional and social loneliness among Dutch older adults. CJA **23**(2), 141–155 (2004)
26. Buchman, A., Boyle, P., Wilson, R., James, B., Leurgans, S., Arnold, S., Bennett, D.: Loneliness and the rate of motor decline in older age: the rush memory and aging projects, a community-based cohort study. BMC Geriatr. **10**, 77–84 (2010)
27. Rosso, A.L., Taylor, J.A., Tabb, L., Michael, Y.L.: Mobility, disability, and social engagement in older adults. J. Aging Health **25**(4), 617–637 (2013)
28. Nap, H.H., de Kort, Y.A.W., IJsselsteijn, W.A.: Senior gamers: preferences, motivations and needs. Gerontechnology **8**, 247–262 (2009)
29. Entertainment Software Association of Canada: Essential Facts 2014. Entertainment Software Association of Canada, Toronto (2014). http://theesa.ca/wp-content/uploads/2015/08/Essential-Facts-2014-EN.pdf
30. Kaufman, D., Sauvé, L., Renaud, L., Sixsmith, A., Mortenson, B.: Digital gameplay by older adults: patterns, benefits, and challenges. S&G **47**(4), 475–489 (2016)
31. Brown, J.A.: Exploring the next generation of older gamers: middle-aged gamers. In: Zhou, J., Salvendy, G. (eds.) ITAP 2016, Part II. LNCS, vol. 9755, pp. 308–318. Springer, Cham (2016). doi:10.1007/978-3-319-39949-2_30
32. Loos, E.F.: Exergaming: meaningful play for older adults? In: Zhou, J., Salvendy, G. (eds.) ITAP 2017, Part II. LNCS, vol. 10298, pp. 254–265. Springer, Cham (2017)
33. De Schutter, B., Brown, J.A., Vanden Abeele, V.: The domestication of digital games in the lives of older adults. New Media Soc. **17**(7), 1170–1186 (2015)
34. De Schutter, B., Maillet, S.: The older player of digital games: a classification based on perceived need satisfaction. Rev. Commun. **39**(1), 67–88 (2014)
35. Delwiche, A.A., Henderson, J.J.: The players they are a-changin': the rise of older MMO gamers. J. Broadcast Electron. Media **57**(2), 205–223 (2013)
36. De Schutter, B.: Never too old to play: the appeal of digital games to an older audience. Games Cult. **6**(2), 155–170 (2011)
37. IJsselsteijn, W.A., Nap, H., de Kort, Y.A.W., Poels, K.: Digital game design for elderly users. In: Kapralos, B., Katchabaw, M., Rajnovich, J. (eds.) Proceedings of the 2007 Conference on Future Play, pp. 17–22. ACM, New York (2007)
38. Goldstein, J., Cajko, L., Oosterbroek, M., Michielsen, M., Houten, O.V., Salverda, F.: Digital games and the elderly. Soc. Behav. Pers. **25**, 345–352 (1997)
39. Hausknecht, S., Schell, R., Zhang, F., Kaufman, D.: Building seniors' social connections and reducing loneliness through a digital game. In: Helfert, M., Restiva, M.T., Svacek, S., Uhomoibhi, J. (eds.) Proceedings of the 7th International Conference on Computer Supported Education, pp. 276–284. Science and Technology Publications, Lda., Setúbal (2015)
40. van Bel, D.T., Smolders, K.C.H.J., IJsselsteijn, W.A., de Kort, Y.: Social connectedness: concept and measurement. In: Callaghan, V., Kameas, A., Reyes, A., Royo, D., Weber, M. (eds.) Intelligent Environments 2009: Proceedings of the 5th International Conference on Intelligent Environments, pp. 67–74. IOS Press, Amsterdam (2009)

41. De Schutter, B., Vanden Abeele, V.: Designing meaningful play within the psycho-social context of older adults. In: Vanden Abeele, V., Zaman, B., Obrist, M., IJsselteijn, W. (eds.) Fun and Games 10: Proceedings of the 3rd International Conference on Fun and Games, pp. 84–93. ACM, New York (2010)

42. Gajadhar, B.J., de Kort, Y.A.W., IJsselsteijn, W.A.: Shared fun is doubled fun: player enjoyment as a function of social setting. In: Markopoulos, P., Ruyter, B., IJsselsteijn, W., Rowland, D. (eds.) Fun and Games 2008. LNCS, vol. 5294, pp. 106–117. Springer, Heidelberg (2008). doi:10.1007/978-3-540-88322-7_11

43. Allaire, J.C., McLaughlin, A.C., Trujillo, A., Whitlock, L.A., laPorte, L., Gandy, M.: Successful aging through digital games: socioemotional differences between older adult gamers and non-gamers. Comput. Hum. Behav. **29**, 1302–1306 (2013)

44. Whitcomb, G.R.: Computer games for the elderly. In: CQL 1990: Proceedings of the Conference on Computers and the Quality of Life, pp. 112–115. ACM, New York (1990)

45. Mahmud, A.A., Mubin, O., Shahid, S., Martens, J.B.: Designing social games for children and older adults: two related case studies. Entertain. Comput. **1**(3–4), 147–156 (2010)

46. Zhang, F., Kaufman, D.: The impacts of social interactions in MMORPGs on older adults' social capital. Comput. Hum. Behav. **51**, 495–503 (2015)

47. Zhang, F., Kaufman, D.: Older adults' social interactions in MMORPGs. Games Cult. **11**(1–2), 150–169 (2016)

48. Nimrod, G.: Seniors' online communities: a qualitative analysis. Gerontologist **50**(3), 382–392 (2010)

49. Khoo, E., Lee, S.P., Cheok, A.: Age invaders: social and physical inter-generational mixed reality family entertainment. Virtual Real. **12**(1), 3–16 (2006)

50. Wollersheim, D., Merkes, M., Shields, N., Liamputtong, P., Wallis, L., Reynolds, F., Koh, L.: Physical and psychosocial effects of wii video game use among older women. IJETS **8**(2), 85–98 (2010)

51. Trepte, S., Reinecke, L., Juechems, K.: The social side of gaming: how playing online computer games creates online and offline social support. Comput. Hum. Behav. **28**, 832–839 (2012)

52. Nimrod, G.: The fun culture in seniors' online communities. Gerontologist **51**(2), 226–237 (2011)

53. Schell, R., Kaufman, D.: Cognitive benefits of digital games for older adults: strategies for increasing participation. In: Svacek, S., Uhomoibhi, J., Costagliola, G., McLaren, B.M. (eds.) Proceedings of the 8th International Conference on Computer-Supported Education, vol. 1, pp. 137–141. Science and Technology Publications, Lda., Setúbal (2016)

54. Astell, A.J.: Technology and fun for a happy old age. In: Sixsmith, A., Gutman, G. (eds.) Technologies for Active Aging, pp. 169–187. Springer, New York (2013)

55. Smith, A.: Older Adults and Technology Use. Pew Research Center, Washington, DC (2014). http://www.pewinternet.org/2014/04/03/older-adults-and-technology-use/

56. Gamberini, L., Alcaniz, M., Barresi, G., Fabregat, M., Prontu, L., Seraglia, B.: Playing for a real bonus: videogames to empower elderly people. J. Cyber. Ther. Rehabil. **1**(1), 37–48 (2008)

57. Buiza, C., Soldatos, J., Petsatodis, T., Geven, A., Etxaniz, A., Tscheligi, M.: HERMES: pervasive computing and cognitive training for ageing well. In: Omatu, S., Rocha, M.P., Bravo, J., Fernández, F., Corchado, E., Bustillo, A., Corchado, J.M. (eds.) IWANN 2009, Part II. LNCS, vol. 5518, pp. 756–763. Springer, Heidelberg (2009). doi: 10.1007/978-3-642-02481-8_115

58. Kari, T.: Explaining the adoption and habits of playing exergames: the role of physical activity background and digital gaming frequency. In: AMCIS 2015: Proceedings of the Twenty-first Americas Conference on Information Systems. AIS Electronic Library (AISeL), vol. 1, pp. 164–176. Curran Associates, Red Hook (2015)
59. Schell, R., Hausknecht, S., Zhang, F., Kaufman, D.: Social benefits of playing wii bowling for older adults. Games Cult. **11**(1–2), 81–103 (2016)
60. Jylhä, M., Saarenheimo, M.: Loneliness and ageing: comparative perspectives. In: Dannefer, D., Phillipson, C. (eds.) Handbook of Social Gerontology, pp. 317–328. Sage, London (2010)
61. Victor, C.R., Scambler, S.J., Bowling, A., Bond, J.: The prevalence of, and risk factors for, loneliness in later life: a survey of older people in Great Britain. Ageing Soc. **25**(6), 357–375 (2005)
62. Marston, H.R.: Digital gaming perspectives of older adults: content vs. interaction. Educ. Gerontol. **39**(3), 194–208 (2013)
63. Renaud, L., Sauvé, L., Kaufman, D., Duplàa, E.: Jouer en ligne chez les ainés améliore leur qualité de vie: résultats du jeu éducatif Pour bien vivre, vivons sainement ! [Online Game for Seniors to Improve their Quality of Life: Results of the Educational Game Live Well, Live Healthy!] CJC (in press)
64. Marston, H.R., Freeman, S., Bishop, K.A., Beech, C.L.: A scoping review of digital gaming research involving older adults aged 85 and older. Games Health J. **5**(3), 157–174 (2016)

Exergaming: Meaningful Play for Older Adults?

Eugène Loos[✉]

University of Amsterdam, Nieuwe Achtergracht 166, 1018 Amsterdam, WV, The Netherlands
e.f.loos@uva.nl

Abstract. Dutch historian Johan Huizinga [1] viewed games as a fundamental aspect of life. As long ago as 1938, he observed that, next to "homo faber" (man the maker), there is also the concept of "homo ludens" (man the player). The aim of this paper is to explore what we can learn from previously conducted empirical studies about the motivation and capability of older adults to use exergames. We were guided by the following questions. To which extent: (1) Are older adults *motivated to* play exergames and why is this the case?, (2) Are older adults *able to* play exergames and why is this the case? and (3) Can the *voices* of the older players be heard in the empirical studies on exergaming in later life? We conducted a narrative literature review to gain insight, not only into the factors relating to older adults' engaging in exergames, but also into the ways older adults themselves experience playing such games. To avoid a mainly functionalist perspective on play, we will also include hedonic aspects of playing exergames.

Keywords: Exergaming · Older adults · Meaningful play · Narrative literature review

1 Introduction

To the left is a *virtual* Tai Chi instructor, while on the right is a representation of an older adult on a computer screen trying to follow the instructions given by the instructor; the number of calories burned (3) are shown in the lower right-hand corner. The miniature table flag next to the screen is from the Dutch senior citizens organisation, ANBO, the host of this research project. The project itself is aimed at understanding how older adults make sense of exergames (Fig. 1).

The next picture shows the *real life* setting (Fig. 2):

The older adult is playing an exergame, which is also known as "active video game, interactive video game, activity promoting video game" [3, p. 10], consisting of an electronic device that allows one or more persons to play a game "requiring physical exertion or movements" [3, p. 10], while receiving immediate digital performance feedback on a screen (see also Primack et al. [4, p. 3]). Kooiman and Sheehan [5, p. 1] state that: "Until recently exergaming was seldom a topic of research. The technology that makes exergaming possible was not available to consumers. In 2006, Nintendo released the Wii gaming system (see also Brown [6]). This new system allowed for interactive physical movement beyond simple hand held play. The Wii system contained hardware and software that responded to movements of the player's body through the tracking of

© Springer International Publishing AG 2017
J. Zhou and G. Salvendy (Eds.): ITAP 2017, Part II, LNCS 10298, pp. 254–265, 2017.
DOI: 10.1007/978-3-319-58536-9_21

hand held controllers and movements of the lower extremities using floor based hardware".

Fig. 1. Screenshot [2]

Dutch historian Johan Huizinga [1] viewed games as a fundamental aspect of life. As long ago as 1938, he observed that, next to "homo faber" (man the maker), there is also the concept of "homo ludens" (man the player). Since then, as Bogost [7] pointed out, we have become as used to playing digital games in the living room as watching television (see also Juul [8] on "casual gaming). Several studies have suggested that playing exergames can, to some extent (the evidence tends to be limited), benefit the wellbeing of *children and young adults*, and hence could form a potential valuable therapeutic instrument (e.g. [9–13]). Other studies have demonstrated that *older adults* are interested in traditional games (e.g. [14, 15]). Hoppes et al. [14] conclude that "Games are a purposeful activity that hold high interest for older adults and consequently have significant value as therapeutic tools for occupational therapists" (p. 71).

Fig. 2. Older adult playing a Tai Chi exergame [2]

The purpose of this study is to explore the role exergames could play in promoting the wellbeing of older adults. In doing so, we were guided by the following questions. To which extent:

(1) Are older adults *motivated to* play exergames and why is this the case?
(2) Are older adults *able to* play exergames and why is this the case?
(3) Can the *voices* of the older players be heard in the empirical studies on exergaming in later life?

To answer these three questions, a narrative literature review was used to gain insight not only into the factors relating to older adults' engaging (or not) in exergames, but also into the ways *older adults themselves experience* playing such games. To avoid a mainly functionalist perspective on play, we will also include hedonic aspects of playing exergames [16–20]. As Iversen [20] states in her paper 'Play and Productivity: The Constitution of Ageing Adults in Research on Digital Games' in which she reviews studies on the impact of digital games for older adults' daily life:

"While there are exceptions, the ageing adults in the examined studies are largely portrayed as ailing, hesitant, in need of encouragement to do what is good for them as well as requiring the care of others. This outlook is coupled with a mainly functionalistic approach to the use of digital games, where the beneficiality of playing in terms of health maintenance is central rather than, for instance, enjoyment, pleasure, or creativity. Importantly, it is not only the researchers who invoke the beneficiality of digital games above other reasons for playing. To the degree that the ageing adults themselves are given voice, they often, too, focus on learning and training elements of digital games." (p. 14)

2   Method

The aim of this paper is to explore what we can learn from previously conducted empirical studies about the capability and motivation of older adults to use exergames for their wellbeing. As Kari et al. [21, p. 30] state: "Physical activity has been shown to have a positive impact on people's well-being. According to WHO [22], regular physical activity can, among others, reduce the risk of diabetes, cardiovascular diseases, depression, breast cancer, and colon [cancer]. It can also improve bone and functional health [23] and have other important health benefits."

Our focus was on exploring how older adults make sense - or do not make sense - of such games. We therefore conducted a narrative literature review [24], the results of which we present in Sects. 3.2, 3.3 and 3.4. We started our search with a recent literature review on the motivation and benefits of digital games for the elderly conducted by Cota and Ishitani [25] and with the paper 'Older Adults' Digital Gameplay Patterns, Benefits, and Challenges. Simulation & Gaming', published in 2016 by Kaufman et al. [26]. We then used the snowball method [27] to search for additional studies more specifically focused on *exer*games that would be suitable for inclusion. The results of the narrative literature review will not only used to present facts and figures, but also to give voice to the ways older adults themselves experience playing such games.

2.1   Results

According to the Entertainment Software Association ESA [28], the number of US older adults playing digital games is considerable: in 2016, 26% of all gamers are aged 50 or older. A similar picture emerges in the countries of Europe. According to Iversen [20], who refers to Bak et al. [29], Nordicom-Sverige [30, p. 2] and Vaage [31], "national surveys on the use of media in Norway, Sweden, and Denmark indicate that - varying between the countries - 5–12% of the population above 60 years of age play digital games at least once a day" (p. 2). Loos et al. [32] confirm this trend for the Netherlands: "New Zoo (the only source for reliable data on Dutch older adults' use of digital games) clearly shows that (...) in 2013 39% of the 51–65 year-olds play digital games." We agree with Pearce [33], who emphasizes that older gamers have "needs and interests that have gone ignored by both the mainstream game industry and the game press" (p. 142). In reviewing the literature in this area, we will therefore aim to gain insight not only into the factors relating to older adults' engaging (or not) in exergames, but also into the extent to which the voices of the older players can be heard in the empirical studies on exergaming in later life.

2.2   Giving Voice to Older Adults' Motivation to Play Exergames

Sherry et al. [34] conducted focus groups with four to eight participants (age 18 to 22, U.S. American undergraduate students, N = 96), adopting a Uses and Gratifications perspective [35]. They concluded that the dimensions arousal, challenge, competition, diversion, fantasy and social interaction were the motivations for the participants to play video games. In this section, we use their classification to gain insight into the motivations of older adults for playing – or not playing - exergames. We used the framework

Table 1. Why older adults play exergames

Dimensions:	Arousal	Challenge	Competition	Diversion	Fantasy	Social Interaction
1. Graves et al. [36]				+		
2. Aarhus et al. [37]			+	+		+
3. Brox et al. [38]						
4. Kari et al. [21]				+		
5. Omholt and Waerstad [39]	+		+	+		+
6. Heuvelink [40]	+	+	+	+	+	+
7. Heuvelink [41]		+		+		+
8. Skalsky Brown [42]			+	+	+	+
9. Cota and Ishitani [25]						+
10. Loos and Zonneveld [43]		+		+		+

developed by Sherry et al. (2006), adding column for dimensions (e.g. exercising) no included in their framework. The results are presented in Table 1. A dimension marked with a + means that the exergames were experienced as enabling wellbeing; a – denotes that this dimension was experienced as a barrier to playing.

The Table above shows that older adults rarely mentioned the motive dimensions in the framework developed by Sherry et al. (2006) of arousal, competition and fantasy; challenge is somewhere in the middle, while diversion and social interaction are mentioned most often (Table 2).

Table 2. Studies on age-related functional limitations due to …

Declining vision: difficulties in seeing and processing cluttered online content and difficulties screen reading	Charness [50]; IJsselsteijn et al. [51]; Lunn and Harper [52]; Billis et al. [53]; Vasconcelos et al.; [54]; Omholt and Waerstad [39]; Skalsky Brown [42]
Useful field of view: difficulties in detecting items in the periphery of screens	Bergstrom et al. [55]
Decreased attention division skills: difficulties in processing multiple forms of information (e.g., text and speech) simultaneously	Czaja and Lee [56]; IJsselsteijn et al. [51]; De Bruin et al. [57]; Aarhus et al. [37]
Hearing: difficulties in detecting high-frequency alerting sounds (beeps)	IJsselsteijn et al. [51], Czaja and Lee [58]; Billis et al. [53]; Omholt and Waerstad [39]
Visualmotor-coor-dination: difficulties in using a computer mouse track	Schueren [60]; Smith et al. [61]; Theng [62]; Diaz-Orueta et al. [63]; Vasconcelos, et al. [54]; Skalsky Brown [42]
Physical constitution: health issues such as arthritis, bad backs, reduced balance	Pearce [33]; Olmholt and Waerstad [39]
Cognition: older adults are much slower than youngers adults	Salthouse [64, 65]; Vercruyssen [66]; Brown and Park [67]; IJsselsteijn et al. [51]; Czaja and Lee [56]; Billis et al. [53]; Aarhus et al. [37]; Vasconcelos et al. [54]; Olmholt and Waerstad [39]; Skalsky Brown [42]

Lastly, we found that only four of the ten studies reviewed gave a voice to older adults, allowing them to explain why they do or do not play exergames. Let us listen to some of these older adults' voices:

Aarhus et al. [37]: *It isn't fun to do it alone. I'd rather have someone to talk to while doing it* (p. 113).

Omholt and Waerstad [39]: *If there is going to be any point in doing something together, it needs to be that you are enhancing each other. Like that you get a better result if you are cooperating* (p. 130).

Skalsky Brown [42]: *I enjoy it [digital games] and it's fun and it's okay to have fun… It's okay for me to relax and have fun and enjoy myself, but that's been a hard thing for me to let go of… that I can cut back on my work. I can slow down some and pick and choose and do what I want to do. So that has been the hard part for me, at this age* (p. 90).

Loos and Zonneveld [43]: *I experienced no pressure while playing, at the most a challenge because it's fun to play and because you're striving to achieve something and you see the scores rising, so that provides the challenge* (p. 335).

2.3   Giving Voice to Older Adults' Capability to Play Exergames

In Sect. 2.1 we saw that older adults in countries such as the USA, Norway, Sweden, Denmark and the Netherlands play digital games. Nevertheless, there are numerous older adults who refrain from doing so. Kari et al. [21, p. 11], in a study among Finnish (non)players of exergames in different age groups, found that: "In the two oldest age groups of 35– 44 years and 45 years or over, the three most significant reasons [for not playing an exergames] were (1) no interest, (2) prefers other forms of exercise, and (3) ownership (…). In the youngest age group, the reason no money was the most significant one. The most significant differences between age groups were in the reasons no money and no interest. No money was more significant the younger the age group was."

In a study among US older adults who did not play digital games, Skalsky Brown [6] found that lack of motivation was by far the most important factor: "Older adults who engage in digital games typically have at least a moderate degree of three domains that interplay with one another: motivation, experience with game-related technology, and functional ability [42]. To assess these domains among non-gamers, I interviewed persons over the age of 60 to explore whether or not any of these aspects surfaced as being deficient. Although most touched upon some concerns pertaining to their functional ability (declining) and limited tech experience, this paled in comparison to their level of motivation to play. Motivations varied widely among the older gamers, yet the strength of the individual motivation was strong enough to negate the other two domains if they were somewhat lacking. With the older non-gamers I interviewed, all but one stated that they simply had no interest in playing, as they believe they had better things to do with their time. Even when I posed the potential of playing as a means of intergenerational play (e.g., playing with grandchildren), this typically wasn't enough of a motivator, which surprised me." (personal communication, 10.10.2016)

Another point to take into consideration is the so-called "I"-methodology. Williams et al. [44] state that the majority of digital games designers (88,5%) are young (average age 31) male adults with highly developed ICT skills. Loos [45] and Loos et al. [46] argue that as typical young male adults, these game designers might have little understanding of the needs of older adults, causing them to fall into the I-methodology trap:

The I-methodology refers to a design practice in which designers consider themselves as representative of the users [47]. Akrich describes the I-methodology as the "reliance on personal experience, whereby the designer replaces his professional that by that of the layman" [47, p. x]. This is often an unconscious process: the designer is not aware of the fact that the user representation he or she is using resembles himself or herself. In contrast to the images created by designers and what people expect, implicit methods are often more powerful than explicit methods in shaping the design. [48, p. 41], Loos [45] and Loos and Romano Bergstrom [49] argue that young male game designers may specifically tend to overlook the aspect of age-related functional limitations due to the factors mentioned in the Table above.

We agree with De Schutter et al. [59] that "Designers must be aware of normative age-related changes and (1) how such aspects can affect technological interaction (e.g. reduced vision and hearing, slower pace, decreased attention division skills, etc., IJssel-steijn et al. [51, p. 1171])."

Of the studies presented in the Table above, quotes from older adults were only found in Skalsky Brown [42]:

I definitely use reading glasses when I game. I find I like to sort of recline when I game in my chair, sort of lean back like this and game. And I find I frequently have to sit up because I can't read the screen, so I have a lot more problems in some kinds of games. Some games are not very good at adjusting font sizes. So if you, say, run the game at high resolutions, the graphics look good. The graphics all scale so things are still the same size or just higher resolution, but all the text gets really small. And that can be very frustrating because I can't read it unless I lean up to the machine. So there are games out there where I actually can find it very hard sometimes to identify what's going on the screen because of the complexity that can now be shown with high-end... you know, high... modern processors and graphics quality (p. 104).

As age-related functional limitations occur with a certain regularity from age 75 on, and are common from age 85 and up [68], these must be taken into account by designers of exergames, to avoid having older adults who are motivated to play exergames (see Sect. 3.2) being hindered by factors due to biological ageing. De la Hera et al. [69] give a specific example of how it would be possible to counter the problem of decreased speed by suggesting that "in-game adjustable speeds might be an option to support older players for whom time-restricted games are a challenge (Nap et al. 2009) [70]."

3   Conclusions and Implications for Future Research

Finally, we answer the research questions formulated in the introduction, and sketch some implications for future research:

(1) To which extent are older adults *motivated to* play exergames and why is this the case?

Older adults are certainly motivated to play exergames. Not only do statistical data from countries such as USA, Norway, Sweden, Denmark and the Netherlands clearly show that a considerable number of older adults play digital games, our narrative literature review also shows which dimensions stimulate older adults to play exergames: diversion, social interaction and user friendliness.

(2) To which extent are older adults *able to* play exergames and why is this the case?

While older adults are definitely able to play exergames, game designers, who are often relatively younger, should take into account age-related functional limitations due to declining vision, useful field of view, hearing, visual motor-coordination and cognition. De la Hera et al. [68] offer a specific example of how the problem of decreased speed could be countered by suggesting that "in-game adjustable speeds might be an option to support older players for whom time-restricted games are a challenge (Nap et al. 2009) [70]."

(3) To which extent can the *voices* of the older players be heard in the empirical studies on exergaming in later life?

Only a very limited number of studies reviewed gave a voice to older adults, allowing them to explain why they do or do not play exergames.

Future research should give voice to the experiences of older adults playing exergames in natural settings, pay attention to differences in the group of older adults (e.g., age, gender, education) and compare the ways older adults make sense of exergames versus traditional approaches. We agree with Kari et al. [21, p. 12] who argue that: "Overall, finding the equilibrium between the hedonic and utilitarian aspects of playing exergames and delivering this message to potential customers seem to be the main challenges facing the exergame designers and the exergaming industry today and most probably also in the future."

Acknowledgement. This paper is based on the research report 'The impact of exergames: A panacea for older adults' wellbeing? Using narrative literature reviews to make sense of exergaming in later life' for the multi-methodological Ageing+Communication+Technologies (ACT) network (http://actproject.ca/). The author would like to thank ACT for financially supporting this research project (grant 895-2013-1018), the chair "Old and New Media in an Ageing Society" at the University of Amsterdam for the research time and Utrecht University Master's student Nynke Meijer for her help with the narrative literature review.

References

1. Huizinga, J.: Homo Ludens: A Study of the Play Element in Culture. Bacon Press, Boston (1938). (1950)
2. Zonneveld, A.: Wat beweegt ouderen? Kwalitatief onderzoek naar het gebruik van exergames onder ouderen (What moves Older People? Qualitative Research on the Use of Exergames among Older People). Unpublished Master thesis. Utrecht University School of Governance, Utrecht, The Netherlands (2013)
3. Oh, Y., Yang, S.: Defining exergames and exergaming. In: Proceedings of Meaningful Play, pp. 1–17 (2010)
4. Primack, B.A., Carroll, M.V., McNamara, M., Klem, M.L., King, B., Rich, M., Nayak, S.: Role of video games in improving health-related outcomes: a systematic review. Am. J. Prev. Med. **42**(6), 630–638 (2012)
5. Kooiman, B., Sheehan, D.D.: Exergaming theories: a literature review. Int. J. Game Based Learn. (IJGBL) **5**(4), 1–14 (2015)
6. Brown, J.A.: Digital gaming perceptions among older adults non-gamers. In: Zhou, J., Salvendy, G. (eds.) ITAP 2017, Part II. LNCS, vol. 10298, pp. 217–227. Springer International Publishing, Switzerland (2017)
7. Bogost, I.: Persuasive Games: The Expressive Power of Video Games. MIT Press, Cambridge (2007)
8. Juul, J.: A Casual Revolution: Reinventing Video Games and Their Players. MIT Press, Cambridge (2012)

9. Daley, A.J.: Can exergaming contribute to improving physical activity levels and health outcomes in children? Pediatrics **124**(2), 763–771 (2009)
10. Papastergiou, M.: Exploring the potential of computer and video games for health and phsyical education: a literature review. Comput. Educ. **53**(3), 603–622 (2009)
11. Biddiss, E., Irwin, J.: Active video games to promote physical activity in children and youth: a systematic review. Arch. Pediatr. Adolesc. Med. **164**(7), 664–672 (2010)
12. Peng, W., Crouse, J.C., Lin, J.H.: Using active video games for physical activity promotion. a systematic review of the current state of research. Health Educ. Behav. **40**(2), 171–192 (2012)
13. Baranowski, T., et al.: Games for health for children—current status and needed research. Games Health J. **5**(1), 1–12 (2016)
14. Hoppes, S., Hally, C., Sewell, L.: An interest inventory of games for older adults. Phys. Occup. Ther. Geriatr. **18**(2), 71–83 (2000)
15. Hoppes, S., Wilcox, T., Graham, G.: Meanings of play for older adults. Phys. Occup. Ther. Geriatr. **18**(3), 57–68 (2001)
16. Lieberman, D.A.: Dance games and other exergames: What the research says. (Internal publication) Santa Barbara University of California (2006). http://www.comm.ucsb.edu/lieberman_flash.htm
17. McLaughlin, A., Gandy, M., Allaire, J., Whitlock, L.: Putting fun into video games for older adults. Ergon. Des. Q. Hum. Factors Appl. **20**(2), 13–22 (2012)
18. De Schutter, B., Brown, J.A.: Digital games as a source of enjoyment in later life. Games Cult. **11**(1–2), 28–52 (2016)
19. Gerling, K., De Schutter, B., Brown, J., Allaire, J.: Ageing playfully: advancing research on games for older adults beyond accessibility and health benefits. In: Proceedings of the 2015 Annual Symposium on Computer-Human Interaction in Play, pp. 817–820. ACM (2015)
20. Iversen, S.M.: Play and productivity: the constitution of ageing adults in research on digital games. Games Cult. **11**(1–2), 7–21 (2014)
21. Kari, T., Makkonen, M., Moilanen, P., Frank, L.: The habits of playing and the reasons for not playing exergames: Gender differences in Finland. In: Lechner, U., Wigand, D., Pucihar, A. (eds.) The 25th Bled eConference "eDependability: Reliable and Trustworthy eStructures, eProcesses, eOperations and eServices for the Future" Research volume, 17–20 June 2012, Bled, Slovenia, pp. 512–526 (2012)
22. WHO: Health topics: Physical activity (2012). http://www.who.int/topics/physical_activity/en/
23. WHO: Global Strategy on Diet, Physical Activity and Health: Physical Activity (2012). http://www.who.int/dietphysicalactivity/pa/en/index.html
24. Lewis-Beck, M., Bryman, A.E., Liao, T.F.: The Sage Encyclopedia of Social Science Research Methods. Sage, London (2003)
25. Cota, T.T., Ishitani, L.: Motivation and benefits of digital games for the elderly: a systematic literature review. Revista Brasileira de Computação Aplicada **7**(1), 2–16 (2015)
26. Kaufman, D., Sauvé, L., Renaud, L., Sixsmith, A., Mortenson, B.: Older adults' digital gameplay patterns, benefits, and challenges. Simul. Gaming **47**, 465–489 (2016)
27. Ridley, D.: The Literature Review: A Step-By-Step Guide for Students. Sage, Los Angeles (2012)
28. ESA 2016: Essential Facts About The Computer And Video Game Industry (2016)
29. Bak, L., Madsen, A., Henrichsen, B., Troldborg, S.: Danskernes Kulturvaner. Danish Ministry of Culture, Copenhagen (2012)
30. Nordicom-Sverige: De första resultaten fra Nordicom-Sveriges mediebarometer 2012. Nordicom-Sverige, Göteborg (2012)

31. Vaage, O.: Norsk Mediebarometer 2012. Statistics Norway, Oslo (2012)
32. Loos, E.F., Kubinsky, P. Romero, M.: The misrepresentation of older players in the world of digital games: grandparents trying to play a digital game
33. Pearce, C.: The truth about baby boomer gamers a study of over-forty computer game players. Games Cult. **3**(2), 142–174 (2008)
34. Sherry, J.L., Lucas, K., Greenberg, B.S., Lachlan, K.: Video game uses and gratifications as predictors of use and game preference. Play. Video Games Motives Responses Conseq. **24**, 213–224 (2006)
35. Ruggiero, T.E.: Uses and gratifications theory in the 21st century. Mass Commun. Soc. **3**(1), 3–37 (2000)
36. Graves, L.E., Ridgers, N.D., Williams, K., Stratton, G., Atkinson, G.T.: The physiological cost and enjoyment of Wii Fit in adolescents, young adults, and older adults. J. Phys. Act. Health **7**(3), 393–401 (2010)
37. Aarhus, R., Grönvall, E., Larsen, S.B., Wollsen, S.: Turning training into play: embodied gaming, seniors, physical training and motivation. Gerontechnology **10**(2), 110–120 (2011)
38. Brox, E., Luque, L.F., Evertsen, G. J., Hernández, J.E.G.: Exergames for elderly: social exergames to persuade seniors to increase physical activity. In: 2011 5th International Conference on Pervasive Computing Technologies for Healthcare (PervasiveHealth), pp. 546–549. IEEE (2011)
39. Omholt, K.A., Waerstad, M.: Exercise games for elderly peope. identifying important aspects, specifying system requirements and designing a concept. Unpublished Master thesis. Norwegian University of Science and Technology, Department of telematics (2013)
40. Heuvelink, A., De Groot, J., Hofstede, C.: Let's Play. Ouderen stimuleren tot bewegen met applied games. TNO & Vita Valley (2014)
41. Heuvelink, A., Tak, Y.R., Van Meeteren, N.: The opinions of people in the Netherlands over 65 on active video games: a survey study. In: Schouten, B., Fedtke, S., Schijven, M., Vosmeer, M., Gekker, A. (eds.) Games for Health 2014, pp. 62–66. Springer, Wiesbaden (2014). doi: 10.1007/978-3-658-07141-7_9
42. Skalsky Brown, J.A.: Let's play: understanding the role and significance of digital gaming in old age. Theses and Dissertations–Gerontology. Paper 6 (2014). http://uknowledge.uky.edu/gerontol_etds/6
43. Loos, E., Zonneveld, A.: Silver gaming: serious fun for seniors? In: Zhou, J., Salvendy, G. (eds.) ITAP 2016. LNCS, vol. 9755, pp. 330–341. Springer, Cham (2016). doi: 10.1007/978-3-319-39949-2_32
44. Williams, D., Martins, N., Consalvo, M., Ivory, J.D.: The virtual census: representations of gender, race and age in video games. New Media Soc. **11**(5), 815–834 (2009)
45. Loos, E.F.: Designing meaningful intergenerational digital games. In: Proceedings of the International Conference on Communication, Media, Technology and Design, Istanbul, pp. 46–51, 24–26 April 2014
46. Loos, E.F, Simons, M., De la Hera, T., Gevers, D.: Setting up and conducting the co-design of an intergenerational digital game
47. Akrich, M.: User representations: practices, methods and sociology. In: Managing Technology in Society. The Approach of Constructive Technology Assessment, pp. 167–184. Pinter, London (1995)
48. Oudshoorn, N., Rommes, E., Stienstra, M.: Configuring the user as everybody: gender and design cultures in information and communication technologies. Sci. Technol. Hum. Values **29**(1), 30–63 (2004)
49. Loos, E.F., Romano Bergstrom, J.: Older adults. In: Romano Bergstrom, J., Schall, A.J. (eds.) Eye Tracking in User Experience Design, pp. 313–329. Elsevier, Amsterdam (2014)

50. Charness, N.: Aging and communication: Human factors issues. In: Charness, N., Parks, D.C., Sabel, B.A. (eds.) Communication, Technology and Aging: Opportunities and Challenges for The Future, pp. 1–29. Springer, New York (2001)
51. IJsselsteijn, W., Nap, H.H., de Kort, Y., Poels, K.: Digital game design for elderly users. In: Proceedings of the 2007 Conference on Future Play, pp. 17–22. ACM (2007)
52. Lunn, D., Harper, S.: Senior Citizens and the Web. School of Computer Science, Manchester (2009)
53. Billis, A.S., Konstantinidis, E.I., Mouzakidis, C., Tsolaki, M.N., Pappas, C., Bamidis, P.D.: A game-like interface for training seniors' dynamic balance and coordination. In: Bamidis, P.D., Pallikarakis, N. (eds.) XII Mediterranean Conference on Medical and Biological Engineering and Computing, pp. 691–694. Springer, Heidelberg (2010)
54. Vasconcelos, A., Silva, P.A., Caseiro, J., Nunes, F., Teixeira, L.F.: Designing tablet-based games for seniors: the example of cogniplay, a cognitive gaming platform. In: Proceedings of the 4th International Conference on Fun and Games (FnG 2012), pp. 1–10. ACM, New York (2012)
55. Bergstrom, J.C.R., Olmsted-Hawala, E.L., Bergstrom, H.C.: Older adults fail to see the periphery in a web site task. Univ. Access Inf. Soc. **15**(2), 261–270 (2016)
56. Czaja, S.J., Lee, C.C.: The impact of aging on access to technology. Univ. Access Inf. Soc. **5**(4), 341–349 (2007)
57. De Bruin, P.D.E., Schoene, D., Pichierri, G., Smith, S.T.: Use of virtual reality technique for the training of motor control in the elderly. Zeitschrift für Gerontologie und Geriatrie **43**(4), 229–234 (2010)
58. Czaja, S.J., Lee, C.C.: Information technology and older adults. In: Sears, A., Jacko, J.E. (eds.) Human-Computer Interaction: Designing for Diverse Users and Domains, pp. 17–32. CRC Press, Boca Raton (2009)
59. De Schutter, B., Brown, J.A., Abeele, V.V.: The domestication of digital games in the lives of older adults. New Media Soc. **17**(7), 1170–1186 (2015)
60. Schueren, B.: Can decline in intellectual functioning be reversed? Dev. Psychol. **22**, 223–232 (1986)
61. Smith, M.W., Sharit, J., Czaja, S.J.: Aging, motor control and the performance of computer mouse track. Hum. Factors **41**(3), 389–397 (1999)
62. Theng, Y.L., Dahlan, A.B., Akmal, M.L., Myint, T.Z.: An exploratory study on senior citizens' perceptions of the Nintendo Wii: the case of Singapore. In: Proceedings of the 3rd International Convention on Rehabilitation Engineering & Assistive Technology, p. 10. ACM (2009)
63. Diaz-Orueta, U., Facal, D., Nap, H.H., Ranga, M.M.: What is the key for older people to show interest in playing digital learning games? initial qualitative findings from the LEAGE project on a multicultural european sample. Games Health Res. Dev. Clin. Appl. **1**(2), 115–123 (2012)
64. Salthouse, T.A.: The processing-speed theory of adult age differences in cognition. Psychol. Rev. **103**(3), 403 (1996)
65. Salthouse, T.A.: What and when of cognitive aging. Curr. Dir. Psychol. Sci. **13**(4), 140–144 (2004)
66. Vercruyssen, M.: Movement control and speed of behavior. In: Fisk, A.D., Rogers, W.A. (eds.) Handbook of Human Factors and the Older Adult, pp. 55–86. Academic Press, San Diego (1997)
67. Brown, S.C., Park, D.C.: Theoretical models of cognitive aging and implications for translational research in medicine. Gerontologist **43**(1), 57–67 (2003)

68. Bouma, H.: Document and interface design for older citizens. In: Westendorp, P., Jansen, C., Punselie, R. (eds.) Interface Design & Document Design, pp. 67–80. Rodopi, Amsterdam (2000)
69. De la Hera, T., Loos, E.F., Simons, M, Blom, J.: Exploring the possibilities of intergenerational digital gaming. a narrative literature review
70. Nap, H., Kort, Y., IJsselsteijn, W.: Senior gamers: preferences, motivations and needs. Gerontechnology 8(4), 247–262 (2009)

Pass the Control(ler): Shifting of Power in Families Through Intergenerational Gaming

Sanela Osmanovic[✉] and Loretta Pecchioni

Department of Communication Studies, Louisiana State University, Baton Rouge, USA
{sosman3,lpecch1}@lsu.edu

Abstract. Interpersonal power, an influential force in relationships, changes over time. Older adults may experience diminishing power as roles in the family shift, leading to negative physical and emotional outcomes. In this study, we examined the potential of joint video gameplay to build or restore power in inter-generational family relationships. Participants (n = 102) were asked to play video games together over a period of six weeks. Participants completed a modified version of the Interpersonal Power Inventory [34] before and after the treatment and responded to a series of open-ended questions post-treatment. Results indicate an increase in referent, expert, and informational power for older adults, and an increase of referent and reward power for younger adults. These findings suggest that with careful design and consideration of current and potential players, video games have the capacity to positively impact families, and social life in general, by generating positive distribution of power among family members.

Keywords: Older adults · Video games · Interpersonal power · Intergenerational gaming · Family relationships · Interpersonal relationships

1 Introduction

Decades of scientific research have placed family communication in a prominent position as the source for a child's attitudes, beliefs, and behaviors. Family members provide a foundation for the development of self, serving as primary socialization agents in the acquisition of interpersonal skills necessary for social wellbeing and relationship development [1, 2], and health behaviors [3] to name a few. While the emphasis in research is usually placed on parent-child relationships, the family as a unit affects the child's development and one of these influential family relationships is that between a grandparent and a grandchild. Distinct due to the usually large generational gap, positive grandparent-grandchild relationships have been shown to produce positive psychosocial outcomes for both parties, where grandchildren gain a source of family values, beliefs, and history, as well as social support, and grandparents gain a source of pride and the feeling of being young again [4]. Studies have shown that young adults have a rather negative view of older adults, holding up the stereotypes of old age—deterioration of physical and mental faculties—undervaluing their competence, their perceived intelligence or abilities [5]. On the other hand, close relationships with grandparents have been found to generate positive stereotyping of older adults [6]. Thus, it is important to

© Springer International Publishing AG 2017
J. Zhou and G. Salvendy (Eds.): ITAP 2017, Part II, LNCS 10298, pp. 266–279, 2017.
DOI: 10.1007/978-3-319-58536-9_22

provide younger and older adults with an opportunity and means to create closer family bonds, improving not only their relationships, but also potentially affecting the views of and interactions among the generations on the whole. In this study, we examine the outcome of joint video gaming on intergenerational relationship development within families, especially as it pertains to an important element of relationships—the role grandparents and grandchildren play in each other's lives.

1.1 Aging Population and Family

Population aging is one of the sturdiest demographic trends of the past few decades, particularly in developed countries. According to the National Institute of Aging [7, p. 2], "in 2006, almost 500 million people worldwide were 65 and older. By 2030, that total is projected to increase to 1 billion—1 in every 8 of the earth's inhabitants." The rise in life expectancy combined with the decline in natality is making older adults an increasingly large fraction of the world's population [7], leaving a significant mark on the relationships and the structure of families. Three and even four generations are now in a position to spend significant parts of their lives together, with older adults having a much larger span of years to perform their family roles [8], and "intergenerational relationships…take on an added dimension as the number of grandparents and great-grandparents increase" [7, p. 10].Thus, it becomes increasingly important to form and maintain strong bonds among older and younger adults in families, especially since these relationships are typically involuntary and tend to be sacrificed on the altar of the all-consuming adolescence and newfound independence. As adolescents become involved in the unforgiving whirlpool of new romantic, academic, and social activities, family ties take a back seat and the frequency and intensity of relationships weakens, especially with the grandparents [9, 10]. One way to maintain important intergenerational relationships within families is through shared activities appealing to both sides of the age spectrum and, potentially, also creating closeness to further strengthen the bonds.

1.2 Video Games as a Relationship-Building Tool

The technological advancements of the past few decades have created a large gap among younger and older adults, alienating them from each other's worlds, and video games are a significant part of that process. While small and large technological miracles have undoubtedly made our lives easier, they have potentially also made a significant part of our daily social routine obsolete. Families and friends still gather, but now around television sets, or even more solitarily in the past decade, around computers, tablets and smartphones. Watching television, the activity on which families spend five hours a day on average [11], does not require nor necessitate much interaction [12]. Thus, those gathered around the screen may share the space but they share little else, either preoccupied by the program or otherwise immersed into social media on other devices and being only physically present. Such lack of communication and interpersonal interaction has led to weaker family ties, distant relationships, and even a breakdown of families and friendships [13].

However, as postulated above, there may be a solution, and it may lie in the technology itself—after all, as the old idiom says, we have to fight fire with fire. The fire of recovery in this case may lie in one of the most controversial and discussed outcomes of the technological golden age—video games. As the biggest entertainment industry in the world, perpetually drawing attention of young adults especially, video games may hold the potential to make people happier and help them maintain a healthy social life within and outside their families. Indeed, research has shown that video gameplay, especially in the circle of friends and family members, can yield positive physical and mental outcomes, as well as improve relationships and promote connectedness [14, 15]. Older adults are increasingly responding to their call as well—between 1999 and 2011, the number of gamers older than 50 has increased from 9 to 26% [16, 17]. Older adults, it transpires, enjoy demanding, intellectually challenging games with rich narratives, and large, involved communities in which they can take part—in short, they just want to have fun [18, 19]. And they especially enjoy the social side of gaming [20, 21], as a means to spending time together, requesting help and attention from children and grand-children, or something to structure the conversation with friends and family. In inter-generational family gaming, in particular, positive emotions such as happiness and enjoyment coalesced with – and stemmed from – the bonding, the conversations, the feeling of being closer to loved ones and of maintaining relationships across distances [15, 22–24].

1.3 Power in Interpersonal Relationships

The findings of the studies on older adults and gaming become especially important as previous research on aging has shown that the loss of habitual roles—being employed, being a spouse, an active parent—results in a feeling of loss of power in existing relationships [25]. According to the social power theory proposed by French and Raven [26], interpersonal power is a structural force in relationships that determines the potential of an individual to exert influence over another person.

Based on the types of influence, French and Raven [26, 27] specified six sources of interpersonal power in relationships:

- *reward power* - the ability to provide the other person with tangible or intangible things they desire (e.g., parents promising the child an ice cream if s/he gets ready for school on time).
- *coercive power* – the ability to punish (another source used frequently by parents, e.g., parents threatening to ground the child if s/he lies).
- *legitimate power* – the ability to influence based on one's formal position (e.g., a boss, a teacher, or a police officer)
- *expert power* – the ability to influence based on perceived special, valuable knowledge and expertise (e.g., a broker managing an investment portfolio).
- *informational power* – the ability to persuade the other person through information, or provide information in decision-making (e.g., a car mechanic providing guidance on what type of engine oil to use).

- *referent power* – the ability to influence based on the other person's admiration and identification with the individual (e.g., a celebrity marketing a product in an advertisement)

Power dynamics in interpersonal relationships fluctuate, with previous research showing that a disbalance or powerlessness can lead to negative physical and psychological outcomes, such as aggression and depression [28, 29]. Greater power equality, however, leads to higher relationship satisfaction [30].

As noted before, family power dynamics may change for older adults with the loss of habitual roles [25]. With the shifts of roles and perceptions during adolescence, older adults may experience weakening or loss of referent, expert and informational power, as well as coercive and reward power when it comes to younger adults in their families. Since interpersonal power signifies influence, the dwindling of power in existing relationships leads to feelings of insignificance and thus social isolationism, which in turn leads to poorer physical and mental health [31]. In two previous studies on intergenerational gaming, older adults have emphasized the satisfaction gained from being able to show their younger family members "that old age still carries knowledge and skill" [15, p. 139, 32]. Thus, intergenerational gaming may not only provide much needed social connection between grandparents and grandchildren, but also have the potential to restore some of the older adults' diminishing interpersonal power and influence within the family.

1.4 Purpose of the Study

How technology and society shape each other in a reciprocal process is the basic question of this study, since video games are both shaped by and shape the lives of those engaging in them. Digital technology has changed the fundamentals of how we interact and bond in society, taking away old and offering new infrastructure through which we can act [33]. Therefore, the aim of this study is to provide an interactional understanding of social video gaming within families. More specifically, what are the effects of social gaming on relationships, and what is its current and potential role as a social leisure activity in everyday family life? The main focus of the research presented here is the intergenerational social interaction in, around, and through video games, and how it potentially changes interpersonal power in family relationships.

2 Method

To fully understand player interactions and relationship development in and around video gameplay, data were collected through a multi-method, six-week study. The participants were recruited from two classes at a large Southern USA university after receiving approval from the appropriate Institutional Review Board. Each participant was asked to select an older adult, age 55 and above, from their immediate family circle who will consent to play video games with him/her at least three hours a week, either in a mediated or co-located setting. Younger adults received partial course credit while older adults did not receive any compensation for taking part in the research. The data from the dyads was collected over a period of six weeks. The duration of six weeks was determined based on the research findings of a pilot study implemented during the summer of 2016.

Participants. The sample consisted of 102 participants: 51 older adults, 32 females and 19 males ($M = 1.63$, $SD = .49$), ages 55–77 ($M = 60.96$, $SD = 5.34$), and 51 younger adults, 31 females and 20 males ($M = 1.61$, $SD = .49$), ages 17–28 ($M = 20.41$, $SD = 2.11$). The older cohort comprised 44 (88%) grandparents, (7.8%) parents, 1 (1.96) stepparent, and 1 (1.96) aunt. The younger cohort comprised 44 (88%) grandchildren, (7.8%) children, 1 (1.96) stepchild, and 1 (1.96) niece. All participants were from the United States.

Data collection. All participants were tasked with completing an initial questionnaire, comprising three sections. The first section contained questions on demographic information. The second section comprised questions on previous gaming experiences (e.g. "Have you ever played video games?", "What games do you play most frequently?"). The third section consisted of questions from the modified Interpersonal Power Inventory [34], measuring participants' perception of their gaming partners' power. Power parameters were measured on a seven-point Likert scale, with predetermined questions for *expert power* (n = 5; sample item: "_____ probably knows the best way to do the task"; $\alpha = 0.83$), *referent power* (n = 5; sample item: "I look up to _____ and generally model myself accordingly"; $\alpha = 0.73$), *informational power* (n = 5; sample item: "_____ gave me good reasons for changing how I did the task"; $\alpha = 0.81$), *legitimate power* (n = 5; sample item: "After all, he/she is my _____"; $\alpha = 0.78$), *reward power*(n = 5; sample item: "I like my _____and his/her approval is important to me"; Cronbach's $\alpha = 0.74$), and *coercive power*(n = 5; sample item: "It would have been disturbing to know that my supervisor disapproved of me"; $\alpha = 0.81$).

The questionnaire was distributed online, together with the digital consent form. The questionnaire took approximately 20 min to fill out.

Younger adults were tasked with, in cooperation with their older gaming partner where possible, selecting a video game or games they would play together. After completing the planned six weeks of playing video games at least three hours a week, participants were asked to fill out the closing questionnaire comprising of four sections. The first section contained questions on demographic information. The second section comprised questions on the games played during the study, location (collocated, remote, or other), and type of play (competitive, collaborative, or other). The third section consisted of the same questions from the modified Interpersonal Power Inventory [34] as listed above, collecting data on the participants' perception of their family members' power post-treatment. The fourth section was reserved for qualitative data collection, allowing the participants to provide detailed and personal accounts pertaining to their gaming experience during the six weeks of the study. The general questions asked the participants to reflect on their gaming ritual, the expectations, outcomes, and plans.

Data analysis. Quantitative data was then examined using pretest-posttest statistical analysis. The first author reviewed the qualitative data, identifying themes in the participants' answers, looking particularly for experiences pertaining to interpersonal power.

Exemplars were identified and placed in a draft file of findings. The second author then reviewed the draft findings and the two researchers discussed them at length. Agreement on the appropriateness of the exemplars was 100%. The researchers then discussed how these findings relate to previous research and agreed on their interpretations of motivations and behaviors which are reported in the next section.

3 Findings

Based on the responses from our participants, we answer our questions about if and in what ways intergenerational game playing may affect the perceptions of interpersonal power in family relationships. Both older and younger adults largely reported positive outcomes from playing video games with family members–while enjoyment was an important aspect, maintaining connections with each other and with the home, and training cognitive and physical abilities were repeatedly emphasized. The shifting of the roles and power was also noted, as both gained more insight into each other's lives, knowledge, and thoughts.

3.1 Older Adults

The majority of the older adults who participated in the study—33 or 64.7%—reported never having previously played video games. None of the remaining 35.3% identified as being active gamers, but stated they have either tried video games in the past or play sporadically. An overwhelming number of the participants (46, 90.2%), however, reported enjoying the experience of playing games with their family members over the course of the study, citing fun, gratification of spending time together, learning something new, as well as feeling happy for being involved and able to help their grandchild with a school assignment.

When it comes to changes in perception of personal power, the results of the paired t-test comparison of the Interpersonal Power Inventory [34] surveys taken before and after the treatment show some statistically significant outcomes. As displayed in Table 1, after the six-week gaming period, older adults perceived their younger family members as having more referent and reward power, with the latter experiencing the largest increase. The perception of younger adults' informational power increased as well and was on the margin of statistical significance with $p = 0.06$. The relevance of these results lies in how this change serves the building of the relationship. As older adults got to spend more time and got to know their post-adolescent family members better—or again—their identification with and admiration of the younger adult increased (referent power), and their perception of the potential for rewards gained from the relationship changed (reward power). They also began perceiving the younger adult as a source of valuable information (informational power), which could be anticipated given that the study generally required them to become proficient in a video game, and their counterparts were the ones who provided the knowledge.

Table 1. Results of pretest and posttest IPI for older adults and their perception of younger family members.

Variable/Results	N	Pretest-posttest diff. of M	SD	t	p
Expert power	51	.94	10.94	0.614	0.541
Referent power*	51	.80	2.26	2.537	0.014
Informational power	51	2.73	10.22	1.905	0.062
Legitimate power	51	1.43	10.83	0.944	0.349
Reward power**	51	8.57	9.25	6.615	0.000
Coercive power	51	-1.20	8.43	-1.012	0.316

Mean difference is statistically significant at: *$p < 0.05$; **$p < 0.01$

Qualitative data supports these findings, underlining the increase in the perception of younger adults' knowledge and admiration of their competence. As a female participant, age 57, explained:

> I was impressed with how much coordination playing the game required, and how good my grandkids were at it. I could never get my figure [character] to do what I wanted them to do, but it became easier to play after a few weeks. My grandson helped me with maneuvers that I had a problem with. It's amazing how quick a person can learn how to master video games, when they have a good teacher.

A female participant, age 63, added:

> I really enjoyed interacting with my granddaughter on the day to day basis, even just through the game. I disliked having to ask her to explain how to play the game several times, but she was very gracious about it and answered all my questions in great detail. Overall, I was impressed how well she was able to explain how to play and I eventually caught on and caught up.

A male participant, age 55, elaborated:

> I used to teach him how to play these games; and now he teaches me. We often spoke about his station in life and his plans, relationships with others and long and short terms goals and achievements. We spoke a lot about politics and life itself.

Conversations and communication were indeed in the center of most responses. More than two-thirds (70.9%) of the participants reported receiving more rewards from the relationship with the younger adult, whether through more frequent communication, getting to discuss topics they do not usually cover, spending more time together, or learning a new skill. A female participant, age 74, said:

> Playing games with my grandson keeps me sharp. We joke and talk and compliment each other on good moves. I love that he treats me as an equal and doesn't hold back. We are worthy opponents because I don't hold back on him either. Playing games has brought us closer, in my opinion. Doing this with [my grandson] is now one of the joys in my life. I feel that playing games together has taught us both different things, we have learned from each other and about each other.

A male participant, age 59, explained:

> Me and my stepson enjoyed playing video games together. We often talked about how life was when I was growing up. How things were so different. It was a great opportunity for us to catch up. We often joked about all kinds of different things, but we also had serious conversations

about how times are changing. It was really a great opportunity to connect with each other, and I can see us playing in the future.

Despite the positive outcomes, though, only about half of older adults (29, 56.9%) plan to continue with the activity and make it a part of their daily or weekly family routine. The cause of this lack of motivation to continue is clear—younger adults have considerably underestimated the technical abilities of their older family members, as well as their capabilities in mastering new forms of electronic entertainment. Such a response was to be expected; after all, even game designers "often view older users as 'old' first and 'users' much further down the proverbial list – somewhere after 'physically impaired', 'socially bereft', 'technically illiterate' and 'struggling to use unmodified versions of mainstream technologies'" [35, p. 27].Thus, younger adults largely selected games based on old tabletop models, such as *Trivia Crack* and *Words with Friends*. Such games have a minimal learning curve and are less involving, which in turn led to older adults soon becoming bored. As one of the older male participants, age 66, said:

If I found a more challenging version of the game that had harder levels of questions, it might be more compelling to play often.

Importantly, of the 29 older adults who plan to continue playing with their family members, 16 either played more challenging games, such as Wii games, or sport and racing simulations, or simply played a variety of easier games. While some concerns about game accessibility may be valid, as many older adults do dread the fast response time requirements and the complex control(ler)s, this concern should be addressed and removed as an obstacle in enjoying the many worlds and stories video games provide. We have discussed related implications of video game accessibility at a greater length and provided recommendations elsewhere [32].

To summarize, older adults who have for the most part never played video games before found the experience enjoyable, rewarding, and bonding. Joint play over the six-week period positively shifted their perceptions of younger adults' reward and reference power. Slightly more than half of the participants wish to continue playing video games with their younger family members. Those who did not express the desire to continue mostly cited boredom as they may have had not been challenged enough by the games selected by their younger family members.

3.2 Younger Adults

An overwhelming number of younger adults who participated in the study (44, 86.2%) reported playing or having played video games, of which 11 (21.6%) identified as active gamers who play six or more hours per week. The majority of the participants (40, 78.4%) reported having enjoyed the experience of playing games with their family members over the course of the study, referencing connectedness, sharing an activity with a family member, and fun.

For the perception of personal power, the results of the paired t-test comparison of the Interpersonal Power Inventory [34] surveys taken before and after the treatment shows statistically significant outcomes for three variables. As presented in Table 2, after the six-week gaming period, younger adults perceived their older family members as having more expert, informational, and referent power, with the latter presenting the largest increase.

Table 2. Results of pretest and posttest IPI for younger adults and their perception of older family members.

Variable/Results	N	Pretest-posttest diff. of M	SD	t	p
Expert power**	51	2.37	6.12	3.6541	0.0004
Referent power**	51	4.87	6.17	7.4430	0.0000
Informational power**	51	3.43	8.54	3.7864	0.0003
Legitimate power	51	.15	12.38	0.1112	0.9117
Reward power	51	.08	5.25	0.1413	0.8880
Coercive power	51	−2.59	17.09	−1.4323	0.1556

**Mean difference is statistically significant at $p < 0.01$

Much like with the outcomes of older adults' data, these results point to changes in and developing of their relationships. Spending time together, talking, and engaging in what is frequently considered a young person's type of activity with the older family member significantly affected younger adults' perception of their gaming partner. The admiration of and identification with the older adult increased (referent power) together with the perception of their family member's knowledge and expertise (expert power). They also began perceiving the older adult as a source of valuable information (informational power), perhaps, as the qualitative data suggests, owing to the conversations, exchange of stories, and the provision of advice.

Similar themes threaded through qualitative data as well, where younger adults expressed regard of their older family members' abilities in the acquisition of new skills. One female participant, age 20, stated:

> I was very surprised that she won every game. I guess I was surprised that my grandmother could be better at this game than me.

A male participant, age 18, had a similar experience:

> I was blown away by how quickly my grandmother grasped game, much faster than I expected from an older person. She was also much more enthusiastic than my brother, and also more competitive.

Others were not quite as flabbergasted, but did find their older family members' competences delightful. A female participant, age 19, explained:

> I liked that I had a great deal of time of playing a game with my grandmother; it kept her and I communicating. She learned how to send me messages through Word with Friends when I could not answer my phone; I thought it was adorable that she learned something I did not know about the game.

Older adults learned fast, and some "students" quickly overtook their "teachers," becoming the experts in the game. Still, younger adults enjoyed the experience, as one male participant, age 20, showed:

I expected playing video games with my father will be challenging, but after I taught him how to play the game, he got good fast and ended up giving me advice on how to play. I liked spending time with him, we would talk and catch up on how our day was while at the same time getting slightly competitive in an endearing way.

A female participant, age 18, added:

My experience playing video games with my dad was fun. We played Words with Friends. I liked having a constant action in the background that kind of forced me to communicate with him every day while I'm away at college because I usually don't. I'm closer to my mom, so I just communicate to him through her. It gave me a constant reminder to talk to him daily. We did talk a lot through the chat mode in the app. Every play, he would usually have a comment on what word I played or why I chose to place it where I placed it on the board. We compared strategies over Thanksgiving while I was home. It gave us something else to talk about while I was home, too. We were competitive and joked about it while playing. I like the challenge of beating him because he has become really good at the game and beats me most of the time.

Other participants also found enjoyment in the communication and conversations with their gaming partner, and learned more about them. As one male participant, age 19, explained:

I liked that we had the ability to communicate and actually play a game together. I feel like I learned more about how my mom thinks, I can understand better our different choices. I did not like that she was really close to beating me every time.

And when the study was over, some were even disappointed they will not "have" to play together anymore, as a female participant, age 18, conveyed:

I liked that we were playing together. It was a nice since the game put us both in position to have conversations about the game and other things in her and my life at the moment. When I told my grandma the six weeks were over, she was disappointed, and so was I. I enjoyed playing with her almost every day. She is about 900 miles away from me so it was a nice way to keep connected and share in each other's lives.

Even with such positive outcomes, only a bit more than one-third of younger adults (19, 37.3%) plan to continue playing video games with older family members, while the remaining 32 (62.7%) either do not plan to engage in gaming at all, or will play at the request of the older adult. Qualitative data shows that the source of this decision is three-fold: the aforementioned and still pervasive view of older adults as struggling with—or dismissive of—new technologies and thus not likely to play more involving games, the disinterest in the games seen as appropriate for older adults due to their simplicity, and the purported lack of time.

To summarize, younger adults found playing video games with their older family members a source of enjoyment, conversation, and social bonding. The six-week gaming assignment shifted their perceptions of older adults' expert, referent, and informational power, gaining more knowledge of their family members and respect for their abilities, skills, and expertise. Only about 37% of them, however, plan to continue gaming with these older family members. Those who did not express the desire to continue cite boredom with simple games, lack of time, and disinclination to put effort into teaching older adults more complex controls and games as main reasons.

Beyond this, an interesting overall trend emerged: for both groups, only coercive power or the perceived ability to punish decreased, while reward, expert, referent, legitimate, and informational power to varying degrees increased over the course of the study. This perhaps points to the relationships becoming closer and the influence of the ability to punish diminishing as each individual stands to offer and gain more positive outcomes from that specific bond.

It is important to note that biological sex, location (collocated vs. mediated play) or type of gaming (collaborative vs. competitive) were not significantly correlated with the difference in any of the sources of interpersonal power for either group. This shows that physical presence is not imperative in gaining benefits from intergenerational gaming, and whether players prefer collaborative or competitive games is not likely to affect the relational outcome of their joint activity.

4   Conclusion

In this study, we explored intergenerational video game playing among family members, seeking to find whether such shared activity provides a platform for building, maintaining, or balancing interpersonal power in relationships. Using a mixed-methods longitudinal design allowed us to collect both power-specific quantitative data and detailed qualitative accounts of the effects of long-term gaming on dyadic family relationships.

Corresponding to the findings of previous studies [15, 32], the social side of gaming, the opportunity for conversation and bonding, drew in both younger and older adults. The older cohort, largely consisting of individuals who have never played video games before, found the experience entertaining, interesting, and gratifying. The younger cohort enjoyed the opportunity to display their expertise to older family members while in turn discovering more about them and receiving the benefit of an interested listener and adviser. While they played video games, in the background their relationships changed. The shift we were looking for materialized in the upward slope of referent power for both sides, each person holding the other in higher esteem after the weeks of joint gaming. Younger adults also gained greater awareness of their older gaming partners' knowledge and capability, while older adults saw their relationships with post-adolescents as more rewarding.

Not all results were positive, and stereotypes of old age as lacking physical and mental acuity to master a new technology like video games influenced the study to a certain measure. Younger adults predominantly selected tabletop-based app games, something they perceived would be easy and accessible to their older family members. In turn, in a lot of cases, both sides at some point became bored with the electronic version of *Scrabble* they were playing, although not bored with the interaction. However, the longer the activity lasts, the less enjoyment both sides would get from playing the game, falling away and thus losing the interaction too.

The social power of video games lies in the backstage, in all the ropes and pulleys that work together to create the experience that is on the surface entertaining, but also affects heart, body, and soul of those who take part in it. The more we know about factors affecting the outcomes of social gaming, which ropes and pulleys work well together, the better we can put new technologies to use in the maintenance of the most important relationships throughout our lives.

5 Implications

With each year, the aging population grows. In the same time, especially in the Western world, the use of technology has led to people living in the same space but rarely spending "quality time together," actually interacting and bonding. While popular media continuously emphasize the importance of meaningful interactions among family members and friends for the strength of the relationships, resulting in calls for sharing meals without distractions, with the wide introduction of personal computers, tablets and smartphones, the silence and distance are becoming more pervasive. In order to enhance lives across generations, the same technology can be used to counter this effect. With careful design and consideration of current and potential players, video games have the capacity to positively impact families, and social life in general, bridging the distance and drowning the silence.

6 Limitations

As with any research, this project has its limitations. The number of participants was relatively small, and they were all from the United States. As a consequence, we should not over-generalize our findings. In addition, for younger adults the participation was a part of the course requirement, which may have impacted their perception of the project —must vs. want—and thus the level of their participation and satisfaction. Future research should address the limitations to this study, as well as examine more specific aspects of personal vs. impersonal powers and influences, examining the effect of existing relationships, family patterns, and emotional and physical states. These additional motivations are important to gaining a more complete picture of power shifts in family relationships and how video games can be used to help balance them.

References

1. Kunkel, A., Hummert, M.L., Dennis, M.R.: Social learning theory: modeling and communication in the family context. In: Braithwaite, D.O., Baxter, L.A. (eds.) Engaging Theories in Family Communication: Multiple Perspectives, pp. 260–275. Sage, Thousand Oaks (2006)
2. Koerner, A.F., Fitzpatrick, M.A.: Toward a theory of family communication. Commun. Theory **12**, 70–91 (2002)
3. Baiocchi-Wagner, E.A.: Future directions in communication research: Individual health behaviors and the influence of family communication. Health Commun. **30**(8), 810–819 (2015)
4. Lin, M., Harwood, J., Bonnesen, J.L.: Conversation topics and communication satisfaction in grandparent-grandchild relationships. J. Lang. Soc. Psychol. **21**(3), 302–323 (2002)

5. Kite, M.E., Stockdale, G.D., Whitley, B.E., Johnson, B.T.: Attitudes toward younger and older adults: an updated meta-analytic review. J. Soc. Issues **61**(2), 241–266 (2005)
6. Pecchioni, L.L., Croghan, J.M.: Young adults' stereotypes of older adults with their grandparents as the targets. J. Commun. **52**(4), 715–730 (2002)
7. National Institute of Aging: Why population aging matters: A global perspective (2015). https://www.nia.nih.gov/publication/why-population-aging-matters-global-perspective/over view-our-aging-world
8. Szinovacz, M.E.: Grandparent research: past, present, and future. In: Szinovacz, M.E. (ed.) Handbook on Grandparenthood, pp. 1–20. Greenwood Press, Westport (1998)
9. King, V., Elder Jr., G.H.: American children view their grandparents: linked lives across three rural generations. J. Marriage Fam. **57**, 165–178 (1995)
10. Roberto, K.A., Stroes, J.: Grandchildren and grandparents: Roles, influences, and relationships. Int. J. Aging Hum. Dev. **34**(3), 227–239 (1992)
11. The Nielsen Company: The total audience report (2015). http://www.nielsen.com/content/dam/corporate/us/en/reports-downloads/2015-reports/total-audience-report-q4-201 4.pdf
12. Kirkorian, H.L., Pempek, T.A., Murphy, L.A., Schmidt, M.E., Anderson, D.R.: The impact of background television on parent–child interaction. Child Dev. **80**(5), 1350–1359 (2009)
13. Segrin, C., Flora, J.: Family Communication. Routledge, New York (2011)
14. Przybylski, A.K., Mishkin, A.F.: How the quantity and quality of electronic gaming relates to adolescents' academic engagement and psychosocial adjustment. Psychol. Popular Media Culture **5**, 145–156 (2015)
15. Osmanovic, S., Pecchioni, L.: Beyond Entertainment: Motivations and Outcomes of Video Game Playing by Older Adults and Their Younger Family Members. Games Cult. Spec. Ed. Games. Ageing **11**, 130–149 (2015)
16. ESA: 2004 essential facts about the computer and video game industry (2004). http://www.theesa.com/facts/pdfs/ESA_EF_2004.pdf
17. ESA: 2016 essential facts about the computer and video game industry (2016). http://www.theesa.com/facts/pdfs/ESA_EF_2016.pdf
18. Pearce, C.: The truth about baby boomer gamers: A study of over-forty computer game players. Games Cult. J. Interact. Media **3**(2), 142–174 (2008)
19. Loos, E., Zonneveld, A.: Silver gaming: serious fun for seniors? In: Zhou, J., Salvendy, G. (eds.) ITAP 2016. LNCS, vol. 9755, pp. 330–341. Springer, Cham (2016). doi: 10.1007/978-3-319-39949-2_32
20. Gajadhar, B.J., Nap, H.H., de Kort, Y.A.W., IJsselsteijn, W.A.: Out of sight, out of mind: co-player effects on seniors' player experience. In: Paper presented at the Proceedings of the Fun and Games Conference, Leuven, Belgium (2010)
21. De Schutter, B.: Never too old to play: the appeal of digital games to an older audience. Games Cult. J. Interact. Media **6**(2), 155–170 (2011)
22. Costa, L., Veloso, A.: Being (Grand) players: review of digital games and their potential to enhance intergenerational interactions. J. Intergener. Relat. **14**(1), 43–59 (2016)
23. Zhang, F., Kaufman, D.: A review of intergenerational play for facilitating interactions and learning. Gerontechnology **14**(3), 127–138 (2016)
24. De la Hera, T., Loos, E.F, Simons, M., Blom, J.: Benefits and factors influencing the design of intergenerational digital games: a systematic literature review (submitted)
25. Krause, N., Herzog, A.R., Baker, E.: Providing support to others and well-being in later life. J. Gerontol. Psychol. Sci. **47**, 300–311 (1992)
26. Raven, B.H., French, J.R.P.: Legitimate power, coercive power, and observability in social influence. Sociometry **21**, 83–97 (1958)

27. French, J.R.P., Raven, B.H.: The bases of social power. In: Asherman, G., Asherman, S.V. (eds.) The Negotiation Sourcebook, pp. 61–74. HRD Press, Amherst (2001)
28. Steil, J.M., Turetsky, B.A.: Is equal better? The relationship between marital equality and psychological symptomatology. Appl. Soc. Psychol. Ann. **7**, 73–97 (1987)
29. Whisman, M.A., Jacobson, N.S.: Power, marital satisfaction, and response to marital therapy. J. Fam. Psychol. **4**, 202–212 (1990)
30. Aida, Y., Falbo, T.: Relationships between marital satisfaction, resources, and power strategies. Sex Roles **24**, 43–56 (1991)
31. Berntson, G.G., Cacioppo, J.T.: Psychobiology and social psychology: Past, present, and future. Pers. Soc. Psychol. Rev. **4**, 3–15 (2000)
32. Osmanovic, S., Pecchioni, L.: Family matters: the role of intergenerational gameplay in successful aging. In: Zhou, J., Salvendy, G. (eds.) ITAP 2016. LNCS, vol. 9755, pp. 352–363. Springer, Cham (2016). doi:10.1007/978-3-319-39949-2_34
33. Castells, M.: The Internet Galaxy: Reflections on the Internet, Business, and Society. Oxford University Press, New York (2001)
34. Raven, B.H., Schwarzwald, J., Koslowsky, M.: Conceptualizing and measuring a power/interaction model of interpersonal influence. J. Appl. Soc. Psychol. **28**, 307–332 (1998)
35. Östlund, B.: Design paradigms and misunderstood technology: the case of older users. In: Jæger, B. (ed.) Young Technologies in Old Hands: An International View on Senior Citizen's Utilization of ICT, pp. 25–39. DJØF Forlag, Copenhagen (2005)

A Mature Kind of Fun? Exploring Silver Gamers' Motivation to Play Casual Games – Results from a Large-Scale Online Survey

Daniel Possler[✉], Christoph Klimmt, Daniela Schlütz,
and Jonas Walkenbach

Department of Journalism and Communication Research (IJK),
Hanover University of Music, Drama, and Media, Hanover, Germany
{daniel.possler,christoph.klimmt,daniela.schluetz,
jonas.walkenbach}@ijk.hmtm-hannover.de

Abstract. Playing video games has become an increasingly popular activity among elderly people. In the present contribution, differences in the motivational profile of these "silver gamers" and younger player segments are investigated. Based on the socio-emotional selectivity theory and age identity theory, it was hypothesized that silver games and younger cohorts differ with respect to the importance of six motivational factors (i.e., challenge, escapism, relaxation, competition, friendship, and collecting/completism). Moreover, it was examined whether these potential age effects interact with gender dynamics in gaming motivations. A large online survey of German players of the casual online game "Farmerama"© (N = 26,109) was conducted. Data analysis revealed that the motivational profile of silver gamers did not differ markedly from the profiles of younger gamer cohorts. Substantial differences between older and younger players were only found for one of the analyzed motivational factors (relaxation). Moreover, no gender-by-age dynamics were identified. Hence, age identity theory and socio-emotional selectivity theory only displayed limited empirical explanatory power to predict specific motivational patterns among silver gamers. Rather, the findings of the present study suggest that older gamers' motivations to play games are mostly congruent with the reasons why younger people turn to gaming.

Keywords: Video games · Motivation · Silver gamers · Casual games · Gender · Age · Development · Farmerama

1 Introduction

Video games left behind the status of a niche medium that only attracts a small segment of society long ago. The great diversity of platforms, genres, and modes of playing that has evolved over the past decades has enlarged the games' audience dramatically [1]. Children and adolescents, the traditionally most loyal gamers, are now being accompanied by large segments of adult and 'silver gamers' [2, 3]. Similar to the diversification of age groups among which gaming has become increasingly popular, market

© Springer International Publishing AG 2017
J. Zhou and G. Salvendy (Eds.): ITAP 2017, Part II, LNCS 10298, pp. 280–295, 2017.
DOI: 10.1007/978-3-319-58536-9_23

data also suggests that gender discrepancies in the affinity towards digital games are vanishing or, at least, declining (cf. for instance [4]). Overall, playing video games is a popular leisure time activity and an integral element of the everyday media menu across virtually all segments of Western (and Asian) societies.

In order to explain the remarkable popularity of video games across such diverse audience segments, games researchers have proposed a variety of systematics to organize the many possible (or demonstrated) motivational attractors of video games and the reasons of pleasant gaming experiences [5–7]. Most of these concepts of game appeal claim psychological universality in the sense that the assumed motivational dynamics underlying game use apply – or can apply – to all gamers. However, scholars also demonstrated that the importance of these motivational factors differ among individuals. For example, motivational differences have been identified between male and female gamers, e.g., [8, 9]. Overall, however, past research on video game motivation has put much more emphasis on the relevance of game elements and gamer-game interactions than on person factors, that is, individual characteristics that gamers bring to the playing process. With the rise of new gamer types, silver gamers in particular [2], the question of individual differences in gaming motivation has acquired greater importance to research on games entertainment and popularity, e.g., [10–14].

While there are explorations on preferences of specific gamer segments, little is known about what different age groups of gamers find appealing in a given game. Past research suggests that the quality of entertainment experiences generated by playing the same game differs among player groups, such as age cohorts [15]. Hence, the question remains, whether older players display systematically different fun experiences and gaming motivations. Is there a 'mature' kind of video game enjoyment that is less appealing or even inaccessible to younger people who are going through earlier developmental stages and possess less life experience than silver gamers?

The present research aims at strengthening the individual difference perspective on game entertainment by exploring possible particularities in silver gamers' motivations to play video games. For this purpose, we review related evidence on aging and age effects in consumption of media entertainment and identify dimensions of fun that should theoretically differentiate the motivational profiles of silver gamers from younger player segments. Moreover, we discuss potential interplays between these age effects and gender differences in gaming motivations. A large-scale online survey among German casual gamers is then reported that tests our hypotheses (see Sects. 2.2 and 2.3) and answers our research question (see Sect. 2.4) empirically.

2 Theoretical Approaches to Aging and Entertainment Motivations

2.1 Motivations to Play Video Games

As video games grew more and more popular in the past decades, a large body of research investigated the motivational processes underlying individual decisions for playing, replaying, and continuing to play games. Multiple conceptualizations of players' motivations have been proposed. For example, based on self-determination theory,

Ryan, Rigby, and Przybylski [5] found that video games satisfy needs for autonomy, competence, and relatedness [16]. Yee [6] selected a different approach and construed a large set of possible gaming motivations mostly from the features of contemporary online games, such as MMOs. He organized the factorial structure of motives in three higher-order dimensions: achievement (e.g., mastering challenges), social (e.g., the joys of companionship in virtual adventures), and immersion (e.g., the suspense of game narrative). Sherry and colleagues [7], in turn, identified six different motives using qualitative focus group interviews: arousal, challenge, competition, diversion, fantasy, and social interaction. Again a different approach was proposed by Klimmt [17], who linked game features to psychological assumptions and suggested three experiential processes that drive video game entertainment: effectance (the sense of causing an impact on the game), suspense and relief (similar to affective responses to linear drama; cf. [18]), and identification with game characters or roles [19]. Still other explanations of video game motivation have been proposed, and this short overview already shows that it is hardly possible to unify all suggestions into one comprehensive model [20]. Hence, in the present paper, we selectively focus on those motivations for which age differences could be predicted by theoretical concepts of emotional development and age identity.

2.2   Emotional Development and Entertainment Gratifications

Past research in communication has identified multiple consequences of human development, including adult development and aging, for media consumption [21]. Of particular relevance in the present context of silver gamers are the dynamics of entertainment use during adult development. Descriptive market research has consistently shown cohort differences in consumption of television entertainment, for instance [21]. Theoretical approaches apply concepts from developmental psychology and acknowledge changes in affective needs and emotional self-regulation as drivers behind the entertainment preferences that shift over the life course. Specifically, Bartsch [22] follows previous studies in building on socio-emotional selectivity theory [23] that explains changes in people's social goal orientations as effect of changing perceptions of one's remaining lifetime. When future time is perceived to be limited (which is often the case with older individuals [23, 24]), people prioritize emotional goals, whereas goals of knowledge acquisition are valued to a greater extent as long as time is perceived as unlimited (i.e., the typical perception of younger individuals [23, 24]). As a consequence, older people prefer states of emotional positivity and balance (e.g., by avoiding rather than engaging in conflict), whereas younger people display greater readiness to go through aversive experiences, which is adaptive when coping skills can be developed from such experiences.

An application of this perspective of socio-emotional selectivity theory [23] to video game motivations suggests that silver gamers are less likely than younger players to seek playing experiences that may result in aversive affects. This can be related to challenging situations featured in many video games (e.g., time pressure to deliver performance). Mastering challenges is a strong driver of enjoyment [25] and, thus, an important motive of video game use [6, 7, 17]. However, the risk of failure may result in suspense and stress during playing [17] and a negative outcome of a challenge is likely to result in aversive emotional experiences such as frustration [25]. Although past studies found, that being challenged is an important motivational factor for playing games for elderly players [11–13], it could be expected that younger cohorts accept the potential aversive elements of challenges to a larger extent. Hence, elderly gamers should evaluate facing challenges as a less important reason to use video games than younger players.

In contrast, silver gamers should value relaxing experiences that provide recovery from aversive conditions more than younger cohorts (e.g., contemplative experiences that are free of time pressure, do not involve immediate risks of failure or loss of achieved progress, and enable mild cognitive stimulation). Hence, the escapist function of games – experiencing the pleasure of temporarily evading real-life problems and sorrows [6, 7, 17] – should be a more important attractor for elderly players. Similarly, to experience relaxation while playing games [6] should attract silver gamers more than younger cohorts. In line with these hypotheses, first exploratory studies found that relaxation and escapism from daily sorrows and duties are important reasons why elderly players use games [10, 12].

- H1. Silver gamers find challenge a less important motivation to play video games than younger players.
- H2. Silver gamers report escapism to be a more important motivation to play video games than younger players.
- H3. Silver gamers find relaxation a more important motivation to play video games than younger players.

Socio-emotional selectivity theory also suggests that older adults are more cautious with their personal relationships in the sense of maintaining positive interpersonal contacts, whereas younger people are relatively more willing to put relationships at risk for other purposes [23]. Bartsch [22] concludes that older people prefer media entertainment that offers positive, non-aversive affective experiences and enables pleasant shared experiences with relevant others. In contrast, younger people would be more likely to also accept challenging, emotionally ambiguous, even aversive entertainment fare that does not necessarily need to contribute to positive peer relations [26, 27].

This element from developmental theory relates to competition motivations in video game use. Many games contain elements of fierce competition, which is often organized as player versus player contests [25, 28]. Older adults should find competitive gaming experiences less enjoyable, as they would threaten their positive interpersonal relationships with co-players or increase aversive elements of stress during game play. Hence, competition should be a less important motivational factor for video game play for elderly users.

- H4. Silver gamers find competition a less important motivation to play video games than younger players.

By the same token, silver gamers should seek playing experiences that involve positive interplayer relations, such as receiving from and giving support to co-players or achieving a sense of community through joint play [6]. In line with these assumptions,

Osmanovic and Pecchino [10] found in an exploratory study that older gamers prefer social collaboration in video games to social competition. Younger players, in contrast, should be less inclined to preserve positive social experiences (see above).

- H5. Silver gamers find positive friendship experiences a more important motivation to play video games than younger players.

2.3   Age Identity and the Place of Entertainment in Life

An alternative theoretical perspective on explaining age differences in entertainment preference looks at media users' self-concept. Harwood [29] argues that media audiences seek for messages that reaffirm their age identity, which means that preferred media content is intended to demonstrate the "prevalence and social significance of their age group". Such experiences of significance support "a positive age identity" [30]. For the case of TV viewing, these considerations have been applied to explain audiences' preference of media characters of similar age; however, the logics of age identity reaffirmation can also be expected to apply to entire media genres or even media types such as video games.

This might imply that players are likely to enjoy gaming experiences that 'fit to' or reaffirm their age identity. While younger players would perceive intense gaming 'action' as well-compatible to their age identity (such as competition, assertiveness, and conflict in games [31]; see the reasoning behind H4 above), older players will rather strive for a gaming experience that is connected to patience, wisdom, and balance – attributes that match well with their self-concept of being experienced and mature. While specific genres fit better to the former or latter intention of playing games (e.g., fast shooter games for the young, puzzle games for older adults [32]), some games with a universally broad appeal may offer incentives for affirming the age identity of different cohorts or generations. In online casual games, for example, patience-focused game play such as collecting items or improving one's base (completism) should, from an age identity perspective, be a more important attractor for older players than for younger gamers.

- H6. Silver gamers find collecting/completism a more important motivation to play video games than younger players.

2.4   Interplay of Age and Gender Differences?

Interestingly, the proportion of females attracted to games has been rising in recent years – especially in older cohorts [4, 33]. Past research has identified substantial gender differences in gaming motivations. Females were found on average to prefer socializing over competition in video games, and were much less attracted by violent content and genres, e.g., [8, 9]. Therefore, explorations of the gaming motivations of silver gamers should also take up the gender perspective and investigate possible interactions between the age effects predicted beforehand and gender dynamics on players' motivations.

So far, little is known about possible interplays of age and gender on players' motivations. It could be assumed that gender patterns of video game motivations are rather stable and do not differ among age groups. Hence, silver gamers may mirror gender differences known from younger cohorts (e.g., females' dislike of competition). However, one could also expect age-gender dynamics. For instance, the combined effects of gender and age identity could render competitive game play particularly repelling for older female players or bring unknown patterns of gratifications sought to the gaming experience. As this does not allow for a clear prediction of the interplay of age and gender on gamers' motivations we decided to explore the gender perspective based on an open research question.

- RQ1. How does the interplay between age and gender influence players' video gaming motivations?

3   Method

During one week in the year 2011, we conducted a multilingual online survey with users of the international casual game "Farmerama"©. To reach out to the game's player base, we cooperated with BigPoint, the German production company of the game. Gamers were invited to the survey by a pop up window that appeared at the end of a game session. Participants were offered raffle tickets to win one out of five "Farmerama" donkey barns (i.e., improvements of their virtual in-game farm). Altogether, 49,973 gamers completed the full survey. However, in the analysis reported here, we focused on participants of the largest nationality group in the data, German users, in order to prevent a potential bias resulting from cross-cultural assessment [34]. Moreover, several cases had to be omitted from further analysis due to unrealistic completion time, implausible response patterns and high numbers of missing values. In addition, few participants reported their age above 70 years. These cases were also excluded from analysis, because they were considered a special group of players that deserves specific attention; however, the case number in the sample was too small to do justice to this group. Ultimately, N = 26,109 complete cases remained for analysis. The sample consisted of 17,579 female (67%) and 8,530 male participants (33%) with an average age of 37.1 years (SD = 13.3; range: 10–70 years).

We captured possible gaming motives by asking about the personal importance of several reasons to play. While the original item list was relatively long, the present research is focused on analyzing the data for selected single-item measures of those dimensions that were hypothesized to contribute to a specific gratification pattern of silver gamers (i.e., challenge, escapism, relaxation, competition, friendship, collecting/completism, see H1 to H6). Items (see Table 1) were partially adapted from existing studies [6, 7] and partially created for the purpose of the present survey. All items were customized to the "Farmerama" case of investigation. We applied a five-point Likert-type scale from 1 'completely disagree' to 5 'completely agree'.

The original questionnaire included further scales that are not relevant here, and demography questions, from which self-reports on gender and age (in years) were taken to explore age and gender effects on video game motivation. In order to be able to compare the importance of the motivational factors between older gamers and younger

Table 1. Items used to assess the importance of reasons to play and their origin (translations of original German wording)

Motivational factor	Item	Item based on
Challenge	I enjoy planning exactly what I grow and built	[7]
Escapism	I play Farmerama because it distracts me from my sometimes stressful day	[6]
Relaxation	I play Farmerama to relax	[6]
Competition	It is important to me to have a higher level than my friends	[6, 7]
Friendship	I play Farmerama because so I can play with my friends	[7]
Collecting/completism	I like to collect tools, different crops and items	-/-

cohorts, players' age was categorized in three groups: adolescents, adults and silver gamers. Although no commonly agreed definition for silver gamers has been proposed, users in their late fifties have mostly been categorized as elderly players, e.g., [10]. Hence, "silver gamers" were defined in the present contribution as players with an age of 55 and above. In addition, adolescents were defined as players with an age of 10 to 24, leaving the age-span of 25 to 54 years for adults.

4 Results

Prior to testing our hypotheses, we investigated the descriptive importance of the motivational factors (see Table 4). Across the entire sample, participants rated collecting/completism to be the most important reason to play "Farmerama" (M = 4.29; SD = 0.92), followed closely by challenge (M = 4.24; SD = 0.93), relaxation (M = 4.14; SD = 1.04) and escapism (M = 4.06; SD = 1.09). Friendship also seems to be a driver of playing "Farmerama", although comparably less important, as participants' mean score of agreement is located just above the scale center of 3 (M = 3.11; SD = 1.41). In contrast, competition turned out as less relevant motivational driver underlying the use of "Farmerama" (M = 2.45; SD = 1.39).

4.1 Effect of Age and Gender Across Motivational Factors

In a next step we calculated a MANOVA to investigate the overall effect of age and gender across the six motivational factors. Challenge, escapism, relaxation, competition, friendship, collecting/completism served as dependent variables, age group (adolescents vs. adults vs. silver gamers) as well as gender were included as independent variables. The multivariate test showed significant main effects for both age (F $(12, 52198) = 134.120$; $p < .001$) and gender (F$(6, 26098) = 70.794$; $p < .001$) as well as a significant interaction effect of both factors (F$(12, 52198) = 19.009$; $p < .001$). While significance is not a very meaningful indicator of the effects' relevance given the large sample size (n = 26,109), the partialized effect sizes (eta^2) indicate that at least both main effects are small but substantial (see Table 2). In contrast, the interaction

Table 2. Multivariate main and interactions effects of age and gender across all motivational factors: challenge, escapism, relaxation, competition, friendship, collecting/completism (MANOVA using Pillai's Trace; N = 26109)

Effect	Df	F	Part. η^2	p
Age group	12	134.120	.030	<.001
Gender	6	70.794	.016	<.001
Age group x gender	12	19.009	.004	<.001

effect explained less than half a percent of the variance across all motivational factors (part. η^2 = .004) and is therefore not substantial. Thus, the following analysis will focus only on the main effects of age and gender.

4.2 Effects of Age and Gender in Detail

To further explore these effects and test our hypotheses, six univariate ANOVAs were conducted – one for each motivational factor (see Table 3). Given the space constraints and the large sample size, we will only focus on substantial effects (partial eta-squared of nearly .01 or more).

Table 3. Main and interaction effects of age and gender on each motivational factor (ANOVA; N = 26,109)

Motivational factor	Effect	Df	F	Part. η^2	p
Challenge	Age group	2	16.037	.001	<.001
	Gender	1	0.764	.000	n.s.
	Age group x gender	2	29.501	.002	<.001
Escapism	Age group	2	46.024	.004	<.001
	Gender	1	87.520	.003	<.001
	Age group x gender	2	39.911	.003	<.001
Relaxation	Age group	2	484.265	.036	<.001
	Gender	1	88.559	.003	<.001
	Age group x gender	2	30.337	.002	<.001
Competition	Age group	2	23.575	.002	<.001
	Gender	1	189.139	.007	<.001
	Age group x gender	2	1.613	.000	n.s.
Friendship	Age group	2	130.903	.010	<.001
	Gender	1	14.323	.001	<.001
	Age group x gender	2	63.892	.005	<.001
Collecting/completism	Age group	2	34.575	.003	<.001
	Gender	1	61.976	.002	<.001
	Age group x gender	2	42.956	.003	<.001

Challenge: In contrast to our prediction (H1) no meaningful age or gender differences were found for challenge (see Table 3). Rather the challenge motivation can be described as remarkably stable across the age groups and both genders. Hence, hypothesis 1 was not supported.

Escapism: Likewise, no substantial age and/or gender dynamics were obtained for the motivation to experience escapism. Thus, hypothesis 2 had to be rejected as well.

Relaxation: While again no robust main effect of gender was found, the main effect of the age groups is small but substantial (F(2, 26103) = 484.265, p < .001, part. η^2 = .036). Post-hoc tests (Tamhane-T2) revealed that silver gamers (55-70 years) rated the relaxation motivation as significantly more important (M = 4.50; SD = 0.84) than adults (25–54 years; M = 4.21; SD = 0.99) and adolescents (10–24 years; M = 3.72; SD = 1.18; see Table 4). In addition, the difference between adults and adolescents is significant as well. Thus, in line with our hypothesis 3, the importance of relaxation as reason to play "Farmerama" increases with participants' age and is more central for silver gamers than for younger player cohorts.

Table 4. Descriptive statistics for the main and interaction effects of age and gender on each motivational factor

Motivational factor		Adolescents	Adults	Silver gamers	Total
		M (SD)	M (SD)	M (SD)	M (SD)
Challenge	Female	4.16 (0.99)	4.25 (0.91)	4.42 (0.88)	4.25 (0.92)
	Male	4.31 (0.96)	4.20 (0.91)	4.27 (0.95)	4.23 (0.93)
	Total	4.23 (0.98)	4.23 (0.91)	4.38 (0.91)	4.24 (0.93)
Escapism	Female	3.86 (1.18)	4.18 (1.03)	4.20 (1.15)	4.13 (1.07)
	Male	3.89 (1.17)	3.92 (1.11)	3.85 (1.20)	3.90 (1.13)
	Total	3.87 (1.18)	4.10 (1.06)	4.09 (1.18)	4.06 (1.09)
Relaxation	Female	3.72 (1.16)	4.28 (0.95)	4.59 (0.78)	4.23 (1.00)
	Male	3.71 (1.19)	4.02 (1.04)	4.32 (0.92)	3.97 (1.09)
	Total	3.72 (1.18)	4.21 (0.99)	4.50 (0.84)	4.14 (1.04)
Competition	Female	2.45 (1.38)	2.28 (1.34)	2.43 (1.44)	2.32 (1.36)
	Male	2.82 (1.49)	2.69 (1.40)	2.72 (1.43)	2.72 (1.43)
	Total	2.62 (1.44)	2.40 (1.37)	2.52 (1.45)	2.45 (1.39)
Friendship	Female	3.14 (1.41)	3.03 (1.42)	3.32 (1.47)	3.07 (1.43)
	Male	3.60 (1.3)	3.00 (1.34)	3.19 (1.41)	3.17 (1.36)
	Total	3.36 (1.38)	3.02 (1.40)	3.28 (1.45)	3.11 (1.41)
Collecting/completism	Female	4.32 (0.94)	4.33 (0.88)	4.35 (0.94)	4.33 (0.90)
	Male	4.39 (0.90)	4.15 (0.95)	4.05 (1.03)	4.21 (0.95)
	Total	4.35 (0.92)	4.27 (0.91)	4.26 (0.98)	4.29 (0.92)

Competition: No substantial differences between the age groups were found for the motive competition, which disconfirms hypothesis 4. However, a small main effect of gender was identified (F(1, 26103) = 189.139; p < .001, part. η^2 = .007). Converging with past research [8], male players rated the importance of competition slightly higher (M = 2.72; SD = 1.43) than female players (M = 2.32; SD = 1.36; see Table 4).

Friendship: While the main effect of gender was not substantial for the motive friendship, we found a small but robust main effect of age (F(2, 26103) = 130.903; p < .001, part. η^2 = .01). Interestingly and in contrast to our assumptions (H5) a post-hoc analysis (Tamhane T-2) revealed that friendship is an equally important driver for playing "Farmerama" for silver gamers (M = 3.28; SD = 1.45) and adolescents (M = 3.36, SD = 1.38; see Table 4). However, both groups rated this motive to be more important than adults (M = 3.02; SD = 1.40). Hence, opposed to our prediction in hypothesis 5, the motive is important for rather young and old players but comparably less for adults.

Collecting/Completism: Similar to challenge and escapism, no robust age and/or gender effect on the importance of the motivational factor "collecting/completism" was found. Hence, in contrast to our prediction in hypothesis 6, silver gamers found this motivation equally important as younger players.

5   Conclusion and Discussion

The present study utilized a massive data set of casual game players from Germany to investigate differences in gamers' motivational preferences between adolescents, adults, and silver gamers as well as between males and females. "Farmerama", a very popular casual online game, served as case of investigation. As expected, the results of the MANOVA reveal that gamers' motivation differ across age and gender, which resonates with past findings [8, 9, 32]. Interestingly, the motivational profile of silver gamers did not stand out as sharply against the profiles of younger gamer cohorts as one may have assumed, however.

5.1   Age and Recovery, Emotional Balance and Stress Motivations

Mixed results were found for the motivations related to recovery and emotional balance (i.e., relaxation, collecting/completism and escapism) as well as stress (i.e., challenges). Relaxation was connected closely to age. Older players find in casual games a welcomed opportunity to recover from daily stress or exhaustion, whereas this relaxation is less important for adults and even less for younger players. This finding converges with assumptions that research on non-interactive entertainment has derived from socio-emotional selectivity theory and age identity theory, as (a) older people value leisure time experiences that provide emotional balance and well-being more than younger individuals do [26], and (b) a relaxed, patient, non-hectic mode of playing is perceived to match with age identity of elderly people. Interestingly and in contrast to these theoretical perspectives, no age differences were found for the motivational factor "challenge". Hence, although elderly players evaluate relaxation as a more important motivational driver of playing "Farmerama" than younger users do, this does not imply that silver gamers regard demands and challenges as unimportant attractors of playing "Farmerama". In addition, no substantial age dynamics were revealed for the motivations "escapism" and "collecting/completism", which are also connected to balance and recovery and should 'fit to' the age identity of elderly players.

Two explanations could be found for these mixed findings. First, one could argue that age differences regarding "relaxation" indeed reflect age-specific preference of entertainment media. The missing effects of age on the motivational factors "challenge", "collecting/completism" and "escapism" could then be explained with the "universality" of these motives. All three motives could be understood as part of the core appeal of casual games like "Farmerama" [1, 35, 36]. This means that all players rate these motivations as important drivers for playing the game. Casual games are 'fun for all', because they offer interactive experiences of collecting virtual objects and solving (light, non-consequential) problems. Such pleasant, mildly active experiences can also function effectively for escapism purposes. Henning and Vorderer [37] argued that television can help particularly individuals with low need for cognition to avoid aversive states of cognitive demand – video games may help other audience segments that actually do not dislike thinking to experience escapism.

Second, an alternative explanation would be that socio-emotional selectivity theory and age identity theory are not useful to explain motivations related to recovery, emotional balance and stress. The effect we found for "relaxation" may then be explained with age dynamics in life circumstances and physical condition that could motivate older players to prioritize recovery-serving activities. For adults and even more for elderly people, work demands and personal responsibility burdens are typically higher than for younger people, which comes with greater needs for recovery, e.g., [38]. As casual games are often played during breaks or as a procrastination activity, the observed greater affinity of older players to the recovery motivation may thus be specific to this game genre and reflect effects of workload and occupational stress rather than age-specific preferences in entertainment quality, see [39, 40]. Given the multiple pathways of explanation and interesting implications for applied health interventions, the observed age dynamics in the recovery motivation to play a casual game certainly warrants further research.

5.2 Age and Social Motivation

Two social motivations to play "Farmerama" were addressed in the present study – the joys of playing together with friends and the positive experience of competing with peers (competition). While both factors do not seem to function as main drivers of "Farmerama" use (average scores range below those obtained for the factors discussed above), an age effect was observed for "friendship". Adolescents and silver gamers value the social component of playing "Farmerama" to a higher extent than adults.

The comparably high importance of the motive for silver gamers is in line with the socio-emotional selectivity theory: Elderly players seek media content that allows them to maintain and strengthen positive interpersonal relationships with co-players. In contrast, the relatively high importance of this motive for adolescents is surprising. A media socialization effect may explain this pattern. Casual games can be treated as a multiplayer experience, but they also work as single-player activity. Currently, young 'digital natives' who grow up with an online-networked media environment may regard multiplayer gaming as a more natural, intuitive pattern of game use and thus be more able to take advantage of social entertainment than older players. In contrast, adults may have adopted "Farmerama" as a single-player game as they are neither psychologically motivated to play in a multiplayer mode (like silver gamers), nor regard multiplayer gaming as default mode of playing online games (like adolescents).

An alternative or possibly additive explanation for younger players' greater valuation of social gaming motivations compared to adults, roots in developmental psychology, where the great importance of peers during adolescence has been documented. The implications of young people's peer orientation for media use have also been shown – social networking and mediated interpersonal communication are particularly appealing to young people precisely because of their great interest to interact with peers, e.g., [41]. Video games and use of multiplayer options fits directly into this pattern of social media use, so younger players' assignment of greater importance to social playing motives compared to adults may also be explained by developmental dynamics of peer orientation. From this perspective, casual games share important features and motivational power with social network sites and instant message services, e.g., [42].

In contrast to our assumptions, no age effect was found for competition. In this regard, the clear theoretical prediction that competitive activities should be more aversive for older people did not translate into an empirical motivational pattern of silver gamers. The most plausible explanation for this null effect of gamer age is the great diversity among older people [43]: Some segments of people aged 50 and older 'still feel young' and are interested in leisure time activities one would typically associate with younger cohorts. Deciding to play video games implies the readiness to engage in competition and performance pressure [25]. So, older people who choose video games for entertainment obviously belong to the fraction of their age group willing to compete and enjoying performance-based entertainment. The fact that silver gamers are equally competitive as younger gamer cohorts would, from this perspective, imply that silver gamers are 'typical gamers', but less 'typical' members of their age group, as they are more playful, active, and interested in competition.

5.3 Gender-by-Age Dynamics in Video Game Motivation

The findings do not show any interaction effects of age and gender on players' video game motivation (RQ1). In contrast, the current study reproduced a rather stereotypical gender pattern of video game motivation, as competition was found to systematically vary between male and female gamers. Male players find competing with other players more motivating than female players, even in a game genre that is not primarily dedicated to competition (like shooter games, for instance, cf. [28]). The stability of the gender discrepancy in the competitive gaming motivation suggests a biological origin and/or a close connection of the competition motivation to male's core self-concept – developmental processes do not seem to extinct the greater competition orientation in male players with increasing age (see [44] for a discussion of biological versus learned factors in media use and effects).

5.4 Limitations and Future Studies

The current findings need to be considered in the light of methodological limitations. First, no probability sample of "Farmerama" players was investigated, but a convenience sample of players who were sufficiently excited by the game to respond to an invitation that popped up at the end of a gaming session (self-selection bias). Moreover, "Farmerama" is only one of many casual online games, and generalizability of findings to other casual games and, even more importantly, to other video game genres can only be claimed with great caution. In addition, we only tested selected motivational factors for which gender and age effects could be assumed on a theoretical basis. Future studies should investigate a larger set of motives.

One important issue that needs to be discussed is that the current study refers to previous work on age dynamics in non-interactive entertainment preferences [22], but those studies inspected audience choices from a broad variety of messages (e.g., sad films versus comedy). The current work, however, looked at motivations of different age groups to play the same game – "Farmerama" was conceptualized as a motivational 'buffet' that can serve very different motivational preferences. This strategy may in fact prevent the detection of age dynamics or age-by-gender dynamics, as these dynamics may not so much become manifest in differences among players of the same game, but rather in developmental (or gender) discrepancies in preferences for different video game genres as indicated by the findings of Scharkow and colleagues [32].

Future work should address these limitations and continue the investigation of age and gender dynamics in video game motivation with improved samples, player audiences of other and different games, alternative research designs that mirror investigations of film or TV preferences (i.e., preferences for different types of games; such as Mares and colleagues [26]), and longitudinal approaches to lifespan developments in gaming motivation.

6 Conclusion

The key finding of the present study is that silver gamers do not seem to be 'special' gamers. Rather, their motivations to play games are mostly congruent with the reasons why younger people turn to gaming. Our findings suggest that there may not exist so much variation among gamers, but great variation among older people in terms of their interests, leisure time activities, and entertainment preferences. Some of those people aged 50 and higher identify themselves as gamers, but this does not mean that they differ substantially from younger gamers. Thus, silver gamers are older people who decide to expose themselves to a "young", challenging, competitive medium.

Therefore, the age identity and socio-emotional selectivity processes [23] that we theorized to predict specific motivational patterns among silver gamers did not display empirical explanatory power. These processes are likely to operate at the level of media choice rather than at the level of how people play or what they seek in games – silver gamers may be a special group of older people (by choosing games as leisure activity), but not a special group of gamers. Future work on gaming motivations should thus work towards typologies of player motivations, e.g., [45], that focus on playing styles, genre preferences, and psychological qualities of entertainment and see whether types (clusters) emerge in which silver gamers are over- or underrepresented. Systematic age comparisons as in the present study suggest, in contrast, that there is no sharp specific entertainment profile of silver gamers as a group in its own right.

References

1. Juul, J.: A Casual Revolution: Reinventing Video Games and their Players. MIT Press, Cambridge (2010)
2. Delwiche, A.A., Henderson, J.J.: The players they are a-changin': the rise of older MMO gamers. J. Broadcast. Electron. Media 57(2), 205–223 (2013). doi:10.1080/08838151.2013.787077
3. Goldstein, J., Cajko, L., Oosterbroek, M., Michielsen, M., van Houten, O., Salverda, F.: Video games and the elderly. Soc. Behav. Pers. 25(4), 345–352 (1997). doi:10.2224/sbp.1997.25.4.345
4. Entertainment Software Association: Essential facts about the computer and video game industry (2016). http://essentialfacts.theesa.com/Essential-Facts-2016.pdf
5. Ryan, R.M., Rigby, C.S., Przybylski, A.: The motivational pull of video games: a self-determination theory approach. Motiv. Emot. 30(2), 344–360 (2006). doi:10.1007/s11031-006-9051-8
6. Yee, N.: Motivations for play in online games. CyberPsychol. Behav. 9(6), 772–775 (2006). doi:10.1089/cpb.2006.9.772
7. Sherry, J.L., Lucas, K., Greenberg, B.S., Lachlan, K.: Video game uses and gratifications as predictors of use and game preference. In: Vorderer, P., Bryant, J. (eds.) Playing Video Games: Motives, Responses, and Consequences, pp. 213–224. Lawrence Erlbaum Associates, Mahwah (2006)
8. Hartmann, T., Klimmt, C.: Gender and computer games: exploring females' dislikes. J. Comp. Mediat. Comm. 11(4), 910–931 (2006). doi:10.1111/j.1083-6101.2006.00301.x
9. Lucas, K., Sherry, J.L.: Sex differences in video game play: a communication-based explanation. Commun. Res. 31(5), 499–523 (2004). doi:10.1177/0093650204267930
10. Osmanovic, S., Pecchioni, L.: Beyond entertainment: motivations and outcomes of video game playing by older adults and their younger family members. Games Cult. 11(1–2), 130–149 (2015). doi:10.1177/1555412015602819
11. de Schutter, B.: Never too old to play: the appeal of digital games to an older audience. Games Cult. 6(2), 155–170 (2011). doi:10.1177/1555412010364978
12. Nap, H.H., Kort, Y.D., IJsselsteijn, W.A.: Senior gamers: preferences, motivations and needs. Gerontechnology 8(4), 247–262 (2009). doi:10.4017/gt.2009.08.04.003.00
13. Diaz-Orueta, U., Facal, D., Nap, H.H., Ranga, M.-M.: What is the key for older people to show interest in playing digital learning games? initial qualitative findings from the LEAGE project on a multicultural european sample. Games Health J. 1(2), 115–123 (2012). doi:10.1089/g4h.2011.0024
14. Loos, E., Zonneveld, A.: Silver gaming: serious fun for seniors? In: Zhou, J., Salvendy, G. (eds.) ITAP 2016. LNCS, vol. 9755, pp. 330–341. Springer, Cham (2016). doi:10.1007/978-3-319-39949-2_32
15. Hartmann, T., Klimmt, C.: The influence of personality factors on computer game choice. In: Vorderer, P., Bryant, J. (eds.) Playing Video Games: Motives, Responses, and Consequences, pp. 115–131. Lawrence Erlbaum Associates, Mahwah (2006)

16. Tamborini, R., Bowman, N.D., Eden, A., Grizzard, M., Organ, A.: Defining media enjoyment as the satisfaction of intrinsic needs. J. Commun. **60**(4), 758–777 (2010). doi:10. 1111/j.1460-2466.2010.01513.x

17. Klimmt, C.: Dimensions and determinants of the enjoyment of playing digital games: a three-level model. In: Copier, M., Raessens, J. (eds.) Level up. Digital Games Research Conference, 4–6 November, 2003, Utrecht University, pp. 246–257. Faculty of Arts, Utrecht University, Utrecht (2003)

18. Zillmann, D.: Mechanisms of emotional involvement with drama. Poetics **23**(1–2), 33–51 (1995). doi:10.1016/0304-422X(94)00020-7

19. Klimmt, C., Hefner, D., Vorderer, P.: The video game experience as "True" identification: a theory of enjoyable alterations of players' self-perception. Commun. Theor. **19**(4), 351–373 (2009). doi:10.1111/j.1468-2885.2009.01347.x

20. Vorderer, P., Bryant, J. (eds.): Playing Video Games. Motives, Responses, and Consequences. Lawrence Erlbaum Associates, Mahwah (2006)

21. Nussbaum, J.F., Pecchioni, L., Robinson, J.D., Thompson, T.L.: Communication and Aging, 2nd edn. Routledge, New York (2011)

22. Bartsch, A.: As time goes by: what changes and what remains the same in entertainment experience over the life span? J. Commun. **62**(4), 588–608 (2012). doi:10.1111/j.1460-2466. 2012.01657.x

23. Carstensen, L.L.: Evidence for a life-span theory of socioemotional selectivity. Curr. Dir. Psychol. Sci. **4**(5), 151–156 (1995). doi:10.1111/1467-8721.ep11512261

24. Carstensen, L.L., Fung, H.H., Charles, S.T.: Socioemotional selectivity theory and the regulation of emotion in the second half of life. Motiv. Emot. **27**(2), 103–123 (2003). doi:10. 1023/A:1024569803230

25. Vorderer, P., Hartmann, T., Klimmt, C.: Explaining the enjoyment of playing video games: The role of competition. In: Marinelli, D. (ed.) ICEC Conference Proceedings 2003: Essays on the Future of Interactive Entertainment, pp. 107–120. Carnegie Mellon University Press, Pittsburgh (2006)

26. Mares, M.-L., Oliver, M.B., Cantor, J.: Age differences in adults' emotional motivations for exposure to films. Media Psychol. **11**(4), 488–511 (2008). doi:10.1080/15213260802492026

27. Hofer, M., Allemand, M., Martin, M.: Age differences in nonhedonic entertainment experiences. J. Commun. **64**(1), 61–81 (2014). doi:10.1111/jcom.12074

28. Jansz, J., Tanis, M.: Appeal of playing online first person shooter games. CyberPsychol. Behav. **10**(1), 133–136 (2007). doi:10.1089/cpb.2006.9981

29. Harwood, J.: Age identification, social identity gratifications, and television viewing. J. Broadcast. Electron. Media **43**(1), 123–136 (1999). doi:10.1080/08838159909364479

30. Mares, M.-L., Sun, Y.: The multiple meanings of age for television content preferences. Hum. Commun. Res. **36**(3), 372–396 (2010). doi:10.1111/j.1468-2958.2010.01380.x

31. Jansz, J.: The emotional appeal of violent video games for adolescent males. Commun. Theor. **15**(3), 219–241 (2005). doi:10.1111/j.1468-2885.2005.tb00334.x

32. Scharkow, M., Festl, R., Vogelgesang, J., Quandt, T.: Beyond the "core-gamer": genre preferences and gratifications in computer games. Comput. Hum. Behav. **44**, 293–298 (2015). doi:10.1016/j.chb.2014.11.020

33. Entertainment Software Association: Essential Facts about the computer and video game industry (2014). http://www.theesa.com/wp-content/uploads/2014/10/ESA_EF_2014.pdf

34. van de Vijver, F., Tanzer, N.K.: Bias and equivalence in cross-cultural assessment: an overview. Revue Européenne de Psychologie Appliquée/Euro. Rev. Appl. Psychol. **54**(2), 119–135 (2004). doi:10.1016/j.erap.2003.12.004

35. Kultima, A.: Casual game design values. In: Lugmayr, A., Franssila, H., Sotamaa, O., Näränen, P., Vanhala, J. (eds.) The 13th International MindTrek Conference: Everyday Life in the Ubiquitous Era, Tampere, Finland, p. 58. doi:10.1145/1621841.1621854

36. Sotamaa, O.: Achievement unlocked: rethinking gaming capital. In: Sotamaa, O., Karppi, T. (eds.) Games as Services, pp. 73–81. University of Tampere, Tampere (2010)

37. Henning, B., Vorderer, P.: Psychological escapism: predicting the amount of television viewing by need for cognition. J. Commun. 51(1), 100–120 (2001). doi:10.1111/j.1460-2466.2001.tb02874.x

38. Jansen, N.W.H., Kant, I.J., van den Brandt, P.A.: Need for recovery in the working population: description and associations with fatigue and psychological distress. Int. J. Behav. Med. 9(4), 322–340 (2002)

39. Reinecke, L.: Games and recovery: the use of video and computer games to recuperate from stress and strain. J. Media Psychol. 21(3), 126–142 (2009). doi:10.1027/1864-1105.21.3.126

40. Reinecke, L., Trepte, S.: In a working mood? J. Media Psychol. 20(1), 3–14 (2008). doi:10.1027/1864-1105.20.1.3

41. Valkenburg, P.M., Peter, J.: Preadolescents' and adolescents' online communication and their closeness to friends. Dev. Psychol. 43(2), 267–277 (2007). doi:10.1037/0012-1649.43.2.267

42. Yang, C.-C., Brown, B.B.: Motives for using Facebook, patterns of Facebook activities, and late adolescents' social adjustment to college. J. Youth Adolesc. 42(3), 403–416 (2013). doi:10.1007/s10964-012-9836-x

43. Stone, M.E., Lin, J., Dannefer, D., Kelley-Moore, J.A.: The continued eclipse of heterogeneity in gerontological research. J. Gerontol. B Psychol. Sci. Soc. Sci. 72(1), 162–167 (2017). doi:10.1093/geronb/gbv068

44. Sherry, J.L.: Media effects theory and the nature/nurture debate. a historical overview and directions for future research. Media Psychol. 6(1), 83–109 (2004). doi:10.1207/s1532785xmep0601_4

45. Bartle, R.: Hearts, clubs, diamonds, spades: players who suit MUDs. J. MUD Res. 1(1), 19 (1996)

Employing a User-Centered Design Process to Create a Multiplayer Online Escape Game for Older Adults

Fan Zhang[✉], Amir Doroudian, David Kaufman, Simone Hausknecht,
Julija Jeremic, and Hollis Owens

Faculty of Education, Simon Fraser University, Burnaby, BC, Canada
{fza26,adoroudi,dkaufman,shauskne,jjeremic,howens}@sfu.ca

Abstract. The purpose of this study was to explore a user-centered design (UCD) process to create a multiplayer online escape game with embedded learning content for older adults. Older adults aged 65 and over were involved in the needs assessment and prototype evaluation. The needs assessment assisted the researchers and developers in understanding older adults' social interaction in real-life escape rooms, which resulted in a list of design recommendations for the online escape game. The findings of prototype evaluation illustrated that older users enjoyed the theme of classical literary work, crossword puzzles, and the format of dual play. It was also found that our UCD process could not effectively address all design challenges of developing a digital escape game for older adults.

Keywords: Older adults · Escape game · Life-long learning · Social interaction · Puzzles

1 Introduction

1.1 Learning in Later Life

The population all over the world is ageing [1]. Later life is defined as "the stage in life when a person is no longer primarily involved in the labour market, raising a family, or both" [2, p. 7]. Terms such as "older adults", "third agers", and "fourth agers" have been used to refer to people at this stage [2]. By review the concepts of active aging, productive aging and successful aging, Merriam and Kee [3] emphasized that older adults should not be considered as uselessness, or frailty. Due to the increasing longevity, good health, and improved quality of life, a large number of older adults are still active and participative [4]. In spite of cognitive decline, older adults are still capable of learning [5]. Real-life learning allows older learners to draw on prior knowledge, expertise, motivation, and strategies, which are products of life experience [6]. Research has suggested that lifelong learning is tightly associated with sustained cognitive function [7, 8], as well as maintained social interaction to society [9]. Participation in learning activities is beneficial to older adults' physical and psychological wellbeing [10]. It provides opportunities to try new things, reduce stress and escape from life temporarily [11].

Learning in later life is qualitatively different from learning experienced in the past and by children and younger people [9]. The time factors are unique to older adulthood

© Springer International Publishing AG 2017
J. Zhou and G. Salvendy (Eds.): ITAP 2017, Part II, LNCS 10298, pp. 296–307, 2017.
DOI: 10.1007/978-3-319-58536-9_24

and influence approaches to learning [12]. Older learners are highly selective and self-directing [13] and prefer to take charge of their learning [10]. Their choice of learning is no longer determined by career goals [14], but is connected to their personal interest and growing [5]. Learning new things about a long-term interest or hobby and for fun and enjoyment (also called leisure learning) is one of the three types of learning needs to older adults [15]. They are less interested in examinations, certificates or degrees [10]. Adult education and life learning is usually through non-formal (e.g., book club) or informal (e.g., a long-held interest) means [3]. Older learners are satisfied when making achievement, and are not concerned about how long it takes them to complete the learning task [12].

1.2   Social Interaction for Successful Aging

Social engagement is a core component of successful aging [16]. It enables older adults to deal with the stress of negative life events [17], as participation in social activities provides a social context for social support, self-regulation of stress and negative emotions, and reappraising lives [18]. People who feel supported during times of need have a stronger sense of meaning in their lives [19]. Both structural (i.e., the number and type of social partners in a given network) and functional (i.e., the perceived receipt of support) aspects of social networks contribute to emotional wellbeing [17] and mental health [20], and are associated with higher levels of cognitive functioning [21]. Research also shows that people with positive emotional experience are at lower risk for morbidity and mortality [22, 23].

1.3   Game-Based Learning

Digital games have a substantial influence on how we spend our leisure time [24]. Playing digital games has become a popular leisure activity for children, adolescents as well as adults [24]. In the last decade, research efforts have been made to explore the potential and benefits of digital games for the purpose of learning and instruction [25]. Digital games are hypothesized to affect learning by increasing intrinsic motivation and stimulating the cognitive processes [25]. Games include the most important factors that intrinsically motivate players to engage in appealing activities which could help them to learn, including challenge, curiosity, and fantasy [26, 27]. Factors such as meaning, autonomy, and competence also contribute to the moment-to-moment experience that is inherently enjoyable and appealing [25], a state which can be described in terms of Csikszentmihalyi's [28] flow experience.

Digital games appear to provide learning activities that are active, experimental, situated, and problem-based [24]. Gee [29] argued that digital games are good for learning and identified sixteen learning principles built into good games. Digital games are also virtual environments where performing the game tasks involves the same cognitive processes that are required for task performance in the real world [30]. Prensky [31] offered examples of what children can learn about real life from games, indicating that skills obtained from games, such as problem-solving, are useful in real life. Digital games for learning have been used across a variety of subject disciplines such as mathematics, engineering, language, history and business [32]. Vogel et al.'s [33] meta-analysis study suggested that digital games yielded higher cognitive outcomes than did conventional learning methods. Wouters et al.'s [25] meta-analysis study found that digital games were more effective in terms of learning and more motivating than conventional instruction methods.

1.4 User-Centered Design

User-Centered Design (UCD) is a broad term for "a philosophy and methods which focus on designing for and involving end users in the creation of computerized system" [34, p. 12]. It was originally used to transform complicated and professional technologies in industry for real-world application and for people without professional knowledge [35]. The users' needs, the goals of the activity and context should guide the development [36]. The creation process should be both iterative and incremental [36]. The iterative design is corresponding with three phases of iterative testing with end users. This usually includes conceptual model evaluation before coding, prototype evaluation to get early feedback about its usability, and product evaluation after the interface is ready [37]. A wide range of methods (e.g., paper sketches, mock-ups and prototypes) can be used to support the creative process, elicit requirements and visualize ideas and solutions, but the principles, methods and the order of activities must be adapted to the particular context [36].

The meaningful participation of end users is important to a UCD approach. However, there has been a lack of a consensus about what constitutes a UCD, and how central users should be in the creation process [38]. Lowdermilk [39] indicated that a UCD does not mean offering users what they want. Users may be experts in terms of usage, but they have little knowledge on how to effectively design complex systems and deliver information [39]. There is a wide range of ways in which end users can participate in a UCD design, and can be involved in one way or another, such as participation in requirements gathering and usability testing, or being involved as partners with designers throughout the design process [34].

2   Research Purpose and Question

The number of older adults who are active gamers has been increasing in recent years [40]. The entertainment and motivating features of digital games and the potential of digital games for effective learning are in line with older adults' needs of leisure learning. Digital games can be designed to contain some elements that have been identified as important to older adults' enjoyment, including mental fitness, competition and winning, fitting their time in a way that provide satisfaction, and a sense of belonging in social games [41]. Civilization and SimCity are two examples of commercial digital games for learning. However, they are not specifically targeted at older adults. There is shortage of practice focusing on designing digital games for older adults' learning.

Real-life escape games are adventure games in which a group of players are locked in a room with the goal of seeking clues and solving puzzles tied to a story or theme to escape the room within a time limit, usually in one hour [42]. The first real-life escape games were developed in the mid-2000s. By 2015, over 2800 room escape venues are in operation worldwide, making it a lucrative game business [43]. Real-life escape games are also viewed as a type of alternate reality games (ARGs). ARGs are "immersive, interactive experiences where players collaboratively hunt for clues, make sense of disparate information, contribute content, and solve puzzles to advance a narrative that is woven into the fabric of the real world" [44, p. 26]. All players are at the center of the story and have direct influence over the actual outcome of the story [45]. Research has shown that in order for a game to promote learning and increase motivation, the design of a game must provoke a sense of autonomy, identity, and interactivity [46]. It should also enable players to strategize actions, test hypotheses, and solve problems [47]. Seeking clues to resolve challenging puzzles collaboratively allows players to immerse in the narrative and escape the room by testing hypotheses, changing strategies, and trying again. Thus, playing escape game provides opportunities to increase older adults' motivation, learning, and social interaction with other players.

The purpose of this study is to explore a UCD process to create a multiplayer online escape game for older adults with learning content embedded. This research can offer insights on the effectiveness of a UCD process that leads to the development of useful products and services for productive aging.

3 Research Design

In this study, the research team who co-authored this paper, along with five game developers and a large group of older adults aged 65 and over, participated in the design, implementation, and evaluation of a multiplayer online escape for older adults. Figure 1 shows the UCD process we employed to create the game. The game developers used Unity game engine and Adobe Photoshop to design and develop the game.

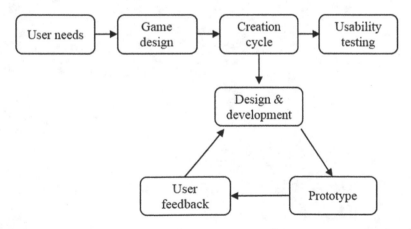

Fig. 1. The UCD process to create a multiplayer online escape game for older adults

This study followed the following steps:

- *User needs assessment*. There is a lack of study examining how players interact with each other in real-life escape rooms. Therefore, a face-to-face escape game study was conducted to understand the needs and interaction of older adults in real-life escape games.
- *Co-designing game ideas*. The research team and the game developers co-designed the game ideas.
- *Creation cycle*. The research team, the game developers, and a group of older adults were engaged in an iterative process to create the game.
- *Usability testing*. A usability test will be conducted to understand how this game meets the needs of older adults.

4   The UCD Process

4.1   User Needs Assessment

The needs assessment of the target users consisted of two phases, in order to explore whether variables such as the number of players in an escape room, their characteristics, and a given escape room design would affect the players' interaction. In the first phase, three groups of older adults played two different real-life escape games: two small groups of four players and a larger group of six players. In the second phase, two intergenerational groups played the same two escape games as those in the first phase. Each intergenerational group included two intergenerational pairs (i.e., grandparents and younger family members). A focus group interview was conducted after every game for each group. Table 1 presents the findings of the needs assessment and corresponding design recommendations for a multiplayer online escape game.

Table 1. Findings of user needs assessment and corresponding design recommendations

Findings of user needs assessment	Design recommendations
Depending on their personalities, some people liked the time limit, but some did not	Allow the players to set the time limit based on their pace and needs
Dim lighting of the room, which was part of its design, made it difficult for older adults to see	Make fonts and other elements large enough so that the players can easily see them
Hints provided by the escape room's staff were useful	Provide hints during the game, so that older adults can search for help when they do not know how to proceed
The players appreciated the realistic historical themes which allowed them to get more immersed into the story	Design puzzles and room elements that are realistic for the story chosen
They tended to enjoy the room more when they achieved more success and proceed in the game	Focus on the successes in the room is just as important as the themes. Gradually increase the difficulty of the puzzles to promote self-efficacy and sense of achievement
The players enjoyed rooms with stories that were immersive	Create an immersive story where they feel they can influence the end result
Different people enjoyed different puzzles. Some liked word puzzles, while others preferred math or sorting puzzles	Include a wide variety of puzzles that include letters, words, numbers, mechanical skills, etc.
Although players were supposed to explore the escape room and seek clues as their own ways, older adults preferred to doing things systematically and exploring the room by following specific steps in comparison to younger people	Provide clear guidance to help older adults understand the purpose of the game
The players enjoyed the experience more when the storyline and the instructions were clear to them before playing the room	Have clear instructions and storyline
The communication among all group members was not well-organized. They did not take up the roles of leaders and followers	For a multiplayer game, a chat function or even a video chat function is useful. Design different roles to allow them to work together to solve the puzzles and facilitate group coordination and collaboration
The players enjoyed moments when the team came together and solved an important puzzle	

4.2 Co-designing Game Ideas

At this stage, older adults did not participate in the design of game ideas for two reasons. On the one hand, the social and emotional meanings of gameplay among older adults are divergent [48]. On the other hand, previous study has already identified the learning interests of older adults such as literature, history, religion, and political/world events [49]. Therefore, the game ideas of this study were co-designed by the researchers and developers. Classic works of literature were chosen as the theme with embedded learning content, because it is familiar and interesting to the older learners [49].

The game is entitled, *A Tale of Tales*. The basic storyline starts with a game character called Ink Monster who drinks the words out of the pages of the players' favorite stories so that they have to seek clues to resolve puzzles in order to recover the stories stolen by the Ink Monster. One room (a maze in this study) is designed after a classic story (e.g. *Alice in Wonderland* and *Sherlock Holmes*) with puzzles that are related to that story. Currently, this game allows two distant players to play synchronously. Once entering a virtual maze, the two players will select the role of either the navigator or the follower. The navigator can see the whole maze and the locations of the puzzles (see the golden stars in Fig. 2), while the follower is situated inside the maze and needs guidance from the navigator. In addition, each player can only see parts of the puzzles and clues distributed in the maze, which requires them to communicate and coordinate with each other to solve the puzzles and escape the maze.

Fig. 2. Follower and navigator

4.3   Creation Cycle

The creation cycle was an iterative process. The game developers met with the research team every two weeks for a period of 13 weeks to show their prototype and receive feedback for the next iteration. Older adults were also involved in the prototype evaluation twice.

The first evaluation by older adults was conducted when the game was relatively playable but some puzzles had not been completed. The purpose of involving older adults at this stage was to receive early feedback about the design elements and the usability of the game. A total of 12 older adults aged 65 and over were paired up and played the prototype for one hour. Ten of them had played a real-life escape game. The two members of each pair were separated and communicated with each other via headphones. Since some puzzles were not completely developed, each older adult was offered a paper sheet including clues for the puzzles. Immediately after the first prototype testing, the 12 older adults completed a questionnaire with both open and closed questions, and then participated in a focus group interview. They mostly enjoyed the theme, crossword puzzles, the sense of accomplishment when resolving a puzzle, and working with their co-players for the same goal. Table 2 summarizes older adults' comments on the prototype and corresponding suggestions for further improvement.

Table 2. Summary of older adults' comments and suggestions for further improvement

Older adults' comments	Suggestions for further improvement
Need more rewards for solving a puzzle	Provide more information and rewards to motivate older adults
Want to know more about the levels and number of puzzles	Provide information about the game mechanism once entering the game, and highlight the puzzles in the maze
Figuring out the sequence was a bit frustrating	Exploring the sequence of the clues, resolving puzzles, and escaping the room are features that make escape games attractive. So, we decided to not provide information about the "steps", but to add a "Hint" button. Older adults can click the "Hint" button for clues when they do not know what to do
The second puzzle was too difficult	Order the puzzles based on difficulty level
Not enough information about what to do next	Explain the purpose of each puzzle; provide more directions once a puzzle is finished; create a tutorial video
Difficult to use the arrow keys	Provide keyboards and mouse so that older adults have more options

The second evaluation by older adults was carried out on a refined version of the game which had new features and fully functional components. The purpose of this evaluation was to get feedback for further refinement before the large-scale usability testing. Twelve older adults aged 65 and over participated in this evaluation. Seven of the participants were also involved in the first test, and five were new to this project. The processes of prototype testing and data collection were the same as the first test. The older adults found the tutorial video helpful to understand the gameplay, although they thought it was fast-paced. The five new participants also enjoyed the theme, the two-player format, and the crossword puzzles. No one had any difficulty in communicating with their partners. Eight of the 12 older adults reported that they would play this game again. Those who said they would not play it again argued that they already knew the puzzles and stories. Five older adults who used arrow keys or touchpads to navigate the game had difficulties with these controllers, while the other older adults who used a mouse did not report any difficulty in navigating the game.

Two shortcomings of the prototype game that most participants reported were lack of direction and insufficient context from the story. First, six older adults, four of whom had participated in the first test, encountered difficulties in understanding what to do next. The majority of participants reported that they still needed some clear, real-time directions and more feedback from the gameplay. For example, the exit door was barely noticeable to them. "If the door had opened automatically, we would know what to do after resolving a puzzle," one participant said. Second, they suggested that the game could include more stories and clues to sustain continued interest. Some older adults also provided feedback for improving the interface design. The following is a list of suggestions for further improvement:

- Provide clearer explanation and instruction
- Expand the game by adding more stories and clues
- Improve the real-time help hints
- Slow down the pace of the tutorial video
- Improve interface design to fit the characteristics of older adults
- Fix the bugs that may cause confusion, such as walking through the bushes

4.4 Usability Testing

The game developers continued working on the prototype for another two weeks to improve it based on the feedback from the second prototype evaluation by older adults. The research team and the game developers held two more meetings during this time to discuss the improvements and plan the next step, which is conducting a large-scale usability testing study to examine the extent to which the game can achieve the goals of this project.

5   Discussion and Conclusion

Escape games have the potential to promote older adults' social interaction and learning activities. However, real-life escape game is a new entertainment for older adults. There is a dearth of practice and research related to the development of digital escape games. Thus, this study aimed at developing a multiplayer online digital game for older adults based on a UCD process. The needs assessment was useful to understand older adults' social interaction in real-life escape rooms, and to generate a list of design recommendations for the online escape game. In this study older adults were not involved in the design of game ideas. Older adults participated in two prototype evaluations: the first one was conducted on an earlier prototype with limited playability, and the second one on a fully functional prototype. The timing of these two evaluations was determined by the research team and the developers. Older adults' comments and suggestions offered insights and directions for further improvement.

In addition, the findings of the two prototype evaluations indicated that they enjoyed the literary theme, crossword puzzles, and interaction with their partners. Crossword puzzle is something older adults are familiar with, and is one of their favorite entertainments. The core feature of this game is one person guiding another one and escaping the maze by communicating and collaborating with each other to resolve the puzzles. It was found that older adults enjoyed this format of playing in pairs because interaction with partners was easy. Each person had different views and could contribute to achieving a common goal.

However, providing useful instruction to help older adults understand the purpose and the tasks of the game was a design challenge. There are also other challenges that need to be addressed in further research. For example, how to enhance the features and core gameplay of escape games, but also make it clear for older adults what they need to do? How to design puzzles that are challenging enough for older adults, but do not frustrate them? How to design a variety of puzzles and individual escape rooms to sustain older adults' attention? What graphics and other audio and visual elements to employ to create an immersive environment that is interesting to older adults with various needs? Some of these problems were already mentioned during the needs assessment (see Table 1), but they have not been completely resolved by the end of this project.

For the current study, the UCD process was useful to help the researchers and developers understand older adults' needs and get feedback for further improvement. However, the UCD process was not the key to resolve all design challenges discussed above. We have not conducted a large-scale test to evaluate the usability of the created game. Therefore, we cannot still assert whether a UCD process leads to usable products and services for older adults. However we argue that creating an online escape game for older adults requires an in-depth understanding of various aspects of the nature of older adults' play, as well as game design principles, such as game thinking, game elements, curve of interest, motivation, aesthetes, and the needs and challenges older adults would face during the game.

Acknowledgement. This work was supported by AGE-WELL NCE Inc., a national research network supporting research, networking, commercialization, knowledge mobilization and capacity building activities in technology and aging to improve the quality of life of Canadians and contribute to the economic impact of Canada. AGE-WELL is a member of the Networks of Centres of Excellence (NCE), a Government of Canada program that funds partnerships between universities, industry, government and not-for-profit organizations.

References

1. Manchester, H., Facer, K.: Digital curation: learning and legacy in later life. E-Learning Digit. Media **12**(2), 242–258 (2015)
2. Anderson, S.: Later Life Learning: a review of the literature (2008). http://www.cpa.org.uk/aea/Lit_review_summary_May_08.pdf
3. Merriam, S.B., Kee, Y.: Promoting community wellbeing: the case for lifelong learning for older adults. Adult Educ. Q. **64**(2), 128–144 (2014)
4. Lindley, S., Harper, R., Sellen, A.: Designing for elders: exploring the complexity of relationships in later life. In: Proceedings of the 22nd Annual Conference of the British HCI Group (HCI 2008), vol. 1, pp. 77–86. British Computer Society Swinton, UK (2008)
5. Chang, D.F., Lin, S.P.: Motivation to learn among older adults in Taiwan. Educ. Gerontol. **37**(7), 574–592 (2011)
6. Jeske, D., Rossnagel, C.S.: Learning capability and performance in later working life: towards a contextual view. Educ. Training **57**(4), 378–391 (2015)
7. Rowe, J.W., Kahn, R.L.: Successful Aging. Pantheon Books, New York (1998)
8. Schaie, K.W.: The course of adult intellectual development. Am. Psychol. **49**(4), 304–313 (1994)
9. Withnall, A.: Improving Learning in Later Life. Routledge, London (2000)
10. Sloane-Seale, A., Kops, B.: Older adults in lifelong learning: participation and successful aging. Can. J. Univ. Continuing Educ. **34**(1), 37–62 (2008)
11. Dattilo, A.E.L., Ewert, A., Dattilo, J.: Learning as leisure: motivation and outcome in adult free time learning. J. Park Recreation Adm. **30**(1), 1–18 (2012)
12. Russell, H.: Time and meaning in later-life learning. Aust. J. Adult Learn. **51**(3), 547–565 (2011)

13. Knowles, M.: The Adult Learner: A Neglected Species, 3rd edn. Gulf, Houston (1984)
14. Illeris, K.: The Three Dimensions of Learning. Roskilde University Press, Frederiksberg (2002)
15. Purdie, N., Boulton-Lewis, G.: The learning needs of older adults. Educ. Gerontol. **29**, 129–149 (2003)
16. Ristau, S.: People do need people: social interaction boosts brain health in older age. J. Am. Soc. Aging **35**(2), 70–76 (2011)
17. Cohen, S., Wills, T.A.: Stress, social support, and the buffering hypothesis. Psychol. Bull. **98**(2), 310–357 (1985)
18. Hutchinson, M.R., Watkins, L.R.: Minocycline suppresses morphine-induced respiratory depression, suppresses morphine-induced reward, and enhances systemic morphine-induced analgesia. Brain Behav. Immun. **22**, 1248–1256 (2008)
19. Krause, N.: Longitudinal study of social support and meaning in life. Psychol. Aging **22**(3), 456–469 (2007)
20. Lang, F.R., Carstensen, L.L.: Close emotional relationships in later life: further support for proactive aging in the social domain. Psychol. Aging **9**(2), 315–324 (1994)
21. Charles, S.T., Carstensen, L.L.: Social and emotional aging. Annu. Rev. Psychol. **61**, 383–409 (2009)
22. Lyyra, T., Keikkinen, R.: Perceived social support and mortality in older people. J. Gerontol. B **61**(3), S147–S152 (2006)
23. Pressman, S.D., Cohen, S.: Use of social words in autobiographies and longevity. Psychosom. Med. **69**(3), 262–269 (2007)
24. Boyle, E.A., Connolly, T.M., Hainey, T.: The role of psychology in understanding the impact of computer games. Entertainment Comput. **2**, 69–74 (2011)
25. Wouters, P., van Nimwegen, C., van Oostendorp, H., van der Spek, E.D.: A meta-analysis of the cognitive and motivational effects of serious games. J. Educ. Psychol. **105**(2), 249–265 (2013)
26. Malone, T.W.: Toward a theory of intrinsically motivating instruction. Cogn. Sci. **4**, 333–369 (1981)
27. Malone, T.W., Lepper, M.R.: Making learning fun: a taxonomy of intrinsic motivation for learning. In: Snow, R.E., Farr, M.J. (eds.) Aptitude, Leaning, and Instruction. Conative and Affective Process Analyses, vol. 3, pp. 223–253. Erlbaum, Hillsdale (1987)
28. Csıkszentmihalyi, M.: Beyond Boredom and Anxiety. Experiencing Flow in Work and Play, 25th Anniversary edn. Jossey-Bass, San Francisco (2000)
29. Gee, J.P.: Good video games and good learning. Phi Kappa Phi Forum **85**(2), 33–46 (2005)
30. Tobias, S., Fletcher, J.D., Dai, D.Y., Wind, A.P.: Review of research on computer games. In: Tobias, S., Fletcher, J.D. (eds.) Computer Games and Instruction, pp. 127–222. Information Age, Charlotte (2011)
31. Prensky, M.: Don't Bother Me Mom - I'm Learning. Paragon House, St. Paul (2005)
32. Connolly, T.M., Boyle, E.A., Macarthur, E., Hainey, T., Boyle, J.M.: Computers & education a systematic literature review of empirical evidence on computer games and serious games. Comput. Educ. **59**(2), 661–686 (2012)
33. Vogel, J.J., Vogel, D.S., Cannon-Bowers, J., Bowers, C.A., Muse, K., Wright, M.: Computer gaming and interactive simulations for learning: a meta-analysis. J. Educ. Comput. Res. **34**, 229–243 (2006)
34. Abras, C., Maloney-Krichmar, D., Preece, J.: User-centered design. In: Bainbridge, W. (ed.) Encyclopedia of Human-Computer Interaction, vol. 37, pp. 445–456. Sage Publications, Thousand Oaks (2004)

35. Keinonen, T.: User-centered design and fundamental need. In: Proceedings of the 5th Nordic Conference on Human-Computer Interaction Building Bridges – NordiCHI 2008, Lund, Sweden, pp. 211–220 (2008)

36. Gulliksen, J., Göransson, B., Boivie, I., Blomkvist, S., Persson, J., Cajander, Å.: Key principles for user-centred systems design. Behav. Inf. Technol. **22**(6), 397–409 (2003)

37. Mayhew, D.J.: The Usability Engineering Lifecycle. Morgan Kaufmann Publishers, Inc., San Francisco (1999)

38. Karat, J., Atwood, M.E., Dray, S.M., Rantzer, M., Wixon, D.R.: User centered design: quality or quackery? In: Proceedings of the Conference Companion on Human Factors in Computing Systems, Vancouver, British Columbia, Canada, pp. 161–162 (1996)

39. Lowdermilk, T.: User-Centered Deign: A Developer's Guide to Building User-Friendly Applications. O'Reilly Media, Sebastopol (2013)

40. Osmanovic, S., Pecchioni, L.: Beyond entertainment: motivations and outcomes of video game playing by older adults and their younger family members. Games Cult. **11**(1–2), 130–149 (2016)

41. Hoppes, S., Wilcox, T., Graham, G.: Meanings of play for older adults. Phys. Occup. Ther. Geriatr. **18**, 57–68 (2001)

42. Miller, S.: The art of the escape room. Newsweek (2015). http://search.proquest.com.proxy.lib.sfu.ca/docview/1675126754?pq-origsite=summon

43. French, S., Shaw, J.M.: The unbelievably lucrative business of escape rooms (2015). http://www.marketwatch.com/story/the-weird-new-world-of-escape-room-businesses-2015-07-20

44. Bonsignore, E., Hansen, D., Kraus, K., Ruppel, M.: Alternate reality games as platforms for practicing 21st century literacies. Int. J. Learn. Media **4**(1), 25–54 (2013)

45. Suellentrop, C.: Gaming Cultures Seeps into Escape Rooms. The New York Times (2014). https://global-factiva-com.proxy.lib.sfu.ca/ga/default.aspx

46. Gee, J.P.: What Video Games Have to Teach Us about Learning and Literacy. Palgrave/Macmillan, New York (2003)

47. Dondlinger, M.J.: Educational video game design: a review of the literature. J. Appl. Educ. Technol. **4**(1), 21–31 (2007)

48. De Schutter, B., Vanden Abeele, V.: Designing meaningful play within the psycho-social context of older adults. In: Vanden Abeele, V., Zaman, B., Obrist, M., IJsselteijn, W. (eds.) Fun and Games 10: Proceedings of the 3rd International Conference on Fun and Games, pp. 84–93. ACM, New York (2010)

49. Benedict, J.: Exploring the learning interests of older adults. https://capilanou.ca/uploadedFiles/Continuing_Education_Students/Eldercollege/Julian%20Benedict%20Learning%20Interests.pdf

Social Interaction Between Older Adults (80+) and Younger People During Intergenerational Digital Gameplay

Fan Zhang[✉], Robyn Schell, David Kaufman, Glaucia Salgado, and Julija Jeremic

Faculty of Education, Simon Fraser University, Burnaby, BC, Canada
{fza26,rmschell,dkaufman,gsalgado,jjeremic}@sfu.ca

Abstract. The objective of this study was to explore the ways in which collaborative digital gameplay facilitates intergenerational interaction between older adults aged 80+ and younger people. Five intergenerational pairs played two Wii games once a week for six weeks. Analyzing participants' conversations during gameplay reveals that guided participation in the form of question-answer is the main way through which the two age groups can maintain shared focus and participate in the meaning-making process. Older adults play the roles of students, followers, and storytellers while younger people play the roles of teachers, leaders, encouragers, and caregivers during the game sessions. The findings also show that intergenerational play facilitates prosocial behaviors in younger people.

Keywords: Older adults · Younger people · Intergenerational interaction · Digital games · Guided participation

1 Introduction

1.1 Understanding the Oldest Old

The oldest-old (80+) has become the fastest growing age segment in most European populations, UK, and North America [1, 2]. The rapid transformation of later life and the increased longevity demand that we change attitudes towards ageing and move towards a strategy that fully integrates the oldest old into an active ageing strategy [3]. Ageing is not a matter of advanced chronological age but is more a consequence of restricted activities [3]. The oldest-old have a higher average loneliness rating than those between 65 and 79. They are also the least likely to have a close friend and confidante [2]. Emotional and social isolation is the result of a number of factors such as loss of family and friends, poor health, decreased mobility, and reduced income. Social trends such as geographical mobility, reduced intergenerational living, and less cohesive communities also play a role [4]. Older adults aged 80 and over need to be supported so they can continue to participate and engage in social life [3]. One's social relationships, social roles and activities all influence the quality of life as one grows older [3].

© Springer International Publishing AG 2017
J. Zhou and G. Salvendy (Eds.): ITAP 2017, Part II, LNCS 10298, pp. 308–322, 2017.
DOI: 10.1007/978-3-319-58536-9_25

1.2 Intergenerational Interaction

Intergenerational separation has become a social issue in industrialized society [5]. A large number of people, including older adults themselves, believe social disengagement with younger people is a natural part of aging [6]. Generativity, the concern for establishing and guiding the next generation [7], reflects older adults' desire to be needed [8]. It is beneficial to wellbeing in later life in the form of assistance to unrelated others and civic engagement [9]. McAdam and de St. Aubin [10] pointed out that the motivational sources of generativity is in the inner desire to do something that transcends one's death and in the cultural demand of devoting personal resources toward the advancement of the next generation. Nowadays, factors such as the fast pace of technological change, the growth of human knowledge, and the changing cultural norms and larger social forces widen the gap between younger people and therefore contribute to the loss of older adults' capacity for generativity [11].

Lloyd [6] suggested positive and strong intergenerational contact and communication were key factors in the transmission and exchange of human capital within society, values, moral codes, culture, and history. Intergenerational ties provide older adults with opportunities to feel younger, share the easiness of the younger generation, rediscover their abilities, and find their way back to be happy, which leads to regeneration and an increased sense of well-being [12]. Through intergenerational contact, younger adults can learn how to take responsibility for other people and find their identity through common cultural activities [5]. As young people build skills and talents they develop personal meaning and direction in their lives [7]. These positive experiences motivate younger people to take part in intergenerational programs [13].

1.3 Intergenerational Digital Gameplay

Play can act as a connecting force between the two age groups, providing opportunities for them to build relationships [14], enjoy each other's company [15], learn together, resolve problems with the help of another perspective, and laugh over shared mistakes or difficulties [16]. While digital games are generally played by younger people, the number of older adults playing digital games is increasing. Based on the findings of ESA 2016, the average game player is 35 years old, and 26% of game players are aged 50 and over [17]. Digital gameplay is an importance source of connectedness for older adults, as it provides opportunities for them to request help and attention from children, or facilitate conversations with friends [18]. Several research studies are focusing on designing digital games to facilitate intergenerational interaction, such as Collage [19], TranseCare [20], Age Invader [21], e-Treasure [18], etc. The goal of these games is to promote intergenerational contact between grandparents and grandchildren over distributed distance, connect older people with younger people, build meaningful intergenerational relationships, facilitate knowledge transfers between younger and older people, and improve the quality of life of older adults [22].

Chua et al. [23] examined the effects of digital gameplay on intergenerational perceptions among 25 older adults and a corresponding 25 younger people. An older person paired with a younger person played Nintendo Wii once a week (30 min) over two months. These video game participants reported greater reduction in intergroup anxiety and an improvement in general attitudes towards the other age group compared to the intergenerational participants who did not play video games together. Chua et al. mentioned that the recreational aspect of gameplay can easily bring about a change in roles between the two age groups. However, this quantitative study did not examine how older adults and younger people interacted with each other during intergenerational play and how they accepted the role reversal. Rice et al. [24] investigated the social interaction and general perceptions of engagement while playing Xtreme Gardener across three user groups (i.e., Young-Young, Old-Old, and Young-Old). Each group consisted of 10 pairs of participants and completed five levels of the game in 30 min. Within the young-old group, the younger players would often help their older partners by physically playing the game for them and assisting them to select certain game features. However, the older partners occasionally followed the body actions of the younger players. The older participants found it difficult to become accustomed to their new social role. One problem of this study is the short duration of game intervention. Rice et al. also recognized that half hour might not be enough to improve the social interactions between the two age groups. Taken together, there is a need for future research with rigorous study design and methods to investigate the social interaction between older adults and younger people during intergenerational play.

1.4   Research Questions

Society is typically organized in peer-groups, which has resulted in an intergenerational gap in industrialized countries [5]. It is important that we find sustainable solutions that overcome this dichotomy and take the needs of both age groups into account [5]. Previous studies have focused on the nature of intergenerational gameplay in the family context. There is still a lack of studies examining how collaborative digital gameplay facilitates non-kin intergenerational relationships, especially between older adults aged 80+ and younger people. The objective of this research was to explore the ways in which collaborative digital gameplay facilitates intergenerational interaction between older adults and younger people.

The research questions were:

- How does intergenerational play facilitate social interaction between older adults and younger people?
- Which roles do older adults and younger people play respectively during intergenerational play?

2   Method

2.1   Research Design

Participants included 11 older adults aged between 65 and 92 from senior and community centers in Greater Vancouver and 11 younger people aged between 18 and 25 recruited from the undergraduate programs at Simon Fraser University in Canada.

Each older adult (O) was paired up with one younger person (Y) based on their schedules. The two players in each pair sat side-by-side (see Fig. 1) and played two Wii Sports Resort games (i.e., Cycling and Canoeing) for two weeks each (45 min per week), followed by playing the two games in the last two weeks. These two games are simple to play, but require the two players to coordinate and communicate with each other in order to win. All participants were new to the two Wii games before this study, but the younger participants had played other digital games at least once a week before our study. The data of this paper are collected from the five intergenerational pairs in senior centers. The five senior participants from senior centers could be considered as oldest-old with an average age 80+. All of these five senior participants and four of the five younger people were females.

Fig. 1. Intergenerational digital gameplay

2.2 Data Analysis

The research team audio recorded the game sessions of each pair rather than videotaping them because of the static nature of their game play which focused mainly on the emerging scenes on the screen. Participants' conversations were analyzed within the conceptual and methodological framework of conversation analysis (see Appendix). Conversation analysis (CA) refers to the study of the systematic analysis of the talk-in-interaction produced in everyday situations [25]. The act of conversation follows a set of rules and is used to accomplish various social orders and goals (e.g., inform, invite, suggest, show emotions) in different contexts [26]. The emphasis of CA is how inter-actants "show their understanding or interpretation of the utterance and orientation to each other using talk as evidence" [27, p. 1079]. The features of talk-in-interaction organization compose the basic work of conversation analysts [28]. Turn-taking is the sequential organization of talk in conversation and is the basic component of talk-in-interaction. Turn form, turn content, and turn length are the interests of CA and are affected by the situation [27]. The turns are comprised of turn construction unit (TCU), which can vary from single lexical items (e.g., "thanks" and "yes") to larger constructs, such as clauses and sentences [28]. The TCUs can project the possible directions and completions of utterances [29]. The next speaker can either self-select or be selected by the current speaker. **Adjacency pairs** are sequences of paired actions, such as question-answer, proposal-evaluation, and invitation-acceptance. They are normatively structured into pairs and the second part is conditionally relevant to the prior turn.

In the following session, specific excerpts will be presented to show how older adults and younger people interact with each other during the six-week intergenerational play. The focus of this study is the interactional opportunities and relationships formed in the course of intergeneration play. The selection criterion is whether the two age groups orient to each other's utterances. The following excerpt is excluded from the analysis because the older player seems to be detached from the conversation and only provides minimal response.

Excerpt 1
1   Y: Oh, we have to change our Wii? (o.3) Ok, you see the pictures? So click.
2   O: This one?
3   Y: It's up to you.
4   (5)
5   Y: So the beginner is easy, and then we go to expert.
6   Oh, we can just pick the same one. Ok, I think we just did that.
7   (3)
8   Y: Whatever you want. We can do easy.

3   Results

3.1   Learning How to Play and Getting into Game Flow

Excerpt 2 comes from a game session at the point where the older adult and younger people finished their first game task in week one. In line 1, the younger player says, "Oh! We are done!". The older player's response ("=What?") indicates she has not realized they finished the game task. In line 3, the younger player is describing their game performance to the older person. The older adult is not sure how to interpret this description and asks her young partner, "So, we did good?" The younger player confirms they have done well and explains that they are at the mid-point position when compared to other competitors. The older adult's question is the first pair part (FPP) of a adjacency pair and the younger player's answer is the second pair part (SPP). This question-answer sequence helps the older adult understand the winning status of the game. Her next turn ("£Oh! This sounds like fun£") is delivered with smiling voice, indicating she feels pleased with the gameplay results. The younger player continues the sequence by highlighting their progress using concrete information (e.g., "last place" and "19th"). In her response to the older player, she expresses her satisfaction with their performance and expresses gratitude to her younger partner ("That is good. Thank you ↑partner.").

The older player then starts another turn-taking sequence by asking her younger player what their next step might be (line 9). The younger player suggests trying another race, but also asks the older player for her opinion (line 11). The older player's response, "Anything you say, I will say yes too", indicates her deferring to the younger player.

The younger player then takes the lead on what they should do next("Okay. °Let's see. °"). In lines 14–16, the older adult explains that she is a novice gamer and her goal at this stage is not to "make a lot of mistakes". In line 17, the younger player does not comment on the older adult's emotional utterances, but based on their good performance decides to try a higher level, directing the older player's attention to the new stage in their gameplay. The older adult's response, "Okay", shows she agrees with the younger player's strategy. In line 19, the older adult starts another round of question-answer sequence by asking for status report on where they are. The younger player explains their current level in the race, and expresses confidently, "But I think we can handle three". The older adult responses, "If you think, I will be with you", confirming her status both as a follower and as a team member. Then, she starts a new round of question-answer sequence to confirm her actions. This excerpt shows how the collaborative play improves. The older adults continues to be more comfortable following the younger player's instructions and her willingness to do so.

Excerpt 2
1   Y: Oh! We are done!
2   O: =What?
3   Y: 19th place.
4   O: So, we did good?
5   Y: Ye:ah! I think we were kind of in the middle ((Laugh))
6   O: £Oh! This sounds like fun£
7   Y: We were on last place and we got to 19th.
8   O: Oh! That is good. Thank you ↑partner ((Laugh))
9   So:, what do we do next?
10 Y: We can try:: (2.2). We can try a different race¿
11   Do you want to try another race?
12 O: Anything you say, I will say yes to it.
13 Y: Okay. °Let's see.°
14 O: I am easy to get along with as long as I do not make a lot of mistakes.
15 Y: Yeah.
16 O: Because I am new.
17 Y: Maybe::. Let's try. I think we were pretty good at this.
18   So, we can move up a level.
19 O: Okay. Where were we?= On the third stage?
20 Y: We were on one stage. (.) But I think we can handle three.
21 O: If you think, I will be with you. (1.2) But, just the same motion all along?
22 Y: Yeah.

Excerpt 3 occurs as the two players finish the last game task of their first game session. In lines 1–3, the older adult doubts her ability to play the game. While she feels she has improved, she looks at her younger partner and becomes discouraged. The younger player encourages the older player by commenting on their good performance and highlights the older player's improvement ("I think you are getting the hang of it"). The older adult's short and minimal response ("Okay") suggests she still doubts her ability. To further develop the older adult's confidence, the younger player again encourages her older partner ("I think you got it"). In line 7, the older player shows that she appreciates her younger partner's positive assessment and starts another turn-taking sequence by verbalizing the in-game instructions. At this point, she still defers to her younger partner and allows the youth to choose what to do next. The younger player tries to engage the older player in the decision making process by saying, "<Let's see what the other options are>". However, the older player verbalizes that she will follow her younger partner's lead (lines 9–10). The younger player does not respond to this turn, but instead offers two options (i.e., "race each other" and "be a team"). The older player chooses to play as a team and repeats she wants to win. This excerpt shows the older player accepts the role as a student and directs the younger player to take the lead, but she also wants to contribute to the team's victory and be an equal partner as she gains more experience.

Excerpt 3

1   O: I do not know what I am doing. I just keep going this way.
2   And now and then that I take a look at you and I say,
3   I am doing the wrong thing.
4   Y: I think we are looking good. I think you are getting the hang of it.
5   O: Okay.
6   Y: I think you got it.
7   O: That sounds ↑good. (.) Play again, (.) change the race. So, what do we do?
8   Y: < Let's see what the other options are>
9   O: You tell me what to do and what kind of game we are playing.
10   And I will listen. Whatever you say, I will try.
11 Y: I think there is one where we can race each other.
12   Do you want to try that one? Or do you still want to be a team?
13 O: Well, I want to be a team until I am sure on myself.
14   And I know if I can beat you or something. I try to win too, you know¿
15   I do not want you to do all the winning. (.) I want to win, too.
16 Y: Okay.

3.2   Encouraging and Building Team Work

Excerpt 4 is selected from the fourth game session. In line 1, the younger player is guiding the older player ("There you go::"). "↑Oh, NO::" signals the failure of the game task. The older adult's turn ("What happened?") is the FPP of a new question-answer sequence. The younger player explains that they run out of time. This question-answer sequence indicates the older adult still does not understand the winning status of the game in the fourth week although she has been improving her game skills. The older adult's next utterances express her worries of "spoiling" the game task. The younger player immediately reassures the older adult ("=No:. I think you are doing Okay") and modifies utterances to direct her to focus on their achievement rather than failure ("We made 155.9 yards"). This strategy seems to be successful because the older player's next turn shows her rebounding, moving forward, and willingness to learn and correct (line 6). She asks the younger player to tell her where she went wrong. The younger player attempts to explain the reason and suggests that the sensor might not register her. The older adult doubts herself ("I haven't go the neck of it") and invites the younger player to the conversation ("you know¿"). The younger player says "Yeah" to accept the invitation and comments on the "hard" task to reassures her. In lines 11–14, the younger player repositions the sensor and directs the older player's attention to the new activities.

The older adult's utterance "Okay" indicates she agrees with the younger player's guidance and is ready to move forward. Then, she asks her younger partner to confirm her action ("So, hold like this?"). The younger player corrects her actions by displaying and explaining the techniques. In line 19, the older adult expresses her understanding of her younger partner's action ("Okay"), and takes leadership to suggest to start the gameplay, which is usually done by the younger player. This excerpts shows how the younger player encourages the older player and builds her confidence in coming new activity. The younger player's unfinished utterances (e.g., "°We just.°" in line 5, "I think sometimes" in line 10) indicates they are learning how to deal with the older adults' negative emotions and problems as well.

Excerpt 4

1   Y: Try. There you go::. (1.7) ↑Oh, NO::!
2   O: >What happened?<
3   Y: We run out of time.
4   O: Oh, no. Because I am not sure. I am spoiling this one.
5   Y: =No:. I think you are doing Okay. °We just.° We made 155.9 yards.
6   O: Well. We will have to go there again. And correct it.
7   Okay, tell me where I went wrong there.
8   Y: I think it was not registering you going on both sides. So, for some reason
9   O: I haven't go the neck of it, you know¿
10 Y: Yeah. It is hard to kind of get it to. (0.7) I think sometimes. (1.8)
11   I am going to try moving this ((sensor)).
12   So, it is facing you a little bit more too.
13   Because sometimes I don't think that picks it up. (3.5)
14   That is where it should be. (1.2) So, it is getting us 165 yards again.
15 O: Okay. So, hold like this?
16 Y: Like THIS. And then arch, (.) like come back and arch kind of,
17   and then bring it up back to the other side.
18   And it should register when you do that.
19 O: Okay. Oh, let's start. Save the energy.

3.3   Coping with Setbacks

Excerpts 5 and 6 show how the two age groups cope with the elusive goal of winning. Excerpt 5 also comes from a game session in week four when the two players failed a game task. The sequence starts with the younger player's comment on the game performance. The utterances are encouraging because instead of mentioning failure, the younger player focuses on the closeness to win (line 1). The word "Look" is an invitation to the conversation. The older player accepts the invitation and suggests to "do this again" and "get it". In lines 3–4, the two players orient to each other's turn and comment on the closeness to win. In line 6, the older player starts another sequence by displaying and verbalizing her game strategy repeatedly. The younger player directs her by highlighting the core action ("Just back (.) and back"). After confirming her correct actions, the older player suggests to "try again" and repeats their goal to build shared focus ("We got get it"). The younger player takes her suggestion and announces starting a new round of gameplay.

Excerpt 6 immediately follows Excerpt 5. The younger player delivers their second failure after a period of quiet collaborative play. In line 2, the older player says, "Time is up again", which is a verbalization of the on-screen information. It shows the older adult is able to concentrate on the emerging core information on the game screen. The younger player continues the sequence by commenting their worse game performance, but immediately says "All right" to close it and starts a new one by asking the older player whether she wants some water. The older adult replies, "Yes. ↑Oh::, boy::. I haven't been taking my deep breath", which suggests she was fully engaged in the previous round of gameplay. It also indicates the younger player takes the role of care-giver.

Excerpt 5
1   Y: <u>Oh</u>::. <u>Look</u>, how ↑<u>close</u> we were.
2   If they just gave us ONE more second, we would have <u>made</u> it.
3   O: <u>Well</u>. We have to do this <u>again</u>. We got <u>get</u> it.
4   Y: <u>Yeah</u>. We were ↑<u>so</u> close on that one.
5   O: I <u>know</u>.
6   I don't know, but I should be just going like this (.) and like this.
7   Y: Yeah. Just <u>back</u> (.) and <u>back</u>.
8   O: Okay, we will try <u>again</u>. We got <u>get</u> it.
9   Y: Yeah. All right. Let's try this. <u>START</u>.

Excerpt 6
1   Y: <u>Oh</u>::. We are not going to get this time.
2   O: Time is up <u>again</u>!
3   Y: Yeah. We did a bit <u>worse</u> on that one.
4   All right. Do you want some <u>water</u>?
5   O: <u>Yes</u>. ↑Oh::, <u>boy</u>::. I haven't been taking my deep breath!
6   After this water, then I take deep <u>breath</u>. That is <u>what</u> I did not do.

Excerpt 7 immediately follows the Excerpt 6. The younger player checks whether the older player is ready to start a new round of gameplay. The older player says "<u>Yeah</u>" and verbalizes her game strategy. The younger player agrees with it, but also makes a little adjustment to improve it ("You can start up <u>here</u>, and then just come down"). The two do not talk with each other during the collaborative play. Then, the younger player delivers the victory with loud voice and raised pitch ("We ↑<u>did</u> it! The deep breaths <u>worked</u>"). Lines 10–13 indicate the older player's enjoyment and excitement of winning the game task. She attributes the winning to "the deep breaths and the water", and mentions this a few times. Her utterances, "I hope you did not count those reckless ones. You did not¿", once again shows her willingness to win and contribute to the team success.

Excerpt 7
1 Y: <u>Ready</u>?
2 O: <u>Yeah</u>. I will start up <u>this</u> way.
3 Y: Yeah. You can start up <u>here</u>, and then just come down.
4   (12.3)
5 Y: We ↑<u>did</u> it! The deep breaths <u>worked</u>.
6 O: It <u>must</u> be the deep breaths and the water.
7   I got blame something good. I am ↑<u>so</u>:: ↑<u>happy</u>.
8   I hope you did not count those reckless ones. You did not¿
9   Because, I like. If it is better ()I won't come.
10   I am ↑<u>so</u> <u>glad</u>. I am <u>happy</u>!
11   <u>Wow</u>. I think that was the deep breath that did it.
12   Because the last time I came the deep breath that helps me.
13   I am going to take some more while I am seating.
14 Y: Okay.

3.4 Downtime Socialization

Four of the five older players shared their life-stories with their younger partners. This usually happened during the break. Excerpt 8 is an example of downtime socialization where the older adult shares her exercise habit and life stories with her younger partner. The older adult's long turns and the younger player's short turns indicate the older adult leads the conversation during this downtime socialization. However, the younger player's short responses (lines 4, 10, 13, 17, 19) stimulate the older adult to talk more. Receiving appreciation, surprise and praise from the younger player encourages her to share more life experience, which also shows the younger player's patience and kindness.

Excerpt 8

1 O: You know. I have got <u>five</u> stents in my heart.
2 Y: <u>Oh</u>, yeah! <u>Wow</u>::, my <u>gosh</u>!
3 O: I go to the specialist every once a year.
4 Y: Once a year?
5 O: That is going to be the <u>4</u>th year now.
6 Y: Okay. Wow.
7 O: I know. But he saw me last time and he said that I was doing good.
8   He said: "What are you doing?" I said: "I am <u>exercising</u>".
9   He said: "<u>Very</u> good."
10 Y: Oh! Great. So, do you do your exercises every morning?
11 O: I love it. I used to live in Ocean Park, and I used to walk <u>twice</u> a day.
12   I hate to be in the house. I am on the road all the time.
13   One time I took my girlfriend and she got breathless,
14   and she said: "I DO NOT want to walk with you".
15   I said, "Okay! Don't. I will do it now,
16   and I won't ask you to come tomorrow. I know".
17 Y: Walking is great though, isn't?
18 O: I have been walking for <u>30</u> years.
19 Y: That is <u>wonderful</u>.
20 O: Have the baby, put the baby aside and go.
21 Y: It is good to take time for yourself to do that too.
22 O: Oh, yeah. Well, I get all my work done, sometimes I do housework at night.
23   So in the morning I am free to go.
24 Y: Yeah. That is good, that is really great.

4 Discussion

The findings of the conversation analysis showed that the joint gaming experience provides a rich social context for guided participation, which means the more experienced users (younger people in this case) would mentor the novices (older adults in this case) through play. The question-answer pair is a main feature of the talk-in-interaction between the two game groups, through which the older adults learn how to co-participate in the joint gaming experience, and at the same time the younger people learn how to interact with older adults. This also indicates the asymmetrical nature of intergenerational play. In order to achieve the shared understanding of the game activities, the younger people make public their understanding of the emerging scenes, addressing problems, displaying actions, providing positive feedbacks to increase their older partners' confidence. The older adults, on the other hand, seek information and follow their younger partners' instruction and guidance.

Digital games are often viewed as the core activities of younger people [23]. The underlying assumption of identified intergenerational programs facilitated by information technologies is kind of younger people as technology teachers and older adults as students [30]. The older participants of this paper could be defined as old seniors who did not grow up in a digital age and might suffer from cognitive decline. Although they improved their gaming skills with the guidance from their younger partners, they were unable to play the game independently. Thus, they verbally accepted their role as learners and followers, and treated their younger partners as technology teachers and leaders from the beginning. As they learned more about the game and felt more comfortable to play the game, the older adults sometimes took the lead to inform upcoming activities, but they still needed their younger partners to confirm their actions. The older adults also took up the role of storytellers during breaks from playing to share their life stories with their younger partners.

Identity formation is regarded as the central motivation for younger people to participate in intergenerational programs [13]. It refers to the search for skills and talents and the development of personal meaning and direction [7]. Kessler and Staudinger [13] indicated that "the motivational sources of identity formation lie in the interplay between physical and cognitive maturation and the societal expectation to take responsibility for oneself and others" [p. 691]. Intergenerational programs offer opportunities for the younger people to learn how to serve and take responsibility for older adults and find their identity through common cultural activities [5]. This study found younger people play more mature roles as instructors, leaders, encouragers, and caregivers. They stay patient when responding to the unexpected questions asked by their older partners, and offered options to engage the older player in the decision making instead of making monologue decision. They always verbally express encouragement and confidence in older players who are discouraged when met challenges. From these perspectives, younger people exhibit prosocial behaviours during intergenerational play which is defined as "behaviour intended to help or benefit another" [9, p. 323].

5   Conclusion, Limitations and Implications for Future Research

Much of the literature to date on the features of intergenerational play focuses on the interactions within the family context, but the current study investigated the interaction between old older adults aged 80 and over and undergraduates. Results indicate that guided participation in the form of question-answer is the main way through which the two age groups can maintain shared focus and participate in the meaning-making process. Older adults play the roles of students, followers, and storytellers while younger people play more mature roles as teachers, leaders, encouragers, and caregivers during the game sessions. The findings also show that intergenerational play facilitates younger people's prosocial behaviors. They learn how to deal with older adults in a friendly and respectful way.

The authors are also aware of the limitations. The participants were mainly females, and the younger participants were well-educated, thereby, limiting the generalizability of the findings. Future research should examine the intergenerational interaction facilitated by digital games with larger and more diverse groups. Although the findings cannot be generalized to other circumstances, this study sheds light on non-kin intergenerational interactions mediated by digital games and contributes to future studies that aim to bridge the intergenerational gap in industrialized societies.

Acknowledgement. This work was supported by AGE-WELL NCE Inc., a national research network supporting research, networking, commercialization, knowledge mobilization and capacity building activities in technology and aging to improve the quality of life of Canadians and contribute to the economic impact of Canada. AGE-WELL is a member of the Networks of Centres of Excellence (NCE), a Government of Canada program that funds partnerships between universities, industry, government and not-for-profit organizations.

Appendix: A List of CA Transcription Symbols

Symbol	Meaning
=	No gap between two utterances; latching
(0.0)	Timed interval (pause) in 1/10 of a second
(.)	A tiny gap
<u>Word</u>	Stress
::	Prolongation of sound
¿	Stronger rise than a comma, but weaker than a question mark
↑↓	Shifts into higher or lower pitch
WORD	Especially loud sounds
°	Quieter sounds (symbol placed before and after)
< >	Slowed down speed
><	Speeding up
£	Smiling voice (before and after the particular words)
()	Inability to hear what was said
(())	Descriptions, e.g. ((laughter))

References

1. Andersen-Ranberg, K., Petersen, I., Robine, J.M., Christensen, K.: Who Are the Oldest-Old (2005). http://www.share-project.org/uploads/tx_sharepublications/CH_2.2.pdf. Accessed
2. Thomas, J.: Insights into Loneliness, Older People and Well-being (2015). https://social welfare.bl.uk/subject-areas/services-client-groups/older-adults/officefornationalstatistics/17 6008dcp171766_418058.pdf. Accessed
3. Age UK: Improving later life. Understanding the oldest old (2012). http://www.ageuk.org.uk/Documents/EN-GB/For-professionals/Research/Improving%20Later%20Life%202%20WEB.pdf?dtrk=true. Accessed
4. Bernard, S.: Loneliness and Social Isolation among Older People in North Yorkshire (2013). http://www.york.ac.uk/inst/spru/research/pdf/lonely.pdf. Accessed
5. Werner, C., Linke, S.K.: The German project called "Triangelpartnerschaften" (triangle partnerships): can music bridge the intergenerational gap? Gifted Talented Int. **28**(1), 239–248 (2013)
6. Lloyd, J.: The State of Intergenerational Relations Today: A Research and Discussion Paper (2008). http://www.ilcuk.org.uk/images/uploads/publication-pdfs/pdf_pdf_66.pdf. Accessed
7. Erikson, E.H.: Identity and the Life Cycle. International Universities Press, Inc., New York (1959)
8. Erikson, E.H.: Childhood and Society, 2nd edn. Norton, New York (1963)

9. Wenner, J.R., Randall, B.A.: Predictors of prosocial behavior: Differences in middle aged and older adults. Personality Individ. Differ. **101**, 322–326 (2016)
10. McAdams, D.P., de St. Aubin, E.: A theory of generativity and its assessment through self-report, behavioral acts, and narrative themes in autobiography. J. Pers. Soc. Psychol. **62**(6), 1003–1015 (1992)
11. Cheng, S.T.: Generativity in later life: Perceived respect from younger generations as a determinant of goal disengagement and psychological well-being. J. Gerontol. Ser. B Psychol. Sci. Soc. Sci. **64**(1), 45–54 (2009)
12. Latz, I.: Musik im Leben älterer Menschen. Dümmler, Bonn (1998)
13. Kessler, E.M., Staudinger, U.M.: Intergenerational potential: effects of social interaction between older adults and adolescents. Psychol. Aging **22**(4), 690–704 (2007)
14. Griff, M.D.: Intergenerational play therapy: the influence of grandparents in family systems. Child Youth Serv. **20**(1–2), 63–76 (1999)
15. Williams, S., Renehan, E., Cramer, E., Lin, X., Haralambous, B.: 'All in a day's play' - an intergenerational playgroup in a residential aged care facility. Int. J. Play **1**(3), 250–263 (2012)
16. Davis, L., Larkin, E., Graves, S.B.: Intergenerational learning through play. Int. J. Early Child. **34**(2), 42–49 (2002)
17. Entertainment Software Association. 2016 Sales, demographic and usage data: essential facts about the computer and video game industry (2016). http://essentialfacts.theesa.com/Essential-Facts-2016.pdf. Accessed
18. De Schutter, B., Vanden Abeele, V.: Designing meaningful play within the psycho-social context of older adults. In: 3rd International Conference on Fun and Games, pp. 84–93. ACM Press, New York (2010)
19. Vetere, F., Davis, H., Gibbs, M.R., Howard, S.: The magic box and collage: responding to the challenge of distributed intergenerational play. Int. J. Hum. Comput. Stud. **67**(2), 165–178 (2009)
20. Derboven, J., Van Gils, M., De Grooff, D.: Designing for collaboration: a study in intergenerational social game design. Univ. Access Inf. Soc. **11**(1), 57–65 (2011)
21. Khoo, E.T., Cheok, A.D., Nguyen, T.H.D., Pan, Z.: Age invaders: social and physical inter-generational mixed reality family entertainment. Virtual Reality **12**(1), 3–16 (2008)
22. Zhang, F., Kaufman, D.: A review of intergenerational play for facilitating interactions and learning. Gerontechnology **14**(3), 127–138 (2016)
23. Chua, P.H., Jung, Y., Lwin, M.O., Theng, Y.L.: Let's play together: Effects of videogame play on intergenerational perceptions among youth and elderly participants. Comput. Hum. Behav. **29**(6), 2303–2311 (2013)
24. Rice, M., Wan, M., Jie, Y. L., Ng, J., Ong, J.: Intergenerational gameplay: evaluating social interaction between younger and older players. In: CHI, Austin, Texas, USA, pp. 2333–2338 (2012)
25. Hutchby, L., Wooffitt, R.: Conversation Analysis, 2nd edn. Polity Press, Cambridge (2008)
26. Sacks, H., Schegloff, E.A., Jefferson, G.: A simplest systematics for the organization of turn taking for conversation. Language **50**(4), 696–735 (1974)
27. Mazur, J.M.: Conversation analysis for educational technologies: theoretical and methodological issues for researching the structures, processes, and meaning of online talk. In: Jonassen, D.H. (ed.) Handbook of Research on Educational Communications and Technology, 2nd edn, pp. 1073–1098. Lawrence Erlbaum Associates, Mahwah (2004)
28. Chepinchikj, N., Thompson, C.: Analyzing cinematic discourse using conversation analysis. Discourse Context Media **14**, 40–53 (2016)

29. Padilha, E.G.: Modelling Turn-taking in a Simulation of Small Group Discussion (Unpublished doctoral dissertation). University of Edinburgh, Edinburgh, UK (2006). http://hdl.handle.net/1842/1679. Accessed
30. Kaplan, M., Sanchez, M., Shelton, C., Bradley, L.: Using Technology to Connect Generations. Penn State University, Generations United, University Park, Washington D.C. http://extension.psu.edu/youth/intergenerational/program-areas/technology/using-technology-to-connect-generations-report. Accessed

Health Care and Assistive Technologies and Services for the Elderly

Distributed User Interfaces for Poppelreuters and Raven Visual Tests

Pedro Cruz Caballero[1], Amilcar Meneses-Viveros[1(✉)],
Erika Hernández-Rubio[2], and Oscar Zamora Arévalo[3]

[1] Departamento de Computación, CINVESTAV-IPN, México, D.F., Mexico
`pcruz@computacion.cs.cinvestav.mx`, `ameneses@cs.cinvestav.mx`
[2] Instituto Politécnico Nacional, SEPI-ESCOM, México, D.F., Mexico
`ehernandezru@ipn.mx`
[3] Facultad de Psicología, UNAM, México, D.F., Mexico
`arevalo@unam.mx`

Abstract. Poppelreuter and Raven tests are used by psychologists to analyze cognitive abilities, mental diseases like visual agnosia, and even dementia syndromes like Alzheimer. It is known that this tests can be applied using mobile devices. However, the natural deterioration of the elderly, particularly visual weakness, may cause problems when using devices, even with Large or Xlarge screens. In order to reduce this problems, we proposed the use of a Distributed User Interface, using a tablet and an smartTV, to support users with visual problems to do Poppelreuter and Raven tests. At the end of our research we confirm that the application of visual tests using a Distributed User Interface is feasible.

1 Introduction

There are different batteries of psychological tests currently used to analyze cognitive abilities, mental diseases, and some other syndromes. Specialists apply tests using printed images, audio, and interviews but lately they are applied using mobile devices, which could also help users, especially older adults, to perform them without having to go to a doctor's office. Nowadays, exist apps for mobile devices to do psychological tests [1,2]. However, their designs do not contemplate the most common deteriorations in advanced ages, visual weakness or even tactile problems [3].

We proposed the use of a Distributed User Interface (DUI) [4], using a tablet and an smartTV, to support users with visual problems to do Poppelreuter and Raven tests. These tests are easy to implement and understand since the participants are not required to have advanced arithmetic or narrative skills. The DUI, that we designed, has got features to help older adults, like text and audio instructions, bigger buttons that are easily identified by its appearance (text and colour), and in some cases users can answer the tests recording their voice or using the tablet to make a draw. The DUI mainly works on a tablet but uses an smartTV to distribute or share some user-interface elements that are displayed in a bigger size.

© Springer International Publishing AG 2017
J. Zhou and G. Salvendy (Eds.): ITAP 2017, Part II, LNCS 10298, pp. 325–338, 2017.
DOI: 10.1007/978-3-319-58536-9_26

In this work we show the results obtained after have tested our DUI prototype, aimed at older adults, developed for iPad and AppleTV. These results include time measures, number of correct answers and number of attempts, all this data were used to measure user's performance. The data was obtained twice, first when users only used iPad to solve the tests, and the second time when using iPad and appleTV together (DUI). Questionnaires, based on Likert and semantic differential scales, were designed to measure the prototype acceptance level [5–7]. We compared the results of both analyzes, performance and acceptance, to corroborate that a higher level of acceptance also reflects a better performance in tests.

Furthermore, we used the questionnaires, to count how many users preferred landscape or portrait mode, and how many of them preferred to use their fingers or an stylus-pen to interact with the touch screen. Our prototype has differences between landscape and portrait orientation mode, not in the mode of interaction but, in how graphic elements are displayed.

These results let us understand what characteristics of our prototype allow users to better solve tests and which ones need to be re-designed. Probably, one of our main targets would be the addition of more elements on appleTV and reduce the number of elements showed on iPad when the DUI mode is being used. During our approaches with real users (older adults between 62 and 90 years that had not used an iPad before) we perceive another uses for the DUI to help specialist's diagnosis procedures. Some other possible future improvements would refer to prevent problems such as shaking hands, which caused unwanted double touch events.

At the end of our research we confirm that the application of visual tests using a DUI is feasible. A mobile device could help patients that cannot easily visit consulting rooms and the specialist could manage battery tests remotely. And in the case that a patient goes to a consulting room the specialist could use the DUI to observe its performance, like in a mirror screen but, additionally he could see other parameters.

2   Related Work

The related work falls into three main lines of research: Neuropsychology testing on mobile devices, mobile applications design for older adults and distributed user interfaces design.

Several traditional neuropsychological tests have been migrated to mobile applications [1,2,8]. There are mobile applications and computer programs that help to identify and treat problems such as Alzheimer's or dementia [9–11]. Other works have been concerned to incorporate the tests of Luria [8,12], these works emphasize the modes of interaction of the older adult with the mobile application depending on the capabilities of the user. Some authors have focused on monitoring, through mobile devices, the degree of deterioration of patients [13,14] y otras apoyan a diversos tratamientos [15–21].

The design of applications focused on the elderly has been developed by different authors along years. Design guides have been developed, and common impairments of older adults have been identified [22,23]. Other studies have focused on analyzing the resistance put by users when using technology for medical purposes, as well as to verify which are the most appropriate or even the most preferable modes of interaction among the elderly [8].

The concept of Distributed User Interfaces have been researched constantly, some papers have reported the developed frameworks and models to support DUIs [24]. Others, have reported particular designs for applications aimed at older adults [25].

3 Distributed User Interface

A user interface (UI) is the set of elements that allow the user to interact with computers. These elements can be categorized as input, output and data control. This definition involves all kinds of technology and interaction mechanisms.

A distributed user interface is a set of UIs that can be implemented in more than one device, or software platform. Based on Gallud [26,27] we know that any single user interface can be cataloged as a distributed user interface if it has some characteristics like portability, fragmentation (also know as decomposition), simultaneity, and continuity. Being the first two characteristics the most important to satisfied the transformation of an user interface to a distributed one.

Portability: Means that a user interface can be completely or partially transferred in order to achieve a better user interaction.
Fragmentation: Any user interface can be fragmented, only if its different fragments can be run independently without losing functionality.
Simultaneity: If an user interface can run in different, software or hardware, platforms and also can be managed at the same time, it means that the UI is a simultaneous system.
Continuity: This characteristic is reachable when a system element can be transfered to another module, that is also a part of our distributed user interface, but always preserving its state.

The use of DUIs is very common in multimedia applications such as music players, video players, image galleries, video games, books or interactive learning materials, but there are still few applications that use it for purposes other than entertainment.

4 Visual Tests

The Soviet neurologist Alexander Romanovich Luria (1902–1977), studied the higher cortical functions in man and his relationship with the cerebral mechanisms. In his book "Higher Cortical Functions in Man" [28] we can learn about the functions and how they are responsible for our human behavior and capabilities. Functions such as perception, memorization, language, thinking, writing, reading and arithmetic can not be considered as isolated or indivisible faculties, since they are usually the result of interaction between different areas of the brain. Luria's ideas have spread widely, especially since a neuropsychological test called Luria-Christensen has been developed [29]. This test was developed by A. Christensen, and is widely used for the diagnosis of various diseases and brain damage. The main purpose of these tests is to analyze and to understand the structure of psychic phenomena. This analysis helps to diagnose abnormalities of the central nervous system, and to rehabilitate superior cortical functions.

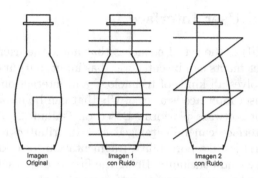

Fig. 1. Example of the Poppelreuter 1 test [28]

Luria visual perception tests are used in the diagnosis of different affections or diseases, for example visual agnosia, which is the inability to recognize objects with the naked eye, but once the patient takes them and manipulates them, recognizes them. This visual condition is due to a dysfunction between the brain and the vision that makes everything around the individual continually new. For example, if a tennis racket is shown to a patient with visual agnosia, he will not know what that object is or what it is used for. Only when using it, the patient will know that it is a racket and that serves to hit a ball. This visual disability is associated with a brain injury caused by traumatic brain injury or stroke and even meningitis.

The application of these tests is carried out by mental health specialists and are usually applied with the help of printed images, audio tracks, interviews, text analysis and even body movements. In this paper we will use three tests, Poppelreuter 1, Poppelreuter 2 and the Raven test. The images that we use for its description were taken from the book of Luria [28].

4.1   Poppelreuters Test 1

This test begins by showing the patient the image of the outline of an object, later it will be shown more images containing the original object, but now the outline is mixed with strokes or lines that can confuse the patient. The specialist will request that the outline of the original object be marked, ignoring the additional

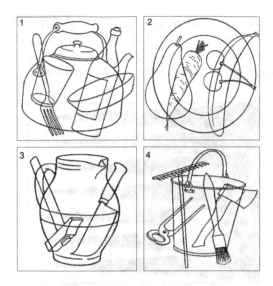

Fig. 2. Example of the Poppelreuter 2 test [28]

lines, which are classified as visual noise. The test consists of displaying different images, with different objects and different types of visual noise. Figure 1 shows an example of test images where the original object is a bottle and next to it we see two images with visual noise, the extra strokes can be straight lines or curves.

4.2   Poppelreuters Test 2

This test consists of displaying images that contain the outline of different objects. Unlike Poppelreuter 1, this test uses visual noise, but it does overlap the contour of different objects. In this test, there are various objects, all the strokes displayed belong to a general drawing and all objects must be identified. The specialist will ask the patient to distinguish objects. In case the patient shows problems to list them he can use his finger and try to point them out. Figure 2 shows four examples with objects that are easily identified. This is important because if uncommon objects are included, the patient will have trouble naming objects and the cause is not a visual disability.

4.3   Raven Tests

The Raven test is used to evaluate visual abilities and cognitive abilities. It consists of the patient observing a certain visual structure, which is incomplete. The patient can choose between six or eight possible options, but only one is correct. In some cases, the specialist will ask the patient to differentiate the answers from the others. To do this, the patient must identify the pattern of each option. The complete Raven test consists of three series, each with twelve different test matrices whose difficulty progressively progresses. The advantage of employing Raven to evaluate cognitive abilities is that no grammatical knowledge or complex mathematical ability is required. For this reason, this test is used in children and adults. Figure 3 shows an example test matrix.

Fig. 3. Example of the Poppelreuter 2 test [28]

5   Prototype

The development of our work uses evolutionary development, "which is based on the idea of developing an initial implementation, exposing it to the user's comments and refining it through the different versions until an adequate system is developed. The activities of specification, development and validation are intertwined with rapid feedback [30]. There are two types of evolutionary development: exploratory development and prototype development; The latter was the way we used it.

5.1   GUI Design for Older Adults

Old age is a natural occurrence in the biological development of humans. It involves a series of physiological changes caused by the sensitive, perceptive, cognitive and motion control impairment in older adults. Humans who reach this stage of life develop diseases of natural degeneration of the body such as Alzheimer and Parkinson, among others [10,16,22,23,31].

Interface design for seniors considered possible natural damage they may have. These impairments are visual, auditory, movement and cognitive.

Vision. Physiological changes to the eye related to aging result in less light reaching the retina, yellowing of the lens (making blue a difficult to discern color), and even the beginning stages of cataracts result in blurriness. The eye muscles are also affected; it can be more difficult for older adults to quickly change focus or get used to fast-changing brightness. Some solutions for design include: conspicuity can be enhanced by enhanced contrast and taking advantage of pre attentive processes, and effortful visual search can be lessened through application of Gestalt laws.

Effect of vision. How the visual aspects of the web can interact with aging to produce difficulties.

Older users vary greatly in their perceptual capabilities; thus interfaces should convey information through multiple modalities (vision, hearing, touch) and even within modalities (color, organization, size, volume, texture). Within a website, consistency should be the highest priority in terms of button appearance and positioning, spatial layout, and interaction behavior. Background images should be used sparingly if at all because they create visual clutter in displays. High contrast should be maintained between important text or controls and the background. Older users are likely to have a reduced tolerance for discovery and quit instead of hunting.

Information should be presented in small, screen-sized chunks so that the page does not require extensive scrolling. If this cannot be helped, alternative ways of navigating (such as table of contents) or persistent navigation that follows the user as they scroll be provided.

Hearing. A wide variety of changes can occur to hearing. A good auditory design considers both the physical changes in sound perception and the cognitive changes in the comprehension that comes from initial perception. Keeping informational sounds above background noise requires a study of the display environments. The loudness of a sound is truly individual, but can be approximated through the sound pressure levels (dB) and frequencies typically maintained in the aging ear. When hearing loss is severe enough that users wear an aid, consider how those aids interact with the interface.

List of general design guidelines that can be used to improve the design of auditory menus. Consider potential background noise. Calculate loudness levels. For tones, use low-tom-mid-range frequencies. When designing a display device, consider physical proximity ti the ear and interactions with hearing aids. Avoid computer-generated voices. Use prosody. Provide succinct prompts. Provide context.

Cognition. The main objective in the design of displays is that they are easy to understand. It is intended that the interface is effective, that is, to help users to complete tasks with less confusion and less possible error. To achieve this, we consider some user skills such as: working memory, spatial skills and perceptual speed. Working memory allows the user to recall situations or things in a short period of time. Spatial ability refers to the user to have a location-based representation of the environment where it interacts, in our case, the state of the application. The perceptual speed indicates the rate at which it perceives and processes information. It is known that these skills decline with age, so the design should not be confused with the instructions or the information presented.

Interface design considerations for older adults with an HCI approach involve: The Display, with large or extra-large screen size to reduce visual limitations and with touchscreen technology. The Information, the text showed, including instructions, must have Sans Serif font and contrast color with backgrounds for a grater understanding. Buttons, big dimensions and must use text instead icons to the user to determine the function of the button more easily. Audio, must exist a volume control for the user, preferably use female voices with a level of acuity below average.

5.2 Prototype Design

Visual tests are applied in phases. In the first phase the patient is shown a set of clear images, and is asked to him to observe and remember them. In the second phase, the patient repeats the previous process, but now seeing more complex or blurred images. In the last phase, the images are even more complex and the patient is asked to identify particular characteristics, such as size, color and some geometric patterns. These tests require different modalities of interaction in computer-human and in human-computer. In computer-human modalities are vision and audition. In human-computer modalities are touchscreen, pointing device and speech recognition.

Poppelreuter 1. In this test, the patient is shown drawings of objects of daily life (e.g., a bottle). Next, a series of images are shown that contain the same object, but superimposed with lines or other strokes (Fig. 1). The patient must distinguish the original object by pointing out its silhouette. This action will be done with the support of the iPad touch screen and drawing events that will allow the user to paint the outline of the image by simply sliding his finger on the screen.

Poppelreuter 2. This test is more complicated than Poppelreuter 1. Now the patient must distinguish a set of objects overlapping together (Fig. 2). The way this test can be solved will be by pointing out the contour of the objects or using voice recording so that the patient responds to the test orally. In case the patient indicates the contours, events of drawing and storage of the image must be implemented. In the case of voice recording, events must be included for recording, playback and high audio responses.

Raven Test. This test begins by showing the patient an incomplete image, with an empty region. This empty region must be completed by choosing one of six options (Fig. 2). The implementation of this test involves the deployment of images belonging to different test arrays. These test arrays contain the main image and its response options. In this case, you only need to add buttons for each of the options and validate the correct answer.

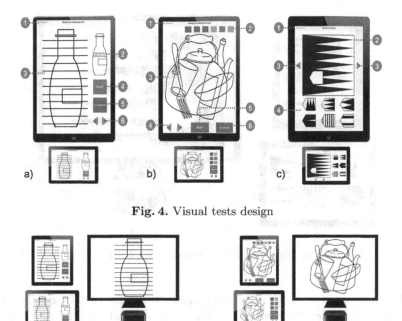

Fig. 4. Visual tests design

Fig. 5. Distributed user interface for Poppelreuter 1 and Poppelreuter 2

Poppelreuters Test 1 Design. In this test Fig. 4(a), six different graphic elements are identified: (1) Button to return to the main menu. (2) The image with the original object. (3) The drawing area, where the outline of the original object must be recognized, simply slide your finger over the image to draw. (4) Button to reset the drawing area, remove any drawing made. (5) Button that stores the image in the drawing area. (6) The buttons to advance or rewind between different tests. This updates (3).

Poppelreuters Test 2 Design. In this test Fig. 4(b), six different graphic elements are identified: (1) Button to return to the main menu. (2) Selection of color to draw. (3) The drawing area, where you must recognize the outline of the different objects, simply slide your finger over the image to draw. (4) The buttons to advance or rewind between different tests. This updates (3). (5) Button to reset the drawing area, delete all drawn drawings. (6) Button that stores the image in the drawing area.

Raven Tests. In this test Fig. 4(c), four different graphic elements are identified: (1) Button to return to the main menu. (2) Main image, which is incomplete. (3) The buttons for forward or backward between different tests. (4) Solution options.

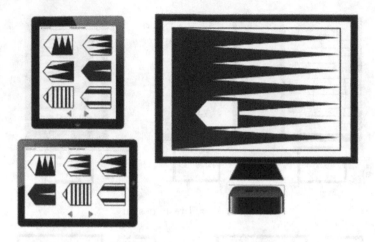

Fig. 6. Distributed User Interface for Raven test

When any of the tests is started, the instructions are visually displayed and displayed to the user. The text and audio of the application is modified according to the language configured on the iPad (currently the Spanish and English language is considered).

When the application distributes the GUI to a device with a larger screen (AppleTV connected to a 27-inch screen), the display of the tests will be as show in Fig. 5. For Poppelreuter 1 and 2 tests, the drawing area is displayed on the AppleTV and the iPad will continue to display the same elements. When you draw on the iPad, you will immediately see the screen.

For Raven test Fig. 6, the appleTV displays the image to be completed. The iPad shows the solution options and navigation buttons. The solution options are displayed in a larger size and the image on the appleTV is also displayed on a larger scale.

6   Test and Results

Usability tests were done. To do this, we use questionnaires. In addition, closed questions were used with Liker scaling [?]. This escalation consists in presenting a set of affirmations or judgments, before which the participant's reaction is requested. That is, each statement is presented and the subject is asked to express their reaction by choosing one of the five points or categories of the scale. Each point is assigned a numerical value. Thus, the participant obtains a score regarding his answer and in the end his total score, adding the scores obtained in relation to all the affirmations. In general terms, a Likert scale is constructed with a high number of affirmations that qualify the attitude object and the obtained score serves as a measurement instrument.

Each of the options receives a score, which ranges from 1 to the number of possible answers. The maximum value is obtained by the answer that shows the highest agreement with the sentence and the minimum value is associated with the answer that denies the sentence. In this way a questionnaire that uses the scale of Likert allows to count the levels of acceptance and, in our particular case, the levels of usability.

6.1 Population

Our tests were performed with the help of a small group of the elderly, belonging to the Mexican National Institute of Older Adults (INAPAM). During 5 days each of the participants performed an individual test session. Starting with a brief explanation, training, resolution of the tests, filling in the questionnaires, and finally if the participant wanted it, a brief interview was conducted. For each of the tests we obtained the number of trials and duration time.

The test group consisted of 25 participants, 22 women and 3 men. 17 of the participants wear eyeglasses, 16 were women and 1 were men. The age of participants was between 62 and 90 years. Being the median 74 years.

6.2 Hardware

The hardware used to do the user's tests were an iPad Mini 2 (8″ Retina Display 2048 × 1536, 16 GB, A7 Chip, Wi-Fi, 1.3 GHz, 1 GB RAM, iOS 9.1), an appleTV 4th generation (H.264 video up to 1080p, 32 GB, A8 Chip, Wi-Fi, Ethernet, 2 GB RAM, tvOS 1.2), and a 24 in. LED Screen (1080p Full HD). The distribution of our application was done using AirPlay services.

6.3 Results

The results were obtained as a result of having qualified the different questionnaires. In general the Landscape orientation was the one that had greater acceptance in the test group. 64% in Poppelreuter 1, 68% in Poppelreuter 2 and 88% in Raven. For the interaction modals, Poppelreuter 1 test consists on drawing, which could be done by tapping or using a stylus. The stylus was the preferred modal of interaction, since it facilitated the correct tracking of the contour of the objects. In Poppelreuter 1, 88% prefered Stylus; In Poppelreuter 2, 80% use dictation; And for Raven test, 72% preferred the Stylus too.

Preferences according to the user interface type show that the distributed user interface was most preferred. In Poppelreuter 1 76% consider it useful. Poppelreuter 2, 72% And in raven 68%.

7 Conclusion

In general, the use of the DUI made that users spent more time to complete the tasks. In the case of Poppelreuter's 1 test, we could not measure the effectiveness, but we could distinguished that the drawings made in the DUI looked more detailed. For poppelreuter's 2 test, we observe that participants preferred the speech mode of interaction and not the drawing mode. Finally, for Raven test, which results and times were obtained with the iPad, we perceive that at least 76 percent of participants showed greater or equal results than doing the test only with iPad. In this case, the responses could not be memorized since the images that formed this test were randomly displayed.

Based on all the data collected and on the experience obtained we can say that the application of these psychological tests can apply in both modes, iPad and DUI mode, but is in DUI mode when better results are obtained.

References

1. Razalgames: Raven test APK. Android, September 2016
2. Games, E.: Raven IQ test. Android, March 2016
3. Calero Valdez, A., Ziefle, M.: Older users' rejection of mobile health apps a case for a stand-alone device? In: Zhou, J., Salvendy, G. (eds.) DUXU 2015. LNCS, vol. 9194, pp. 38–49. Springer, Cham (2015). doi:10.1007/978-3-319-20913-5_4
4. Luyten, K., Coninx, K.: Distributed user interface elements to support smart inter-action spaces. In: Seventh IEEE International Symposium on Multimedia, 8 pp. IEEE (2005)
5. Love, S.: Understanding Mobile Human-Computer Interaction. Butterworth-Heinemann, Newton (2005)
6. Rossiter, J.R.: Measurement for the Social Sciences: The C-OAR-SE Method and Why It Must Replace Psychometrics. Springer Science & Business Media, New York (2010)
7. Narens, L.: Introduction to the Theories of Measurement and Meaningfulness and the Use of Symmetry in Science. Psychology Press (2013)
8. Hernández-Rubio, E., Meneses-Viveros, A., Mancera-Serralde, E., Flores-Ortiz, J.: Combinations of modalities for the words learning memory test implemented on tablets for seniors. In: Zhou, J., Salvendy, G. (eds.) ITAP 2016. LNCS, vol. 9754, pp. 309–319. Springer, Cham (2016). doi:10.1007/978-3-319-39943-0_30
9. Cristancho-Lacroix, V., Wrobel, J., Cantegreil-Kallen, I., Dub, T., Rouquette, A., Rigaud, A.S.: A web-based psychoeducational program for informal caregivers of patients with Alzheimer's disease: a pilot randomized controlled trial. J. Med. Internet Res. **17**(5) (2015)
10. Mandala, P.K., Saharana, S., Khana, S.A., Jamesa, M.: Apps for dementia screening: a cost-effective and portable solution. J. Alzheimers Dis. **47**, 869–872 (2015)
11. Sawyer, P., Sutcliffe, A., Rayson, P., Bull, C.: Dementia and social sustainability: challenges for software engineering (2015)
12. Miranda, J.A.H., Hernàndez Rubio, E., Meneses Viveros, A.: Analysis of Luria memory tests for development on mobile devices. In: Duffy, V.G. (ed.) DHM 2014. LNCS, vol. 8529, pp. 546–557. Springer, Cham (2014). doi:10.1007/978-3-319-07725-3_54

13. Pereira, C., Almeida, N., Martins, A.I., Silva, S., Rosa, A.F., Oliveira e Silva, M., Teixeira, A.: Evaluation of complex distributed multimodal applications: evaluating a telerehabilitation system when it really matters. In: Zhou, J., Salvendy, G. (eds.) DUXU 2015. LNCS, vol. 9194, pp. 146–157. Springer, Cham (2015). doi:10. 1007/978-3-319-20913-5_14

14. Hackney, M.E., Hall, C.D., Echt, K.V., Wolf, S.L.: Multimodal exercise benefits mobility in older adults with visual impairment: a preliminary study. J. Aging Phys. Act. 23(4), 630–639 (2015)

15. Jang, W.: An iPad application prototype to enhance memory of older adults. In: Stephanidis, C. (ed.) HCI 2015. CCIS, vol. 528, pp. 299–304. Springer, Cham (2015). doi:10.1007/978-3-319-21380-4_51

16. Czaja, S., Beach, S., Charness, N., Schulz, R.: Older adults and the adoption of healthcare technology: Opportunities and challenges. In: Sixsmith, A., Gutman, G. (eds.) Technologies for Active Aging, pp. 27–46. Springer, New York (2013). doi:10.1007/978-1-4419-8348-0_3

17. Sixsmith, A., Johnson, N.: A smart sensor to detect the falls of the elderly. IEEE Pervasive Comput. 3(2), 42–47 (2004)

18. Demiris, G., Rantz, M.J., Aud, M.A., Marek, K.D., Tyrer, H.W., Skubic, M., Hussam, A.A.: Older adults' attitudes towards and perceptions of "smart home" technologies: a pilot study. Medical Informatics and the Internet in Medicine 29(2), 87–94 (2004)

19. Sorwar, G., Hasan, R.: Smart-TV based integrated e-health monitoring system with agent technology. In: 2012 Proceedings of the 26th International Conference on Advanced Information Networking and Applications Workshops (WAINA), pp. 406–411. IEEE (2012)

20. Aal, K., Ogonowski, C., von Rekowski, T., Wieching, R., Wulf, V.: A fall preventive iTV solution for older adults, Siegen, Germany (2014)

21. Demongeot, J., Virone, G., Duchêne, F., Benchetrit, G., Hervé, T., Noury, N., Rialle, V.: Multi-sensors acquisition, data fusion, knowledge mining and alarm triggering in health smart homes for elderly people. C.R. Biol. 325(6), 673–682 (2002)

22. Pak, R., McLaughlin, A.: Designing Displays for Older Adults. CRC Press, Boca Raton (2010)

23. Fisk, A.D., Rogers, W.A., Charness, N., Czaja, S.J., Sharit, J.: Designing for Older Adults: Principles and Creative Human Factors Approaches. CRC Press, Boca Raton (2009)

24. Kovachev, D., Renzel, D., Nicolaescu, P., Koren, I., Klamma, R.: Direwolf: a framework for widget-based distributed user interfaces. J. Web Eng. 13(3–4), 203–222 (2014)

25. Cruz Caballero, P., Viveros, A.M., HernándezRubio, E.: Distributed user interfaces for Luria's tests for older adults. In: Stephanidis, C. (ed.) HCI 2016. CCIS, vol. 617, pp. 413–419. Springer, Cham (2016). doi:10.1007/978-3-319-40548-3_69

26. Gallud, J.A., Peñalver, A., López-Espín, J.J., Lazcorreta, E., Botella, F., Fardoun, H.M., Sebastián, G.: A proposal to validate the user's goal in distributed user interfaces. Int. J. Hum. Comput. Inter. 28(11), 700–708 (2012)

27. Vanderdonckt, J., et al.: Distributed user interfaces: how to distribute user interface elements across users, platforms, and environments. In: Proceedings of the XIth Interacción, vol. 20 (2010)

28. Luria, A.: Las funciones corticales superiores del hombre. Martínez Roca, Barcelona (1983)

29. Hamster, W., Langner, W., Mayer, K.: Tübinger-Luria-Christensen Neuropsychologische Untersuchungsreihe: TÜLUC. Beltz Test (1980)
30. Sommerville, I.: Software Engineering. International Computer Science Series. Addison Wesley, Reading (2004)
31. Yamagata, C., Kowtko, M., Coppola, J.F., Joyce, S.: Mobile app development and usability research to help dementia and Alzheimer patients. In: 2013 IEEE Long Island Systems, Applications and Technology Conference (LISAT), pp. 1–6. IEEE (2013)

Adaptation of the Model for Assessment of Telemedicine (MAST) for IoT Telemedicine Services

George E. Dafoulas[1(✉)], Georgios Pierris[2], Santiago Martinez[3], Lise Kvistgaard Jensen[4], and Kristian Kidholm[4]

[1] Faculty of Medicine, University of Thessaly, Larisa, Greece
gdafoulas@med.uth.gr
[2] National Centre for Scientific Research 'Demokritos', Athens, Greece
gpierris@iit.demokritos.gr
[3] Faculty of Health and Sport Sciences, University of Agder, Grimstad, Norway
santiago.martinez@uia.no
[4] Center for Innovative Medical Technology, Odense University Hospital, Odense, Denmark
{lise.kvistgaard.jensen,kristian.kidholm}@rsyd.dk

Abstract. Internet of Things (IoT) based solutions and services may be used to support and extend the independent living of older adults in their living environments by responding to real needs of caregivers, service providers and public authorities. Telemedicine and telehealth platforms are among the various types of IoT services that could support the provision of health services. Current Health Technology Assessment (HTA) models that are used for the evaluation of telehealth and telemedicine services do not consider IoT aspects. HTA models would ideally need to be extended to include IoT platforms, for an optimal introduction of IoT in everyday provision of health and care services. This paper presents an initial adaptation of the Model for Assessment of Telemedicine (MAST) for IoT Telemedicine services based on a literature review of IoT, telemedicine and telehealth services characteristics. MAST involves assessment of outcomes within the following seven domains: Health problem and characteristics of the application, Safety, Clinical effectiveness, Patient perspectives, Economic aspects, Organizational aspects, Socio-cultural, ethical and legal aspects. The domains of the characteristics of the application, socio-cultural, safety and ethical and legal aspects were identified as those to be adapted to cover new challenges associated to IoT services.

Keywords: Internet of Things · Telemedicine · Health Technology Assessment

1 Background

The 2015 Ageing Report [1] stated that one out of three Europeans would be over 65 years old, with a ratio of "working" to "inactive" population of 2 to 1 by 2060. For the European countries, the fact that their populations are ageing represents a great challenge for the sustainability, quality and demand coverage of their current health and social care

© Springer International Publishing AG 2017
J. Zhou and G. Salvendy (Eds.): ITAP 2017, Part II, LNCS 10298, pp. 339–349, 2017.
DOI: 10.1007/978-3-319-58536-9_27

systems. In this line, the European Commission has proposed the introduction of Information and Communication Technologies (ICT) for the management of eHealth and e-care services, prioritizing telemedicine and telehealth [2, 3]. However, the organizational challenges, legislation aspects, cost of technological infrastructures and technological updates, reimbursement policies and issues related with privacy, safety and security, constitute significant barriers for the development of ICT services at scale, where telemedicine and telehealth services play a substantial role. Health Technology Assessment (HTA) has been introduced to systematically evaluate properties, effects and impact of health technology from a multidisciplinary perspective. HTA has already become "an important part of evidence-based health decision-making in most EU countries" [4].

2 Introduction

The Institute of Electrical and Electronics Engineers (IEEE) recently produced an extensive report tapping on numerous research directions of IoT to provide a formal definition of IoT [5]. In general, IoT is often referred to as an idea, vision, infrastructure or paradigm that proposes, in a rather indistinct form, multiple future internet technologies where everyday objects exploit their inherent networking capabilities allowing them to communicate bi-directionally with other networked devices. Presently, various IoT solutions are being deployed in Europe for sensing, measuring and controlling indoor and outdoor smart connected objects to different emerging IoT platforms available in the market that have the aim to support the independent living idea of older users. IoT platforms are more numerous when compared to existing telemedicine platforms and therefore it is necessary an unequivocal interpretation that dictates what and how IoT telemedicine service solutions could be used for a specific purpose. Health technologies are essential for a modern health system, and among them emerging IoT medical equipment and devices have the potential to support the prevention, diagnosis, and treatment of disease, as well as patient rehabilitation. HTA is aimed at improving the uptake of cost-effective new technologies, by preventing or slowing the uptake technologies that seem promising but have persistent uncertainties or may cause an unjustified burden for the health system [6]. Available HTA models for the evaluation of IoT telehealth and telemedicine services need to be examined to ensure cover of IoT platforms, prior to their effective introduction to everyday provision of health and care services.

A few comprehensive HTA frameworks have been introduced for the evaluation of Telemedicine and Telehealth services [7, 8]. Among them the aim of the HTA Model for Assessment of Telemedicine (MAST) [7] is to provide a structure for assessment of effectiveness and contribution to quality of care of telemedicine applications which can be used as a basis for decision making. In other words, the aim is that clinical, administrative and political decision makers in hospitals, communities, regions, government department etc. will use the model as a structure for the description of the outcomes of telemedicine and as an important basis for decisions on whether to implement telemedicine services in the health care systems. Similarly, the producers of telemedicine, the biotech industry, can use MAST as a structure for description of the outcomes of their products for patients, hospitals etc. It is the overall aim that MAST will improve the possibilities for decision makers to choose the most appropriate technologies to be used in the most cost-effective way by providing a multidisciplinary assessment based on scientific methods and results. MAST was developed within a project that was funded by the EU under SMART 2008/0064 and was conducted as part of the MethoTelemed study.

3 Objective

This objective of this paper is to examine if the HTA framework MAST can be used to evaluate IoT based telemedicine services and identify any adaptation required for MAST to this direction. In addition an effort to identify potential synergies and complementary functions of MAST with existing HTA frameworks used for the evaluation of IoT supported telemedicine services, was made.

4 Methods

The definition of IoT telemedicine and telehealth solutions in accordance with the current literature [5–10] was identified together the characteristics that could interact with the domains of the MAST framework. Due to the vast heterogeneity of definitions of IoT in the literature, the definition [5] provided by the major technical professional organization for the advancement of technology, the Institute of Electrical and Electronics Engineers (IEEE) and the definition [9] from agency of the United Nations (UN) whose purpose is to coordinate telecommunication operations and services throughout the world, the International Telecommunication Union (ITU), were used. In addition, a respective survey on IoT definition highly cited in the literature was used [10].

MAST involves assessment of outcomes within seven domains as described in Fig. 1. When using the model, the assessment starts with several preceding considerations. The focus should be on the determination of the purpose of the telemedicine application, the relevant alternatives that should be compared in the assessment, the level in the health care system (local, regional, national) at which the assessment should be produced and whether the telemedicine application is a mature technology. Finally, MAST also includes assessment of the transferability of the results found in the multidisciplinary assessment, e.g., across borders or when going from a small-scale pilot to a large-scale implementation.

Preceding consideration
- Purpose of the telemedicine application?
- Relevant alternatives?
- International, national, regional or local level of assessment?
- Maturity of the application?

Multidisciplinary assessment
1. Health problem and characteristics of the application
2. Safety
3. Clinical effectiveness
4. Patient perspectives
5. Economic aspects
6. Organisational aspects
7. Socio-cultural, ethical and legal aspects

Transferability assessment
- Cross-border
- Scalability
- Generalizability

Fig. 1. The elements in MAST

5 Results

Out of the seven domains of the MAST model and their subtopics (Table 1), the domains of Clinical effectiveness, Patient perspectives, Economic aspects and Organizational are based on methodologies and Key Performance Indicators that focus on the service provision rather than the technical platform itself. Therefore, we concluded that MAST framework can cover the HTA related to the specific domains for IoT telemedicine services.

On the other hand, the following domains were identified as those that need careful consideration when applying MAST to evaluate IoT based telehealth and telemedicine solutions.

Table 1. The domains and topics in MAST

Domain	Definition	Topics
1. Health problem and description of the application	Description of health problem of patients expected to use the telemedicine application and the application being assessed, including description of current use	• Health problem • Description of application • Technical characteristics Current use of application
2. Safety	Identification and assessment of harms	• Clinical safety (patients and staff) • Technical safety (technical reliability)
3. Clinical effectiveness	Effects on patient's health	• Effects on mortality • Effects on morbidity • Effects on health-related quality of life (HRQL) • Behavioral outcomes Utilization of health services
4. Patient perspectives	Issues related to patient's perception or relatives of telemedicine application including patients and relatives' acceptance of technology	• Satisfaction and acceptance • Understanding of information • Confidence in treatment • Ability to use application • Access and accessibility Empowerment, self-efficacy
5. Economic aspects	A societal *economic evaluation* comparing a telemedicine application with relevant alternatives in terms of costs and consequences. A *business case* describing expenditures and revenues for healthcare institutions using telemedicine application	• Economic evaluation: • Amount of resources used when delivering application and comparators • Prices for each resource • Related changes in use of healthcare • Clinical effectiveness Business case: • Expenditures per year Revenue per year
6. Organizational aspects	Assessment of type of resources mobilized and organized when implementing a new technology, and changes or consequences technology use can further produce in the organization	• Process • Structure • Culture • Management
7. Socio-cultural, ethical and legal aspects	Socio-cultural aspects include places where patient lives and acts during use of application. Ethical analysis appraises ethical questions raised by application itself and by the consequences of implementing it or not. Legal aspects focus on legal obligations which must be met and any specific legal barriers that may exist to implementation of application.	• Ethical issues • Legal issues • Social issues

5.1   Description of the Application

The aim of MAST as a model for assessment of telemedicine is to provide a structure for the assessment of effectiveness and contribution to quality of care of telemedicine applications which can be used as a basis for decision making. In the MAST domain of description, the description of the health problem of the patients expected to use the telemedicine application and the description of the application being assessed. These two issues are included in one common domain because the description of the patients and the telemedicine application serve as an overall description of the background for the assessment. Even today, almost 20 years after the IoT term was coined, it remains a difficult exercise to formally define the broad vision of IoT.

IoT enables the development at a global scale of advanced services by interconnecting, both physical and virtual "things" based on interoperable information [9]. Atzori et al. [10] highlighted the pervasive nature of the technology to enable the interaction and cooperation of "things" to reach common goals. A more systematic definition of an IoT system is by validating a list of features that the things in an IoT system should exhibit, namely, the Interconnection of Things, Connection of Things to the Internet, Uniquely Identifiable Things, Ubiquity ("anywhere" and "anytime" referring to where and when it is needed), Sensing/Actuation capability, Embedded Intelligence, Interoperable Communication Capability, Self-Configurability, and Programmability [5]. Starting from things as low in complexity as an RFID-tagged "thing" and up to smart devices with embedded intelligence offering even advanced analytics on the edge, the IoT paradigm entails the necessary ingredients to drive another transformation of telemedicine. Therefore, a careful description of the content and aim of the IoT application becomes crucial, as does the description of the type of patients' needs to be addressed, their health problem and the aim of using a specific IoT technology.

5.2   Safety

IoT telemedicine solutions include unprecedented capabilities and data from sensing, measuring, controlling smart connected objects and personal health systems. The remotely monitor of a patient's health with the use of network of sensors, actuators and other mobile communication devices, is referred to as the Internet of Things for Medical Devices (IoT-MD) [11]. The IoT-MD provides a platform that allows patient's vital parameters to get transmitted by medical devices via a gateway onto secure cloud based platforms where it is stored and analyzed. Thus, new challenges regarding patient's safety for liability issues are expected for health professionals. The framework of definition and reporting of adverse events of IoT connected medical devices is regulated by the respective Medical Devices Directives in EU and different bodies in other countries (e.g., Food and Drug Administration in US). The IoT-MD capabilities could set additional safety challenges for service based on the connected medical devices and therefore in the respective MAST domain the assessment could focus on these challenges. This domain of MAST focuses on the legal obligations which must be met and will identify any specific legal barriers that may exist to the implementation of the application.

5.3   Ethics and Privacy

IoT telehealth services are characterized by pervasive computing aiming to make devices "smart," thus creating a sensor network capable of collecting, processing and sending data, supporting a comprehensive platform to improve the human experience and quality of life. However, the data sharing capabilities of IoT platforms raise serious concerns regarding privacy of patients' personal health data. In the EU, the Working Party on the Protection of Individuals about the processing of personal data, set up by Directive 95/46/EC of the European Parliament and of the Council of 24 October 1995, has adopted the opinion 8/2014 on the Recent Developments on the Internet of Things [12].

In the respective domain, MAST considers the prevalent morals, values and behavioral models of society relevant for assessment of telemedicine applications in ethical analysis in this domain. These values, moral principles and social rules (norms) form the basis of social life as well as national laws and consequently it is important to understand them. These factors play a key role in shaping the context in which telemedicine applications are used. The moral rules of the society reflect the values of the society and the values may be weighted differently in various societies. Evident cultural (e.g. religious) and economic (e.g. gross national product) differences also have a major impact on the moral value of the consequences that the implementation of a telemedicine application can have.

The MAST domain on ethics and privacy could include the following subtopics to state the main principles arising from respective regulations for an IoT telemedicine service:

- Informed consent: Informed consent is required for data collection, data storage, data processing and publication of raw or processed data. Before consent is sought, information must be given, specifying the alternatives, risks, and benefits for those involved, in a way users understand.
- Voluntary participation: Participation must be on a voluntary basis.
- Participation of disabled people: It is essential that every IoT telemedicine service provision, should deal with the challenges of ethical nature, such as personal autonomy and integrity regarding citizen rights and especially confidentiality aspects.
- Minimal risk: Patients should not be exposed to more than minimal risk.
- Anonymity: Patients have the right to remain anonymous. All data analyses must be performed on an anonymous basis.
- Feedback: Participants shall be provided with the possibility to retrieve feedback on the results of research.
- Privacy: Health professionals must ensure that the way outcomes of patients' monitoring are reported does not contravene the right to privacy and data protection.
- Confidentiality: Confidentiality is different from the patient's right to privacy and it refers to how data will be stored.
- Data control: The data subject has the right to access all data processed about him or her, and has the right to demand the rectification, deletion or blocking of data that is incomplete, inaccurate or is not being processed in compliance with the data protection rules.

- Informed stakeholders: Informing stakeholders in detail on ethical aspects of research and evaluation/validation in reporting activities.
- Incentives (financial inducements, etc.) for participation in a telemedicine service provision should be stated clearly, whenever they are allowed by the regulatory and legal framework.

6   Discussion

MAST has been used in several European telemedicine projects, including more than 25,000 patients [13]. Based on this, MAST can be considered the most widely used assessment framework in studies of telemedicine in Europe. The adaption of MAST framework for IoT services needs to be validated via quantitative and qualitative methods, as it was the case for a recent Delphi study for the validity of the standard version of MAST [13].

The emergence of remote IoT telemedicine services has motivated the need in measuring the impact and evidence of the benefits of these relatively modern practices in the health sector. Some of them are focused on specific application domains (e.g. telemedicine), others are related to specific aspects (e.g. technology user acceptance, socioeconomic impact). Apart from MAST, other specific selected methodologies have been developed with relatively different focus (e.g. MAFEIP Monitoring and Assessment Framework for the European Innovation Partnership on Active and Healthy Ageing services (EIPonAHA) [14], ASSIST Assessment and Evaluation Tools for Telemedicine [8]).

These methodologies have proved their reliability and scientific-based approach to help decision makers about future investments in the Smart Living and telemedicine domains, which have a strong parallelism with the IoT technologies for active and healthy ageing. For example, MAST has been already used in integrated care pilots with large number of users (BEYOND SILOS, SMARTCARE, MASTERMIND, RENEWING-HEALTH, etc.). MAST is very much focused in the assessment of the outcomes of telemedicine solutions, and may be more clinically oriented when compared to other contexts of IoT for ageing well.

The European Commission has recently decided to co-fund and launch the Horizon 2020 Large Scale IoT project ACTIVAGE (http://www.activageproject.eu/).

ACTIVAGE is in line with the strategic vision on evaluating and scaling up IoT-based solutions to support independent living and active and healthy ageing. It is a flagship H2020 project (25.000.000 Euros budget, 50 partners, pilots with 7,000 expected users). One of the most important objectives of ACTIVAGE is the implementation of a reference evaluation framework for Smart Living for aging well solutions. Attention has been dedicated to raise specific indicators related not only to QoL, Economic, Acceptability and Usability but also to deployment scale and service model achieved during the pilots. The evaluation framework reports together with the analysis of enabling factors and potential barriers, includes the ambition to shape the foundations for the mobilization of investment at public and private levels, not only in Europe but also worldwide, to start the way for massive adoption of IoT solutions in the European market.

ACTIVAGE has a pilot ecosystem, characterized by heterogeneous and complex scenarios, both at service and technological level. Some of the use cases will include telemedicine services.

The evaluation framework of the IoT services will be based on the ACTIVAGE "GLOCAL" evaluation framework based on element of frameworks, such as MAST. A key aspect is the multilayer and multidimensional evaluation strategy, which can catch and integrate Global and Local specific features (GLOCAL approach). Each pilot site will measure not only global indicators related to domain standard reference parameters able to contribute to demonstrate effectiveness of the implemented solution (impact on citizens' Quality of Life, sustainability, innovation), but also local socio-economic indicators that will attract the mobilization of investment by public and private entities in each site according to the actual socioeconomic context.

This framework will be applied to specific use-case implementation of the related stakeholders involved who will address the assessment of GLOCAL framework Key Performance Indicators (KPIs) in an aggregated reference evaluation integrated framework. Certain aspects of GLOCAL are similar to MAST framework and therefore the two HTA models are expected to be complementary for certain use cases. ACTIVAGE will not reinvent methods and approaches but will rather build on top of existing best practices and experiences, among which MAST is included.

The GLOCAL evaluation framework is based on three main evaluation categories referring to the main Triple Win indicators of the EIPonAHA: impact on QoL, Sustainability, Innovation and Growth [14]. Every category is composed of sub-criteria focused on specific aspects. Both global and local indicators will be detailed in terms of measurement tool, target and reference methodology. The skeleton of the GLOCAL approach is the following. ACTIVAGE demand side partners have initially listed specific KPIs, measurement tools and reference methodology of the GLOCAL evaluation framework.

Specific ACTIVAGE pilot targets will be described for each KPI at local level according to background and expected impact. Evaluation data concerning every GLOCAL KPI per sites will be collected in a global data-repository called "ACTIVAGE Evidence Open Data Base" that will be specifically implemented and exploited by the ACTIVAGE project.

ACTIVAGE Evidence Open Data Base will complement the role of the marketplace tailored to offer direct access to resources and applications. Specific goal of the project is to raise the "ACTIVAGE Evidence Open Data Base" as Reference Framework for evaluating IoT solutions in the AHA domain, acting as dashboard to collect evaluation data and as well as advisor tool for stakeholders and company that want to access ranking of IoT solutions in the AHA domain. ACTIVAGE exploitation plan will address a specific business model and will collaborate with the AHA key players to make ACTIVAGE Evidence Open Data Base a sustainable service. The ACTIVAGE Evidence Open Data Base aims to provide orientation and advisory services to a variety of users, including of course end-users of pilots, and motivate fieldwork players and manufacturing and product distributing companies to participate in enriching the collective knowledge which it represents. The outcome of such ACTIVAGE Public Evidence website is to be able to provide an evaluation data collection tool and at the same time to make available quantitative and qualitative KPI values reported by pilots and different initiatives.

7   Conclusion

Based on the characteristics of MAST as a comprehensive HTA model, it seems it can be used for the evaluation of IoT telemedicine services, by adaptation of those MAST domains referring to the detailed description of the IoT platform and the MAST domains related to ethics, safety and privacy aspects. Due to focus of MASTon telemedicine applications, it could be used for the evaluation of IoT telemedicine services, as long as a detailed description of the IoT platform will be provided, given their heterogeneity. The MAST domains related to ethics, safety and privacy issues require extra focus in order to address the related challenges posed by an IoT telemedicine service.

Acknowledgements. This paper is part of the ACTIVAGE project that has received funding from the European Union's Horizon 2020 research and innovation program under grant agreement No 732679.

References

1. European Commission: The 2015 ageing report, underlying assumptions and projection, methodologies, Joint Report prepared by the European Commission (DG ECFIN) and the Economic Policy Committee (AWG). European Commission, Brussels (2014)
2. Commission of the European Communities, COM: 245 Communication from the Commission to the European Parliament, the Council, the European Economic and Social Committee and the Committee of the Regions, A Digital Agenda for Europe. European Commission, Brussels (2010)
3. Commission of the European Communities, COM: 689 communication from the Commission to the European Parliament, the Council, the European Economic and Social Committee and the Committee of the Regions on telemedicine for the benefit of patients, healthcare systems and society. European Commission, Brussels (2008)
4. European Commission: Public Health, Health Technology Assessment (2017). https://ec.europa.eu/health/technology_assessment/policy_en. Accessed 10 Feb 2017
5. Minerva, R., Biru, A., Rotondi, D.: Towards a definition of the Internet of Things (IoT). IEEE Internet Initiative. Telecom Italia, Torino (2015)
6. WHO: Health technology assessment of medical devices, WHO Medical device technical series. WHO Press, Geneva (2011)
7. Kidholm, K., Ekeland, A.G., Jensen, L.K., Rasmussen, J., Pedersen, C.D., Bowes, A., Flottorp, S.A., Bech, M.: A model for assessment of telemedicine applications: MAST. Int. J. Technol. Assess. Health Care **28**(1), 44–51 (2012). doi:10.1017/S0266462311000638
8. Empirica: ASSIST - Assessment and evaluation tools for telemedicine and telehealth (2012). http://assist.empirica.biz. Accessed 7 Nov 2016
9. ITU-T: Overview of the Internet of Things, ITU-T Y.4000/Y.2060 (2012). http://handle.itu.int/11.1002/1000/11559. Accessed 2 Jan 2017
10. Atzori, L., Iera, A., Morabito, G.: The internet of things: A survey. Comput. Netw. **54**, 2787–2805 (2010). doi:10.1016/j.comnet.2010.05.010

11. Ashok, K., Prattep, M.: White Paper: The internet of Things for Medical Devices-Prospects, Challenges and the way forward, TCS' Life Sciences Business Unit (2014). http://www.tcs.com/resources/white_papers/Pages/Internet-of-Things-Medical-Devices.aspx. Accessed 2 Jan 2017

12. Working Party on the Protection of Individuals with regard to the processing of personal data. 14/EN WP 223 Opinion 8/2014 on the on Recent Developments on the Internet of Things. European Commission, Brussels (2014)

13. Kidholm, K., Jensen, L.K., Kjølhede, T., Nielsen, E., Horup, M.B.: Validity of the model for assessment of telemedicine: A delphi study. J. Telemed. Telecare (2016). doi: 10.1177/1357633X16686553

14. European Commission, Joint Research Centre. MAFEIP (2009). http://is.jrc.ec.europa.eu/pages/TFS/MAFEIP.html. Accessed 2 Jan 2017

Harvesting Assistive Technology Vocabularies: Methods and Results from a Pilot Study

Yao Ding[1], J. Bern Jordan[2], and Gregg C. Vanderheiden[2(✉)]

[1] University of Wisconsin-Madison, Madison, WI, USA
ding@trace.wisc.edu
[2] University of Maryland, College Park, MD, USA
{jbjordan, greggvan}@umd.edu

Abstract. A terminology gap is one of the leading difficulties faced by consumers and practitioners in selecting assistive technology (AT). As we design and develop a decision support tool for people to discover and choose AT, it is crucial to better understand the language that the users can interpret and prefer to use when referring to and searching for AT. This paper presents a study that aims to harvest vocabulary of people describing access technologies, access needs and difficulties. We describe the method of eliciting user-generated, domain-specific vocabulary; analyze data collected from 44 participants during the pilot phase; and discuss potential use of the vocabulary to improve interface design and product findability.

Keywords: Assistive technology · Terminology · User-generated vocabulary

1 Introduction

Computer access has become essential for all people to fully and equally participate in almost every aspect of everyday life. Many people need assistive technology to achieve full access due to disability, aging, literacy or computer literacy related barriers. Assistive technology (AT) is an umbrella term that includes "any item, piece of equipment, or product system, whether acquired commercially, modified, or customized, that is used to increase, maintain, or improve functional capabilities of individuals with disabilities" [1]. Examples of AT for computer access—or computer access technology or access technology/products, interchangeably used in this paper—include text-to-speech that reads screen content aloud for people who are blind or have low vision, word prediction and completion that makes text input easier for people with learning or physical disabilities, and many others.

However, it is estimated that fewer than 15% of people who need special interfaces are getting them [2]. Many potential clients cannot find or get professional evaluations due to the shortage of sufficiently trained providers [3]. Also, individual consumers face many difficulties in choosing AT by themselves, which results in many ill-fitted products being selected and abandoned prematurely. It is found that one of the most common difficulties is a terminology gap [3]. Consumers find themselves in the situation of "you don't know what you don't know", and thus are not able to search for and find what fits their needs.

© Springer International Publishing AG 2017
J. Zhou and G. Salvendy (Eds.): ITAP 2017, Part II, LNCS 10298, pp. 350–361, 2017.
DOI: 10.1007/978-3-319-58536-9_28

An open-source, joint collaborative tool is under development to use data federated from multiple AT databases (EASTIN, AbleData, GARI, etc.) to help people with disabilities find access technology with best fit, and assist practitioners in both clinical selections and keeping up with technology advances [2]. As part of this endeavor, this paper presents a vocabulary study that aims to reduce the terminology gap by studying the language people use in describing access technologies, and access needs and difficulties. We describe the method of eliciting user-generated, domain-specific vocabulary; analyze data collected from 44 participants during the pilot phase; and discuss potential use of the vocabulary to improve interface design and product findability.

2   Background and Related Works

2.1   The GPII Initiative, the Unified Listing, and the Shopping/Alerting Interface

This study is being conducted as part of the Global Public Inclusive Infrastructure (GPII) initiative. The goal of the GPII is to "create an infrastructure that would simplify the development, delivery and support of access technologies and provide users with a way to instantly apply the access techniques and technologies they need, automatically, on any computers or other ICT they encounter" [4]. From a user's viewpoint, the GPII will help them discover what features or technologies they need to make ICT usable. This information will form a set of user's needs and preferences, which can then be stored in the cloud or in a personal device. The needs & preferences set will be used by the GPII's "auto-personalization from preferences" (APfP) capability to cause any interface or e-content to change into a form that the user can use.

The *Unified Listing* is a critical component of the GPII, which allows users to search and find AT that meet their needs. It is a listing of assistive technologies federated from multiple data sources [5]. For example, AbleData (http://www.abledata. com), and the EASTIN AT database (http://www.eastin.eu).

For end users to be able to effectively browse and search, we are developing an interface usable and understandable to people with all levels of knowledge in AT—from experts and clinicians to users who know nothing about these technologies. The interface allows the user to explore not only by product categories (as in most shopping sites) but also by user needs and difficulties. In addition to discovering and shopping, the interface will alert users, at their requests, to new products that meet their needs and preferences. This interface is thus called the *Shopping/Alerting Interface*.

In designing the Shopping/Alerting Interface, the terminology gap has become a big challenge. The vocabulary used to describe access needs and access features are hard for end users to understand when they appear on the interface, and hard for the system to interpret when they are composed by the user for searching. This study aims to better understand users' vocabulary to inform interface design and improve product findability.

2.2   Terminology Gap and Solutions

The problems of terminology gaps have been studied since early research in information systems. It is observed that a user must refer to a desired object by the same
name given by the system designer (an exact match) to find the object (for example, a
person might have to specifically search for a "screen reader" when they want to find
AT software that reads aloud the text and metadata of a graphical user interface). One
attempt to improve object findability was to increase the system's vocabulary richness
by having experts generate keyword descriptors for system content [6]. In their
experiment, Gomez and Lochbaum used a culinary information system with 188
recipes indexed by keywords generated by 8 expert cooks. They varied the vocabulary
richness by combining keywords generated by one, two, four, or eight experts.
Compared to the leaner vocabulary, richer vocabularies significantly (1) retrieved more
results, (2) returned target results more often, (3) reduced unrecognized queries, and
(4) required fewer attempts to identify the targets.

In addition to enriching system vocabularies, later research explored *enriching
query-target relationships* on top of "exact matching". A study observed differences in
vocabulary of the user and the interactive system, which hinders the use of a built-in
"Help" function [7]. For example, searching "black and white" in a graphic editing
software to achieve the effect of black-and-white film did not yield the desired results,
since the software uses "desaturate", "grayscale", or "channel mixer" features for such
effect. The authors tried to solve the problem by bridging possible search queries and
system features. They harvested search queries related to the software from
auto-completion services (e.g., "Google Suggest"), enumerated all the system features,
and associated each pair of query-feature with a relevancy score by automatically
evaluating the retrieved documents. Compared to simple term matching, query-feature
matching search is superior in all measures of relevancy [7].

In the field of AT, enriching both the system vocabulary and query-feature relationships may be helpful in improving product findability. This study will take both
measures. However, using prior studies' methods of populating vocabulary and
query-feature relationships in our study poses a few challenges. First, experts may use
different vocabularies than lay people. Expert-generated keywords may not be as
representative as those that might be used by novice consumers in product searching.
Second, it requires many experts to generate a comprehensive set of vocabulary. In
Gomez's study [6], the agreement between the eight experts in the words they used to
describe the same objects was about one in 20 times. We can anticipate much more
than eight experts in the AT field be required until the vocabulary reaches saturation.
Third, the automatic enrichment from existing content will not be able to associate user
"needs and difficulties" with product features if such descriptions are lacking. For
example, "shaky hands" is a common access-related difficulty. Ideally, it could be
associated with products such as big-key keyboards, keyguards, tremor filtering mouse
or software, etc. Unfortunately, such colloquial, need/difficulty-oriented descriptions
are rare in product descriptions. Any search using such queries is not likely to lead to
many desirable results.

We also reviewed existing vocabularies or taxonomies that contain AT-related
terms, and assessed how much they can be used in the Shopping/Alerting Interface.

ISO 9999:2011 is the International Organization for Standardization's categorization of assistive technology. It is comprehensive but not fine-grained enough for our purpose. For instance, it contains only one category for keyboards of all kinds, while there are many kinds of alternative keyboards. There are also taxonomies of medical and clinical terms that contain some AT-related terms; the Unified Medical Language System Metathesaurus (UMLS, https://www.nlm.nih.gov/research/umls/), and the Systematized Nomenclature of Medicine-Clinical Terms (SNOMED CT, https://www.nlm.nih.gov/healthit/snomedct/). In a quick search by names of 50 common AT features in the two taxonomies, no results were found in more than 40 of the searches. Search by access needs was worse. The scarcity and coarseness in AT-related terms render the existing vocabularies less useful to our project. We need an AT-focused, fine-grained vocabulary that contains both technology terms and user needs/difficulties language.

2.3   Feature-Based and Need-Based Searching

Seventy-six percent (76%) of the top-grossing shopping sites have adopted feature-based searching and browsing [8]. Feature-based tools usually index and present information in a way that allows searching and browsing by product types, names, features, attributes, etc. This usually works well for commonly known products, and for power users within a niche market. However, for most AT consumers—unaware of available options, unfamiliar with product properties, and vague about their needs—this approach requires domain knowledge, and shifts users' focus from their needs to unfamiliar features. This can lead users to "tunnel vision" focusing on limited (and potentially inadequate) options.

The Shopping/Alerting Interface will provide a need-based taxonomy, in addition to the common feature-based taxonomy. It will allow users to explore access features without having to know any technology jargon. For instance, the interface will filter and display products based on user needs and difficulties: "make visual content easier to see", "help with entering letters, words, numbers" and so on.

Besides the needs/difficulty taxonomy, the Shopping/Alerting Interface will also be able to understand free-text search queries in laypersons' language. Feature-based search usually works well for consumers with some knowledge of the potential purchases. For example, one may start off searching for "digital camera", then for "camera full frame", followed potentially by "Sony A7 reviews". However, this may not be the case for shoppers with little or no domain knowledge. An amateur might search by "travel camera", "lightweight HD camera", and the like, without going into depth in searching for features. AT consumers reported not knowing what products or features to look for and thus have great difficulty constructing effective search keywords [3].

The provision of a need-based taxonomy and enriched search engine requires a better understanding of both consumer and AT professional vocabulary. We need to know what words or phrases consumers and professionals might use to describe access needs and difficulties. The research questions of this study are: what language do consumers and professionals use to describe AT and needs for AT; and what are the methods to harvest the vocabulary. The rest of the paper describes the pilot testing of this vocabulary study from three aspects:

- developing an operational method for collecting domain-specific, topic-specific vocabulary;
- collecting vocabulary on computer access related needs, difficulties, and technology from both laypeople and professionals;
- discussing potential use of the vocabulary to improve product findability;

3 Participants

To gather consumer and AT professional vocabulary, study participants included individuals with disabilities; family, friends or caregivers of individual of disabilities; and occupational therapists, speech-language pathologists, physical therapists, and assistive technology practitioners. The screening process excluded participants under 18, who are not able to provide informed consent independently, and those whose first language was not English.

During the pilot phase, participants were recruited through flyers posted in public libraries in Wisconsin and Pennsylvania, online posters, and email listservs. As of February 2017, 44 participants were recruited; 40 have completed all the questions. Participant demographics are shown in Table 1.

Table 1. Participant demographics

Gender	• males 11 • females 33
Age	• average 48.20 • standard deviation 14.62

Self-reported Disabilities	• blind 16
	• low vision 4
	• hard of hearing 3
	• speech 2
	• physical 4
	• cognitive or learning 1
	• no disability 18
	• others
	  − balance disorder 1
	  − multiple sclerosis 1
	  − seizure 1

Education	• some college 10 • college 22 • graduate 12
Clinicians or experts (OT, PT, SLP, ATP, etc.)	• clinicians 15 • non-clinicians 29

4   Procedures

Potential participants who responded to the recruitment flyer were given a link to complete a screening questionnaire. Eligible participants received another link to the consent form followed by online survey questions. Before the survey began, participants were instructed that they could skip any questions, pause at any time and return to where they left off at any time, or withdraw from the study at any time.

The online survey instrument presented 30 questions to each participant. The 30 questions were randomly selected from a question bank of 104 questions. The first 15 questions were "need" questions that polled participants' vocabulary on describing access needs/difficulties. The latter 15 questions were "feature" questions that asked participants to "name" access features or solutions using their own language. Each group of 15 questions were preceded by a sample question for the participants to become familiarized. A need question (Fig. 1) presents a use case describing a person's difficulty with certain kind of computer access. The participant will be asked to search for a solution and type in possible search queries. A feature question (Fig. 2) describes how a solution helps a person with his/her access difficulty, and asks what words/phrases the participant may use to call this solution.

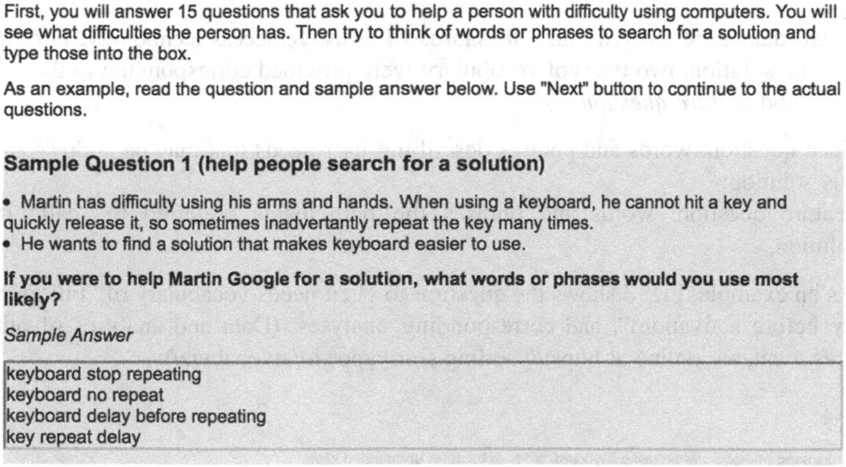

First, you will answer 15 questions that ask you to help a person with difficulty using computers. You will see what difficulties the person has. Then try to think of words or phrases to search for a solution and type those into the box.

As an example, read the question and sample answer below. Use "Next" button to continue to the actual questions.

Sample Question 1 (help people search for a solution)

• Martin has difficulty using his arms and hands. When using a keyboard, he cannot hit a key and quickly release it, so sometimes inadvertantly repeat the key many times.
• He wants to find a solution that makes keyboard easier to use.

If you were to help Martin Google for a solution, what words or phrases would you use most likely?

Sample Answer

keyboard stop repeating
keyboard no repeat
keyboard delay before repeating
key repeat delay

Fig. 1. Sample "Need" Question (how a user might search for a solution to particular problems and needs)

Participants could take the survey on the web or in person. All took it on the Web. They were encouraged to provide as many answers as they could. On the web questionnaire, there is no limit in the answer input field, and no time limit.

Participants who took part in the study were entered into a drawing to win a Kindle Fire tablet with 1:15 odds of winning.

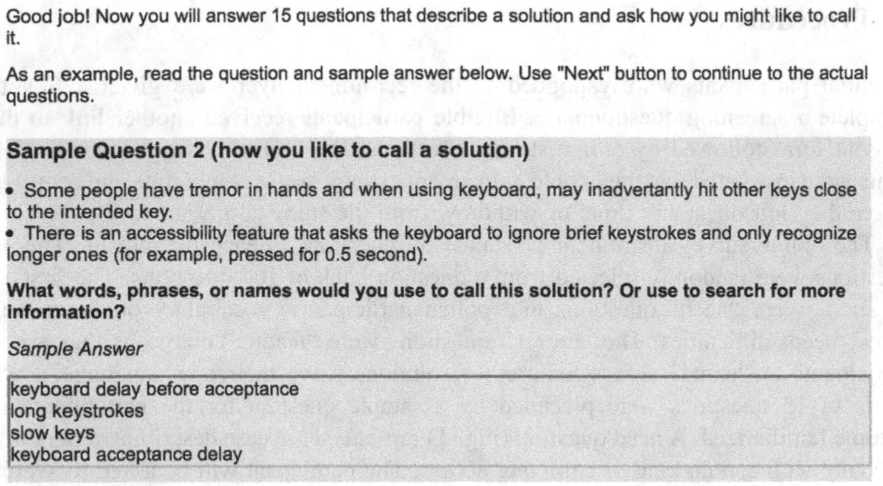

Good job! Now you will answer 15 questions that describe a solution and ask how you might like to call it.

As an example, read the question and sample answer below. Use "Next" button to continue to the actual questions.

Sample Question 2 (how you like to call a solution)

• Some people have tremor in hands and when using keyboard, may inadvertently hit other keys close to the intended key.
• There is an accessibility feature that asks the keyboard to ignore brief keystrokes and only recognize longer ones (for example, pressed for 0.5 second).

What words, phrases, or names would you use to call this solution? Or use to search for more information?

Sample Answer

keyboard delay before acceptance
long keystrokes
slow keys
keyboard acceptance delay

Fig. 2. Sample "feature" question (what a user might call a solution)

5 Data Analysis

Collected data were entered into a thesaurus of assistive/access technology. For each AT feature/solution, two types of vocabulary were provided corresponding to the *need question* and *feature question*:

• Need question: words and phrases describing user needs that may be addressed by this solution;
• Feature question: words and phrases the participants preferred to "call" this solution.

As an example, Fig. 3 shows the question to elicit needs vocabulary of "FilterKeys (delay before activation)", and corresponding analyses. (Data and analyses of other features available online at https://yaoding.shinyapps.io/atvocabviz/):

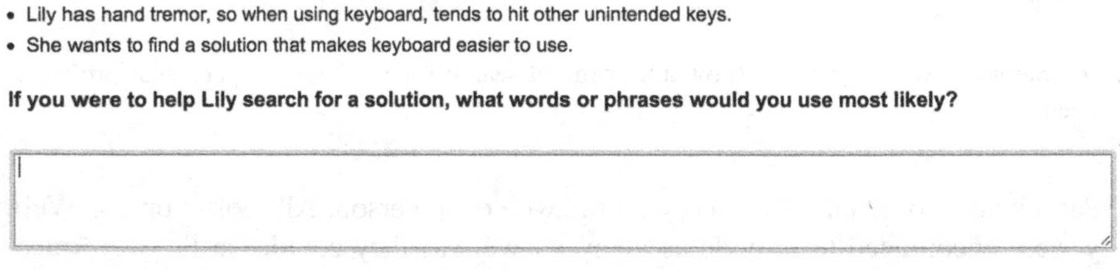

• Lily has hand tremor, so when using keyboard, tends to hit other unintended keys.
• She wants to find a solution that makes keyboard easier to use.

If you were to help Lily search for a solution, what words or phrases would you use most likely?

Fig. 3. Question to elicit vocabulary of needs/difficulties that may be addressed by "FilterKey (key delay before activation)"

Original queries. These are participants' input without any editing (Table 2).

Table 2. Participants' original queries in respond to need and feature questions of "FilterKeys"

Feature	Queries (Terms describing user needs)	Queries (Terms used to call this feature)
filterkeys delay before activation	program keyboard modifications	ignore brief keytstrokes
filterkeys delay before activation	adjust keyboard sensitivity	delay keyboard
filterkeys delay before activation	keyboard with larger keys	hold keyboard
filterkeys delay before activation	keyboard with keys spaced further apart	Sticky keys
filterkeys delay before activation	typing with tremors	SlowKeys or "slow keys"
filterkeys delay before activation	key guards	long press keyboarding
filterkeys delay before activation	Keyboard delay or latency	keypress acceptance level
......	......(25 more queries omitted due to limited space)......	......(10 more queries omitted due to limited space)......

Word stems and frequencies. Word stems are word "roots" of original queries after congregating, cleansing (changing to lowercase, removing punctuations and white spaces), removing stop words (e.g., the, at, which), and stemming (e.g., reducing "disability", "disabled", "disabling" to "disabl") (Table 3). Frequencies can be used to calculate weight factors of query-feature relationships, which indicate the likelihood of a search keyword leading to a feature.

Table 3. Word stems and frequencies of needs vocabulary of "FilterKeys"

Terms	Frequency
keyboard	23
key	8
tremor	6
delay	4
access	4
type	3
hand	2
......(45 more word stems omitted due to limited space)......	

Correlation with other features. These are correlation coefficients between FilterKeys-related terms and terms used to describe access needs for other features. The coefficients were calculated based on the set of terms (weighted by frequency) that the two solutions have in common (multiplication of the two vectors formed by *word stems and frequencies* of two solutions). The coefficients show the degree of "similarity" of two solutions in their user generated vocabularies (Table 4).

Table 4. Correlations between FilterKeys-related terms and terms used to describe other access features

Other access features	Correlation with "FilterKeys"
large key keyboard	0.88
bouncekey ignore rapid repeated	0.84
chorded keyboard	0.73
keyguard	0.71
keyboard adjust delay before repeat	0.68
onscreen keyboard	0.62
mousekeys	0.54
stickykeys	0.44
abbreviation expansion	0.29
......(40 more features omitted due to limited space)......	

Other features that may address the same needs (need vocabulary only). These are original queries that the participant thought could address the same need/difficulty as the selected feature does (Table 5). For example, given a use case of "font size", participants used search terms such as "screen magnification", "high contrast", "screen resolution", etc. This information can help us understand feature-feature relationships from the aspect of user needs. This will then inform organization of products based on user needs—an important feature of the Shopping/Alerting Interface. Some products may not be grouped together from a technological aspect, but become closely related in consideration of the user needs they may address. This information may be also used to strengthen the system's capability of recommending similar products.

Table 5. Other access features that participants think can address the same needs in the use case of "FilterKeys"

Other features	
filterkeys delay before activation	on screen keyboard
filterkeys delay before activation	key guard
filterkeys delay before activation	large keys
filterkeys delay before activation	speech to text technology
filterkeys delay before activation	sticky keys
filterkeys delay before activation	Extra large keyboard for reducing tremors
filterkeys delay before activation	keyboard with keys spaced further apart

Word cloud. This is a visual representation of *word stems and frequencies* of the solution, with text size associated with frequency (Fig. 4).

Fig. 4. Word cloud for needs vocabulary of "FilterKeys"

Saturation plot. This is a line plot showing the increasing number of collected terms as the number of participants increases (Fig. 5). It helps us observe data saturation when the line chart "plateaus", indicating that more participants are not likely to contribute significantly more new terms

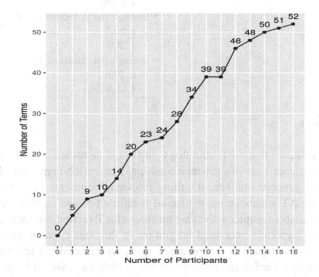

Fig. 5. Saturation plot for needs vocabulary of "FilterKeys"

Table 6 presents descriptive statistics of the pilot testing data. Complete responses from 40 participants are included. A total of 102 questions (use cases) polled 2005 search queries, resulting in 3264 terms.

Table 6. Descriptive statistics

Number of completed surveys	40
Number of questions (use cases)	total 102 • needs 51 • features 51
Search queries	• total 2005 – n 1301 – f 704 • average per participant 50.1 – n 32.5 – f 17.6 • average per question 19.7 – n 12.8 – f 6.9
Terms (word stems)	• total 3264 – n 2106 – f 1158 • average per participant 81.6 – n 52.7 – f 28.9 • average per question 32 – n 20.6 – f 11.4

6   Conclusion

Past research has shown that the terminology gap could be remedied with richer system vocabularies and richer query-target relationships. The enrichment could be achieved by having experts generate indexes, or culling relevant documents from the web. When trying to populate AT vocabularies, we found it difficult to use similar methods given the scarcity of available resources, the vast number of AT-related products and features, and the need for laypeople-generated language. In this study, we used made-up use cases to elicit search queries that consumers might use in real-world situations. This method is especially effective in eliciting "needs" vocabulary, which is rare in existing resources but crucial to need-oriented search for novice users.

In addition to enriched query-feature pairs, this method can also provide data on feature-feature relationships. We found similar queries (high correlation coefficients) used to search different features—sometimes remotely related features if we categorize them technologically. When we discover more about which features are inherently similar in terms of addressing access needs, we can organize products based on needs and difficulties.

The use of use cases solved the problem of lacking "seed data" in populating vocabularies, but it also introduced biases. The participants were more likely to use the words and phrases in a use case. Even though we tried to use plain language and to avoid any technical terms, it is inevitable that the participants become guided by what they just read about. Future research may explore using pictures and videos to present use scenarios and minimizing textual elicitations.

As data collecting is still ongoing, we will monitor each question's status of saturation. Next steps are to integrate the vocabularies into the system to realize need-based searching, and replace (or add explanations to) technical terms with user-friendly language. Once implemented, the need-based searching and browsing will be empirically evaluated to assess its ability to improve product findability and users' selection of AT. With more data, we will also compare consumers' vocabulary and clinicians' vocabulary, and explore the use of vocabularies that adapt to the user's expertise.

Acknowledgement. The contents of this paper were developed with funding from the National Institute on Disability, Independent Living, and Rehabilitation Research, U.S. Department of Health and Human Services, grant number H133E080022 (RERC on Universal Interface & Information Technology Access). However, those contents do not necessarily represent the policy of the Department of Health and Human Services, and you should not assume endorsement by the Federal Government.

References

1. Section 508 Standards, 36 C.F.R Section 1194. USA (2017)
2. Vanderheiden, G., Treviranus, J.: Creating a global public inclusive infrastructure. In: Stephanidis, C. (ed.) UAHCI 2011. LNCS, vol. 6765, pp. 517–526. Springer, Heidelberg (2011). doi:10.1007/978-3-642-21672-5_57
3. Ding, Y., Chourasia, A., Anson, D., Atkins, T., Vanderheiden, G.: Understanding decision requirements for selection of assistive technology. In: 59th Annual Meeting of the Human Factors and Ergonomics Society, pp. 160–164. SAGE Publications (2015)
4. Vanderheiden, G.C., Treviranus, J., Gemou, M., Bekiaris, E., Markus, K., Clark, C., Basman, A.: The evolving global public inclusive infrastructure (GPII). In: Stephanidis, C., Antona, M. (eds.) UAHCI 2013. LNCS, vol. 8009, pp. 107–116. Springer, Heidelberg (2013). doi:10. 1007/978-3-642-39188-0_12
5. Anson, D., Ding, Y.: Federated databases and supported decision making. In: Stephanidis, C., Antona, M. (eds.) UAHCI 2014. LNCS, vol. 8516, pp. 337–347. Springer, Cham (2014). doi:10.1007/978-3-319-07509-9_32
6. Gomez, L.M., Lochbaum, C.C.: People can retrieve more objects with enriched key-word vocabularies; But is there a human performance cost? In: INTERACT 84 - 1st IFIP International Conference on Human-Computer Interaction, pp. 257–261, London, UK (1984)
7. Fourney, A., Mann, R., Terry, M.: Query-feature graphs: Bridging user vocabulary and system functionality. In: Proceedings of the ACM Symposium on User Interface Software and Technology, pp. 207–216 (2011)
8. Appleseed, J.: Deconstructing E-Commerce Search: The 12 Query Types. http://baymard. com/blog/ecommerce-search-query-types

Understanding Acceptance Factors for Using e-care Systems and Devices: Insights from a Mixed-Method Intervention Study in Slovenia

Vesna Dolničar[1(✉)], Andraž Petrovčič[1], Mojca Šetinc[1], Igor Košir[2], and Matic Kavčič[1]

[1] Faculty of Social Sciences, University of Ljubljana, Ljubljana, Slovenia
vesna.dolnicar@fdv.uni-lj.si
[2] ENERGOCOSM raziskave d.o.o., Ljubljana, Slovenia

Abstract. An increasing number of scholars have been recently exploring the role of factors that foster the adoption of different types of assistive technologies among older adults. Our study contributes to this field with a mixed-methods intervention study that combines a baseline and follow-up telephone survey with semi-structured interviews to evaluate the user experience and potentially identifies additional acceptance factors of e-care systems and relations among them. Different assistive technologies were tested and evaluated by three groups of participants: (1) older adults testing mobile and wearable devices and (2) informal carers who remotely monitored events recorded by e-care systems installed in the homes of (3) care receivers. The findings indicate heterogeneous needs and expectations these three groups have towards the use of e-care systems. Moreover, the results also unveil the fear of not getting help quickly in case of an emergency, and perception of safety and peace of mind as important predictors of the use of e-care systems among informal carers and care receivers. Indirectly, the results also reveal the importance of intervention and mixed methods design studies as a means of a more comprehensive understanding of acceptance factors of assistive technologies.

Keywords: e-care · Assistive technology · Acceptance factors · Mixed methods design · Intervention study · Older adults · Informal carers

1 Introduction

The new generation of information and communications technology (ICT)-based assistive technologies has the potential to increase quality of living, safety, wellbeing, and interpersonal relationships for older adults and their informal carers [1–3]. However, assistive technologies have rarely been upscaled, so an increasing number of studies has explored the barriers to use as experienced by older adults [4], such as individual (e.g., resistance toward technology) and contextual issues (e.g., socio-economic status, family support), as well as design demands concerning age-related issues with older adults' perceptual, cognitive and movement difficulties [5]. Several conceptual models exist that study user acceptance and behavior among older adults related to assistive systems or technology in general, including the USE–Model [6], the STAM model [7],

© Springer International Publishing AG 2017
J. Zhou and G. Salvendy (Eds.): ITAP 2017, Part II, LNCS 10298, pp. 362–377, 2017.
DOI: 10.1007/978-3-319-58536-9_29

McCreadie and Tinker's model [8], the ecological model [9], the Smart Home Technology Acceptance Model [10], as well as a model of factors influencing the level of technology used by older adults who are aging in place [11]. As such, informal carers are becoming more important, as access to paid assistants and public services is limited [12, 13]. Moreover, informal carers have been shown to play a central role in decision-making processes related to adopting assistive systems for care receivers' homes [12].

The aim of this study is to evaluate user experience and potentially identify additional factors that influence acceptance. The study will further examine the relationships among the acceptance factors for e-care systems and devices aimed at enhancing the security and independence of community-dwelling older adults within their home environments, as well as relieving informal carers' burden and concerns. The study is comprised of three groups of participants: (1) older adults testing mobile and wearable devices, (2) informal carers who remotely monitor events recorded by e-care systems installed in the homes of (3) care receivers[1], typically being family members of informal carers. Mobile and wearable devices included two smartphones with an SOS button and two fall detectors with an SOS button adapted for older adults. The four tested e-care systems encompassed various combinations of sensors and gadgets such as wearable SOS buttons, movement sensors, door sensors, fall detectors linked to the main unit, which enables informal carers (and service providers via a care assistance center) to monitor activities and trends in care receivers' homes via smartphone or web app.

Drawing on an intervention study consisting of two telephone surveys and semi-structured interviews, we first present results of the quantitative evaluation of the e-care systems and mobile and wearable devices among older adults and informal carers, which is based on the American Costumer Satisfaction Index (ACSI) [14] and a block of open-ended survey questions regarding positive and negative experiences with the tested system/device. Afterwards, satisfaction and experiences with the e-care systems are further explored with semi-structured interviews, the results of which demonstrate in-depth insight into the experiences of informal carers and care receivers with the tested e-care systems. This information contributes to further elaboration of the complex and broad array of acceptability factors.

2 Research

2.1 Research Design

In order to gain insight and evaluate e-care systems as well as mobile and wearable devices provided by the largest telecommunications company in Slovenia, an interventional study was designed. The telecommunications provider purposefully selected a number of e-care systems and a convenient sample of participants who volunteered to test the devices/systems from three weeks to two months, depending on the type of device/system. The intervention was carried out by the provider, whose staff members

---

[1] Hereafter, for the sake of simplicity, we refer to older adults with installed e-care systems in their homes as "care receivers" (given the fact that they receive care in terms of using e-care systems), irrespective of whether they receive any other form of help or care.

installed, monitored, maintained and removed the e-care systems/devices. The evaluation was based on a panel design consisting of a baseline and follow-up telephone survey, lasting approximately 10 min, conducted before and at the end of the e-care system/device testing period. Also, semi-structured interviews with a subsample of participants, lasting 30 to 90 min, were conducted after the end of the testing period (see Fig. 1). While e-care systems have been tested by care receivers and informal carers, only the latter were involved in the baseline and follow-up survey. In the semi-structured interviews, however, both types of users in the dyad of informal carer and care receiver were interviewed. Thus, our approach to collect data on user experiences can be characterised as sequential explanatory mixed methods design [15].

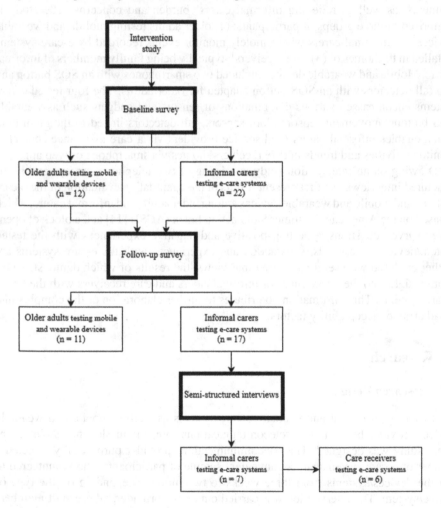

Fig. 1. Sample structure and design of the mixed methods intervention study.

Surveys were conducted among informal carers testing e-care systems (e.g., movement sensors) and older adults testing mobile and wearable devices (two types of age-friendly smartphones with an SOS button and two fall detectors). The baseline survey aimed at gaining insight into participants' expectations regarding the tested systems/devices prior to the testing period. Accordingly, the follow-up survey measured users' satisfaction and experiences with the tested system/device at the end of the testing period. In addition to topics under investigation herein, the baseline survey covered the following topics: use of new technologies; provision (for informal carers)/reception (for older adults) of help regarding (instrumental) activities of daily living; technology acceptance factors; price sensitivity; care receivers' (for informal carers)/older adults' recent need for emergency help; his/her health condition; and socio-demographics.

Further, informal carers were asked about their relationship with care receivers. Likewise, in the follow-up survey, participants were asked about use of the tested system/device, technology acceptance factors, and purchasing decision.

2.2 Apparatus

Participants involved in the intervention study tested four e-care systems and four mobile and wearable devices. The e-care systems consisted of Sensara, Essence, LivOn and CMIP. With e-care systems we refer to remote monitoring systems enabling family members and (informal) carers to check the wellbeing of a care receiver living on their own through the web or mobile app. A set of sensors, linked to the main unit, transmits the data to the cloud and triggers alarms in case of any deviation from the routine. Furthermore, e-care system provider's care assistance center monitors events, provides support and assistance to informal carer and care receiver and deals with critical events. Mobile and wearable devices included two fall detectors (i.e., IN LIFE smartwatch, PERS FD) and two age-friendly smartphones (i.e., Doro 8031, Emporia Smart). All tested devices are described in detail below.

Mobile and Wearable Devices

Doro 8031. Doro is a smartphone built to be as easy to use as possible. Its features are large icons and large buttons, an age-friendly user interface, loud and clear sound, hearing aid compatibility, GPS, a step-by-step tutorial, and an assistance button. Furthermore, the My Doro Manager application enables the user to get remote help from a relative or carer who can read the device and write/make changes to it. Charging the battery is simplified due to the attached charging cradle [16].

EmporiaSMART. EmporiaSMART is the second tested adapted smartphone. Its main difference in comparison to other smartphones is a removable keypad display cover that enables entering numbers, scrolling through the telephone book, or writing and reading messages. Moreover, the included stylus pen that can be attached directly to the device makes using the touchscreen easier. A charging station simplifies battery charging. In addition to the age-friendly user interface, large icons and buttons, loud and clear sound, compatibility with hearing aids, and the device's emergency call function enable the user to feel safe [17].

IN LIFE Smart Watch. The IN LIFE smartwatch is a device with fall-recognizing algorithms that initiate an automatic call in case of a fall. The watch has built-in GPS and allows the user to trigger the emergency call, whereby location data is transmitted to the call recipient. Further, the watch monitors users' activity and automatically generates daily reports on device and user status. Carers can access the watch and manage it remotely through a user-friendly web interface. The watch has been developed in Slovenia as an output of the Horizon 2020 project IN LIFE [18].

PERS FD. The Personal Emergency Response System Fall Detection (PERS FD) is a wearable fall detector that can be worn as a wrist strap or pendant. An SOS button enables the user to activate an emergency call. When a fall is detected, the alarm with location data is forwarded to predetermined numbers and voice communication is enabled without any user action required. For an example of PERS FD, see [19].

e-care Systems

Sensara. Sensara (see Fig. 2a) is a remote monitoring system.[2] It uses small, unobtrusive sensors to help provide support for care receivers living on their own. Through use of a smartphone app, family members or (informal) carers can stay up to date on the care receivers' wellbeing. The app provides the user with information on the care receiver's current status and detailed long-term information. The system contains one gateway device, two or three door sensors, three or five activity sensors, and all the equipment necessary for installation. The front door and back door sensors monitor activities such as entering and leaving the house. The kitchen sensor keeps track of activity in the kitchen and can be installed on the refrigerator door. Activity sensors are supposed to be installed to the toilet/bathroom, living room, and hallway. All these sensors were included in the test period.

It takes approximately two weeks for Sensara to learn the resident's behavior fully. Over time, the system learns what behavior is normal and what is abnormal. When there is anything suspicious seen in the app, the care receiver can be called through the app's speed-dial button [20].

Essence. Essence (see Fig. 2b) is a system for home-care providers. It indicates hazards and worsening scenarios and triggers alarms automatically. Family member or (informal) carer can monitor care receivers' daily activities by using the monitor app on a smartphone or computer. The control panel supports up to 32 peripherals/sensors such as cameras, door/window sensors, smoke detectors, and more. It also includes an emergency button and two-way audio communication capability for the care service provider to communicate with the user [21].

Sensors used in this study were motion detectors that identified entrance and alerted for extreme temperatures, door/window sensors reporting the status of door and

---

[2] None of the interviewees tested the Sensara system.

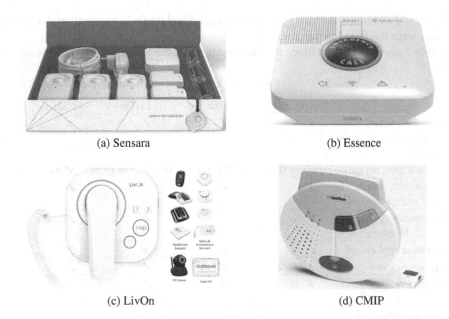

(a) Sensara

(b) Essence

(c) LivOn

(d) CMIP

Fig. 2. Tested e-care systems.

windows to determine whether someone enters or leaves the premises, and a portable emergency button that can be worn as a pendant or wrist strap. Essence can be further extended with a fixed emergency button, flood detector to warn of water leakage, smoke detector, and cameras. These extensions, however, were not tested in this study.

LivOn. LivOn (see Fig. 2c) is a wireless monitoring system that automatically identifies changes in the activities of daily living. Through online and mobile apps, it keeps family members and (informal) carers informed about care receivers' activities and triggers alarms. The system consists of a wireless base unit with a telephone handset and sensors connected with a service platform [22].

The tested system in this study was composed of a base unit, activity sensors, and a help trigger (i.e., emergency button). LivOn can be extended with additional (not tested in this study) telecare sensors (i.e., fall detector, temperature and humidity sensor), safety sensors (i.e., fire detector, gas detector, intrusion detector, flood detector), and healthcare sensors (i.e., glucose meter, pulsimeter, blood pressure gauge, thermometer, weighing scale and pedometer).

CMIP. CareMobile IP (see Fig. 2d) is the fourth monitoring system tested. It operates using GSM communication and does not require a telephone line. During the testing period, the main Carephone unit was supplied with a wrist radio trigger and a fall detector. An alarm on the CMIP can be activated on the main unit or by the wearable radio trigger. The main unit also enables two-way communication. The CMIP system can be extended with additional sensors and services, such as door alarm, smoke detector, and additional alarm triggers to meet individual needs (additional products and services were not tested in this study) [23].

Table 1 concisely summarizes the main features of the four e-care systems tested.

Table 1. Comparison of the e-care systems' features

	Sensara	Essence	LivOn	CMIP
Sensor system for monitoring changes in the daily routine	✓	✓	✓	✗
Communication network	Fixed (Ethernet)	Mobile (SIM)	Mobile (SIM)	Mobile (SIM)
Base unit with integrated speaker and microphone	✗	✓	✓	✓
Battery backup power supply of the base unit	✗	✓	✓	✓
Smartphone application	✓	✓	✗	✗
Online application	✗	✓	✓	✓
Healthcare sensors (optional)	✗	✓	✓	✗
Direct emergency call activation	✗	✓	✓	✓

2.3 Sample and Methods

Baseline Survey. Baseline survey data collection took place in September 2016. A total of 22 informal carers testing e-care systems[3] and 12 older adults testing mobile and wearable devices participated in the baseline telephone survey. Surveyed informal carers were between 27 and 72 years of age (average age of 45 years) with an almost equal proportion of males and females. A large majority of informal carers were employed; they were experienced ICT users, and had obtained a university or high education diploma. On average, informal carers spent eight hours weekly providing informal care and did not perceive it as a burden.

The average age of surveyed older adults was 77 years, with age ranging between 70 and 83 years. Eight were women, and four were men. All but one were retired, and half had a secondary education. On average, they assessed their health status as good and mostly lived alone or with a partner or spouse in a house or apartment building. Three out of four received some help with (instrumental) activities of daily living in the past 12 months. The majority of them were able to move unassisted (i.e., did not use a wheel chair, rolator or a walking stick).

Follow-Up Survey. Follow-up survey data collection took place in October 2016. Out of 22 informal carers and 12 older adults who completed the baseline survey, 17 informal carers and 11 older adults also completed the follow-up survey (see Fig. 1). Among 17

---

[3] Only informal carers were involved in the baseline and follow-up surveys (see Sect. 2.1 for details).

informal carers, seven of their care receivers had installed the Essence system in their home, three used Sensara, four tested LivOn, and three were using CMIP. Among 11 older adults, one was using the Doro smartphone, four were using the smartphone emporiaSMART, two tested PERS FD, and four had been wearing the IN LIFE smart watch.

Semi-structured Interviews. To further examine user experiences and acceptance factors, semi-structured interviews were carried out in November 2016 with 13 users of e-care systems. Among them, seven interviews were carried out with informal carers (who participated in the follow-up survey) and six with their respective care receivers. All interviewees gave consent to participate in the qualitative research phase earlier in the survey. In all cases except one[4], we collected data from both members in the dyad (i.e., care receiver and informal carer) who used the same e-care systems during the testing period. Among the interviewees, three dyads were testing the Essence system, two LivOn, and two the CMIP system. None of them tested the Sensara system.

Informal carers who participated in the semi-structured interviews were between 27 and 57 years old, with an average age of 45 years. Interviews were conducted with two women and five men. All the interviewed informal carers were employed. They considered themselves to be experienced ICT users and had obtained a university or high education diploma. During the last 12 months, four of them provided informal care to their care receivers.

The care receivers interviewed were between 61 and 93 years old. Their average age was 80 years. Four of them were males, and two were females. All were retired, and most had a secondary education. Four lived alone in a house or apartment building, and two care receivers lived together with another person. Three care receivers could move unassisted, while three used mechanical transfer aids such as walking stick or rolator. Furthermore, in the last 12 months, four were receiving informal help.

All interviews were audio recorded and fully transcribed.[5] Personal information was anonymized. They were carried out in the setting of interviewees' choosing (their home or office) and lasted 30 to 90 min. A qualitative thematic content analysis was used to analyze the data gathered from the interviews [24, 25]. Standard coding procedures based in grounded theory [26] were used in collaboration between six researchers to develop concepts and themes emerging from the gathered materials. We strictly adhere to the ethical guidelines of the University of Ljubljana.

3   Results

3.1   Quantitative Evaluation of e-care System Use by Informal Carers

The quantitative evaluation of e-care system use (Table 2) – based on data collected in the follow-up survey – showed that the older adults on average rated their satisfaction

---

[4] One informal carer declined the interview with his care receiver due to her medical condition.
[5] All interviews were carried out in the spoken Slovene language and were transcribed verbatim. Quotations presented later in the paper were then translated into English by a native speaker.

with the tested device (M = 6.5) slightly higher than they did the overall quality of the device (M = 6.4) and the extent to which it met their personal requirements (M = 6.4). Somewhat lower were their average rates of recommending the tested device to friends and/or family (M = 6.1) and of purchase likelihood (M = 5.1). Furthermore, they assessed the occurrence of difficulties in operation as not too often (M = 3.8).

Table 2. Results of quantitative evaluation of e-care systems and mobile and wearable devices

Variables[a]	Informal carers[b]	Older adults[c]
Overall quality of tested e-care system/device	8.1	6.4
How often things with tested system/device went wrong	1.9	3.8
Satisfaction with tested system/device	8.6	6.5
How well tested system/device met personal requirements	8.1	6.4
Probability of recommending tested system/device to friends and/or family	8.1	6.1
Likelihood of purchasing tested system/device in the near future	6.8	5.1

[a]Responses were measured on a scale ranging from 1 to 10, with higher values indicating stronger agreement. [b]N = 14–17. [c]N = 8.

On the other hand, informal carers attributed the highest average scores (both M = 8.6) to satisfaction with the tested system and to probability of recommending it to friends and/or family. Overall quality of the system and personal requirements met were also, on average, rated high (both M = 8.1). Considerably lower average scores were attributed to purchase likelihood (M = 6.8). Likewise, difficulties in operation were also rated low (M = 1.9).

Further, in the follow-up survey, additional information on positive and negative user experiences was also gathered with a set of open-ended questions. The answers were coded and categorized in a way that reflected positive/negative user experiences of participants with the system/device. The results are presented in Tables 3 and 4. On one hand, among the most-frequently-expressed positive aspects were feelings of safety and security, being able to monitor the care receiver remotely, as well as specific functionalities of the tested devices/systems. On the other hand, the most-often-mentioned negative experiences were specific technical or physical characteristics of the devices/systems and, interestingly, their (limited) functionalities. Informed by previously presented findings, the researchers decided to explore these issues in detail in the ensuing qualitative phase.

Table 3. Positive experiences with tested systems/devices

Coded answers	N (%)
Safety and security when using system/device	40
Monitoring care receiver remotely	30
System's/device's functionalities	25
Importance of the assistance center	20
Technical/physical properties of system/device	20
Quality of life when using system/device	20
Usability of system/device	15
Entertainment and relaxedness when using system/device	15
Relationship between informal carer and care receiver	10
User interface of the system/device	5
Other aspects/factors/reasons	5

N = 20.

Table 4. Negative experiences with tested systems/devices

Coded answers	N (%)
Technical/physical characteristics of system/device	39
System's/device's functionalities	22
User interface of the system/device	17
Compatibility of system/device with lifestyle	6
Respondent has not stated any aspect/factor/reason	28

N = 18.

3.2 Qualitative Evaluation of e-care System Use by Informal Carers and Care Receivers

The initial analysis of data collected through semi-structured interviews showed that a frequently mentioned and often-determining factor in considering and deciding to adopt an e-care system is the occurrence of (potential) critical events related to serious health issues and corresponding consequences, such as fall, stroke, and similar. Fear of recurrence of critical and potentially dangerous events, together with the concern of not getting rapid and appropriate assistance, are major sources of worry for care receivers and informal carers. Increasing needs for personal safety and wellbeing stem from age-related health declines that diminish the care reciever's ability to live at home independently. Accordingly, health problems considerably increase the need for care and control (monitoring) of older adults by their carers. An older female, for instance, explained what it means to her to use an e-care system:

Care receiver, 81 years: *I feel more sure, more safe, don't I?*
Interviewer: *Something else maybe?*

Care receiver, 81 years: *Well, I don't know. So that I'm not, how should I put it, always tense everywhere. When I came home from hospital, I said, oh no! Now it will throw me out. Now it will throw me out* [referring to stroke], *and then what? That fear, right, that you are alone, right.*

Further, the results reveal that use of the e-care system should lead to a feeling of relief among informal carers and care receivers. This "relief" affects both the psychological and behavioral aspects of the relationship between the two groups. On one hand, psychological relief is reflected in reduced anxiety and apprehension, which leads to a greater sense of safety and reassurance. On the other hand, the behavioral aspects of relief refer the actual physical and logistic burdens of informal carers that might be alleviated by the fact that with the e-care system, they can remotely check and monitor the condition of care receivers. For example, an interviewed informal carer explained:

Informal carer, 44 years: *You don't have to ring dad to see if everything is okay with him, because you simply look at the application. /.../ So, that /.../ part of the communication fades away since you simply look at the telephone and see what was happening.*

However, both informal carers and care receivers shared a concern that the remote access provided by the e-care systems would lead to a decrease in the number and quality of in-person visits between them. The possibility of fewer visits is perceived as a potential disadvantage, since the systems provide care receivers with the feelings of safety and emotional reassurance. Also, in-person contacts play a role in socializing, as they allow for opportunities to maintain and strengthen personal support networks. In this sense, the factors presented above regarding e-care system utilization demonstrate a wider impact on users' daily lives. Carers also realize these concerns, and one pointed out:

Informal carer, 56 years: *Now, I remembered just then, when you said before, potentially, what could negatively affect these people, the users of that...would maybe be feeling they are going to lose attention as a result.*

If the care receivers and carers perceive that an e-care system can provide them with a feeling of relief and safety, while, at the same time, decrease the actual burden placed on the informal carers, then it is likely that both groups would be motivated to use e-care in the future. However, other important factors shape interest in using an e-care system in the future. First, the system should be designed to accommodate the everyday needs, customs, and routines of users. Second, the system should not be disruptive; its presence in the home and/or its use should not substantially alter the care receivers' daily lives. Third, the e-care system should be error-free. In other words, users learn to trust the system and never lose confidence about the e-care system's operation and reliability. Fourth, the e-care system should have an age-friendly design and system features in order to be appreciated as useful and easy to use. It is important to note that one interviewee commented on the sensor bracelet's design:

Informal carer, 56 years: *Currently, it's a rugged thing, a little bit, still, isn't it? But okay, with time, this will change, so it will get a nicer shape, as such.*

On one hand, usability is, by and large, related to adapting to the user interface and ergonomically designed devices that are part of an e-care system (e.g., central unit, sensors, wearables). On the other hand, the essential feature of the system for it to be perceived as useful seems to be a physical emergency button or a panic button that should be available on the central unit. Moreover, care receivers prefer a button that enables two-way communication with a care assistance center. Also, interviewees would prefer a wearable, emergency button that can be used both inside and outside of the home. The wearable, emergency button would allow automatic detection and activation of alarms in case of critical events (e.g., fall, stroke). Likewise, mobile-based e-care systems should enable an automatic alert to carers through a push notification in the mobile app.

The e-care system should be equipped with features that enable timely and responsive provision of assistance to care receivers by allowing remote monitoring of their actions in the home and support voice communication with the care receivers. In this context, a fully operational care assistance center is a key factor, and the most important added value, of an e-care system. In fact, both informal carers and care receivers recognized its central role in providing prompt support and assistance to care receivers. In particular, an e-care system's efficacy is expected in the management of emergencies. Thus, it seems to be vital that the care assistance center is responsive, reliable, provides appropriate feedback to the user, and/or is able to inform informal carers about the care receiver's conditions. However, there are some indications that both groups do not expect that an assistance center support is focused solely on dealing with life-threatening events. Instead, the assistance center should play a supportive role in fulfilling at least the most basic needs of care receivers regarding socializing and emotional exchange, as illustrated below:

Informal carer, 35 years: *Positively. I am more positively surprised that the service was complete. Primarily, this human factor was very…it just balanced out with a positive opinion like that.*

Whenever possible, the assistance center's role should be aligned with the expectations, needs, and heterogeneous requirements of system users. In addition, users should be thoroughly familiar with the operation of the e-care systems and equipment installed in their homes. An e-care system's most significant technical characteristics, as well as the assistance center's role and the subsequent handling in activating the aid (e.g., What happens in emergency cases regarding access to the apartment?). In this context, the results indicate the critical role of technical staff who monitor and maintain the equipment in the care receiver's home. During installation, users must be informed about the system's features and equipment in a user-friendly manner. Namely, technical staff should be able to explain and show users how the equipment and system work, its features, and how to establish a connection with the assistance center and their (informal) carers (e.g., how to activate an emergency call). Manuals should be adapted to match the cognitive, sensory, and memory-processing abilities of care receivers and highlight the most relevant instructions and illustrations. Preferably during the installation, users should be introduced to the e-care system with assistance from video tutorials and simulations.

In general, the informal carer has a central role in the decision to adopt and use an e-care system. The trial period in this study indicates that such systems come into play (and, due to their features, are most suitable for use) in family situations where a care receiver lives alone and has a solid, close relationship with the informal carer. Emotional attachment and the burden (actual and/or perceived) associated with providing care means that the person who advocated for purchasing the e-care system will most likely be an informal carer in the care receiver's family. However, this situation of one person taking responsibility for the system does not imply that he or she is the only decision-maker. In fact, due to the complexity and heterogeneity of life situations emerging from the multi-layered relationships in later life between care receivers and their informal carers, both sides can make decisions. Also, significant others outside the care receiver's family, such as general practitioners, neighbors, and/or professional (formal) carers might take part in the decision and purchase process. However, since relatives are expected to provide help in the decision, purchase, and installation processes and will be closely involved with the system, it is crucial that they demonstrate adequate digital skills in order to be able to benefit from the system's features.

Finally, yet importantly, the results indicate that the purchase and maintenance costs of an e-care system are important factors (illustrated in the following excerpt):

> Informal carer, 56 years: *Ah, depends on the price.*
> Interviewer: *Mmm, so, the price...*
> Informal carer, 56 years: *Mainly. The determining factor is the price. A need, an urgent need for that, we don't have at the moment. That could change tomorrow, right? No one knows that. If there was some normal, acceptable price, right, then I would decide. 'Cause it is, after all, quite a big addition.*

The initial purchase price should be set at an affordable level, considering the financial capacities of care receivers and informal carers. Otherwise, both sides might not become actively involved in the purchase process. In this sense, what is critical from the informal carer's and care receiver's point of view is the trade-off between costs and perceived value added through using the e-care system for enhanced safety, security, release of burden, health management, and more. This is particularly true when compared with technologies and services both groups already use for care provision. In this context, the perceptions of (potential) users are meaningfully shaped by their existing experience with assistive technology, as well as expectations for their current and future needs.

4   Discussion and Conclusion

The intervention study enabled us to examine "real life" experiences with tested e-care services and mobile and wearable devices. Quantitative evaluation showed that various aspects of the tested e-care systems were, on average, rated positively by informal carers. However, the likelihood of purchasing the tested system in the near future was not very high. From another perspective, older adults who tested mobile and wearable devices rated them, on average, less favorably, but still quite positive. Although satisfaction with the system/device during the testing period received a higher average score among informal carers and older adults, open-ended questions asked during the second survey revealed important discrepancies. Interestingly, system functionalities were often mentioned among the positive as well as negative aspects of the testing period.

Results from the semi-structured interviews unveiled the full complexity of the phenomenon. The results indicate the heterogeneous needs and expectations users have towards using e-care systems. Moreover, alleviating the fear of not getting help quickly in an emergency increased the perception of safety and peace of mind; both were assessed as important factors for further use of the service. In order to attain further use, we recognized various design and service features as important factors in the purchasing decision. Some concerns about the e-care system potentially creating less contact between the carer and the care receiver were also raised.

Furthermore, the results of this study underline the importance of intervention research design for researching assistive technology. Accordingly, the results indicate the importance of a more in-depth examination, confirmed by the rich data gathered in semi-structured interviews. While various modifications of the Technology Acceptance Models (TAM) (e.g., [7, 8, 10]) typically include several acceptance factors[6], these factors turned out to be non-exhaustive when studying the intention to use the tested e-care system by both informal carers and care receivers. Our inductive orientation uncovered new and not-yet-reflected issues by quantitative TAM studies of smart technology for independent living of older adults at home. The phenomenon under examination demonstrated a complex mix of interrelated factors (system characteristics and functionalities, service management, [overlap of] informal carers' and care receivers' needs, characteristics, expectations and perceptions), which should all be considered when studying technology acceptance in this field. Technology anxiety, for example, was brought out as a minor inhibiting factor. Furthermore, fear that the e-care system would be substituting for human contact and thus negatively influence the caregiving relationship, was clearly identified in the semi-structured interviews [27, 28]. Hence, further and more detailed analysis of the qualitative data will be carried out in the future. This finding should prove useful also for providers launching e-care products in the rapidly growing and highly competitive market. In addition, mixed methods design enabled us to "tap different domains of knowing" [29], where different (also more sensitive) issues related to experiences with the e-care systems were provided in the semi-structured interviews compared to those raised in the open-ended questions of the follow-up survey.

However, our mixed methods intervention study has some limitations concerning the convenient sample of participants who volunteered to test the devices/systems. During the interviews conducted with care receivers and their informal carers, the researchers noticed that participants' motives for being involved in the intervention study were not only related only to a current need to use the e-care system, but by other motives as well. Most informal carers were technologically skilled employees of the telecommunication provider. This fact might have partially influenced the narrative of the semi-structured interviews. Also, the study is limited by a rather small sample size that prevented us from studying statistically significant differences, for instance, in perceived and actual satisfaction with e-care systems, as reported in the baseline and follow-up surveys. A longer testing and intervention period could also enable care receivers and informal carers to evaluate the systems' and assistance center's function in a more informed way. An extended testing and intervention could also result in more urgent interventions regarding the need for immediate help and assistance. Nevertheless,

---

[6] Besides perceived ease of use and perceived usefulness, acceptance factors examined in TAM studies are: social influence, compatibility with lifestyle, availability of resources, enjoyment, technology anxiety, and resistance to change.

the rich materials gathered in this intervention study will enable us to analyze the complex relations between acceptance factors in greater detail in the future, particularly difficulties related to the actual e-care systems. Additionally, users' ideas for additional functionalities were identified, providing a sound basis for further exploration of the findings.

Acknowledgments. The study was funded by Telekom Slovenije, d. d., Cigaletova 15, 1000 Ljubljana. The authors extend their appreciation to Peter Pustatičnik and Elena Nikolavčič for their useful feedback on an early version of the manuscript and to Anja Tuš and Otto Gerdina for their assistance in the data collection and analysis.

References

1. Chiatti, C., Fry, G., Hanson, E., Magnusson, L., Socci, M., Stückler, A., Széman, Z., Widéhn, N., Barbabella, F., Lamura, G.: Deliverable 4.3. Final report containing case-by case detailed description and analysis of selected 12 good practices. Vienna (2011)
2. Dolničar, V., Müller, S., Santi, M.: Designing technologies for older people: a user-driven research approach for the Soprano Project. In: Colombo, F. (ed.) Broadband Society and Generational Changes, 5th edn., pp. 221–246. P. Lang
3. Kidholm, K., Dinsen, B., Dyrvig, A.K., Schnack, R., Yderstraede, K.B.: Results from the World's Largest Telemedicine Project – The Whole System Demonstrator. Ugeskr Læger, Denmark (2014)
4. Czaja, S.J., Charness, N., Fisk, A.D., Hertzog, C., Nair, S.N., Rogers, W.A., Sharit, J.: Factors predicting the use of technology: findings from the Center for Research and Education on Aging and Technology Enhancement (CREATE). Psychol. Aging **21**, 333–352 (2006). doi: 10.1037/0882-7974.21.2.333
5. Fisk, A.D., Rogers, W.A., Charness, N., Czaja, S.J., Sharit, J.: Designing for Older Adults: Principles and Creative Human Factors Approaches, 2nd edn. CRC Press, Boca Raton (2009)
6. Dewsbury, G., Clarke, K., Rouncefield, M., Sommerville, I., Taylor, B., Edge, M.: Designing acceptable "smart" home technology to support people in the home. Technol. Disabil. **15**, 191–199 (2003)
7. Renaud, K., van Biljon, J.: Predicting technology acceptance and adoption by the elderly: a qualitative study. In: Proceedings of the 2008 Annual Research Conference of the South African Institute of Computer Scientists and Information Technologists on IT Research in Developing Countries: Riding the Wave of Technology, pp. 210–219. ACM, New York (2008)
8. McCreadie, C., Tinker, A.: The acceptability of assistive technology to older people. Ageing Soc. **25**, 91–110 (2005). doi:10.1017/S0144686X0400248X
9. Sixsmith, A.J., Gibson, G., Orpwood, R.D., Torrington, J.M.: Developing a technology "wishlist" to enhance the quality of life of people with dementia. Gerontechnology **6**, 2–19 (2007). doi:10.4017/gt.2007.06.01.002.00
10. Bierhoff, I., Müller, S., Schoenrade-Sproll, S., Delaney, S., Byrne, P., Dolničar, V., Magoutas, B., Verginadis, Y., Avatangelou, E., Huijnen, C.: Ambient assisted living systems in real-life situations: experiences from the SOPRANO project. In: Sixsmith, A., Gutman, G. (eds.) Technologies for Active Aging, pp. 123–153. Springer, US (2013)
11. Peek, S.T.M., Rijnaard, M.D., Nieboer, M.E., Van Der Voort, C.S., Aarts, S., Wouters, E.J.M., Van Hoof, J., Luijkx, K.G., Vrijhoef, H.J.M.: Older adults' reasons for using technology while aging in place. Gerontology **62**, 226–237 (2016). doi:10.1159/000430949

12. Carretero, S., Stewart, J., Centeno, C.: Information and communication technologies for informal carers and paid assistants: benefits from micro-, meso-, and macro-levels. Eur. J. Ageing **12**, 163–173 (2015). doi:10.1007/s10433-015-0333-4
13. Hlebec, V., Srakar, A., Majcen, B.: Care for the elderly in Slovenia: a combination of informal and formal care. Revija za Socijalnu Politiku **23**, 159–179 (2016). doi:10.3935/rsp.v23i2.1317
14. The Regents of University of Michigan: American Customer Satisfaction Index (ACSI): Methodology report. Michigan, United States (2001)
15. Creswell, J.W., Plano Clark, V.L.: Designing and Conducting Mixed Methods Research. Sage, Los Angeles (2011)
16. Doro 8030. https://www.doro.co.uk/doro-8030.html. Accessed 6 Feb 2017
17. telecom emporia emporia telecom - emporiaSMART. http://www.emporia.eu/en/products/overview/emporiasmart. Accessed 6 Feb 2017
18. Bizjak, J., Gjoreski, H.: Gams M Projekt IN LIFE v Sloveniji. In: Bela knjiza EMZ. Institut "Jožef Stefan," Ljubljana, Slovenija, pp. 32–34
19. Personal Emergency Response System - Bay Alarm Medical. https://www.bayalarmmedical.com/medical-alert-system/in-home/. Accessed 6 Feb 2017
20. Sensara|Beter weten, beter zorgen. In: Sensara. https://sensara.eu/. Accessed 6 Feb 2017
21. Smart Care. http://www.essence-grp.com/smart-care. Accessed 6 Feb 2017
22. LivOn. http://www.hidea.kr/hidea/livon/livon.html. Accessed 6 Feb 2017
23. Doro Care|Social security services for elder and disabled. http://care.doro.co.uk/. Accessed 6 Feb 2017
24. Boyatzis, R.E.: Transforming Qualitative Information: Thematic Analysis and Code Development. Sage Publications, Thousand Oaks (2005)
25. Braun, V., Clarke, V.: Using thematic analysis in psychology. Qual. Res. Psychol. **3**, 77–101 (2006). doi:10.1191/1478088706qp063oa
26. Corbin, J.M., Strauss, A.L.: Basics of qualitative research: techniques and procedures for developing grounded theory. Los Angeles, Calif. [u.a.] (2015)
27. Huber, L.L., Shankar, K., Caine, K., Connelly, K., Camp, L.J., Walker, B.A., Borrero, L.: How in-home technologies mediate caregiving relationships in later life. Int. J. Hum. Comput. Interact. **29**, 441–455 (2013). doi:10.1080/10447318.2012.715990
28. Wild, K., Boise, L., Lundell, J., Foucek, A.: Unobtrusive in-home monitoring of cognitive and physical health: reactions and perceptions of older adults. J. Appl. Gerontol. **27**, 181–200 (2008). doi:10.1177/0733464807311435
29. Mathison, S.: Why triangulate? Educ. Res. **17**, 13–17 (1988). doi:10.3102/0013189X017002013

Sensor-Driven Detection of Social Isolation in Community-Dwelling Elderly

Nadee Goonawardene[✉], XiaoPing Toh, and Hwee-Pink Tan

SMU-TCS iCity Lab, Singapore Management University, Singapore, Singapore
{nadeeg,xptoh,hptan}@smu.edu.sg

Abstract. Ageing-in-place, the ability to age holistically in the community, is increasingly gaining recognition as a solution to address resource limitations in the elderly care sector. Effective elderly care models require a personalised and all-encompassing approach to caregiving. In this regard, sensor technologies have gained attention as an effective means to monitor the wellbeing of elderly living alone. In this study, we seek to investigate the potential of non-intrusive sensor systems to detect socially isolated community dwelling elderly. Using a mixed method approach, our results showed that sensor-derived features such as going-out behavior, daytime napping and time spent in the living room are associated with different social isolation dimensions. The average time spent outside home is associated with the social loneliness level, social network score and the overall social isolation level of the elderly and the time spent in the living room is positively associated with the emotional loneliness level. Further, elderly who perceived themselves as socially lonely tend to take more naps during the day time. The findings of this study provide implications on how a non-intrusive sensor-based monitoring system comprising of motion-sensors and a door contact sensor can be utilized to detect elderly who are at risk of social isolation.

Keywords: Non-intrusive sensors · Ageing-in-place · Social isolation

1 Introduction

According to the United Nations, countries across the world are facing an upward trend of population ageing [1]. Along with this, is the upward trend towards the elderly living alone. In order to meet rapidly changing elderly needs, nations are increasingly adopting cost effective home and community based care models to substitute costly and labor intensive institutionalized elderly care system. Community care models allow elderly to age-in-place, i.e., to live in their own home, thus giving them the freedom and independency in life. Although such care models would alleviate the resource shortfall in care facilities, it could also lead to various social and health issues.

The risks faced by elderly people living alone could range from their safety and health to their psychological well-being. Further, as the elderly are living alone and often have a limited network of family and friends, they may be at a high risk of social deprivation, which could lead to pertinent issues such as loneliness and social isolation. Social isolation has been often identified as an objective measure of network size and diversity,

© Springer International Publishing AG 2017
J. Zhou and G. Salvendy (Eds.): ITAP 2017, Part II, LNCS 10298, pp. 378–392, 2017.
DOI: 10.1007/978-3-319-58536-9_30

and frequency of interpersonal contact. On the other hand, loneliness is a qualitative, subjective evaluation related to one's expectations and satisfaction with the frequency and closeness of interpersonal contacts [3]. However, both loneliness and social isolation have often been associated with various negative health repercussions, such as greater risk of cardiovascular disease [4], cognitive impairment [5, 6] and worsened sleep quality [7]. They have also been found to be correlated with higher mortality rates among the elderly [8, 9].

The prevalence of social isolation and loneliness amongst older people aged 60 or above is substantial, (estimated to be up to 17% [10–12]) and loneliness is reported to be experienced by approximately 40% within this age group [13]. The trend towards elderly living alone, and the impact of social isolation on individuals' health highlight the need to target social isolation as an emergent societal issue. However, challenges to care provision and social interventions could arise when identifying the elderly who are lonely and socially isolated. Direct self-reported methods are most commonly used to measure the loneliness and social isolation of an individual. However, these subjective responses may not be accurate as existing social stigmas associated with being lonely can be potential obstacles.

In Singapore, elderly aged 65 and above who live alone has grown exponentially from 14,500 in 2000 to 42,100 in 2015 [2]. From 2007 to 2011, at least 50 elderly living alone have passed away in their own homes, only to be discovered after a prolonged period [2]. Past studies have shown the potential of sensor technologies to identify elderly with physical, psychological and cognitive impairments [14, 15]. Sensor-enabled 'Smart Homes' have the ability to effectively monitor the wellbeing of elderly living alone. Therefore, in recent years, many technology-based initiatives have been carried out to transform the face of ageing [17] in Singapore. However, past studies have acknowledged that privacy concerns with installing monitoring cameras in the elderly's homes and memory lapses in remembering to put on their wearables are some challenges in building a sensor-enabled smart home environment [16].

The Smart Homes and Intelligent Neighbors to Enable Seniors (SHINESeniors) project aims to create up to 100 sensor-enabled homes in support of ageing-in-place, through the use of non-intrusive and non-participative sensor technologies such as passive infrared (PIR) motion and door contact sensors. In this study, we use a mixed method approach with data gathered from surveys, observations and objective measures derived from PIR sensors to present an all-encompassing approach for caregivers to detect socially isolated elderly who are living in their own homes.

2   Methodology

2.1   Data Collection

The data in this study was collected from sensor-enabled homes of 50 elderly participants in the SHINESeniors project. These participants were selected on a voluntarily basis if they meet the following criteria: living alone in government-subsidized flats, aged 65 or above and affiliated to a Voluntary Welfare Organization (VWO) operating in the neighborhood. All the participants agreed to have the sensors installed in their homes and the consent to obtain data for research purposes was obtained prior to the installation.

The sensor-based monitoring system was deployed in early 2015 for 50 flats [18]. Specifically, passive infrared (PIR) motion sensors have been installed in every room of the apartment, including the living room, bedroom, kitchen and bathroom. Each sensor, at 10 s intervals, reports if motion has been detected within its coverage area. Additionally, a door contact sensor has been installed on the main door to report every door opening or closing event. Together with the motion sensors, we can monitor if the elderly is in or out of home, as well as their daily living patterns observed by sensor data at home, in an unobtrusive manner.

In order to obtain ground truth such as daily routines, unusual events etc., two researchers conduct home visits to the elderly homes twice a month from the day of the installation of the system. Further, a survey has been conducted in early 2016 to gather information pertaining to participants' demographics and wellbeing. The survey comprised of questions to assess participants in terms of both the physical and mental health wellbeing. The main aspects of the survey include: demographic characteristics, social isolation, depression, cognition, physical health status and subjective wellbeing. Although the system has been installed since 2015, we limit the scope of this study to 7 months (January 2016 to July 2016). Further, at the quantitative data analysis stage, we have considered sensor data from two months prior to the survey date of the particular elderly.

Social isolation. Social isolation has been defined and explored in myriad ways in past literature. It is often referred to the lack of interpersonal contacts with the society [11]. On the other hand, loneliness refers to the subjective state of negative feelings associated with perceived social isolation [19]. In this study we measure social isolation as a combination of three factors: (1) relative lack of a social network, including both family and friends, (2) the subjective loneliness and (3) attendance in social activities. All dimensions were assessed using self-reported measures.

First, the presence of a social network was measured using the Lubben Social Network Scale [20]. This scale includes questions to evaluate the family and friendship network of individuals. The scale includes questions such as: 'How many relatives do you see or hear from at least once a month?' and 'How many friends do you feel close to such that you could call on them for help?' Second, loneliness of elderly was subjectively measured using the De Jong Gierveld Loneliness Scale [3]. All items were measured using a five-point likert-scale with anchors from 'strongly disagree' to 'strongly agree'. It is a multidimensional measure of loneliness, which consists of two factors encompassing 6 emotional loneliness items and 5 social loneliness items. In this study, we refer to emotional loneliness as the absence of an attachment figure in one's life and someone to turn to. On the other hand, social loneliness refers to the absence of an acceptable social network that can provide a sense of belonging, of companionship and of being a member of a community [3, 21].

Items under emotional loneliness include questions such as: 'I miss having people around me' and 'I miss the pleasure of the company of others,' and social loneliness items include: 'There are plenty of people I can lean on when I have problems' and

'There are enough people I feel close to.' Finally, elderly's frequency of attendance in four activities was surveyed to derive a score on their social functions. Specifically, the survey included questions on their frequency of meeting friends, visiting family, attending religious activities and having meals outside.

Geriatric depression. Loneliness and depression are often identified to be correlated [22]. The subjective feeling of loneliness as a result of lack of interpersonal contact could lead to the development of depressive symptomatology in the elderly. On the other hand, symptoms of depression could also result in avoidance behavior. Thus, the reciprocal relationship between the depression and the lack of social contact could result in an upward spiral, causing the elderly to become more socially isolated. The geriatric depression was measured using the 15 item Geriatric Depression Scale (GDS) and a cutoff score of 5 was used to screen for the elderly with depressive symptoms [23].

Cognition. Perceived social isolation has been extensively recognized in the literature as a contributing factor to poorer overall cognitive performance, faster cognitive decline and poorer executive functioning [6]. In this study, we assess the cognition using the Abbreviated Mental Test score [24]. The scale is popularly used to assess the elderly for the possibility of cognitive impairment. A score above 7 out of 10 is considered normal.

Other wellbeing indices. Other wellbeing indices that were measured in the survey include subjective sleep quality, chronic conditions, Activities of Daily Living (ADL) and Instrumental Activities of Daily Living (IADL). Past studies have shown the association between social isolation and the quality of sleep [7]. Therefore, factors such as sleep duration, daytime tiredness, napping and the quality of night time sleep can be used as important indicators when detecting the socially isolated elderly. In our survey, we measure the subjective sleep quality using the items of Pittsburgh Sleep Quality Index (PSQI) [25]. Independence in performing activities of daily living and instrumental activities of daily living were assessed using the Katz, et al. [26] and Lawton and Brody [27] respectively.

2.2 Feature Extraction

There are several aspects of elderly daily living that can be inferred using an in-home sensor-based monitoring system. In SHINESeniors project, we have designed algorithms to derive elderly's behavioral patterns such as sleep, going out and toileting from sensor readings. Then we use different features derived from sensor data to examine the association with elderly's social isolation level.

Going out. We consider that the elderly has gone out if the flat is empty, i.e., no motion is detected between consecutive door contact events of duration longer than 30 min but less than 24 h. Two measures were derived based on the going-out pattern: average daily away duration and the number of times the elderly went out (away count).

Sleep. The sleep duration was calculated based on the bedroom sensor and personalized to living habits of the elderly. If the elderly is sleeping in the room, the number of sensor firings should be very low. Assuming one sleep event last for at least 30 min, the elderly is identified as sleeping if there is no motion detected in any other area of the flat other than the bedroom for 30 min. After identifying the sleep intervals objectively, findings were compared against the subjective data collected through surveys and ground truth data collected regularly through observations. Two features were derived from the sleep intervals: (1) day time napping duration was calculated using the sum of all sleep durations between 7 am and 7 pm and (2) night time sleeping duration was calculated based on the sleep durations after 7 pm and before 7 am.

Time spent in the living room. Individuals who are alone may spend prolonged periods of time in the living room watching TV, reading or just relaxing on the sofa. Therefore, the time spent in the living room could be an indicator of the elderly's overall activity level and thus may relate to their subjective isolation level. As with the sleep duration assessment, the time spent in the living room was determined based on the sensor signal in the living room, but without considering minimum time duration.

Activity level in the kitchen. The ability to perform activities of daily living is often related to the perceived loneliness level of individuals [28]. Elderly who are fully independent in performing activities of daily living are likely to perform more household chores, thus triggering more sensor signals. Therefore, the total count of sensor firings from the kitchen sensor was captured as an indicator of the activities elderly perform in the kitchen area. When the elderly is active in a particular area of the flat, the number of sensor firings has to be higher than when the elderly is stationary.

2.3 Data Analysis

The main analysis has been carried out in two stages: (1) analysis of the relationship between the sensor-derived features, wellness indices and social isolation measures and (2) qualitative analysis of elderly's daily living patterns observed by sensor data. First, the Pearson product-moment r correlation is computed to investigate the factors associated with social isolation dimensions, as it provides a bivariate measure of the relationship strength between two variables. The association of social isolation dimensions with the survey indices and sensor-derived features were examined at this stage of the analysis. Second, a more in-depth qualitative analysis has been carried out to validate the findings of the quantitative analysis. Specifically, individual elderly profiles which are generated using data gathered by periodic observations, interviews and the survey were examined against the long-term sensor-derived daily living patterns to identify trends of socially isolated elderly. Figure 1 illustrates the process of data analysis and validation.

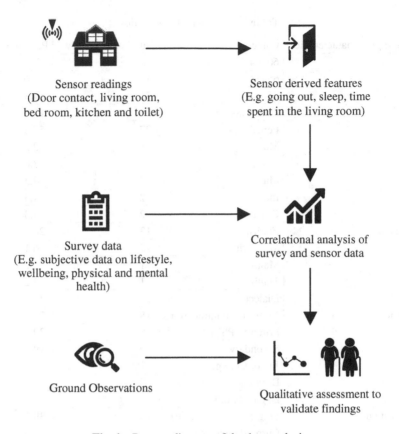

Fig. 1. Process diagram of the data analysis

3   Results and Findings

3.1   Descriptive Statistics

Table 1 illustrates the demographic characteristics of 46 elderly who participated in the survey, out of 50 elderly participants of the project. All 46 elderly were within the age range of 60 to 91 and 27 were female and 19 were male. The majority of the elderly were of Chinese descent (87%), had no formal (39%) or only primary (39%) education and only 3 were married at the time of the survey. Further, only one elderly performed poorly in AMT (<5) test, indicating cognitive impairment, while 16 elderly showed GDS score of 5 or above. Therefore, in subsequent quantitative analysis, we have not considered the AMT scores of the elderly.

Table 1. Demographic statistics

Demographic characteristic	Category	Number of elderly	Percentage %
Age group	60–64	3	6.5
	65–74	12	26.0
	75–84	25	54.3
	85 and above	6	13.0
Gender	Female	27	57.8
	Male	19	42.2
Race	Chinese	40	87.0
	Malay	2	4.3
	Indian	2	4.3
	Others	2	4.3
Language	English	13	28.2
	Mandarin	12	26.1
	Malay	1	2.2
	Tamil	1	2.2
	Dialect	19	41.3
Education	No formal qualifications	18	39.1
	Primary (PSLE)	18	39.1
	Secondary	9	19.6
	Junior College	1	2.2
	Diploma	0	–
	Degree or higher	0	–
Marital status	Single (never married)	18	39.1
	Currently married	3	6.5
	Separated	1	2.2
	Divorced	9	19.6
	Widowed	15	32.6

The distribution of the loneliness score and the social networking score is presented in the Fig. 2. The total loneliness score was calculated based on two factors, subjective social loneliness and emotional loneliness levels. The Fig. 2 illustrates the normalized scores of total loneliness level and social networking. According to the graph, elderly who have a low social network tend to perceive higher loneliness levels.

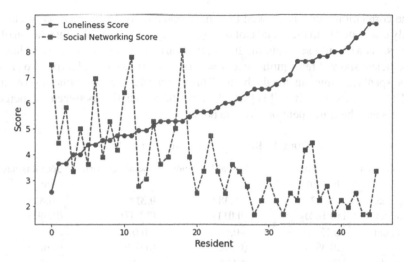

Fig. 2. Distribution of the loneliness and social network

3.2   Social Isolation and Sensor-Derived Features

Table 2 shows the results of the correlation analysis. The table shows the correlations between the sensor-derived features, wellness indices derived by the survey and the social isolation dimensions (i.e., emotional loneliness, social loneliness and social networking scores). The overall social isolation score was calculated based on the loneliness scores (emotional and social loneliness), social network and attendance in social activities. A composite score of social isolation was computed based on the standard loadings of each dimension. Thus, the composite social isolation is a weighted score of three dimensions which could measure one's overall isolation level.

Results showed that the average daily away duration is negatively correlated with the social loneliness score ($p < 0.05$) and the social isolation score ($p < 0.01$) and positively correlated with the social networking score ($p < 0.05$). In a related work by Austin, et al. [29], the time out duration was related to the overall perceived loneliness level using the UCLA loneliness scale [30], a unidimensional measure of the perceived loneliness [21]. However, according to our results, average daily away duration is associated with the social loneliness, a component of the multi-dimensional loneliness, but did not show a strong association with the emotional loneliness.

Further, time spent in the living room is significantly correlated with the emotional loneliness score ($p < 0.05$). This suggests that the elderly who lack of an attachment figure or who do not have anyone to turn to when they need emotional comfort, would spend more time in the living room. Daytime napping duration showed a significant and positive correlation with social loneliness ($p < 0.05$), suggesting that the elderly who lack a sense of belonging or companionship tend to sleep more during the day time.

Geriatric Depression Score (GDS) showed a significant positive correlation with all social isolation dimensions and the overall social isolation score. IADL and the sleep quality (PSQI) scores showed significant correlation with the emotional loneliness score.

The correlation analysis showed that the average daily away duration of elderly is strongly associated with the social isolation score. Figure 3 shows the correlation of both variables. As we could see from the figure, two variables are negatively correlated and the coefficient shows high significance ($r = -0.43$, $p < 0.01$), i.e., elderly who are more isolated spent less time outside the home. This is consistent with the findings of Austin, et al. [29] and Petersen, et al. [31] which show the association between the perceived loneliness and the time spent outside the home.

Table 2. Results of the correlation analysis

Sensor-derived feature	Emotional loneliness	Social loneliness	Social network	Social isolation score
Average daily away duration	−0.22 (0.144)	**−0.38*** **(0.011)**	**0.31*** **(0.037)**	**−0.42**** **(0.005)**
Away count	0.13 (0.392)	−0.10 (0.503)	−0.07 (0.656)	0.08 (0.606)
Napping duration	−0.08 (0.597)	**0.32*** **(0.038)**	−0.26 (0.101)	−0.05 (0.777)
Night time sleep duration	−0.12 (0.448)	0.24 (0.133)	−0.14 (0.373)	−0.16) (0.297
Average time spent in the living room	**0.31*** **(0.049)**	−0.01 (0.973)	−0.23 (0.149)	0.17 (0.292)
Kitchen activity	−0.11 (0.48)	0.03 (0.854)	0.03 (0.852)	0.10 (0.508)
Gender	0.09 (0.534)	−0.08 (0.611)	0.14 (0.374)	0.17 (0.255)
Geriatric Depression Score (GDS)	**0.49**** **(0.001)**	**0.50**** **(0.000)**	**−0.34*** **(0.021)**	**0.59**** **(0.000)**
Instrumental activities of daily living (IADL)	**−0.31*** **(0.042)**	−0.15 (0.33)	0.20 (0.193)	−0.27 (0.067)
Sleep Quality (PSQI)	**0.35*** **(0.021)**	0.25 (0.101)	−0.25 (0.092)	0.29 (0.053)

P values are in parenthesis
***p < 0.001, **p < 0.01, *p < 0.05

The correlation analysis highlighted the factors that are associated with social isolation dimensions. Next, a qualitative analysis of the daily living patterns of elderly, based on the sensor-derived features and ground truth data gathered through the survey and periodic visits, was carried out to validate the findings of the correlation analysis.

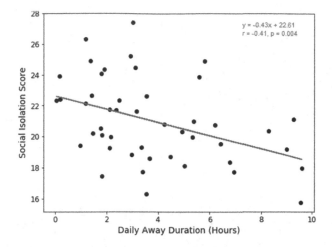

Fig. 3. The relationship between the social isolation score and the daily away duration

3.3 Qualitative Analysis

Going Out Patterns and Social Isolation. Long-term trends of the elderly's going out patterns, defined by the away frequency and durations, could reveal changes in their perception of social isolation. Further, our quantitative analysis revealed a significant correlation between the away duration and the social isolation level. Hence, to gain a relative idea of one's social isolation level with respect to the community, we can compare the going out patterns of each elderly against the average going out pattern of all the elderly in the sample. As all the elderly live in the same neighborhood, external factors such as community activities, seasonal effect and weather changes, which could influence the going out behavior, are common for all the elderly.

The case of two elderly is illustrated in this section using multiple data sources to triangulate the results. Figure 4 illustrates their weekly going out frequency and away duration. As can be seen in Fig. 4, going out trend consistently lies below the average of the community, except for one week. The social and emotional loneliness levels of elderly 1 were 21 and 23 respectively (community medians: 15 and 17), which were significantly above the average loneliness level of the community. Further, the GDS score showed that she suffers from mild depression. Face-to-face interviews revealed that the elderly had suicidal thoughts and would like to stay home and watch TV during the day. On the other hand, elderly 2 perceived a moderately well loneliness level (social loneliness 19 and emotional loneliness 14), but had a poor social network. The going out duration of the elderly showed a downward trend over time. Ground observations revealed that the elderly suffers from lack of social connections as her children have stopped visiting or calling her. Such qualitative observations provide ground truth evidence for the association between the going-out pattern and the social isolation level.

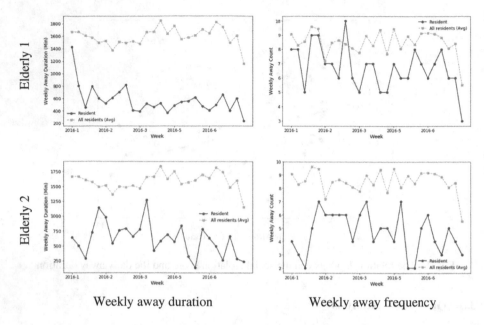

Weekly away duration   Weekly away frequency

Fig. 4. Going out pattern

Daily In-home Living Patterns and Social Isolation. In this section, we analyze the elderly's in-home daily living patterns observed by sensor data and the social isolation dimensions. Our correlation analysis revealed that, the time spent in the living room is associated with the emotional loneliness and the day-time napping duration (sleep between 7:00 am and 7:00 pm) is associated with the social loneliness level. Therefore, we have qualitatively examined elderly's in-home behavior detected by PIR sensors (i.e. bedroom, bathroom, living room and kitchen sensors) to identify how different loneliness levels can be reflected in their daily living patterns.

As discussed above, elderly 2 showed moderately high loneliness levels and a poor social networking score and a going out pattern that was below the community average. Therefore, we have analyzed elderly 2's daily living pattern in-depth to apply our findings. The heat maps in Fig. 5 show the daily living patterns of the elderly 2 captured by each sensor. Signals of sensors in each area was aggregated on an hourly basis to generate the heat maps. Thus, areas with lighter shades represent high activity time periods. From the heat map of the bed room sensor, it is evident that this elderly had consistently stayed in the bedroom from midnight until after 10:00 am. The survey data revealed that, the elderly usually wakes up at 8:00 am but frequently goes back to sleep after waking up in the morning, thus starting the day very late. After waking up in the morning and using the bathroom, she would mostly stay in the living room area and the kitchen.

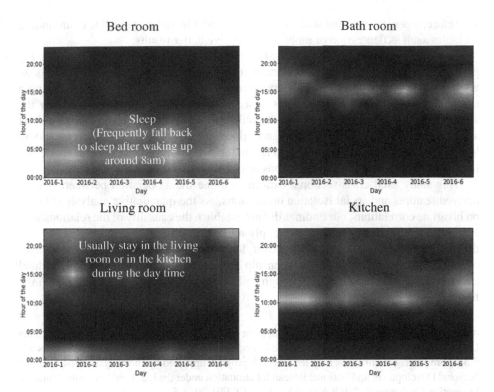

Fig. 5. Daily living pattern of elderly 2

4 Conclusion

This study used a mixed method approach to detect elderly who are at risk of social isolation using in-home sensors. Our results showed that the average time spent outside home is associated with the social loneliness and the social networking score of the elderly. Further, elderly who perceived themselves as socially lonely have taken more naps during the daytime. Average time spent in the living room was significantly associated with the perceived emotional loneliness level of the elderly. We also correlated the overall social isolation level calculated based on the social and emotional loneliness, social network and attendance in social activities, with the daily away duration and results showed a linear negative relationship.

The qualitative analysis of the in-home daily living patterns observed by sensor data validated the findings of the correlation analysis. In-home behavior and going out behavior captured by the motion sensors and the door contact sensor revealed different patterns for elderly with different perceived social isolation levels. However, there can be other confounding factors, which influence both the social isolation and their behavioral patterns. Further, as highlighted by Petersen, et al. [31], it is also possible that some elderly do not experience loneliness but display somewhat similar daily living patterns.

Therefore, when determining social isolation, a model including plausible confounding variables such as depression or mobility could give better results.

The ability to detect socially isolated elderly, solely by observing their daily living patterns through sensor data, is important for the provision of care. Our study is an attempt to detect socially isolated, community dwelling elderly living alone, using a minimum number of in-home sensors. Our results provide implications on how the sensor-based monitoring systems can be utilized to detect elderly who are at risk of social isolation, using motion-sensors and a door contact sensor. The caregivers should look into the individual daily living patterns and specific circumstances in order to design interventions to improve social functions of elderly living alone.

This study used cross-sectional data to examine the association between sensor-derived features and social isolation dimensions. As the quantitative analysis is based on bivariate correlations, our findings did not establish the causality of the relationships. Future research will be carried out to apply multivariate estimation models to identify the predictors of social isolation. Moreover, longitudinal analysis using multiple waves of data could establish the causal relationship between variables. Therefore, longitudinal analysis using the data gathered through follow-up surveys will be carried out in the future.

Acknowledgements. This research was supported by the iCity Lab, a partnership between Tata Consultancy Services (TCS) and Singapore Management University (SMU). SHINESeniors is a Singapore Management University led research project supported by the Singapore Ministry of National Development and National Research Foundation under the Land and Livability National Innovation Challenge (L2NIC) Award No. L2NICCFP1-2013-5.

References

1. World population ageing: United Nations Department of Economic and Social Affairs, Population Division (2015)
2. The straitstimes: Old and home alone in Singapore (2015). http://www.straitstimes.com/singapore/old-and-home-alone-in-singapore. Accessed 3 Feb 2017
3. De Jong-Gierveld, J., Kamphuls, F.: The development of a Rasch-type loneliness scale. Appl. Psychol. Meas. **9**(3), 289–299 (1985). doi:10.1177/014662168500900307
4. Kawachi, I., Colditz, G.A., Ascherio, A., Rimm, E.B., Giovannucci, E., Stampfer, M.J., Willett, W.C.: A prospective study of social networks in relation to total mortality and cardiovascular disease in men in the USA. J. Epidemiol. Commun. Health **50**(3), 245–251 (1996). doi:10.1136/jech.50.3.245
5. Luanaigh, C.Ó., Lawlor, B.A.: Loneliness and the health of older people. Int. J. Geriatr. Psychiatry **23**(12), 1213–1221 (2008). doi:10.1002/gps.2054
6. Cacioppo, J.T., Hawkley, L.C.: Perceived social isolation and cognition. Trends Cogn. Sci. **13**(10), 447–454 (2009). doi:10.1016/j.tics.2009.06.005
7. Cacioppo, J.T., Hawkley, L.C.: Social isolation and health, with an emphasis on underlying mechanisms. Perspect. Biol. Med. **46**(3), S39–S52 (2003). doi:10.1353/pbm.2003.0049
8. Patterson, A.C., Veenstra, G.: Loneliness and risk of mortality: a longitudinal investigation in Alameda County, California. Soc. Sci. Med. **71**(1), 181–186 (2010). doi:10.1016/j.socscimed.2010.03.024

9. Shiovitz-Ezra, S., Ayalon, L.: Situational versus chronic loneliness as risk factors for all-cause mortality. Int. Psychogeriatr. **22**(03), 455–462 (2010). doi:10.1017/S1041610209991426

10. Iliffe, S., Kharicha, K., Harari, D., Swift, C., Gillmann, G., Stuck, A.E.: Health risk appraisal in older people 2: the implications for clinicians and commissioners of social isolation risk in older people. Br. J. Gen. Pract. **57**(537), 277–282 (2007)

11. Dickens, A.P., Richards, S.H., Greaves, C.J., Campbell, J.L.: Interventions targeting social isolation in older people: a systematic review. BMC Public Health **11**(1), 1 (2011). doi: 10.1186/1471-2458-11-647

12. Hawthorne, G.: Measuring social isolation in older adults: development and initial validation of the friendship scale. Soc. Indic. Res. **77**(3), 521–548 (2006). doi:10.1007/s11205-005-7746-y

13. Savikko, N., Routasalo, P., Tilvis, R.S., Strandberg, T.E., Pitkälä, K.: Predictors and subjective causes of loneliness in an aged population. Arch. Gerontol. Geriatr. **41**(3), 223–233 (2005). doi:10.1016/j.archger.2005.03.002

14. Hayes, T.L., Riley, T., Pavel, M., Kaye, J.A.: Estimation of rest-activity patterns using motion sensors. In: Annual International Conference of the IEEE Engineering in Medicine and Biology. IEEE (2010). doi:10.1109/IEMBS.2010.5628022

15. Cacioppo, J.T., Hawkley, L.C., Berntson, G.G., Ernst, J.M., Gibbs, A.C., Stickgold, R., Hobson, J.A.: Do lonely days invade the nights? Potential social modulation of sleep efficiency. Psychol. Sci. **13**(4), 384–387 (2002)

16. Smith, J.R., Fishkin, K.P., Jiang, B., Mamishev, A., Philipose, M., Rea, A.D., Roy, S., Sundara-Rajan, K.: RFID-based techniques for human-activity detection. Commun. ACM **48**(9), 39–44 (2005). doi:10.1145/1081992.1082018

17. Action plan for successful ageing: Ministry of Health. https://www.moh.gov.sg/content/dam/moh_web/SuccessfulAgeing/action-plan.pdf

18. Bai, L., Gavino, A., Lee, W.Q., Kim, J., Liu, N., Tan, H., Tan, H., Tan, L.B., Toh, X., Valera, A.C., Yu, E., Wu, A., Fox, M.: SHINESeniors: personalized services for active ageing-in-place. In: 2015 IEEE First International Smart Cities Conference (ISC2). Research Collection School of Information Systems (2015)

19. Wenger, G.C., Davies, R., Shahtahmasebi, S., Scott, A.: Social isolation and loneliness in old age: review and model refinement. Ageing Soc. **16**(03), 333–358 (1996). doi:10.1017/S0144686X00003457

20. Lubben, J., Blozik, E., Gillmann, G., Iliffe, S., von Renteln, K.W., Beck, J.C., Stuck, A.E.: Performance of an abbreviated version of the Lubben Social Network Scale among three European community-dwelling older adult populations. Gerontologist **46**(4), 503–513 (2006). doi:10.1093/geront/46.4.503

21. Dahlberg, L., McKee, K.J.: Correlates of social and emotional loneliness in older people: evidence from an English community study. Aging Ment. Health **18**(4), 504–514 (2014). doi: 10.1080/13607863.2013.856863

22. Weeks, D.G., Michela, J.L., Peplau, L.A., Bragg, M.E.: Relation between loneliness and depression: a structural equation analysis. J. Pers. Soc. Psychol. **39**(6), 1238 (1980). doi: 10.1037/h0077709

23. Herrmann, N., Mittmann, N., Silver, I.L., Shulman, K.I., Busto, U.A., Shear, N.H., Naranjo, C.A.: A validation study of the Geriatric Depression Scale short form. Int. J. Geriatr. Psychiatry **11**(5), 457–460 (1996). doi:10.1002/(SICI)1099-1166(199605)11:5<457:AID-GPS325>3.0.CO;2-2

24. Hodkinson, H.: Evaluation of a mental test score for assessment of mental impairment in the elderly. Age Ageing **1**(4), 233–238 (1972). doi:10.1093/ageing/1.4.233

25. Buysse, D.J., Reynolds, C.F., Monk, T.H., Berman, S.R., Kupfer, D.J.: The Pittsburgh Sleep Quality Index: a new instrument for psychiatric practice and research. Psychiatry Res. **28**(2), 193–213 (1989). doi:10.1016/0165-1781(89)90047-4

26. Katz, S., Ford, A.B., Moskowitz, R.W., Jackson, B.A., Jaffe, M.W.: Studies of illness in the aged: the index of ADL: a standardized measure of biological and psychosocial function. JAMA **185**(12), 914–919 (1963). doi:10.1001/jama.1963.03060120024016

27. Lawton, M., Brody, E.M.: Assessment of older people: self-maintaining and instrumental activities of daily living. Nurs. Res. **19**(3), 278 (1970). doi:10.1093/geront/9.3_Part_1.179

28. Hacihasanoğlu, R., Yildirim, A., Karakurt, P.: Loneliness in elderly individuals, level of dependence in activities of daily living (ADL) and influential factors. Arch. Gerontol. Geriatr. **54**(1), 61–66 (2012). doi:10.1016/j.archger.2011.03.011

29. Austin, J., Dodge, H.H., Riley, T., Jacobs, P.G., Thielke, S., Kaye, J.: A smart-home system to unobtrusively and continuously assess loneliness in older adults. IEEE J. Transl. Eng. Health Med. **4**, 1–11 (2016). doi:10.1109/JTEHM.2016.2579638

30. Russell, D.W.: UCLA Loneliness Scale (Version 3): reliability, validity, and factor structure. J. Pers. Assess. **66**(1), 20–40 (1996). doi:10.1207/s15326934crj1701_4

31. Petersen, J., Austin, D., Kaye, J.A., Pavel, M., Hayes, T.L.: Unobtrusive in-home detection of time spent out-of-home with applications to loneliness and physical activity. IEEE J. Bio-Med. Health Inf. **18**(5), 1590–1596 (2014). doi:10.1109/JBHI.2013.2294276

Understanding Middle-Aged and Elderly Taiwanese People's Acceptance of the Personal Health Information System for Self-health Management

Pi-Jung Hsieh[1], Hui-Min Lai[2], Hsuan-Chi Ku[3], and Wen-Tsung Ku[4(✉)]

[1] Department of Hospital and Health Care Administration, Chia Nan University
of Pharmacy and Science, Tainan, Taiwan, R.O.C.
beerun@seed.net.tw
[2] Department of Information Management, Chienkuo Technology University,
Changhua, Taiwan, R.O.C.
hmin@cc.ctu.edu.tw
[3] National Chiayi Senior High School, Chia-Yi, Taiwan, R.O.C.
kwt2056@gmail.com
[4] Department of Physical Medicine and Rehabilitation, St. Martin De Porres Hospital,
Chia-Yi, Taiwan, R.O.C.
kib56265@gmail.com

Abstract. With the increasingly aging population and advances in information technology, self-health management has become an important topic. Middle-aged and elderly people are considered to have higher risks of contracting multiple chronic diseases and complications, thus increasing their need for healthcare. Personal health information systems provide middle-aged and elderly people with their personal healthcare information, enable them to exercise their right to know their healthcare information, and ultimately enhance measures that increase users' convenience in managing their own health. Although several prior studies have focused on the factors that influence the adoption of personal health records and electronic medical records, the literature on middle-aged and elderly people's attitudes toward the use of personal health information systems in self-health management is scarce. Thus, this study proposes a theoretical model to explain middle-aged and elderly people's intention to use a personal health information system in self-health management. A field survey was conducted in Taiwan to collect data from middle-aged and elderly people. A total of 240 valid responses were obtained, constituting a response rate of 88.89%. The results indicate that perceived severity, perceived benefits, self-efficacy, and cues to action have positive effects on usage intention. However, perceived susceptibility and perceived barriers do not significantly affect behavioral intention. The study has implications on the development of strategies to improve personal health IT acceptance.

Keywords: Technology acceptance · Health belief · Self-health management · Personal health information

© Springer International Publishing AG 2017
J. Zhou and G. Salvendy (Eds.): ITAP 2017, Part II, LNCS 10298, pp. 393–403, 2017.
DOI: 10.1007/978-3-319-58536-9_31

1   Introduction

It has been two decades since Taiwan's National Health Insurance (NHI) system was launched in 1995 to provide universal and quality healthcare to citizens at an affordable cost. To date, over 99% of the population are covered by this public program [1]. The insured have access to more than 20,000 healthcare facilities around the country providing inpatient, ambulatory, and home care. With Taiwan now considered an aging society, the NHI Administration (NHIA) intends to build a health information platform where everyone's health records will be stored in the personal health information system (PHIS). The PHIS provides insured persons with their personal healthcare information, enables them to exercise their right to know their healthcare information, and ultimately enhances measures that increase users' convenience in managing their own health. Despite this potential, as of 2015, only about 0.57% of Taiwanese citizens were using the PHIS for queries regarding personal medical records. The PHIS can play a crucial role in healthcare by providing patient information that supports numerous healthcare applications such as the diagnosis, treatment, and prevention of disease. For these information technology (IT)-enabled benefits to manifest in Taiwan, citizens must first adopt the PHIS.

The adoption and use of health IT among middle-aged and elderly people is an important issue in the field of medical informatics. Despite an emerging interest in the field of medical informatics and studies that have identified barriers to personal health record adoption [2, 3] and acceptance factors among citizens [4, 5], the understanding of middle-aged and elderly people's self-health management behavior is limited. Since health technology services are used to promote, protect, or maintain health, health technology acceptance behavior should be considered health behavior [6]. Therefore, a better understanding of health technology acceptance behavior can be gained from a health behavior perspective. A variety of health behavior theories can be used to explain the health technology acceptance phenomenon. Among these theories, the health belief model (HBM) is the most widely used. The HBM suggests that individuals decide whether to take a health-related action based on their evaluations of the perceived health threat of not taking the action and the net benefits of taking the action [7]. Thus, this study aims to propose and empirically validate the HBM depicting the factors that influence middle-aged and elderly people's adoption of the PHIS in the context of self-health management.

2   Literature Review

2.1   Personal Health Information System

Population aging, intensified by the low birth rate, is affecting the rate of economic growth and national health expenditure. To improve the general public's understanding of personal health and treatment conditions, the NHIA established the PHIS to enable people to check their medical records anytime and anywhere. Individuals can use their password-registered NHI card or citizen digital certificate to get information on hospitalization, vaccination, preventive care, dental health, drug allergies, discharge summaries, pathological test reports, medical image reports, personal outpatient visits, and organ donation and palliative care wishes. Thus, the PHIS bridges the medical information gap between medical personnel and patients to make treatment safer and more effective. The PHIS can also be used to check and download one's personal NHI card status and records as well as insurance fees and premium records. By allowing people to quickly and conveniently obtain personal healthcare data, the PHIS makes self-health management easier. For example, an elderly patient with diabetes will be directed to a list of competent medical institutions that treat diabetes, with attached quality indicators for people to choose from. An elderly patient with chronic hepatitis B or C will be directed to the website of the liver disease prevention, treatment, and research foundation, which offers rich health information, prompting timely and appropriate actions. For these health IT–enabled benefits to materialize, middle-aged and elderly people must first adopt the PHIS. A number of previous studies regarding users' health IT adoption behaviors developed technology characteristic constructs to better understand patients' unique features [3, 8, 9]. However, studies that examine middle-aged and elderly people's willingness to use a PHIS are rare.

2.2 The Health Belief Model

The HBM was developed in the 1950s. It tries to explain people's preventive health behaviors and considers health behavior a function of two basic mechanisms: threat perception and behavioral evaluation [10]. Perceived threat is assessed according to perceived susceptibility and perceived severity. Perceived susceptibility is an individual's assessment of his or her risk of contracting a condition, whereas perceived severity is an individual's assessment of the seriousness of the disease and its consequences. Behavioral evaluation is based on the perceived benefits and perceived barriers. Perceived benefits refer to an individual's assessment of the positive consequences of adopting a health behavior, including the extent to which it reduces the risk of the disease or the severity of its consequences. Perceived barriers refer to an individual's assessment of the influences that discourage the adoption of the health action.

Other important cognitive components of the HBM are self-efficacy and cues to action. Self-efficacy is an individual's confidence in his or her ability to perform the health action [11, 12]. This concept originates from the social cognitive theory [13]. Cues to action are triggers that stimulate an individual to take health action, such as health education and advice from others. Cues to action may be internal (e.g., perception of bodily states) or external (e.g., physician's advice, interpersonal interactions, and the impact of the communication medium). High susceptibility, high severity, high benefits, low barriers, high self-efficacy, and high cues to action are assumed to lead to a high probability of adopting the recommended action [11, 14–16]. Prior studies have also shown that the HBM has good explanatory power in predicting users' health IT acceptance [14, 16]. Therefore, this study applies the HBM to explain middle-aged and elderly people's intention to use the PHIS for self-health management.

3 Research Model

Prior studies have argued that behavior intentions are more appropriate than actual behavior because the former are measured contemporaneously with beliefs [17–19]. Certain studies have also chosen behavior intentions instead of actual behavior as the dependent variable to investigate users' health IT acceptance [20]. Therefore, we considered it appropriate to use middle-aged and elderly people's behavior intentions as the dependent variable of this study. Previous studies have empirically proven that the effect of the original HBM variables on behavior can be mediated by behavior intentions [14, 21]. Thus, we linked the six HBM constructs (i.e., perceived susceptibility, perceived severity, perceived benefits, perceived barriers, self-efficacy, and cues to action) to behavior intentions. Figure 1 shows the proposed research model, which details the various dimensions and the development of the theoretical arguments.

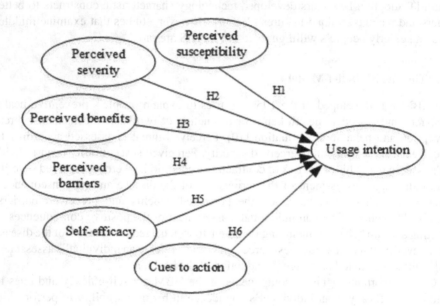

Fig. 1. Research framework

In the HBM, when users consider themselves more likely to suffer a health-related threat (i.e., high perceived susceptibility) and/or perceive the threat as likely to cause serious harm (i.e., high perceived severity), they tend to adopt the health IT that can prevent or reduce the risk of contracting a condition or disease [16]. Prior studies have provided support for the positive effect of perceived susceptibility and perceived severity on behavior intentions [14, 22]. Thus, we posit the following hypotheses:

H1. Perceived susceptibility is positively related to the intention to use the PHIS.
H2. Perceived severity is positively related to the intention to use the PHIS.

As indicated in the HBM, perceived benefits refer to the evaluation of the effectiveness of taking health actions to reduce the threat of a disease. Thus, if users believe that using health IT enables them to reduce the threats to their health, then they will be more likely to adopt this health technology. Prior studies have provided support for the positive effect of perceived benefits on behavior intentions [14, 16]. On the other hand, costs and negative perceptions pertaining to system usage, such as inconvenience, time consumption, and the considerable expense of system usage, also affect the possibility of action by functioning as perceived barriers. The stronger the perceived barriers, the more difficult it would be for one to take health action [16, 23]. Thus, we posit the following hypotheses:

H3. Perceived benefits are positively related to the intention to use the PHIS.

H4. Perceived barriers are negatively related to the intention to use the PHIS.

According to social cognitive theory, individuals with greater confidence in their abilities are more likely to initiate challenging behaviors such as healthy eating behavior [12]. In the health technology acceptance context, when users are confident in their ability to use the health IT, they are more likely to use that technology. Conversely, the lack of competence to use the health IT may become a major barrier to middle-aged and elderly users' new technology acceptance [6]. Prior studies have provided support for the positive effect of self-efficacy on behavior intentions [6, 12, 14, 23]. Therefore, we propose the following hypothesis:

H5. Self-efficacy is positively related to the intention to use the PHIS.

Based on the HBM perspective, cues to action—including internal cues (e.g., physical discomfort and appearance of symptoms) and external cues (e.g., physician's advice, impact of media education, encouragement from friends and relatives, and family members or relatives who suffer from health problems)—directly move people to undertake health behaviors. These cues positively affect the chances of health action [16]. Prior studies have provided support for the positive effect of cues to action on behavior intentions [14, 23]. Thus, we posit the following hypothesis:

H6. Cues to action are positively related to the intention to use the PHIS.

4 Research Method

4.1 Questionnaire Development

The questionnaire is divided into two parts. The first part includes nominal scales and five-point Likert scales ranging from *strongly agree* to *strongly disagree*. The first part of the questionnaire was used to collect basic information about the respondents' characteristics, including age, gender, education, occupation, experience in computer use, and mobile device usage experience. The second part of the questionnaire was developed based on the constructs of perceived susceptibility, perceived severity, perceived benefits, perceived barriers, self-efficacy, and cues to action. Although previous studies have validated the questionnaire items, we conducted pretests by requesting three healthcare professionals to evaluate each item. To ensure validity and reliability, we conducted a pilot test with a sample that was representative of the actual respondents.

4.2   Data Analysis

We conducted structural equation modeling using partial least squares (PLS) estimations for the data analysis because the PLS method requires a minimal sample size and has few residual distribution requirements for model validation [24]. We tested the reliability and validity of the proposed model. The model was deemed reliable if the construct reliability was greater than 0.8 [25]. Convergent validity was assessed based on the following criteria: (a) statistically significant item loading greater than 0.7, (b) composite construct reliability greater than 0.8, and (c) average variance extracted (AVE) greater than 0.5 [24]. The discriminant validity of the constructs was assessed based on the criterion that the square root of the AVE for each construct should be greater than the corresponding correlations with all the other constructs [26].

4.3   Sample and Data Collection

The target participants were the middle-aged and elderly in Taiwan. This study employed an online survey for data collection because online surveys provide researchers with various benefits such as saving time and reducing expenses by over-coming geographic distance [27, 28]. Moreover, online surveys assist in accessing unique subjects. For improving generalization of our results, the participants in this study must consider different target groups by gender and geographical. A total of 270 questionnaires were distributed through an online survey company, and 240 questionnaires were returned. We assessed the nonresponse bias by comparing early and late respondents (i.e., those who replied during the first three days and the last three days, respectively). We found no significant difference between the two respondent groups based on the sample attributes (e.g., gender and age).

5   Research Results

The 240 valid questionnaires constituted a response rate of 88.89%. Slightly more than half (53.8%) of the respondents were females. The majority of respondents (56.7%) were between the ages of 40 and 49 years. The education level for 50.8% of the respondents was college or below. Nearly all (92.5%) the respondents had more than five years of computer experience, and 52.1% of the respondents had more than five years of mobile device usage experience. In this study, the construct reliabilities are all greater than 0.9. For the convergent validity, the item loadings are all greater than 0.7, and the AVEs range from 0.63 to 0.89. For the discriminant validity, the square root of the AVE for each construct is greater than its corresponding correlations with the other constructs. Table 1 shows the descriptive statistics of the principal constructs and the correlation matrix. These results indicate acceptable reliability, convergent validity, and discriminant validity.

Table 1. Reliability and validity of the scale

Construct	Item loading	CR	AVE	Correlation						
				CA	BA	BE	SE	PS	SU	US
CA	0.74–0.83	0.91	0.63	**0.79**						
BA	0.78–0.91	0.91	0.72	−0.08	**0.85**					
BE	0.70–0.94	0.94	0.75	0.01	0.24	**0.87**				
SE	0.93–0.96	0.97	0.89	0.48	−0.07	0.11	**0.95**			
PS	0.92–0.94	0.95	0.87	0.28	0.04	0.01	0.30	**0.94**		
SU	0.93–0.94	0.97	0.89	0.17	0.16	0.26	0.01	0.25	**0.94**	
US	0.94–0.96	0.98	0.89	0.62	−0.12	−0.18	0.56	−0.30	0.12	**0.95**

Leading diagonal shows the square root of AVE of each construct. AVE = average variance extracted, CR = construct reliability, CA = cues to action, BA =perceived barriers, BE = perceived benefits, SE = self-efficacy, PS = perceived severity, SU = perceived susceptibility, US = usage intention

Figure 2 presents the test results for the structural model. The statistical test conclusions partially support this research model. In this study, the intention to use the PHIS was predicted by perceived severity ($\beta = 0.13$, p < 0.05), perceived benefits ($\beta = 0.18$, p < 0.01), self-efficacy ($\beta = 0.31$, p < 0.001), and cues to action ($\beta = 0.58$, p < 0.001). Together, these variables explained 53% of the variance in the intention to use the PHIS. These results support Hypotheses 2, 3, 5, and 6. Perceived susceptibility ($\beta = 0.05$, p > 0.05) and perceived barriers ($\beta = -0.05$, p > 0.05) did not significantly affect the intention to use the PHIS. Hence, Hypotheses 1 and 4 are not supported.

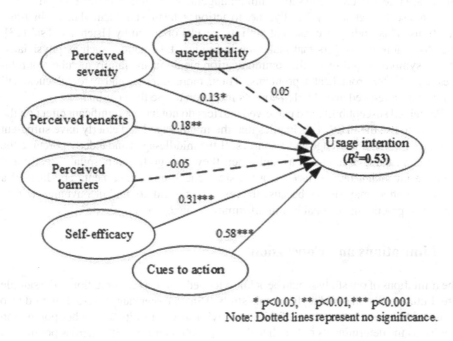

* p<0.05, ** p<0.01,*** p<0.001
Note: Dotted lines represent no significance.

Fig. 2. Results of the structural model

6   Discussion

We explored how the selected variables affected middle-aged and elderly people's intention to use the PHIS for self-health management. The study results indicate that the HBM provides an adequately explains middle-aged and elderly people's intention to use the PHIS, as the R-square of usage intention is 0.53. This implies that the HBM might be a robust research model for predicting middle-aged and elderly people's intention to use information systems. This result is consistent with the theoretical model of Rosenstock [10] and a number of other studies [14, 22, 23].

The results indicate that perceived severity, perceived benefits, self-efficacy, and cues to action are key determinants of middle-aged and elderly people's usage intentions. First, perceived severity is an influential factor in the intention to use the PHIS, although its effect is smaller than that of perceived benefits, self-efficacy, and cues to action. This finding is consistent with the result obtained by Ivanov et al. [22]. Thus, individuals who perceive a higher degree of severity are more likely to know their healthcare information so that they can manage their own health status. Second, perceived benefits also have a direct positive effect on behavior intentions, which is consistent with the findings of Huang [16]. As such, higher perceived benefits will increase middle-aged and elderly people's intention to use the PHIS. If the middle-aged and elderly believe that using the PHIS will improve their self-health management, then they will use it. Thus, the PHIS should be designed and developed to deliver value to them. Third, self-efficacy has a significant positive effect on behavior intentions. This result coincides with the findings of previous studies on IT adoption [11, 16, 23] and suggests that the middle-aged and elderly are likely to engage in self-health management when they believe they have the ability to use the technology. Finally, cues to action is the most influential factor in usage intentions. This finding is consistent with the results obtained by Hsieh and Tsai [23]. Cues to action are triggers that make the individual take action, such as physicians' advice, symptoms of disease, the communication medium, and family members or relatives who suffer from health problems. Thus, more internal and external cues will increase middle-aged and elderly people's intention to use the health IT.

Perceived susceptibility and perceived barriers do not have a significant effect on the intention to use the PHIS. This implies that the middle-aged and elderly have sufficient health promotion knowledge and resources. If the middle-aged and elderly perceive the risk of contracting a condition as high, then they may go to the hospital directly and meet the physician face to face for a physical check-up or treatment. The lack of a significant effect may also be because the respondents did not find inconvenience in or barriers to practicing personal health information management.

7   Limitations and Conclusion

The limitations of our study should be acknowledged. First, a key limitation is the sample size. Future research could replicate this study using a larger sample size. It would also be useful to compare the results of this study with survey results from other population groups, as the determinants of health technology behavior may differ across population groups. Second, the relevance of this study is confined to the health technology acceptance behavior of the middle-aged and elderly. The findings and implications drawn from this study cannot be generalized to other groups such as medical personnel. A study targeting medical personnel, who might have different information needs and different levels of computer support and abilities, could generate different results. The main contribution of this study is that it is the first to use existing health belief theory to explore middle-aged and elderly people's usage behavior. Compared with other theories, the HBM approach which was adopted for the model, provides a more complete set of antecedents that better explain the intention to employ a specific technology (i.e., personal health IT), thereby enhancing the practical contributions of this study. Several practical implications can be derived from the study. First, as perceived severity has a significant impact on adoption intention, the NHIA and healthcare providers should carry out strategies to promote the PHIS among the middle-aged and elderly with chronic diseases. This will increase middle-aged and elderly people's tendency to adopt self-health management, which can reduce the seriousness of their disease and its consequences. Second, perceived benefits is an important factor in the adoption of personal health IT; thus, service providers should try their best to improve their system performance to attract more middle-aged and elderly people. Third, self-efficacy is an important factor influencing behavior intentions. Therefore, the NHIA and healthcare providers should adopt user-friendly design features to ensure that the PHIS can be easily learned and used; they should also provide training on PHIS use for the middle-aged and elderly. Fourth, since cues to action can positively affect user behavior, the NHIA and healthcare providers should implement promotion strategies to attract adopters and then expand the number of PHIS users through internal cues and external cues. Finally, we hope that this study will stimulate interest in the health IT acceptance phenomenon and motivate researchers to examine in greater depth this unexplored yet potentially fertile area of research.

References

1. Ministry of Health and Welfare: 2015 Taiwan Health and Welfare Report (2011). http://www.mohw.gov.tw/EN/Ministry/DM2.aspx?f_list_no=475&fod_list_no=845. Accessed 25 Oct 2016
2. Househ, M.S., Borycki, E.M., Rohrer, W.M., Kushniruk, A.W.: Developing a framework for meaningful use of personal health records (PHRs). Health Policy Technol. **3**, 272–280 (2014)
3. Dontje, K., Corser, W., Holzman, G.: Understanding patient perceptions of the electronic personal health record. J. Nurse Pract. **10**(10), 824–828 (2014)
4. Lemire, M., Par'e, G., Sicotte, C., Harvey, C.: Determinants of Internet use as a preferred source of information on personal health. Int. J. Med. Inform. **77**(11), 723–734 (2008)
5. Andrews, L., Gajanayake, R., Sahama, T.: The Australian general public's perceptions of having a personally controlled electronic health record (PCEHR). Int. J. Med. Inform. **83**, 889–900 (2014)

6. Sun, Y., Wang, N., Guo, X., Peng, Z.: Understanding the acceptance of mobile health services: a comparison and integration of alternative models. J. Electron. Commer. Res. **14**(2), 183–200 (2013)
7. Rosenstock, I.M.: What research in motivation suggests for public health. Am. J. Public Health Nations Health **50**, 295–301 (1960)
8. Lapsia, V., Lamb, K., Yasnoff, W.A.: Where should electronic records for patients be stored? Int. J. Med. Inform. **81**, 821–827 (2012)
9. Greenhalgh, T., Morris, L., Wyatt, J.C., Thomas, G., Gunning, K.: Introducing a nationally shared electronic patient record: case study comparison of Scotland, England, Wales and Northern Ireland. Int. J. Med. Inform. **82**, e125–e138 (2013)
10. Rosenstock, I.M.: Why people use health services. Milbank Mem. Fund. Q. **44**(3), 94–127 (1966)
11. Ng, B.Y., Kankanhalli, A., Xu, Y.: Studying users' computer security behavior: a health belief perspective. Decis. Support Syst. **46**, 815–825 (2009)
12. Orji, R., Mandryk, R.L.: Developing culturally relevant design guidelines for encouraging healthy eating behavior. Int. J. Hum Comput Stud. **72**(2), 207–223 (2014)
13. Bandura, A.: Self-efficacy: towards a unifying theory of behavioral change. Psychol. Rev. **84**(2), 191–215 (1977)
14. Nundy, S., Dick, J.J., Solomon, M.C., Peek, M.E.: Developing a behavioral model for mobile phone-based diabetes interventions. Patient Educ. Couns. **90**, 125–132 (2013)
15. Melzner, J., Heinze, J., Fritsch, T.: Mobile health applications in workplace health promotion: an integrated conceptual adoption framework. Procedia Technol. **16**, 1374–1382 (2014)
16. Huang, J.C.: Remote health monitoring adoption model based on artificial neural networks. Expert Syst. Appl. **37**, 307–314 (2010)
17. Agarwal, R., Prasad, J.: Are individual differences germane to the acceptance of new information technologies? Decis. Sci. **30**(2), 361–391 (1999)
18. Chang, M.K.: Predicting unethical behavior: a comparison of the theory of reasoned action and the theory of planned behavior. J. Bus. Ethics **17**(16), 1825–1834 (1998)
19. Chau, P.Y.K., Hu, P.J.H.: Investigating healthcare professionals' decisions to accept telemedicine technology: an empirical test of competing theories. Inform. Manag. **39**(4), 297–311 (2002)
20. Hung, S.Y., Ku, Y.C., Chien, J.C.: Understanding physicians' acceptance of the medline system for practicing evidence-based medicine: a decomposed TPB model. Int. J. Med. Inform. **81**(2), 130–142 (2011)
21. Brijs, K., Brijs, T., Sann, S., Trinh, T.A., Wets, G., Ruiter, R.A.C.: Psychological determinants of motorcycle helmet use among young adults in Cambodia. Transp. Res. Part F **26**, 273–290 (2014)
22. Ivanov, A., Sharman, R., Rao, H.R.: Exploring factors impacting sharing health-tracking records. Health Policy Technol. **4**, 263–276 (2015)
23. Hsieh, H.L., Tsai, C.H.: An empirical study to explore the adoption of telehealth: health belief model perspective. J. Eng. Sci. Technol. Rev. **6**(2), 1–5 (2013)
24. Chin, W.W.: Issues and opinion on structural equation modelling. MIS Q. **22**(1), 7–16 (1998)
25. Fornel, C., Larcker, D.: Structural equation models with unobservable variables and measurement error: algebra and statistics. J. Mark. Res. **18**(3), 382–388 (1981)

26. Chin, W.W., Marcolin, B.L., Newsted, P.R.: A partial least squares latent variable modeling approach for measuring interaction effects: results from a Monte Carlo simulation study and an electronic-mail emotion/adoption study. Inform. Syst. Res. **14**(2), 189–217 (2003)
27. Wright, K.B.: Researching Internet-based populations: advantages and disadvantages of online survey research, online questionnaire authoring software packages, and web survey services. J. Comput. Mediat. Commun. **10**, 00 (2005). doi:10.1111/j.1083-6101.2005.tb00259.x
28. Alharbi, S., Drew, S.: Using the technology acceptance model in understanding academics' behavioural intention to use learning management systems. Int. J. Adv. Comput. Sci. Appl. **5**(1), 143–155 (2014)

To Capture the Diverse Needs of Welfare Technology Stakeholders – Evaluation of a Value Matrix

Ella Kolkowska[1](✉), Anneli Avatare Nöu[2], Marie Sjölinder[2], and Isabella Scandurra[1]

[1] Örebro University School of Business, Örebro, Sweden
{ella.kolkowska,isabella.scandurra}@oru.se
[2] SICS Swedish ICT, Kista, Sweden
{anneli,marie}@sics.se

Abstract. Welfare technology (WT) is often developed with a technical perspective, which does not involve important ethical considerations and different values that come up during the development and implementation of WT within elderly care. This paper presents a study where we have applied an ethical value matrix to support systematic ethical assessments of WT intended for personal health monitoring. The matrix consists of values in a checklist and a number of stakeholders and it is possible to analyze which values are emphasized by which stakeholders. The aim was to assess the matrix and find out how the matrix supports identification of values and interests that drive the various stakeholders in the development and implementation of WT. We have realized that several values specified by different actors as especially important were not included in the matrix and that the values in the matrix did not visualize or enable identification of value conflicts.

Keywords: Ethics · Elderly · Welfare technology · Stakeholders · Values

1 Introduction

Welfare technology (WT) is often developed with a techno-centric perspective that does not deliberate important ethical considerations and different values that come up in development and implementation of WT in elderly care or elderly person's life.

Welfare technology is defined as *digital technologies aimed at maintaining or increasing safety, activity, participation and independence for a person who has or is at increased risk to have a disability*. This technology can be used by the person him/ herself, or by formal or informal caretaker(s); a relative, staff or any other person close to the person with a disability. The large variation and reduced cost of WT along with technology increased efficiency creates almost limitless possibilities. However the technical focus often applied in development and implementation of these technologies do not consider the ethical implications that these technologies may have on the different categories of stakeholders.

Many different stakeholders, such as elderly, relatives, home care personnel, healthcare professionals, programmers, system designers, and commercial companies may be involved in the development of WT [1]. These different stakeholders often have their

© Springer International Publishing AG 2017
J. Zhou and G. Salvendy (Eds.): ITAP 2017, Part II, LNCS 10298, pp. 404–419, 2017.
DOI: 10.1007/978-3-319-58536-9_32

own, sometimes conflicting interests and values that they want to realize through the new technology [2]. Usually not all values and interests may be realized and consequently the new technology does not address all stakeholders' needs and values [2]. This in turn lead to ethical considerations such as, which stakeholders should be supported and why as well as, which values and interests should be realized and why. These ethical considerations must be highlighted already in the beginning of development projects because it may be too expensive and too difficult to modify the technical solution in the end of the project [3]. For that reason ethical assessments aiming at identifying and understanding the different values and interests that drive the different stakeholders during the development process need to be conducted regularly already from the beginning of the early stages of the development process.

Recently Nordgren [4] proposed an ethical matrix, which aims to support identifying values that are important to various groups of stakeholders in relation to WT, used for personal health monitoring (PHM). The vertical axis of the matrix includes a checklist of values identified in earlier studies as important in this context and the horizontal axis suggests a number of stakeholders that may be relevant to include in the analysis. Nordgren [4] claim that the matrix may be used as a tool for ethical reflection by people involved in the development and practical use of WT. The aim of this study is to apply and evaluate the value matrix proposed by Nordgren in two projects aiming to develop WF for elderly care. We want to find out how the matrix supports identification of the values and interests that come up during the development and implementation of WT.

The paper is structured as follows. Section 2 describes the value matrix suggested by Nordgren. In Sect. 3 we present our research method. Section 4 reports on our analysis of the case studies. The paper ends with a discussion and conclusions in Sect. 5.

2   The Value Matrix for Ethical Evaluation of Welfare Technology

Because ethical and legal aspects can be a hindering factor for the WTs' adoption within health care [5] a number of ethical checklists supporting ethical analysis have been suggested in the literature [3]. Beauchamp and Childress [6] propose an ethical assessment framework based on four principles: (1) the principle of beneficence, (2) the principle of non-maleficence, (3) the principle of respect for autonomy, and (4) the principle of justice. Although these principles may be use for evaluations of WT aimed for health care sector [7] they are criticized for being too general for this purpose. More adopted for this purpose are principles suggested by Collste [8]: (1) doctor–patient relationship, (2) responsibility, and (3) respect for autonomy. Another attempt to address ethical considerations is the "eHealth Ethics Draft Code" emphasizing aspects such as privacy, user consent and accountability. Recently Nordgren [4] proposed an ethical value matrix to support systematic ethical assessments of WT aimed for personal health monitoring. The matrix consists of values in a checklist and a number of stakeholders so it is possible to analyze which values are emphasized by which stakeholders. The proposed matrix includes nine groups of stakeholders: patients, relatives, friends, health care professionals, social care professionals, public care providers, private care providers, technology developers (companies) and regulators. The values in the checklist are divided into three groups: (1) Practical values (Reliability, Ease of use, Affordable price), (2) Quality of life values (Health, Independence, Safety, Social contact), (3) Moral values (Autonomy, Privacy, Justice).

The *Quality of life values* were identified based on earlier empirical studies [9–11] of elderly peoples' and patients' expectations on PHM technologies. In addition to health (prevention of future medical conditions), the studies highlight values such as *independence, safety, and social contact*.

Practical values are the technical and economic requirements that a PHM technology must fulfill in order to be able to promote the quality of life values. Practical values found in earlier studies [12, 13] and included by Nordgren in his ethical matrix are *reliability, ease of use and affordable price*. Finally, *moral values: autonomy, privacy, justice* that Nordgren included in the matrix are derived from ethical principles [6, 14], health care legislations, conventions and declarations. Below, follow the descriptions of the values in line with Nordgren [4].

Reliability value is about measurement, which means that the measurement (for example blood pressure) provided by a technical device must be correct. When it comes to *Ease of use*, a technical unit needs to be user friendly and easy manageable by the users.

Regarding the price of the technology, it must be *affordable*. It must be economically justifiable for caregivers (both private and public). In some cases, municipalities are reluctant to invest in advanced technology because of the high initial costs. In some cases, patients pay a fee for the technical device. Again, it is important that the price is affordable.

In health care, *quality of life* is an important measurement. It may be the patients themselves who appreciate the quality of life. It is noted that other values may influence the quality of life.

Regarding *health*, it is often compared how the number of visits to the health center and the hospital can be reduced when the patient has a PHM device and how the patient's quality of life is improved. Furthermore, it is pointed out that it is neither desirable nor possible to replace meetings with healthcare professionals with health monitoring technology. It must be an individual adaption.

The value of health can be compared with the values of independence and safety (see below). We all want to be *independent* as far as possible when it comes to residents and everyday lives. It is pointed out that PHM, which is designed to support independence, can have a negative meaning when visits by staff from the clinics or hospitals are reduced.

Safety regarding personal health monitoring is that patients and their families do not feel any concern over health risks when the patient is continuing to stay at home instead of staying at a nursing home. Of course, safety is perceived differently from person to person.

The value *autonomy* is an important value for the elderly people. A common way to describe autonomy is to talk about informed consent. It is very important that the elderly can give his/her consent to the use of a PHM, but in some circumstances it may be difficult to determine what the elderly think and perceive. See [4] for a discussion about informed consent when it comes to health related actions. It is significant that the elderly understand how technology should be used, for example, it is important that the elderly person understands that he/she should press the red button on the social alarm when he/she needs help.

When it comes to value *privacy* PHM can provide more privacy but at the same time it may be too much supervision that leads to reduce privacy. This problem can be addressed by building privacy into the monitoring techniques (Privacy by Design).

The last value is about *justice* in health care. An important reason for introducing PHM is to improve the quality of life for people. Another reason is that health monitoring is expected to reduce health care costs for an aging population, as for example fewer visits to health centers, the time of hospitalization is reduced. This leads to questions about priorities in health care and in the end it's about justice. Who is entitled to PHM?

3   Research Method

Nordgren (2013) points out that the matrix may be used descriptively or normatively depending of the context (p. 169). The matrix may be used descriptively for a systematic ethical analysis of various stakeholders' views on particular WT. In this case, descriptive statements of the stakeholders' views are filled into the slots in the matrix. The matrix can also be used normatively for instance in the technology assessment carried out by governmental or other agencies. In this case the agencies can fill in normative recommendations regarding the technology in relation to various stakeholders (p. 170). We evaluated the matrix by applying it descriptively in two case studies [15] and by discussing the matrix with various stakeholders during two seminars. One of the case studies was conducted in four Swedish municipalities and was focused on outdoor social alarms as an example for WT (Case 1). In this study we used the matrix to present the values that the involved stakeholders emphasized as particularly important when introducing outdoor social alarms for elderly within municipalities. In the second case study we used

Table 1. Empirical datasets in the two cases studies

	Case 1	Case 2
Focus	To present the values that the involved stakeholders emphasized as particularly important when introducing outdoor social alarms within municipalities	To present which values various stakeholders considered as particularly important during development of a system supporting independent living
Method	Case study, open-ended interviews, focus group interviews	Case study, semi-structured interviews, focus group interviews, documents analysis
Subjects	Users (elderly people), relatives, home care personnel, alarm operators	Municipalities officers, home care personnel, health care professionals, relatives, elderly people, system developers
N	16 open-ended interviews, 3 focus group interviews (approx. 5 in each group)	11 semi-structured interviews, 4 focus groups (approx. 10 in each group), reports

the matrix to illustrate which values various stakeholders considered as particularly important during development of a system supporting independent living (Case 2). Mixed methods approach [16] was adopted in for data collection within each case study. Details for data collection for each case are presented in Table 1 and were earlier described in [18].

3.1 Case 1: Outdoors Social Alarms

WT focused in this study is outdoor social alarms. A traditional social alarm is an alarm device that is installed in a user's home and makes it possible for a user to call for help in urgent situations at home. In previous studies [17, 18] we have described how important it is to understand the entire alarm chain (it starts when an alarm holder presses the alarm button and ends when staff from home care visits the alarm holder) is working. There is also a need for the elderly to be more active and feel safe outdoors as well. An outdoor alarm could help people to feel safe even when outdoors, and thereby enable them to have an active life with better health and improved quality of life. An outdoor alarm communicates typically via mobile networks and has a GPS (Global Positioning System) receiver to locate a person. There are several outdoor alarms on the market that can locate a person via GPS. This kind of social alarm enables an alarm receiver to see where the person is located. With this service, you can enter a geographic security zone for a person. When the person goes outside the zone, an alarm is sent to the alarm receiver's mobile phone to indicate the user's position. Relatives can either call or seek the user at the given position if they become anxious.

The work was conducted as a collaboration between SICS Swedish ICT and four municipalities in Sweden (see Table 2) [17]. The municipalities in the case study were selected to reflect the social alarm field from diverse needs and different circumstances.

In the first part of the study [17] we could see there was a great need for an outdoor alarm. Both users and staff (welfare administration, home care) highlighted the need for better alarm solutions. The weakness of the traditional alarm is that the alarm holder cannot alert outside home, outdoors. The problems regarding the traditional social alarms in terms of being unable to use the alarm outdoors had the effect that some elderly people hesitated to leave their homes. Open-ended interviews were conducted with managers in the municipalities, home care staff and alarm holders. Approximately 2–3 alarm holders, in each municipality, 1–2 managers, and staff members were interviewed. The focus was to find the values that were important for various stakeholders when introducing outdoor social alarm. During all interviews, the researchers took notes.

In the second part of the study, we also investigated needs among elderly people and their relatives regarding outdoor social alarms to identify challenges and important values. The material was gathered in two ways, through focus groups and open-ended interviews. Focus groups were used to gather new ideas from a broad perspective. The objective was to encourage the participants to evolve new ideas together with others. Interviews were chosen to detect phenomena, properties, and meanings of using outdoor social alarms with respect to safety. In the interviews, 15 participants from three user categories were included: elderly, middle-aged next of kin who took care of their elderly

Table 2. The case study in four municipalities

Municipality	Location	No of citizens	No of social alarms	Alarm centre
Botkyrka	Suburb to Stockholm	85 000	800	Connected to a large central alarm centre
Värmdö	Municipality in the archipelago (rural and urban)	38 000	275	Connected to a large central alarm centre
Örnsköldsvik	Small town and rural	57 000	1 300	Local alarm centre
Pajala	Rural area	6 000	144	Connected to a large central alarm centre

relatives, and younger people who assisted a grandfather or a grandmother. During the focus group and the interviews, the researchers took notes.

3.2 Case 2: System Supporting Independent Living

WT focused in this study is a system supporting independent living [19, 20]. The system consists of a number of sensors for used for monitoring and a robot with a Skype-like interface used for communication with caregivers, family and friends. The sensors can be placed in the home as well as attached to the elderly person's body to collect different type of data such as the blood pressure, a fall or whether a door is closed or opened. The collected data is then sent by the system to relevant caregivers who can take relevant actions in case of emergency. The system supports four types of monitoring: (1) Physiology monitoring, (2) Social interaction monitoring (3) Activity monitoring and (4) Home monitoring.

We identified the relevant stakeholders involved in the development of the system by reviewing the project documents and interviewing the project manager. Then, we reviewed the project documents in order to understand the different stakeholders' values and interests regarding the system. The documents (User Requirements and Design Principles System Reference, Architecture Technological Component Specification, Evaluation Report. Intermediate Evaluation Report) were reviewed with the focus on what interest and values were particularly highlighted by different stakeholders during the design process.

As a complement to the document reviews, focus group interviews [21] and the indepth interviews with the key stakeholders were conducted (see Table 1). Individual interviews lasted approximately one hour, focus group interviews lasted approximately two hours. All interviews were recorded and transcribed.

3.3 Evaluation Seminars

Finally, two seminars were organized to discuss the ethical matrix with various stakeholders usually involved in development and implementation of WT. Each seminar group consisted of about ten people and lasted approximately two hours. The discussion was structured around the following questions: which groups of stakeholders are often involved the projects, what values and interest are particularly emphasized by these different stakeholders, can these values come in conflicts, if yes who decides which values are realized and which are not. The discussions were recorded.

4 Applying of the Value Matrix in the Context of Elderly Care – Empirical Investigations

The aim of this paper was to evaluate the value matrix and find out how the matrix supports identification of the values and interests that drive different stakeholders during the development and implementation of WT. Thus in this section we describe our experiences from applying Nordgren's (2013) value matrix in two cases (see Sect. 3: Research method).

4.1 Case 1: Outdoor Social Alarms

We have used the matrix to find important values that stakeholders see as their interests/challenges when introducing outdoor social alarms within municipalities. In this case there were three stakeholders (see Table 3). We have included all values in the matrix even if stakeholders did not raise some values. The starting point was to test the matrix as it is and not add or remove values. Detailed descriptions of the values as well as citations from the respondents in the study are provided in the text below the table.

Table 3. The matrix shows the values for outdoor social alarm.

Values	Stakeholders		
	Elderly	Relatives	Home care staff/Managers
Practical			
Reliability			X
Ease of use	X	X	X
Affordable price	X		X
Quality of life			
Health	X		X
Independence	X	X	
Safety			
Social contact	X	X	X
Moral			
Autonomy			X
Privacy	X		
Justice			X

4.1.1 Practical Values

Relatives pointed out that the outdoor alarm must be easy to use. They argued that the outdoor alarm should be integrated with the traditional safety alarm that works indoors. It would be easier for the user if she/he only needs to carry an alarm device (alarm button). *The problem with indoor and outdoor alarms is that they are based on different technologies and they are not integrated in the same alarm system.*

In the study, both managers for elderly care and home care staff talked about the price and they thought that it must be affordable. The municipality could not require users to pay the full cost of the outdoor alarm. *The outdoor alarm is expensive, what can the municipality pay and what is reasonable for the user to pay?* Managers for the elderly care in all municipalities (that took part in the study) talked about the additional costs they would get if they would offer outdoor alarms for the elderly. *Who will act on alarm that occur outdoors? Extra costs for the municipality/home care.*

4.1.2 Quality of Life Values

Both relatives and home care staff noted that many of the elderly who had social alarm did not felt safety when they were outdoors because they could not raise the alarm. The relatives also felt certain insecurity when their related went out for a walk or for shopping. *The elderly people are precarious outdoors when the alarm (the traditional security alarm) is not working. The result is that the elderly people are not going out for walks, and this in turn affects their health.*

The elderly would be able to live a more social active life if they could use an outdoor alarm. Both the elderly and home care staff considered it. *Social alarms also need to work outdoors with regard to enabling elderly people to live an active life and be able to move in a safe way. If I could use the alarm button even outdoors, I would go out often to meet friends.*

We all want to live an independent life as far as possible. For people with dementia it can be a sense of independence to have the possibility to go out for a walk. For relatives, it is reassuring to know that the person can be found, if he/she wears an outdoor alarm. *Outdoor alarm would be good for people with dementia who may have trouble to find home.* It is a quality of life to be able to go out on your own.

4.1.3 Moral Values

In terms of autonomy and informed consent, it is important that the elderly themselves can decide if they want to use social alarm (both indoor and outdoor alarm) or not and give his/her consent to the use of an alarm. It is important that information is provided so that the user understands how the alarm works. *The user must understand that he/she should press the button to raise the alarm. It is important that an elderly should not feel compelled to choose an outdoor alarm if he/she does not want.*

Privacy regarding usage of outdoor social alarms was discussed with the participants in the focus group. The participants did not consider the use of their geographical location as an invasion of privacy. The benefits were seen as far greater than the disadvantages to be located using GPS. *I do not think the use of my geographical position would feel like an intrusion into my privacy. I would like to have an outdoor alarm with GPS so I can get help if I get into trouble.*

If there is a lack of knowledge about how technology is used, it is also difficult to get the proper consents and understand the context for how the information is used from a privacy perspective.

4.1.4   Reflections from Applying the Value Matrix in Case 1

We saw that some values where missing in order to be able to take a comprehensive approach to the new technology and also of the systems to be procured. In this section we discuss examples of additional values that need to be considered.

The first value we want to highlight is *knowledge*. The technology for outdoor social alarms is complex and required considerable expertise in the area. Staff in eldercare pointed out themselves that they needed more knowledge and skills to be able to procure the right technology. *The outdoor social alarm is complex and requires expertise that is usually missing.*

It becomes much more complicated when the elderly can alert outside the home. Municipalities had not the resources to acting on alarm outside the home. Process/ working method is another important value. New *processes/working methods* need to be developed when outdoor alarms shall be introduced in a municipality. New models for responsibility, for acting on alarm, for payment models etc., are needed to get this kind of complex structure to work. *Who shall act on alarm that occur outdoors (home care, relatives)? Can relatives assist when an alarm is activated outdoors?*

We believe that users' *needs* are a very important value, which must be considered in order to succeed in developing and introducing new technologies. Usually the municipalities had no methods to include user needs in the process when social alarms were procured. Mangers for social alarms within the municipalities needed more knowledge about the technology and user needs to be able to offer tomorrow's new technology to its population. Better dialogue with users about their needs, and new methods in gathering these needs are required to be successful in introducing new types of alarms. *It is difficult for staff at the municipality to know/understand users' needs. We (home care staff) need better methods for capturing user needs in terms of social alarms and safety but we see that there is a need for outdoor alarm system (GPS) for the elderly.* Relatives stressed the need of a unit for both indoor and outdoor social alarm. *The problem with indoor and outdoor alarms is that they are based on different technologies and they are not integrated in the same alarm system.* Users also expressed the needs. *The portable alarm device must be something other than a mobile phone (a user needs).*

Responsibility is also a value that can be included when we look to the outdoor alarm. Could it be a shared responsibility to act on alarms that occur outdoors? Both middle-aged and young relatives wanted to be there for their elderly relative, but to be responsible for receiving and acting on alarm calls was too great of a responsibility with too many difficult decisions to make.

Finally, we summarize several values quality of life, safety, independence, and participation when we emphasize the benefits of outdoor alarm. This type of alarm is expected to lead to increased safety (both for the user and relatives), independence and continued participation in community life as well as maintaining health of the elderly. One must also consider that if you do not have enough knowledge about the outdoor alarm in order to feel comfortable with its use, it is also likely that you will not understand exactly what impact/consequences the outdoor alarm may have for privacy.

4.2   Case 2: System for Monitoring and Social Interaction

Table 4 show results from applying the value matrix in case 2. We included six key stakeholders: municipalities officers (MO), home care personal, called here formal caregivers (FCG), health care professionals (HCP), relatives, called here informal caregiver (ICG), elderly people (EP) and system developers (SD) in the analysis, as shown in Table 4. Because of the space limitation the table only shows which values are emphasized by the different stakeholders, while detailed description of the values as well as citations from the discussions are provided in the text below the table.

Table 4. Values and stakeholders identified in case 2

Values	MO	FCG	HCP	ICG	EP	SD
Practical						
Reliability			X			X
Ease of use		X		X	X	X
Affordable price						
Quality of life						
Health	X	X	X	X	X	X
Independence	X	X	X	X	X	X
Safety	X	X	X	X	X	X
Social contact	X	X	X	X	X	X
Moral						
Autonomy	X	X		X	X	
Privacy	X	X	X	X	X	X
Justice						

4.2.1   Practical Values

Reliability was emphasized by all the stakeholders but especially by SD and HCP. The stakeholders stressed the importance of correct measures provided by the system, but also robustness of the system itself, meaning that the system must always be functional. Robustness of the system was pointed out as important especially regarding monitoring of physiological data.

Ease of Use was an important value considered during the development process. For that reason all kinds of users (EP, HCP, ICG, FCG) were involved in the design of the system. The users played an important role in the selection (i.e., priority and definition) and development of the system's features and functionality. Usability was emphasized by most of the stakeholders: *The technology must be introduced in the right way, many of the staff are not familiar with the technology, they have not chosen this profession to manage technology, so they can be stressed if the technology is too complicated or too difficult to handle.*

Affordable price. This value was not pointed out as an important in the discussions. Rather the danger of focusing on costs and economic efficiency was discussed: *It is important the technology is not only introduced with efficiency in mind. It should increase the quality of care and quality of life for the elderly.* However EP were worried that their social contact will be reduced because of the costs related to implementation of the new technology. ICG were worried that the implementation of the new technology will result in reduced amount of personnel.

4.2.2   Quality of Life Values

Health was extended discussed during the developing process. Focus was on identification of what activities, events, physiological/psychological data and behaviors could be important to observe (measure) for an early detection of a deteriorating health condition. EP, HCPs as well as FCG and ICG were involved in the process. All groups of users (EP, HCP, FCG, ICG) claimed that a decrease of bodily functions is something important and relevant to observe early, and also for an acute detection of a decline of health. Some examples suggested by these stakeholders as important to monitor, are: general health deterioration, cardiovascular functions, blood sugar, and so on. As one of our respondents put it: *The functionality in the system allowing elderly to measure blood pressure or body temperature at home instead of going to the hospital is only positive. I think this possibility is beneficial for both the elderly and all the involved caregivers.*

Monitoring aiming at detecting falls was also emphasized by all the user groups (HCP, FCG, ICG, and EP). Monitoring of changes in daily activities and routines were mostly emphasized by HCPs. EP on the other hand pointed out privacy concerns related to this extended monitoring and subsequent access to the collected data (*privacy*).

Independence. To support independent leaving was one of the main goals for the system, thus was emphasized by all the stakeholders. However there were some differences between the different stakeholders' opinions regarding this value. Both FCG and EP pointed out a number of concerns related to how the monitoring information should be used and who should eventually decide about the implementation and the extent of these services. FCG expressed, for instance, several concerns related to how they should interpret and react to the information they get from the system. They raised questions such as: to what extent should they be able to influence the elderly's way of living? When should they act on the information? What right do they have on deciding what should be considered as normal and what not? Should they, for example, react if an elderly eats candies while suffering from diabetes? The elderly people emphasized the importance of consulting the monitored person about how the information should/could be interpreted before the caregivers react on it (*autonomy*).

Safety is also one of the main values emphasized during the project by all the stakeholders group. Monitoring of bodily functions increases safety and physiological parameters as well as home monitoring and in some extend activity monitoring. In relation to safety EP, FCG and ICG emphasized for instance the need to reduce potential risks related to environmental factors. Hence, the system includes different sensors to detect, for instance smoke, fire and gas leaks. It is important to notice that this extensive monitoring raised several privacy concerns.

Social contact. Maintaining relationships, especially with family and friends was considered as important for the elderly's well-being. Thus, social interactions using the robot should decrease the elderly's feeling of isolation and loneliness. Our respondents mainly experienced these services as useful and needed. However FCG pointed out a number of concerns regarding using technology as a means for social interaction: *all communication cannot go through machines, a nurse is a very important person for older people's lives, and the technology cannot reduce the real-life interaction with the staff, people need other people to feel good, an image on the screen cannot replace it!*

4.2.3   Moral Values

Autonomy regarding this value, the elderly's ability to control the technology was an important factor especially highlighted by FCG. The EP also emphasized the need for a facility to switch off the monitoring when it would feel uncomfortable or to completely abort monitoring if it does not feel right any more. FGC argued that it is impossible to generalize what is acceptable or not regarding monitoring. They stated that the EP are a very heterogeneous group and every person needs a different kind of help and to a different extent. According to ICG, many of the elderly would experience such monitoring as controlling and, hence, restricting their independent life. Thus the elderly's informed consent regarding the suggested services was emphasized as extremely important.

Also the elderly highlighted several concerns regarding the presence and use of the robot in their homes. The robot is part of the system, as described in Sect. 3.2. The robot allows HCP and other caregivers (ICG and FCG) to virtually visit the elderly in his/her home. The visitor can communicate with the elderly and at the same time move the robot in the home. The elderly emphasized the importance of having control over the robot itself and its movements at home. As one of the elderly users expressed: *It is extremely important to feel that you can control the technology! It's important that I can steer the robot and switch it off. I would like the robot to react on a voice commando "please follow me now". This is a completely different feeling, because it is me who is in charge.* An important aspect emphasized in relation to this value was also, a proper introduction of the technology. The elderly pointed out that they often do not understand the technology being implemented. They do not understand how the monitoring works, what it allows others to see and whether the technical devices are on or off. This lack of understanding makes them feel anxious and helpless.

In relation to autonomy MO and FCG especially emphasized the elderly's freedom of choice when it comes to implementation of technical solutions. They stressed that: *alternative options must exist be for the elderly to choose from, the municipality must offer different possibilities, WT can be one of them.*

Privacy. Although many of our respondents seemed to be convinced that monitoring of home activities clearly has benefits, they also pointed out serious privacy concerns related to such functionality. While HCP and ICG saw these services as necessary, EP, FCG and MO experienced them as useful but also often as invasive to the privacy of care takers. These groups of stakeholders argued that these concerns need to be considered and taken care of before the system is put into use. While SD emphasized in this context the protection of personal data during transmission and storage, the other stakeholders understood privacy in a broader sense. They included in this dimension also aspects such as the purpose for which the data is collected, how long the data should be stored, how the data should be interpreted, etc. This broader way of perceiving privacy influences the view of privacy problems and solutions in this context. For instance, installing cameras in the elderly person's bedroom is a violation of the elderly's privacy and encrypting the images during transmission and storage cannot solve it.

4.2.4   Reflections from Applying the Value Matrix in Case 2

All values suggested by Nordgren in the value checklist besides affordable price and justice was discussed in the project. The values were considered as very important in the development process and were emphasized by the different stakeholders. We noticed that the same value can be interpreted differently by the different stakeholders, like for instance value of privacy described above. It is thus important to discuss these values in groups where different stakeholders are represented.

We also noticed that some values emphasized as particularly important by various stakeholders are not included in the checklist. For instance value of *participation and/or co-determination* are not included in the checklist, but strongly emphasized by MO, FCG. The stakeholders stressed that people who are affected by the WT need to be involved in the development and implementation of this WT. *All concerned parties [organizations, individuals, and personnel] must be informed and involved in the development process.* Another value that is not clearly included in the checklist is utility, meaning satisfaction of individual needs and preferences and individualization. This value was pointed out as especially important by several groups of stakeholders. As one of the MO stated: *It is important to take into account the individual, special needs in development and implementation of WT in elderly care. It is important to identify the individual's specific needs and to adjust the solutions to these needs.*

An individual adjustment of the services and a prior and formal approval of these services were also emphasized as crucial by all the stakeholders. Other values that were emphasized in relation to the system were: flexibility (of the solution), personalization of the services, and awareness (knowledge) of the implemented technology and services.

FCG emphasized importance of synchronization of the technology and *processes/working methods* existing in the organization. Otherwise, according to this stakeholder group, there is the risk that the technology will not be usable or reliable.

We also noticed that several of the values come in conflicts. For instance, the robot was designed such that it was moved by a remote control around in the elderly persons' home by a formal caregiver or an informal caregiver (easy to use). However according to our analysis the fact that the elderly are not able to control the robot was experienced by them as a limitation of their autonomy. The elderly emphasized the importance of having control over the robot itself and its movements at home. Several other conflicts are highlighted earlier in this section.

5   Discussion and Conclusions

In this section we describe the experiences gained from applying the value matrix in the two cases as well as the results from the discussion seminars.

Based on our experiences we claim that the value matrix supports ethical discussion and allow identifying what values the various stakeholders consider as especially important when WT is developed or implemented. During the analysis we could also see that various stakeholders interpret/define the same value in different ways, see, for example, the discussion about privacy in Sect. 4.2.3. The example shows that both system developers, elderly people and caregivers emphasize the value of privacy, however the interpretation of this value among the stakeholders is different. If we were not aware about these differences, probably system developers' interpretation would be realized in the system, resulting in insufficient privacy protection seen form the other stakeholders' perspective. We applied the matrix descriptively and filled descriptions of the stakeholders' views on which values are particularly important into the slots in the matrix. In this way we could clearly see possible differences between different stakeholders' interpretations of the same value by looking at the rows in the matrix. Hence we argue that one benefit from using the value matrix is possibility to identify the different stakeholders' values regarding WT and another benefit is a possibility to understand how the different stakeholders interpret/define the values in the checklist.

When applying the value matrix in the case studies (see Sect. 4) we realized that several values that were emphasized by the different stakeholders as especially important were not included in the value checklist in the matrix. For instance health care staff, in case 1 pointed out the importance of having expertise (*knowledge*) regarding outdoor social alarms to be able to precise the requirements concerning usability and functionality for this WT. Lack of sufficient knowledge can results in insufficient functionality and consequently in a solution that cannot realize *quality of life* values. Another value highlighted by stakeholders in case 1 is responsibility. Clear responsibility structures are important to be able to ensure that outdoor social alarms are reliable i.e. that someone actually response on alarms calls. Home care personnel in both cases emphasized also the importance of harmonization of the technology and *processes/working methods* existing in the organization to be able to ensure reliability of the developed solution as a whole. We believe that all these values could be placed in: *practical values* category. As explained earlier, practical values must be fulfilled to be able to support fulfillment of the quality of life values. Besides new practical values our stakeholders also emphasized values such as *participation and/or co-determination, utility, flexibility* (of the solution) and *personalization* of the services. We believe that these values are also important to consider in ethical analysis. Nordgren [4] admit that the suggested checklist may be incomplete and may result in simplified analysis, but including more values would make the tool (the value matrix) too complicated and difficult to use. We claim that this problem could be partially solved if the values in each value category are presented as examples that may be complemented by additional values relevant for the specific context instead for presenting them as a completed value list.

Another finding form our study is that the value matrix does not visualize or support identification of value conflict. According to stakeholders participating in the discussion seminars, value conflicts are very common during development and implementation of WT. The conflict may exist between different stakeholders that emphasize different values, but also between different values. We identified several such conflicts in our cases (see Sect. 4.2). Conflicts existed for instance between safety and independence, individual adjustment and affordable price, safety and privacy. Nordgren [4] also highlighted a number of possible value conflicts imbedded in the matrix. The participant in discussion seminars stressed that the matrix shows a harmonized picture of the values important to consider in development or use of WT, while the reality is different. They argued that it would be better to analyze what values are prioritized by which stakeholders when important decisions are made during development or implementation of WT. They meant that first in these situations we could rally see which values are emphasized by which stakeholders. We argue that the value matrix could be better supported for ethical analysis if it in a clearer way visualized the existing value conflicts.

References

1. Sponselee, A.-m., Schouten, B., Bouwhuis, D., Willems, C.: Smart home technology for the elderly: perceptions of multidisciplinary stakeholders. In: Mühlhäuser, M., Ferscha, A., Aitenbichler, E. (eds.) AmI 2007. CCIS, vol. 11, pp. 314–326. Springer, Heidelberg (2008). doi:10.1007/978-3-540-85379-4_37
2. Friedman, B., Kahn Jr., P.H.: Human Values, Ethics, and Design. Lawrence Erlbaum Associates, Mahwah (2003)
3. Palm, E., Nordgren, A., Verweij, M., Collste, G.: Ethically sound technology? Guidelines for interactive ethical assessment of personal health monitoring. In: Schmidt, S., Rienhoff, O. (eds.) Interdisciplinary Assessment of Personal Health Monitoring, pp. 105–114. IOS Press, Amsterdam (2013)
4. Nordgren, A.: Personal health monitoring: ethical considerations for stakeholders. J. Inf. Commun. Ethics Soc. **11**, 156–173 (2013)
5. Liu, L., Stroulia, E., Nikolaidis, I., Miguel-Cruz, A., Rincon, A.R.: Smart homes and home health monitoring technologies for older adults: a systematic review. Int. J. Med. Inf. **91**, 44–59 (2016)
6. Beauchamp, T.L., Childress, J.F.: Principles of Biomedical Ethics, 6th edn. Oxford University Press, Oxford (2009)
7. Whitehouse, D., Duquenoy, P.: Applied ethics and eHealth: principles, identity, and RFID. In: Matyáš, V., Fischer-Hübner, S., Cvrček, D., Švenda, P. (eds.) Privacy and Identity 2008. IAICT, vol. 298, pp. 43–55. Springer, Heidelberg (2009). doi:10.1007/978-3-642-03315-5_3
8. Collste, G.: Ethical, Legal, and Social Issues in Medical Informatics. IGI Global, Hershey (2008)
9. Hanson, J., Percival, J., Aldred, H., Brownsell, S., Hawley, M.: Attitudes to telecare among older people, professional care workers and informal carers: a preventative strategy or crisis management? Univ. Access Inf. Soc. **6**, 193–205 (2007)
10. Essén, A.: The two facets of electronic care surveillance: an exploration of the views of older people who live with monitoring devices. Soc. Sci. Med. **67**, 128–136 (2008)
11. Harrefors, C., Axelsson, K., Savenstedt, S.: Using assistive technology services at differing levels of care: healthy older couples' perceptions. J. Adv. Nurs. **66**, 1523–1532 (2010)

12. Marzegalli, M., Lunati, M., Landolina, M., Perego, G.B., Ricci, R.P., Guenzati, G., Schirru, M., Belvito, C., Brambilla, R., Masella, C., Di Stasi, F., Valsecchi, S., Santini, M.: Remote monitoring of CRT-ICD: the multicenter Italian carelink evaluation - ease of use, acceptance, and organizational implications. Pacing Clin. Electrophysiol. **13**, 1259–1264 (2008)
13. Charness, N., Fox, M., Papadopoulos, A., Crump, C.: Metrics for assessing the reliability of a telemedicine remote monitoring system. Telemed. J. e-Health **19**, 487–492 (2013)
14. Gillon, R.: Medical ethics: four principles plus attention to scope. BMJ **309**, 184–188 (1994)
15. Myers, M.D.: Qualitative Research in Business & Management. Sage Publications, London (2009)
16. Patton, M.Q.: Qualitative Research & Evaluation Methods. Sage Publications, Inc., Thousand Oaks (2002)
17. Sjölinder, M., Avatare Nöu, A.: Indoor and outdoor social alarms: understanding users' perspectives. JMIR Mhealth Uhealth **2**, e9 (2014)
18. Kolkowska, E., Avatare Nöu, A., Sjölinder, M., Scandurra, I.: Socio-technical challenges in implementation of monitoring technologies in elderly care. In: Zhou, J., Salvendy, G. (eds.) ITAP 2016. LNCS, vol. 9755, pp. 45–56. Springer, Cham (2016). doi: 10.1007/978-3-319-39949-2_5
19. Kolkowska, E., Kajtazi, M.: Privacy dimensions in design of smart home system for elderly people. In: AIS SIGSEC Workshop on Information Security & Privacy, 13 December 2015, Fort Worth, USA (2015)
20. Kolkowska, E.: Understanding privacy in smart homes systems used in elderly care. In: European, Mediterranean & Middle Eastern Conference on Information Systems 2016 (EMCIS2016), 23–24 June 2016 (2016)
21. Stewart, D.W., Shamdasani, P.N., Rook, D.W.: Focus Groups: Theory and Practice. 2. uppl. Sage Publications, Thousand Oaks (2007)

Technology and Service Usage Among Family Caregivers

Chaiwoo Lee[(⊠)], Carley Ward, Dana Ellis, Samantha Brady,
Lisa D'Ambrosio, and Joseph F. Coughlin

Massachusetts Institute of Technology AgeLab, Cambridge, MA, USA
chaiwoo@mit.edu

Abstract. Family caregivers often assist their care recipients with a wide variety of activities ranging from basic personal care to transportation, medication management, finances and more. Furthermore, many caregivers live apart from the loved ones that they provide care to, and have responsibilities outside of caregiving including work and family. Use of technologies and services designed to make life easier for the general population can also be leveraged to reduce the burden and stress related with caregiving. In this study, 30 family caregivers were surveyed in depth to learn about their experiences with various technologies and services. Questions covered caregivers' use of technologies and services, perceived usefulness and ease of use, reasons for use and non-use, and ideas for new and improved tools. Many caregivers were currently using a technology or service for caregiving, but most of the technologies and services presented in the questionnaire were only used by a limited number of participants. While usage was limited, those that currently used technologies and services generally found them helpful for making caregiving duties easier. Responses showed that technologies and services were not being widely used mainly due to limited awareness and availability, and less because of lack of interest.

Keywords: Technology adoption · Family caregiving · Home services

1 Introduction

It is estimated that almost four in ten American adults are providing care to someone [1]. The National Alliance for Caregiving & AARP Public Policy Institute [2] reported that a large majority (85%) of its estimated 43.5 million adult caregivers in the United States are providing care to a family member. These caregivers are mostly unpaid individuals assisting a spouse, parent(s), or other relative.

Family caregiving is an important and difficult job for many and encompasses tasks in domains including health care, transportation, preparing meals, eating, housework, home maintenance, coordinating services, personal hygiene, managing finances, and keeping company. The National Alliance for Caregiving & AARP Public Policy Institute [2] found that the majority of caregivers assist their care recipient with one or more basic Activities of Daily Living (ADLs) and help with 4.2 of 7 Instrumental Activities of Daily Living (IADLs) on average. ADLs are defined as fundamental

© Springer International Publishing AG 2017
J. Zhou and G. Salvendy (Eds.): ITAP 2017, Part II, LNCS 10298, pp. 420–432, 2017.
DOI: 10.1007/978-3-319-58536-9_33

personal care tasks such as functional mobility, including walking, getting in and out of beds and chairs, getting dressed, toileting and dealing with incontinence or diapers, bathing or showering, feeding, and personal hygiene. IADLs include activities required for independent living in the community, such as transportation, grocery or other shopping, housework, preparing meals, managing finances, taking medications, and arranging outside services using different forms of communication. In addition to caregiving responsibilities, the majority of family caregivers are likely to be employed and/or have other family-related obligations. Six in ten caregivers are employed, the majority of whom work full-time [2]. Additionally, 46% of caregivers reported being a parent of one or more children under 18 years of age [1].

Due to demands from caregiving, work, family and other responsibilities, caregivers often find it difficult to manage their time, well-being and stress levels. As a result, caregivers often experience high physical, emotional and financial strain, poor health, and are in need of help with managing caregiving burdens. For instance, while only about 10% of the general population describes their health as fair or poor [3], 17% of caregivers reported their health as fair or poor [2]. Hoffman and Rodrigues [4] also stated that caregivers are more likely to experience social isolation, psychological distress, and depression, partly due to the intensity of caregiving and a lack of personal time.

Many technologies and services developed to make life easier for the general population also have potential to assist older adults, as well as individuals who are charged with providing care to them. For example, Fox et al. [1] found that caregivers are more likely, than non-caregivers, to look for health information using their cell phone, and that many caregivers use the internet to find online resources for caregiving and managing stress. In addition, a variety of technologies and services specifically designed for caregivers and care recipients have been found to be beneficial. In a review of existing telephone-based caregiver interventions, Glueckauf and Noël [5] found those interventions for education, behavioral modification, and exercise and nutrition counseling were effective in improving the emotional and physical well-being of caregivers. Tindall and Huebner [6] demonstrated the effectiveness of a videophone-based therapy program in reducing caregiving time and financial burden. Kinney et al. [7] studied family caregivers of dementia patients and found internet-based monitoring technology to be potentially beneficial. Mortensen et al. [8] found a significant decrease in caregiver burden with the use of assistive technology. Blusi et al. [9] found caregiver support services offered through information and communication technologies contributed to improving the quality of life of older caregivers caring for their spouses, and had a positive influence on family relationships and perceptions of independence, competence and social inclusion. Gaugler et al. [10] found that the use of adult day programs, which provide a variety of services ranging from health monitoring and medical care to socialization and transportation, was effective in reducing caregivers' emotional and psychological distress and decreasing the amount of time they assisted their care recipients with basic ADLs, behavioral problems and memory issues.

Little is known, however, about how the family caregiver population is utilizing various technologies and services, what their perceptions are of different solutions available to them, and what their unmet needs are. Furthermore, studies have found that many existing technologies and services currently are not widely adopted and used by caregivers. For example, Fox et al. [1] found that while medication management is a common task among caregivers, a very small percentage of caregivers use tools to help manage their care recipient's medications. Glueckauf and Noël [5] reported that while internet-based and mobile tools are increasingly available, telephone-based interventions remain a popular form of service delivery, especially in rural areas. Gaps often exist between caregiver needs and types of available services. Based on a study of services offered by the Area Agencies on Aging in California, Whittier et al. [11] found that existing services mostly offered institutional care, while other services needed by caregivers, such as transportation and financial assistance, were less available. Kinney et al. [7] also found gaps between the needs of family caregivers and the tools that they currently have available. In a survey of smartphone-based tools for behavior management, clinical treatments, symptom tracking and education, Luxton et al. [12] noted possible issues related to acceptance, security and privacy, and related policy that need to be addressed for widespread use. A review of networked technologies for caregiver decision support, communication and education by Powell et al. [13] demonstrated moderate benefits, but also found low usage rates. Brodaty et al. [14] identified that only a limited portion of the caregivers providing care to people with dementia utilize services available to them, and also reported on reasons for lack of use including reluctance on the part of the care recipient, lack of awareness and knowledge, and limited understanding of their own needs.

The objective of this study is to better understand family caregivers' use of technologies and services that can potentially improve their caregiving experiences as well as their quality of life. In this study, the types of technologies and services used by caregivers, the reasons and purposes for use, and level of satisfaction and perceived usefulness are described based on a survey of 30 family caregivers in the United States. Open responses on unmet needs and suggestions for improvement of existing tools, as well as ideas for future services, are presented in this paper.

2 Data Collection

2.1 The MIT AgeLab Caregiver Survey

A series of in-depth online diaries and questionnaires as well as phone interviews were completed as part of a larger study on understanding the caregiving experience. In this study conducted by the Massachusetts Institute of Technology AgeLab, 30 adult family caregivers in the United States were surveyed over a 3-month period. At the beginning of the study period, caregivers participated in a phone interview about their demographics, characteristics as a caregiver, characteristics of the family member for whom they provide care, and the overall caregiving situation. During the study, caregivers were asked about various aspects of their caregiving experiences, including how they assist their care recipients with different tasks, how they manage time and stress, how they seek help and support, how caregiving affects their work and family life, and how they use tools and resources to make their caregiving jobs easier.

In one questionnaire, caregivers were asked about their use of technologies. Specifically, caregivers answered questions about their overall technology experience, knowledge of new technologies, use of various technologies for personal use and for caregiving, reasons for use and non-use, and level of satisfaction with technologies that they use for caregiving. In another questionnaire that focused on management of time and task priorities, caregivers were asked about their use of services that could help with their caregiving responsibilities. They reported on which services they used for caregiving, reasons for use and lack of use, frequency of usage, perceived usefulness, perceived importance and ease of use. In both questionnaires, caregivers were provided with spaces to describe their unmet needs, suggestions for improving existing technologies and services, and ideas for future systems. These questionnaires were completed online.

2.2 Data Profile

All of the caregivers who participated in the study were providing unpaid care to a family member and employed for pay in addition to their caregiving responsibilities at the time of study enrollment. The convenience sample had a median age of 53 and was mostly female (90%). The majority of the sample was employed full-time (87%), married or living with a partner (57%), and caring for a parent or parent-in-law (87%). Table 1 summarizes the characteristics of the participating caregivers, their care recipients, and the overall caregiving situation.

Table 1. Participant profile (N = 30)

Category	Characteristics	Descriptive statistics
Caregiver characteristics	Age	Median: 53, Range: 35–63
	Gender	Female: 27, Male: 3
	Employment	Employed full-time: 26, Part-time: 4
	Marital status	Married or living with partner: 17, Single: 13
	Household	Average size: 2.5 including the caregiver Living with child(ren): 6
Care recipient characteristics	Age	Median: 83, Range: 33–98
	Gender	Female: 19, Male: 11
	Relationship to caregiver	Parent or parent-in-law: 26, Grandparent: 1, Uncle/aunt: 1, Spouse: 1, Adult child: 1
	Living arrangements	Caregivers living with care recipient: 15, Living within walking distance: 4, Living at a short driving distance: 8, Living at a far distance: 3
	Conditions	Long-term physical condition: 23, Memory problem: 19, Emotional or mental issue: 15, Behavioral issue: 8, Short-term physical condition: 3, Developmental or intellectual issue: 2

(*continued*)

Table 1. (*continued*)

Category	Characteristics	Descriptive statistics
Caregiving situation	Caregiving load	Average: 30.8 hours per week providing direct care
	Duration of care	Less than 1 year: 2, 1 year or more but less than 5 years: 15, 5 years or more but less than 10 years: 11, 10 years or more: 2
	Caregiving tasks and responsibilities	Number of caregivers helping with... taking and managing medications: 30, transportation and getting to places: 27, grocery and other shopping: 27, arranging services and appointments: 26, seeking information and resources: 26, social activities and interactions: 23, preparing meals and eating: 23, housework and home management: 22, managing finances: 22, using technology: 18, personal hygiene and getting dressed: 16
	Effect on family life	Negative effect: 11, Positive effect: 7, Both negative and positive effects: 5, No effect: 5, Not sure or not applicable: 2
	Effect on work and career	Negative effect: 16, Positive effect: 3, Both negative and positive effects: 3, No effect: 7, Not sure or not applicable: 1
	Effect on caregiver's own health	Negative effect: 14, Positive effect: 3, No effect: 11, Not sure or don't know: 5
	Need for help	A total of 29 caregivers reporting need for help in... keeping care recipient safe at home: 19, managing their own emotional and physical stress: 18, making end-of-life decisions: 14, managing care recipient's toileting problems: 8, managing care recipient's challenging behaviors: 7, other: 20 (finding resources, coordinating between doctors, understanding insurance terms, finding assistive tools, finding available services, etc.)

As shown in Table 1, most of the caregivers in this study were experiencing some difficulties and negative effects of caregiving. Very few reported positive effects of caregiving. Many caregivers reported a severe burden associated with caregiving and difficulties balancing various responsibilities in life. For example, the majority of the sample said that they had gone to work late, left early or had to take time off during the work day (25 participants), been unable to do housework (22 participants), missed family events (21 participants), and gotten involved in arguments with family due to caregiving (20 participants). Many also reported that they had fallen behind in managing their own finances (13 participants), had to stay out of their home for several days or longer for caregiving duties (13 participants), cut their work hours or changed to part-time (9 participants), took a leave of absence from work (5 participants), or turned down a promotion (4 participants). In addition, while all 30 caregivers in the sample were helping their care recipients with medication management, 25 of them were also taking daily prescribed medications themselves. The sample characteristics suggest that caregivers can potentially benefit from use of technologies and services that can ease their burden by making caregiving tasks easier, less stressful and more efficient.

3 Results

3.1 Caregivers' Use of Technology

A series of questions was asked about caregivers' experiences with various technologies (e.g., mobile devices, monitoring systems, computers, entertainment technologies, smart home appliances and more). Questions were asked about caregiver's use of given technologies generally (i.e., personal use for purposes other than caregiving), as well as in relation to their caregiving responsibilities. Figure 1 shows a selection of technologies included in the questionnaire, along with a summary of responses.

A total of 25 caregivers reported currently using some form of technology to assist with their caregiving responsibilities. As shown in Fig. 1, the most commonly used form of technology for caregiving was smartphones (currently used for caregiving by 20 participants), followed by laptop computers (13 participants), wireless home internet networks (12 participants), and televisions (11 participants). While the majority of caregivers were providing care to a parent with memory issues and/or long-term physical conditions, few reported currently using an emergency call system (6 participants) or GPS trackers (2 participants). When asked about the effect of using technologies for caregiving on a scale from 1 (not at all easier) to 5 (very much easier), the 25 caregivers currently using technologies said that technology has made caregiving somewhat easier for them (average score: 3.44). Also, on a scale from 1 (not a strain at all) to 5 (very much a strain), caregivers said that technology use is not too much of a strain for them physically (average score: 1.32), financially (2.16), or emotionally (1.64).

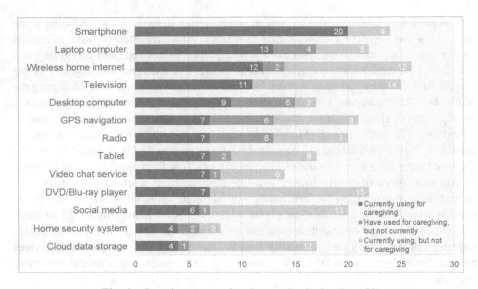

Fig. 1. Caregivers' use of various technologies (N = 30)

When caregivers indicated current use of a technology, they received additional questions on reasons for using that technology. Caregivers' responses to these questions – reasons for use in terms of task domains and anticipated benefits – are summarized across technologies in Fig. 2. As shown in Fig. 2, technologies currently used by caregivers were mostly used to assist with health care and management (47.0% of chosen technologies), followed by information search (42.4%), social interactions and communication (36.4%), intellectual stimulation (31.8%), shopping and retail (30.3%), entertainment (24.2%) and personal care (24.2%). Responses indicated that caregivers were mostly using technologies to save time (54.5% of chosen technologies). Many caregivers also used technologies to ease their emotional burden (36.4%), but less to ease their physical (16.7%) or financial (4.5%) burden.

As shown in Fig. 1, several caregivers reported that they had used some technologies for caregiving before, but that they stopped using them. For example, some said that they used digital cameras (7 participants), desktop computers (6 participants), GPS navigation systems (6 participants), radios (6 participants) and basic mobile phones (6 participants) for caregiving at one point, but not currently. Furthermore, while use of various technologies in caregiving was limited, caregivers were utilizing them in other situations and for personal use outside of caregiving. For example, smartphones, laptop computers, wireless home internet networks, televisions, GPS navigation systems, DVD or Blu-Ray players, social media, USB flash drives and radios were used for purposes other than caregiving by at least 20 participants. When asked why they had not used or have stopped using these technologies for caregiving, caregivers reported the primary reason as that they had never thought of using them for caregiving (34.7% of technologies not currently used for caregiving). Other reasons reported were that caregivers found the selected technologies costly (9.5%), that they did not find them useful (9.5%), and that they found them difficult to learn or use (3.2%).

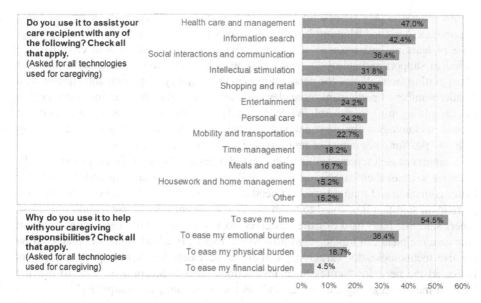

Fig. 2. Reasons for caregivers' use of technologies (aggregated across all technologies used)

The study also identified characteristics that caregivers look for when they decide to get and/or use new technologies for caregiving, and compared the results against technologies for personal use. Caregivers were presented with a list of criteria adapted from a multidimensional set of technology adoption factors defined in [15] and were asked to choose all factors that applied in their decisions. Results are summarized in Fig. 3.

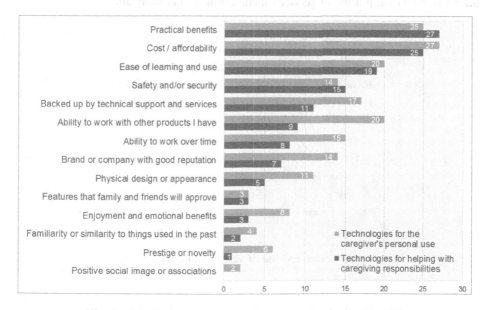

Fig. 3. Criteria for getting and using new technologies (N = 30)

As shown in Fig. 3, practical benefits and cost or affordability were the most important criteria for adopting both technologies for personal use and for caregiving. Ease of learning and use was also considered to be important in both cases. While technical support and ability to work with other products were considered important when getting technologies for personal use by the majority of participants, however, a smaller number of participants considered these key criteria when getting technologies for caregiving use. In general, while a variety of different factors were considered around technologies for personal use, caregivers' decisions for getting and using technologies for caregiving seemed focused on a smaller number of criteria.

Caregivers also reported difficulties and challenges that they faced in using technologies to assist their caregiving responsibilities. Caregivers emphasized the need for better education and training, and the need for improved ease of use. For example, one participant said that it is "hard to teach the care recipient how to use technology", and others said that it is "hard (for the caregiver) to learn to use at the beginning" and that "the care recipient can't understand how to use them". In addition, they explained how the use technologies for caregiving can be made easier for them. Again, caregivers indicated the need for "professional instructions" and "education on how to use the tools to make caregiving easier", as well as the importance of "simplicity".

3.2   Caregivers' Use of Services

Caregivers also provided insight on their use of and perceptions about a variety of available services (e.g., delivery services, housekeeping, retail services, healthcare services and more). First, questions asked about caregivers' current and past use of various services with regard to their caregiving responsibilities. Figure 4 summarizes the results with the full list of services included in the questionnaire.

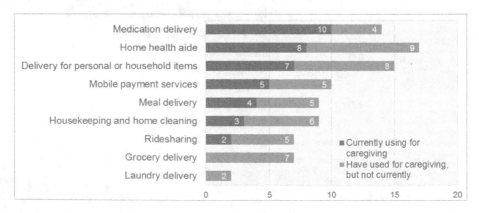

Fig. 4. Caregivers' use of various services (N = 30)

A total of 19 caregivers reported currently using at least one of the services presented in the questionnaire to assist with their caregiving duties. As shown in Fig. 4, services for medication delivery were most common (10 participants), followed by the use of home health aides (8 participants), delivery for personal or household items (7 participants) and use of mobile payment services (5 participants). It is evident, however, that even the most common services were only used by a minority of caregivers.

When asked about reasons for using services to help with their caregiving responsibilities, caregivers reported that 68.4% of selected services were currently used to save time. Another main reason for use of services was to ease caregivers' emotional burden (36.8% of chosen services). Services were less used to ease physical burden (21.1%) or financial burden (13.2%).

Questions on perceived importance, usefulness and ease of use explored how caregivers felt about the services that they were currently using. While only a limited number of participants were using given services, current users found these services to be important, useful and easy to use. On a scale from 1 (not important at all) to 5 (very important), the overall average perceived importance score was 4.31, and ranged from 3.71 for delivery for personal products or household items to 4.75 for home health aides. Perceived usefulness, on a scale from 1 (not useful at all) to 5 (very useful), was also very high with an overall average of 4.49 and ranged from 4.00 for ridesharing to 5.00 for home health aides. Caregivers also rated the services they currently use as very easy to use, with an overall average score of 4.69 on a scale from 1 (very difficult) to 5 (very easy). Average scores for ease of use ranged from 4.00 for ridesharing to 5.00 for mobile payment services.

While 11 caregivers said that they were not currently using any of the given services for caregiving, many said that they had used or tried using some of the given services for caregiving before but had stopped doing so, as shown in Fig. 4. For example, while no participant reported current use of grocery delivery services, 7 participants said that they had used these types of services before. While 8 participants said that they currently used home health aides, a larger portion of the sample (9 participants) said that they had stopped using them. When asked why they had stopped using or had not tried these services, the main reason was that they replaced the services with something else (15.7% of selected services), and that they found the services too expensive to use (11.8%). Other reasons included that the services were or became unavailable to them (9.8%), that they did not enjoy using the services (7.8%) and that the services did not fit into the caregivers' lifestyles (5.9%).

Caregivers were encouraged to provide any ideas or suggestions to improve existing services. Responses addressed the need for better and easier ways of scheduling services and being reminded on time. These suggestions included receiving "email reminders", getting "notifications on time", and making "online scheduling" available. Caregivers also discussed their unmet needs for better tools to manage time and resources, with options such as "a user-friendly scheduling application", "something that would combine work, home and caregiving information together securely to keep track of everything in one place", "a digital day planner", "a database of local agencies combined with shopping and errand services that link automatically to your calendar", and "alerts and timers to move along faster".

4 Discussion and Conclusion

The family caregiving experience entails a broad spectrum of tasks, needs and pain points. Technologies and services available to the general public have the potential to ease the challenges that family caregivers manage (e.g., balancing between caregiving tasks and responsibilities outside of caregiving, managing stress and well-being). In order to better understand the current state of technology and service usage among caregivers, this study looked at responses from 30 unpaid family caregivers to questions on use of technologies and services, perceptions of importance and usefulness, reasons for use, criteria for adoption, and unmet needs.

While the majority of participants reported using at least one technology for caregiving, smartphones were the only technology that most of the caregivers in this study were currently using. While many of the technologies in the questionnaire were widely used by caregivers for personal use outside of their caregiving responsibilities, they were only used by a limited number of caregivers to assist with caregiving duties. Similarly, when asked about the use of services to help with caregiving responsibilities, it was found that the services presented in the questionnaire were used only by a small number of participants. Furthermore, several caregivers had used some of the technologies and services asked about in the questionnaire at some point in the past, but had stopped using them.

Even though technologies and services were used by only a fraction of caregivers surveyed, those who used them were generally satisfied with them, as indicated by high ratings for perceived importance, usefulness and ease of use for services, and by self-reported scores indicating that the use of technologies have made caregiving easier. Additionally, reasons for stopping use of or not having tried these technologies and services were connected more to limited awareness and accessibility, including cost and expense, rather than to a lack of interest or minimal perceived usefulness. For example, during interviews and in response to open-ended questions, many caregivers expressed interest in exploring and experimenting with new technologies and services that would potentially help them manage their time, save money and access information, as well as ease the physical, financial and emotional burdens associated with caregiving. Also, several caregivers showed interest in using a caregiving robot, even though the technology is new, potentially expensive, and unfamiliar to them. Many caregivers also discussed the need for better instructions, education programs and professional support for using technology and service solutions generally.

Future research can explore ways to improve access to various technologies and services so that caregivers can more easily access the tools they may need to ease their burden. Better coaching and education may be necessary to enable caregivers to learn about ways that they can use existing and new technologies and services to assist with their caregiving responsibilities, as well as to save time and balance caregiving with work and family life. There are also avenues of research open around caregiving in the workplace, as many participants expressed concerns related to the cost of getting and using technologies and services, and workplace benefits and insurance subsidization are possible means to support and ease the demands on working caregivers.

Addressing these awareness and accessibility barriers may encourage caregivers to adopt more caregiving technologies and adapt more general technologies for caregiving purposes. Increased technology use may provide support to the 43.5 million American unpaid family caregivers and help them manage their physical, financial, and emotional caregiving burden, improving their well-being and quality of life.

Acknowledgments. The authors would like to thank the caregivers who put their time and effort into sharing their experiences. This study was funded by CVS Caremark.

References

1. Fox, S., Duggan, M., Purcell, K.: Family caregivers are wired for health (2013). http://pewinternet.org/Reports/2013/Family-Caregivers.aspx. Accessed 20 Oct 2016
2. National Alliance for Caregiving & AARP Public Policy Institute: Caregiving in the U.S. 2015 – executive summary (2015). http://www.caregiving.org/caregiving2015. Accessed 20 Oct 2016
3. National Center for Health Statistics: Health, United States, 2014: With special feature on racial and ethnic health disparities (2016). https://www.cdc.gov/nchs/data/hus/hus15.pdf. Accessed 11 Jan 2017
4. Hoffman, F., Rodrigues, R.: Information carers: who takes care of them? European Centre for Social Welfare Policy and Research (2010). http://www.euro.centre.org/detail.php?xml_id=1714. Accessed 4 Jan 2017
5. Glueckauf, R.L., Noël, L.T.: Telehealth and family caregiving: developments in research, education, policy and practice. In: Toseland, R.W., et al. (eds.) Education and Support Programs for Caregivers, pp. 85–105. Springer, New York (2011)
6. Tindall, L.R., Huebner, R.A.: The impact of an application of telerehabilitation technology on caregiver burden. Int. J. Telerehabilitation **1**(1), 3–8 (2009)
7. Kinney, J.M., Kart, C.S., Murdoch, L.D., Ziemba, T.F.: Challenges in caregiving and creative solutions: using technologies to facilitate caring for a relative with dementia. Ageing Int. **28**(3), 295–314 (2003). doi:10.1007/s12126-002-1009-x
8. Mortensen, W.B., Demers, L., Fuhrer, M.J., Jutai, J.W., Lenker, J., DeRuyter, F.: Effects of an assistive technology intervention on older adults with disabilities and their informal caregivers: an exploratory randomized controlled trial. Am. J. Phys. Med. Rehabil. **92**, 297–306 (2013). doi:10.1097/PHM.0b013e31827d65b
9. Blusi, M., Asplund, K., Jong, M.: Older family carers in rural areas: experiences from using caregiver support services based on information and communication technology (ICT). Eur. J. Ageing **10**, 191–199 (2013). doi:10.1007/s10433-013-0260-1
10. Gaugler, J.E., Jarrott, S.E., Zarit, S.H., Stephens, M.P., Townsend, A., Greene, R.: Adult day care service use and reductions in caregiving hours: effects on stress and psychological well-being for dementia caregivers. Int. J. Geriatr. Psychiatry **18**, 55–62 (2003). doi:10.1002/gps.772
11. Whittier, S., Scharlach, A., Dal Santo, T.S.: Availability of carevier support services: implications for implementation of the national family caregiver support program. J. Aging Soc. Policy **17**(1), 45–62 (2005). doi:10.1300/J031v17n01_03
12. Luxton, D.D., McCann, R.A., Bush, N.E., Mishkind, M.C., Reger, G.M.: mHealth for mental health: integrating smartphone technology in behavioral healthcare. Prof. Psychol. Res. Pract. **42**, 505–512 (2011). doi:10.1037/a0024485

13. Powell, J., Chiu, T., Eysenbach, G.: A systematic review of networked technologies supporting carers of people with dementia. J. Telemedicine Telecare **14**, 154–156 (2008). doi:10.1258/jtt.2008.003018
14. Brodaty, H., Thomson, C., Thompson, C., Fine, M.: Why caregivers of people with dementia and memory loss don't use services. Int. J. Geriatr. Psychiatry **20**, 1–10 (2005). doi:10.1002/gps.1322
15. Lee, C.: User-centered system design in an aging society: an integrated study on technology adoption. Dissertation, Massachusetts Institute of Technology (2014)

Change in the Relationship Between the Elderly and Information Support Robot System Living Together

Misato Nihei[1(✉)], Yuko Nishiura[2], Ikuko Mamiya[2], Hiroaki Kojima[4], Ken Sadohara[4], Shinichi Ohnaka[3], Minoru Kamata[1], and Takenobu Inoue[2]

[1] Department of Human and Engineered Environmental Studies,
The University of Tokyo, Tokyo, Japan
{mnihei,mkamata}@k.u-tokyo.ac.jp
[2] Research Institute of National Rehabilitation Center for the Persons
with Disabilities, Saitama, Japan
{nishiura-yuko,mamiya-ikuko,inoue-takenobu}@rehab.go.jp
[3] NEC Corporation, Tokyo, Japan
shinoonaka@nec.co.jp
[4] National Institute of Advanced Industrial Science and Technology, Ibaraki, Japan
{h.kojima,ken.sadohara}@aist.go.jp

Abstract. We developed an interactive communication robot to support the elderly who have mild cognitive impairment with their daily schedule. In this study, we examined how elderly people receiving information from a robot behave according to the robot's interaction protocol, through an experiment providing schedule information for several days. In addition, we examined the interaction between humans and robots through long-term life intervention experiments and analyzed the quantitative and qualitative changes in their reactions.

Keywords: Mild cognitive impairment · Support robot · Interaction · Memory assist aid

1 Introduction

The number of elderly and persons with dementia are increasing worldwide [1]. More specifically, the number of persons with mild dementia is predicted to rise markedly as a result of the medical progress that slows down the course of the dis-ease, and the advances in diagnostic technologies that facilitates its early detection. Based on these perspectives, there are greater expectations from assistive technologies to support persons with mild dementia, due to the insufficient number of caregivers. For this reason, it is also important for these persons to be able to maintain self-reliance and to live independently.

In our project, we developed the prototype of an information support robot for persons with dementia, using field-based methodology [2]. The communication robot produced by NEC Corporation, called "PaPeRo," was chosen as the platform for this system. In order to keep persons with dementia informed of their daily schedule and to prompt them into action, interactive verbal communication algorithms were

© Springer International Publishing AG 2017
J. Zhou and G. Salvendy (Eds.): ITAP 2017, Part II, LNCS 10298, pp. 433–442, 2017.
DOI: 10.1007/978-3-319-58536-9_34

programmed into the robot. The results of the experiments, which were conducted in our previous studies, with five dementia sufferers, showed that this system has an information acquisition rate of over 90%. In addition, a life support demonstration confirmed that the robot could successfully prompt the users into taking action.

During these experiments, we observed changes in the relationship between the elderly and the information-support robot system that they lived with. In this study, we examine how the elderly people receiving information behave according to the robot's interaction protocol, and how to modify the relationship with the robots. For this, we analyze the interaction between robots and humans, both quantitatively and qualitatively, using long-term experiments in everyday life.

2   Concept of Information Support Robot System

2.1   Platform Robot System Used in the Experiments

The platform for the robot system, called "PaPeRo" (Partner Personal Robot) [2] is shown in Fig. 1. The robot is equipped with speech recognition, speech synthesis, facial image recognition, autonomous mobility, head motion, light indication functions, and tactile sensing capabilities. In this research, we limited these functions to adopt to our system concept.

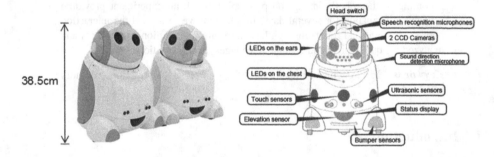

Fig. 1. PaPeRo (R500) (NEC)

PaPeRo also has some preinstalled content to make the interaction between the robot and the user enjoyable, such as quiz, games, riddles, mimics, songs, and greetings. This content also includes functions that generate sound, light, or motion in response to a registered voice when a user calls the robot. In this research, we utilized these preinstalled content to increase affinity.

2.2   System Concept [2]

The key functions of the proposed information-support robot system are as follows:

– To provide required information to the users
– To prompt actions/activities in the users

– To attract the attention of users
– To communicate with the users through interactive conversation

A method for interactive information support based on the nature of the interaction between humans, was adopted for the following interactions: the most basic way of starting a conversation, which involves an attention-seeking cue (an "alert" (a)), and "pre-sequence" information support, which facilitates the eventual ex-change ("communication" (b)) that extends to the end of the conversation, as shown in Fig. 2(i). The proposed information support algorithm, which is based on the evaluation experiments conducted in the previous studies, is shown in Fig. 2(ii).

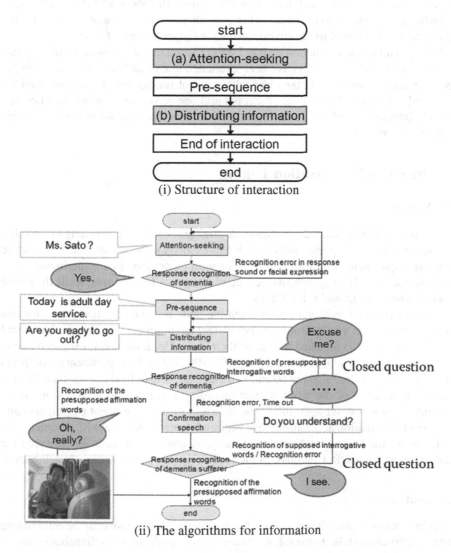

(i) Structure of interaction

(ii) The algorithms for information

Fig. 2. Structure of interaction and the algorithms for information [2]

In this algorithm, two conditional branches are provided. One is for an alerting interaction that judges whether it responds by reply (sound), when it is difficult to direct attention to the robot at the start of the dialogue due to deterioration of the attention function. The second is for distributing information, as an information interaction for confirming that the user has acquired the information, depending on whether the answer is affirmative (*yes*, *understood*, etc.), negative (*no*, *do not know*, etc.), or doubtful (*what?*, *eh?*, etc.).

2.3 Human-Robot Interaction

There are many cases in which the social interactions of robots with the elderly were evaluated in laboratory environments. However, there are few cases of evaluations that were conducted in actual living environments for longer periods of time.

Robots with tactile interaction such as PARO [3] and mobile robots used in hospitals such as Care-O-bot [4], etc [5] have been evaluated alongside humans in actual living environments. However, it is not clear what kind of relationship was established for dialogue-based interaction between the robot and one person living alone, and how the person's interaction with the robot is modified. In this research, we will focus on this point and examine it.

3 Change in Conversation Timing

3.1 Method

An experiment was conducted to evaluate the change in conversation timing of the robot and the participant. The participants included five elderly persons with mild to moderate cognitive impairment, who were not familiar with computers. Five experiments were conducted per day. The experiments were conducted on A for five days, while they were conducted on B, C, D, and E for 3 days.

The experimental environment involved the daily living environment, and for this the target participant's own room or an equivalent environment was chosen. The sound environment was also matched to that of their daily life; however, it excluded sound sources such as television, audio, and radio. The distance of the experiment participants from the robot was fixed at about 60 cm, and the dialogue was held face-to-face. For the voice characteristics of the robot, a male recording voice was adopted and the basic utterance volume was set to 80 [dB]. The reactions of the experiment participants and the state of information acquisition were captured using webcam and IC recorder.

To record the basic characteristics of the participants, professionals measured the cognitive function (CDR: Cognitive Dementia Rating [6]) and the average hearing level.

3.2 Evaluation

In this interactive system, it is necessary for the interlocutor to answer at the right timing when the participant talks to the robot while the robot speaks or when the robot performs sound/speech recognition. In this experiment, we analyzed the responses to each inter-action and investigated the utterance timing of the experiment participants.

In the dialog system proposed in this research, the robot speaks first. During this time, the robot does not perform sound/speech recognition. After completion of utter-ance, it performs sound/speech recognition for 10 [s]. In the case where the speech recognition interval is $t_0 - t_t$, and $t_0 = 0$ [s], the dialogue start time t_a, t_b of the interlocutor takes a negative value. If the participant does not reply until it exceeds the recognition section of 10 [s] or does not respond to it while the robot is speaking (R_a in Fig. 3), the robot does not recognize the utterance of the reply and calls repeatedly (R_d in Fig. 3). On the other hand, when the reply is related to the speech recognition interval, it can be correctly recognized (R_b, R_c in Fig. 3). Since the details of these systems are not explained to the experiment participants, the replies are given at an arbitrary timing by the experiment participants.

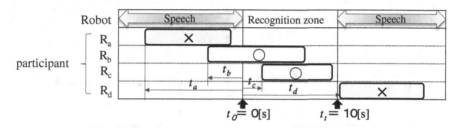

Fig. 3. Definition of reaction time of the dialog system

3.3 Results

The profile of the participants are shown in Table 1. Figure 4(a) shows the change in response timing of participant A. The average response time was calculated by averaging the reaction time for each experiment day of attention interaction and information support interaction. Although variations are observed, it can be seen that the timing of the sound/speech recognition is within the speech recognition interval and approaches the t_0 value both in replying to the call for attention and in response to the information transmission. Figures 4(b)–(e) show the change in the response timing of participants B, C, D, and E. A similar tendency as that of participant A was observed.

Table 1. Profile of participants [2]

Participant	Age	Gender	Disease	Care level	MMSE	CDR
A	97	Female	AD	1	17	1
B	79	Female	CVA	1	17	2
C	83	Female	AD like	1	16	1
D	89	Female	AD like	1	17	1
E	81	Female	AD	1	23	1

*Care Level shows the typical scale used in Japan with long term care insurance.

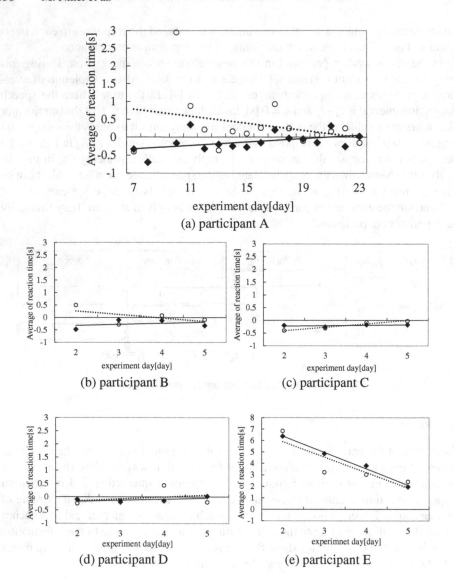

Fig. 4. Temporal change in response time of participants

4   Change in Quality of Relationships Between Robot and Human

4.1   Method

(i)   Intervention method

The robot was set in the living room of the participant for one month and the information support functions were carried out every day. The introduction was conducted step by step, only during daytime, every day for one week or more, considering the opinion of the participant and a key person. The support functions included schedule and medication support, and the schedule was input by the key person based on the interview with the participant. The preliminary interview determined the requirements of information, forbiddance and precautions, confirmation of input information, attitudes at the time of regular information support (wording and the way of responding to support information from regular staff). The execution timing of the information support depends on the data and time recorded using dedicated software.

The target participants were recruited from a paid nursing home. The condition of the target participants were: there was a need for information support, they found it difficult when disturbed, and the staff often had to support their actions by word.

Cognitive function tests and average hearing level tests were conducted before and after the introduction.

(ii) Experimental system

The robot, which was installed with the proposed information support system, was used for the experiment. The robot activated the preinstalled contents (described previously) in order to enhance the affinity, in addition providing information support depending on the time. Specifically, when a participant speaks or touches the robot and the meaning cannot be recognized, it operates a function that returns a nod and some reaction.

The robot was installed in the place that the participant wanted and video cameras, microphones, sensors, etc. installed for recording. When the experiment was set up, particular attention was given to ensure that the power supply, wiring, and the mechanical devices were blinded as much as possible to blend in with the participant's daily life. The video camera was set to record for 3 [min] before and after the robot performed the information support functions and the pre-installed reaction tasks.

4.2 Results

The participants were two females living alone in a paid nursing home. Their profiles are listed in Table 2. The information support implemented based on the needs of participant A was about 240[times], while that of B was about 75[times], during a period of about 1 month. The support items were classified into the following four categories: meal time (breakfast, lunch, supper); living information (garbage disposal, bathing, other schedule); health care (blood pressure measurement, medication, visit); and leisure and customary activities (walking, reading, watching TV).

Table 2. Profile of participants

Participant	Age	Gender	MMSE
F	77	Female	27
G	81	Female	30

Except for information support, communication with the robot were voluntarily carried out by the participant. Figure 5(a) shows the daily change in interactions of participant A, and Fig. 5(b) shows the weekly change in interactions of participant B.

Overall, participant A had more interactions than B, and it was done frequently. In both cases, an increase in the number of interactions was observed after the initial stage of introduction.

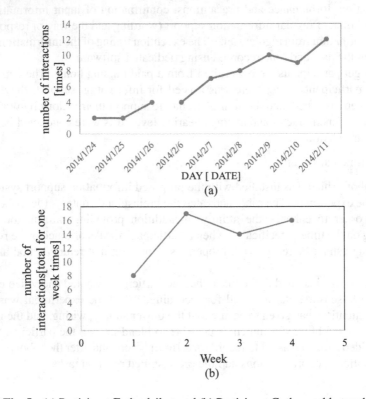

Fig. 5. (a) Participant F: the daily trend (b) Participant G: the weekly trend

Table 3 lists the contents of the interactions made by the participants with the robot. Despite the fact that the robot performs only built-in reactions, it was observed that the participants took care of the robot as if it were a pet or a small child.

(iii) The day to say good-bye

In the morning of the last day of the one-month intervention experiment, the robot told the participant that it would say goodbye that day. The goodbye said by the participant to the robot was recorded.

Participant A: *"Thank you for everything PaPeRo. It is kind of painful to think that this is the end, PaPeRo. Thank you Pr. PaPeRo. Thanks. It was fun, wasn't it? You went to a house somewhere and worked as Mr. PaPeRo. Good luck with. Good luck do your best. Hang in there. Good luck PaPeRo."*

Participant B: *"Bye bye, huh, I enjoyed having a new experience. Thank you."*

Particularly, participant A shed tears during parting, and it seemed that trust relationship had grown during the interaction for one month.

Table 3. Lists the contents of the interactions made by the participants with the robot

Type	Regarding to schedule support	Free interaction
Detail	Thanks and responses	Concern for robot
	thank you/it is snowing, today is a day off/	*tired?/boring?/cold?/hot?*
	I'm the one who should be thanking you.	Praise the robot
	Report	*cute/good child./c\cleverness*
	I'm going out for a meal./I'm back home.	Question
	I ate dinner. It was delicious./please keep	*understand?/can you hear me?/you know*
	your answer.	*what?/you are surprised, don't you?*
	Urge robot to do work	Taking care of the robot
	It's time for work./Good job/your work	*I will wipe you/tickle tickle*
	time will finish soon./you didn't say	
	anything but what did I do.	

5   Discussion

The participants were able to acquire the reaction time of the robot empirically and were able to respond to the timing of speech recognition. It is possible to assume that the protocol of dialogue was learned through dialogue, even if there was mild cognitive impairment, allowing natural interaction without any computer knowledge.

Long-term intervention experiments on information-supporting robots showed that the relationship between humans and robots are changing both quantitatively and qualitatively. This can be considered to be a new human relationship established by the role of information support and sympathy, which is a reaction to the participant's speech.

On the other hand, through their responses, robots can deepen their relationships with people and form an irreplaceable relationship. However, they are likely to be dependent.

6   Conclusion

In this research, we conducted an intervention experiment using an interactive communication robot to provide schedule information to elderly people with mild cognitive impairment who live independently. It was shown that the elderly who receives the information improves the timing of the response according to the interaction protocol of the robot. In addition, a long intervention experiment for one month showed that the amount of free interactions increased and its quality changed to an irreplaceable existence.

Acknowledgements. We would like to thank Seikatsu Kagaku Un-Ei Co., Ltd. and the participants of experiments for their cooperation in this study.

References

1. Alzheimer's disease International: World Alzheimer Report 2015. The Global Impact of Dementia, ADI (2015)
2. Inoue, T., Nihei, M., Narita, T., Onoda, M., Ishiwata, R., Ikuko, M., Shino, M., Kojima, H., Ohnaka, S., Fujita, Y., Kamata, M.: Field-based development of an information support robot for persons with dementia. Technol. Disabil. **24**, 263–271 (2012)
3. Shibata, T.: Mental commit robot (paro). http://www.paro.jp
4. Webster, M., Dixon, C., Fisher, M., Salem, M., Saunders, J., Koay, K.L., Dautenhahn, K.: Toward reliable autonomous robotic assistants through formal verification: a case study. IEEE Trans. Hum. Mach. Syst. **46**(2), 186–196 (2016)
5. Cory, D.K., Will, T., Sherry, T.: A social robot to encourage social interaction among elderly. In: Proceedings of the 2006 IEEE ICRA, pp. 3972–3976 (2006)
6. Huges, C.P., Berg, L., Danziger, W.L., Coben, L.A., Martin, R.L.: A new clinical scale for the staging of dementia. Br. J. Psychiatry **140**, 566–572 (1982)

Digital Storytelling and Dementia

Elly Park[1(✉)], Hollis Owens[2], David Kaufman[2], and Lili Liu[1]

[1] Department of Occupational Therapy, University of Alberta, Edmonton, Canada
{elly1,lili.liu}@ualberta.ca
[2] Faculty of Education, Simon Fraser University, Burnaby, Canada
{howens,dkaufman}@sfu.ca

Abstract. Digital storytelling is a form of narrative that creates short films using media technology such as downloading still photos, sound, music, and videos. Past research has indicated benefits of storytelling for persons with dementia to include enhanced relationships and communication. The purpose of this research was to explore and understand digital storytelling as perceived and experienced by the storytellers themselves.

Using a multi-site case study design, the study was conducted in Edmonton, and will continue in Vancouver and Toronto. This paper presents preliminary data collected in Edmonton, the first site to commence. The study involved participants with dementia in a seven-session workshop over the period of six weeks, where they created digital stories with the help of researchers and care partners. Participants then discussed the experience of meeting with researchers, sharing stories and using technology including digital media. Lastly, there was an opportunity for participants to share their digital stories with loved ones and the public.

Data was collected through observational field notes and audio recorded workshop sessions and interviews. The recordings were transcribed and analyzed using NVivo 10 software and using a thematic analysis protocol.

Findings showed that overall participants enjoyed the process of creating digital stories, despite some challenges with communication, memory and using technology. Findings also provided insight into the best practices for a digital storytelling workshop as expressed by the storytellers with dementia. Digital storytelling has the potential for persons with dementia to share and preserve stories in a meaningful and rewarding way.

Keywords: Digital storytelling · Persons with dementia · Qualitative research

1 Background

Currently, 564,000 Canadians live with dementia. By 2031 it is estimated that this number will increase to 937,000 [1]. Challenges experienced by persons with dementia include difficulties with communication, memory loss, and loss of sense of identity [2].

Digital storytelling can be an effective method for communicating important information because it does not rely on one method for telling the story but provides multiple ways. The visuals, spoken words and music are selected independently but work collectively to impart messages to audiences. Since digital stories are so personal, they not

© Springer International Publishing AG 2017
J. Zhou and G. Salvendy (Eds.): ITAP 2017, Part II, LNCS 10298, pp. 443–451, 2017.
DOI: 10.1007/978-3-319-58536-9_35

only tell us what happened but also how it happened [3]. Having understood another person's experience, audiences are then able to relate it to their own narrative through the power of shared archetypal knowledge and wisdom contained in the human psyche [4]. This can make it possible for healthy adults to better understand and connect with the experiences of people with dementia.

A literature review of the use of digital storytelling for persons with dementia indicates that sharing stories has a positive impact on the persons with dementia, their family members and other caregivers [2, 5–9]. The definition of digital storytelling, however, varies in the literature and includes reminiscence therapy, the use of communication assistive devices, and ambient assistive technology. For the purposes of this study, digital storytelling is operationally defined as a form of narrative that creates short movies using simple media technology [10]. Potential for learning and using technology is possible for persons with dementia and is a growing area of research [11, 12].

Specific benefits discussed in the literature for persons with dementia include: improved well-being, increased confidence, communication, connection with others, and a sense of purpose [2, 5–7]. Likewise, the use of technology or digital media allows participants to look at or listen to stories repeatedly at their convenience [8]. Storytelling is a way to appreciate the "beauty of the present moment" [9, p. 421] but also to leave a "legacy for families and future generations" [9, p. 425]. Relationships between the participant and care partner, as well as relationships with others show positive changes including deeper conversations [6–8], and an increased sense of trust [5].

Currently, technological advances have made it possible for stories to be preserved digitally using multimedia to increase the potential for dissemination as well as improve the likelihood of stories being heard by a broader audience. In addition, the stories may be kept and passed down to loved ones as a legacy.

The purpose of this project was to gain a better understanding of the benefits of storytelling and the use of digital media for persons with dementia. We began with a digital storytelling curriculum developed for the Simon Fraser University Elder's Digital Storytelling project for older adults [13]. This curriculum was created in September of 2014 using principles gathered from the Center for Digital Storytelling in California (now called StoryCenter), and the Digital Storytelling Cookbook [13].

We have identified some potential benefits from our own past research. The positive outcomes we found in previous digital storytelling workshops with older adults include: empowered participants; assisted social connections among workshop participants, friends, and family; provided a means for legacy creation; increased digital storytelling, technology, and internet skills; provided an opportunity to share stories with others and to learn something new [13, 14]. This study used the core elements of the digital storytelling curriculum because of the positive outcomes generated from the earlier Elder Digital Storytelling project, as well as the potential benefits discussed in the literature.

2 Theoretical Framework

The paradigms that influenced this study included Bruner's [15] notion of 'narrative knowing' and constructivism. In Making Stories, Bruner [15] discusses the etymology of narrative-derived from 'telling' and 'knowing' in some particular way. Stories are one way of conveying a perspective, an idea, or a certain experience to others, but are also a way to convey the knowledge that comes with the telling. Narrative knowledge provides the storyteller with an understanding of others and themselves through the storytelling process.

Constructivism is based on the notion that there are multiple truths based on perspective and the meanings that individuals place on objects, experiences, and others [16–18]. A constructivist paradigm is maintained in this study as the participants share their perspectives through stories of experience. There is a close collaboration between participants and researchers to authentically portray their views and foster understanding of their lives and actions. Hancock and Algozzine [19] note that a case study approach can "capture multiple realities that are not easily quantifiable" (p. 72) and is a way to collect information in natural settings. The case study approach takes individual stories as a way of conveying experiential knowledge and provides a viewpoint that is based on the participant's understanding of reality [18].

3   Research Questions

1. What is the experience of the digital storytelling workshop for adults with early stage dementia?
2. How does digital storytelling affect their quality of life in terms of relationships and sense of identity?

4   Methods

4.1   Research Team

The researcher team includes six researchers from the University of Alberta, Simon Fraser University, and University of Toronto in Edmonton, Vancouver and Toronto respectively, as well as a care partner consultant in Toronto. Data collection is being staggered over the three sites beginning with Edmonton. Collaborators were all involved in the design of the study, and provided input regarding the digital storytelling workshop and data collection process. The remainder of this paper focuses on the data and findings from the Edmonton site.

4.2   Participants

Eight participants were recruited from the Alzheimer Society in Edmonton. Four males and three females were part of this study. Participants had a diagnosis of dementia and were categorized as being in the early disease stage. All participants lived in the community with a care partner. One participant was unable to complete the digital story due to time constraints (she was leaving on holidays for two months before she finished) but expressed that she would like to participate in the future if there is another opportunity to do so. The other seven participants were able to complete their digital stories. Participants received a copy of their digital stories on a USB key at the end of the study.

4.3 Workshop Details

The digital storytelling workshop took place over seven sessions in six weeks. Participants were involved in the discussion of the workshop and storytelling process and shared about their experience. By providing their perspectives about digital storytelling throughout the process, the participants were able to have a direct impact on the future direction of the project in terms of adaptations and modifications at the subsequent sites in Vancouver and Toronto to improve and enhance the experience of digital storytelling for persons with dementia.

4.4 Workshop Modifications

The Elder's Digital Storytelling workshop conducted by researchers at Simon Fraser University consists of ten weekly two hour sessions for nine weeks. A tenth week is then scheduled for viewing of the stories by participants, their families and friends. The present study with participants with dementia had shorter, condensed sessions over a span of six weeks. We have shortened the duration of the workshop to minimize any effects related to the progression of dementia on workshop participation.

An initial session included a pre-study interview to gather demographic information, as well as baseline information about a participant's use of technology, storytelling practices, and other pertinent information. The initial interview included questions to stimulate the discussion of stories from their past and present life. Two sessions involved conversations about stories that were meaningful to the participant. Participants were encouraged to think about which story they would like to develop in more detail. The remaining sessions involved a step-by-step process to create digital stories using a video editing program called WeVideo (https://www.wevideo.com/). After the digital stories were created, the participants had an opportunity to share their stories with a broader audience including friends and family. During the last session, each of the participants talked about their experience of participating in the workshop.

During one of the first sessions, the Standardized Mini Mental Status Examination (SMMSE) was administered to the participants to provide additional information regarding their cognitive state [20]. The SMMSE is a cognitive assessment which can be used to estimate the level of cognitive impairment and dementia severity [21]. The following scores are used to estimate dementia severity out of a total score of 30: *21–25* (mild), *11–20* (moderate), and *0–10* (severe) as outlined in the literature [22]. In this study, the SMMSE was part of the protocol across the three sites.

Another modification made in this study was reducing the number of participants per workshop from 5 to 10 participants [13] down to 2 to 4 participants. This modification was made to give the participants with dementia more individual attention. Care partners were also invited to attend workshop sessions if the participant requested their support. In most sessions the participant did not ask for the care partner to be present.

Last, the sessions were not all carried out as a group, but there was a combination of one-on-one and group sessions. In Edmonton, several of the participants and care partners expressed concerns with getting to and from the workshop site. Likewise, all of them requested to meet in their own home where they felt comfortable. As a result, the researcher and workshop facilitator[1] went to their homes for a majority of the sessions.

4.5 Technology

The digital storytelling curriculum required participants to use computers to create their digital stories. The video editing software used, WeVideo, is available for free online. This program includes several features including uploading pictures, adding layers of voice and music recordings, animation, and publishing. The participants were engaged in the entire process, although depending on their abilities, the facilitator worked closely with them. Two participants did not have computers and were unable to use the program without assistance. Other participants were able to navigate the program with help from their care partners. None of the participants were able to use the program independently.

The stories were recorded using a Yeti Blue microphone to enhance the quality of the audio recordings. Six of the participants were able to read the stories they had created. One participant had difficulty reading the story that she had created because of visual impairment. In this case the facilitator read the story and the participant repeated it line by line.

5 Ethics

This study received ethics approval from the University of Alberta (Pro00066310) for the Edmonton site.

6 Data Collection

Data collection occurred across the three sites beginning with Edmonton, and continuing on in Vancouver and then Toronto. Data collection commenced in Edmonton from January, 2017.

The workshop facilitator took field notes, observational notes and audio recorded the workshop sessions as part of data collection. The audio recordings were transcribed and used to clarify and support the field notes on what was said by participants during the workshop. Stake [18] also recommends that observations for a qualitative case study focus on "finding the good moments to reveal the unique complexity of the case" (p. 63). The observational field notes included thick descriptions of the context of the case including the physical environment and the participants [18].

---

[1] The researcher and/or workshop facilitator discussed in this study refers to the first author (Elly Park).

7 Data Analysis

The interview recordings were transcribed by the researchers and coded using NVivo 10 software for analyzing qualitative research. Findings were independently coded by the facilitator in Edmonton with the intention to reanalyze with the researchers from the other two sites to refine and establish themes. At this preliminary stage, the analysis focused on the experience of creating digital stories from the participants' perspective, as well as the modifications made to the current digital storytelling workshop to possibly implement in Vancouver and Toronto to optimize the benefits for persons with dementia.

Thematic analysis as described by Braun and Clark [23] was used to analyze our interview transcripts and field notes. The six steps of data analysis include: familiarization with the data, coding, searching for themes, reviewing themes, defining and naming themes, and writing up the report [23].

The facilitator transcribed all the audio recordings and documented observations. Coding entailed grouping phrases from participants and field notes into modes and then into themes. Themes determined from the codes will be discussed with the other researchers after analysis is independently completed at the three sites. Findings will be reviewed collectively at a later date.

8 Findings

Modifications made to the original digital storytelling workshop curriculum, such as a change in the number of participants in the workshop, the number of sessions, as well as a change in the style of sessions from all group sessions to a combination of one-on-one and group sessions seemed to enhance the level of interaction and engagement of individual participants, especially those who were quieter in group settings. Likewise, including the care partner in the digital storytelling process when the participant requested support was an effective way of maintaining flow and alleviating any sense of pressure the participant may have felt to recall details.

On the Standardized Mini Mental Status Examination (SMMSE), six of the participant scores varied from 20–29 out of 30. One participant was unable to complete the assessment because of poor visual acuity. The SMMSE was administered in the participants' homes, after meeting one or two times. One of the care partners commented that her husband scored higher than he would have at a doctor's office because of the context and setting. She stated that he knew who the person administering the assessment was and he was in his home, making it much easier for him to relax.

Overall, the participants enjoyed the sessions; they commented that they looked forward to the meetings. Their receptive demeanour and willingness to talk indicated that they were engaged in the process. One participant stated that she felt incredibly lonely since receiving her diagnosis and she enjoyed the social interaction this workshop offered. They were able to share stories, choose a particular story or topic that was meaningful to them, and take part in creating the digital story with support from their care partners and facilitator. The participants were attentive and put a great deal of care and consideration into the stories they chose, as well as the way they wanted to present them. The care partners were mindful to be involved without controlling or taking over the process to enhance the experience for the participant. Using the web-based WeVideo program was difficult for all participants but together with the facilitator, the participant was still able to provide input about the images, music and style of the digital story.

Participants were not always able to explicitly express how they felt or what they enjoyed during the sessions, but there was a level of participation and enthusiasm that indicated interest. The participants all recognized the facilitator at each of the sessions, even if they had difficulty recollecting the content discussed during previous sessions. The sense of accomplishment that came from developing and creating digital stories was observable to the facilitator and care partners. One care partner noted that when her husband shared the story he wrote with her he was "beaming." Another care partner exclaimed to her husband during the session when he had recorded his story, "I am so proud of you!" One of the participants expressed that this was "above and beyond anything [he] thought was possible"when he saw the video for the first time.

9   Discussion

Preliminary findings from the Edmonton site are consistent with the literature pertaining to digital storytelling with persons with dementia in terms of enhanced relationships between participants and caregivers, as well as an increase in communication and inter-actions [5–9]. The relationship between the participants and facilitator also improved with time leading to a greater sense of trust and comfort [5].

There was a variability in symptoms among participants depending on the partici-pant, time of day, and setting. One participant noted that he has good days and bad days. For him, a bad day meant his aphasia was worse than usual and he would struggle to get his words out. For another participant, she noted that her life had changed drastically since she was diagnosed with dementia and she knew she was not able to remember details about what we talked about during each workshop session, so she kept a notebook with her where she wrote down anything she felt was important to remember.

Although participants seemed to have slightly varying levels of dementia and presented different symptoms, they were all able to share distinct and meaningful stories. With encouragement from their care partners, the participants also prepared for work-shop sessions by looking at photos, talking about the stories they wanted to focus on, and writing down notes to remind them of which stories they had shared. The participants were not comfortable using the technology without support from the facilitator, but expressed their appreciation when they were asked to provide input in choosing the images, songs and special effects that were all part of the digital story. Care partners played a critical role in the process as well by providing support in a loving and unin-trusive way.

Themes that emerged from the data analysis consistently related to engagement. The participants were engaged with the process, the stories and in the relationships with their care partners as well as the facilitator. Participants were clearly proud of the stories they had created and care partners were also pleased with the end product. Being able to complete the workshop gave them a sense of accomplishment while helping them think about and share meaningful stories.

Participants had difficulty explicitly stating what they enjoyed or what the benefits were, but they all thought that despite the amount of work and effort involved, the time had been well spent. The opportunity to create a story as a legacy was one benefit that participants stated, which was also part of the literature review findings [9]. Some stated that they liked being able to access their stories whenever they wanted, in line with what past research noted [8]. Overall, the process of thinking about, sharing and creating a digital story was a positive experience, as a present moment memory [9].

The benefits of creating digital stories are promising and warrant further study. Follow-up with the participants after the end of the workshop could also provide insight into the lasting impact of digital storytelling for persons with dementia and should be part of future workshops.

10 Limitations

This study is still in the preliminary stage of analysis at the Edmonton site only. Therefore, the results shared here may not reflect the overall findings from all three sites. The relatively small number of participants at each site was necessary given the modifications made to the workshop to accommodate the needs of the participants.

11 Conclusion

Communication and preservation of memories are two significant challenges for persons with dementia. It can be daunting for them to reach out for social contact, to reflect on and talk about life experiences. When given the opportunity, people with dementia were able to share meaningful stories and provide input into creating digital stories that involve the use of computers, audio, and images. The use of technology was challenging, but an essential part of the process as it allowed the participants to share their stories in a provocative and stimulating way. This digital storytelling workshop can provide persons with dementia and their care partners with both a tool for creating stories and the opportunity to interact with others through their stories.

References

1. Chambers, L.W., Bancej, C., McDowell, I.: Prevalence and monetary costs of dementia in Canada: population health expert panel. Alzheimer Society of Canada (2016)
2. Alm, N., Dye, R., Gowans, G., Campbell, J., Astell, A., Ellis, M.A.: Communication support system for older people with dementia. Computer **40**, 35–41 (2007)
3. Gray, B., Young, A., Blomfield, T.: Altered lives: assessing the effectiveness of digital storytelling as a form of communication design. Continuum **29**(4), 635–649 (2015). doi: 10.1080/10304312.2015.1025359
4. Frank, A.: The Wounded Storyteller: Body, Illness, Ethics. University of Chicago Press, Chicago (1995)

5. Capstick, A., Ludwin, K., Chatwin, J., Walters, E.R.: Participatory video and well-being in long-term care. J. Dement. Care **24**(1), 26–29 (2016)
6. Massimi, M., Berry, E., Browne, G., Smyth, G., Watson, P., Baecker, R.M.: An exploratory case study of the impact of ambient biographical displays on identity in a patient with Alzheimer's disease. Neuropsychological Rehabil. **18**, 742–765 (2008). doi: 10.1080/09602010802130924
7. Stenhouse, R., Tait, J., Hardy, P., Sumner, T.: Dangling conversations: reflections on the process of creating digital stories during a workshop with people with early-stage dementia. J. Psychiatr. Ment. Health Nurs. **20**, 134–141 (2013). doi:10.1111/j.1365-2850.2012.01900.x
8. Crete-Nishihata, M., Baecker, R.M., Massimi, M., et al.: Reconstructing the past: personal memory technologies are not just personal and not just for memory. Hum. Comput. Interact. **27**, 92–123 (2012). doi:10.1080/07370024.2012.656062
9. Savundranayagam, M.Y., Dilley, L.J., Basting, A.: StoryCorps' memory loss initiative: enhancing personhood for storytellers with memory loss. Dementia **10**, 415–433 (2011). doi: 10.1177/1471301211408123
10. Rule, L.: Digital storytelling has never been so easy or so powerful. Knowl. Quest **38**(4), 56–57 (2010)
11. Rossiter, M., Garcia, P.A.: Digital storytelling: a new player on the narrative field. New Dir. Adult Continuing Educ. **126**, 37–48 (2010)
12. Nygård, L., Starkhammar, S.: The use of everyday technology by people with dementia living alone: mapping out the difficulties. Aging Ment. Health **11**, 144–155 (2007)
13. Hausknecht, S., Vanchu-Orosco, M., Kaufman, D.: Sharing life stories: design and evaluation of a digital storytelling workshop for older adults (2016). Manuscript submitted for publication
14. Hausknecht, S., Kaufman, D., Vanchu-Orosco, M. (n.d.): Digitizing the wisdom of our elders: Connecting life learning through digital storytelling. Manuscript in preparation
15. Bruner, J.: Making Stories: Law, Literature, Life. Farrar, Straus and Giroux, New York (2002)
16. Baxter, P., Jack, S.: Qualitative case study methodology: study design and implementation for novice researchers. Qual. Rep. **13**(4), 544–559 (2008)
17. Stake, R.E.: The Art of Case Study Research. Sage Publications, New York (1995)
18. Yin, R.K.: The case study crisis: some answers. Adm. Sci. Q. **26**, 58–65 (1981)
19. Hancock, D.R., Algozzine, B.: Doing Case Study Research: A Practical Guide for Beginning Researchers. Teachers College Press, New York (2015)
20. Molloy, D.W., Standish, T.I.: A guide to the standardized Mini-Mental State Examination. Int. Psychogeriatr. **9**(1), 87–94 (1997)
21. Mitchell, Alex J.: The Mini-Mental State Examination (MMSE): update on its diagnostic accuracy and clinical utility for cognitive disorders. In: Larner, A.J. (ed.) Cognitive Screening Instruments, pp. 37–48. Springer, Cham (2017). doi:10.1007/978-3-319-44775-9_3
22. Perneczky, R., Wagenpfeil, S., Komossa, K., Grimmer, T., Diehl, J., Kurz, A.: Mapping scores onto stages: mini-mental state examination and clinical dementia rating. American J. Geriatr. Psychiatry **14**(2), 139–144 (2006)
23. Braun, V., Clarke, V.: Using thematic analysis in psychology. Qual. Res. Psychol. **3**, 77–101 (2006)

From Noticing to Suspecting: The Initial Stages in the Information Behaviour of Informal Caregivers of People with Dementia

Ágústa Pálsdóttir[✉]

Department of Information Science, School of Social Sciences,
University of Iceland, Reykjavík, Iceland
agustap@hi.is

Abstract. The information behaviour of informal caregivers of people with dementia was explored, from when the first symptoms of dementia were noticed until a decision to seek medical attention was made. Qualitative methods were applied and interviews conducted with 21 caregivers. Their information behaviour went through a sequence of three stages, in line with Holly Skodol Wilson's temporal model [27]: (1) Information about the disease is noticed; (2) Interpretation of information – Normalizing and discounting; (3) Suspecting – Purposive information seeking begins. As their information need developed, as described by Taylor [15], the caregivers moved from relying on opportunistic information seeking at the first two stages, to using both opportunistic and purposive seeking on the third stage. After they had fully developed their information need, they could seek information that was useful for bridging their knowledge gap, which allowed them to move forward to the decision to seek medical advice for the patients. The second stage of the process was particularly complicated as the caregivers misinterpreted the information about dementia that they came across as signs of something else. More public discussion by professionals about dementia could provide the caregivers and the patients with a better understanding of the disease. This in turn might help to shorten the time spent at the second stage, making it possible for the caretakers to enter the third stage more quickly, and thereby to come to the decision to seek medical advice.

Keywords:: Dementia · Informal caregivers · Information behaviour

1 Introduction

Today's information environment consists of a variety of information sources that can be accessed in various ways and by different means [1]. However, not all members of the society are able to benefit from it and people with dementia are in urgent need for support from their informal caregivers, that is, people who provide assistance outside the framework of organized, paid, professional work [2].

The growing number of elderly people has led to an increase in the number of people with dementia, a disease which has been declared a priority within public health [3]. As a result, the need for research investigating how the burden of their informal caregivers'

© Springer International Publishing AG 2017
J. Zhou and G. Salvendy (Eds.): ITAP 2017, Part II, LNCS 10298, pp. 452–466, 2017.
DOI: 10.1007/978-3-319-58536-9_36

can be eased has been emphasised [3]. This calls for awareness of the caregivers' information behaviour and how they assist people at using information for their own advantage. The period leading up to the decision to seek medical advice can be particularly difficult for the caregivers, as it may be filled with uncertainty and concern about what is happening to their family member. At the same time, the benefits of having dementia diagnosed at an early stage have been stressed. An early diagnosis opens up for various possibilities at treatment and care, and allows the patients and the caretakers to make plans for the future [4].

The paper will report from a study about the information behaviour of informal caregivers of patients with dementia, with focus on the time from when they begin to notice signs of the disease, until the conclusions that the patients need medical attention has been reached.

1.1 Informal Caregivers and Information Behaviour

The importance of the work that informal caregivers provide is well known [5]. Several studies exists of the information needs of informal caregivers of different groups [see e.g. [6–8], as well as various aspects of the information behaviour of caregivers of elderly people [9, 10] and patients in palliative care [11].

Information behaviour is an encompassing and multifaceted concept including all aspects of human interaction with information, provoked by the information need of a person who is situated in a certain context [12]. Information need has been described as a cognitive gap [13], or an anomalous state of knowledge of a person [14].

Taylor [15] has identified the advancement of the information need as a gradual development in four levels: (1) the visceral need, or a "vague sort of dissatisfaction", which cannot be expressed in words; (2) the conscious need, which is ill-defined, and can only be expressed in an "ambiguous and rambling statement"; (3) the formalized need, when it is possible to describe it in statements that are "qualified and rational"; (4) compromised need, when the information need has developed so that can be express clearly enough, in terms that fit the information system.

Although Taylor [15] based the model on experience from reference work at libraries but not on a systematic research approach, it is nevertheless believed by the researcher that it may apply to different situations and to be of value for the current study. The first two levels of the model subscribe what happens when people start to notice that there is a gap in their knowledge and gradually attempt to clarify and formulate what it is that they need to know. As such, these levels can relate to people in various contexts, such as the informal caregivers of people with dementia, and are not restricted to those who end up seeking reference service at a library. At the third level peoples thoughts on the subject have developed enough for them to be able to explain their need for information to others in a rational way. In Taylors model this would be to a reference librarian, but it is believed here that it could in fact be to anyone who is believed to be in a position to help the caregivers at solving their information needs, for example a relative or a close friend. The fourth and final level involves an interaction with an information system, when the caregivers have developed their information needs enough for them to be able to reword their questions so that it fits the system. This could be by doing an internet search, for example by using Google or search engines at specific websites, it could also involve the use of a library system, or any other way that allows them to retrieve information.

The sense-making theory [13] further describes what happens when people find themselves in situations where they experience a cognitive gap, and as a result perceive an information need. The theory assumes that life is a journey where people take steps through experiences. At certain moments, when they are unable to make sense of what is happening, they are faced with a discontinuity, their path forward is blocked. To be able to continue their movement through time and space they need to create a new or changed sense. The strategies that people use to find answers and solutions, or the methods they employ for information seeking, serve as a bridge over the cognitive gap. Information is seen here as constructed by those involved, it can be anything that allows them to make sense of the experiences, and thereby continue their process through daily life. Similarly, in the Information Search Process (ISP) model [16] it is assumed that, based on previous knowledge, each person understands information in her own unique way. However, for people to be able to come to the conclusion that their previous knowledge is not adequate, they must have received information in some form that allows them to understand this.

Although purposive information seeking, when people set out to seek information with the goal to fulfil their information need, or close their cognitive gap, is well known [12, 17–19], other modes of information seeking have also been identified. This entails opportunistic information seeking, that is when people unexpectedly come across information which they had not intended to seek [12, 17–19]. Including what [17] has been termed as by proxy, or when people receive information through another person.

With few exceptions [20–24], studies that explore the role of information in relation to the support provided by informal caregivers of people with dementia, have mainly focused on the caregivers information needs, in particular at the time when the disease is being diagnosed or after the diagnoses. Thomsell and Lodestone [20] explored how well the information needs of relatives who are living far from the patients are met, compared with the patients caregivers. The findings suggest that, distant relatives' access information less frequently and are more dissatisfied with the information that they receive. The findings from a study by Wald, Faheem, Walker and Livingston [21] indicate that what kind of information the caregivers require differs, depending on the time from diagnosis. While information about the disease, the symptoms and treatments are regarded important at the time of diagnosis, the caregivers want information about the disease process, reaction in crisis and formal services, at a later stage. This was, later on, followed by a need for financial and legal information, as well as support groups. Finally, information about psychological and complimentary therapies were required. Other studies support the existence of these information needs. Wackerbartha and Johnson [22] reported that information about diagnosis and treatment options were most important, and after that legal and financial information, which were of particular importance to less experienced caregivers. Hirakata, Kaseya, Enki and Emera [23] found that the primary concern was to get information about how the disease might progress, how to provide care, and availability of formal care service. A study by Komarahadi, Ruf, Hüell and Härter [24] revealed the importance of information about symptoms, the course and treatment of dementia, as well as financial support, daily care and interaction with patients.

The findings from the above mentioned studies provide important understanding of the topics that caregivers of people with dementia need knowledge about, at the time of and after the diagnosis of dementia. Less attention has, however, been paid to what happens during the period leading up to the time of diagnosis. In addition, the various aspects of the caregivers' information behaviour has received relatively little academic attention. From the information science perspective, models and theories which relate not only to dementia but also health information in general have been discussed [25]. The review provides a thorough overview of the main information models, and how they can be used to enhance comprehension of the information behaviour of patients and their caregivers. Furthermore, the information behaviour of caregivers suffering from depression, who participated in a training and support research project, have been investigated. Through the program the caregivers were offered an opportunity to share their experiences under circumstances and received professional guidance which were aimed at enhancing their problem-solving skills. The findings shed a light on how caregivers can be helped and strengthened in their role by professionals, through training and support programs [26].

The emphasis of previous studies has been on the information needs of the caregivers of people who are in the process of being diagnosed with dementia or have already received a diagnosis. The present study, however, aims at investigating the initial stages in the informal caregivers' information behaviour, in the period when the first signs of dementia appear, until they realize that medical advice is needed. The important of detecting the disease at an early stage has been stressed, and for various reasons. This includes for example the possibility of the patients to optimise the benefits of any available treatment, care and support, as well as allowing them to make plans for their future [4]. Thus, shedding more light on the issue at hand might prove useful for health specialists who are responsible for providing information about dementia, and help to support both the patients and the caregivers when making the decision to seek medical attention.

An answer to the following research question will be sought: What characterizes the initial stages in the information behaviour of informal caregivers of people with dementia?

The study draws on the temporal model by Holly Skodol Wilson [27]. The model describes the process of the Alzheimer's disease from the perspective of informal caregivers in eight stages. The first three stages in the model are of interest for the present study. At the first stage "Noticing", the caregivers gradually became aware of something unusual in the patients behaviour. This stage was only recognized in retrospect, as it was no particular cognitive defect or behaviour change had alerted them, instead it came as a result of a cumulative behaviour, which eventually led them to move on to the second stage. The second stage is called "Discounting and normalizing", although [28] it has been pointed out that the sequence of what happens is that the caregivers first normalize the behaviour and after that discount it. Therefore, the term "normalizing and discounting" is more appropriate. At this stage the caregivers had recognised that the patients' behaviour had changed and wondered what might be happening. However, they normalized the behaviour by seeking a rationalized explanation, usually the patients' old age, and as a result discounted it. This stage lasted until the patients' behaviour either became seriously worse, or a particular incident took place, which was too severe to discount. This lead to the third stage, "Suspecting", when the caregivers realized that something serious was happening and began to observe the patient more closely in order to determine how they should react on it, which brought about the decision to seek medical advice.

The conceptual basis for the study is, furthermore, formed by theoretical knowledge about information seeking and models from information science. In particular, Taylors [15] phase model will be used to explain how the caregivers information needs advances in four levels, as they experience the first three stages in the process of the disease, as well as the sense-making theory by Dervin [13], which further helps to describe how the way that the caregivers used to get information and interpreted it, gradually allowed them to create a new sense about the situation, and thereby move on to the conclusion to seek medical attention for the patients.

2   Method

With the purpose of gaining a deep understanding of various aspects related to the participants' information behaviour, from their own point of view, it was decided to employ qualitative methods, inspired by grounded theory [29]. One of the main methods used in qualitative research is interviewing, which seeks to describe the meanings of central themes in the life world of the participants and how they make sense of their daily life experiences [30].

In the study open-ended interviews were conducted with informal caregivers of people with dementia. The interviews sought to address a broad range of issues related to the nature of the caregivers information behaviour, their information needs, how the support was provided and their experience as informal caregivers, supporting their relatives with information. A convenience sample was used, and the participants were recruited through the assistance of an association of interest groups and relatives of people with Alzheimer and related diseases. A group of 21 people participated, 18 women and three men, aged 36 to 76, living in the capital area and smaller towns in the country. Seven of them were supporting their spouses, 13 their parents and one participant supported her sibling.

The interviews were carried out from February to August 2014 and lasted 50–110 min. They were digitally recorded, transcribed verbatim, and the transcriptions checked against recordings. To be able to modify the following interviews and examine more closely any ideas or themes that began to emerge, initial analysis started as soon as each interview had been conducted. The data was analysed as described by Strauss [31]. Open coding was used to question the data at the early stage. Key remarks and concepts were noted, incidents compared and grouped, and some initial themes developed. The data were reanalysed at a later stage with the themes in mind. Axial coding was used and questions asked about the conditions, actions/interactions, and consequences of the themes, and the data organized by making connections between the main themes and subthemes.

3   Results

In line with Wilsons [27] temporal model about how the Alzheimer's disease developed, from the perspective of informal caregivers, three stages were identified in their information behaviour process: *Stage 1: Information about the disease is noticed*; *Stage 2: Interpretation of information – Normalising and discounting*; and *Stage 3: Suspecting – Purposive information seeking begins*. In the study, the term patients is used, although the participants did not know, at the time, that their relatives had dementia. Likewise, the participants are called caregivers, even though at the initial stage they may, or may not, have considered themselves as such.

3.1   Stage 1: Information About the Disease Is Noticed

The initial stage describes the process when the caregivers began to notice symptoms of dementia. At this stage, they occasionally detected something unusual in the patients' appearance. But as their thoughts about it were too indistinct, they were not able to put a finger on what might be happening. One of them described it so: *Something that I felt at the time to be incomprehensible.* Another caretaker said that she had started to notice small discrepancies in her mother's behaviour: *She was perhaps in tights that didn't quite fit to the dress.* Thus, the caregivers sporadically came across unexpected information, which caused them an uneasy feeling. However, their ideas at this stage were very unclear, and as a result they were not able to formulate what they needed to know to resolve it. What happened at this state may be compared to what Taylor [14] defined as the first level of an information need, as a vague need for information. A dissatisfaction which the caregivers could not at the time express in words. It was only at a later stage, when they thought back, as is described in Wilson's model [27], that they understood that the patients had in fact been showing signs of dementia. One of them expressed this so: *When I think back, she definitely had symptoms around the age of sixty.* The duration of the first stage varied across the caregivers. In some cases it could last for a considerable time as is well illustrated by one of the caregivers: *In retrospect, this was almost certainly…I could think two years back.*

After the incidents started to increase and the caregivers stopped viewing them as separate happenings, they were able to move on to the second stage in Wilsons [27] temporal model "Interpretation of information – Normalising and discounting".

3.2   Stage 2: Interpretation of Information – Normalising and Discounting

When the caregivers began to connect the isolated incidents' which they had been observing together and interpret it, they became aware that the patients' behaviour had changed. One of them stated: *There were all these weird things that I began to observe.* Another caregiver said: *I think many people had started to notice something.* At this point the caregivers were in a situation where they lacked an overview and understanding of what was happening. Nevertheless, by recognising that something might be wrong and that they needed to find an explanation for it, they had developed what can be describe as an ill-defined need for information, or what Taylor [15] defined as a second level of an information need.

The caregivers received information by way of opportunistic seeking, in the form of the patients altered behaviour patterns. But rather than interpreting what they noticed as symptoms of dementia, they ascribed it as something else, they normalized and discounted it.

Normalizing and discounting. The subtheme *normalizing and discounting* describes how the caregivers interpreted the information and tried to find what they, at the time, considered a rational explanation.

Patients' characteristics. Some of the caregivers believed that the symptoms that they observed could be explained by the patients' characteristics, such as their age, other medical conditions, personality traits or even their abilities. Wilson [27] found that the patients' old age was the main reason why symptoms of Alzheimer were normalized and discounted. In the present study there were indeed examples of the caregivers interpreting what they noticed as normal symptoms of a person who had reached an old age. One of them noted: *They are just elderly people, they were in their eighties*. But although the likelihood of getting dementia increases with age, it is not confined to old age. In the findings there were examples of the opposite, with the caregivers normalizing and discounting the symptoms, because they considered the patient to be too young to have dementia. One of them said that she had discussed changes in her mother's behaviour with other family members. They did, however, dismiss the possibility of dementia to begin with. She shared her experience as follows: *She was also so young. We were so focused on it. She was just a little over sixty, maybe 62, when all kinds of warning signs started to appear*. As a result, some time passed before the caregivers realised that the patients might have dementia.

In some cases the patients had other medical conditions which made it difficult for the caregivers to interpret correctly what they observed. One of them said, that although she had noticed that her mother was losing some abilities, the thought of dementia did not cross her mind to begin with. She noted: *There was so much there that lead me to think that this was nothing unnatural and not linked to dementia*. The following further illustrates how a caregiver explained why his father's medical conditions had confused him: *He has hereditary hypertension...I thought maybe this could be because he was getting some bleeding or something*. In these cases, the caregivers had a tendency to explain the symptoms of dementia as the signs of another disease.

There were, furthermore, examples of the caregivers mentioning that the personality traits or abilities of the patients had hindered them from interpreting what they noticed correctly. One of the symptoms of dementia can be that the patients start to withdraw from social activities. However, when a patient had not been considered to enjoy interacting with others this personality trait could make it difficult for the caregivers to notice the change in his behaviour, as the following illustrates: *She never was a very social person, so you may not realize it...* Another symptom is that patients may start to misplace things. For caregivers of patients who had always been regarded as careless, it could be problematic to recognize this symptom. One of them explained this so: *...just since I was a kid, she's the women who lost her gloves, she lost her keys.* Thus, when the caregivers know and are accustomed to certain character traits which are similar to the symptoms of dementia, they may normalise and discount what they notice as a typical behaviour of that person. In addition, there was an example of a caregiver who stated that she and her family had not considering dementia a possibility because of the abilities of the patient:: *The idea never came to us that this active and clever woman who had achieved so much...That she was beginning to lose her memory, it was just not an option, it never occurred to us.* In this case the patient's reputation of being a very competent and talented person had influenced the caregiver's interpretation.

Slow progression of the disease. The speed at which dementia gets worse varies, there are differences from person to person and between the different types of dementias. In some cases the caregivers said that the symptoms had started out slowly and gradually become worse and that had made it difficult for them to realize what was happening. One of them explained his experience so: *This starts perhaps just once, and then a long time goes until something else happens that provokes you to think: "Wait, why don't you remember this?" Because it's natural for us to forget perhaps a thing or two.* Hence, the caregivers had to piece together information about disperse incidents over time. Until it was possible for them to get a more complete picture of what was happening, they described the incidents as normal and discounted them.

Denial. There were also examples of the caregivers stating that they had not been ready to acknowledge that the patient might be showing signs of dementia. This is well illustrated by the following: *We always found some excuse. And I think this was just the fear and the grief. This just could not be.* Because the family found it emotionally too difficult to face up to the fact that the patient might have dementia, they tried to interpret the symptoms as signs of something else.

Lack of knowledge. Finally, some of the caregivers claimed that, because they lacked knowledge about dementia, they had not been able to interpret the symptoms correctly. One of them noted that he had not reacted on his father's worries about his mother: ... *he starts to complain that she is so forgetful and this and that. And I didn't realize that this was memory loss.* Hence, the caregivers needed more knowledge about the symptoms, as one of them said: *...it would be good to get much more education and information about it.* Another caregiver added that there was a particular need for information in the beginning of the disease process: *...to identify early symptoms.* Furthermore, some of them called for more public discussion about dementia: *...they need to write a lot more in the papers, bring much more to the radio...,* but at the same time it was stressed that this should be done professionally and that the debate must be based on knowledge and respect.

At this second stage in Wilsons [27] model, the caregivers thoughts about what was happening with the patents were still unclear and as a result their need for information poorly defined [15]. Although they did come across information that made them realize that there were changes in the patients' behaviour, their interpretation of the information, or the sense that they made of it, did not provide them with answers that eventually proved to be helpful at bridging their knowledge gap and allow them to move on [13].

This stage lasted until the patients' condition either became seriously worse, or a particular incident took place, which was too critical to normalise and discount. The change lead to the third stage, "Suspecting – Purposive information seeking begins".

3.3   Stage 3: Suspecting – Purposive Information Seeking Begins

When the patients conditions had worsened so much that the caregivers had realized that something serious was happening with their health the caregivers moved on to the third stage in Wilsons model [27]. One of them explained what made her suspect that something severe was happening with her husband's health so: *Because there was so much personality change. He started to come with all sorts of ideas, all kinds of conspiracy theories...* While another caregiver described what got her thinking about her mother's condition in the following way: *Her behaviour mostly...and stopped doing things that she was used to do...and we noticed that she got anxiety attacks which we had not experienced before.* Thus, the information that the caregivers detected, and which made them ask themselves if something more serious was happening to their family members than they had understood previously, vary.

In some cases the caregivers together with the patient recognized that they needed to understand better what was going on: *Both we and she herself had realized that there was something, her brain was failing,* said one of them. In other cases, the information were provided by proxy, when persons outside the family alerted the caregivers about how severe the situation was, or as one of them stated: *...others had noticed that something was happening.* Another caregiver said that her father had been recovering from a different disease, when his doctor noticed the symptoms: *She had just started to notice that he had begun to forget his keys and something like that, but nothing serious.* There was, furthermore, an example of a patient who was the first one to understand that something was seriously wrong. Her husband described this so: *In the beginning our friends were joking and saying "well you have Alzheimer" or "it's just the age". But she realized that this was more...*

After the caregivers had acknowledged that they could no longer interpret the behaviour changes of the patients in the way that they had done before, they realized that more information was needed about what might be happening. As a result they began to express their thoughts more clearly and ask questions that could better help them to understand what was going on. By doing so, they managed to develop the third level of information need (formalized need) when it is possible to use "qualified and rational" statements to describe what information is needed [15].

At this stage the caregivers used both opportunistic and purposive seeking, to get information that could help them to clarify what might be happening. They monitored the patients with the purpose of collecting information about their behaviour, before making a decision about the next step: *So when we had been checking her for a while we had realize that this was something strange...,* said one of them. Some described information seeking by proxy, or as one of them noted: *...she immediately contacted me and said: "Something is happening to your mother".* They also communicated and shared information with other members of the family, or their close friends, and compared information in an attempt to clarify what should be done. Sometimes they searched in information sources to learn about the symptoms that they had noticed and what it might mean. This could be books or other printed sources: *Of course I had been reading and reading, because I was beginning to suspect this*, stated one of them. Some of them used online sources as the following illustrates: *I completely lost myself online… the FAAS site and international websites.* To do this, the caregivers needed to reach the fourth level of information need, the compromised need, when they were able to express what they were seeking clearly enough to fit the information system [15].

Hence, various ways were used by the caregivers, to try to find an explanation, or some confirmation, in order to reach a conclusion about what could possibly be wrong, and what should be done about it. As they sought to create a new sense of what was happening, the caregivers used whatever strategy they possessed to seek information that could help them to bridge their cognitive gap, in order to be able to move on [13].

When the caregivers entered the third stage, the disease had sometimes progressed so much that it took a relatively short time before they reached the conclusion that a medical advice was needed. In other cases, this stage could last for some years.

A few of the caregivers reported that knowledge about dementia had existed within their families, which had helped them to interpret the information. One of them explained this so: *He has several siblings and two of them had been diagnosed with this before they died.* There were also a few examples of caregivers who worked within the health system and therefore had some knowledge about aging diseases. One of them said: *I naturally come from the health sector and I was perhaps the first one who realized that this was not alright, it was not just like a normal old age degradation.* Thus, knowledge about dementia can help people to recognize the symptoms of dementia, which in turn allows them to act more quickly on it and seek medical attention.

4   Discussion and Conclusion

The aim of the study was to explore the information behaviour of informal caregivers of people with dementia, from the time when they first notice a change in the patients' behaviour, until a decision is made that medical attention is needed. The study indicates that Wilson's temporal model [27], together with Taylor's [15] model of the development of the information need and Dervin's sense making theory [13], was helpful at explaining what happens at these initial stages in the caregivers information behaviour. The analysis revealed a certain correspondence between how the caregivers' information behaviour developed and the initial stages in Wilson's temporal model of how caregivers experience the process of the Alzheimer's disease [27]. In line with the model, three stages were identified in the caregivers' information behaviour: (1) Information about the disease is noticed; (2) Interpretation of information – Normalizing and discounting; (3) Suspecting – Purposive information seeking begins.

During the first two stages, "Information about the disease is noticed" and "Interpretation of information – Normalising and discounting", Taylors [15] model was useful at explaining how the caregivers information needs advanced from vague ideas that something might be happening to the patients, to realizing that this was indeed the case and that they needed somehow to explain it. However, as their thoughts regarding this were very unclear, the caregivers were not able to form questions and seek answers about it, or seek information on purpose. Thus, they only received information that something might be wrong through opportunistic seeking [12, 17–19], as they unexpectedly witnessed the patients altered behaviour patterns. When they sought to interpret the information, they normalized and discounted it as a sign of something else than dementia. As a result, the caregivers attempts to define their knowledge gap and how it might be resolved were not successful. They were in fact stuck in time and space, incapable of bridging the gap in their knowledge and move forward, as described by the sense making theory [13].

When the caregivers understood that they could not normalize and discount the information which they encountered, they moved on to the third stage in their information behaviour "Suspecting – Purposive information seeking begins". It was during this stage, that the caregivers managed to reach the level of formalized information need [14], when they could begin to ask more direct questions about what might we wrong with the patients, discuss their thoughts about it and compare it with the ideas of others. By doing so, the caregivers were able to reach the fourth level of information need and translate what they wanted to know into a search strategy (compromised need) [14]. This made it possible for them to use more various ways of information seeking, both opportunistic and purposive seeking [11, 17–19], to acquire information that they could make sense of. Thus, it was first after they had fully developed their information need that the caregivers were able to get information that they could use to bridge their knowledge gap, and move forward to the decision that a medical advice was needed for the patients [13].

According to Wilson [27], old age is the main reason why symptoms of Alzheimer are being normalized and discounted at the second stage in the temporal model. Keady and Nolan [28] also found this often to be the case. The findings of the present study show that age could act as a hindrance for interpreting the information encountered as signs of dementia, either because the changes that the caregivers noticed were believed to be normal for a person of old age, or because the patients were considered too young to have dementia. Although the likelihood of getting dementia increases with age it is not confined to old age. The need to be aware of young-onset dementia, where the traditional criteria has been patients younger than 65 years, has been stressed [32]. However, several other factors that lead the caregivers to interpret the information wrongly were identified in the study, such as the patients other medical conditions, their personality traits or even the abilities or talents that they had possessed. In particular, when the disease progressed slowly, it became difficult for the caregivers to piece the information about disperse incidents together to get a more complete picture of what was going on. While lack of knowledge could lead the caretakers to normalize and discount the information that they noticed at the second stage of the information behaviour process, caregivers who had prior knowledge about dementia reported that at the third stage in the process it had helped them to interpret the information that they detected correctly.

It needs to be kept in mind that the findings are from small scale qualitative study, and cannot be generated to the wider population of caregivers of patients with dementia. Nevertheless the findings may help to shed light on what characterizes the initial stages in the caregivers' information behaviour.

To conclude, having dementia diagnosed as early as possible allows people to benefit from potential treatments, care and support that is available, in addition to making plans about the future [4]. It is therefore essential that informal caregivers and patients have knowledge about the symptoms of dementia so that they can react on it. From the time when the informal caregivers first began to notice symptoms of dementia, until they reached the decision to seek medical attention for the patients, their information behaviour went through a sequence of three stages, where their information need gradually developed from a vague idea about a cognitive gap at the first stage, "Information about the disease is noticed", to become a formalized need at the third stage, "Suspecting – Purposive information seeking begins". During these stages the caregivers unexpectedly discovered information. To be able to seek information and knowledge on purpose, and subsequently realize that the patients needed medical attention, it was necessary for them to reach the third stage in the information behaviour process and fully develop their information need. The second stage of the process, "Interpretation of information – Normalizing and discounting", was particularly complicated as the caregivers misinterpreted the information about dementia that they came across as signs of something else.

More public discussion by professionals about dementia could provide the caregivers and the patients with a better understanding of the disease. This in turn might help to shorten the time spent at the second stage, making it possible for the caretakers to enter the third stage more quickly, and thereby to come to the decision to seek medical advice.

5   Limitations and Implications for Future Research

As noted above, the findings from the study cannot be generalized to the population of informal caregivers of patients with dementia. The purpose with using qualitative methods was to gain a deep understanding of various aspects related to the information behaviour and the support provided by the participants, from their own point of view [28]. Furthermore, since aspects of the information behaviour of informal caregivers of people with dementia were examined which few studies have investigated so far, qualitative methods were chosen because they are considered useful for better understanding phenomena which little knowledge exists about [33]. In future it might be of interest to examine the topic by using quantitative methods in order to find out how findings about information behaviour relate to the wider population of informal caregivers of people with dementia. Achieving more specific knowledge concerning the most important factors regarding the dissemination of information about the early signs of dementia, as well as the disease itself, might of significance for the health professionals who are responsible for providing this information.

The emotional aspect of the caregivers' information behaviour would also be worth consideration. Previous studies suggest that worries about dementia is widespread in Western populations [34]. Furthermore, there are indications that negative feelings, such as fear of the disease, can lead to people refusing to face up to the possibility that their family members may have dementia and avoid talking about it [35]. Although the participants in the current study did express various feelings, this was not systematically analyzed, nor was it a specific focus of the study. Nevertheless, in the second stage of the caregivers information behaviour, Interpretation of information – Normalizing and discounting, it was clear that negative emotions were acknowledged and that they played a role in delaying the recognition that the patients may have dementia. Thus, studies aimed at understanding how psychological factors, such as negative emotional reactions towards dementia, affect the caregivers' information behaviour may be useful for identifying how it can be countered.

The focus of the study was limited by the period of examination, from when the signs of dementia began to appear until a decision to seek medical advice was made. In future, it would be of significance to examine the information behaviour of the informal caregivers during and after the time of diagnosis of dementia. How well does the health system, for example, meet the informal caregivers needs for information while the diagnosis is being made? Likewise, how are they supported with information and knowledge after the diagnosis?

As people with dementia are expected to make up an increasing proportion of the population [3], it becomes of increasingly significant for future research to be aimed at how the patients with dementia, and their relatives who care for them, can be supported. Attaining better knowledge and understanding about the complex nature of the informal caregivers' information behaviour, and the diverse factors related to it, can aid to achieve this.

References

1. Loos, E.F., Haddon, H., Mante-Meijer, E.A. (eds.): The Social Dynamics of Information and Communication Technology. Ashgate, Aldershot (2008)
2. Triantafillou, J., Naiditch, M., Repkov, K. et al.: Informal Care in the Long-Term Care System: European Overview Paper. European Centre for Social Welfare Policy and Research, Athens, Vienna (2010). http://www.euro.centre.org/data/1278594816_84909.pdf
3. World Health Organization: Global Age Friendly Cities: A Guide. World Health Organization, Geneva (2007). http://www.who.int/ageing/publications/Global_age_friendly_cities_Guide_English.pdf
4. Prince, M., Bryce, R., Ferri, C.: World Alzheimer Report 2011: The Benefits of Early Diagnosis and Intervention: Executive Summary. Alzheimer's Disease International (ADI), London (2011)
5. Finkel, S.: Introduction to behavioural and psychological symptoms of dementia. Int. J. Ger. Psyc. 15, 2–4 (2000)
6. Alzougool, B., Chang, S., Gray, K.: The nature and constitution of informal carers' information needs: what You don't know You need is as important as what You want to know. Inf. Res. 18(1), paper 563 (2013). http://InformationR.net/ir/18-1/paper563.html
7. Hepworth, M.A.: Framework for understanding user requirements for an information service: defining the needs of informal carers. J. Am. Soc. Inf. Sci. Technol. 55(8), 695–708 (2004)
8. Odhiambo, F., Harrison, J., Hepworth, M.: The information needs of informal carers: an analysis of the use of the micro - moment time line interview. Libr. Inf. Res. 27(86), 19–29 (2003)
9. Pálsdóttir, Á.: Elderly peoples' information behaviour: accepting support from relatives. Libri Int. J. Libr. Inf. Serv. 62(2), 135–144 (2012a)

10. Pálsdóttir, Á.: relatives as supporters of elderly peoples' information behavior. Inf. Res. **17**(4), paper 546 (2012b). http://InformationR.net/ir/17-4/paper546.html
11. Fourie, I.: information needs and information behaviour of patients and their family members in a cancer palliative care setting: an exploratory study of an existential context from different perspectives. Inf. Res. **13**(4), paper 360 (2008). http://InformationR.net/ir/13-4/paper360.html
12. Wilson, T.D.: Human information behaviour. Informing Sci. **3**(2), 49–55 (2000). http://inform.nu/Articles/Vol3/v3n2p49-56.pdf
13. Dervin, B.: From the mind's eye of the user: the sense-making qualitative-quantitative methodology. In: Glazier, J., Powell, R.R. (eds.) Qualitative Research in Information Management, pp. 61–84. Libraries Unlimited, Englewood (1992)
14. Belkin, N.J., Oddy, R.N., Brooks, H.M.: ASK for information retrieval: part I. Background and theory. J. Documentation **38**(2), 61–71 (1982)
15. Taylor, R.S.: Question-negotiation and information seeking in libraries. Coll. Res. Libr. **29**, 178–194 (1968)
16. Kuhlthau, C.: Seeking Meaning: A Process Approach to Library and Information Services. Libraries Unlimited, London (2004)
17. McKenzie, P.J.: A model of information practices in accounts of everyday-life information seeking. J. Documentation **59**(1), 19–40 (2003)
18. Pálsdóttir, Á.: The connection between purposive information seeking and information encountering: a study of Icelanders' health and lifestyle information seeking. J. Documentation **66**(2), 224–244 (2010)
19. Erdelez, S.: Information encountering: a conceptual framework for accidental information discovery. In: Vakkari, P., Savolainen, R., Dervin, B. (eds.) ISIC Proceedings of an International Conference on Research in Information Needs, Seeking and Use in Different Contexts, Tampere, Finland, 14–16 August 1996, pp. 412–431. Taylor Graham, London (1996)
20. Thompsell, A., Lovestone, S.: Out of sight out of mind? Support and information given to distant and near relatives of those with dementia. Int. J. Geriatr. Psychiatry **17**, 804–807 (2002)
21. Wald, C., Fahy, M., Walker, Z., Livingston, G.: What to tell dementia caregivers: the rule of threes. Int. J. Geriatr. Psychiatry **18**, 313–317 (2003)
22. Wackerbartha, S.B., Johnson, M.M.S.: Essential information and support needs of family caregivers. Patient Educ. Couns. **47**(2), 95–100 (2002)
23. Hirakawa, Y., Kuzuya, M., Enoki, H., Uemura, K.: Information needs and sources of family caregivers of home elderly patients. Arch. Gerontol. Geriatr. **52**, 202–205 (2011)
24. Komarahadi, F.L., Ruf, D., Hüell, M., Härter, M.: Information needs of physicians, professional carers and family carers for an evidence-based dementia website. Psychiatr. Prax. **39**(1), 34–39 (2012)
25. Harland, J.A., Bath, P.A.: Understanding the information behaviours of carers of people with dementia: a critical review of models from information science. Aging Ment. Health **12**(4), 467–477 (2008)
26. Kazmer, M.M., Glueckauf, R.L., Ma, J., Burnett, K.: Information use environments of african-american dementia caregivers over the course of cognitive-behavioral therapy for depression. Libr. Inf. Sci. Res. **35**(3), 191–199 (2013)
27. Wilson, H.S.: Family caregivers: the experience of Alzheimer's disease. Appl. Nurs. Res. **2**(1), 40–44 (1989)
28. Keady, J., Nolan, M.R.: The dynamics of dementia: working together, working separately, or working alone? In: Nolan, M.R., Lundh, U., Grant, G., Keady, J. (eds.) Partnerships in Family Care: Understanding the Caregiving Career, pp. 15–32. Open University Press, Maidenhead (2003)

29. Taylor, S.J., Bogdan, R.: Introduction to Qualitative Research Methods: A Guide-Book and Resource. Wiley, New York (1998)
30. Kvale, S.: Doing Interview. Sage Publication, London (2007)
31. Strauss, A.L.: Qualitative Analysis for Social Scientists. Cambridge University Press, Cambridge (1987)
32. Rossor, M.N., Fox, N.C., Mummery, C.H., et al.: The diagnosis of young-onset dementia. Lancet Neurol. 9(8), 793–806 (2010)
33. Strauss, A., Corbin, J.: Basics of Qualitative Research: Grounded Theory Procedures and Techniques. Sage, Newbury Park (1990)
34. Kessler, E.-M., Catherine, E., Bowen, C.E., Baer, M., Lutz, F., Wahl, H.-W.: Dementia worry: a psychological examination of an unexplored phenomenon. Eur. J. Ageing 9(4), 275–284 (2012)
35. Corner, L., Bond, J.: Being at risk of dementia: fears and anxieties of older adults. J. Aging Stud. 18, 143–155 (2004)

Usability Evaluation on User Interface of Electronic Wheelchair

Cheng-Min Tsai[1(✉)], Chih-Kuan Lin[2], Sing Li[1],
and Wang-Chin Tsai[2]

[1] Department of Creative Product Design and Management,
Far East University, Tainan, Taiwan
ansel.tsai@gmail.com
[2] Department and Graduate School of Product and Media Design,
Fo Guang University, Jiaoxi, Taiwan

Abstract. The purpose of this study is to focus on "User Interface Design of Electronic Wheelchair." Two stages were set for this study. First, the questionnaire survey was used to discuss the interface design of an electronic wheelchair; second, the observation method was used to understand the participant's operation of the electronic wheelchair and its operation time was measured. There were 27 participants in the first stage with convenience sampling from a design college in Far East University. In this stage, 49 icons were designed by the focus group, and the icons were divided based on the following functions: power, alarm, direction, speed adjustment, battery, and stop icon. In the second stage, there were 20 undergraduates with convenience sampling from the same college. All of them had no operation experience of the electronic wheelchair. The results showed that the power icon, alarm icon, speed adjustment icon, and the battery icon demonstrated that the new icons were better than the present icons. The results also showed that there was no significant variation in the usage of the wheelchair between the male and female participants. On the other hand, the correlation analysis performed for the operation concept revealed that the operation of power and the operation of speed adjustment exhibited a high correlation. The left/right operation and the forward/backward operation exhibited a significant direct correlation.

Keywords: Electronic wheelchair · Icon design · User interface design

1 Introduction

Taiwan is the one of most important countries that manufactures electronic wheelchairs. The major sales of the wheelchairs are through exports to the European Union and USA. For most users facing difficulty in travel, it is one of the common ways of assistance through the mobility assistive technology (Souza *et al.* 2010). Therefore, more time must be invested in the development and design of electronic wheelchairs and the future of intelligent auxiliary system. However, when users operate the electronic wheelchair, they should be able to accurately sense the surrounding environment

© Springer International Publishing AG 2017
J. Zhou and G. Salvendy (Eds.): ITAP 2017, Part II, LNCS 10298, pp. 467–474, 2017.
DOI: 10.1007/978-3-319-58536-9_37

and predict possible obstacles or hazards. For most users, electronic wheelchair control is still difficult. The manufacturing process for an electronic wheelchair would include (1) seat and posture transformation mechanism system; (2) drive system: drive motor, reducer (gear group), electromagnetic brake, clutch, anti-tilting wheel, etc.; (3) electronic control system: control mode, input mode, controller, monitor, and power supply; (4) human-computer interface: input device and output device. The key aspect in operating an electronic wheel chair are accessibility and maneuverability. According to the World Health Survey in 2015, approximately 785 million people are suffering from disability and living inconvenience globally (Mortenson *et al.* 2015). National Institute on Aging, NIA (2010) points out that more than 38% of the people with difficulty in walking are over 65 years of age. From 2000 to 2010, approximately 3.1% of disabled people changed their traditional wheelchairs to electronic wheelchairs (Loraine *et al.* 2010). There are approximately 2 million new wheelchair users every year. The traditional wheelchair industry revenue grew at an average annual rate of 2.5% from 2009 to 2014. Approximately 1.825 million wheelchair users are of the age of 65 or are older. Particularly, 11.2% of adult wheelchair users are graduates, compared to the 21.6% of the general adult population (Reznik 2015).

Karma Co. Ltd. is the one of the most important companies that manufactures electronic wheelchairs in Taiwan. Karma's product occupation in the market of Spain was 50%, Japan was 20%, Taiwan was 80%, Singapore was 60%, and Thailand was 80% in 2016. Karma's KP-25.2 electronic wheelchair was suitable for both indoor and outdoor use in Taiwan. Figures 1 and 2 show the appearance, user interface, and size of an electronic wheelchair. As the research report of Transparency Market Research (TMR) shows that the Global electronic wheelchair market was valued at USD 1.23 billion in 2013, growing at an estimated CAGR of 19.2% over the forecast period from

Fig. 1. Karma KP-25.2 electronic wheelchair (on the right side is the user interface of the electronic wheelchair)

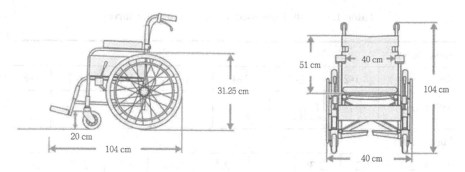

Fig. 2. KP-25.2 electronic wheelchair

2014 to 2020. Electronic wheelchairs are the battery supported wheelchairs which reduce the user's dependence on any external human assistance for movement (TMR 2017).

In 1993, Nielsen defined the concept of 'Usability Engineer' (Nielsen and Kaufmann 1993; del Galdo and Nielsen 1996). Nielsen stated that usability is a measurement of the quality that the user experiences when interacting with a system. He also states that good usability is composed of learnability, low error rate, memorability, efficiency, and satisfaction (Preece *et al.* 1994). To understand the experience of a user operating an electronic wheelchair, the usability evaluation for the user interface of an electronic wheelchair is presented in this study.

2 Research Method

The study was conducted in two stages. First, the questionnaire survey was set for the interface design of the electronic wheelchair; second, participants operating the electronic wheelchair were observed.

2.1 Image Stimuli

Table 1 shows the 49 icons used in the questionnaire survey. The following six group icons were included: power icons, alarm icons, direction icons, speed adjustment icons, battery status icons, and stop icons. All the icons were monochromatic shapes. A total of 27 participants assessed these 49 icons on a scale of 10 ('1' indicated a poor icon; '10' indicated the best icon) on the questionnaire.

Table 1. The 49 icons used in the questionnaire survey.

Power icons							
No.	1-1	1-2	1-3	1-4	1-5	1-6	1-7	1-8
Icon								

Alarm icons								
No.	2-1	2-2	2-3	2-4	2-5	2-6	2-7	2-8	2-9
Icon									

Speed adjustment icon							
No.	3-1	3-2	3-3	3-4	3-5	3-6	3-7	3-8
Icon								

Direction icon							
No.	4-1	4-2	4-3	4-4	4-5	4-6	4-7	4-8
Icon								

Battery status icon							
No.	5-1	5-2	5-3	5-4	5-5	5-6	5-7	5-8
Icon								

Stop icon							
No.	6-1	6-2	6-3	6-4	6-5	6-6	6-7	6-8
Icon								

2.2   Observation

In the second stage, 20 undergraduates from Department of Creative Product Design and Management at Far East University in Taiwan were selected on the basis of convenience sampling. Those with less than perfect vision used glasses or contact lenses to correct their vision; hence, all subjects were able to see normally. All of them had no experience in operating the electronic wheelchair. The procedure of operation included task introduction, operation of electronic wheelchair, and questionnaire

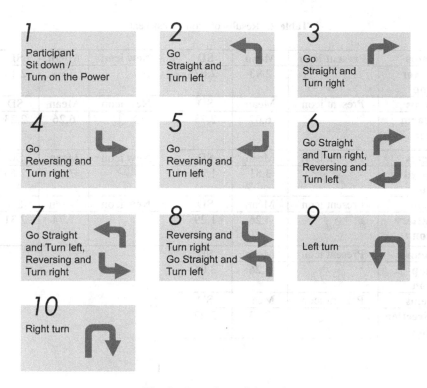

Fig. 3. Procedure of the task

survey (subjective satisfaction). The experiment for observing participants' operation experience of the electronic wheelchair was divided into ten steps (see Fig. 3). One-way ANOVA was used to analyze the operation time between the male and female participants by using SPSS software. Figure 3 shows the procedure of the task.

3 Data Analysis and Results

3.1 Subjective Assessment Analysis

Data analysis was done according to the participants' subjective assessment of the icon cognitive. The analysis of mean and standard deviation (SD) results demonstrated that the new icons are better than present icons. The power icon, alarm icon, speed adjustment icon, and the battery icon showed that the new icons are better than the present icons. Norman (1988) pointed out that a good interface (or feedback) provides good user experience (Shackel 1990). These subjective assessment results suggest that new icons will lead to a correspondingly better experience. The power icon, alarm icon,

Table 2. Results of icon assessment

Items	Present icon	Mean	SD	New icon	Mean	SD
Power Icon		2.93	2.02		7.93	2.13
Items	Present icon	Mean	SD	New icon	Mean	SD
Alarm Icon		6.07	2.73		6.26	2.23
Items	Present icon	Mean	SD	New icon	Mean	SD
Speed Icon		3.81	1.78		7.00	2.65
Items	Present icon	Mean	SD	New icon	Mean	SD
Battery Icon		4.26	1.29		7.74	2.31
Items	Present icon	Mean	SD			
Stop Icon		6.26	3.05			
Items	Present icon	Mean	SD			
Direction Icon		7.63	2.27			

speed adjustment icon, and battery icon received relatively high scores from the participants. Since the present electronic wheelchair had no stop function, the direction-control was based on the control lever. Conversely, when the participants performed the stop icon and direction icon assessment tasks, the participants gave icon 6 a score of 4 and icon 4 a score of 7. (see Table 2).

3.2   Results of Analysis

Generally, when participants used the electronic wheelchair, they could easily navigate forward and backward, as well as turn right and left by using the control lever (see Fig. 4). The results showed that there was no significant variation between the usage by male and female participants ($F_{(1, 198)} = .065$, $p > .05$). The correlation analysis performed between the tasks revealed that the operation of power and of speed adjustment exhibited significant direct correlation ($r = .63$, $p < .001$). The left/right and forward/backward operations exhibited a significant direct correlation ($r = .97$, $p < .001$).

Fig. 4. Operation of electronic wheelchair

3.3 Suggestion for Icons Design

The new icons were selected from the icons that received a higher score in the questionnaire. As shown in Table 2, this study developed the user interface of the electronic wheelchair, as shown in Fig. 5. The right side of Fig. 5 shows the new icons of the user interface; the icons from top to bottom are the power switch, alarm, speed adjustment, and the battery icon. The speed adjustment should replace the layout from left/right to top/bottom. The upper part of the speed adjustment icon is for increasing the speed, and the lower part is for decreasing the speed. The battery icon should be integrated into LED's backlight to indicate battery life to help the user understand the battery status at night.

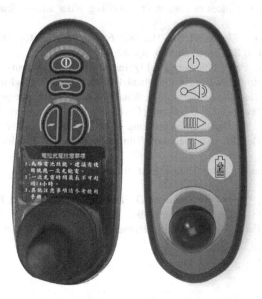

Fig. 5. Simulated icon for user interface of electronic wheelchair

4 Discussion

Norman (1988) observed that the mental model included the user's model, design model, and system image. He had advocated that the user interface should be based on user-centered design. In this study, we found that the user interface, which included the power icon, alarm icon, speed adjustment icon, and the battery icon, should be redesigned to provide good user experience. This study suggests a new power icon, alarm icon, speed adjustment icon, and battery icon. The 7 Principles of Universal Design guide the design of environments, products, and communications. The following 7 principles were included: 1. equitable use; 2. flexibility in use; 3. simple and intuitive use; 4. perceptible information; 5. tolerance for error; 6. low physical effort; 7. size and space for approach and use. In the second stage, we found that the electronic wheelchair could be operated easily. It was observed that the electronic wheelchair is very simple and intuitive in terms of direction operation for a novel user. KP-25.2 is in accordance with items 1, 2, 3, and 6 of the 7 Principles of Universal Design.

Acknowledgments. The authors would like to thank the participants for supporting this research and providing insightful comments.

References

Souza, A., Kelleher, A., Cooper, R., Cooper, R.A., Iezzoni, L.I., Collins, D.M.: Multiple sclerosis and mobility-related assistive technology: systematic review of literature. J. Rehabil. Res. Dev. **47**(3), 213–224 (2010)

Mortenson, W.B., Hammell, K.W., Luts, A., Soles, C., Miller, W.C.: The power of power wheelchairs: mobility choices of community-dwelling, older adults. Scand. J. Occup. Ther. **22**, 394–401 (2015)

Loraine, A., West, S.C., Goodkind, D., He, W.: 65 + in the United States: 2010, Current Population Reports, U.S. Census Bureau, pp. 23–212 (2010)

Reznik, R.: Wheelchair, Facts, Numbers and Figures, Healthcare Company, USA (2015). http://kdsmartchair.com/blogs/news/18706123-wheelchair-facts-numbers-and-figures-infographic

Transparency Market Research, Electric Wheelchair Market – High Degree of Technological Advancements in Developed & Developing Countries, Transparency Market Research (2017)

Nielsen, J., Kaufmann, M.: Usability Engineering (1993). ISBN: 978-0-12-518406-9

Norman, D.: The Design of Everyday Things. Doubleday Business (1988). ISBN: 978-0-465-06710-7

del Galdo, E., Nielsen, J.: International User Interfaces. Wiley, New York (1996). ISBN: 0-471-14965-9

Preece, J., Rogers, Y., Sharpe, H., Benyon, D., Holland, S., Carey, T.: Human – Computer Interaction. Addison – Wesley, Boston (1994)

Shackel, B.: Human Factors and Usability, Human-Computer Interaction Selected Readings, pp. 27–41 (1990)

Fall Detection Based on Skeleton Data

Tao Xu[1,2(✉)] and Yun Zhou[3]

[1] School of Software and Microelectronics, Northwestern Polytechnical University,
127 West Youyi Road, Xi'an 710072, Shaanxi, People's Republic of China
xutao@nwpu.edu.cn

[2] State Key Laboratory for Manufacturing Systems Engineering, Xi'an Jiaotong University,
99 Yan Cheung Road, Xi'an 710054, Shaanxi, People's Republic of China

[3] School of Education, Shaanxi Normal University, 199 South Chang'an Road,
Xi'an 710062, Shaanxi, People's Republic of China
zhouyun@snnu.edu.cn

Abstract. Fall is one of most threats to elders' health when their living alone. We propose a fall detection method based on skeleton data getting from Kinect. This method choose biomechanics equilibrium as main feature and adopt Long Short-Term Memory networks (LSTM) to detect a fall. It does not require elders to wear any other sensors and can protect elders' privacy comparing with other vision-based methods. The performances show that it can detect 95% fall. Our method provides a feasible solution for fall detection.

Keywords: Fall detection · Skeleton data · Biomechanics equilibrium

1 Introduction

With the advancement of medical technology, the life span of human beings have been significantly prolonged, and the aging of population has become a serious problem faced in China. Data from Ministry of Civil Affairs of China shows that China's population over the age of 60 is more than two hundred million, and will reach 243 million accounted for 17% of the total population by 2020. Due to disease, age and other factors, many elderly people cannot take good care of their selves. One of the kinds of dangerous behavior is a fall, which is one of the main threats to elders' health [1]. According to the WHO Global Report on Falls Prevention in Older Age [2], about 28%–35% of 65-year-olds fall every year, and for 70-year-olds this number will rise to 32–42%. The frequency of falls increases year by year with age and physical debility [3]. Vellas et al. [4] conducted a follow-up study of 482 elderly people who lived independently in the community for 24 months. The study showed that the accidental fall was the leading cause of accidental death in elderly people over 85 years of age. 61% of participants (53.7% of men and 65.7% of women) experienced at least one fall during a two-year study. Detecting a fall can effectively reduce the risk of injury for the elderly, which is a very significance condition for the elderly healthy living at home.

© Springer International Publishing AG 2017
J. Zhou and G. Salvendy (Eds.): ITAP 2017, Part II, LNCS 10298, pp. 475–483, 2017.
DOI: 10.1007/978-3-319-58536-9_38

Fall has a widely accepted definition by scholars: non-deliberate movements toward the ground or lower (except for continuous blows, loss of consciousness, paralysis, and epileptic consequences) [5]. There are many researchers' attempts to separate the fall behavior from normal daily behaviors. This is a difficult task, because many normal daily behaviors, such as sitting down, Lying down, are very similar with falling [3]. In recent years, with the advancement of sensor technology, more and more scholars explored on the fall detection problems. Initially researchers use wearable acceleration sensor to distinguish a fall from different behaviors based on change of the acceleration [6–8]. These methods can effectively identify some kinds of fall behavior. Then many scholars detect a fall according to different falling end posture (Ending Posture) feature by using image-processing technology [9–11]. Due to the two-dimensional image data's limitations, the accuracy of recognition has been affected by different kinds of issue like how to distinguish between foreground and background, how to accurately track human behavior and so on.

Falls in biomechanical research can be seen as an uncontrolled imbalanced movement of the human body. An imbalance is an important feature of fall behavior. Kinect, a three-dimensional somatosensory vision sensor, provides a new possibility for the study of fall behavior. It can dynamically capture the motion of human body in three-dimensional space so that researchers can analyze human posture more accurately, which greatly improve the ability of human behavior analysis. In addition, differing from the traditional vision sensor, Kinect provides dynamic position information of skeletal nodes in the three dimension. It can protect users' privacy while analyzing behavior based on skeleton data.

We study fall detection based on changes of human balance by skeleton data. The research includes three aspects, shown in Fig. 1:

1. Building a human bionic dynamic mass model by skeleton joints data from Kinect and human mass distribution and computing dynamic positions of Center of Mass (COM);
2. Determining balance by calculating the region of Support of Base (SOB) and Line of Gravity (LOG);
3. A fall detection algorithms based on the recurrent neural networks (RNN) by imbalanced posture features.

Uncontrollable imbalance behavior will result in a fall, but the controllable will not, like sitting or lying. Posture and body movement speed is significant different between controllable and uncontrollable imbalance behavior. Skeleton joints' relative position and speed are used to describe body's postures as input features. The Short-Term Memory networks (LSTM) is used to detect fall based on these features.

We have evaluated our fall detection method on the existing database [12]. The results show that our fall detection algorithm by studying human biomechanics equilibrium and posture recognition can detect a fall (95%).

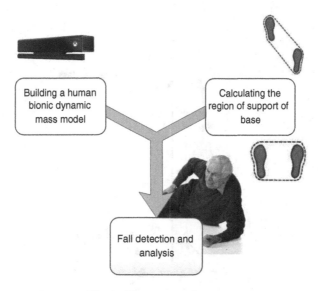

Fig. 1. Three research aspects

2 Human Body Balance Study

According to a detailed analysis of the lack of the current fall detection methods mentioned above, our paper provides a fall detection method based on skeleton data by studying status of human body balance. Firstly, we will investigate human body balance in this section.

2.1 Balance Definition

Body balance refers to the ability of an individual to maintain the Center of Mass (COM)'s Line of Gravity (LOG) within the body's Base of Support (BOS) region shown in Fig. 1. Fall starts from an imbalance situation of human body. When imbalance of human body can be detected, the fall might be detected. Imbalance is a key feature of imminent fall. The basic idea of fall detection is to determine whether the body balance by relative position of LOG and BOS, (most of the actions in daily life, such as standing and walking, belong to a state of equilibrium). If imbalance: (fall is an action of imbalance, sitting down and lying are not equilibrium either.) we will try to find whether human will fall or not by LSTM (Fig. 2).

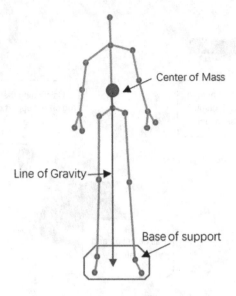

Fig. 2. The features of body balance

2.2 Balance Feature Extraction

Determining COM. The balance situation depends on position relationship between COM and BOS. COM is the unique point where the weighted relative position of the distributed mass sums to zero [13]. COM of human body depends on the gender and the position of the limb [14] in a standing posture, it is typically about 10 cm lower than the navel, near the top of the hip bones. However, COM of human body is not concentrated in a particular point during human moving. COM cannot be get directly. The main idea to get COM of human has four steps [15]:

1. Calculating the center of mass location of each segment of the body
2. Calculating the torque about the reference point due to each segment based on the segment's mass and position.
3. Summing the torques about the reference point for all the segments.
4. Dividing the sum of the torques by the total body mass to determine the center of mass location with respect to the reference point.

In real situations, we employ skeleton data from Kinect and Demspter's body segment parameters [16] to estimate COM position. Kinect is a line of motion sensing input devices by Microsoft, which can detect up to six users at the same time and compute their skeletons in 3D with 25 joints representing body junctions like the feet, knees, hips, shoulders, elbows, wrists, head. COM of segment can be determined from the proximal and distal point coordinates and the segment length percent, all the parameter mentioned above can get from [16] (Table 1).

Table 1. The mass and coefficient of human segment [16]

Body segment	Segmental mass/Total body mass (m/M)	CM/Segment length	
		Proximal	Distal
Head and neck	0.081	1.000	N/A
Thorax and abdomen	0.355	0.500	0.500
Upper arms	0.028	0.436	0.564
Forearms	0.016	0.430	0.570
Hands	0.006	0.506	0.494
Pelvis	0.142	0.105	0.895
Thighs	0.100	0.433	0.567
Legs	0.0465	0.433	0.567
Feet	0.0145	0.500	0.500

We improve the method [17] to get COM of human from two dimensions to three dimensions. In short, the method can be summarized in the equation for two steps:

1. Computing COM of each body's segment by following formulas:

$$x_{sCOM} = x_p l_p + x_d l_d \tag{1}$$

$$y_{sCOM} = y_p l_p + y_d l_d \tag{2}$$

$$z_{sCOM} = z_p l_p + z_d l_d \tag{3}$$

where x_{sCOM}, y_{sCOM}, z_{sCOM} are coordinates of COM of segmental body; x_p, y_p, z_p are coordinates of proximal ends; x_d, y_d, z_d are coordinates of distal ends; and the percentage of segmental length from the proximal and distal ends are represented by l_p, l_d.

2. Calculating COM of all body by following formulas:

$$x_{COM} = \frac{\sum m_i x_{s_i com}}{M} \tag{4}$$

$$y_{COM} = \frac{\sum m_i y_{s_i com}}{M} \tag{5}$$

$$z_{COM} = \frac{\sum m_i z_{s_i com}}{M} \tag{6}$$

where x_{COM}, y_{COM}, z_{COM} are coordinates of body; m_i is the mass of the ith segment; M is the whole mass of body.

Calculating LOG and SOB. The LOG is important to understand and visualize when determining a person's ability to maintain balance. When the LOG is within the BOS, the person is considered as balance. When the LOG falls outside the BOS, the person is considered as imbalance [18]. Since the direction of the force of gravity through COM is downward, towards the earth, the LOG can be computed by vertical projection of COM.

The BOS refers to the area beneath a person that includes every point of contact that the person makes with the supporting surface [19]. We estimate the BOS by the eclipse covering humans' feet skeleton, shown in Fig. 3.

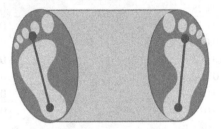

Fig. 3. Support of base estimation

3   Fall Detection Based on LSTM

Fall detection can be convert to sequential data classification problem. Recurrent Neural Networks (RNN) is a very powerful method for dealing with classification for sequence data, but training them has proved to be problematic because the back-propagated gradients either grow or shrink at each time step, so over many time steps they typically explode or vanish [20]

LSTM has been introduced by [21], which have become a crucial ingredient in recent advances with recurrent networks since they are good at learning long-range dependencies [20] and not affected by vanishing and exploding gradient problems. The structure of LSTM is shown in Fig. 4. It introduces a new structure called a memory cell, which is composed of four main elements: an input gate, a forget gate, an output gate and cell activation vectors. The gates serve to modulate the interactions between the memory

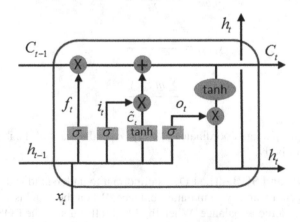

Fig. 4. The structure of LSTM in sequence [23]

cell itself and its environment. The input gate allows incoming signal to alter the state of the memory cell or block it. The output gate allows the state of the memory cell to have an effect on other neurons or prevent it. The forget gate modulates the memory cell's self-recurrent connection, allowing the cell to remember or forget its previous state [22].

The formulas 7 to 12 describe how a model of LSTM works, as shown in below:

$$f_t = \sigma(W_f \cdot [h_{t-1}, x_t] + b_f) \tag{7}$$

$$i_t = \sigma(W_i \cdot [h_{t-1}, x_t] + b_i) \tag{8}$$

$$\tilde{C}_t = \tanh(W_C \cdot [h_{t-1}, x_t] + b_C) \tag{9}$$

$$C_t = f_t * C_{t-1} + i_t * \tilde{C}_t \tag{10}$$

$$o_t = \sigma(W_O \cdot [h_{t-1}, x_t] + b_O) \tag{11}$$

$$h_t = o_t * \tanh(C_t) \tag{12}$$

where i, f, o and C denote input gate, forget gate, output gate, and cell activation vectors respectively, and σ denotes the logistic sigmoid function.

In our fall detection method, we employ that skeleton data per frame is as input of LSTM. When imbalance occurring, LSTM is employed to classify human's activities based skeleton data.

4   Experiments and Evaluation

We employ database [12] to evaluate our fall detection method. In this database, Kinect is employed to record human's actions, which are grouped two main categories: Activity of Daily Living (ADL) and fall. ADL has four types of actions: sit, grasp, walk, lay; and fall has four types of actions depending on direction: front, back, side, and end-up-sit. It contains 11 healthy volunteers from 22 to 39 years old with different height and weight. Every action is recorded in database three times from 11 health volunteers. We random choose 224 actions as training set and the remaining's are testing set.

Gasparrini et al. proposed three algorithms to detect a fall based on this database. First one used variation in the skeleton joint position from Kinect and acceleration of the wrist accelerometer; Second one used the same parameters as first one, but it got data from the accelerometer placed on the waist; Third one added a parameter: distance of the spine base joint from the floor. Comparing with theirs, our method's only use data from one sensor: Kinect, which does not require human to wear any other sensors on the body, and our accuracy is much better than algorithm one and two, a little weaker than algorithm three, as shown in Table 2 below.

Table 2. Results comparison

Name	Data type	Accuracy
Algorithm one	• Skeleton joints • The wrist accelerometer	79%
Algorithm two	• Skeleton joints • The wrist accelerometer	90%
Algorithm three	• Skeleton joints • The waist accelerometer • Distance of the spine base joint from the floor	99%
Ours	• Skeleton joints	95%

5 Conclusion and Future Work

In this paper, we propose a fall detection method based on skeleton data by analyzing human's biomechanics equilibrium. The LSTM is adopted to distinguish fall from other activities. Our method uses only skeleton data from Kinect, it does not require elder to wear any other sensors and get a good performance. It provides a feasible solution for fall detection.

References

1. Noury, N., Fleury, A., Rumeau, P., Bourke, A.K., Laighin, G.O., Rialle, V., Lundy, J.E.: Fall detection - principles and methods. In: 29th Annual International Conference of the IEEE Engineering in Medicine and Biology Society, 2007, EMBS 2007, pp. 1663–1666 (2007)
2. WHO Global Report on Falls Prevention in Older Age. World Health Organization, Geneva, Switzerland (2008)
3. Igual, R., Medrano, C., Plaza, I.: Challenges, issues and trends in fall detection systems. Biomed. Eng. OnLine. **12**, 66 (2013)
4. Vellas, B.J., Wayne, S.J., Garry, P.J., Baumgartner, R.N.: A two-year longitudinal study of falls in 482 community-dwelling elderly adults. J. Gerontol. A Biol. Sci. Med. Sci. **53**, M264–M274 (1998)
5. The prevention of falls in later life. A report of the Kellogg International Work Group on the Prevention of Falls by the Elderly. Dan. Med. Bull. **34**(Suppl 4), 1–24 (1987)
6. Tamura, T., Yoshimura, T., Sekine, M., Uchida, M., Tanaka, O.: A wearable airbag to prevent fall injuries. IEEE Trans. Inf. Technol. Biomed. **13**, 910–914 (2009)
7. Bianchi, F., Redmond, S.J., Narayanan, M.R., Cerutti, S., Lovell, N.H.: Barometric pressure and triaxial accelerometry-based falls event detection. IEEE Trans. Neural Syst. Rehabil. Eng. **18**, 619–627 (2010)
8. Zhang, T., Wang, J., Xu, L., Liu, P.: Fall Detection by wearable sensor and one-class SVM algorithm. In: Huang, D.-S., Li, K., Irwin, G.W. (eds.) Intelligent Computing in Signal Processing and Pattern Recognition, pp. 858–863. Springer, Heidelberg (2006)
9. Vishwakarma, V., Mandal, C., Sural, S.: Automatic detection of human fall in video. In: Ghosh, A., De, R.K., Pal, S.K. (eds.) PReMI 2007. LNCS, vol. 4815, pp. 616–623. Springer, Heidelberg (2007). doi:10.1007/978-3-540-77046-6_76

10. Hazelhoff, L., Han, J., With, P.H.N.: Video-based fall detection in the home using principal component analysis. In: Blanc-Talon, J., Bourennane, S., Philips, W., Popescu, D., Scheunders, P. (eds.) ACIVS 2008. LNCS, vol. 5259, pp. 298–309. Springer, Heidelberg (2008). doi:10.1007/978-3-540-88458-3_27

11. Rougier, C., Meunier, J., St-Arnaud, A., Rousseau, J.: Robust video surveillance for fall detection based on human shape deformation. IEEE Trans. Circ. Syst. Video Technol. **21**, 611–622 (2011)

12. Gasparrini, S., Cippitelli, E., Gambi, E., Spinsante, S., Wåhslén, J., Orhan, I., Lindh, T.: Proposal and experimental evaluation of fall detection solution based on wearable and depth data fusion. In: Loshkovska, S., Koceski, S. (eds.) ICT Innovations 2015. AISC, vol. 399, pp. 99–108. Springer, Cham (2016). doi:10.1007/978-3-319-25733-4_11

13. Center   of   mass   (2016).   https://en.wikipedia.org/w/index.php?title=Cener_of_mass&oldid=752653442

14. Boundless: Center of Mass of the Human Body. Boundless. (2016)

15. Center   of   Mass.   https://www.d.umn.edu/~mlevy/CLASSES/ESAT3300/LABS/LAB8_COM/cm.htm

16. Winter, D.A.: Biomechanics and Motor Control of Human Movement, 4th edn. Wiley (2009)

17. Yeung, L.F., Cheng, K.C., Fong, C.H., Lee, W.C.C., Tong, K.-Y.: Evaluation of the Microsoft Kinect as a clinical assessment tool of body sway. Gait Posture **40**, 532–538 (2014)

18. Centre of Gravity - Physiopedia, universal access to physiotherapy knowledge. http://www.physio-pedia.com/Centre_of_Gravity

19. Base of Support - Physiopedia, universal access to physiotherapy knowledge. http://www.physio-pedia.com/Base_of_Support

20. LeCun, Y., Bengio, Y., Hinton, G.: Deep learning. Nature **521**, 436–444 (2015)

21. Hochreiter, S., Schmidhuber, J.: Long short-term memory. Neural Comput. **9**, 1735–1780 (1997)

22. LSTM Networks for Sentiment Analysis — DeepLearning 0.1 documentation. http://deeplearning.net/tutorial/lstm.html

23. Understanding LSTM Networks – colah's blog. http://colah.github.io/posts/2015-08-Understanding-LSTMs/

Aging and Learning, Working and Leisure

The STAGE Project: Tailored Cultural Entertainment for Older Adults via Streaming Technology

Luigi Biocca[1(✉)], Nicolò Paraciani[1], Francesca Picenni[2], Giovanni Caruso[1],
Marco Padula[2], Riccardo Chiariglione[3], Agnieszka Kowalska[4], Monica Florea[5],
and Ilias Kapouranis[6]

[1] ITABC-CNR, Area della Ricerca RM 1, Via Salaria Km 29,300,
00015 Monterotondo Scalo, RM, Italy
{luigi.biocca,nicolo.paraciani,giovanni.caruso}@itabc.cnr.it
[2] ITC-CNR, via A. Corti 12, 20133 Milan, Italy
{picenni,padula}@itc.cnr.it
[3] CEDEO SAS, via Borgionera 103, 10040 Villar Dora, TO, Italy
riccardo@cedeo.net
[4] ASM Market Research and Analysis Centre, ul. Grunwaldzka 5, 99-300 Kutno, Poland
a.kowalska@asm-poland.com.pl
[5] SIVECO Romania SA, 73 – 81 Ploiesti Drive, Complex Victoria Park, Bucharest, Romania
Monica.Florea@siveco.ro
[6] GEORAMA L.L.C, Georgiou Seferi 6 – 102, 1076 Nicosia, Cyprus
i.kapouranis@georama.com.cy

Abstract. In recent years, Ambient Assisted Living (AAL) solutions for older people have been increasingly focusing on leisure and educational activities, as opposed to healthcare assistance.

In this framework, the European research project STAGE – Streaming of Theatre and Arts for old aGe Entertainment, was recently approved and funded by the Active and Assisted Living - AAL programme, in the context of Call for Proposals 2015.

STAGE aims at developing an easy-to-use ICT platform to deliver cultural and educational content to older people via video streaming technology. This content will be provided through customized interfaces and will include events such as theatre plays, concerts, opera performances and museum exhibits.

In order to accomplish this, it will employ a co-design methodology, involving older users in the design and development of the platform from the beginning of project activities. Users will also test the platform prototype and provide feedback, in order to define a final fully customized version.

The ultimate goal of the project is to provide older people who are interested in culture but find difficulties accessing it, with a facilitated and affordable way to enjoy this type of content.

Keywords: Assisted Living · Co-design · Cultural entertainment · Video streaming · ICT platform

© Springer International Publishing AG 2017
J. Zhou and G. Salvendy (Eds.): ITAP 2017, Part II, LNCS 10298, pp. 487–500, 2017.
DOI: 10.1007/978-3-319-58536-9_39

1 Introduction

Older people, as shown by some studies, are generally interested in participating in cultural and recreational activities [1]. This interest can also be fostered by the increased free time that is available to them as a consequence of retired life.

However, a substantial percentage of older adults in Europe find difficulties in accessing cultural events [2].

The nature of these impediments varies: they could be related to mobility, financial or health problems. As a consequence, many older people feel discouraged or are unable to attend such events.

Furthermore, cultural and social activities have been shown to be beneficial for the mental health of older people, reducing the risk of cognitive illness and contributing to a sense of active and fulfilling lifestyle [3–5].

Therefore, the possibility of attending this type of events would represent an opportunity for their personal enrichment and social engagement, and would increase the perceived level of satisfaction.

The STAGE project (*Streaming of Theatre and Arts for old aGe Entertainment*) was conceived to find a remedy to problems hindering the participation of older people in cultural events, and help them keeping an active lifestyle, through the employment of ICTs.

The main goal of the project, in fact, is to design and develop an easy-to-use, cross-device ICT platform to deliver videos of cultural events via streaming technology that can be easily accessed by older people at home or in any other context where an Internet connection is available.

The platform will provide a diverse selection of offers, by liaising with cultural associations and event providers worldwide, including (but not limited to) theatres, concert halls, opera houses and museums.

Digital tickets of events would be sold through the platform at a reduced price, and in some cases even for free, with a facilitated and secure payment system.

This will not only enable older people to enjoy culture in a comfortable and affordable way, but also give them the opportunity to access events from countries far away from where they live, which would be impossible with traditional means.

The STAGE project was approved by the Active and Assisted Living programme in 2015, and started in March 2016 [6].

It is being developed by a European research consortium led by the Construction Technologies Institute of the National Research Council of Italy (ITC-CNR). The other partners are: CEDEO and ANCS from Italy, SIVECO from Romania, ASM from Poland, MATERIA and GEORAMA from Cyprus, and PBN and Karma Interactive from Hungary.

ITC-CNR is a public research body, it will coordinate the project and assess and evaluate user requirements.

CEDEO, GEORAMA, Karma Interactive and SIVECO are ICT enterprises, in charge of developing the software platform, including interface design and implementation of user requirements.

ANCS, MATERIA and PBN are end user organizations, with the role of involving older users in the project and ensuring that privacy and ethics are respected.

ASM is an SME specialized in socio-economic surveys and analysis; marketing and business planning that will develop the business plan of the project, in addition to coordinating dissemination activities.

In its initial phase, the project is concerned with defining user requirements, which will be analyzed and implemented in the platform design and development activities.

To this end, two questionnaires were prepared and administered to selected groups of possible older users, belonging to three end user organizations from Cyprus, Hungary and Italy (MATERIA, PBN and ANCS), who volunteered to be involved in the project.

The first questionnaire aimed at outlining a general user profile by collecting data about personal information, health conditions, education level, attitudes and cultural interests. The second one concerned users' preferences in reference to the STAGE application graphical user interface (GUI). It was administered jointly with mock-up images of the GUI, developed by GEORAMA.

Older users were asked to answer specific questions about the layout and the intelligibility of the interface elements, as well as to suggest improvements where needed.

An outline of the platform characteristics, together with a detailed description of the questionnaires and an analysis of the obtained answers will be provided in the following sections.

2   Project Scope and ICT Platform for Streaming Events

The ICT platform the project intends to develop will be able to run on the majority of technological devices, such as PC/laptop, tablet, smartphone and Smart TV. Therefore, it will be compatible with most popular operating systems, such as Windows, Mac OS, Android, iOS and WebOS.

In addition to the main video streaming feature, the STAGE solution will also include eLearning elements with informative content about the events being viewed or scheduled, and a dedicated social network. This latter will allow users to exchange comments and opinions about events, as well as to engage in online conversations. All the features of the platform will be designed and implemented according to accessibility principles (such as WCAG – Web Content Accessibility Guidelines [7]), using an approach based on co-design. (Co-design, or participatory design, is a methodology based on involving end users and other stakeholders in the conception and design of a product or technology targeting them [8]).

The interface will be initially translated at least into three of the five languages spoken in the consortium – i.e., Greek, Hungarian and Italian –, plus English.

A facilitated payment procedure to purchase event tickets will also be included.

The first prototype of the platform will be tested with volunteer users – involved through informed consent – during a one year-long pilot trial. This trial will be instrumental in collecting a significant amount of user feedback, in order to produce a final version of the platform responding to their needs and requirements as much as possible.

2.1   The Video Streaming Platform

The STAGE video streaming platform is a Java-based Web application offering a range of services exposed by API (Application Programming Interface): content management, import/export, show time, live streaming, trading and payment.

Each service is organized, by means of suited APIs, into a number of sub-services. For instance, the Showtime API includes:

- List Videos;
- Detail Video;
- Post Video;
- Remove Video;

while the Live streaming API includes:

- Create Event;
- List Events;
- Stream Event;
- EPG (Electronic Program Guide).

The platform runs a number of docker containers that ensure flexibility and scalability. (A docker container is a software that allows running an application within a self-contained environment, ensuring interoperability, regardless of the hosting platform [9]). The docker containers are used for content ingestion, transcoding, database management, scheduled services, payment, streaming, statistics and log aggregation.

The video streaming platform forms the main server-side component on which the STAGE software is based.

2.2   The Service Platform

The STAGE service platform will be built under Drupal 7 CMF (Content Management Framework). Drupal 7 is an open source content management platform powering millions of websites and applications. It is built, used and supported by an active and diverse community of people around the world and offers high delivery performance, stability and high security features when using its API [10].

The used database is MySQL, one of the most popular open source database management systems.

Drupal CMF accepts load balancing between application servers using a MySQL database. Load balancing is the practice of evenly distributing work among multiple computers.

This technique provides several important benefits, including:

- reducing load on individual systems and minimizing response time;
- increasing network utilization and maximizing throughput;
- improving reliability;
- facilitating scaling.

The STAGE software is based on the interoperation of a server-side platform and a client-side application. This latter, in addition to the GUI specifically designed for older people, will have another interface for cultural event providers.

This will be managed through Drupal 7, which will be used as the client side platform where cultural institutions will have the possibility to interact with the video streaming platform (that is, the server side).

The interoperability of the two platforms will be assured by secured Web services and will allow the following actions:

- connect to an account on the streaming platform;
- upload, describe and publish new videos;
- set access conditions for each published video (free, creative commons, pay per view);
- given a list of videos, publish those of choice on your website;
- insert videos anywhere on the page;
- choose the skin and the size of the video player;
- choose whether to make videos visible to everyone or only to certain users;
- create a new video playlist and publish it on the pages and posts of the site;
- create live streaming events to be published on the pages of your site;
- record videos of live events that have already been broadcasted;
- synchronize videos with your streaming platform account (if you posted a video with some conditions, these are also updated on the streaming platform);
- control and monitor access analytics for your content.

See Fig. 1 for a schematic representation of the service platform.

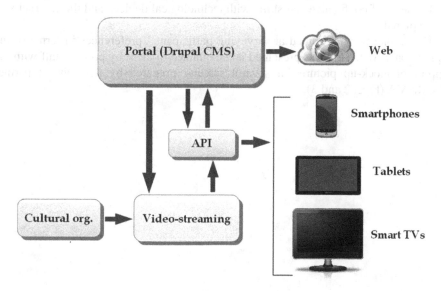

Fig. 1. Diagram of the STAGE service

3   User Involvement and Co-design Methodology

As mentioned above, a central element of the project's research approach is the active role of users in the design and implementation of the platform.

To this purpose, the very first phase of STAGE concerned the involvement of older people in the project activities, on the basis of informed consent.

This was accomplished with the help of end user partner organizations, which organized meetings with older persons who previously expressed an interest in the project. These meetings had the purpose of better explaining the project's aims and expected results, as well as to administer dedicated questionnaires to explore their preferences and requirements.

The user sample participating in these meetings, in addition to the prerequisite of willingness and interest, was also selected according to the following criteria:

- being 65+ years old;
- not having serious cognitive diseases (though mild cognitive impairment was not excluded);
- being of varied social and cultural background;
- being gender balanced.

Two sets of meetings were organized in three partner countries (Cyprus, Hungary and Italy), involving a total of 71 participants.

In the first meeting, users provided answers to a questionnaire targeting their personal and social profile, cultural and recreational interests and preferences, as well as a first survey of their opinions about the perspectives offered by the STAGE platform.

The level of confidence and skills with technological devices and the Internet was also explored.

The second meeting aimed at surveying participants' preferences in terms of the application's GUI. This was presented and explained to them by project staff with the support of mock-up pictures of several screens, prepared by the Cypriot partner GEORAMA (Figs. 2 and 3).

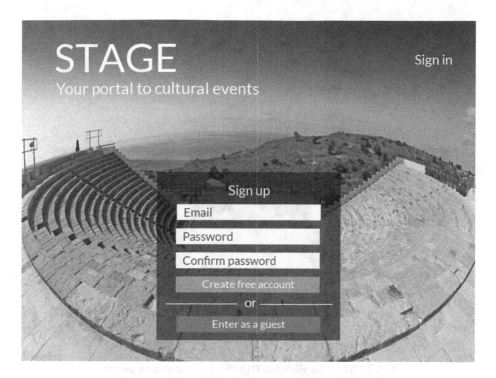

Fig. 2. STAGE application GUI mock-up: home page

The questions were focused on the intelligibility of text, color contrast, layout, font size and clarity of purpose, structure and size of buttons and menus.

The questionnaire allowed users to suggest improvements where they found shortcomings in the way the mock-up interface was designed.

These suggestions will be used to define and implement the first version of the actual GUI of the STAGE platform, thus complying with co-design principles.

This approach will be also adopted on a larger scale when the pilot trials with users will start, based on the first prototype that will be released in early 2017.

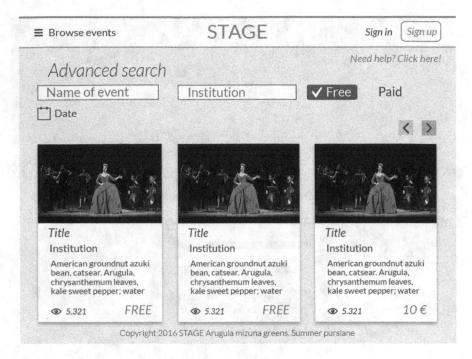

Fig. 3. STAGE application GUI mock-up: search for events

4 First Outcomes of the Survey on End Users

The sample of 71 involved volunteers that took part in the survey were on average 72 years old; 47.89% of them were females and the remaining 52.11% males (Fig. 4 shows the distribution of users by age groupings).

Data were gathered through two paper questionnaires filled out by users, that were later anonymized. The first one was formed by five main sections focused on different topics:

- residence information (4 questions);
- personal information (6 questions);
- social participation and recreational activities (15 questions);
- STAGE platform preferences (6 questions);
- technical information (5 questions).

These questions were conceived with the purpose of defining a general user profile that would be the basis for the project use cases and scenarios. For this reason, users' personal information and data on their level of social participation and engagement were collected.

Specific questions on STAGE platform preferences were drafted to probe the average interest on cultural activities, as well as users' preferences regarding the type of cultural content to be provided by the project.

Technical information gathered by means of the questionnaire, instead, will be central in the development of the first prototype of the software platform.

Its design, in fact, will have to take into account users' requirements concerning technological devices and their average ability and confidence when using them.

The questionnaires were digitized and the data were transferred into an Excel database file to be subsequently analyzed.

According to the results, over half of users (55.71%) had a primary or intermediate education level, while 30% have attended either high school or a trade/technical/vocational training; 14.29% of them achieved a higher degree.

As mentioned above, the STAGE platform was conceived to bring cultural entertainment to older adults' homes: indeed, some data collected in the first questionnaire have highlighted the necessity of this type of service as people grow older.

In fact, 18.84% of surveyed users live alone and 59.42% with a partner (only 21.74% live with two or more people).

Older people living alone can in general be prone to boredom and exposed to the risk of loneliness [11, 12], while those who live in couple might wish - more than people living in bigger families - to find new activities to do with their partner.

Moreover, though more than 50% of them declared to be healthy, 46.48% suffer from minor disabilities (motor, hearing, visual or multiple) and only 2.82% of major ones. This kind of issues is likely to inhibit older people to leave their houses for a long time and especially by night (the time of the day when most cultural events - such as theatre shows and concerts - take place).

Indeed, when potential end users were asked to specify the frequency of engaging in 17 selected leisure activities, it turned out that the most frequent activities (done at least once a week) are all indoor or home activities, such as watching TV, reading or watching movies.

Activities qualified as "cultural" (i.e. attending conferences, cinema shows, theatre plays, concerts, opera and museum exhibits) appear to be carried out less than twice a month and some, such as going to the opera, tend to never be carried out (Fig. 5).

According to these results, it can be assumed that the possibility of attending various and heterogeneous cultural events and happenings which take place worldwide - ranging from pop music to opera concerts, from theatre shows to guided tours and museum exhibits - thanks to streaming technologies, would constitute a major improvement in users' quality of life. It is not just a matter of entertainment, but rather a way to keep the mind active by providing users with knowledge in various forms - visual and textual contents -, and making them interact with a multimedia environment. When directly asked about the relevance of such a possibility, the large majority of the users (85%) showed their interest.

As the STAGE platform is being developed to work on devices such as smart TVs, tablets, smartphones, desktop PCs and laptops, one possible weakness could concern the lack of technological skills in older adults.

The IT literacy level of end users was investigated as well. The data show that they are distributed in three categories: 39.13% of respondents regularly use the main social networks and Web applications, 21.74% know them - though are not familiar with them - and 39.13% do not use them at all.

The most used devices for online activities are, in decreasing order: computers, smartphones, tablets and laptops. Furthermore, 53% of the interviewees do not feel confident handling tablets (just 6% do feel very confident), and 28% feel confident or even very confident in using smartphones. This data indicates the tendency of the target STAGE user to approach this kind of devices, but also their difficulties when facing complex user interfaces. It will be therefore essential to design a simple, linear and intelligible interface in order to optimize the platform usability and make users feel confident while browsing it.

This is why the second questionnaire, whose data are currently being analyzed, was based on mock-ups of the interface which is being developed through a co-design approach.

The analysis of the most used social networks and Web apps provided another significant result: Facebook is the most frequently used one - on average once a week; this means that users are already familiar with its graphics and functionalities. Since one of the features of the STAGE platform will be a dedicated social network where users could exchange information and opinions on the cultural contents they have already enjoyed - or want to enjoy -, it would be clearly sensible to build an environment along the lines of Facebook - though of course not identical to it, in order to avoid ambiguity.

Vaguely evoking features, graphics and mechanisms people already know - or at least have already approached - is a way to speed up the initial learning curve, to let the users handle the platform easily and to make them have fun using it, which means engaging and motivating them to come back [13].

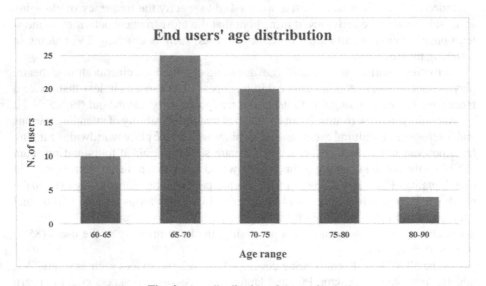

Fig. 4. Age distribution of respondents

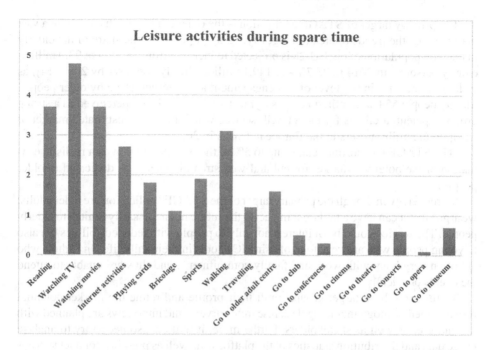

Fig. 5. Frequency of leisure activities done by end users; the frequency scale is: 0 = "never", 1 = "less than two times a month", 2 = "twice a month", 3 = "once a week", 4 = "three/five times a week" and 5 = "everyday"

5   Future Directions and Scenarios

The next phases of the project will concern mainly the development and implementation of the first prototype of the ICT platform, along with the involvement of cultural organizations as event providers.

In fact, before the beginning of pilot trials with users, it will be necessary to recruit content providers on a voluntary basis.

At the moment, two cultural associations have been involved in Italy, by signing a letter of support.

These organizations will provide video streaming of cultural events, both live and recorded, that will be available to users through the platform. These will be free events for the entire duration of the project.

When the final version of the platform will be released, it is expected that it will represent a working example of a customized ICT application, fully tailored to older users' needs and preferences. It could also be considered as a successful implementation of co-design principles in the specific field of video streaming platform, and generally web-based applications.

To ensure that the STAGE service will operate successfully after the project end, resources are planned as well to perform detailed market analysis and elaborate the most suitable and effective business model for this type of innovation.

The primary target of STAGE application is the older adults which constitute a vast market given the trends related to longevity, aging population (the share of the elderly in the total population of the EU-28 is projected to increase from 18.5% - or 93.9 million elderly persons - in 2014 to 28.7% - or 149.1 million elderly persons - by 2080 [14]) as well as an increase in the level of arts engagement and Internet usage by older people. Mainly people 55+ and retired persons (typically 65+) in EU are perceived as a strong group of potential clients for the STAGE service which means an estimated market of ca. up to 6.2 million users in the European Union in 2020.

(The STAGE Consortium claims up to 5% of the 65+ population as a realistic estimation of the potential market for cultural web streaming services dedicated to older people).

Moreover, even though the primary target of the STAGE application are older adults, we argue that it can have a far larger impact in the future not necessarily limited to elderly people. The service could be of interest not only to people with reduced abilities but also to young people who are very fond of using ICT tools in their daily life, and adults who are often very busy with work and family commitments and thus are unable to attend the events physically.

To research these target groups, draft their profile and refine the market potential research methodology including desk research, surveys and interviews are planned with the end user as well as stakeholders. Furthermore, it will be also necessary to analyse usage data and distribution statistics of the platform, as well as possibly conduct surveys to assess the satisfaction of users in terms of usability, accessibility and quality of the cultural offer.

As a result, carefully planned market and stakeholder's analysis will ensure that the new service will be implemented in the market effectively and older adults could start benefiting from it within two years after the project end.

6   Conclusions

In this paper the European research project STAGE - Streaming of Theatre and Arts for old aGe Entertainment, recently approved and funded by the AAL Programme, is presented. It is devoted to the development of an easy-to-use ICT platform for streaming cultural and educational events, like concerts, theatre shows, conferences and museum visits, to older people.

A co-design methodology is being employed for developing the platform, in order to meet the specific needs of the users and be as much user-friendly as possible.

For this reason, the very first phase of the project concerned the involvement of older people in the design phase by selecting groups of possible users in three partner countries. Two questionnaires were delivered to the selected users, one concerning social profile, interests and confidence level with technological devices, the second investigating user preferences with respect to the application's GUI.

The main outcomes of this initial phase are the following:

- both older persons living alone and with a partner may wish to find new activities for entertainment;

- though more than 50% of the involved older people declared to be healthy, 49% experience some degree of disability, which may prevent them from having an active life out of their houses;
- the most frequent activities performed by the potential users are indoor activities (watching TV, reading, bricolage). Out-of-home cultural activities are rarely carried out.

According to the survey outcomes, it turns out that the possibilities offered by the STAGE project can yield a major improvement for the quality of life of older people.

Of course, it will be essential to design an easy-to-use and accessible platform, in order to make users feel comfortable when using it.

Also the feature of endowing the STAGE platform with a dedicated social network for exchanging information and opinions on the cultural contents appear to be a very interesting and promising opportunity for the potential users.

The next phase of the project will be the development of the first platform prototype, and the recruitment of event providers on a voluntary basis for testing the platform with the selected user sample.

Furthermore, a detailed market analysis will be conducted, by considering the possibility of extending STAGE to other categories of users, in addition to older people.

Acknowledgements. The STAGE project was approved by the European research funding programme "Active and Assisted Living" (AAL, http://www.aal-europe.eu/) on September 30 2015, in the framework of Call for Proposals 2015 "Living actively and independently at home" (project number AAL-2015-1-014).

Partners in the project receive funding from their respective National Funding Bodies, listed below by partner country:

- Ministry for Education, University and Research – MIUR, Italy (ANCS, CEDEO and CNR);
- Executive Unit for Financing Higher Education, Research, Development and Innovation – UEFISCDI, Romania (SIVECO);
- Research Promotion Foundation, Cyprus (GEORAMA and MATERIA);
- National Centre for Research and Development – NCBR, Poland (ASM);
- National Research, Development and Innovation Office, Hungary (Karma Interactive and PBN).

References

1. Zentrum Für Kulturforschung (Centre For Cultural Research): 'Cultural Participation and the 50+ Generation - A new study and perspectives of an international comparative research project' (2008)
2. http://www.comres.co.uk/polls/arts-council-england-older-people-poll/. Accessed July 2016
3. Ragheb, M.G., Griffith, C.A.: The contribution of leisure participation and leisure satisfaction to life satisfaction of older persons. J. Leisure Res. **14**(4), 295 (1982)
4. Toepoel, V.: Cultural participation of older adults: investigating the contribution of lowbrow and highbrow activities to social integration and satisfaction with life. Int. J. Disabil. Hum. Dev. **10**(2), 123–129 (2011)
5. Toepoel, V.: Ageing, leisure, and social connectedness: how could leisure help reduce social isolation of older people? Soc. Ind. Res. **113**(1), 355–372 (2013)

6. http://www.aal-europe.eu/projects/stage/. Accessed July 2016
7. https://www.w3.org/WAI/intro/wcag.php. Accessed July 2016
8. Muller, M.J., Kuhn, S.: Participatory design. Commun. ACM **36**(6), 24–28 (1993)
9. https://www.docker.com/what-docker. Accessed July 2016
10. https://www.drupal.org/about. Accessed July 2016
11. Conroy, R.M., Golden, J., Jeffares, I., O'Neill, D., McGee, H.: Boredom-proneness, loneliness, social engagement and depression and their association with cognitive function in older people: a population study. Psychol. Health Med. **15**(4), 463–473 (2010)
12. Victor, C., Scambler, S., Bond, J., Bowling, A.: Being alone in later life: loneliness, social isolation and living alone. Rev. Clin. Gerontol. **10**(4), 407–417 (2000)
13. Venkatesh, V., Thong, J.Y., Xu, X.: Consumer acceptance and use of information technology: extending the unified theory of acceptance and use of technology. MIS Q. **36**(1), 157–178 (2012)
14. http://ec.europa.eu/eurostat/statistics-explained/index.php/People_in_the_EU_%E2%80%93_population_projections. Accessed July 2016

Facilitating Remote Communication Between Senior Communities with Telepresence Robots

Atsushi Hiyama[1](✉), Akihiro Kosugi[2], Kentarou Fukuda[2], Masatomo Kobayashi[2], and Michitaka Hirose[1]

[1] The University of Tokyo, 7-3-1 Hongo, Bunkyo, Tokyo 113-8656, Japan
hiyama@star.rcast.u-tokyo.ac.jp, hirose@cyber.t.u-tokyo.ac.jp
[2] IBM Research – Tokyo, 19-21 Hakozaki, Nihonbashi, Chuo, Tokyo 103-8510, Japan
{a1kosugi,kentarou,mstm}@jp.ibm.com

Abstract. Rapid aging and low birthrate of the society is a big issue especially in suburban district of Japan. Since social participation is one of the major factors of well being, online communication helps the elderly in suburban community maintain social relationships by receiving various kinds of services provided from urban area. Our research group introduced a remote IT classroom for senior citizens as an example of local senior communities support each other by connecting those communities through the Internet. This remote IT classroom is based on video conferencing system, and the IT lecturer and his assistants in urban district taught participants live in suburban district how to use tablet devices. From previous study, assistants pointed out that they had difficulties in establishing conversation with the students. Thus we propose the use of telepresence robots in order to overcome this issue. Results from the remote IT classroom indicated that the application of telepresence robots lowered the barrier for initiating conversation between remote assistants and local students.

Keywords: Telepresence · Elderly workers · Remote classroom · Human-robot interaction

1 Introduction

Japan is known as the first country that became a hyper-aged society. The percent of people aged 65 year and above in Japan has exceeded 25% in 2013. Friedman et al. described one of the key factors to successful aging as being the maintenance of an active relationship with the surrounding community [1]. During the 1970s and 1980s, many new towns were constructed in the suburbs and the aging rate of the population in these districts is especially rapid. Many of these areas have an elderly population already above 30% and they are going to become marginal villages in near future. The major reason is that younger generations in those areas are likely to move to urban areas when they grow up. Though the elderly living in urban district can still benefit various kinds of relationships in the local communities, the elderly living in suburban districts are facing the risk of losing active relationships in local communities. Information technology (IT) is considered a powerful tool to maintain a social presence for the elderly [2]. Comparison

© Springer International Publishing AG 2017
J. Zhou and G. Salvendy (Eds.): ITAP 2017, Part II, LNCS 10298, pp. 501–515, 2017.
DOI: 10.1007/978-3-319-58536-9_40

between an older Internet user and an older non-user showed that Internet use has a positive effect on the user's psychological well-being [3]. Our research group aims to develop a model wherein local senior communities support each other by connecting those communities through the Internet.

Takagi et al. proposed a system that connects an urban senior community and a suburban senior community using video conferencing to offer a lifelong learning service —IT classrooms—from urban area to suburban area. IT classrooms are mainly located in certain urban areas. Therefore, senior communities in suburban areas, like the new towns mentioned earlier, have difficulty accessing such classes. In contrast, many older adult IT experts do not have opportunities to use their skills in their own communities [4]. From this study, participants mentioned that it would be helpful if it were possible to convey and receive non-verbal information to remote participants and to grab their attention.

One possible solution to this issue is the application of a telepresence robot. A telepresence robot is the strongest media that enables embodied interaction with a distant person. Application of telepresence robots has begun and has made it possible to expand the interaction of the elderly with family or close friends. Many kinds of telepresence robots have become commercially available and are easy to develop from off-the-shelf robot platforms [5]. Remote elderly care is expected to be one of the most promising applications of service robots [6]. The ExCITE project focused on designing a social telepresence system for elderly care using the mobile telepresence robot Giraff [7]. Many studies have been done that examine the effect of telepresence systems in education or communication environments with younger participants. Tanaka et al. compared the difference in communication using a video conferencing system and a mobile telepresence robot in remote foreign language class for children [8, 9]. In this study, application of the telepresence robot encouraged vocalization by the children. Rae et al. explored how the height of the mobile telepresence robot [10] and the task conducted by the robot [11] affects working efficiency and the form of communication. Social presence of the remote operator can also be improved even if a remote operated system is designed without mobility [12, 13]. Tsui et al. examined cases of actual office meetings and found that the telepresence robot fit more in the situation like informal meetings [14]. From previous research, the telepresence robot will be a useful tool for remote communication. Beer et al. assessed that older adults are eager to control telepresence robot for having communications or experiences in distant location, however, the presence of robot in their private space make them feel awkward [15]. This implies that public space is more acceptable place for installing telepresence robot than private space.

This study aims to explore the feasibility of telepresence robots to facilitate communication between distant senior communities in public situation. In Sect. 2, we describe conditions of the application field. Then, in Sect. 3, we introduce the designed system, which uses telepresence robots for remote IT education between distant senior communities followed by the evaluation and discussion of the system in Sects. 4 and 5.

2   Application Field

We applied the system to a remote IT course between Sendai City and Kiyosedai Town in Nishinomiya City. The locations of each place is shown in Fig. 1. The distance between these two sites is about 625 km. Students in this course are residents of Kiyosedai. Kiyosedai is one of the new towns in Japan, and it has a high ratio, estimated at around 35%, of people over the age of 65. There is no available IT classroom for the elderly in Kiyosedai therefore the residents' association of Kiyosedai decided join this remote IT education course. Lecturers and assistants are members of Sendai Senior Net Club, an IT training organization for the elderly in Sendai. About 100 members have teaching experience in IT classes. Detailed information about these two sites is described in [4].

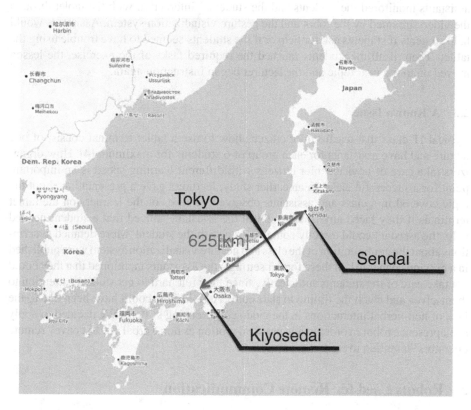

Fig. 1. Location of learners' site Kiyosedai, and lecturers' site Sendai

2.1   Participants

Learners were from Kiyosedai and lecturers and assistants were from Sendai Senior Net Club. Classes were mainly held on Sunday mornings and afternoons. There were 12 people who registered as students (7 women and 5 men in their 60s and 70s) in Kiyosedai.

Students were divided into two groups (each group had six students). All students owned a laptop or desktop computer but only one student owned a tablet terminal. There were 2 lecturers (both men in their 60s and 70s) and 7 assistants (4 women and 3 men in their 60s and 70s) in Sendai.

2.2 Procedure

The course used for the evaluation of the proposed system started from August 24th 2013 and ended on October 7th. One course was composed of five lessons. Each lesson began with a greeting from the lecturer and an introduction of the day's topic followed by the lecturer's presentation and demonstration of how to use the tablet terminal. After the lecture, students began an exercise involving their tablet. During the exercise, remote assistants monitored the students and the students' interaction with the tablet through the video streamed by the robot and the gesture visualization system. Assistants would help students if students ask for help or if the students seemed to have trouble using the tablet. Then, if all the students finished the required tasks of the exercise, the lesson moved on to the next topic and the lecturer began instruction again.

2.3 A Known Issue

Typical IT class that teach senior citizens how to use a tablet terminal consist of one lecture and have assistants for each group of 6 students for maximum [4]. How organizers take care of novice senior citizens with different learning speed is an important point for a successful class. In an earlier study, lecturers gave a presentation about the topic covered in a class and assistants observed gestures of the learners on the tablet terminals if they faced any troubles. Once the assistant noticed that a student needed help, the assistant could directly communicate with the student. More detailed descriptions about the configuration of the class and gesture visualization system were published in a previous paper [4]. In these former settings, the assistants mentioned that they could not take care of the students sufficiently, since they felt hard to get students attention to themselves and catch the timing to start conversation. This could have been due to the lack of non-verbal interactions in the video conferencing system. We decided to apply a telepresence robot in order to add physical motion as non-verbal cue to convey remote operators' intention to start conversation.

3   Robots Used for Remote Communication

3.1   System Requirements

Each class had 1 lecturer and 2 assistants. An assistant took care of a group of students. We needed 3 telepresence robots for a class. The telepresence robot for the lecturer needed to be operated in hands free since the lecturer must give a presentation and demonstration of how to use the tablet terminal. On the other hand, the telepresence robots for assistants needed to be operated manually. Assistants are needed to move the camera directly towards the students' face. Based on related research, different sizes and the mobility of the robot affect the social presence of the remote operator in a different way [10–13]. For a comparison, we adopted 2 types of telepresence robots for assistants. One was a mobile type robot that allowed the remote operator to move around the class; the other robot was a desktop type robot that the operator could pan and tilt in the direction of a camera. Figure 2 illustrates the overall system configuration of the system used in the IT classroom.

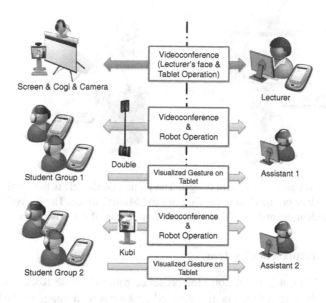

Fig. 2. System overview

3.2 Cogi: Lecturer Telepresence System

Cogi receives commands, including the angles of the arm using serial connection over a Bluetooth from PC or mobile devices. In our study, we have built our own video conferencing system based on Web-RTC with the capability to detect the head position of the user in front of the camera. Cogi is linked to this video conferencing system both as a video streaming source and as a receiver of commands transmitted from a remote site. Cogi has two mode to be linked with the videoconference:

- "Master" mode, which tracks and follows the head of the operator in front of the camera, and sends the movement of the user to the remote Cogi in "Slave" mode.
- "Slave" mode, which pans and tilts the camera and screen according to the movement sent from Cogi in "Master" mode.

In our study case, the lecturer joins the videoconference with Cogi linked in "Master" mode. Cogi tracks the head of the lecturer and sends the angles of the lecturer's face from the screen. In the remote classroom, there is another Cogi joining the videoconference that is linked in "Slave" mode. This Cogi directs its face to the angles sent by the Cogi in "Master" mode. For example, when the lecturer looks into the screen from the left, the Cogi in the remote classroom faces to the right. In this way, the lecturer can look around in the remote classroom just by moving his/her head as if he/she were looking through an observation window [16] (Fig. 3).

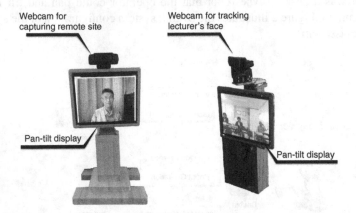

Fig. 3. Lecturer telepresence system (Cogi). The picture on the left is the Cogi set to "Slave" mode and the picture on the right is the Cogi set to "Master" mode. The "Slave" mode Cogi is placed at the Student site and the "Master" mode Cogi is placed at the Lecturer's site.

3.3 Mobile Telepresence System

The left part of Fig. 4 is the mobile telepresence robot (Double Robotics Double) we used and the right part of Fig. 4 is the captured desktop screen image of the telepresence

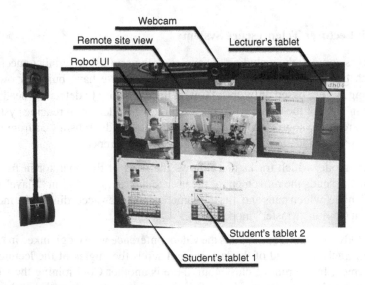

Fig. 4. Mobile telepresence robot (Double) and its control interface for remote assistant.

robot's control interface. The control interface is a web browser based system. The interface consists of a video window captured by a robot that is then displayed on a robot user interface (UI). Assistants can move the robot with a cursor key on a keyboard. Remote site view is the video from the wide-angle camera placed in the classroom in the community center. The lecturer's tablet view is a captured video that displays how the lecturer is operating a tablet terminal. In the lower side of the window, the students' tablet view is displayed. Gesture interaction of a student is overlaid on the captured screen image of a student's tablet terminal. In order to avoid cross talk, an assistant uses headset for audio communication. A webcam that captures an assistant's face is attached to the top of the display.

3.4 Desktop Telepresence System

Figure 5 shows the desktop telepresence robot (Evolve robotics Kubi) we used and the screen image of the robot's control interface. Only the robot UI view is different from the mobile robot's interface. Assistants can control the desktop telepresence robot by clicking the cursor button on the screen. In addition, assistants can move the display, mounted on a Kubi, toward each learner's face or tablet by clicking the buttons placed under the video image of the robot UI. Also, the webcam is attached on top of the display.

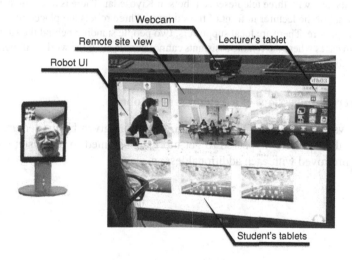

Fig. 5. Desktop telepresence robot (Kubi) and its control interface for remote assistant.

4 Evaluations

Evaluation of the system was made from participants in 5 lessons (Fig. 6). Each lesson held twice during a course. Students are divided into two groups, which supported by either Kubi or Double. Number of attended students in each lesson was 7 in lesson 1 (3 assisted through Kubi, 4 assisted through Double), 8 in lesson 2 (4 assisted through Kubi, 4 assisted through Double), 7 in lesson 3 (3 assisted by Kubi, 4 assisted by Double), 7 in lesson 4 (4 assisted by Kubi, 3 assisted by Double), and 8 in lesson 5 (4 assisted through Kubi, 4 assisted through Double). After each lesson, we asked all lecturers, assistants, and students to answer the questions. We also observed the recorded videos of the lessons and examined the differences in communication among participants from previous remote IT courses.

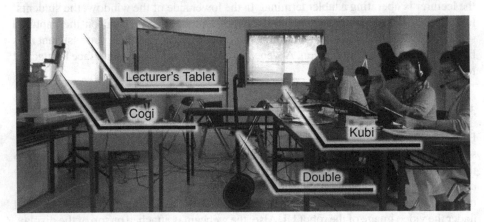

Fig. 6. Students' site with three telepresence robots in Kiyosedai. There is a screen that displays the tablet terminal of the lecturer in front of the students. Three robots are placed in the room as indicated in the picture. There are local supporters, two people standing behind the students, that help students in cases where the remote assistants cannot handle all of the work or if there is audio connection trouble.

4.1   Lecturers' Impressions of a Telepresence Robot

Figure 7 shows the answers to the evaluation questions given by the lecturers. From these results, the lecturers' appeared to get more accustomed to the system and their impressions improved with each additional lesson.

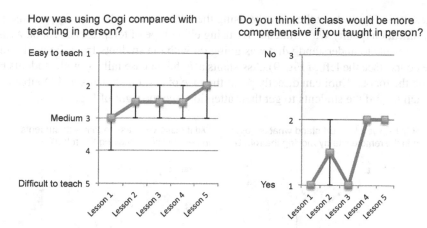

Fig. 7. The lecturers impression compared with teaching in person. From the beginning they felt that they could teach better if they gave a lecturer in person. As lessons went on, they get used to the system and they thought that they can teach as well as face to face.

4.2   Remote Assistants' Impressions of Telepresence Robots

Figure 8 shows the overall impressions of the class as given by the assistants in Sendai. Impressions of assistants, those who use Double, seem gradually get used to operating a robot. Impression of assistants, those who use Kubi, marked a negative impression on the first and the last lessons. They mentioned that time lag of the Internet connection made them difficult to understand the context of remote site. However, Kubi had a good reputation on its pan and tilt motion, since assistants can observe both students face and hands. They also felt some awkwardness at the beginning of the course and they gradually became accustomed to giving support to the students through the robot.

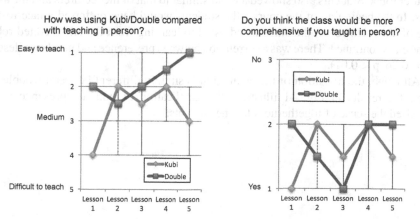

Fig. 8. Impressions of assistants giving technical support to students through both types of telepresence robot.

510   A. Hiyama et al.

Results in Fig. 9 show the effect of using the telepresence robots for improving the communication quality with students. By using either type of telepresence robot, assistants were able to understand what was going on with the students from the beginning of the course (see the left of Fig. 9). Assistants also felt at ease talking with students by moving the robots. Kubi can directly point the face of certain students and Double can approach toward the students to get their attention (see the right of Fig. 9).

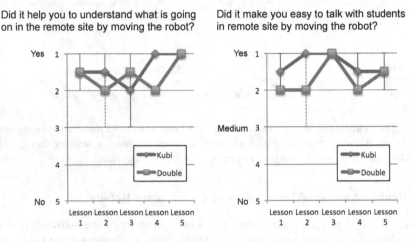

Fig. 9. Two evaluation questions indicating that the telepresence robots improved understanding at the remote site and helped smooth lecturer and assistant communication with students.

4.3 Students' Impressions of Telepresence Robots

Figure 10 shows the impressions that students developed from Cogi, the telepresence lecturer robot. Students also showed a trend similar to that of the lecturers and the assistants. In the beginning of the course, the students would have preferred a face-to-face type of class. However, the students adjusted to learning from the teleoperated robots as the class continued. There was a correlation between preference and number of lessons ($r2 = 0.26$, $p < 0.01$).

Although, the transition of the evaluation is slightly different between Double and Kubi, the results in Fig. 11 illustrate that application of both telepresence robots increased the sense of togetherness for the students.

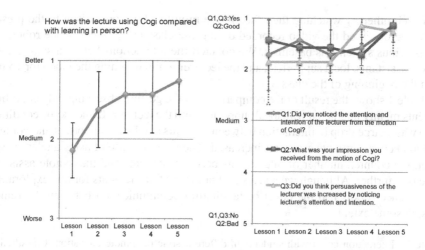

Fig. 10. Answers to evaluation questions indicating the students' impressions toward the lecturer telepresence system, Cogi.

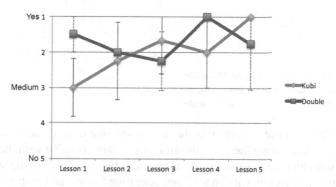

Fig. 11. Evaluation of togetherness by applying telepresence robots.

4.4 Did Telepresence Robots Facilitate Communications?

We compared the remote education with telepresence robots and the previous systems in terms of communication facilitation. In previous systems two different types of remote assistance were conducted. The first type was remote assistance by only observing a gesture visualization system [4]. In this case, the assistants just observed a gesture visualization system and if they found that the students were facing some difficulties, they could communicate via audio with the Students' site. In most cases, the assistants in Sendai asked local supporters in Kiyosedai to take care of the students. The second type of remote assistance was a Skype based remote assistant. In addition to monitoring the gesture visualization system, the assistants and the students could communicate directly with each other by watching their face in the monitor. For comparison to the present study, we observed the video recorded during the class using telepresence robot, and two previous systems as baselines. We counted the interactions between students and remote assistants, local supporters, and the lecturer while watching the video for 15 min from the beginning of the class.

Table 1 shows the result of the comparison. In the gesture observing only condition, students mainly interacted with local supporters and the lecturer. In the Skype condition, there was a large drop in interaction between students and local supporters and communication between remote assistants increased. Then, for the case of using a telepresence robot, the counted number of interactions between students and the remote assistants increased further. Although we had a small number of participants for this exploration, telepresence robots had the effect of facilitating communication between the remote sites, to some extent.

Table 1. Interaction count with students in different style of remote education. Classified by whom addressed.

Communication with students started by	Conditions of remote assistants		
	Only observing gesture visualization system[a]	*Skype*[b]	*Telepresence robots*[c]
Students	3	3	5
Remote assistants	3	8	14
Local supporters	10	2	3
Lecturer	13	10	10

[a] 5 students were in the class. 2 for one assistant and 3 for another.

[b] 5 students were in the class. 2 for one assistant and 3 for another.

[c] 4 students were in the class. Each assistant took care of 2 students.

One remarkable difference between remote education using telepresence robots and the former system is that, during the class, the students became familiar with the robots and remote assistants and made some idle conversation. Figure 12 shows the students taking a commemorative picture with an assistant operating Double and with a lecturer. Additionally, during the exercise period, when students were practicing with their tablet terminal without any trouble, an assistant who was operating Double went for a walk inside the classroom and watched students in other groups or had idle conversation with the local supporters.

Fig. 12. Students enjoying embodied communication with Cogi (left) and Double (right).

5 Discussion

From the results, the elderly in remote IT education classes accepted the application of telepresence robots. Telepresence robots also served to better facilitate communication between the students' side and the lecturer's side compared with conventional video conferencing styles of remote education. From observations, successful facilitation of communication was found to be subject to the assistant's outgoing characteristics, not to their IT skills. We adopted Double and Kubi as remote assistant telepresence robots in this study. We could not find a remarkable difference between Double and Kubi, in terms of their practical effect on communication, except that some assistants mentioned Kubi's tilt motion was useful for observing students' hands while the students operated the tablet terminal. One particular difference we found was that Cogi and Double had an eye-catching motion so that they could participate in informal communication with the students in spare time, however this was not the case with Kubi. Although evaluations of the impressions of the class were dependent on the condition of the audio connection quality, its affect to the students is getting smaller. We had frequent audio connection trouble especially in the first and the second lessons; students' evaluation to the class is improving. From the discussion with lecturer side, it was mentioned that it would be useful if assistants could have UI support to distinguish the speaker's location at the local site.

6 Conclusion

In this paper, we introduced a system using telepresence robots in remote IT education classes for the elderly, in order to facilitate communication between senior communities on the lecturer's side and the students' side. From use in an actual class, we confirmed that the telepresence robot is applicable in the class and it also promotes interactions between students and assistants.

Acknowledgments. This research was partially supported by Japan Science and Technology Agency, JST, under Strategic Promotion of Innovative Research and Development Program. We would like to thank Sendai Senior Net Club and the residents' association of Kiyosedai, Nishinomiya City for cooperation and participation in the IT classroom.

References

1. Friedman, H.S., Martin, L.R.: The Longevity Project: Surprising Discoveries for Health and Long Life from the Landmark Eight-Decade Study. Hudson Street Press, NY (2011)
2. Moser, C., Fuchsberger, V., Neureiter, K., Sellner, W., Tscheligi, M.: Elderly's social presence supported by ICTs: investigating user requirements for social presence. In: 2011 IEEE Third International Conference on Privacy, Security, Risk and Trust (PASSAT) and 2011 IEEE Third International Conference on Social Computing (SocialCom), pp. 738–741, 9–11 October 2011
3. Chen, Y., Persson, A.: Internet use among young and older adults: relation to psychological well-being. Educ. Gerontol. **28**(9), 731–744 (2002)
4. Takagi, H., Kosugi, A., Ishihara, T., Fukuda, K.: Remote IT education for senior citizens. In: Proceedings of the 11th Web for All Conference (W4A 2014). ACM, New York (2014). Article 41, 4 pages
5. Lazewatsky, D.A., Smart, W.D.: An inexpensive robot platform for teleoperation and experimentation. In: 2011 IEEE International Conference on Robotics and Automation (ICRA), pp. 1211–1216, 9–13 May 2011
6. Schroeter, C., Mueller, S., Volkhardt, M., Einhorn, E., Huijnen, C., van den Heuvel, H., van Berlo, A., Bley, A., Gross, H.-M.: Realization and user evaluation of a companion robot for people with mild cognitive impairments. In: 2013 IEEE International Conference on Robotics and Automation (ICRA), pp. 1153–1159, 6–10 May 2013
7. Kristoffersson, A., Coradeschi, S., Loutfi, A., Severinson Eklundh, K.: Assessment of interaction quality in mobile robotic telepresence: an elderly perspective. Interact. Stud. **15**(2), 343–357 (2014)
8. Tanaka, F., Takahashi, T., Matsuzoe, S., Tazawa, N., Morita, M.: Child-operated telepresence robot: a field trial connecting classrooms between Australia and Japan. In: 2013 IEEE/RSJ International Conference on Intelligent Robots and Systems (IROS), pp. 5896–5901, 3–7 November 2013
9. Tanaka, F., Takahashi, T., Matsuzoe, S., Tazawa, N., Morita, M.: Telepresence robot helps children in communicating with teachers who speak a different language. In: Proceedings of the 2014 ACM/IEEE International Conference on Human-Robot Interaction (HRI 2014), pp. 399–406. ACM, New York (2014)
10. Rae, I., Takayama, L., Mutlu, B.: The influence of height in robot-mediated communication. In: Proceedings of the 8th ACM/IEEE International Conference on Human-Robot Interaction (HRI 2013), pp. 1–8. IEEE Press, Piscataway (2013)
11. Rae, I., Mutlu, B., Takayama, L.: Bodies in motion: mobility, presence, and task awareness in telepresence. In: Proceedings of the 32nd Annual ACM Conference on Human Factors in Computing Systems (CHI 2014), pp. 2153–2162. ACM, New York (2014)

12. Nakanishi, H., Murakami, Y., Kato, K.: Movable cameras enhance social telepresence in media spaces. In: International Conference on Human Factors in Computing Systems (CHI 2009), pp. 433–442 (2009)
13. Yankelovich, N., Simpson, N., Kaplan, J., Provino, J.: Porta-person: telepresence for the connected conference room. In: CHI 2007 Extended Abstracts on Human Factors in Computing Systems (CHI EA 2007), pp. 2789–2794. ACM, New York (2007)
14. Tsui, K.M., Desai, M., Yanco, H.A., Uhlik, C.: Exploring use cases for telepresence robots. In: Proceedings of the 6th International Conference on Human-Robot Interaction (HRI 2011), pp. 11–18. ACM, New York (2011)
15. Beer, J.M., Takayama, L.: Mobile remote presence systems for older adults: acceptance, benefits, and concerns. In: Proceedings of the 6th International Conference on Human-Robot Interaction. ACM (2011)
16. Kosugi, A., Kobayashi, M., Fukuda, K.: Hands-free collaboration using telepresence robots for all ages. In: Proceedings of the 19th ACM Conference on Computer Supported Cooperative Work and Social Computing Companion. ACM (2016)

Reopening the Black Box of Career Age and Research Performance

Chien Hsiang Liao[✉]

Department of Information Management, Fu Jen Catholic University,
New Taipei City, Taiwan
jeffen@gmail.com

Abstract. Prior studies have a debate on whether research performance will be affected by age. Some researchers suggest that scientist's career age will positively affect research performance. For instance, for senior faculty with the later career years, their publications only slightly decline than highly productive faculty members, suggesting the statement of "Matthew effect" in science. In contrast, some studies point out that research productivity will decline with age, showing "a loss of vigor" in scientific research. This research question is still remain unanswered. The purpose of this study is to reexamine this association between career age and research performance, measured by number of publications, top-tier publications, and the h-index. The empirical study was conducted on a sample of 137 scholars from the *Web of Knowledge*. The results indicate that the relationship between career age and research performance is not a linear, nearly an inverted U-shaped curve.

Keywords: Research performance · Age · Tenure · H-index · Cognitive capital

1 Introduction

During the academic life, research plays a crucial role for scholar. Higher research performance not only inspires scholars to continue their research, but also it increases the possibility of a higher research funding from sponsors (Liao 2011). Research performance is related to a scholar's reputation and future promotions. Dean et al. (2011) posed an interesting question about what level of journal publication productivity is required for tenure. By using actual successful tenure-case data from faculty at several institutions, they found that productivity in top-tier journals clearly plays an important role in determining tenure for scholars. Nevertheless, even the professor who receives tenure from the university should retain the research quality to come up to the expectation of the university. Otherwise, he or she would be asked to give more lectures, which leads to lack of time for research. Therefore, keeping better research performance is always an important topic for researchers (Clark and Warren 2006; Gulbrandsen and Smeby 2005).

However, age is an unavoidable factor for scholar. Most importantly, Prior studies have different opinions on whether research performance will be influenced by age. In Gingras et al. (2008)'s study, they found there are two turning points in the professor's

© Springer International Publishing AG 2017
J. Zhou and G. Salvendy (Eds.): ITAP 2017, Part II, LNCS 10298, pp. 516–525, 2017.
DOI: 10.1007/978-3-319-58536-9_41

career. A first turning point is at age 40 years, where their productivity increases at a slower pace. A second turning point is around age 50, older scholars publish fewer first-authored papers and move closer to the end of the list of co-authors. Their productivity decreases linearly until about age 50. Similarly, Blackburn et al. (1978) indicate that research productivity tends to decrease with increasing age. But this decrease is only relative. Interest in research for high productive scholars remain rather high throughout the career when compared to medium or low productive scholars.

In contrast, Pelz and Andrews (1976) suggest that for lowly productive scholars, their productivity decrease with increasing age, but highly productive scholars tend to remain relatively high producers over time. Additionally, Allison and Stewart (1976) report that because of feedback through professional recognition and resources, highly productive scholars maintain or increase their productivity. The distribution of productivity increases as a cohort of scholar's ages. They conclude that research productivity, resources, and esteem will increase as career age increases, showing possible effect of accumulative advantage in the discipline or 'Matthew effect' (Merton 1968). Indeed, Blackburn et al. (1978) found that tenured faculty had a higher rate of productivity with 24.2% publishing five or more articles compared to only 12.8% of untenured faculty. Perhaps resources are usually focused on senior or tenured faculty.

With the respect to the effects of faculty aging, there are some contradictory results which report both positive and negative effects. Little empirical evidence is available on the relationship between age and academic performance (see Bayer and Dutton 1977). To enrich our understanding and fill the void in the literature, this study aims to reexamine the association between career age and research performance, which measured by the number of publications, top-tier publications, and h-index.

2   Theoretical Background

2.1   Career Age and Cognitive Capital

Nahapiet and Ghoshal (1998) proposed that there are three dimensions of social capital facilitating the creation of knowledge in communities, including structural capital, cognitive capital, and relational capital. The combination and exchange of knowledge is facilitated when individuals are motivated to engage in its exchange, there are structural links or connections between individuals (structural capital), individuals have the cognitive capability to understand and apply the knowledge (cognitive capital), and their relationships have strong, trust, reciprocal benefits (relational capital). In this study, I only focus on cognitive capital because it is strongly related to career age or seniority. More specifically, cognitive capital represents that individuals have a shared language and understanding in order to apply the intellectual capital. An individual's cognitive capital develops as he or she interacts over time with others sharing the same practice and learns the skills, knowledge, specialized discourse, and norms of the practice (Wasko and Faraj 2005). For instance, suppose scholars x and y work together for several years. When they want to conduct a new research project, they can communicate with each other more easily and effectively due to the high level of shared understanding and expertise. That is, the shared understanding and expertise (i.e., cognitive capital) has been developed from their prior experience. Likewise, scholars' sophisticated experience in a discipline will definitely be useful for producing their shared language, understanding, and expertise. Indeed, cognitive capital consists of mastering the application of expertise, which takes experience. Individuals with longer tenure in the shared practice are likely to better understand how their expertise is relevant, and are thus better able to share knowledge with others (Wasko and Faraj 2005).

In addition, career age or seniority is associated with prior experience. That is, prior experience has been empirically shown to be correlated with performance (Pajares and Miller 1994; Potosky 2002; Wood and Bandura 1987). For instance, Pajares and Miller (1994) found that prior experience with mathematics in high school and college have direct effects on mathematics self-efficacy and further affect problem solving performance in mathematics. Therefore, perhaps sophisticated scholars might achieve greater research performance than junior scholars because they have much more cognitive capital or prior experience to refine research.

2.2 Research Performance

In bibliometric studies, many indicators can be used to measure the research performance of an individual scholar (van Raan 1993). Totally, this study incorporates three factors as the manifestation of research performance, including the number of research publications, the number of top-tier journal publications and the H-index. Firstly, the number of research publications or so-called research productivity has been widely used to capture the efficiency of research work (Auranen and Nieminen 2010). This number is calculated as the articles published in academic journals with a peer-reviewed process.

To further distinguish the difference between these journal publications, this study also counts the number of top-tier journals specifically, aiming to trace a scholar's research productivity in terms of premier IS journals. Considering six previous studies about IS journal ranking, Li et al. (2013) develop a mean ranking for each IS journal. More specifically, they selected six prior studies that provide IS-related journal rankings. Next, they limited the journals to a selected set of IS research journals that were included in at the least three of the six studies. If a journal was ranked in only one or two prior studies, that journal was not included because it lacks enough evidence for ranking. Finally, they calculated the mean rank of these selected journals and sorted the journals by mean rank (see Appendix A). They concluded that the top five pure IS journals are *MIS Quarterly (MISQ), Information Systems Research (ISR), Journal of Management Information Systems (JMIS), Information & Management (I&M)*, and *Decision Support Systems (DSS)*. In this vein, this study also regards these five journals as being top-tier journals. Therefore, the number of top-tier publications is counted as the number of these five journals.

In addition, the H-index has been widely applied to measure individual research performance (e.g., Bornmann and Daniel 2005; Cronin and Meho 2006; van Raan 2006). Hirsch (2005) proposes the H-index as a simple and useful way to characterize the scientific output of a researcher. He defines the index as follows: "*a scientist has index h if h of his/her N_p papers have at least h citations each*". Interestingly, the H-index is a stable and consistent estimator of scientific achievement (Henzinger et al.

2010), because increasing the number of publications alone does not have an immediate effect on this index (Bornmann and Daniel 2007; Glänzel 2006).

3   Methodology

3.1   Data Source

Totally, 137 scholars are selected from the Social Science Citation Index (SSCI) database provided by Web of Knowledge. Following the data collection procedure by Li et al. (2013), 101 prolific or productive scholars who published three more articles and 36 ordinary scholars who published two articles from 1999 to 2003 in top five IS journals are targeted. These five IS journals are *MISQ*, *ISR*, *JMIS*, *I&M*, and *DSS*, which are highly determined as the top-tier IS journals (Clark and Warren 2006; Lowry et al. 2013). To further measure the future research performance of these scholars, their total number of publications, top-tier journal publications, and h-index during the period of 2004–2012 are collected. These data are collected from the SSCI database as well.

3.2   Measurement

Career age is measured as the duration time from the publication year of scholar's first publication in the SSCI database to 2012, because the time period of research accomplishment is up to 2012. For instance, if a scholar published his or her first article in 1990, the value for his or her publishing age or tenure is 22.

Research performance includes three measures in this study. The number of publications is calculated using search engineer of the SSCI database by given specific scholar. It should be noted that the publications are limited to the publication coverage of *Web of Knowledge*; the other publication sources may not be included. Similarly, the number of top-tier journals can be computed as well, which is limited to top five IS journals as aforementioned. Moreover, the h-index is calculated from all articles of given author during 2004–2012 and citation counts for these articles.

4   Results and Discussions

The associations between career age and research performance are tested by using regression analyses. This study firstly uses linear regression to test their associations. The results show that career age is not positively related to the number of publications and h-index (see Table 1).

The F values of career age on these two measures of research performance are 1.927 ($p > .05$) and 2.453 ($p > .05$). Nevertheless, career age is strongly associated with the number of top-tier publications ($F = 7.253$; $p <= .01$). According to the results, the linear associations between career age and research performance is partially supported. One plausible explanation is that the association from career age to accumulative advantage is not a simple linear relationship, contrary to Allison and Stewart (1976)'s expectation. Not necessarily all scholars can cumulative advantages or obtain required resources year by year, resulting this resource shortage cannot be reflected on the number of publications (research productivity) and h-index (i.e., research novelty or attracting more citations). The exception is the number of top-tier journal publications, because top-tier journals ask for high-quality articles, merely experienced scholars comprehend how to meet such standards or requirements of high-quality article.

Table 1. The results of regression analysis

Mode	Linear		
Dependent variable	The number of publication	The number of top-tier publication	H-index
F value	1.927	7.253**	2.453
P value	.167	.008	.120
R square	.014	.051	.018
Mode	Quadratic		
Dependent variable	The number of publication	The number of top-tier publication	H-index
F value	2.497+	4.058*	2.756+
P value	.086	.019	.067
R square	.036	.057	.040

Predictor: Career age
$^+$:$p < .1$; *:$p < .05$; **:$p < .01$

As listed in Table 1, this study also tests quadratic associations between career age and research performance. Corresponded with the statement by Gingras et al. (2008), there are two turning points in scholar's career age. As shown in Figs. 1, 2 and 3, these quadratic associations are approached significant and supported. More specifically, the F values of career age on the number of publications, top-tier journal publication, and h-index are 2.497 ($p = .086$), 4.058 ($p < .05$), and 2.756 ($p = .067$), respectively. These results show that when scholars were young or junior faculty, their performance grow exponentially. With middle ages, their performance came to a peak. But, their perform-ance will decline after middle age. The association is an inverted U-shaped curve. Inter-estingly, career age not only positively affects the number of top-tier journals, but also has a quadratic relationship with it. Both linear and quadratic relationships are supported. This finding reveals that the number of top-tier journals is highly affected by career age, which can be treated as an important antecedent or predictor for future research.

The number of publications

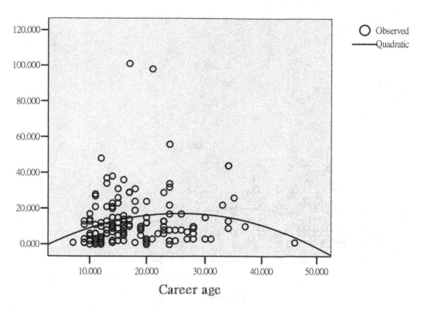

Fig. 1. Curve estimation (the number of publications)

The number of top-tier journals

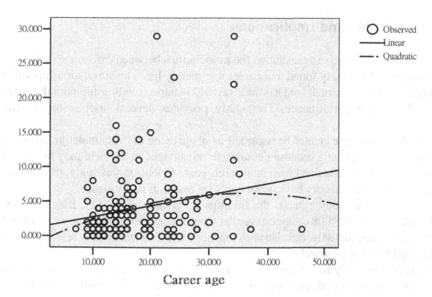

Fig. 2. Curve estimation (the number of publications)

H-index

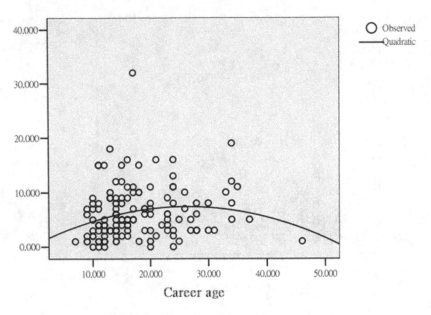

Fig. 3. Curve estimation (h-index)

5   Conclusion and Implications

The aim of this study is to reexamine the associations between career age and research performance. This study found that career age merely has a linear relationship with the number of top-tier journals, but has an inverted U-shaped relationship with three measures of research performance. This study provides several implications to future research.

Firstly, career age cannot be regarded as a surrogate of "accumulative advantage" or the "Matthew effect", because cumulative advantages in the field may not be long-term sustained or maintained with increasing year. At least in this study, prolific senior scholars do not necessarily have advantages on research performance.

Secondly, this study extends the findings by prior studies (e.g., Blackburn et al. 1978; Gingras et al. 2008), suggesting that career age not only has curve relationship with research productivity, but also with top-tier journals (high-quality research productivity) and h-index (research novelty).

Finally, this study found that loss of vigor seems to be inevitable for research when scientists are at advanced age. How to extend the growth period or postpone the recession period of research performance are worth to discuss. This study encourages future researchers could shed light on the related issues. It will definitely enrich our understanding and fill the void in the literature.

Appendix A

The results of journal ranking by Li et al. (2013)

Journals	[A]	[B]	[C]	[D]	[E]	[F]	Mean rank	Rank of mean
MISQ	1	1	2	1	1	2	1.33	1
ISR	3	2	3	2	3	1	2.33	2
CACM	2	3	1	5	2		2.6	3
JMIS	4		6	3	5	4	4.4	4
MS	5		7	4	4		5	5
DS	8		5	6	7		6.5	6
HBR	7		4	15	6		8	7
I&M	10	14	9	9	12	9	10.5	8
DSS	9	20	11	7	8	8	10.5	9
EJIS	11	14	8	11	13	10	11.17	10
ACM T	13	10	18	10	9		12	11
CAIS	18		10		23	6	14.25	12
SMR	12		17		16		15	13
IEEE TSE		5	24	22	10		15.25	14
Database	14		14		30	5	15.75	15
JAIS	30		20	12		3	16.25	16
OS	15		22	14			17	17
ISJ	16	17	23	13			17.25	18
ACM CS	24	12	16		20		18	19
JSIS	20	22		18	28	7	19	20
IEEE Computer	19	16	19	25	19		19.6	21
ASQ	21		15		24		20	22

[A]: Mylonopoulos and Theoharakis (2001);
[B]: Katerattanakul et al. (2003);
[C]: Peffers and Ya (2003);
[D]: Lowry et al. (2004);
[E]: Rainer and Miller (2005); and
[F]: Ferratt et al. (2007)
Source: Li et al. (2013)

References

Allison, P.D., Stewart, J.A.: Productivity differences among scientists: evidence for accumulative advantage. Am. Sociol. Rev. **39**(4), 596–606 (1976)

Auranen, O., Nieminen, M.: University research funding and publication performance - an international comparison. Res. Policy **39**(6), 822–834 (2010)

Bayer, A.E., Dutton, J.E.: Career age and research-professional activities of academic scientists: tests of alternative nonlinear models and some implications for higher education faculty policies. J. Higher Educ. **48**(3), 259–282 (1977)

Blackburn, R.T., Behymer, C.E., Hall, D.E.: Research notes: correlates of faculty publications. Sociol. Educ. **51**(2), 132–141 (1978)

Bornmann, L., Daniel, H.-D.: Does the h-index for ranking of scientists really work? Scientometrics **65**(3), 391–392 (2005)

Bornmann, L., Daniel, H.-D.: What do we know about the h-index? J. Am. Soc. Inform. Sci. Technol. **58**(9), 1381–1385 (2007)

Clark, J.G., Warren, J.: In search of the primary suppliers of IS research: who are they and where did they come from? Commun. Assoc. Inf. Syst. **18**(1), 296–328 (2006)

Cronin, B., Meho, L.: Using the h-index to rank influential information scientists. J. Assoc. Inf. Sci. Technol. **57**(9), 1275–1278 (2006)

Dean, D.L., Lowry, P.B., Humpherys, S.L.: Profiling the research productivity of tenured Information Systems faculty at U.S. institutions. MIS Q. **35**(1), 1–15 (2011)

Ferratt, T.W., Gorman, M.F., Kanet, J.J., Salisbury, W.D.: IS journal quality assessment using the author affiliation index. Commun. Assoc. Inf. Syst. **19**, 710–724 (2007)

Gingras, Y., Larivière, V., Macaluso, B., Robitaille, J.P.: The effects of aging on researchers' publication and citation patterns. PLoS ONE **3**(12), e4048 (2008)

Glänzel, W.: On the opportunities and limitations of the H-index. Sci. Focus **1**(1), 10–11 (2006)

Gulbrandsen, M., Smeby, J.C.: Industry funding and university professors' research performance. Res. Policy **34**(6), 932–950 (2005)

Henzinger, M., Suñol, J., Weber, I.: The stability of the h-index. Scientometrics **84**(2), 465–479 (2010)

Hirsch, J.E.: An index to quantify an individual's scientific research output. Proc. Natl. Acad. Sci. U.S.A. **102**, 16569–16572 (2005)

Katerattanakul, P., Han, B., Hong, S.: Objective quality ranking of computing journals. Commun. ACM **46**(10), 111–114 (2003)

Li, E.Y., Liao, C.H., Yen, R.H.: Co-authorship networks and research impact: a social capital perspective. Res. Policy **42**(9), 1515–1530 (2013)

Liao, C.H.: How to improve research quality? Examining the impacts of collaboration intensity and member diversity in collaboration networks. Scientometrics **86**(3), 747–761 (2011)

Lowry, P.B., Romans, D., Curtis, A.: Global journal prestige and supporting disciplines: a scientometric study of Information Systems journals. J. Assoc. Inf. Syst. **5**(2), 29–80 (2004)

Lowry, P.B., Moody, G.D., Gaskin, J., Galletta, D.F., Humpherys, S.L., Barlow, J.B., Wilson, D.W.: Evaluating journal quality and the association for information systems senior scholars' journal basket via bibliometric measures: Do expert journal assessments add value? MIS Q. **37**(4), 993–1012 (2013)

Merton, R.K.: The Matthew effect in science. Science **159**, 56–63 (1968)

Mylonopoulos, N.A., Theoharakis, V.: Global perceptions of IS journals. Commun. ACM **44**(9), 29–33 (2001)

Nahapiet, J., Ghoshal, S.: Social capital, intellectual capital, and the organizational advantage. Acad. Manag. Rev. **23**(2), 242–266 (1998)

Pajares, F., Miller, M.D.: Role of self-efficacy and self-concept beliefs in mathematical problem solving: a path analysis. J. Educ. Psychol. **86**(2), 193–203 (1994)

Peffers, K., Ya, T.: Identifying and evaluating the universe of outlets for information systems research: ranking the journals. J. Inf. Technol. Theory Appl. **5**(1), 63–84 (2003)

Pelz, D.C., Andrews, F.W.: Scientists in Organizations. Wiley, New York (1976)

Potosky, D.: A field study of computer efficacy beliefs as an outcome of training: the role of computer playfulness, computer knowledge, and performance during training. Comput. Hum. Behav. **18**(3), 241–255 (2002)

Rainer Jr., R.K., Miller, M.D.: Examining differences across journal rankings. Commun. ACM **48**(2), 91–94 (2005)

van Raan, A.F.J.: Advanced bibliometric methods to assess research performance and scientific development: basic principles and recent practical applications. Res. Eval. **3**(3), 151–166 (1993)

van Raan, A.F.J.: Comparison of the Hirsch-index with standard bibliometric indicators and with peer judgment for 147 chemistry research groups. Scientometrics **67**(3), 491–502 (2006)

Wasko, M.M., Faraj, S.: Why should I share? Examining social capital and knowledge contribution in electronic networks of practice. MIS Q. **29**(1), 35–57 (2005)

Wood, R., Bandura, A.: Social cognitive theory of organizational management. Acad. Manag. Rev. **14**(3), 361–384 (1987)

Intergenerational Techno-Creative Activities in a Library Fablab

Margarida Romero[✉] and Benjamin Lille

Laboratoire d'Innovation et Numérique pour l'Éducation (#fabLINE),
Université de Nice Sophia Antipolis, 89, Avenue George V, 06 046 Nice, France
margarida.romero@unice.fr, benjamin.lille.1@ulaval.ca

Abstract. A growing number of libraries are introducing maker spaces for facilitating the access of a diverse audience to the activities and tools that can foster the development of digital co-creativity and learning by making artefacts. In this paper, we introduce the intergenerational techno-creative activities we have co-designed in the context of the EspaceLab makerspace under the project #smartcitymaker, and we then analyze the potential of intergenerational techno-creative activities to overcome the gender and age stereotypes related to creative uses of technologies. We observe that intergenerational learning does not occur spontaneously in most cases and makerspace facilitation must promote intergenerational collaboration for achieving the objectives of facilitating learning across the lifespan by taking advantage of the forces of each age group.

Keywords: Intergenerational learning · Library · Digital creativity · Makerspace · Makerculture

1 Introduction

In the past few decades, libraries have been a popular place for sharing books and, more recently, multimedia documents. In the past few years, we have observed the emergence of makerspaces in public spaces such as libraries. Makerspaces are physical spaces, often in educational or public spaces, which aim to interconnect people who want to engage in constructing and tinkering with objects, new technologies and digital tools [1]. While the term "makerspace" is widely used in North America, the term "FabLab" (Fabrication Lab) is sometimes used to describe it in Europe. In both cases, the spaces unite people interested in technological tinkering and in the co-construction of artefacts [2]. For Capdevila [3], "hacker spaces, makerspaces, living labs, fablabs or co-working spaces are common denominations of localized spaces of collaborative innovation (LSCI) where knowledge communities meet to collectively innovate spaces of collaborative innovation". For this author, common features of these spaces include openness to the public and shared norms related to the way they share information, tools and knowledge among the different participants sharing these collaborative spaces of innovation. According to Dougherty [1], the community and the makers' interconnectedness are at the basis of the maker movement and an essential trait of the makerspaces reuniting makers of different ages for learning and creating artefacts together. Intergenerational makerspace activities could help overcome creative and digital ageism (which will be

© Springer International Publishing AG 2017
J. Zhou and G. Salvendy (Eds.): ITAP 2017, Part II, LNCS 10298, pp. 526–536, 2017.
DOI: 10.1007/978-3-319-58536-9_42

later defined) by engaging older adults in the techno-creative makerspace activities. Engaging teens, young and older adults in a joint techno-creative activities, such as digital game design, allows each of the age groups to know each other better and ensure their own representativeness in the game design process and product they develop together [4, 5]. Makerspace activities consider a larger type of activities than digital game design, to include 3D modelling and printing, and electronic and wood tinkering among others. The high diversity of activities that are usually developed in the maker-spaces allows the older participants to value their know-how in a wide range of skills: from woodworking, to electrical tinkering to the different techniques of sewing, older participants can share a wide range of diverse skills that could be required when partic-ipants are engaged in complex making projects such as the #smartcitymaker project we will introduce in this paper. We introduce the #smartcitymaker project and the way teen participants are engaged towards the design and making and of a city model, which integrates both analogic and digital techniques and materials to develop the different components of the city. The weekly activities developed with the teen participants engaged in the Québec city EspaceLab invite their parents and grandparents to help with the activities in order to promote intergenerational learning and learning between learners of different ages (from 8 to 16 years old). The informal context of the EspaceLab in the Monique Corriveau library (Québec, Canada) contributes to blurring some of the age-specific lines usually found in formal education contexts. In the next section, we introduce creative and digital ageism as one of the stereotypes to tackle through inter-generational learning experiences in the makerspace. Afterwards, we introduce inter-generational learning and the potential for both younger and older adults, specifically in the context of maker educational projects [6]. Then, we introduce the activities in the EspaceLab Junior and the project #smartcitymaker and the potential of the project for engaging participants in intergenerational learning activities. Finally, we introduce different game mechanics, which can help in promoting intergenerational making (Fig. 1).

2   Creative and Digital Ageism

Makerspaces located in libraries can provide the opportunity to unite different genera-tions and help fight some of the age-related stereotypes, such as the spontaneous crea-tivity of younger children [7] and digital and creative ageism. For Butler [8] ageism is the "systematic stereotyping and discrimination against people because they are old, just as racism and sexism accomplish this with skin colour and gender". In this paper we consider two types of ageism: creative ageism and digital ageism. Creative ageism assumes that older people are less creative because of their age. Romero and Hubert [9] consider digital ageism as a "form of discrimination appearing through the use of tech-nologies that have not been adapted for older adults or that conveys a negative image of older adults through their representation of older adults" (Fig. 2).

Fig. 1. EspaceLab open door activity reuniting intergenerational participants

Fig. 2. EspaceLab Junior techno-creative activities

Different authors have pointed to the interest of intergenerational activities as a way to reduce age-related stereotypes [10, 11]. Not only can younger participants value an older person's knowledge and know-how, but they can be inspired by their less impulsive attitudes towards the use of technology. Working with older adults can also offer learning opportunities for younger learners, as they are able to develop skills and acquire topic-related knowledge through collaborative work. Intergenerational collaboration can also foster broader personal development amongst younger learners, as interactions between adults and adolescents are characterized by warmth and acceptance. Adults expressing an interest in the youngsters and promoting autonomy may contribute to the development of their identity and their sense of responsibility. Intergenerational collaboration could also play a role in breaking down some of the age-based stereotypes that younger learners may have towards older adults and how they interact with digital technologies (Fig. 3).

Fig. 3. EspaceLab Junior intergenerational collaboration potential

2.1 Intergenerational Learning

While some intergenerational learning programs are designed to foster a one-sided transfer of knowledge and competencies from youth to the elderly and vice versa, effective intergenerational learning describes the way by which individuals from different generations are able to come together and learn from one another. It is a "systematic transfer of knowledge, skills, competencies, norms and values" that allows both the generations to stay gain a deeper understanding of the other generation's culture [12]. While this concept originated in the context of the family, intergenerational learning has evolved and expanded in contemporary society as a function of non-familial social groups. Due to a geographical shift where families are relocating and separating farther from relatives, the familial intergenerational shift is wavering. Also, economic and social changes have resulted in changes in the social contract and evolving expectations about the relative position of generations in society [13, p. 52]. To some, older adults are more considered as a burden than as a resource. That shift combined with ageism may result in low social capital, which is defined by Balatti and Falk [14] as the resource and access to network and communities, as older adults sometimes don't have access to their initial source of social capital: the family. Therefore, the symbiotic relationship that exists, which centres on growth and learning, social insights, and new technological skills faces a concerning hit and should therefore be explored between non-biologically related individuals to bolster social and emotional growth. Many programs related to intergenerational learning are grounded in Erikson's theory on life span development [15]. He postulated that children and older adults have parallel developmental needs, and this unique relationship fosters personal growth and agency. When younger and older generations join together for a shared activity, they are able to share their own personal experiences related to aging, experiences, values and aspirations. Older learners may feel after these events that they have more autonomy than originally realized can actively influence the community, and have a deeper understanding of younger generations and newer technologies. Younger learners may walk away with higher self-esteem and self-efficacy, a deeper understanding of adults, a belief that they can be appreciated and respected, and that they can even trust others more fully. Younger learners may also have the possibility to develop a more positive attitude towards aging. The effects of this reciprocity between older and younger individuals' opens minds to new skills and insights as well as new social structures and technologies influences both parties so that they can feel empowered and have a new perspective on lifelong learning. Intergenerational learning may also increase participants' social capital as learning, a social activity, creates condition that can foster social capital development by extending, enriching, and reconstructing social networks and by building trust and relationships. Intergenerational learning also aims to influence the development of tolerance, understanding, and respect between participants to encourage individual behaviours and attitudes that influence community participation [14, 16]. Granville [17] demonstrates the social and educational potential of intergenerational learning in his case study where young offenders in rehabilitation were provided placements to work in a community service centre with older adults with physical abilities or dementia. Interviews showed presence of intergenerational learning as the young offenders developed employability competencies while older adults developed a more positive attitude towards youth and a better opinion on their own agency as older adults with physical disabilities or dementia. Intergenerational learning therefore possesses a strong potential in addressing ageism while also offering learning opportunities for younger and older learning to develop valuable competencies (Fig. 4).

2.2 Intergenerational Making

The maker movement culture based on sharing, giving, participating and supporting [6] could facilitate intergenerational learning. By encouraging democratic cyberculture that is available to everyone, maker culture and maker spaces can provide opportunities for intergenerational learning. It provides chances for participation that act as a mediator of transformation of knowledge and the ability to practice learning within and between generations [6]. Maker space activities can bring together parents, grandparents and youngsters to tinker and create together while also understanding not only science and technology concepts but also those of the arts and social sciences. Intergenerational making activities, like intergenerational learning, can provide opportunities to learn from one another and share new knowledge. Maker spaces are open to do-it-yourselfers of varied backgrounds and ages. Maker space activities that combines digital technologies with crafts and more traditional technologies such as a sewing machine can therefore require different a variety of competencies and skills that can be attained by collaboration of younger and older learners. Using maker spaces for joint projects requiring both experience-based and technological know-how could be an opportunity not only for different types of intergenerational learning but also for achieving the goal of inclusive design. Moreover, the sharing of knowledge, projects and achievements encouraged in maker space activities can foster family and community involvement for younger and older participants. Intergenerational making activities therefore possess a great potential for participating in the improvement of cross-generational relationships and for sustaining learning across the lifespan.

3 #Smartcitymaker Project in the EspaceLab Junior

3.1 EspaceLab, an Intergenerational Makerspace Situated in a Public Library

EspaceLab is the first Québec fablab to be part of the MIT FabLab network. For Debaque, president of EspaceLab, we must stress the desire to develop a "culture of pooling" resources. The location of EspaceLab within the Quebec City library network facilitates is key strategic aspect to support the access to the makerspace for everyone, independently of their age or their technological skills. EspaceLab is an open and intergenerational makerspace that brings citizens closer to design and techno-creative manufacturing. In the image below we can appreciate an informal team composed by adults, a teen and a toddler who had informally engaged in understanding the functioning of a Sparki robot. By being open to all the public, EspaceLab also offers the opportunity for

Fig. 4. City model developed through the #SmartCityMaker in the EspaceLab

underprivileged children to have access to digital technologies that would be harder to have access to.

3.2 EspaceLab Junior

While the EspaceLab offers general services such as introductory workshops and tutorials aiming to develop participants' comprehension of the digital tools available at the fablab, EspaceLab also offers EspaceLab Junior which offers the opportunity for participants, learners from eight to sixteen years old, to co-design techno-creative projects. EspaceLab Junior has an intergenerational learning objectives which aims to extend Quebec library services to an intergenerational audience composed of teens, their parents, other young and older adults and provide them the opportunity and context to learn and engage in digital creative and educational activities. EspaceLab Junior activities aims to promote the 21st century competencies, in a playful and practical way. Among these skills, problem solving, digital creativity, collaboration and computational thinking could be developed through the co-design and achievement of techno-creative projects such as #smartcitymaker. 21st century competencies could be developed not only for younger learners, but also for older adults that are engaged in the project.

By being an environment open to all the public, EspaceLab Junior allows adults and older adults to engage in the #smartcitymaker project. Engagement is facilitated because many of the parents of the children work in techno-creative fields [18], such as engineering and computer science, and therefore can instill in their children a thirst for these types of activities. While most adults come from techno-creative fields, not all of them have a working knowledge of the tools available at EspaceLab Junior. For example, one grandmother only wanted to transport her grandchildren to the library where EspaceLab Junior was held, but when she saw the types of activities that the children were engaged in, she first decided to watch and observe and progressively engaged in the learning activities. While, at first, she wanted to understand the digital and tangible technologies for her own interest, she was soon offering her own input and insights to children on project progression. Maker activities therefore offer a collaborative setting where all participants are aiding one another in order to solve complex problems, such as the co-creation of or the tinkering with tangible and digital artefacts. The informal setting of EspaceLab Junior also allows for any willing children or adults that wish to join an activity to do it at any time. The informal setting aims to encourage intergenerational collaboration.

3.3 #SmartCityMaker Projet

The #SmartCityMaker is a research project that aims to develop learners' 21st-century competencies by proposing a theme-immersed techno-creative project in which learners are engaged in a learning-by-making approach through co-designing and co-constructing a model of a city. #SmartCityMaker is composed of pedagogical sequences where technology is used to foster learners' design thinking [19] by placing learners in a complex task that requires a high level of creativity. #SmartCityMaker adopts an approach that offers digital resources that are combined with a tangible model of a smart city. Townsend [20] defines the smart city as "places where information technology is combined with infrastructure, architecture, everyday objects, and even our bodies to address social, economic, and environmental problems". In that context, participants in EspaceLab Junior are building a smart city model with recycled and affordable material (construction paper, tape, painting), electrical components (smart city lighting system), electronic components (Makey Makey electronic system linked with Scratch visual coding software) and pedagogical robots (cars of the smart city). The combination of digital and tangible objects could offer an opportunity for learning through embodied cognition, as learners are able to physically interact with the pedagogical artifacts. Intertwining craft with digital artifacts could foster learners' engagement in complex programming concepts and practices. As Peppler and Kafai [21] valued, these three aspects are important in media art practices. #SmartCityMaker aims to foster creativity, collaboration and computation. Constructing a city model in the classroom is a complex based activity, which requires a certain number of sessions to be completed. The city theme has been chosen by the potential for interdisciplinary projects to build on the city model. Cities are complex systems, which engage all the curriculum disciplines at different stages. From geography technic for being able to read and transpose a plan, to history and mathematics required to reconstruct a building, all the disciplinary objectives of the Québec curriculum [22] can be related to the city theme. Moreover, the concept of a smart city "as a city that uses digital technology, data analysis and connectivity to create value and address its challenges" [15, p. 2]. The smart city theme offers a large diversity of possible projects, which requires digital solutions to improve the problems identified by the students in their daily lives.

#SmartCityMaker project is also carried out in the required course "ICT uses for preschool and elementary school," offered at the third year of the pre-service teachers program in Université Laval (Canada). Constructing a city model in the classroom is a complex based activity, which requires a certain number of sessions to be completed. In the first sessions of the project, the #SmartCityMaker is constituted of activities, which are developed with a higher degree of teacher regulation. The first activities engage the learners as city planners, and each small team should define the urban rule to design and build the building in their neighborhood. Buildings are assembled within the team, and the different neighborhoods are merged at the end of the second session of the course. Students carry out the second part of the project in parallel through team-based projects. Each team is required to address an educational issue that they may face in their career and analyze it. They are then asked to design a pedagogical intervention considering Technology Enhanced Learning (TEL) possibilities. Subsequently, students are invited to discuss the educational limit of their activity and the potential transferability of the activity in another educational context. Figure 5 introduces the different phases and tasks within the #SmartCityMaker project. In the initiation phase, students are organized in teams based on their level of confidence on the use of ICTs in order to ensure teams are homogeneous from this perspective. The first activities aim to develop the team building (forming and storming) and the norming stage (Tuckman and Jensen, 1977). Norming is orchestrated through the urban rules definition task where the teammates decide together how they will work as a team and what are the urban rules of their neighborhood in the #SmartCityMaker project.

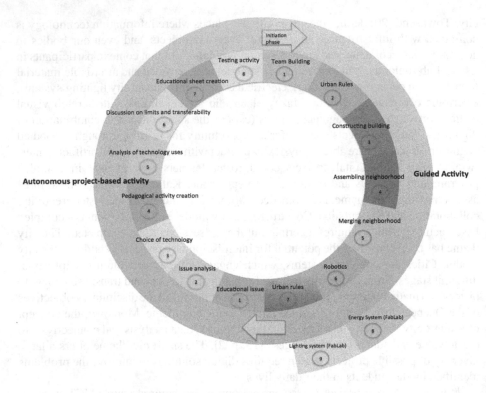

Fig. 5. #SmartCityMaker iterative process

Within the #SmartCityMaker class-based projects, students are asked to transfer class-developed competencies in the community. One of the modalities of transfers accepted is to participate in an intergenerational maker activity in EspaceLab Junior.

4   Cues for Fostering Intergenerational Making in the EspaceLab

By encouraging intergenerational collaboration in which people from all ages and gender are engaged in techno-creative activities, maker activities can help in overcoming gender and age stereotypes related to creative uses of technologies. Despite an important potential for informal intergenerational learning of competencies and topic-oriented knowledge through the values of the maker movement culture shared in the EspaceLab, and the #smartcityprojet EspaceLab Junior initiative, the dynamic is not systematic and only some of the adults and older persons engage spontaneously with the teens engaged in the activities. We need to go further in the active promotion of intergenerational learning opportunities by ensuring a climate which foster collaboration in risk-free and judgment free context. For this we should encourage the values of mutual aid, positive interdependence [23, 24] and attitudes of initiative taking, flexibility, leadership, accountability, conflict management and collaborative and complex problem solving competencies [25–27]. We also need to further orchestrate some activity designs that encourage intergenerational collaboration by identifying competencies possessed by participants from every generation and by taking them into account in activity design. Participation could also be elicited by implementing gaming mechanics in maker activities such as collaborative competition and by adding a narrative to maker activities. Such structuration of maker activities would also need to respect values of maker culture such as openness, democratization and inclusion of all. Like other scholars [6, 28–30], we believe that it is important to move away from top-down approach in analyzing and implementing intergenerational maker activity and instead analyze how all participants can be directly involved in maker activity design as well as analyzing their motives for participating in making activities. Older adults and youngsters could therefore discuss and design their own making activities. We also need to ensure that adults and older adults that are not comfortable with the tools used at EspaceLab feel secure in taking part in maker space activities. Also, we need to identify adults' and older adults' skills that could be invested in maker space activities so that anyone can contribute to the progression of maker projects. Creating two open questionnaires that would be given before the activity could be the first step in understanding motives, representation and beliefs of participants in intergenerational making activities that could then help us encourage intergenerational collaboration.

References

1. Dougherty, D.: The maker movement. Innovations. **7**, 11–14 (2012)
2. Suire, R.: La Performance Des Lieux De Co-Création De Connaissances: Le cas des Fablab (The Performance of Co-Creation Knowledge Places: The Case of Fablab). SSRN 2,671,713 (2015)
3. Capdevila, I.: Typologies of localized spaces of collaborative innovation. SSRN 2,414,402 (2013)
4. Loos, E.: Designing meaningful intergenerational digital games. In: International Conference on Communication, Media, Technology and Design, pp. 46–51 (2014)
5. Romero, M.: Intergenerational digital storytelling pairing teens as multimedia facilitators with an elder as narrative director. In: Bira, M., Ivan, L., Daba-Buzoianu, C. (eds.) International conference Qualitative Research in Communication 2015. Book of abstracts, p. 30, Bucharest, Romania (2015)
6. Barma, S., Romero, M., Deslandes, R.: Implementing maker spaces to promote cross-generational sharing and learning. In: Romero, M., Sawchuk, K., Blat, J., Sayago, S., Ouellet, H. (eds.) Game-Based Learning Across the Lifespan. AGL, pp. 65–78. Springer, Cham (2017). doi:10.1007/978-3-319-41797-4_5
7. Romero, M., Hyvönen, P., Barberà, E.: Creativity in collaborative learning across the life span. Creat. Educ. **3**, 422 (2012)
8. Butler, R.N.: Age-ism: another form of bigotry. Gerontologist **9**, 243–246 (1969)
9. Romero, M., Ouellet, H.: Scaffolding digital game design activities grouping older adults, younger adults and teens. In: Zhou, J., Salvendy, G. (eds.) ITAP 2016. LNCS, vol. 9754, pp. 74–81. Springer, Cham (2016). doi:10.1007/978-3-319-39943-0_8
10. Romero, M., Loos, E.: Intergenerational Game Creation. Engaging elders and secondary level students in intergenerational learning about immigration through participative game design. In: Presented at the European Distance and E-Learning Network 2015, Barcelona (2015)

11. Cucinelli, G., Davidson, A.-L., Romero, M.: Participatory game design in intergenerational contexts: co-designing digital games for intergenerational learning using Scratch. In: ACG2016: Favoriser l'innovation en recherche sur le vieillissement/ CAG2016: Fostering Innovation in Research on Aging. Canadian Association on Gerontology, Montréal, Québec, Canada (2016)
12. Newman, S., Hatton-Yeo, A.: Intergenerational learning and the contributions of older people. Ageing Horiz. **8**, 31–39 (2008)
13. Icenogle, R.S.H.M.: Preparing for an age-diverse workforce: intergenerational service-learning in social gerontology and business curricula. Educ. Gerontol. **27**, 49–70 (2001)
14. Balatti, J., Falk, I.: Socioeconomic contributions of adult learning to community: a social capital perspective. Adult Educ. Q. **52**, 281–298 (2002)
15. Erikson, E.H.: Childhood and Society. WW Norton & Company, New York (1993)
16. Schuller, T., Brassett-Grundy, A., Green, A., Hammond, C., Preston, J.: Learning, Continuity and Change in Adult Life. Wider Benefits of Learning Research Report. ERIC, London (2002)
17. Granville, G.: An 'unlikely alliance': young offenders supporting elderly people in care settings. Educ. Ageing **16**, 9–25 (2001)
18. Florida, R.: The Rise of the Creative Class—Revisited: Revised and Expanded. Basic books, New York (2014)
19. Bowler, L.: Creativity through "maker" experiences and design thinking in the education of librarians. Knowl. Quest. **42**, 58 (2014)
20. Townsend, A.M.: Smart Cities: Big Data, Civic Hackers, and the Quest for a New Utopia. WW Norton & Company, New York (2013)
21. Peppler, K.A., Kafai, Y.B.: Collaboration, computation, and creativity: media arts practices in urban youth culture. In: Proceedings of the 8th International Conference on Computer Supported Collaborative Learning, pp. 590–592. International Society of the Learning Sciences (2007)
22. PFÉQ, Gouvernement du Québec: Programme de formation de l'école québécoise, Québec (2011)
23. Collazos, C.A., Guerrero, L.A., Pino, J.A., Ochoa, S.F.: Collaborative scenarios to promote positive interdependence among group members. In: Favela, J., Decouchant, D. (eds.) CRIWG 2003. LNCS, vol. 2806, pp. 356–370. Springer, Heidelberg (2003). doi: 10.1007/978-3-540-39850-9_30
24. Johnson, D.W., Johnson, R.T.: Cooperation and Competition: Theory and Research. Interaction Book Company, Edina (1989)
25. OECD: PISA 2015 Collaborative Problem Solving Framework. OECD Publishing (2013)
26. Steiner, G.: The concept of open creativity: collaborative creative problem solving for innovation generation—a systems approach. J. Bus. Manag. **15**, 5–33 (2009)
27. Neubert, J.C., Mainert, J., Kretzschmar, A., Greiff, S.: The assessment of 21st century skills in industrial and organizational psychology: complex and collaborative problem solving. Ind. Organ. Psychol. **8**, 238–268 (2015)
28. Hedegaard, M.: Strategies for dealing with conflicts in value positions between home and school: influences on ethnic minority students' development of motives and identity. Cult. Psychol. **11**, 187–205 (2005)
29. Rogoff, B.: The Cultural Nature of Human Development. Oxford University Press, Oxford (2003)
30. Monk, H.: Learning and development across the generations: a cultural-historical study of everyday family practices (2011)

'Industrie 4.0' and an Aging Workforce – A Discussion from a Psychological and a Managerial Perspective

Matthias Schinner[1], André Calero Valdez[2(✉)], Elisabeth Noll[1],
Anne Kathrin Schaar[2], Peter Letmathe[1], and Martina Ziefle[2]

[1] Chair of Management Accounting, RWTH Aachen University,
Templergraben 64, Aachen, Germany
{schinner,noll,letmathe}@controlling.rwth-aachen.de
[2] Human-Computer Interaction Center, RWTH Aachen University,
Campus-Boulevard 57, Aachen, Germany
{calero-valdez,schaar,ziefle}@comm.rwth-aachen.de

Abstract. The aging workforce is already impacting on companies, particularly those in countries of the industrialized Western world. Furthermore, Western companies are coming under the increasing influence of technological developments, such as 'Industrie 4.0', which are in the process of completely changing traditional working environments. In order to maintain their industrial competitiveness, companies need to synchronize these technological developments with their own organizational requirements and in particular with the requirements of an aging workforce. We show how different types of competencies may be categorized in order to enable a successful synchronization. In addition, we take a look at recent developments in the domain of 'Industrie 4.0' and derive future research areas for solving the challenges involved.

Keywords: Complexity · Industrie 4.0 · Competence management · Collaboration · Communication · Internet of Things

1 'Industrie 4.0', Internet of Things, and an Aging Workforce: Their Pitfalls for Employees and Employers

The aging of the world's population is having an impact on all areas of daily life. As a result, the United Nations describe this demographic change as *"one of the most significant social transformations of the twenty-first century"* [1].

To underline this development in numbers: By 2050 every fifth person of the world's population will be aged 60 years or older. In 2015 only every eighth person belonged to this age group [1]. Especially companies in high-wage countries are affected by the effects of an aging workforce [2,3].

The main trends which are driving this development are the expansion of life expectancy as well as a decline in birth rates, the latter resulting from better education and birth control [4]. The number of young employees entering the

© Springer International Publishing AG 2017
J. Zhou and G. Salvendy (Eds.): ITAP 2017, Part II, LNCS 10298, pp. 537–556, 2017.
DOI: 10.1007/978-3-319-58536-9_43

workforce will fall, and a considerable number of older employees will leave their working lives as a result of the extended age pyramid [2].

Especially companies are struggling with these changes in the age structure of their workforce. Well-trained and highly-skilled employees are the key factor to the success of the German economy [5,6]. With the retirement of these workers, important knowledge for maintaining industrial competitiveness will leave the companies [7]. Therefore, companies increasingly depend on the knowledge, skills, and experience of their older workers. This will force companies to find ways to keep older workers employed for a longer period of time and also to retrain them to meet the challenges of the future through new technological developments. Thus, there is a need to reconsider current workforce training methods and to adapt them to the needs of an older workforce [4]. Although age management seems to be a big topic, Fornalczyk et al. [2] showed that knowledge about age management might be relatively weak among young workers.

Further trends to affect companies are so-called 'Digitization' and 'Automation'. One of the most cited studies on the influence on jobs from these developments is the study by Frey and Osborne concerning the possible loss of jobs due to automation over the next twenty years in the US. As a consequence, 47 % of US workers are in great danger of being replaced by robots [8]. For Germany, Bonin et al. conducted a comparable study based on different types of activities in companies. As a result, only 12 % of tasks are in danger of being automated. Nevertheless, the content of a lot of tasks will change, and many activities will become more complex [9].

Related technologies, e.g., for Digitization and Cyber Physical Systems, will lead to significant economic and social changes and challenges [10]. Furthermore, the trend of an aging workforce is present. In combination this could be a big challenge for companies in the industrialized Western world. Therefore, we should take a closer look at the consequences. In order to describe and summarize these developments, in Germany the term 'Industrie 4.0' has become popular [11], so we will use this term hereafter.

2   Changes and Challenges in Organizations Posed by 'Industrie 4.0'

In this section we describe the main technological trends of 'Industrie 4.0' and highlight some changes in the workplace of the future.

2.1   Digitization, Cyber Physical Systems, 'Industrie 4.0', and Big Data

Digitization and Cyber Physical Systems are well-known and often cited buzzwords in both academia and industry, as e.g. the related term Big Data [3]. Scientists and practitioners call these technological changes the "fourth industrial revolution" [4–7]. Some other authors claim that this development will change our lives more than any other developments of the past 40 years [8]. But what do these buzzwords involve? According to Mauro et al. [3], Digitization is the *"process of converting continuous, analog information into discrete, digital and machine-readable format"*. Mayer-Schönberger and Cukier [9] define Digitization as *"making analog information readable by computers, which also makes it easier and cheaper to store and process"*. This development is driven by performance improvements of hardware, e.g., increased computer memory or increased packing density of microprocessors [10]. In this context also the term 'Datafication' occurs. Datafication describes the collection of all available data, their transformation into formats in order to quantify them and to generate new helpful information through the analysis of these data [9]. Pattern recognition for logistic systems based on huge data which are analyzed by multivariate statistics or predictive data analytics are examples of these new technical possibilities [12]. This leads to another frequently used term in this context: Big Data. It is a phenomenon related to the actual technological possibilities to generate, transform, analyze, and store big amounts of data. For instance, devices are able to steadily produce user data about behavioral patterns from their users [3].

These new opportunities make the implicit value of the information visible and help to improve decision processes in many areas or help to understand complex relationships. Analytical methods for transforming data into value are, e.g., Machine Learning, Natural Language Processing, and Pattern Recognition [9]. On the other hand concerns about the collection of these data amounts are obvious. One of the main challenges will be to protect the privacy and the personal data of the users. Furthermore, it has to be clarified who will have access to data amounts and who will control the data in order to avoid misconduct [13].

According to Hirsch-Kreinsen and ten Hompel [10], there are two phases of Digitization. In the first phase, the production, communication, and consumption of goods are based on digital processes which are intangible and themselves based on data and information. The second phase is the connection between physical things through Digitization. In the future, physical elements like machines, storages, or materials will be connected throughout the whole value chain. These connected systems are so called Cyber Physical Systems [11]. According to Lee [14], *"Cyber-Physical Systems (CPS) are integrations of computation and physical processes. Embedded computers and networks monitor and control the physical processes, usually with feedback loops where physical processes affect computations and vice versa"* [14]. At best, Cyber Physical Systems collect data worldwide through sensor systems from other physical systems and actors and respond to them in order to optimize the whole system. Also humans are able to communicate via human-computer interfaces. Figure 1 shows a typical architecture of a Cyber Physical System which includes embedded systems, sensors, and electronic hardware and software. These systems communicate with other systems and humans and are often 'Systems of Systems'. Together, they build superordinate systems [15].

The focus of this development is the creation of smart and agile factories which use the intelligence of the 'Internet of Things' for planning and execution of production [5,7]. According to Xia et al. [17], Internet of Things *"refers to*

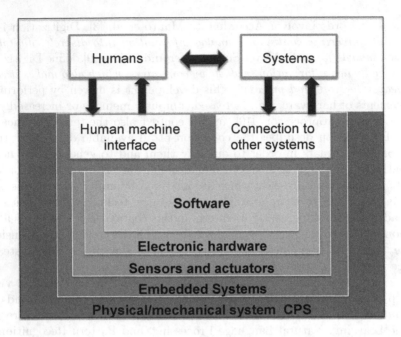

Fig. 1. Architecture of a Cyber Physical System (based on [8,16])

the networked interconnection of everyday objects, which are often equipped with ubiquitous intelligence". Schlick et al. [18] summarize the main criteria within production environments which will change in the next years: comprehensive networking, the use of Internet standards for communications, adaptive and agile production systems, smart objects, and a change in the role of the employee. One example of this change will be the opportunity to work from different locations all over the world, which means being independent from any particular location. In this context, it is not necessary to be at the manufacturing site, and it is possible to steer the production processes from outside the factory [19]. Important for the success of Cyber Physical Systems are their design and usage. Specific requirements arise in the fields of safety, usability, or trust in the system [20].

2.2   Changes in the Digital Workplace

To use the full potential of 'Industrie 4.0', organizations have to adapt to the new technological trends. Furthermore, they also have to find the balance between human and technological factors [21]. Dworschak and Zaiser [21] developed two scenarios to describe the extreme for organizing the work and technology within production companies of the future using Cyber Physical Systems (see Table 1). In the automation scenario, the technology guides the employees. Highly skilled employees are just necessary for installing the system, for implementing changes within the system, or for maintenance reasons. For the rest of the time, the system is running the production and the employees have a limited decision-making power. Within the tool scenario, the employees steer the systems and have a higher degree of freedom in their decision making. As a result, there is a higher need for skilled employees in order to handle the complexity.

Table 1. Scenarios in CPS [21]

Automation scenario	Tool scenario
– CPS guide skilled workers – Work is determined by technology – Emergence of a skill gap: Skilled workers cannot develop/build up the know-how for dealing with problems anymore – High-skilled employees are responsible for installation, modification and maintenance of CPS	– Skilled workers guide CPS – CPS supports the decision-making of skilled workers – A successful performance requires the provision of crucial information and suitable approaches of vocational education and training due to an increasing demand for IT, electronic and mechanical knowledge

Kölmel et al. [20] distinguish in this context between a technological and a contextual complexity (see Table 2). Within technological complexity, the employees are confronted with more complex interaction characteristics through Digitization, e.g. systems stability or interfaces [22]. Within contextual complexity, employees are confronted with a change of the task type. For instance, the tasks of the future will have a higher degree of freedom and less structure than before because simple tasks can be automated. As a result, the workforce will experiencing a change of role. That is, typical tasks will be the supervising of the production and the solving of unexpected problems. In these cases, the employee acts as a problem-solver [27]. Also Autor and Dorn [28] highlight the changes within human tasks in the future workplace. According to them, the content of the tasks will change more and more into collaboration, communication, or creative problem-solving.

Through Digitization, communication in the workplace has already been altered and might be altered even more in the future. Today, plenty of communication channels exist for communication between employees. Besides conventional face-to-face communication, digital communication channels are upcoming (or have already been established), such as email or platform communication [29,30]. In a study by Jäckel and Würfel [31], the majority of employees in an organization (71.5% to 83.8% of the respondents) state that their daily work routine depends strongly on email communication [31]. Moreover, platform communication has developed into an important communication channel for organizational communication within a few years [30]. Nonetheless, there is general agreement in the literature that traditional face-to-face communication is irreplaceable [32]. Face-to-face communication allows employees to clarify uncertainties and to give feedback immediately as well as to transfer non-verbal contents. In conversations, these non-verbal elements play an important role because they can modify or even change completely the verbal message.

Table 2. Technical and contextual complexity of CPS task characteristics from [23]; based on [21, 24–26]

	Technological complexity	Contextual complexity
Increasing challenges of CPS for the workforce	– Interaction characteristics of technology (interfaces, coordination, information exchange, systems stability) – System architecture and variety of different systems, agents, architectures, devices, or data-bases	– Broader tasks, roles, or jobs – Open-ended and unstructured tasks (problems) – Less structure – Abstractness – Interpretation and use of information – Collaboration – Information overload

Digital communication channels, such as emails, are not or only to a limited extent able to transfer these important non-verbal elements [33].

Also, collaboration will change in the workplace of the future. One example of the change will be the freedom to work from different locations all over the world and to steer the machines simply via virtual dashboards [19, 34]. Furthermore, teams will use more technological tools for knowledge-sharing and collaborative problem-solving when they work in different offices or manufacturing sites [35]. As a result, they will need different skills for using these collaboration tools. For example, Slack could be used for communication in teams or Google Drive to create text documents in teams on a shared project [34]. Knowledge-sharing technologies could be a powerful tool for solving organizational problems. The use of such technologies is crucial for maintaining industrial competitiveness when knowledge gets lost with retiring employees [36–38]. The control of the physical world by the employees and also the interaction between employees will be changed by the introduction of Cyber Physical Systems [39]. That is, sensors will be able to measure all kinds of movements from the employees and these data can be shared worldwide in real time [15]. In the end, it will be a matter of employee acceptance [40]. Additionally, the need for new collaboration concepts will occur because more and more diverse groups from different cultural and professional backgrounds will be involved in interaction processes [41, 42] in order to solve problems collaboratively [43]. Schuh et al. [44] hypothesize that collaboration and its different dimensions (communication, cooperation, coordination) can be levers for 'Industrie 4.0' (see Table 3). Analogously, challenges within collaboration will occur, which will, in this case, be the organizational driver for meeting the requirements of technological developments. For cooperation, also concepts such as open production and open innovation will attract more attention [45]. Highly-skilled and specialized employees will collaborate in new organizational forms to find solutions for complex problems which could not be solved by algorithms or by one discipline alone [42]. As a result, companies have to develop competencies for their workforce with a stronger focus on technological change than before to prepare their employees for the digital age. Especially so-called soft skills, e.g. communication, problem-solving, or self-organization, will become more important [45, 46].

Table 3. Exemplified levers of 'Industrie 4.0' in the context of collaboration [33]

	Challenges of Collaboration	Levers of 'Industrie 4.0'
Communication	**Information sharing:** Delay between obtaining and interpreting data	**High resolution real-time communication** for obtaining real-time data directly from the source and exactly when needed
	Sense-making: Inadequate knowledge regarding the global effects of local decisions	**Large-scale simulation** for assessing the impact of action alternatives in context of the chosen optimization criteria
Coordination	**Resource-pooling:** Allocation of best- fitting and available resources in production network	**Self-forming system-of-systems** for the ad-hoc linkage of dispersed resources
	Goal-congruence: Ensuring coherent goals in organizations	**End-to-end standardization of reporting** for instating consistent objectives throughout all hierarchies
Cooperation	**Cross-functional activities:** Interdivisional and cross-company cooperation	Virtual representations of physical objects for collaboration without the limitations of the physical world
	Empowerment: Implementing decentralized leadership and decision-making	**Automatic control and pre-processing of data** for unburdening employees from routine activities in order to put focus on policymaking

3 Characteristics of an Aging Workforce in a Digitized Workplace

Besides the changes in the workplace, also the workforce itself will be changing in the near future. Demographic changes, technology generations [47], and changes in generational values will shape the future work design.

3.1 How Aging Affects the Worker

Aging is a highly individual process, which predominantly strengthens preexisting differences in physical, psychological, and socio-economic backgrounds [48]. This means that inter-individual differences are stronger between older adults than between younger ones [49]. Still, there are systematic processes that do correlate with age. With increasing age, several changes occur in the human body and brain—some of them highly relevant for the working environment.

For example, sensory, senso-motoric, and cognitive capabilities degrade with age. They do so very individually and at different speeds, although some evidence hints at an interrelated degradation process [50,51]. As a result, employees work at different speeds. This means that older employees might be very individually affected by their aging process. Some might still be able to perform complex motoric tasks, while others may only perform well in tasks that require cognitive skills. Matching the task to the working is even more critical for older employees [52,53].

One must note, though, that these skills also still show high plasticity [54], meaning that it is necessary to use and foster the usage of these capabilities even when first signs of degradation occur, in order to prevent further loss.

Social interaction has been shown to prevent the loss of cognitive functions to some extent; Thus, keeping an employee integrated in a social environment such as work is also helpful for retaining capabilities [55].

When looking at job performance and age, no direct correlation can be found [56]. However, older employees statistically tend to be absent more often than younger ones. Older employees do not necessarily get sick more often, but they are often more affected by an illness and also more often struck by illnesses that lead to loss of working capabilities [56].

Older adults often apply compensatory action in order to counteract (e.g. writing things down, planning further ahead [56]) a slowdown in their information processing. This decrease of performance in information processing also shows itself when looking at the learning of new skills. People of higher age have a harder time learning new skills and processing information than younger adults do. Nevertheless, age has no effect on the act of forgetting. Older adults do not forget new knowledge more quickly than younger adults do [56].

3.2   Age as a Resource

One benefit of not forgetting more quickly than younger employees also yields the basis for a strong benefit of older employees. They excel at tasks where knowledge and experience are crucial. The cognitive and affective changes that occur after conducting a task several hundred times (also referred to as 'expertise') is beneficial for job performance. Older employees often have more declarative and procedural knowledge about tasks [56], which enhances their capabilities and their sense of security in performing a knowledge-intensive task.

In particular, skills that were ingrained during early adulthood and strengthened on the job [57] tend to show equally high performance in older adults as in younger ones, even when cognitive skills are required that show signs of degradation. It seems to be the case that older adults develop strategies to arrange mental tasks in order differently to optimize the task by using less cognitive load (e.g., looking further ahead, writing things down, pruning options through experience) [56].

When it comes to relatively simple tasks (tasks that require low cognitive load), age is not relevant, as for example primary memory is unaffected by age. Older and younger adults alike remember facts and information equally well [56] and can apply them to simpler tasks. Furthermore, spontaneous imagination is unaffected by age. This means that tasks that involve creativity can very easily be conducted by older adults.

Overall, older adults show effects of domain specialization [56]. This means that older adults pick and choose where to apply cognitive effort which is more strictly based on experience. This leads to very high performance in areas of specialization and disinterest in other areas. Even when a high information processing speed is required, older adults may outperform younger adults when they can apply more specialized skills. If traversing an option space is necessary for a task (e.g. as in a game of chess), older adults tend to look as equally ahead as younger ones, but prune some options more quickly based on experience. This compensates for the slower information processing speed [56]. When motor-skills are needed, older adults may compensate for lower skill levels by looking further ahead and pre-planning their tasks [56]. This can also lead to higher performance in information-seeking tasks, even when spatial cognition shows signs of degradation [58].

The largest set of skills unaffected by age is the language domain. Older adults are as able to use language [59] as competently as younger ones are.

3.3 Possible Mitigation Strategies

Aging, on its own, is neither a pure benefit nor a pure drawback for individual employees or employers. It is how age and employee demographics are managed that defines organizational performance.

When adding digital media to the equation, the challenge seemingly becomes more simple: Use social media for knowledge exchange from old to young and use age-diverse teams for creativity tasks! However, especially the usage of such technology is different between technology generations [60]. Older users are accustomed to a more formal way of communicating in social media, while younger users tend to carry over their behavior from private social media to work-related settings. These etiquette mismatches may lead to an unfruitful use of digital media and a lack of motivation [61].

To enable successful knowledge transfer in the social media, one must identify benefits and barriers for the individual users and must regard user diversity (incl. age) respectfully [62]. If the individuality of users is disregarded, knowledge sharing might be reduced [63].

Beyond these technological means, it is necessary to adopt processes that ensure successful collaboration in heterogeneous teams. For example, mentoring programs can be used to transfer tacit knowledge from older employees to new hires. This serves a double purpose, as it utilizes capabilities (expertise in older adults and fast learning in younger adults) and ensures protection against crucial knowledge loss. Furthermore, this addresses the motivational differences of the two age groups. Older employees want to share their knowledge and put it to use, while younger employees want to invest in learning and invest in their careers [64].

Overall, it is necessary to value the differences present in the workforce and to match tasks to employees, while allowing growth and knowledge transfer. This can only be achieved by addressing training on the job to match individual preferences, capabilities and task requirements, and necessities.

4   Competence Management

Companies should address these changes in order to maintain competitiveness [6]. To coordinate their resources for training and development, they need tools to analyze the requirements of their technology, their organization, as well as their workforce. For this reason, we discuss competence management as the basis for the management of the aging workforce in the age of 'Industrie 4.0'. There is no commonly accepted definition of the construct 'competence'. Erpenbeck and von Rosenstiel [65] argue that competencies of an individual person are *"dispositions for self-organization activities"*. Unlike qualifications, competencies are not measurable with standardized tests. The results of the tests simply show knowledge, but not whether the knowledge could be applied in real-world situations and different contexts. However, competence is also the ability to convert knowledge and qualifications into situation-adequate action [65]. This is similar to the competence definition by Reinhardt and North [66]: *"Competence basically describes a relation between requirements placed on a person/group or self-created requirements and these persons' skills and potentials to meet these requirements. Competencies are concretized at the moment knowledge is applied and become measurable in the achieved results of the actions."*[1] It becomes clear that Reinhardt and North highlight, among other things, the application of knowledge and that competencies lead to a measurable use. Besides, there are not just individual competencies of a person. Wilkens et al. [67] underline that competence management should go far beyond pure personnel and educational management and cover the individual and organizational levels of competencies. This is in line with North et al. [68], who argue that individual competencies should be aligned with the technological requirements. Furthermore, competence management should be developed and matched with other organizational requirements, such as e.g. strategic and market decisions, organizational structure, processes, projects, or technologies. This so-called competence adaption can help to coordinate between technologies as organizational requirements and individual competencies [66]. According to Freiling [69], competence is an *"organizational, repeatable, learning-based and therefore non-random ability to sustain the coordinated deployment of assets and resources enabling the firm to reach and defend the state of competitiveness and to achieve the goals"*. So they highlight especially the importance of organizational competencies for the competitiveness of companies [69]. Mills et al. [70] emphasize in the context of organizational competencies the dynamic capabilities of an organization for the adaption of relevant competencies as a main competitive advantage. This concept is linked to resources which are important for change. Individual competencies are often divided into

---

[1] All direct quotes are translated from German by the authors, where applicable.

professional competencies (technological and, in part, methodological competencies), personal, and soft competencies (in part, methodological, self-management, and social competencies) to describe competencies. In addition, we adopt the approved approach dividing competencies into technical, methodological, social, and self-management competencies (see Fig. 2). Moreover, this classification is often used to develop competence models and frameworks within companies [46, 68, 71, 72].

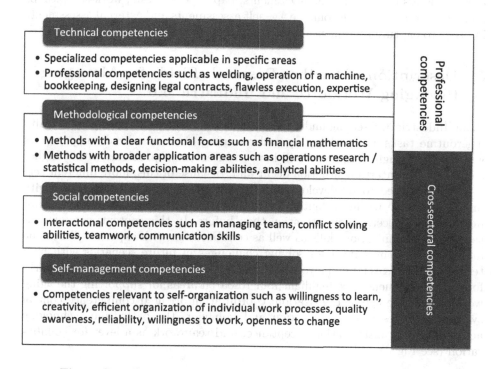

Fig. 2. Competence classification (based and extended) [23, 68, 71–73]

Having developed a competence model to describe the required competencies for the fulfillment of organizational requirements, it is important to use adequate measurement instruments for determining different levels of the respective competence. As a result, a clear classification of the requirements and the status quo of the individual employees should be possible and should constitute the basis for an analysis of the resulting gap. Unfortunately, no commonly accepted model for measuring competencies and their classification exists.

North et al. [68] propose a simple scale with different dimensions for the assessment (knowledge and experience, task complexity, autonomous work and self-management, and capability of reflection) and based on experience (Levels: Connoisseur, Experienced and Advanced, Expert) to describe the different levels of the respective competence. The experienced-based scale could be subdivided into six proficiency level (A1, A2, B1, B2, C1, C2), like the European

Language Portfolio. Letmathe and Schinner [23] proposed an extension to this scale. They divide the task complexity into two fields: technological complexity of the task and contextual complexity of the task. Furthermore, they divide the newly introduced category 'contextual complexity of the task' into three already mentioned dimensions which are relevant for 'Industrie 4.0': structure of the task, content of the task, and interaction and collaboration. Examples of methods for measuring competencies and classifying employees on these scales are: self-assessments, external assessments, paper-pencil tests, work-samples, or holistic approaches which combine e.g. self-assessments and external assessments in order to capture all dimensions of competencies [74].

5   Description of Further Research Fields for Managing the Aging Workforce and 'Industrie 4.0'

In an 'Industrie 4.0' setting under the influence of quickly fluctuating staff, training routine tasks and building up and retaining of standardized competencies will not be enough. Employees will have to intervene if problems with a higher complexity in uncertain situation occur and, because of this, more different sets of skills will need to be developed and trained to ensure sufficient adaptivity in the workforce within a digitized world. Especially personal and social competencies will receive more attention than before. In this context, communication and communication skills as well as collaboration with experts will become more and more important for solving challenges in future scenarios with high technical challenges for employees resulting from Digitization and an aging workforce. In consequence, we highlight four research areas for supporting the aging workforce in the age of Digitization: coordination-oriented competence control systems, changes in communication and behavior, the path from technology acceptance to transformation acceptance, and teamwork as a lever for collaboration (see Fig. 3).

5.1   Competence Control Systems

Companies have to analyze their current organizational competence portfolio as well as the individual competencies of their aging employees in order to make these transparent for an efficient coordination of their resources. Coordination-oriented competence control systems which help to steer the adaption between technologies as well as organizational requirements and individual competencies are a key instrument for maintaining industrial competitiveness. Furthermore, they can help to keep the employability of the aging workforce despite extensive automation through Cyber Physical Systems and robots. The aim should be to coordinate the human resources of companies at the best place—for the employee as well as for the organization. For this reason, it is necessary to know the experience-based professional competencies as well as the methodological, social, and self-management competencies of the employees. Competence control systems can map the special experiences as well the capabilities of the aging

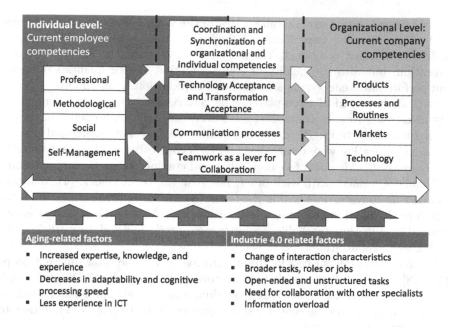

Fig. 3. Ensuring employability of the aging workforce in the age of 'Industrie 4.0'

workforce in order to use them most effectively for the organization as well to prevent them from engaging in tasks which are too challenging. Companies also should pay attention to the individual characteristics of their employees for the design of effective learning processes [75] in order to build competencies. With the identification of the competence gap between technological as well as organizational requirements it is possible to develop competence-oriented tailored learning programs for synchronizing organizational and individual competencies. Organizational competencies are often induced by the product portfolio, processes, markets, or used technology. For the transfer to competencies on the level of the individual, it is necessary to develop measurement instruments for the description and analysis of organizational and technological requirements as well as individual competencies. These measurement instruments should include measurement scales which also describe the special experiences of the aging workforce as well as the technological requirements which arise through 'Industrie 4.0' developments. However, human development through competence management is limited. In this case, communications as well as collaboration with experts and other coworkers can help older employees to solve problems and to remain competitive.

5.2 Teamwork as a Lever for Collaboration

More important than the individual for success is the complete team and team organization requires increased communication. Pentland [76] found that the style of communication explains about 50% of the variation in a team's successes. Good communication outperformed individual factors such as intelligence, personality, and talent combined. Yet it is not only about the amount of communication, but also the quality of communication. Three qualities influence team performance: energy, engagement, and exploration. Pentland even goes as far as to derive an ideal team-player. The "charismatic connector" democratically invests his time in connecting with everyone on a high energy basis, yet listens more than talks. Besides these quality characteristics, five patterns of good communication were established: (1) Everyone talks and listens in roughly equally much. (2) Members face each other and conduct energetic conversations. (3) Members connect with each other, not just the team leader. (4) Members carry on side conversations within the team. (5) Members break out of the team to explore the outside and bring information back. Making these competencies measurable, and thus teachable, requires sociometric methodology [76,77] and graph-based visualization.

When establishing success in groups, groups as a whole show different properties [78]. Successful groups show indicators of groupthink orientation, which reveals itself as risk-taking behavior, cohesion, and strongly opinionated leaders. Unsuccessful teams on the contrary show signs of vigilance (e.g., internal debate to the point of factionalism).

In times when innovations are being made by small teams within larger company settings, innovators are needed. One personality trait beneficial to entrepreneurial thinking is tolerance for ambiguity [79,80]. Situations in the fast-changing digitized world require from leaders that they adapt quickly to new contexts and that they tolerate that outcomes will not always be either black or white. Sometimes, requirements established carefully can become obsolete during the production process, as change appears quickly in a globalized, digitally interconnected world. But not only the leaders have to deal with a changing world; employees will have to adapt to change as well. When changes of strategy and procedures are conducted, it pays off to integrate the employees into the process [81].

Both the requirements from communication and organizational transformation call for shallower hierarchies, a new form of trust and sense-making between leadership and employees, and a development of competencies required in these new settings. A deeper understanding of these aspects of collaboration is needed.

5.3   Changes in Communication and Behavior

As mentioned above, organizational communication behavior has changed, as more and more digital communication channels are being used nowadays. Nonetheless, in the literature it is argued that conventional face-to-face communication cannot be completely replaced by digital communication channels [32]. During face-to-face communication, also non-verbal elements are transferred, which express the relationship between the conversation partners [82]. If there is a lack of attention to this element, communication might be distracted [33]. Therefore, attention must be paid to how to define and to teach management competencies in order to overcome this lack of experience with digital communication channels. Additionally, one should not implement upcoming digital communication channels without investigating the (dis-)advantages of their implementation for the organization [83]. More research is needed for evaluating situations where innovative communication channels might be useful for the organization and situations where conventional communication channels should remain unchanged.

Another change in the field of communication incurred by 'Industrie 4.0' is that more and more data are being stored and becoming available for decision support systems. Employees have to decide within a complex environment of, e.g. time stress, interruptions, and digital requirements, which information to select and to employ as a decision basis. Further research should investigate the competencies needed for dealing with huge information amounts in decision-making situations.

5.4   From Technology Acceptance to Transformation Acceptance

When bringing together modern individual competence management and demographically aware human-resource management (see Fig. 3), use of technology-mitigated processes is inevitable. Typically, technology acceptance modeling is used to predict the future success of such systems. Technology acceptance models typically include individual user factors, such as age, gender, prior experience, technical self-efficacy, as well as social factors (e.g., social norms, influence, etc.), and technological factors (e.g., ease of use, usefulness, etc.) [84,85]. And even the influence of cultural effects has been investigated [86,87]. However, emergent effects of change processes in teams and the willingness to adapt under rapidly changing conditions have not been integrated into the models yet. If we see technology as an integrative part of a socio-technical system, not only does the technology need acceptance [88]. To ensure that the efforts in communication, cooperation, collaboration, and coordination are fruitful, it is necessary to understand acceptance of transformation processes from a holistic point of view. For this purpose, it is important to address these questions interdisciplinarily. The utilization of results from these four research areas will ultimately help with successfully managing the challenges posed by 'Industrie 4.0'.

Acknowledgments. The authors thank the German Research Council DFG for the friendly support of the research in the excellence cluster "Integrative Production Technology in High Wage Countries".

References

1. World Health Organization, et al.: World report on ageing and health. World Health Organization, Geneva (2015)
2. Fornalczyk, A., Stompór-Świderska, J., Ślazyk-Sobol, M.: Age management within organizations-employees' perceptions of the phenomenon - research report. J. Intercultural Manage. **7**(3), 39–51 (2015)

3. De Mauro, A., Greco, M., Grimaldi, M., Giannakopoulos, G., Sakas, D.P., Kyriaki-Manessi, D.: What is big data? A consensual definition and a review of key research topics. In: AIP Conference Proceedings, vol. 1644, pp. 97–104. AIP (2015)

4. Bauernhansl, T.: Die Vierte Industrielle Revolution – Der Weg in ein wertschaffendes Produktionsparadigma. In: Bauernhansl, T., ten Hompel, M., Vogel-Heuser, B. (eds.) Industrie 4.0 in Produktion, Automatisierung und Logistik, pp. 5–35. Springer, Wiesbaden (2014). doi:10.1007/978-3-658-04682-8_1

5. Becker, K.-D.: Arbeit in der Industrie 4.0 – Erwartungen des Instituts für angewandte Arbeitswissenschaft e.V. In: Botthof, A., Hartmann, E.A. (eds.) Zukunft der Arbeit in Industrie 4.0, pp. 23–29. Springer, Heidelberg (2015). doi:10.1007/978-3-662-45915-7_3

6. Monostori, L.: Cyber-physical production systems: roots, expectations and R&D challenges. Procedia CIRP **17**, 9–13 (2014)

7. Kagermann, H., Helbig, J., Hellinger, A., Wahlster, W.: Recommendations for Implementing the strategic initiative INDUSTRIE 4.0: securing the future ofbreak German manufacturing industry; Final report of the Industrie 4.0 working group. Forschungsunion (2013)

8. Broy, M.: Cyber-physical systems–Wissenschaftliche Herausforderungen bei der Entwicklung. In: Broy M. (ed.) Cyber-Physical Systems: Innovation Durch Software-Intensive Eingebettete Systeme. acatech DISKUTIERT (ACATECHDISK), pp. 17–31. Springer, Heidelberg (2010). doi:10.1007/978-3-642-14901-6_2

9. Mayer-Schönberger, V., Cukier, K.: Big Data: A Revolution That Will Transform How We Live, Work, and Think. Houghton Mifflin Harcourt, Boston (2013)

10. Hirsch-Kreinsen, H., ten Hompel, M.: Digitalisierung industrieller Arbeit: Entwicklungsperspektiven und Gestaltungsansätze. In: Vogel-Heuser, B., Bauernhansl, T., ten Hompel, M. (eds.) Handbuch Industrie 4.0 Bd. 3, pp. 357–376. Springer, Berlin (2017). doi:10.1007/978-3-662-53251-5_21

11. Hirsch-Kreinsen, H.: Einleitung: Digitalisierung industrieller Arbeit. In: Digitalisierung industrieller Arbeit, pp. 10–31. Nomos Verlagsgesellschaft mbH & Co. KG (2015)

12. Wehberg, G.: Big Data-Mustererkennung als Erfolgsfaktor der Logistik 4.0. In: Vogel-Heuser, B., Bauernhansl, T., ten Hompel, M. (eds.) Handbuch Industrie 4.0 Bd. 3, pp. 377–392. Springer, Berlin (2017). doi:10.1007/978-3-662-53251-5_92

13. Boyd, D., Crawford, K.: Critical questions for big data: provocations for a cultural, technological, and scholarly phenomenon. Inf. Commun. Soc. **15**(5), 662–679 (2012)

14. Lee, E.A.: Cyber physical systems: design challenges. In: 2008 11th IEEE International Symposium on Object Oriented Real-Time Distributed Computing (ISORC), pp. 363–369. IEEE (2008)

15. Geisberger, E., Broy, M.: agendaCPS: Integrierte Forschungsagenda Cyber-Physical Systems, vol. 1. Springer, Heidelberg (2012)

16. Brettel, M., Friederichsen, N., Keller, M., Rosenberg, M.: How virtualization, decentralization and network building change the manufacturing landscape: an industry 4.0 perspective. Int. J. Mech. Ind. Sci. Eng. **8**(1), 37–44 (2014)

17. Xia, F., Yang, L., Wang, L., Vinel, A.: Internet of things. Int. J. Commun Syst **25**(9), 1101–1102 (2012)

18. Schlick, J., Stephan, P., Zühlke, D.: Produktion 2020 - Auf dem Weg zur 4. Industriellen Revolution. Inf. Manage. Consult. **27**(3), 26–34 (2012)

19. Krenz, P., Wulfsberg, J.P., Bruhns, F.L.: Unfold Collective Intelligence! Erschließung neuer Wertschöpfungspotenziale durch Entfaltung kollektiver Intelligenz. ZWF-Zeitschrift für Wirtschaftlichen Fabrikbetrieb **107**, 152 (2012)

20. Kölmel, B., Bulander, R., Dittmann, U., Schätter, A., Würtz, G.: Usability requirements for complex cyber-physical systems in a totally networked world. In: Camarinha-Matos, L.M., Afsarmanesh, H. (eds.) PRO-VE 2014. IFIP AICT, vol. 434, pp. 253–258. Springer, Heidelberg (2014). doi:10.1007/978-3-662-44745-1_25

21. Dworschak, B., Zaiser, H.: Competences for cyber-physical systems in manufacturing-first findings and scenarios. Procedia CIRP **25**, 345–350 (2014)

22. Golightly, D., D'Cruz, M., Patel, H., Pettitt, M., Sharples, S., Stedmon, A., Wilson, J.: Novel interaction styles, complex working contexts, and the role of usability. In: Evaluation of User Interaction, Usability of Complex Information Systems, pp. 281–304 (2011)

23. Letmathe, P., Schinner, M.: Competence management in the age of cyber physical systems. In: Jeschke, S., Brecher, C., Song, H., Rawat, D.B. (eds.) Industrial Internet of Things. SSWT, pp. 595–614. Springer, Cham (2017). doi:10.1007/978-3-319-42559-7_25

24. Frey, B., Osborne, C.: The future of employment: how susceptible are jobs to computerisation? (2015)

25. Bonin, H., Gregory, T., Zierahn, U.: Übertragung der Studie von Frey/Osborne (2013) auf Deutschland. Technical report 57, ZEW Kurzexpertise (2015)

26. Dworschak, B., Zaiser, H., Martinetz, S., Windelband, L.: Logistics as a domain of application for the "Internet of Things" in the early identification initiative of the German Federal Ministry of Education and Research (BMBF). Technical report, Fraunhofer IAO (2013)

27. Gorecky, D., Schmitt, M., Loskyll, M.: Mensch-Maschine-Interaktion im Industrie 4.0-Zeitalter. In: Bauernhansl, T., ten Hompel, M., Vogel-Heuser, B. (eds.) Industrie 4.0 in Produktion, Automatisierung und Logistik, pp. 525–542. Springer, Wiesbaden (2014). doi:10.1007/978-3-658-04682-8_26

28. Autor, D.H., Dorn, D.: The growth of low-skill service jobs and the polarization of the US labor market. Am. Econ. Rev. **103**(5), 1553–1597 (2013)

29. Voigt, S.: E-Mail-Kommunikation in Organisationen: eine explorative Studie zu individuellen Nutzungsstrategien. Reinhard Fischer, München (2003)

30. Mast, C.: Unternehmenskommunikation - Ein Leitfaden. 4. neue und erw. Auflage. Lucius & Lucius Verlagsgesellschaft mbH, Stuttgart (2010)

31. Jäckel, M., Würfel, A.M.: "Und sie mailten was sie tun": Erfahrungen mit neuen Informations- und Kommunikationstechnologien in Unternehmen und Verwaltungen. Competence Center E-Business an der Univ., Trier (2004)

32. Rusch, G.: From Face-to-Face to Face-to-"Face". Zehn Schritte von der mündlichen Kommunikation zum Cyberspace, Siegen (1998)

33. Franken, S.: Verhaltensorientierte Führung: Individuen - Gruppen - Organisationen. Gabler Verlag, Wiesbaden (2004)

34. Colbert, A., Yee, N., George, G.: The digital workforce and the workplace of the future. Acad. Manage. J. **59**(3), 731–739 (2016)

35. Haas, M.R., Criscuolo, P., George, G.: Which problems to solve? Online knowledge sharing and attention allocation in organizations. Acad. Manag. J. **58**(3), 680–711 (2015)

36. Argote, L., McEvily, B., Reagans, R.: Managing knowledge in organizations: an integrative framework and review of emerging themes. Manage. Sci. **49**(4), 571–582 (2003)

37. Reagans, R., McEvily, B.: Network structure and knowledge transfer: the effects of cohesion and range. Adm. Sci. Q. **48**(2), 240–267 (2003)
38. Sambamurthy, V., Subramani, M.: Special issue on information technologies and knowledge management. MIS Q. **29**(1), 1–7 (2005)
39. Rajkumar, R.R., Lee, I., Sha, L., Stankovic, J.: Cyber-physical systems: the next computing revolution. In: Proceedings of the 47th Design Automation Conference, pp. 731–736. ACM (2010)
40. Geisberger, E., Cengarle, M., Keil, P., Niehaus, J., Thiel, C., Thönnißen-Fries, H.J.: Cyber-Physical Systems - Driving force for innovation in mobility, health, energy and production, acatech-Deutsche Akademie der Technikwissenschaften (2011)
41. Linke, A.: Management der Online-Kommunikation von Unternehmen: Steuerungsprozesse, Multi-Loop-Prozesse und Governance. Springer, Wiesbaden (2014)
42. Hirsch-Kreinsen, H.: Entwicklungsperspektiven von Produktionsarbeit. In:break Botthof, A., Hartmann, E.A. (eds.) Zukunft der Arbeit in Industrie 4.0, pp. 89–98. Springer, Heidelberg (2015). doi:10.1007/978-3-662-45915-7_10
43. Basmer, S., Buxbaum-Conradi, S., Krenz, P., Redlich, T., Wulfsberg, J.P., Bruhns, F.L.: Open production: chances for social sustainability in manufacturing. Procedia CIRP **26**, 46–51 (2015)
44. Schuh, G., Potente, T., Varandani, R., Hausberg, C., Fränken, B.: Collaboration moves productivity to the next level. Procedia CIRP **17**, 3–8 (2014)
45. Moraal, D., Lorig, B., Schreiber, D., Azeez, U.: Ein Blick hinter die Kulissen der betrieblichen Weiterbildung in Deutschland. Daten und Fakten der nationalen CVTS3-Zusatzerhebung [Electronic Version]. BIBB Report **7**(09), 1–12 (2009)
46. Meyer, G., Brünig, B., Nyhuis, P.: Employee competences in manufacturing companies-an expert survey. J. Manage. Devel. **34**(8), 1004–1018 (2015)
47. Oblinger, D., Oblinger, J.: Is it age or IT: First steps toward understanding the net generation. Educ. Net Gener. **2**(1–2), 20 (2005)
48. Schieber, F.: Human factors and aging: Identifying and compensating for age-related deficits in sensory and cognitive function. In: Impact of Technology on Successful Aging, pp. 42–84 (2003)
49. Jakobs, E.M., Lehnen, K., Ziefle, M.: Alter und Technik - Eine Studie zur alters-bezogenen Wahrnehmung und Gestaltung von Technik (2008)
50. Li, K.Z., Lindenberger, U.: Relations between aging sensory/sensorimotor and cognitive functions. Neurosci. Biobehav. Rev. **26**(7), 777–783 (2002)
51. Craik, F.I., Salthouse, T.A. (eds.): The Handbook of Aging and Cognition. Psychology Press, New York (2011)
52. Czaja, S.J., Charness, N., Fisk, A.D., Hertzog, C., Nair, S.N., Rogers, W.A., Sharit, J.: Factors predicting the use of technology: findings from the Center for Research and Education on Aging and Technology Enhancement (CREATE). Psychol. Aging **21**(2), 333 (2006)
53. Arning, K., Ziefle, M.: Effects of age, cognitive, and personal factors on PDA menu navigation performance. Behav. Inf. Technol. **28**(3), 251–268 (2009)
54. Goble, D.J., Coxon, J.P., Wenderoth, N., Van Impe, A., Swinnen, S.P.: Propriocep-tive sensibility in the elderly: degeneration, functional consequences and plastic-adaptive processes. Neurosci. Biobehav. Rev. **33**(3), 271–278 (2009)
55. Lövdén, M., Ghisletta, P., Lindenberger, U.: Social participation attenuates decline in perceptual speed in old and very old age. Psychol. Aging **20**(3), 423 (2005)
56. Warr, P.: Age and job performance. In: Work and Aging: A European Perspective, pp. 309–322 (1995)
57. Charness, N., Campbell, J.I.: Acquiring skill at mental calculation in adulthood: a task decomposition. J. Exp. Psychol. Gen. **117**(2), 115 (1988)

58. Downing, R.E., Moore, J.L., Brown, S.W.: The effects and interaction of spatial visualization and domain expertise on information seeking. Comput. Hum. Behav. **21**(2), 195–209 (2005)

59. Alwin, D.F., McCammon, R.J.: Aging, cohorts, and verbal ability. J. Gerontol. Ser. B: Psychol. Sci. Soc. Sci. **56**(3), S151–S161 (2001)

60. Calero Valdez, A., Kathrin Schaar, A., Ziefle, M.: Personality influences on etiquette requirements for social media in the work context. In: Holzinger, A., Ziefle, M., Hitz, M., Debevc, M. (eds.) SouthCHI 2013. LNCS, vol. 7946, pp. 427–446. Springer, Heidelberg (2013). doi:10.1007/978-3-642-39062-3_27

61. Calero Valdez, A., Brell, J., Schaar, A.K., Ziefle, M.: The diversity of why - a meta-analytical study of usage motivation in enterprise social networks. Universal Access in the Information Society (accepted, 2017)

62. Calero Valdez, A., Schaar, A.K., Ziefle, M.: State of the (net) work address - developing criteria for applying social networking to the work environment. Work **41**(Suppl. 1), 3459–3467 (2012)

63. Schaar, A.K., Calero Valdez, A., Ziefle, M.: The impact of user diversity on the willingness to disclose personal information in social network services. In: Holzinger, A., Ziefle, M., Hitz, M., Debevc, M. (eds.) SouthCHI 2013. LNCS, vol. 7946, pp. 174–193. Springer, Heidelberg (2013). doi:10.1007/978-3-642-39062-3_11

64. Schaar, A.K., Calero Valdez, A., Ziefle, M., Eraßme, D., Löcker, A.-K., Jakobs, E.-M.: Reasons for using social networks professionally. In: Meiselwitz, G. (ed.) SCSM 2014. LNCS, vol. 8531, pp. 385–396. Springer, Cham (2014). doi:10.1007/978-3-319-07632-4_37

65. Erpenbeck, J., von Rosenstiel, L.: Handbuch Kompetenzmessung: Erkennen, verstehen und bewerten von Kompetenzen in der betrieblichen, pädagogischen und psychologischen Praxis, 1st edn. Schäffer-Poeschel, Stuttgart (2007)

66. Reinhardt, K., North, K.: Transparency and transfer of individual competencies - a concept of integrative competence management. J. UCS **9**(12), 1372–1380 (2003)

67. Wilkens, U., Sprafke, N., Nolte, A.: Vom Kompetenzmanagement zum Kompetenzcontrolling. Controlling **27**(10), 534–540 (2015)

68. North, K., Reinhardt, K., Sieber-Suter, B.: Kompetenzmanagement in der Praxis: Mitarbeiterkompetenzen systematisch identifizieren, nutzen und entwickeln Mit vielen Fallbeispielen. Springer, Heidelberg (2012)

69. Freiling, J.: A competence-based theory of the firm. Manage. Revue **15**(1), 27–52 (2004)

70. Mills, J., Platts, K., Bourne, M., Richards, H.: Strategy and Performance - Competing Through Competencies. Cambridge University Press, Cambridge (2002)

71. Grote, S., Kauffeld, S., Billich, M., Frieling, E.: Implementierung eines Kompetenzmanagementsystems: Phasen, Vorgehen und Stolpersteine. In: Kompetenzmanagement-Grundlagen und Praxisbeispiele, pp. 33–58. Schäffer-Poeschel Verlag für Wirtschaft Steuern Recht, Stuttgart (2006)

72. Gerst, D.: Designing workplaces from a work organizational perspective by detlef gerst. In: Wiendahl, H.-P., Reichardt, J., Nyhuis, P. (eds.) Handbook Factory Planning and Design, pp. 169–195. Springer, Heidelberg (2015). doi:10.1007/978-3-662-46391-8_7

73. Kauffeld, S.: Kompetenzen messen, bewerten, entwickeln: Ein prozessanalytischer Ansatz für Gruppen. Schäffer-Poeschel, Stuttgart (2011)

74. Nickolaus, R., Seeber, S.: Berufliche Kompetenzen: Modellierungen und diagnostische Verfahren. In: Handbuch berufspädagogischer Diagnostik, pp. 166–195. Beltz (2013)

75. Letmathe, P., Zielinski, M.: Determinants of feedback effectiveness in production planning. Int. J. Oper. Prod. Manage. **36**(7), 825–848 (2016)
76. Pentland, A.: The new science of building great teams. Harvard Bus. Rev. **90**(4), 60–69 (2012)
77. Cillessen, A.H.: Sociometric Methods. Guilford Press, New York (2009)
78. Peterson, R.S., Owens, P.D., Tetlock, P.E., Fan, E.T., Martorana, P.: Group dynamics in top management teams: groupthink, vigilance, and alternative models of organizational failure and success. Organ. Behav. Hum. Decis. Process. **73**(2–3), 272–305 (1998)
79. Norton, R.W.: Measurement of ambiguity tolerance. J. Pers. Assess. **39**(6), 607–619 (1975)
80. Schere, J.L.: Tolerance of ambiguity as a discriminating variable between entrepreneurs and managers. Acad. Manage. Proc. **1982**(1), 404–408 (1982)
81. Sagie, A., Elizur, D., Koslowsky, M.: Effect of participation in strategic and tactical decisions on acceptance of planned change. J. Soc. Psychol. **130**(4), 459–465 (1990)
82. Schulz von Thun, F.: Miteinander reden 1: Störungen und Klärungen. Allgemeine Psychologie der Kommunikation. Rowohlt Taschenbuch, Hamburg (2001)
83. Letmathe, P., Noll, E.: Ökonomische Bewertung von Kommunikationsflüssen am Beispiel von Führungsimpulsen. Controlling: Zeitschrift für erfolgsorientierte Unternehmensführung (accepted, 2017)
84. King, W.R., He, J.: A meta-analysis of the technology acceptance model. Inf. Manage. **43**(6), 740–755 (2006)
85. Venkatesh, V., Thong, J.Y., Xu, X.: Consumer acceptance and use of information technology: extending the unified theory of acceptance and use of technology (2012)
86. Oshlyansky, L., Cairns, P., Thimbleby, H.: Validating the Unified Theory of Acceptance and Use of Technology (UTAUT) tool cross-culturally. In: Proceedings of the 21st British HCI Group Annual Conference on People and Computers: HCI... but not as we know it-Volume 2, pp. 83–86. British Computer Society (2007)
87. Alagöz, F., Ziefle, M., Wilkowska, W., Valdez, A.C.: Openness to accept medical technology - a cultural view. In: Holzinger, A., Simonic, K.-M. (eds.) USAB 2011. LNCS, vol. 7058, pp. 151–170. Springer, Heidelberg (2011). doi:10.1007/978-3-642-25364-5_14
88. Calero Valdez, A., Brauner, P., Ziefle, M.: Preparing production systems for the internet of things - the potential of socio-technical approaches in dealing with complexity. In: Competitive Manufacturing (COMA) (2016)

Towards Extracting Recruiters' Tacit Knowledge Based on Interactions with a Job Matching System

Kaoru Shinkawa[1]([✉]), Kenichi Saito[2], Masatomo Kobayashi[1], and Atsuhi Hiyama[3]

[1] IBM Research - Tokyo, 19 – 21 Hakozaki, Nihonbashi, Chuo, Tokyo 103–8510, Japan
{kaoruma,mstm}@jp.ibm.com
[2] Circulation Co., Ltd., 2-2-1 Marunouchi, Chiyoda, Tokyo 100–0005, Japan
kenichi.saito@circu.co.jp
[3] The University of Tokyo, 7-3-1 Hongo, Bunkyo, Tokyo 113–8656, Japan
hiyama@star.rcast.u-tokyo.ac.jp

Abstract. Finding good job matches for elderly workers is becoming a big challenge for aging society. To secure the labor force population, it is necessary to improve the employment rates of the elderly workers and utilize their accumulated knowledge and skills. Matching relies on each recruiter's tacit knowledge of what we assume as word association information in matching experts' mind based on their experience. In order to conduct effective job matching for elderly workers, retrieving word associations from the matching experts' tacit knowledge is necessary for the purpose of generating domain-specific ontology. In this paper, we propose an interactive job matching system that collects recruiters' interaction data to find word association specific to job matching for elderly workers. Our system is designed for recruitment operations as to acquire the real interaction data with real job opportunity. Our experimental results indicate that the interaction data are effective for identifying word associations that can be used to extract the recruiters' tacit knowledge.

Keywords: Job matching · Elderly workers · Ontology · Word association · Interactive information retrieval · Human computer interaction

1 Introduction

In aging countries, employment of elderly workers has been a long-standing issue. Elderly workers are a valuable and productive economic resource [1]. Increasing employment opportunities for elderly workers is essential to allow utilizing their accumulated knowledge and skills. Therefore, the job matching method that can allocate their special abilities is required.

Job matching means matching of job opportunities with qualified workers. In most cases, open job descriptions and workers' resumes are written in text. Workers' resumes may not always be in a structured format, and most information in them is written in natural language. Despite this, we can adapt information retrieval techniques to enable us to rank all workers for a given job opportunity from their resumes.

© Springer International Publishing AG 2017
J. Zhou and G. Salvendy (Eds.): ITAP 2017, Part II, LNCS 10298, pp. 557–568, 2017.
DOI: 10.1007/978-3-319-58536-9_44

Yamada et al. indicated that the use of natural language is effective, but just considering the frequency of words is a hard way to match diverse candidates, as the context of the sentences in a resume does not appear as text. They also pointed out that the tacit knowledge of the recruiter is important for job matching [2, 3].

Our discussions with a senior consultant in the recruitment market led us to conclude that the task of searching for appropriate elderly workers for job opportunities has special characteristics. It is different from ordinary document searches, as it does not have an exact answer. Recruiters find workers by trial-and-error and by making comparisons, such as by changing keywords, adjusting weights of the word, comparing resumes, and so on. With this in mind, we developed a job matching system called "JINZAIScouter", which has an interactive interface to adjust search queries by adding, deleting, and changing weights of extracted keywords. We conducted an experiment at a recruitment agency that collected interaction data from their daily recruitment operations. We extracted word associations from the interactions of recruiters in charge of job matching. Word associations can be considered attributes with which to retrieve a recruiter's tacit knowledge of job matching. Continuous interaction data and improvements considering associations should improve the quality of job matching systems.

2   Related Work

There have been many approaches to automate various aspects of the recruitment process. Popular approach is to use information retrieval techniques to rank candidates for a given job opportunities.

Singh et al. created a system called PROSPECT in which resumes and job requests are automatically matched and recruiters can conduct filtering interactions by adding search options [4]. For each job description, the system ranks candidates based on the similarity between job description and candidates' resumes and the ranking can be refined by adding filtering criteria. This refining procedure is repeated until the recruiter is satisfied with the system generated ranking. The system also has automatic skills suggestion. If required skills are missing from job description, the system estimates the required skills by assuming that most of the candidates who have applied for the job have the relevant skills. This suggestion is helpful if recruiter is not well versed in the job domain. Our work also provides keyword weighting interactions, which is similar to filtering interactions in PROSPECT. Our purpose of interaction is to extract tacit knowledge of recruiters from their searching operation, not for filtering.

Ontology is widely used due to its efficient knowledge representation. Kumaran et al. created EXPERT, an intelligent tool for screening candidates for recruitment using ontology mapping [5]. EXPERT has three phases in screening candidates for recruitment. In first phase, the system collects candidates' resumes and constructs ontology document for the features of the candidates. Job requirements are represented as ontology in the second phase and in third phase, EXPERT maps the job requirement ontology onto the candidate ontology document and retrieves the eligible candidates. Use of ontology is effective, however, automatic ontology generation approaches typically require a large set of training data with prior domain-specific knowledge. Our research is focusing on extracting word associations which are specific to job matching for elderly workers, for the use of building domain-specific ontology in the future.

Yamada et al. developed an interactive job matching system that can match diverse elderly candidates by changing weights on the job experience profiles in searching process [2, 3]. Tags for job category, job content and job position are added to the candidates' resume manually and these tags are used to search for candidates interactively. They pointed out that the tacit knowledge of recruiter is important for job matching and it can be extracted from user interaction on the job matching system. They defined a person's profile (job experience) as attributes and introduced an interface that helps recruiters to find appropriate elderly workers by adjusting the values and weights of these attributes. We defined word associations as attributes and developed an interactive job matching system that can retrieve word associations from recruiters' interactions with the system.

3 Preliminary Investigation

To investigate information retrieval approach, we conducted an initial experiment using Apache Solr[1], which defines a job opportunity as a query and a workers' resume as data source. The job opportunity and workers' resume were provided by a Japanese recruitment agency specializing in highly skilled elderly workers. Past job matching results were also provided in order to evaluate the usability of the text search engine for job matching.

We evaluated the number of relevant results on the first 10 search results (P@10), and 73% was applicable. We conducted a failure analysis of the job matching results and came up with three failure patterns: (1) the criteria for making a decision are not explicitly shown in the job description (e.g., the person's characteristics); (2) the vocabulary used in the workers' resumes differs from that of the job description and matching concept is described in a different vocabulary; (3) necessary keywords are extracted, but the search engine gives unimportant words priority over important words. In the case of the first failure pattern, non-verbal information is considered the most important information, such as the impression of the interview. The second pattern points to need to have an ontology built for a specific domain. In the case of the third pattern, there is no interaction to adjust the query.

We expanded the experiment in order to evaluate the effect of word similarities on the ranking results. Similarities were calculated using word2vec[2], which is a popular neural word embedding method for defining word similarities. We generated word2vec by combining Wikipedia data and data from actual resumes of elderly workers. However, we did not observe any improvement in the ranking results when word similarity was incorporated. We also built word vectors using open job offerings for people over the age of 65 in a public employment security office (known as "Hello Work"), but the extracted words were not useful for job offerings for highly skilled elderly people.

---

[1] http://lucene.apache.org/solr/.
[2] https://code.google.com/p/word2vec/.

The above results indicate that an ontology for each specific domain is needed to improve the quality of job matching engines. In particular, the recruiters' interactions with a search system when they are searching for elderly workers are useful for retrieving tacit knowledge and are essential for building ontologies for job matching of elderly workers.

4 Proposed System

4.1 Methodology

The methodology of the system is shown in Fig. 1. Our system is currently being used by recruiters in the recruitment agency. The recruitment process is as follows:

(1) Job offering information is sent to the agency from the client company (by e-mail).
(2) The job offerings are allocated to recruiters, and the recruiters copy & paste the job descriptions written in natural language into our system. Keyword search is also available.
(3) The system returns workers who match the job offerings along with the top ten keywords scored by the system.
(4) The recruiters select the workers who seem to be appropriate for the offering. In order to find a diverse group of candidates, recruiters can change the keywords and weights and select multiple workers.
(5) The recruiters review the workers selected in the previous step and download their profiles.
(6) The recruiters introduce the matching workers to the client company.

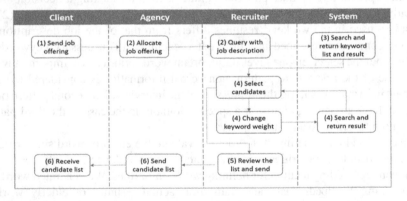

Fig. 1. System methodology

The main purpose of the system is to collect interaction data to retrieve recruiters' tacit knowledge. Therefore, the system needs to be compatible with the recruiter's daily business operations. We implemented a final review process and downloading feature (step 5), so that the system could be easily incorporated in the business.

4.2 Architecture

Figure 2 shows the architecture of the system deployed on the recruiter's environment. The relational database, Job matching server, and client are deployed on Amazon Web Services (AWS)[3], a cloud computing service. Workers' resumes are stored in a MySQL[4] database and imported to Apache Solr. The job matching server calls Solr for the initial search, and the extracted keywords and matching results are sent to the JINZAIScouter server. The JINZAIScouter server scores and prioritizes the extracted keywords and generates Solr queries by using the adjusted keywords. The results of the query are sent to the JINZAIScouter client, together with keyword information. The interface supports keyword interactions (e.g., a slider to adjust the weights) so that users can seek various types of workers through trial-and-error. The interaction data and matching information are collected and stored in a MySQL database. The interaction information can be used in keyword scoring and prioritization on the server side. If the added keyword does not exist in the index, it is stored in the user dictionary of the JINZAIScouter server. This enables user defined keywords to be used in post queries without any time lag.

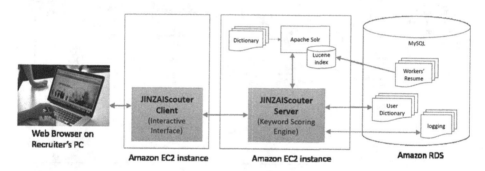

Fig. 2. System architecture

4.3 System Flow

Figure 3 shows the system flow of the job matching operation. The user inputs a job opportunity description in natural language or by entering keywords and starts searching (1). The system extracts keywords from the job description text by tokenizing sentences and filtering noun words based on the results of the morphological analysis (2). Keyword scores are calculated from the average term scores included in the top 100 documents matching the query. Keyword score is based on the Solr/Lucene scores of BM25 similarity algorithm[5]. The scoring of BM25 uses both term frequency and document length normalization. Based on the calculation, top ten keywords are selected (3). System

---

[3] https://aws.amazon.com/.

[4] https://www.mysql.com/.

[5] https://lucene.apache.org/core/6_0_0/core/org/apache/lucene/search/similarities/BM25Similarity.html.

searches the documents using selected top 10 keywords (4) and normalizes the returned document score (5). The system lists the top ten keywords and has a slider bar covering the matched people entries (6, 10). Users can delete, add, and change the weights of the keywords to adjust the query (7, 8, 9). Based on the modified keyword settings, the system generates a Solr query and executes it (5). The matching people list is dynamically updated (10), and the user can interactively change the keyword weights to find appropriate candidates (6, 7, 8, 9). Since the user can adjust the keywords in the application, the people list changes each time he or she does so. In order to keep track of candidates who look appropriate for the job, the system provides buttons to score each candidate as "Good" (means probably a good match) and "Super!" (best match); in this way, the user can check the list of selected people for final review and adjustment. The selected people list in CSV format can be downloaded by selecting "Download CSV", and this operation signals to the system that a final decision was made and the matching results are to be used for analysis.

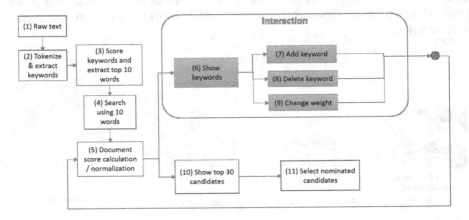

Fig. 3. System flow

4.4 Interface

Figures 4 and 5 show the system interface after conducting the user operation of the system and selection of candidates. The data shown in the figure is dummy personal data fetched from Wikipedia. In Fig. 4, resume summaries of the matching workers are listed on the left side of the window, and the keyword interaction field is on the right side. The maximum number of matching people is 30, segmented with pagination. Each page consists of ten worker resume summaries. When the ID number in the summary field is clicked, the whole list of worker resumes is shown. If the recruiter finds an interesting worker while viewing the summaries, he/she is able to decide whether to put the worker on the candidate list by reviewing the whole information.

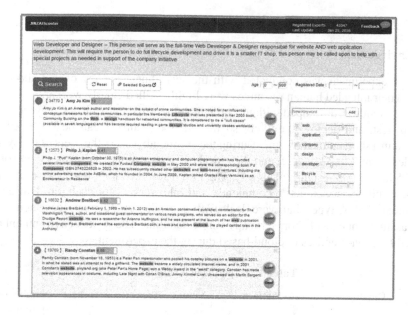

Fig. 4. Search window

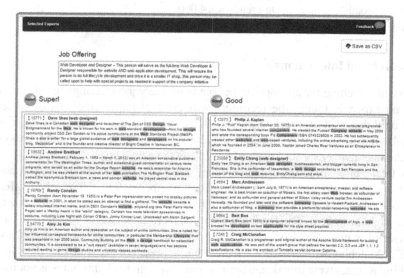

Fig. 5. Matching window

5   Experiments and Results

5.1   Environment

The pilot experiment was conducted with the recruitment agency over a six-month period. Their intended human resources were highly skilled elderly workers.

The system was developed with the agile development approach, i.e., get feedback, develop, test, and deploy iteratively so that all the feedback can be reviewed and collected in a short amount of time. During the six-month period, the users of the system expanded from 2 to 32 people, and the elderly worker resumes grew as a data source from 2,500 to 5,000 resumes (Table 1). The initial searched job offerings were from a micro-consulting service that recommends multiple workers for each job. During the experiment, the job types that were dealt with expanded to other services such as the single assignment type of short-term advisory consulting. The system environment also changed from on-premises to cloud-based during the experiment.

Table 1. Experiment environment

	Duration	Platform	Number of registered workers	Number of system users
Phase I	3 month	On-premises	2,500	2
Phase II	2 month	On-premises	4,000	10
Phase III	1 month ~ on going	Cloud	5,000	32

5.2   Search and Interactions

The way of searching for appropriate people is to query job offerings in full-text first, and if no expert is found, the recruiters will conduct the interactions discussed in Sect. 4 until they find appropriate experts. The selected experts considered to be well-matched to the job are scored "Super!" or "Good". When experts are selected, the system stores the interaction data for keyword scoring in the next query.

The total number of job offerings searched during the six months was 1,010, and the interactions collected from matched offerings numbered 920. Unmatched offerings included a case that matching workers were found, but users did not create or download a list through the system. The feedback from the recruitment agency indicated some of the reasons for unmatched offerings, e.g., "No matching people were found by the system", "Matching workers were selected, but list was not generated by the system", "Matching workers were found, and their resume was sent to clients but was not marked as selected on the system", or "The search was interrupted". Further consultations with the customer indicated that in most cases, users did not score "Good" or "Super!" on the resume summaries of the matched workers. There were also cases in which resumes of workers were marked as candidates, but the final review and CSV downloading were not completed, and hence, the result could not be considered a completed query by the system. In phase III (Table 2), 283 workers were selected in a one month period, but only 154 worker resumes were downloaded. Figure 6 shows the cumulative number of queries and interactions conducted in the experiment. The angle of inclination in the last two weeks is larger than in the other periods, because the system was deployed in a production environment and the number of users became three times larger. An interview with the customer indicated that users tended to use the system without saving the selected workers' list. We found that the types of operations varied with the types of services. For the micro-tasking consulting services, recruiters were requested only to provide multiple candidates. In this case, they used the "Good" and "Super!" buttons to keep track of appropriate candidates and download worker lists to be sent to the client. Therefore, in this case, the search operation was the expected usage for the system. However, finding workers for short-term advisory consulting services may not require a final review or downloading process. The reason is that such a service requires only the single best matched candidate not multiple candidates. When the recruiter finds a matching worker, he/she copy & pastes the resume from the result to an e-mail and starts exchanging e-mails with clients. In this case, no selection or downloading operation is conducted, meaning that system cannot consider the query as matched. In order to collect all available interaction data of the matched queries, the system needs to get completed state information in all cases.

Table 2. Number of worker selection in phase III (1 month)

	Number of workers
Selected candidate workers	283
Unselected candidate workers	81
Deleted workers	15
Selected as recommended workers	154

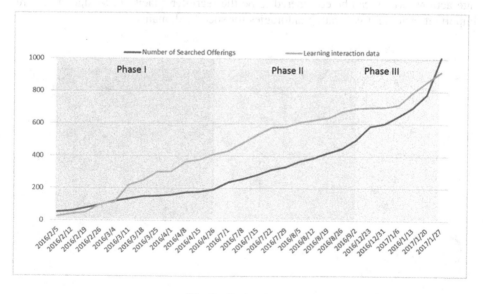

Fig. 6. System usage

5.3 Interaction Data Analysis

The most-used interactions were adding a new keyword and weighting the interaction by using the slider interface. Since the operating process of dealing with some job offerings was to get an exhaustive list of candidates, the trial-and-error process of adjusting the keyword weights was a suitable interaction to get the list of matching candidates. Figures 7 and 8 show examples of query interactions. The horizontal axis shows the keywords used in the query, while the vertical axis is the interaction count. The cell value is the weight assigned to the keyword (an empty cell means the keyword is not used in the interaction). In the example of Fig. 7, two workers are selected from the first query. Here, the recruiter is trying to find a person who has experience in car body design. The recruiter found two workers in first query and selected them as candidates. Even though the job opportunity description mentioned "car", the recruiter expanded the query by adding "flight" as a keyword. The recruiter may knew from his recruiting experience, that person who has expertise in airplane design also has expected skills. The recruiter actually selected three workers as candidates after expanding the scope. He/she also expanded the scope to motorcycle design. Therefore, the recruiter had expanded the query because he had a knowledge of searching the different field which is not actually describe in the job offering. Figure 8 shows another query expansion example. The job opportunity description was a search for workers who have resource management experience in research and development of air-conditioners. The system selected keywords that did not return the expected results, so the recruiter added semantically similar words, such as "R&D" for research and development and "ventilation", "heating & cooling" for air-conditioners. Word association can be retrieved from interactions, which can be considered to be the recruiters' tacit knowledge. They are important factors for generating ontologies for specific domains.

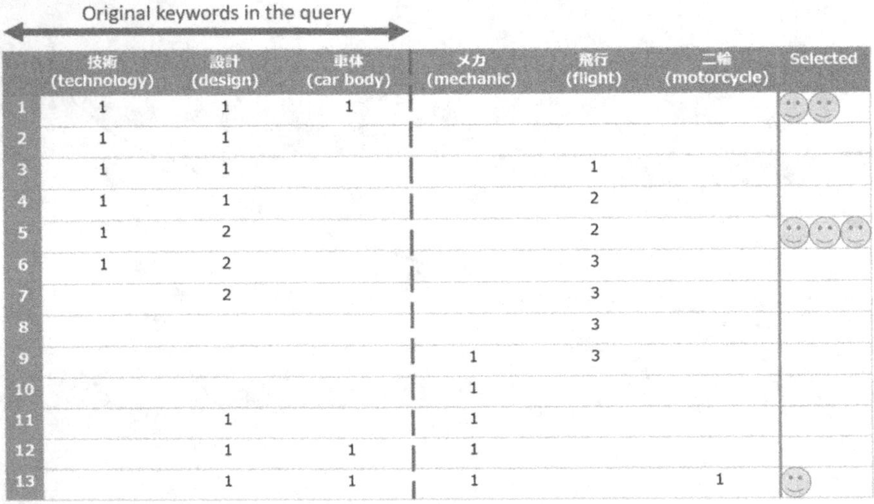

Original keywords in the query

	技術 (technology)	設計 (design)	車体 (car body)	メカ (mechanic)	飛行 (flight)	二輪 (motorcycle)	Selected
1	1	1	1				☺ ☺
2	1	1					
3	1	1			1		
4	1	1			2		
5	1	2			2		☺ ☺ ☺
6	1	2			3		
7		2			3		
8					3		
9				1	3		
10				1			
11		1		1			
12		1	1	1			
13		1	1	1		1	☺

Fig. 7. Example query interaction of adding a new factor

Original keywords in the query

	エアコン (air-Conditioner)	研究 (research)	メーカ (manufacturer)	マネジメント (management)	開発 (development)	管理 (manage)	空調 (ventilation)	R&D	冷暖房 (heating & cooling)	Selected
1	1	1	1	1	1	1				
2	1	1	1	1	1					
3	4	1	1	1	1					
4	4	1	1	1	1					
5	4	3.5	1	1	1					
6	4	3.5	1	1	4					
7	4	3.5	1	1	4		1			
8	4	3.5	1	1	4		4			
9	4	3.5	1	1	4		4	1		
10	4	3.5	1	1	4		4	3.5		☺☺
11	4	3.5	1	1	4		4		1	
12	4	3.5	1	1	4		4		2.5	☺

Fig. 8. Example query interaction of adding semantically similar words

5.4 Keyword Characteristics

By analyzing the keywords used in the search query, we could identify different characteristics between job opportunities for highly skilled elderly workers and public employment for elderly workers. The public employment opportunities were fetched from open job opportunities listed in Hello Work. Figure 9 shows examples of keywords used in the job descriptions. There are no "Advisory" or "Executive" keywords in the public employment domain. Even though a huge number of Hello Work jobs exist, an ontology built on this data would not be able to be applied to the task of recruiting highly skilled workers.

High-skilled elderly workers

Keyword	Translation
有識者	Advisory
役員	Board member
執行役員	Executive Officer
経営理念	Corporate Identity
経営企画	Corporate Planning
アドバイザリー	Advisory
リーソースマネージメント	Resource Management

Public employment for elderly workers

Keyword	Translation
パート	Part-time
事務	Office work
清掃	Cleaning
調理	Cooking
接客	Server
自動車免許	Drivers License
パソコン	Personal Computer

Fig. 9. Keyword differences between high-skilled job queries and public employment queries

6 Conclusions and Future Work

We presented a method that allows recruiters to search for highly skilled elderly workers interactively. By doing so, interaction data which may reflect recruiters' tacit knowledge are fetched through the query operation. We found that the recruiters' interaction is an important factor in generating an ontology for highly skilled elderly workers. This ontology should be used for query generation in order to improve the quality of the search results.

Our experiment in an actual production environment has just started. We have already found that the system flow needs to be re-considered so that it can fetch all the useful interaction data since the flow did not fit into the recruitment process of the advisory consulting service which only requires single candidates. There are also some queries in which candidates are not marked as matched due to burden of having to do many operations We are in process of changing the flow of the system in order to collect the interaction data more effectively. Furthermore, we should develop an algorithm for applying analyses of small sets of interaction data to the keyword extraction. Huge datasets are required to build ontologies, therefore, a different approach to utilizing interaction data should be considered so that results of interaction data analyses can be applied to the system in real time.

Acknowledgements.   This research was partially supported by the Japan Science and Technology Agency (JST) under the Strategic Promotion of Innovative Research and Development Program.

References

1. Clark, R., Ogawa, N., Lee, S.H., Matsukura, R.: Older workers and national productivity in Japan. Popul. Dev. Rev. **34**, 257–274 (2008). Population Aging, Human Capital Accumulation, and Productivity Growth
2. Yamada, H., Hiyama, A., Yamaguchi, M., Kobayashi, M., Hirose, M.: Job Matching Interface for Searching Elderly Workers. LIFE 2015 (2015)
3. Yamada, H., Shinkawa, K., Hiyama, A., Yamaguchi, M., Kobayashi, M., Hirose, M.: Interactive searching interface for job matching of elderly workers. In: Antona, M., Stephanidis, C. (eds.) UAHCI 2016. LNCS, vol. 9739, pp. 436–445. Springer, Cham (2016). doi:10.1007/978-3-319-40238-3_42
4. Singh, A., Catherine, R., Visweswariah, K., Chenthamarakshan, V., Kambhatla, N.: PROSPECT: a system for screening candidates for recruitment. In: CIKM2010, pp. 659–668 (2010)
5. Kumaran, V.S., Sankar, A.: Towards an automated system for intelligent screening of candidates for recruitment using ontology mapping (EXPERT). Int. J. Metadata Semant. Ontol. **8**(1), 56–64 (2013). doi:10.1504/ijmso.2013.054184

The Influence of Mental Model Similarity on User Performance: Comparing Older and Younger Adults

Bingjun Xie[✉] and Jia Zhou

Department of Industrial Engineering, Chongqing University, Chongqing 400044, China
alwansmiths@gmail.com, zhoujia07@gmail.com

Abstract. The objective of this study is to investigate the effect of mental model similarity on the performance of older adults. A total of 14 older adults were recruited and their performance was observed. The results of the experiment indicate that mental model similarity, which measures the gap between older adults' mental models and designers' mental models, differed among information structures. Specifically, directional similarity was marginally affected by information structure while directionless similarity was not affected by information structure. There was no evidence that directionless similarity influenced user performance, whereas directional similarity had a marginally significant effect on the task completion time. An age effect was observed—younger adults had higher mental model similarity than older adults, and younger adults took less time and clicks to complete tasks than the older adults. The results of this study may give researchers an insight into the extent to which mental models affect performance.

Keywords: Directional similarity · Directionless similarity · Information structure · User's performance · Age effect

1 Introduction

Currently, two major characteristics are shaping modern society. The first characteristic refers to the profound demographic change that is marked by an increasingly aging population. The population of senior adults is getting larger. The second characteristic is the ongoing proliferation of information technology products, such as web pages, in many parts of daily life [1]. The Internet is no longer inaccessible for older adults and they can also enjoy the convenience of the Internet. Despite the various appearances of Internet resources, seniors still have some disadvantages in effectively using Internet resources such as web pages. A previous study has shown that older people face more difficulties than younger people finding information on a website [2]. Meanwhile, a survey has found that a substantial portion of the senior population will never join the Internet community due to disability or the difficulty of using a web page [3]. This phenomenon has led to a number of studies. In particular, the mental model has been widely used to explain this phenomenon and it has been applied to human-computer interaction (HCI).

Many researchers have used the mental model to explore user performance. Some researchers have found that the mental model was positively correlated with user

© Springer International Publishing AG 2017
J. Zhou and G. Salvendy (Eds.): ITAP 2017, Part II, LNCS 10298, pp. 569–579, 2017.
DOI: 10.1007/978-3-319-58536-9_45

performance [1, 4–6] while others have found that the mental model either has an adverse effect or no significant effect on user performance [7, 8]. There may be two explanations for why these researchers have different and even conflicting results. The first is the method of eliciting mental models. The traditional method to elicit mental models of hierarchical systems is card sorting [9]. However, card sorting cannot be used to elicit the mental model of information structure considering the directional relationship, which is a key element of information structure. The second is that most researchers have explored the effects of mental models qualitatively.

In a previous study, Schmettow and Sommerr [7] had proposed an index called mental model similarity to investigate the effect of the mental model through a quantitative perspective and found that the match between mental model and website structure has no effect on browsing performance. However, Huang et al. [10] found that information structure had a significant effect on older adults' performance and the mental models of older adults were positively correlated with user performance. Another previous study has found that users will have navigational issues when the information structure does not match the users' mental model [11]. The reason why these results are different may be the method used to elicit mental models, which was card sorting. This method failed to be used to elicit mental models of information structures with the directional relationship. Getting a better understanding of the impact of mental model similarity on user performance is important for academics and practitioners alike.

This study aims to investigate the effect of mental model similarity on older adults' performance as well as the age effect. Given that researchers have already investigated the mental model similarity effect on younger adults [12], this study mainly intends to investigate whether mental model similarity has an effect on the performance of older adults. The methods which were used to elicit mental models were card sorting and path diagram. The path diagram can be used to elicit mental models of information structures with the directional relationship, which had been verified in previous work. Specifically, in the experiment the older participants are asked to navigate three web pages built with a net structure, tree structure, and linear structure. The results of this study may give researchers an insight into the extent to which mental models affect performance.

2 Literature Review

2.1 Mental Model and User's Performance

Since it was applied to HCI, the mental model has been widely used to analyze user performance. Studies on mental models can be approximately divided into two branches. The first branch is qualitative and the second branch is quantitative. There have been many qualitative studies on mental models. Some researchers have found that the mental model has a positive effect on the user's performance. For example, Ziefle and Bay [4] found that users had better performance using the devices when they had better mental models of navigations menus. Slone [5] pointed out that the user's website performance was affected by their mental model. Converse et al. [6] found that shared mental model was related positively to Team Decision Making (TDM). Huang.et al. [10] found that information structure had a significant effect on older adults' performance and that mental models of older adults were positively correlated with user's performance. Previous studies have also found that the users will have navigational issues when the information structure does not match their mental model [11]. However, some researchers have found that mental models have no significant effect on user performance. For example, Borgman [8] found that a mental model made no difference to the user's performance of routine tasks. Furthermore, Payne [13] found that users who had the wrong mental model were still able to use the device well.

Compared with the qualitative studies, there are far fewer quantitative studies of mental models. The existing studies have focused on the match degree between the user's mental model and website information structures. Schmettow and Sommer [7] introduced an index that they called mental model similarity to investigate whether or not the match degree between the mental model and website structure had an effect on user's browsing performance. They found that there was no significant difference between mental model similarity and performance. However, researchers have already investigated the effect of mental model similarity on younger adults [12] and found that mental model similarity had a significant effect on the user's performance.

2.2 Methods of Eliciting Mental Models

Many methods have been used to elicit mental models. Among them, card sorting is the most widely used method of eliciting mental models of hierarchical systems [4]. However, card sorting is not effective for eliciting mental models of information structure when the directional relationship among various elements of information structure is considered. In the previous work, researchers have proposed a path diagram to elicit the mental model [12]. This method adds the directional relationship based on the card sorting and it can be used to describe the understanding of a hierarchical system.

2.3 Age Difference

Age has been studied as a factor affecting use of new technologies and many studies have investigated the effect of age. For example, Phang et al. [14] found that older adults who perceived themselves in declining physical condition reported that e-government services are less easy to use. Zaphiris [15] has found that older adults have particular difficulties with deep menu structures and they tend to get more easily lost in broad or deep menus than young people. Ziefle and Bay [4] demonstrated that younger participants who had a fairly correct mental model have better performance than older participants, none of whom had a correct mental representation of the information structures. Kolodinsky [16] pointed out that the reasons why older people tend to shy away from the Internet is the lack of understanding from web developers that older people have different needs from their younger counterparts, both in the reasons for which older people use the Internet and also in the way that older users interact with it (mostly due to ageing-related functional impairments).

However, there have not been enough studies of age. In one of the few examples, Arning and Ziefle [1] pointed out that the factor 'chronological age' cannot be used as an explaining variable itself when it comes to usability research and design for older users. Consequently, this study aimed at a detailed examination of the age effect on mental model similarity.

3   Methodology

An experiment was conducted to investigate the effect of mental model similarity on older adults' performance. Mental model similarity was calculated from card sorting and the path diagram using the mathematical formula that has been verified in the previous work [12].

3.1   Equipment and Materials

A notebook computer with a touch screen (ThinkPad YogaS1) was used. A Morae Recorder was used to present the task specification for the participants. Cards with the name of the nodes of three websites were used to place card sorting and a whiteboard was used to draw path diagrams. A phone was used to record the card sorting and the path diagram for analysis.

Web pages with net, tree and line structures were used. To avoid the learning effect, the knowledge about ancient inventions, books, and historical figures were used as the content of the websites and this knowledge was uncommon to see in daily life. The users' spatial ability was tested by a KJ-I spatial location memory span tester.

3.2   Participants

A total of 14 older adults from urban and rural areas of Chongqing, China were recruited as participants. Older adults who were literate and aged above 60 were eligible for this study. The age of the participants ranged from 62 to 85 years old (Mean = 71.9, SD = 7.42). In total, there were nine male participants and five female participants. The experience of using computers, tablets, and smartphones (see Table 1) was investigated.

Table 1.   The participants' experience of using technology products (hours per day)

	Mean	SD
Computers	0.36	0.63
·Tablets	0.29	0.61
Smartphones	0.86	1.10

3.3   Task

There were six tasks for each website and the tasks were focused on finding an item hidden in the web page. The participants firstly watched the task specification. They then found the target according to the task specification by touching the hyperlink in the web page. Finally, they answered two questions according to the content, which were used to check whether they had read the content carefully.

3.4 Dependent Variables

There are two dependent variables: task completion time and the number of clicks. The task completion time is the average value of the completion time of six tasks under each information structure. The number of clicks is the average value of the number of clicks to complete the six tasks under each information structure. Both the task completion time and the number of clicks were recorded by Morae Recorder.

3.5 Independent Variables

There are three independent variables: website information structure, mental model similarity between older adults and designers, and age. The mental model similarity was calculated from the card sorting and the path diagram using the mathematical formula, which has been verified in previous work [12]. Specifically, the directionless similarity was calculated from card sorting, and the directional similarity was calculated from the path diagram. The website information structure has three levels: net, tree and linear, which are commonly seen in daily life.

Age here was regarded as one independent variable and this study investigated the effect of age on mental model similarity through a quantitative perspective.

The demographic variables included technology product experience and spatial ability. The technology product experience was measured through a questionnaire. The participants' spatial ability was tested through the spatial location-memory span tester. To avoid memory and learning effects, the order of the task was randomized.

3.6 Procedure

The experiment took each participant about 90 min. First, each participant filled out a consent form and a general questionnaire about his/her demographic information and experience with technology products. Second, a spatial ability test was conducted by using a spatial location–memory span tester. Third, training about how to place card sorting and draw path diagram was conducted. The training only ended when the participants got a full understanding of how to place card sorting and draw the path diagram. Finally, the participants completed tasks on each web page. After completing all six tasks of each page, the participants were required to place card sorting and draw a path diagram on a whiteboard. During the whole process, the participants were encouraged to complete the tasks individually. They could ask for help but it would be recorded.

3.7 Quantifying Mental Model Similarity

The method of quantifying mental model similarity has been well elaborated in previous work [12]. The method consists of two parts: the first part is used to calculate the directionless similarity and the second part is used to calculate the directional similarity. The formulae that are used here are drawn from Xie and Zhou [12]. The directionless similarity measure a^{ij} can be obtained using:

$$a^{ij} = \frac{e^{ij}}{e^{ij} + b^{ij} + b^{ji}}. \tag{1}$$

Equation (1) was used to calculate the directionless similarity through card sorting. The directionless similarity can be calculated by calculating the number of identical and different elements of the information structure between two different card sortings.

The directional similarity measure r^{ij} can be obtained using the following formulae:

$$c^{ij} = \sum_k \sum_l \min\{h^i_{kl}, h^j_{kl}\} \tag{2}$$

$$d^{ij} = \sum_k \sum_l |h^i_{kl} - h^j_{kl}| \tag{3}$$

$$r^{ij} = \frac{c^{ij}}{c^{ij} + d^{ij}} \tag{4}$$

The adjacency matrix was used to describe the path diagram. Equation (2) was used to calculate the identical parts of two different path diagrams (mainly the directed segments in path diagram) and Eq. (3) was used to calculate the different parts of two different path diagrams. Equation (4) was used to calculate the directional similarity. These formulae were used to quantify the match degree between the user's mental model and the information structure. See previous work [12] for a detailed description of these formulae.

4   Results and Discussion

4.1   Descriptive Statistics

There were a total of 14 participants in this experiment (nine males, five females). About 43% of the participants used multiple technology products—such as a computer or smartphone—and the rest had no experience of these products.

4.2   Information Structure and Mental Model Similarity

The directional similarity and directionless similarity were calculated using the formulae. The descriptive analysis results of directional similarity and directionless similarity are shown in Table 2.

Table 2. The descriptive analysis results of directional similarity and directionless similarity

	Mean	SD
Directional similarity	0.27	0.25
Directionless similarity	0.60	0.29

Table 2 indicates that the mean of directional similarity was lower than the mean of directionless similarity. One possible reason for this is that card sorting did not take the directional relationship of information structure into account, which makes it easier for users to elicit mental models. Once more details such as directional relationship are considered, the mental model similarity is changed. This verified that it is incorrect to elicit mental models without considering the directional relationship of the information structure.

Repeated variance analysis was conducted. The dependent variables were directional similarity and directionless similarity, the independent variable was information structure. The results of repeated variance analysis are shown in Table 3.

Table 3. The influence of information structure on mental model similarity

	Directional similarity				Directionless similarity			
	Type-III SS	df	MS	F	Type-III SS	df	MS	F
IS	0.18	2	0.09	3.37*	0.20	2	0.10	1.06

Note. IS refers to information structure.
*$p<0.05$

A regression analysis was then conducted. There were three independent variables: information structure, technology product experience, and spatial ability. The dependent variables were directional similarity and directionless similarity. The results of the regression analysis are shown in Table 4.

Table 4. Regression analysis results of information structure on mental model similarity

	Directional similarity			Directionless similarity		
	B	t	p	B	t	p
IS	0.08	1.71	0.09	-0.01	-0.19	0.85

Note. IS refers to information structure.

Table 4 indicates that the information structure had a marginal effect on directional similarity while it had no effect on directionless similarity. One possible reason for this is that the path diagram is more effective than card sorting when researchers elicited mental models of information structure. In addition, the number of subjects here was only 14, which is small. Different results may be found after expanding the number of subjects.

4.3   Mental Model Similarity and User Performance

A linear regression was conducted. The dependent variables were the task completion time and the number of clicks. The independent variables were directional similarity and the directionless similarity. The demographic variables were spatial ability and technology product experience. The results of the regression are shown in Table 5.

Table 5. The influence of mental model similarity on user's performance

	The task completion time			The number of clicks		
	B	t	p	B	t	p
Directional similarity	−10.97	−1.77	0.08	−0.59	−0.27	0.79
Directionless similarity	−5.71	−0.52	0.61	−4.60	−1.24	0.22

According to Table 5, the directional similarity was marginally linearly related to the task completion time. The participants took less time when the directional similarity was higher. The directional similarity's mean under net structure (Mean=0.19, SD=0.15) was lower than the tree (Mean=0.28, SD=0.25) and the linear structure (Mean=0.35, SD=0.31), which means that it took less time to complete a task in the net-structure web page than the other two web pages. These results are in agreement with those of Huang [10].

The effect was marginal and one possible reason is that the information structure had a significant effect on the user's performance. Repeated ANOVA was conducted to investigate the effect of information structure on user's performance. The dependent variables were the task completion time and the number of clicks, and the independent variable was information structure. The results indicated that the information structure had a significant effect on the task completion time and it had no impact on the number of clicks. One possible reason for this is that the older participants tended to focus on the content of the web page, and they would have more meaningless clicks to find the target item. The results of the repeated ANOVA are shown in Table 6.

Table 6. The effect of information structure on the user's performance

	The task completion time				The number of clicks			
	Type-III SS	Df	MS	F	Type-III SS	df	MS	F
IS	3492.15	2	1746.07	5.25**	239.78	2	119.89	2.66

Note. IS refers to information structure.
**p<0.01

4.4 Age Effect

To investigate the influence of age on mental model similarity, one-way ANOVA was conducted. The age and the mental model similarity were categorized by the average. The dependent variables were directional similarity and directionless similarity. The independent variables was age. The results of one-way variance analysis are shown in Table 7.

Table 7. The influence of age on mental model similarity

	SS	df	MS	F
Directional similarity	1.42	1	1.42	5.91*
Directionless similarity	6.67	1	6.67	49.16**

Note. **p<0.01, *p<0.05.

Table 7 shows that age had significant influence on mental model similarity. The extent to the effect of age on mental model similarity was investigated and the results are shown in Table 8. Table 8 indicates that age had different degrees of influence on mental model similarity. Younger adults had higher mental model similarity than older adults, showing that younger adults had a better understanding of information structure than the older adults. One possible reason for this is that younger adults have more experience using technological products such as a computer or smartphone. The older participants who had enough experience of technology products acted as well in the test as the younger adults. Table 8 also indicates that the effect of age on directional similarity is larger than the effect of age on directionless similarity. One possible reason is that drawing path diagram is more difficult for older adults.

Table 8. The difference of mental model similarity between younger and older adults

	Younger adults		Older adults		Diff%
	Mean	SD	Mean	SD	
Directional similarity	0.75	0.31	0.27	0.25	94%
Directionless similarity	0.95	0.14	0.60	0.29	46%

Note: Diff% means percentage difference, Diff% = (M1 − M2)/[(M1 + M2)/2]

The influence of age on user's performance was investigated. The results of one-way ANOVA showed that age had a significant effect on the task completion time ($F_{(1,132)} = 103.34$, $p = 0.00$) and the number of clicks ($F_{(1,132)} = 4.25$, $p = 0.41$). The extent to the effect of age on user's performance was investigated and the results are shown in Table 9.

Table 9. The difference of user's performance between younger and older adults

	Younger adults		Older adults		Diff%
	Mean	SD	Mean	SD	
Task completion time	17.36	6.63	41.08	20.19	82%
The number of clicks	8.73	5.18	10.95	6.92	22%

Note: Diff% means percentage difference, Diff% = (M1 − M2)/[(M1 + M2)/2]

Table 9 indicates that younger adults took less time and clicks that older adults. In addition, the effect of age on the task completion time is larger than the effect of age on the number of clicks. One possible reason is that older adults had to take more time to read the content in the experiment.

5 Discussion

First, the method which was proposed to elicit the mental model in previous research [12] is effective for eliciting the mental model of older adults. The results indicated that the information structure had marginal effects on directional similarity while it had no effect on directionless similarity. This is a little bit different from the results of a previous study which found that the information structure had a significant effect on directional similarity [12]. One possible reason for this is that there were 14 older participants in the present study, which is smaller than the number of younger adults. Hence, expanding the number of older adults may give different results.

Second, the directional similarity had a marginal impact on the task completion time while it had no impact on the number of clicks. One possible reason for this is that in this experiment the older participants tended to focus on the content of the web page while always ignoring the relationship between each page. Thus, the older participants would have more meaningless clicks to find the target item while the younger adults would not. Another possible reason is that the information structure had a significant effect on the user's performance. The results of repeated ANOVA indicated that the information structure had a significant effect on the task completion time while it had no impact on the number of clicks.

Third, an age effect was observed. The results showed that age had a significant effect on mental model similarity and user's performance. Younger adults had higher mental model similarity than the older adults. In addition, younger adults took less time and clicks to complete tasks than the older adults.

6   Conclusion

This study investigated the effect of mental model similarity on the older adults' performance, as well as the age effect. There were three main findings:

First, information structure had a marginal impact on the directional similarity while it had no significant effect on directionless similarity. This is almost same as the previous finding of younger adults, which indicated that the information structure had a significant effect on the directional similarity while it had no significant effect on directionless similarity.

Second, the directional similarity had a marginal effect on the task completion time while it had no impact on the number of clicks. Directionless similarity had no effect on the task completion time or the number of clicks.

Third, an age effect was observed. Younger adults had higher directional similarity and directionless similarity than older adults. Younger adults also took less time and clicks to complete tasks than the older adults.

Future work should be conducted in order to: (i) increase the number of older participants in order to get a full understanding of the mental model similarity's impact on; and (ii) expand the types of tasks and information structure.

Acknowledgement.   National Natural Science Foundation of China (Grants nos. 71401018 and 71661167006) and Chongqing Municipal Natural Science Foundation (cstc2016jcyjA0406).

References

1. Arning, K., Ziefle, M.: Effects of age, cognitive, and personal factors on PDA menu navigation performance. Behav. Inf. Technol. **28**(3), 251–268 (2009)
2. Kurniawan, S.H., Zaphiris, P.: Web health information architecture for older users. It Soc. **1**(3), 42–63 (2003)
3. Rheingold, H.: Look who's talking. Wired, 7.1 (1999)
4. Ziefle, M., Bay, S.: Mental models of a cellular phone menu. comparing older and younger novice users. In: Brewster, S., Dunlop, M. (eds.) Mobile HCI 2004. LNCS, vol. 3160, pp. 25–37. Springer, Heidelberg (2004). doi:10.1007/978-3-540-28637-0_3
5. Slone, D.J.: The influence of mental models and goals on search patterns during web interaction. J. Am. Soc. Inform. Sci. Technol. **53**(13), 1152–1169 (2002)
6. Converse, S.: Shared mental models in expert team decision making. In: Individual and Group Decision Making: Current issues, p. 221 (1993)
7. Schmettow, M., Sommer, J.: Linking card sorting to browsing performance – are congruent municipal websites more efficient to use? Behav. Inf. Technol. **35**(6), 452–470 (2016)
8. Borgman, C.L.: The user's mental model of an information retrieval system. In: Proceedings of the 8th Annual International ACM SIGIR Conference on Research and Development in Information Retrieval, SIGIR 1985, New York, NY, USA, pp. 268–273. ACM (1985)
9. Hsu, Y.-C.: The effects of metaphors on novice and expert learners' performance and mental-model development. Interact. Comput. **18**(4), 770–792 (2006)
10. Huang, J., Zhou, J., Wang, H.: Older adults' usage of web pages: investigating effects of information structure on performance. In: Zhou, J., Salvendy, G. (eds.) ITAP 2015. LNCS, vol. 9193, pp. 337–346. Springer, Cham (2015). doi:10.1007/978-3-319-20892-3_33
11. Selwyn, N.: The information aged: a qualitative study of older adults' use of information and communications technology. J. Aging Stud. **18**(4), 369–384 (2004)
12. Bingjun, X., Jia, Z., Huilin, W.: How influential are mental models on interaction performance? Exploring the gap between users' and designers' mental models through a new quantitative method. IEEE Access (2016, in press)
13. Payne, S.J.: Mental models in human-computer interaction. In: The Human-Computer Interaction Handbook, pp. 63–75 (2007)
14. Phang, C.W., Sutanto, J., Kankanhalli, A., Li, Y., Tan, B.C.Y., Teo, H.H.: Senior citizens' acceptance of information systems: a study in the context of e-government services. IEEE Trans. Eng. Manag. **53**(4), 555–569 (2006)
15. Zaphiris, P., Kurniawan, S.H., Ellis, R.: Age related differences and the depth vs. breadth tradeoff in hierarchical online information systems. In: Carbonell, N., Stephanidis, C. (eds.) UI4ALL 2002. LNCS, vol. 2615, pp. 23–42. Springer, Heidelberg (2003). doi: 10.1007/3-540-36572-9_2
16. Kolodinsky, J., Cranwell, M.: Bridging the generation gap across the digital divide: teens teaching internet skills to senior citizens. J. Extension **40**(3) (2002)

Author Index